A HISTORY OF THE WORLD

Volume II

A HISTORY OF THE WORLD

Volume II

Stanley Chodorow
University of California, San Diego

Hans W. Gatzke
Yale University

Conrad Schirokauer
The City College of The City University of New York

Harcourt Brace Jovanovich, Publishers

San Diego New York Chicago Atlanta Washington, D.C.

London Sydney Toronto

Cover art by John Dawson

Maps by Jean Paul Tremblay

ISBN: 0-15-538332-9
Library of Congress Catalog Card Number: 85-80082
Printed in the United States of America

Copyrights and Acknowledgments and illustration credits appear on page 1017, which constitutes a continuation of the copyright page.

A Note on the Paperback Edition

This volume is a part of a variant printing, not a new or revised edition, of *A History of the World.* The two-volume paperbound version enables users of the text to fit it into the particular patterns of their teaching and scheduling. This printing exactly reproduces the text of the one-volume version of *A History of the World.* The first of these volumes, which contains Chapters 1 to 28, begins with the development of the human species, of culture, and of civilization and examines events through the seventeenth century. The second volume repeats the last six chapters of the first volume and carries the account forward to the present day in Chapters 23 to 46. The variant printing, then, is intended as a convenience to those instructors and students who have occasion to use either one part or the other of *A History of the World.* Consequently, the pagination and index of the one-volume version, as well as its time lines, illustrations, maps, and other related materials, are retained in the new printing. The difference between the one-volume and the two-volume versions of the book is a difference only in form.

Preface

In this book we have tried to provide a basis for year-long courses in world history. Our intent has been to present a global perspective rather than a history of the West with chapters on other cultures added for comparative purposes only. Out of 46 chapters, 18 are devoted to nonwestern cultures — China, Japan, India, Islam, Africa, pre-Columbian America, and Southeast Asia. Only when we deal with the period of European domination of the world (from the seventeenth century through the nineteenth) do we focus on the West.

The writing of a new world-history textbook is a difficult task. We have tried to provide a framework of political history while primarily giving the reader an idea of the character and dynamics of different civilizations. To accomplish this we have tried to show the interrelationships of the artistic, intellectual, economic, social, and political life of cultures. Recognizing that the major world civilizations did not develop in isolation, we have examined the relationships among cultures, as well.

In the modern period the various parts of our globe have become so closely interconnected that we may say that modern history *is* world history; but we may also say that ancient history began as world history. The earliest discernible stage in the development of culture was common to human communities wherever they existed. Only later did geographical and political isolation produce the characteristics of distinctive cultures. The first chapters of the book are, therefore, worldwide in vision and approach. They treat both the development of human beings and their culture and the origins of civilization. The chapters that follow trace the history of individual civilizations — Greece, Rome, Islam, China, Japan, India. The later chapters, which discuss the seventeenth century and after, then show how European domination integrated world civilizations and, slowly, created our current world in which all regions are now interdependent.

It is natural that the measure of detail is greater in the later chapters than in the earlier ones. We have been concerned with showing how earlier civilizations shaped and influenced later ones — in other words, how the past shaped the future. Our historical interest in change and cross-cultural influences becomes increasingly specific as we approach the present. Although we are interested in the general sources of medieval European religious institutions and those of classical Chinese philosophy, we want to know the specific sources of twentieth-century fascism and independence movements. Because of this natural intensification of interest in the history of modern events and movements, the pace of treatment slows as we approach the present, and the chapters cover their subjects in greater depth than do earlier chapters.

This book is merely a starting point for the study of history. We hope that it will stimulate readers to explore the reference works cited at the end of each chapter, and even to enroll in additional specialized courses. As an introductory work, this book is *about* history, as well as *of* history. It tells something of the story of the past, but it also treats historical method and introduces the reader to problems of historical evidence and interpretation.

We have been fortunate in being able to base this book on the successful work *The Mainstream of Civilization*, and, where appropriate, *A Brief History of Chinese and Japanese Civilizations*. *Mainstream* gave us a framework for developing the new book, and we owe thanks to Joseph Strayer for permission to use it.

We would also like to thank the following scholars, who read the typescript of *A History of the World* and gave us valuable advice and suggestions: Edward Anson, University of Arkansas, Little Rock; Lester J. Bilsky, University of Arkansas, Little Rock; Margery Ganz, Spelman College; Cho-yun Hsu, University of Pittsburgh; Peter Mellini, Sonoma State University; Robert Roeder, University of Denver; and Joseph E. Schwartzberg, University of Minnesota.

Stanley Chodorow
Hans W. Gatzke
Conrad Schirokauer

Contents

List of Maps

Introduction

The study of history is an intellectual activity based on the common ways that we explain ourselves and relate to others. How often do we explain what we have done or said by referring to something that happened in the past? How often do new acquaintances exchange life stories as they get to know one another? Such actions reveal an assumption—very widespread in our culture—that to know and understand a person requires a knowledge of his or her past. At least with individuals, we assume that knowledge of the past is necessary for explaining the present, and our expectations of people rest on what we know of their past. Unexpected behavior is surprising because it contradicts this historical knowledge. It usually leads us to look again at what we know of a person's past.

This interest in the life histories of individuals also forces us to gather information about the collective past of the people who make up our community. This broader historical knowledge makes it possible for us to judge the commonness or uniqueness of a person's life experience.

Thinking in historical terms, therefore, is common to everyone. The historical work of everyday existence is one of the foundations of our dealings with others and with the world at large. Our basically historical mindedness is what makes news gathering a good business. We continually read newspapers and listen to news programs on radio and television because we assume that knowing the immediate past is the best way to understand the present and to prepare for the future.

This interest in news falls between the informal collection of information about the past of other individuals and the formal study of history. News reporters usually reveal the sources of their stories, but sometimes they do not. The formal study of history as an academic subject focuses our attention not only on the story of the past, but also on how we know it—on the sources of our knowledge. In the study of history, the commonplace gathering of historical information becomes an intellectual activity in which we think about what we want to know about the past and how we are going to learn it.

The study of history sharpens intellectual skills that we use in many parts of our lives. It forces us to realize that how we tell a story depends on the purpose it is to serve. What details must we include to make the story coherent and effective? Judgment and choice are essential to learning anything. Given a library of historical documents, what we might read depends on our preconceptions of the subject—that is, on what we want to know. These preconceptions provide us with questions and preliminary ideas about how to answer them. As we read, our conception and questions lead us from one body of material to another until we form an account of the subject that appears to be true and coherent—that is, understandable by others. This is a basic pattern of intellectual work.

Once we have become aware of how we know things and of our own role in shaping that knowledge, we become cautious about what we know. Historians are always conscious of the evidence they lack. A political historian may have an account of events from one side of a conflict, but not from the other. An economic historian may have accounts of wheat sales, but no way of knowing what the terms of measurements or monetary units mean. Much of the progress in historical studies is made by scholars who discover or point out the distortions in the evidence used less perceptively by earlier scholars. A new view of the evidence may produce a new interpretation or a search for material that can remedy the defect in the foundation of knowledge about the subject.

The progress of historical scholarship has tended to emphasize the relationships of all aspects of human existence. Early histories relied on narrative sources, such as chronicles and annals, and focused on political events and personalities — the things the chroniclers wrote about. In the twentieth century, historians have learned to use a wide variety of evidence. Estate records, tax rolls, records of law cases, kitchen accounts — all have served as the basis for histories that provide the social and economic context of political events. These works also show how political, economic, and social conditions influenced one another and shaped human affairs. Furthermore, recent works have shown how these conditions affected intellectual activity. They have elucidated the sociology, economics, and politics of art and scholarship and, conversely, the influence of artistic and intellectual culture on society, economics, and politics. Historical studies give us, therefore, an opportunity to think formally about the interrelationship of all human activities.

The study of history also has a social purpose. It not only teaches us how information is gathered and used, but gives us the independent power to judge the quality of historical information put forth by governments or other social agencies. To those who want to manipulate information to their own advantage, the study of history is a dangerous activity.

It is clear why studying a country's or region's history is socially and politically useful, but why should we study world history? The daily news provides one answer: The world's populations are economically interdependent and tied together by light-speed communications, effective and fast transportation systems, and international political organizations, such as the United Nations. But this has not always been true. For most of recorded history, people have been limited by the horizons of their own particular culture.

The study of world history provides us with an opportunity to enrich our mental lives by expanding our own cultural horizons beyond the specific time and place of our own physical circumstances. More than that, studying world history provides an essential perspective on what it means to be a human being. We are all shaped by the culture into which we are born. Clearly, if we are to understand the human animal, we must study its cultures.

Although cultures differ very much from one another, they share certain basic characteristics, and understanding these similarities is crucial for understanding humans themselves. The study of world history is a comparative study of cultures. Anthropologists engage in this comparative study by going from culture to culture to distinguish the universal from the particular. But cultures exist in time as well as in place, and the present and immediate past make up only a tiny fraction of the life of human cultures. To discover basic patterns of culture and to see culture in all its variety, we must study the life histories of cultures. In its fullest form, this must be a study of world history.

A HISTORY OF THE WORLD

Volume II

	1200		1400			
SOUTHWEST ASIA AND AFRICA	***ca.* 1200–1546** Mali Empire, West Africa **1204–61** Latin Empire of Constantinople **1220** Mongol invasion of Southwest Asia	**1242** Mongol armies reach Adriatic **1260** Mongols defeated by Mamluks ***ca.* 1300** Rise of Yoruba states, West Africa	**1370–1405** Timur	***ca.* 1450–1528** Songhai Empire, West Africa **1453** Ottomans capture Constantinople	**1453–1918** Ottoman Empire **1488** Bartholomeu Dias rounds Cape of Good Hope	**1501–1722** Safavid Empire **1520–66** Sultan Suleiman **1571** Battle of Lepanto
EUROPE	**1215** *Magna Carta* ***ca.* 1225–74** Thomas Aquinas **1265–1321** Dante Aligheri **1276–1337** Giotto **1305–77** Avignon Papacy	**1340–1453** Hundred Years' War **1340–1400** Geoffrey Chaucer **1348** Bubonic Plague **1378–1417** Great Schism	**1452–1519** Leonardo da Vinci **1453** Gutenberg Bible **1462–1505** Ivan III, first Russian Tsar **1469–1527** Niccolò Machiavelli	***ca.* 1469–1536** Erasmus **1492** Granada falls; Christopher Columbus sails west **1504–64** John Calvin **1517** Martin Luther's 95 theses	**1519** Magellan sets sail around world **1529** Turks besiege Vienna **1558–1603** Elizabeth I **1561–1626** Sir Francis Bacon	**1566** Netherlands Revolt **1534** Luther translates Bible into German **1534** Henry VIII heads English Church **1545–63** Council of Trent
SOUTH AND SOUTHEAST ASIA	**1206–1526** Delhi Sultanate **1293** Mongol expedition to Java	**1398** Timur invades India	**1483–1530** Babur, founder of Mughal Empire **1499** Vasco da Gama reaches India		**1511** Portuguese capture Malacca	
EAST ASIA	**1215–23** Mongols conquer Central Asia, Russia, North China **1260–90** Khubilai Khan **1271–95** Marco Polo in China	**1274, 1281** Mongols attack Japan **1279–1368** Yüan dynasty **1336–1408** Ashikaga Shogunate	**1368–1644** Ming dynasty	**1405–33** Ming maritime expeditions **1467–77** Onin War **1472–1529** Wang Yangming, Neo-Confucianism		
THE AMERICAS AND PACIFIC		**1325** Rise of Aztec Empire	**1460** Rise of Inca Empire **1492** Columbus discovers New World	**1493** First Spanish colony, Hispaniola **1493** Treaty of Tordesillas	**1510** First African slaves in New World **1519** Hernando Cortés conquers Aztecs **1520** Magellan crosses Pacific	**1533** Francisco Pizarro conquers Incas **1571** Spanish conquer Philippines **1580** Virginia Company founded

Aztec calendar stone, *ca.* 1324-1521.

Timur, 1370-1405.

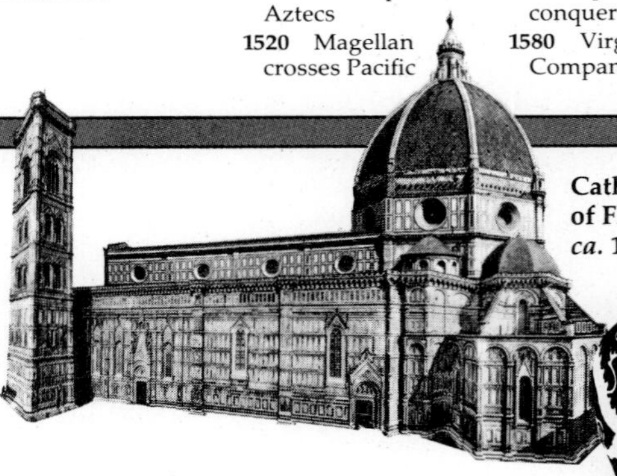

Cathedral of Florence, *ca.* 1296-1436.

Dante, 1265-1321.

Ivory belt mask, Benin, *ca.* 1500.

Ming vase.

1648	
1571 Portuguese found Angola **1588–1629** Shah Abbas I	
1572 St. Bartholomew's Day Massacre **1588** Spanish Armada **1600** British East India Company founded	**1602** Dutch East India Company founded **1618–48** Thirty Years' War **1624–42** Richelieu **1640–49** Puritan Revolution
1526–1739 Mughal Empire	**1556–1605** Akbar, Mughal emperor **1619** Dutch colonize Indonesia **1641** Dutch capture Malacca from Portuguese
1573–1600 Unification of Japan **1592, 1597** Japanese expeditions to Korea	**1600–1868** Tokugawa Shogunate **1630** Japan closed to foreigners **1638** Russians reach Pacific **1644–1911** Qing dynasty
1607 Jamestown settled **1608** Quebec founded **1609** Henry Hudson explores Hudson River	**1620** Puritans land in Massachusetts **1624** Dutch found New Amsterdam **1636** Harvard College founded **1642** Dutch discover New Zealand

Portuguese caravel, ***ca.*** **1400**

Incan silver figurine, ***ca.*** **1400.**

23 China and Japan: *Fourteenth to Seventeenth Centuries*

In the fourteenth century both China and Japan acquired new governments that set the course for each for the following two centuries. But China's Ming dynasty (1368–1644) proved more enduring than the Ashikaga Shogunate, which was paramount only from 1334 until 1467 even though the shogunal line did not come to an end until 1573. As this suggests, the inner dynamics of Chinese and Japanese history and society continued to be very different.

CHINA

The Early Ming (1368–1414)

Zhu Yuanzhang (Chu Yuang-chang, r. 1368–98), the founder of the Ming dynasty, began life in poverty and in his youth spent time in a Buddhist monastery and as a beggar before rising to a military command in a popular rebellion against the Mongol Yüan dynasty. He then went on to become the leader of his own rebellion. By abandoning the messianic radicalism of earlier rebels and by demonstrating his intention to reconstruct the traditional kind of imperial government, he was able to gain valuable support among the gentry (see pp. 353–55). Once in power he proved to be a very able autocrat capable of farsighted statesmanship but also of terrible cruelties. As a Qing (Ch'ing) dynasty scholar put it, "The Founder of the Ming combined in his person, the nature of a sage, hero, and robber."

Emperor Tai-zu (T'ai-tsu), to use his official, posthumous title, abolished the post of chancellor and concentrated all power in his own hands. This took an enormous amount of paper work, and he also held three audiences a day. In earlier times officials at such audiences had been allowed to sit or stand; now they knelt. And they were subjected to beatings in open court. Always painful and terribly humiliating, the beating was sometimes so severe that the man died. Merciless in exterminating those who stood in his way or were suspected of doing so, Tai-zu obtained information through a secret service provided with its own prison and torturing apparatus.

At the same time, the emperor energetically furthered the work of reconstruction and relief for the poor, some of whom were resettled. He conducted a great land survey and fixed the land tax at a low rate. Furthermore, he reestablished the imperial university, founded many schools, and reinstituted the civil service examination system. Confucianism again became the official state doctrine. But the emperor rejected the antiauthoritarian aspects of the thought of Mencius and expurgated about one-third of the text of *The Mencius.*

Tai-zu's work of laying the foundations of the dynasty was completed by his son Cheng-zi (Ch'eng-tsu, r. 1402–24—also known as Yongle or Yung-lo), the third emperor. Cheng-zi, however, moved the capital from Nanjing (Nanking) in the south back north to Beijing (Peking), which he largely rebuilt and reconstructed the Grand Canal. He sponsored major works of Confucian scholarship as well as the publication of Buddhist works and allowed the complete, unexpurgated *Mencius* to reappear.

Both emperors pursued vigorous foreign policies. By the end of his reign Tai-zu had won control of all of China and dominated the frontier region from Hami in Xinjiang (Sinkiang) north through Inner Mongolia and into northern Manchuria. The Ming had also won the subjugation of Korea and various Central and Southeast Asian states sent tribute. Cheng-zi himself led five expeditions against the Mongols, intervened in northern Vietnam (Annam) and then incorporated it into the empire, and sent out great maritime expeditions, which established China as a naval power.

There were seven great expeditions (1405–33). The first included 27,800 men on 62 or 63 large ships and 255 smaller vessels. They sailed not only to various areas of Southeast Asia but also visited the Indian Ocean, Arabia, and the east coast of Africa. The voyages were unique in their scope and official sponsorship, but the technology that made them possible had previously been employed by private ventures not considered worth recording by official historians. Thus it is interesting to note that the Ming fleet had dealings with Chinese settlers in Sumatra.

As a result of the expeditions, foreign regimes acknowledged the Ming's suzerainty and Southeast Asian rulers such as those of Malacca and Brunei (on Borneo) traveled to China to do homage. Also arriving from abroad were exotic objects and animals—giraffes caused a particular stir. It is

The Complaints of the Ming Founding Emperor

In the morning I punish a few; by evening others commit the same crimes. I punish these in the evening and by the next morning again there are violations. Although the corpses of the first have not been removed, already others follow in their path. The harsher the punishment, the more the violations. Day and night I cannot rest. This is a situation which cannot be helped. If I enact lenient punishments, these persons will engage in still more evil practices. Then how could the people outside the government lead peaceful lives?

What a difficult situation this is! If I punish these persons, I am regarded as a tyrant. If I am lenient toward them, the law becomes ineffective, order deteriorates, and people deem me an incapable ruler. All these opinions can be discerned in the various records and memorials. To be a ruler is indeed difficult.

Proclamation of the Hung Wu Emperor from Patricia B. Ebery, *Chinese Civilization and Society: A Sourcebook* (New York: The Free Press, 1981), p. 125.

likely that a desire for trade also figured among the motives for the expeditions, and it certainly was a major factor in inducing foreign lands to send tribute. The Ming government, however, did not consider this trade as intrinsically worthwhile. From the official Chinese point of view, these expeditions did not have an economic rationale. On the contrary, they were expensive, and the fact that they were led by a Muslim eunuch certainly did nothing to win them friends among the Chinese officials. Furthermore, the maintenance of strength along the land frontier was, as always, of crucial importance whereas ocean expeditions were a luxury. Consequently they were discontinued by Xuan-zong (Hsüan-tsung, r. 1426–35), the fourth Ming emperor, with the result that ultimately it was left for Europeans to take the lead in world navigation and discovery.

The Middle Ming (1425–1590)

The first seventy-five years of the middle Ming were generally peaceful and prosperous. The government was stable under emperors less ambitious for military glory and personal power than Tai-zu and Cheng-zi. While there were new troubles with the Mongols and one emperor even suffered the ignominy of being captured by them, there was a resurgence of military strength in the 1460s and 1470s. The Great Wall was strengthened and extended for six hundred miles. Although the wall was first built in the third century B.C., the wall as it stands today owes much of its imposing mass and length to the Ming.

To preserve himself from drowning in official business, Xuan-zong selected certain officials to screen memorials, draft edicts, and the like. This informal group of two to six officials became increasingly influential during the last quarter of the fifteenth century and became known as the Grand Secretariat. However, unlike the heads of the government ministries, the grand secretaries had no real roots in the bureaucracy and thus represented imperial rather than bureaucratic power. Of particular concern to Confucian officials was the growth of eunuch influence. Tai-zu had warned against allowing eunuchs a political role, even installing a plaque in the palace stating, "Eunuchs must not interfere in government business. Violators will be beheaded." But even during his reign there were complaints of an increase in the number of eunuchs. Under Xuan-zong a school for eunuchs was established, but this did not prevent the continuing hostility of Confucian officials, who seem to have criticized even honest and able eunuchs as a matter of principle. Eunuchs enjoyed unique opportunities for informal, relaxed conversation with emperors who often turned to them for advice or entrusted them with important missions.

The Ming emperors believed in doing things in grand style. For example, it is reported that in 1425 the court had 6,300 cooks in its employ, preparing meals not only for the large palace population but also for government officials on set occasions. To please the eye there were fine bronzes and especially porcelain. It was during Xuan-zong's reign that the blue-and-white ware produced by the royal kilns reached its height of artistic excellence. Ming blue-and-white had such appeal that it went on to win admiration and stimulate imitation not only in East Asia but in such distant lands as Persia

***Kittens*, detail of a scroll painting copied after a painting by Emperor Xuan-zong.**

Blue-and-white porcelain (eighteenth-century copy after a Ming design). This kind of porcelain has been popular ever since it was first produced under the Ming.

Ming China   Middle Sixteenth Century

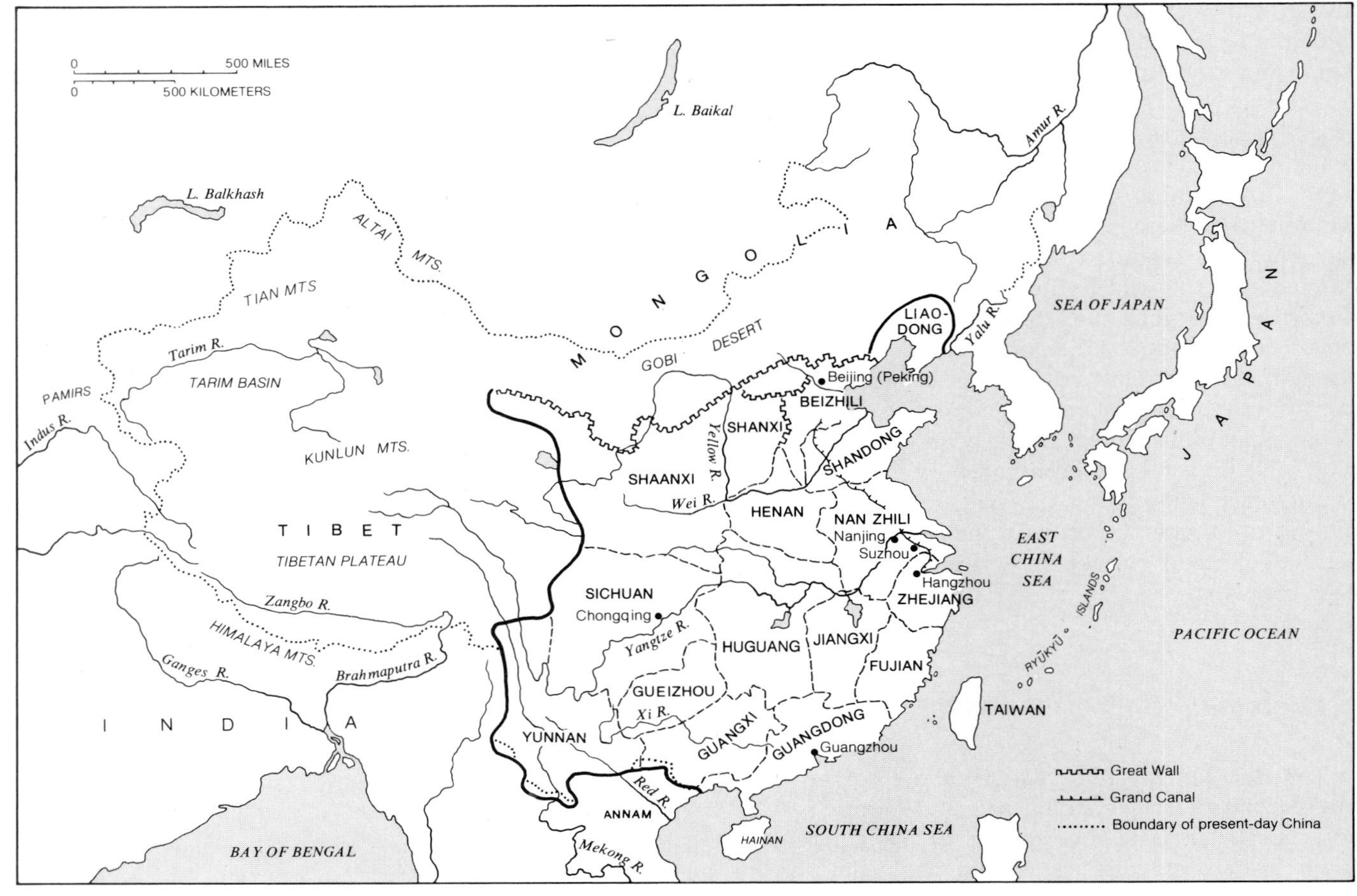

and Holland. The porcelain of each reign had its own characteristics, and the color range was broadened with the use of a variety of enamel colors.

By the early sixteenth century the dynasty showed signs of wear. Between 1506 and 1572 three emperors reigned who paid greater attention to their private concerns than to public business, and they were followed by Shen-zong (Shen-tsung, r. 1573–1620), who was a minor until 1590. Grand secretaries and eunuchs wielded great power. A decline in government honesty and efficiency was apparent both at the center and in the provinces. On the district level, the gentry increasingly abused their local power and influence. For example, they bought land but forced the seller to remain responsible for the taxes, or, conversely, sold land and made the buyer assume a disproportionate share of the tax burden. Such activities harmed both the small peasant proprietors and the government's coffers.

But there were also reformers. Most notable was Hai Rui (Hai Jui, 1513–87) famed for his concern for the common people as well as his courage in criticizing the emperor, which very nearly cost him his life. After his death he was idealized as the perfect official incarnate. A very different, hard-headed reformer was Zhang Juzheng (Chang Chü-cheng, 1525–82) who dominated government from about 1567 until his death. Among his achievements were repair of the Grand Canal, reform of the courier system, new regulations designed to strengthen central government control over provincial officials, a reduction in the total number of officials, the elimination of eunuch influence, and a reform of the examination system. He also conducted a land survey and consolidated tax obligations into a single annual bill, with silver used as the basis for calculating tax assessments. The silver tael (ounce) remained the standard monetary unit into the twentieth century.

These reforms demonstrated the dynasty's ability to rally and stem the process of decline. But Zhang made many enemies. They had their revenge after his death when his family property was confiscated and his sons tortured. Yet he left the regime in sound financial condition at a time when it was sustaining heavy military expenses, fighting Mongol invasions between 1550 and 1570 and maintaining military preparedness thereafter.

Economy and Society

Peace and stability made for prosperity. In the North agriculture was rehabilitated, but the South remained the most prosperous and populous region. The gradual spread of superior strains of rice, which had begun during the Song (Sung), permitted a steady increase in China's population so that by 1600 the population had doubled from the 60 million people at the start of the Ming. In the sixteenth century, the introduction of new crops from the Americas—maize (corn), sweet potatoes, and peanuts—laid a foundation for still further population increases to follow during the Qing.

It is difficult to find in the Ming major technological or industrial breakthroughs such as those of the Song, but the population increase, the flourishing of commerce, and the expanding use of money reveal this period to have been far from stagnant. Nourished by trade, such great lower Yangtze cities as Nanjing, Suzhou (Soochow), and Hangzhou (Hangchow) prospered. Among the important industries of the period were porcelain and ceramics, cotton, and silk. Indigo and sugar cane, along with cotton and some varieties of rice, were important cash crops grown for the market.

Despite economic growth, the Ming fiscal system remained geared to a grain economy. Nor did government impinge much on local society. At the local level the central government was represented by the magistrate, who in theory was responsible for everything that happened in his district. He was supposed to supervise tax collection, provide for public security, administer justice, and see to the economic as well as moral needs of the population. However, because his staff was small and the average Ming district had a registered population of over 50,000 the magistrate's control and influence were restricted.

It was the local gentry who presided over provincial life. There were no doubt important regional variations, but research to date suggests that gentry lineages were able to perpetuate themselves generation after generation by maintaining solid economic roots in local landownership and investing their income in education, which provided them with local status as well as permitting them to compete in the civil service examinations. Members of a lineage who secured office could use their political influence to the lineage's advantage, but even lineages lean in successful examinations managed to maintain themselves. This suggests that local social and economic status was the primary source of their power and that there was greater continuity in the family background of the local elite than among those capable and fortunate enough to gain access to a career in the imperial bureaucracy.

Among the means to secure cohesion of a lineage were the periodic compilations of genealogies, the maintenance of ancestral halls and graveyards, the performance of ceremonial sacrifices to lineage ancestors financed by income from lineage lands, and the perpetuation of lineage rules and guides for the behavior of lineage members. One penalty for severe infraction of the rules was expulsion.

Ming porcelain showing ladies playing *weiqi* (called go in Japan).

Individual gentry lineages profited from participation in a complicated network of marriage relationships. They also had great influence on government officials assigned to their districts. For one thing, they moved in the same social and cultural circles; they were of the same class. Even if uninfluenced by personal associations, government officials could hardly disregard the power and influence of the local gentry.

At least in the more prosperous and urbanized parts of China gentry tended to move to district capitals and, as absentee landowners, to abuse their power by charging high rents, allocating taxes unfairly, demanding exorbitant interest on mortgage loans, and so on. A rift developed between the gentry and the peasant tenants who worked their lands. Hostilities between the groups led to rebellions during the Late Ming. However, at least some lineages survived the upheavals of the Late Ming. Sobered by the lesson, they apparently were more ready to observe the frugality enjoined on them by ancestral admonitions and to conform to accepted standards of behavior.

Literacy and Literature

Along with prosperity came an increase in literacy, not only among the well-educated and ambitious but also among the more humble and less sophisticated. Bookshops did a brisk trade. Among their best sellers were collections of model examination papers used by candidates to cram for their tests. But they also sold encyclopedias, colored prints, novels, and collections of short stories. There were also guides that explained the classics in simple language, and books of moral instruction illustrated with tales of wrongdoing and retribution. The audience for wood block prints was even wider than for books. Colored prints, as well as black-and-white, were widely used to illustrate texts ranging from Buddhist sutras to books of erotica.

The Ming is known for its short stories but even more so for its novels. Reflecting its roots in a much older tradition of oral storytelling, the novel remained essentially episodic in construction and often included passages of poetry. Despite their literary excellence, it was not until the twentieth century that novels won respectability in China as a form of high literature. In Japan the novel was an honored part of literary culture, but in China reading a novel was a surreptitious pleasure indulged in by students when their teacher was not looking—or vice versa.

The four major novels that have come down to us from the Ming illustrate the range of subject matter treated in Chinese prose. *The Romance of the Three Kingdoms* is a historical novel depicting in lively prose the brilliant stratagems and heroic deeds of some leaders and the foibles and weaknesses of others during the third century A.D. when, after the collapse of the Han Dynasty, China was divided into three states. A different kind of history provided the materials for *The Water Margin,* also known as *All Men Are Brothers.* It is set in the closing years of the Northern Song and recounts the deeds of 108 bandit heroes, men driven by the cruel corruption of a decadent government to take justice into their own hands; these outlaws champion the oppressed and avenge the wronged. Numerous episodes tell of feats of strength and daring, clever tricks, and acts of savage but righteous vengeance.

The third major Ming novel, *Journey to the West,* translated also as *Monkey,* is based on the trip to India by the famous Tang monk Xuan Zhuang (see p. 184). The trip is transformed into a fantastic journey, a heroic pilgrimage, and a tale of delightful satire and high comedy. Monkey is one of three supernatural disciples assigned by the Buddha to accompany the monk and protect him from the monsters and demons that threaten him along the way. Monkey frequently saves the day, for he is endowed with penetrating, although mischievous and restless, intelligence and has acquired many magical gifts. The novel can be enjoyed as sheer fantasy, or for its satirical accounts of the bureaucratic organization of Heaven and the underworld, or as a religious (or today Marxist) allegory.

The fourth great Ming novel, *The Golden Lotus* is an erotic novel still widely considered pornographic. In one hundred chapters it gives a detailed account of the dissipations of a wealthy lecher providing a naturalistic tableau of amorous intrigues within a household and beyond, of parties and feasts, and portraits of go-betweens, fortune-tellers, doctors, mendicants, singing girls, venal officials, and so on. After a life of sex without love, the hero, reduced to an empty shell, meets a fitting death, and the novel rolls on for another twenty chapters to recount the unraveling of the household.

Landscape in the Style of Ni Zan, **by Shen Zhou (1484).**

Ming Thought

Although the government supported Confucianism, the world in which Ming thinkers lived was far removed from the Confucian ideal. Furthermore, just as the growth of commerce had an impact on social values, the spread of literacy undercut the monopoly of classical thought, classical values, and the status of those with a classical education. Also disturbing was the perception that in a post-classical age perhaps the only way a scholar could make a personal contribution was through specialization—a marked departure from the traditional aim of universal knowledge. These were just some of the considerations stimulating an effort by Ming literati to define their personal and social roles and to probe into the essence of human nature. Thus they were not merely concerned with working out the ramifications of the Neo-Confucian synthesis but also intensively occupied with a quest for wisdom, a striving for sagehood.

The foremost Ming thinker was Wang Yangming (Wang Shouren, Wang Shou-jen 1472–1529) who identified human nature with the mind-heart (a single entity in Chinese), which he in turn identified with principle (*li,* see pp. 360–61). Everyone is endowed with natural goodness and has an innate capacity to know good. The truth is in and of the mind. For Wang Yangming, as for all Neo-Confucians, this truth was at once metaphysical and moral. It is not just to be grasped intellectually but must be lived: A person can no more know filial piety without practicing it than he can know the smell of an odor or understand pain without experiencing them. Knowing and acting are not only inseparable, they are two dimensions of a single process: "Knowledge in its genuine and earnest aspect is action, and action in its intelligent and discriminating aspect is knowledge."

A philosophy that focuses on the inner person is conducive to diversity because people differ. It was echoed in the paintings of Late Ming individualists for whom art was an experience of self-expression, a chance to allow free play to their genius and sensibility, as Dong Qichang (Tung Ch'i-ch'ang, 1555–1636), China's foremost art historian, said it should be. In social thought and private life it could, and did, make for quietism but also had a radical potential realized by some of Wang Yangming's Late Ming followers. Li Zhi (Li Chih, 1527–1602) carried the individualism implicit in Wang Yangming's thought to the point of defending selfishness and in other ways too offended the literati to such a degree that in the end he died a suicide in prison.

Li Zhi shocked not only members of the establishment but also activist Confucians, who were appalled by the radical subjectivism of this line of thought. Such men also saw it as their duty to protest forcefully against political abuses and un-Confucian conduct. Early in the seventeenth century, the Donglin (Tung-lin) Academy in Wuxi (Wu-hsi), northwest of Suzhou, became a center for such "pure criticism," which cost many Donglin men their lives. Conflict between pro-Donglin and anti-Donglin factions persisted through the last thirty years of the dynasty.

The Late Ming (1590–1644)

During its last fifty years the Ming evidenced clear signs of dynastic deterioration. From 1590 until he lay dying in 1620 Shen-zong only saw the grand secretaries five times. Except for matters of taxation and defense, he left memorials unanswered with the result that much of the business of government did not get done and many major government posts were left vacant for years. The emperor did take an interest in military matters. From the 1580s on there was fighting in the southwest against various tribal peoples, Thais, and especially the Burmese. In the nineties there were campaigns in Inner Mongolia, and large Ming armies fought a Japanese invasion of Korea. These military operations were generally successful but enormously expensive. Also costly but not as successful was the military effort in Manchuria, where the Manchu chief Nurhachi founded a state and fought the Ming to a draw.

Emperor Shen-zong was apparently intelligent and sensitive but distressed by a controversy over the designation of an heir apparent and bored by court ritual and bureaucratic paperwork. His successor, however, was distinctly odd: He never learned to write and spent all his time on carpentry, creating much fine furniture. Factionalism, bad under Shen-zong, now turned vicious as a very capable and unscrupulous eunuch Wei Zhongxian (Wei Chung-hsien, 1568–1627) gained such influence over the emperor that he was able to purge all opponents, foremost among them members of the Donglin faction. Wei, not content with the realities of power, also thirsted for public glory. He heaped honors on himself and even

A Ming Parable

WHERE THE MONK WAS

A village chief was conducting a convicted monk to frontier duty. By design, the monk suggested a drink one night on the road. After the village chief, dead drunk, had fallen into a snoring sleep, the monk took a knife and shaved the chief's head, loosened the cords around himself, transferred them to the neck of the chief, and fled.

At daybreak the village chief awoke and looked for the monk without finding him. Feeling his own head and the cords around his neck, he was astonished and said, "The monk is still here; now where am I?"

Men set up forms in the world at the expense of their own minds. How can the village chief be the only one who does not recognize his true "I"?

Liu Yuanqing, *Yingxie lou* (Joke collection) trans. in John Meskill, *Academies in Ming China: A Historical Essay* (Tucson: The University of Arizona Press, 1982), pp. 112–13.

Hills on a Clear Autumn Day, after Huang Gongwang, by Dong Qichang (early seventeenth century).

had a nephew take the emperor's place in performing sacrifices in the imperial temple. He also encouraged a movement to have temples housing his own image built throughout China. But he did not survive his emperor for long, and the temples perished shortly after the man. The succeeding emperor attempted reform during his reign (1627–44), but the regime lacked a consistent policy as indicated by frequent shifts of personnel at the highest level.

With deteriorating leadership at the center and an inadequate fiscal system, the delicate balance between the central government and the local elite was upset. The dynasty was making too many concessions to the local gentry. Too much was given away, too many fields were removed from the tax rolls. Large landowners were able to find tax shelters, and only peasant freeholders remained to pay taxes. Resentment against the gentry grew in the villages, while shortage of funds forced the government to neglect vital public works. Emergency grain was sold off, the postal system was shut down, and troops went unpaid.

Military deserters and dismissed postal employees were among those who took the lead in forming the outlaw gangs that appeared first in Northern Shenxi (Shensi) and then spread from there. In 1644 Li Zicheng (Li Tzu-ch'eng, *ca.* 1605–45), a rebel leader who had once been a postal attendant, seized Beijing, and the last Ming emperor committed suicide. But Li was unable to establish a new dynasty, for, unlike the Ming founder, he did not take the necessary steps to win over the scholar-official elite. For them he represented at best an unknown, but no one could rule China without their cooperation. This was understood by Li's most powerful and capable competitors, even though they came from Manchuria. When they established their own Qing dynasty, they did so as heirs to the Ming, and they made extensive use of Ming precedents. Nevertheless, the Ming was to be China's last native dynasty.

JAPAN

The Ashikaga Shogunate

The weakening of the Kamakura shogunate in decline provided an opportunity for the throne to assert itself. Taking advantage of this situation, Emperor Go-Daigo (1288–1339) defied Kamakura and mustered sufficient warrior support to overcome the *bakufu* (the shogun's headquarters) and put an end to the power of the Hōjō family. Briefly, during the so-called Kemmu Restoration (1333–36) the emperor managed to restore the authority of the throne. But, in the final analysis, he remained dependent on the power of the warriors who were not inclined to submit to him and were, furthermore, themselves divided by conflicting interests and ambitions. Fighting continued even after Go-Daigo was forced to abdicate. The ultimate outcome was the establishment of Japan's second shogunate when the victor, Ashikaga

Takauji (1305–58), received the coveted title of shogun from an emperor he himself installed in Kyoto. Nevertheless, for another half a century (1336–92) a rival court south of Kyoto in Yoshino served as a focus for opposition to the Ashikaga. It was Yoshimitsu (1358–1408), the third and most capable of the Ashikaga shoguns, who finally secured the reunification of the imperial line.

Unlike their predecessors, the Ashikaga shoguns did not attempt to establish a new center of power but conducted their affairs from Kyoto and appointed a deputy to look after their interests in the East, with other deputies in Kyushu, west-central Japan, and in the North. Although the shoguns held the highest civil offices, their actual power depended on a system of family and feudal loyalties.

The Military Protectors of the Kamakura period developed into military governors, although their title *shugo* remained the same. In the days of its vigor, the Kamakura *bakufu* had tried to limit the power of the *shugo* by assigning men to provinces where they had no family roots or property, and by asserting its right to dismiss and confirm the *shugo,* even though the positions eventually became hereditary. These military governors received virtually unlimited rights of taxation and adjudication but held only very limited proprietary rights within their provinces of assignment. Moreover, the shogunate was able to pressure most of the *shugo* to reside in Kyoto.

The Ashikaga depended on the *shugo* families for support and appointed some of their leaders to important positions in their own *bakufu* organization. A council of important *shugo* contributed to the *bakufu*'s decision-making process. The system involved a complicated balance of power which all tried to manipulate to their own advantage. In 1441, when a shogun tried to encroach on the power of the *shugo,* he was assassinated by one of his senior vassals. Until the Onin War (1467–77) the fulcrum of power remained in Kyoto.

Kyoto now developed into an economic as well as political and cultural center. The basis of the Japanese economy remained agrarian, and an increasing agrarian yield provided the means for growth. Improvements in farm technology, new crops, new strains of rice, and greater use of draft animals all helped to increase the productivity of the land. This had a positive impact on commerce and manufacturing. Technical progress in such endeavors as mining, sake brewing, and paper production, to mention just a few, further contributed to this process.

An added stimulus came from trade with China and Korea initiated by Yoshimitsu. This shogun's admiration for Chinese culture extended to Chinese dress, for he liked to wear Chinese clothes as well as contemplate Chinese paintings. The trade with China, in which Zen monasteries played a major role, continued, with minor interruptions, to flourish under Yoshimitsu's successors. To control this commerce and keep the number of ships within agreed upon limits, the Ming issued official tallies valid for trading at specified ports. This system also helped to control piracy by restricting the pirates' ability to trade stolen goods; it lasted until the middle of the sixteenth century. Japanese imports included cotton from Korea, and from China great quantities of copper coins as well as porcelain, paintings, medicine, and books. A major Japanese export was fine swords. Japan also exported copper, sulphur, folding fans (a Japanese invention), screens, and so forth. The ability to export products of sophisticated craftsmanship is one index of Japanese accomplishments during this period.

With the growth of commerce, of markets, and of market towns, guilds *(za)* were formed by merchants and artisans to exercise monopoly rights over the exchange and production of various commodities. To safeguard their rights and privileges, and to obtain protection, these guilds turned to the great religious institutions and power-

Japan *ca.* 1200–1600

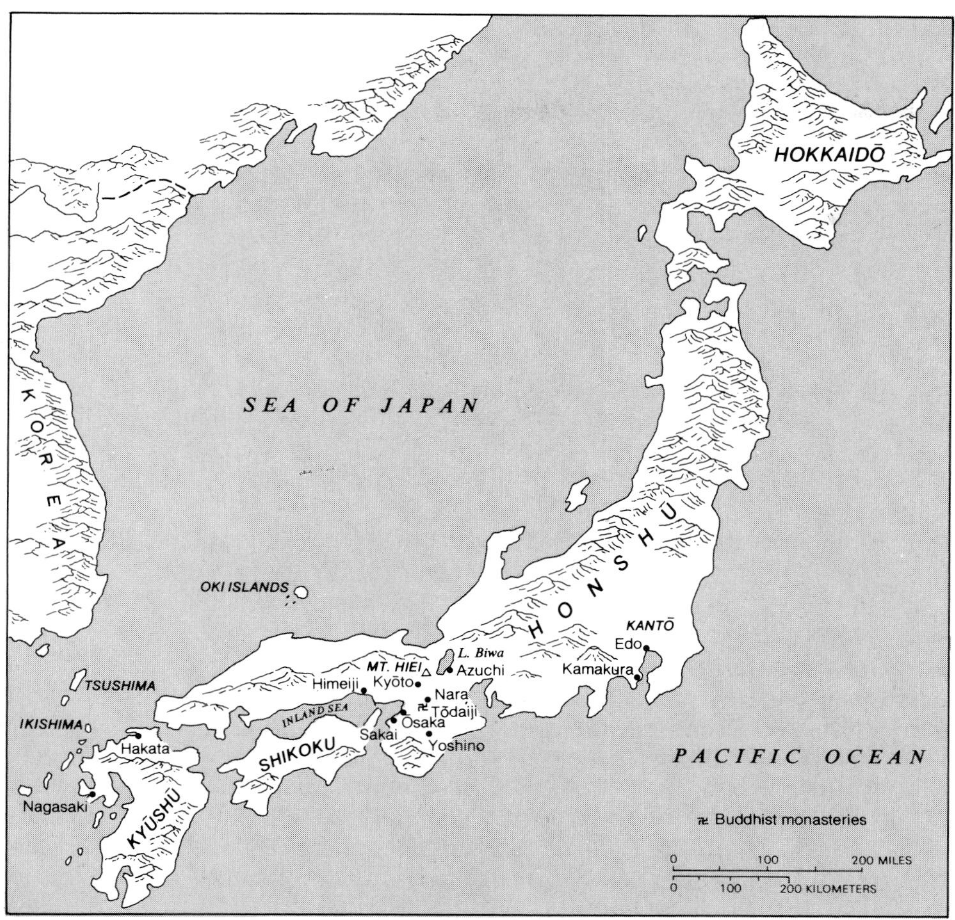

ful families. Temples and shrines, the great families, and the *bakufu* itself welcomed the guilds as a source of revenue and became increasingly dependent on income from this source. Ever since the *bakufu* had begun taxing Kyoto's wealthy pawnbrokers and sake merchants under Yoshimitsu, revenue from commercial sources remained a crucial factor in the shogunate's finances. The prosperity of the pawnbrokers is only one sign of the increasing use of money, a development that was both a product of and a stimulant to commercial growth. To facilitate transactions between distant places, bills of exchange came into use.

Kyoto was not the only urban center to benefit from these developments. Most impressive was the growth of Sakai, near modern Osaka, which became an autonomous political unit governed by a group of elders who were mostly merchants. Hakata in Kyushu, the center for trade with Korea, also flourished as did a number of other well-placed cities. The growth of these cities suggests parallels with European history, but such parallels hold only to a limited degree, for Japanese cities did not achieve sufficient power to undermine the prevailing order; rather, the merchants provided a source of revenue for the feudal lords. Social and political institutions were not shattered, but society was enriched by the emergence of a new urban population. One result of political decentralization combined with economic growth was the diffusion of higher culture to the provinces. Conversely, the arts of the elite were reinvigorated by

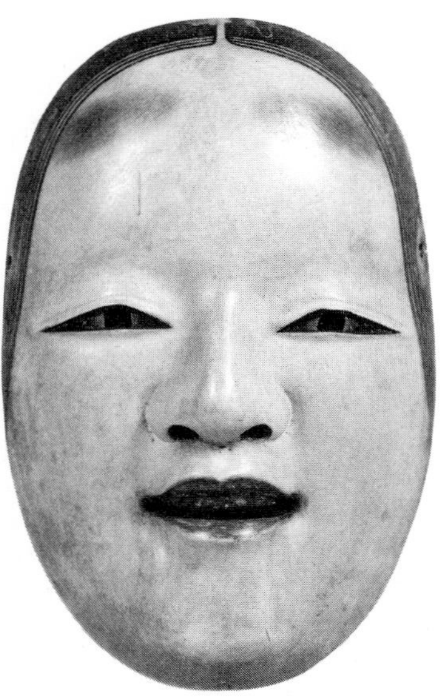

Nō mask.

the influence of popular culture; many of those who molded elite tastes were themselves of commoner background.

Cultural Florescence

Yoshimitsu was the first Ashikaga shogun born and raised in Kyoto and sought to combine his warrior heritage with the values long cherished in the capital. In gratifying his taste for fine architecture and gardens, he spared no expense. He believed in doing things in truly royal style: Once he entertained the emperor with twenty days of banqueting, music, and theatrical performances. This entertainment took place in Yoshimitsu's estate in the northern hills just beyond Kyoto, graced by the Golden Pavilion. Built in a style combining aristocratic and Buddhist, Japanese and Chinese elements, this building was a symbol of the shogun's good taste as well as his affluence.

Among the entertainments Yoshimitsu provided for the emperor were performances of Nō, the classic drama of Japan. The tone is serious; the presentation symbolic. Some, but not all, of the actors wear highly stylized and exquisitely fashioned masks. By subtle body movements and just the right tilt of the head, a great actor can suggest remarkable nuances of mood and emotion, while the frozen faces of the unmasked actors attain a mask-like effect. Attired in elegant costumes, the actors move with deliberate grace, unfolding gestures as full of meaning to the cognoscenti as those employed in the religious observances of esoteric Buddhism. It is an art that avoids realism and aspires to convey a sense of profound meaning beyond the words and scenes on stage.

A full program of Nō would take about six hours, but a tone of grave sadness is hard to sustain for hours on end. Comic relief was provided by *kyōgen* performed in the interlude between Nō plays. Often in the nature of a farce, they show a fondness for broad humor and foolery. Livelier than the Nō, the *kyōgen* are less demanding on the audience, but they lack the aura of poetic mystery that has sustained the Nō tradition.

As great a patron of the arts as Yoshimitsu but lacking that shogun's political skills was Yoshimasa (1436–90, shogun 1443–73). He too was very fond of Nō. As a counterpart of Yoshimitsu's Gold Pavilion, there is Yoshimasa's Silver Pavilion, more subdued and intimate than its predecessor, but also combining Chinese and native elements in its architecture. A Chinese theme is also echoed in its sand garden, a rendition of the West Lake outside Hangzhou, but near one bank stands a volcano, also of sand—a miniature Mt. Fuji.

At the Silver Pavilion there is also a small hall, the interior of which is divided between a Buddhist chapel and a new element—a room for the performance of the tea ceremony. The accent in the classic tea ceremony, as developed in Yoshimasa's time, is on simplicity and tranquility. Through a small doorway no bigger than a window, the guests crawl into a room about nine feet square, there to enjoy in silent calm the movements of their host as he prepares the tea with motions as deliberate as those of a Nō actor. After they have drunk the deep green tea, they may exchange a few remarks on the bowl or the flower arrangement prepared for the ceremony. When performed with the easy grace of a master, the tea ceremony can convey Japanese good taste at its best.

Seami on the Nō

Among those who witness Nō plays, the connoisseurs see with their minds, while the untutored see with their eyes. What the mind sees is the essence; what the eyes see is the performance. That is why beginners, seeing only the performance, imitate it. They imitate without knowing the principles behind the performance. There are, however, reasons why the performance should not be imitated. Those who understand the Nō see it with their mind and therefore imitate its essence. When the essence is imitated, the performance follows of itself.

From Ryusaku Tsunoda, Wm. Theodore de Bary, Donald Keene, *Sources of Japanese Tradition* (New York: Columbia University Press, 1958), p. 302.

Influenced by the tea ceremony, secular architecture adopted many of the features of the tea room. Rush matting *(tatami)* covered the whole floor—previously individual mats had been placed on wooden floors as needed to provide a place for people to sit. Sliding doors consisting of paper pasted on a wooden frame *(shoji)* came into common use, supplementing the sliding partitions *(fusuma)* with their painted surfaces. Another standard feature is the alcove *(totonoma)* with its hanging scroll and flower arrangement. Flower arranging, like the tea service, became an art, with its own rules and regulations passed on through generations by the masters of distinct schools.

Painting and poetry played an important part in cultural life, and here the influence of Zen was particularly marked. The era's most renowned poet, Sōgi (1421–1502), was a Zen monk of commoner background. The foremost ink monochrome painters were also Zen monks. In developing their art, these monks could draw on a tradition in Japan of painting in the Chinese manner going back to the Kamakura period. Some might also see Chinese paintings kept in Japan, above all the shogun's own collection. The most fortunate, like the great master Sesshū (1420–1506), were able to travel to China itself. Sesshū painted in a variety of styles. One of his masterpieces is a landscape scroll over fifty-two feet long, guiding the viewer on a leisurely trip through scenery and seasons. Another famous masterpiece is in the ink-splash technique.

Also contributing to the artistic scene were professional painters organized into schools that, like those of Nō and the other arts, were continued from father to son or, if necessary, to adopted son, perpetuating traditions much like warrior or merchant families, guarding their professional secrets as carefully as sake brewers or pharmacists guarded their formulas. One famous school, the Tosa, worked in the old native narrative style. Another, the Kano, painted in a predominantly Chinese manner.

The Silver Pavilion, Kyoto.

Common to the aesthetics of Nō, the sand garden, the tea ceremony, and a Sesshū landscape was a taste for the old *(sabi)*, the solitary and poor *(wabi)*, the astringent (*shibui)*, and the profound *(yūgen)*, a taste best expressed in its own vocabulary. The prestige of Chinese culture was enormous, and Sinophiles versified and painted in Chinese. But, unlike their predecessors of the Nara period, they were selective in borrowing and rapidly assimilated the new. In later ages this aesthetic sensibility was challenged, assailed, and even displaced, but it never disappeared completely.

Tea bowl, Raku ware.

The Rise of the Daimyo

The Onin War (1467–77) signaled not only the end of the balance between the shogunate and the *shugo* but demolished the very constituents of the

Haboku **(broken ink)** *Landscape,* **by Sesshū (1494).**

old order. It left the *bakufu* with its effective authority restricted to the capital area, but the *shugo* were also in dire straits, threatened by those who held proprietory control in the provinces. Most of the latter were the successors of the former Kamakura Military Land Stewards *(jitō),* who had transformed their *shiki* into proprietary rights, thereby bringing the old *shōen* system to an end (see pp. 345–46, 364).

Ironically, a major source of instability was a practice adopted by powerful families seeking to maintain family stability. The old tradition of dividing an estate equitably among heirs was abandoned as too dangerous in a period of constant fighting when families needed to muster all their economic and human resources to survive. To secure the family's future, the property was left intact and passed on to a single heir designated by the family head. This was not necessarily the eldest son, but it was always a son: A daughter would be unable to protect the property militarily. Far from functioning smoothly, however, this system frequently led to bitter rivalries and hard-fought succession disputes. A dispute over who should succeed Yoshimasa set off the Onin War, but the Ashikaga was merely the most prominent family to be undermined in this manner.

The Onin War became merely the first decade of a century of warfare during which Japan was fragmented into countless separate principalities, directed by *daimyo,* military lords whose power exceeded that of the *shugo* for they had proprietary rights in their domains and could grant and confirm fiefs. In return for the fiefs, vassals of the *daimyo* (lords) were obliged to render military service to their lord and to provide the service of a set number of their own fighting men.

The *daimyo* competed with each other to preserve their territories and, if possible, to expand them. The size of the principalities varied widely; some were no larger than a small castle town while others might be as large as one of the old provinces. Regardless of the size of his holding, the lord's fate depended on his success in the field of battle. What counted was power. Although some of the mid-sixteenth century *daimyo* belonged to the old families, many emerged out of the class of local warriors. In these strenuous, difficult times, capable, ambitious, and unscrupulous men struggled to the top using any means at hand; frequently, betrayal was the price of upward mobility. The introduction of formal oaths, unnecessary in an older and simpler age, did not change the situation. Vassals could be counted on for their loyalty only as long as it was in their own interest to remain loyal.

In the long run, success went to those lords who could most effectively mobilize the resources of their domains, turning them into small states. The ultimate consequence of the breakdown of central unity was the creation of smaller but more highly integrated political entities. The *daimyo* asserted their authority over the succession of their vassals and, because political combinations were involved, they also had a say concerning their vassals' marriages. Some asserted rights to tax the land in their territory and to regulate economic activities. And many employed spies to keep a watch on the vassals.

A potent force for territorial integration was the changing nature of warfare. The *daimyo* found that massed foot soldiers recruited from the peasantry and armed with spears and the like were effective against the traditional, proud, and expensive mounted warriors. Armies grew larger, and vassals tended to serve as officers commanding commoner troops. To defend against these new armies, the *daimyo* built castles. The typical castle was often built on a hill, crowned with a tower, protected by walls and surrounded by a moat or natural body of water. In concept and function they were much like the castles of Europe.

The castles often served as the center for their principalities, and increasingly warriors were gathered there, thus removing them from direct supervision of their own land. This resulted in the transformation of villages into peasant communities left to manage their own affairs as long as they provided the payments and services required of them. This is not to suggest that the peasantry was docile during this period of fighting and social unrest. On the contrary, there were many peasant uprisings, often led by low-ranking warriors or organized by religious sects. In one case peasants held power for eight years, but nowhere could they establish more permanent peasant power.

Himeiji Castle.

Unification

The restoration of central authority was a cumulative process begun by Oda Nobunaga (1534–82), practically completed by Toyotomi Hideyoshi (1536–98) and consolidated by Tokugawa Ieyasu (1542–1616) who, after winning a crucial battle in 1600, organized what was to be Japan's last premodern government, the Tokugawa Shogunate (1600–1868).

Nobunaga was fortunate in inheriting a strategic territorial base in central Honshu, but his military and political skills, applied with complete ruthlessness, account for his success. Militarily he was an innovator as well as a bold tactician. Quick to understand the use of firearms, introduced by the Portuguese in 1543, Nobunaga won one major battle through the superior firepower of his three thousand musketeers. Politically he managed to keep his enemies divided and to retain and increase his followers and allies. Encouragement of trade, reorganization of land administration and tax collection, the initiation of a land survey and of the disarming of the peasantry were among the measures he undertook in trying to stabilize his territories. By the time he died, betrayed by one of his own generals to avenge a wrong, Nobunaga had mastered about a third of Japan.

Hideyoshi was born a peasant but rose to be one of Nobunaga's foremost generals and defeated other contenders for the succession. He then continued to increase his power by warfare and diplomacy. Hideyoshi married his sister to the strongest *daimyo,* Tokugawa Ieyasu, and assigned him very substantial holdings in eastern Japan in exchange for domains of less value in central Japan. In this way he saw to it that Ieyasu was both content and at a distance. Unlike Nobunaga whose unlimited quest for power frightened the *daimyo,* Hideyoshi reassured them as a group by working out a federal system, that is "the union of semi-autonomous domains under an integral authority." Involving adjustments on both sides, this secured the *daimyo* in their domains even as it provided Hideyoshi necessary support as, in effect, overlord of all Japan, for by 1590 all *daimyo* had sworn loyalty to him.

Hideyoshi's settlement did not stop at the *daimyo* level. One of his most important acts was the great "sword hunt" of 1588, when all peasants who had not already done so were ordered to surrender their weapons. His purpose was not only to deprive peasants of weapons they might use in riots and rebellions, it was also to draw a sharp line between peasant and samurai, to create an unbridgeable gulf between the tiller of the soil and the bearer of arms, where previously there had been low-ranking samurai who worked the land. Similarly Hideyoshi's great land survey, completed in 1598, listed the names of the peasant proprietors and effectively separated farmers and fighters. An edict of 1591 carried the process still further. The first of its

Portrait of Hideyoshi, with an inscription by his son (early seventeenth century).

Western "barbarian" in Japan, as depicted on a section of a sixfold screen (*ca.* 1610).

three articles prohibited fighting men from becoming peasants or townsmen, and the second forbade peasants to leave their fields and become merchants or artisans and prohibited the latter from becoming farmers. The third and final article prohibited anyone from employing a samurai who had left his master without permission. In this way, Hideyoshi, himself of peasant background, did his best to make sure that henceforth everyone would remain within a hereditary social status.

Hideyoshi's vision of the world and his place in it extended well beyond Japan. He took an active interest in overseas trade and also had visions of empire. Motivated in part by a need to satisfy his vassals' land hunger and find employment for his warriors but also expressing his own exaggerated pride, he made plans to conquer China and dispatched 150,000 men to Korea in 1592 after Korea had refused him free passage for his armies. The Japanese had great initial success but were then stopped by a combination of Korea's superior seamanship, Chinese military intervention, and Korean guerrilla fighting. In 1597 Hideyoshi sent another force of 140,000 men that met with strong resistance and was recalled immediately after his death in 1598.

Hideyoshi's grandiose scheme for conquering China failed, and his Korean venture came to naught. Nor was he able to found a dynasty at home. Before he died, he made his most powerful vassals solemnly swear allegiance to his five-year-old son. But this proved useless, and in the ensuing struggle for power Ieyasu emerged the winner. Ieyasu inherited Hideyoshi's power, but unlike Hideyoshi, he concentrated on building a lasting state at home, thereby ushering in a new epoch of Japanese history.

Alessandro Valignano, S.J., Comments on the Japanese

They also have rites and ceremonies so different from those of all the other nations that it seems they deliberately try to be unlike any other people. The things which they do in this respect are beyond imagining and it may truly be said that Japan is a world the reverse of Europe; everything is so different and opposite that they are like us in practically nothing. So great is the difference in their food, clothing, honours, ceremonies, language, management of the household, in their way of negotiating, sitting, building, curing the wounded and sick, teaching and bringing up children, and in everything else, that it can neither be described nor understood.

Now all this would not be surprising if they were like so many barbarians, but what astonishes me is that they behave as very prudent and cultured people in all these matters. To see how everything is the reverse of Europe despite the fact that their ceremonies and customs are so cultured and founded on reason, causes no little surprise to anyone who understands such things. What is even more astonishing is that they are so different from us, and even contrary to us, as regards the senses and natural things; this is something which I would not dare to affirm if I had not had so much experience among them. Thus their taste is so different from ours that they generally despise and dislike the things we find most pleasing; on the other hand, we cannot stand the things which they like.

From Michael Cooper, *They Came to Japan: An Anthology of European Reports on Japan, 1543–1640* (Berkeley: University of California Press, 1965), p. 229.

Western Contacts

Maritime contacts between Europe and East Asia began in the sixteenth century. Here, as elsewhere, the Portuguese were the pioneers, reaching China in 1514 and Japan, where they were shipwrecked, in 1543. In China the unruly behavior of these "ocean devils" started relations off badly, but the Portuguese were permitted informally to establish themselves at Macao in exchange for an annual payment.

Trade and booty were not the only objectives of the Europeans. Missionary work was of equal importance, and most impressive among the missionaries were the Jesuits. In 1549 one of the founders of the order, St. Francis Xavier (1506–52), landed in Japan. First impressions were favorable on both sides, and the Jesuits did their best to accommodate themselves to Japanese culture, learning how to squat Japanese style, dress and speak properly, and even mastered the art of tea. Furthermore, some of the *daimyo* were attracted by the prospects of trade. Both Nobunaga and Hideyoshi were personally well disposed to the fathers. Hideyoshi even liked to dress up in Portuguese clothes complete with rosary. While it is true that in 1578 he ordered the expulsion of the foreign monks, he did not actually enforce this decree. Yet it foreshadowed the expulsion and persecution that was to come in the early Tokugawa period.

In China, with its official distrust of trade, it was more difficult for the Jesuits to gain access, but this was finally accomplished by Matteo Ricci (1551–1610). A student of law, mathematics, and science, he also knew a good deal about cartography and something of practical mechanics. Once in the East, he was also able to master the Chinese language and the classics. In Beijing he impressed the Chinese with his erudition. His successors were able to build on these foundations and by demonstrating the superior accuracy of European astronomy established themselves in the Bureau of Astronomy. One of the Jesuit chief astronomers even helped cast cannon for the Ming, although that did not save the dynasty. Cordial relations continued initially under the new Qing dynasty. The missionary presence in China, as in Japan, carried with it potentialities for friction and conflict, but, in both cases, these did not come to the surface immediately. But when China and Japan decided to reject the missionaries (see pp. 549, 558), it was easily accomplished, for this initial encounter between East Asia and post-medieval Europe was conducted on the terms of the host country, where it had little immediate effect; even the introduction of firearms accelerated rather than molded the course of history. Perhaps these earliest contacts can best be viewed as an overture to later momentous developments.

Suggestions for Further Reading

A basic resource for the study of the Ming is the monumental *Dictionary of Ming Biography 1368–1644* (1976). An excellent analysis of the Ming state is Charles O. Hucker, *The Traditional Chinese State in Ming Times, 1368–1644* (1970). For the early Ming see the same author's *The Ming Dynasty: Its Origins and Evolving Institutions* (1978). An important book on the late Ming is Ray Huang, *1587, a Year of No Significance: the Ming Dynasty in Decline* (1981). Also see the same author's *Taxation and Government Finance in 16th Century Ming China* (1974). Also recommended for economic history is Evelyn Sakakida Rawski, *Agricultural Change and the Peasant Economy of South China* (1972).

A major advance in the study of Ming thought was achieved with the publication of *Self and Society in Ming Thought* (1970) by Wm. Theodore de Bary et al. Literature provides an excellent source for the study of Ming society. Recommended in addition to the novels mentioned in the text is Cyril Birch, trans., *Stories for a Ming Collection: The Art of the Chinese Story-Teller* (1958).

An excellent collection of essays dealing with the political, social, economic, cultural, and religious history of Ashikaga Japan is John W. Hall and Toyoda Takeshi, eds. *Japan in the Muromachi Age* (1977). H. Paul Varley has contributed studies of two of the major events of the period: *Imperial Restoration in Medieval Japan* (1971) and *The Onin War* (1967). For the period after the Onin War see George Elison and Bardwell L. Smith, *Warlords, Artists, and Commoners: Japan in the Sixteenth Century* (1981). Mary E. Berry, *Hideyoshi* (1982), is outstanding.

A good collection of Nō plays is Donald Keene, trans., *Twenty Plays of the Nō Theater* (1970). These plays were intended for the stage, not the library. A most welcome reminder of this is Monica Bethe and Karen Brazell, eds., *Nō as Performance: An Analysis of the Kuse Scence of Yamamba* (1978). For a general survey of Japanese cultural history see H. Paul Varley, *Japanese Culture: A Short History* (1973, expanded 1977).

	1200		1400			
SOUTHWEST ASIA AND AFRICA	*ca.* 1200–1546 Mali Empire, West Africa 1204–61 Latin Empire of Constantinople 1220 Mongol invasion of Southwest Asia	1242 Mongol armies reach Adriatic 1260 Mongols defeated by Mamluks *ca.* 1300 Rise of Yoruba states, West Africa	1370–1405 Timur	*ca.* 1450–1528 Songhai Empire, West Africa 1453 Ottomans capture Constantinople	1453–1918 Ottoman Empire 1488 Bartholomeu Dias rounds Cape of Good Hope	1501–1722 Safavid Empire 1520–66 Sultan Suleiman 1571 Battle of Lepanto
EUROPE	1215 *Magna Carta* *ca.* 1225–74 Thomas Aquinas 1265–1321 Dante Aligheri 1276–1337 Giotto 1305–77 Avignon Papacy	1340–1453 Hundred Years' War 1340–1400 Geoffrey Chaucer 1348 Bubonic Plague 1378–1417 Great Schism	1452–1519 Leonardo da Vinci 1453 Gutenberg Bible 1462–1505 Ivan III, first Russian Tsar 1469–1527 Niccolò Machiavelli	*ca.* 1469–1536 Erasmus 1492 Granada falls; Christopher Columbus sails west 1504–64 John Calvin 1517 Martin Luther's 95 theses	1519 Magellan sets sail around world 1529 Turks besiege Vienna 1558–1603 Elizabeth I 1561–1626 Sir Francis Bacon	1566 Netherlands Revolt 1534 Luther translates Bible into German 1534 Henry VIII heads English Church 1545–63 Council of Trent
SOUTH AND SOUTHEAST ASIA	1206–1526 Delhi Sultanate 1293 Mongol expedition to Java	1398 Timur invades India	1483–1530 Babur, founder of Mughal Empire 1499 Vasco da Gama reaches India		1511 Portuguese capture Malacca	
EAST ASIA	1215–23 Mongols conquer Central Asia, Russia, North China 1260–90 Khubilai Khan 1271–95 Marco Polo in China	1274, 1281 Mongols attack Japan 1279–1368 Yüan dynasty 1336–1408 Ashikaga Shogunate	1368–1644 Ming dynasty	1405–33 Ming maritime expeditions 1467–77 Onin War 1472–1529 Wang Yangming, Neo-Confucianism		
THE AMERICAS AND PACIFIC		1325 Rise of Aztec Empire	1460 Rise of Inca Empire 1492 Columbus discovers New World	1493 First Spanish colony, Hispaniola 1493 Treaty of Tordesillas	1510 First African slaves in New World 1519 Hernando Cortés conquers Aztecs 1520 Magellan crosses Pacific	1533 Francisco Pizarro conquers Incas 1571 Spanish conquer Philippines 1580 Virginia Company founded

Aztec calendar stone, *ca.* 1324-1521.

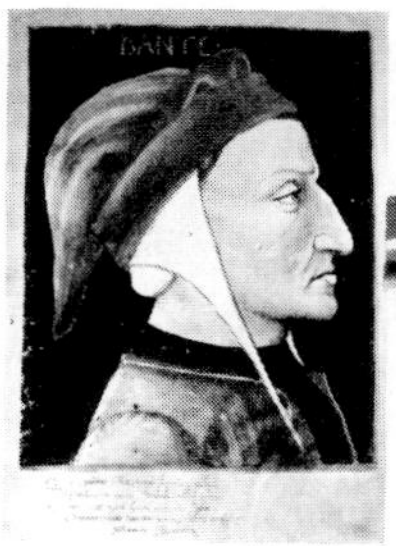

Timur, 1370-1405.

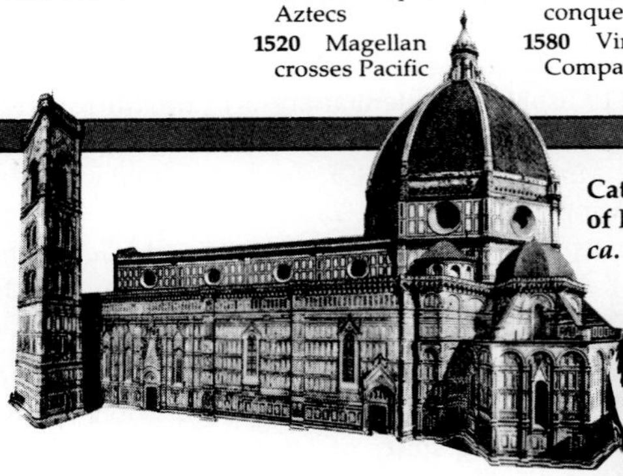

Cathedral of Florence, *ca.* 1296-1436.

Dante, 1265-1321.

Ivory belt mask, Benin, *ca.* 1500.

Ming vase.

1648	
1571 Portuguese found Angola **1588–1629** Shah Abbas I	
1572 St. Bartholomew's Day Massacre **1588** Spanish Armada **1600** British East India Company founded	**1602** Dutch East India Company founded **1618–48** Thirty Years' War **1624–42** Richelieu **1640–49** Puritan Revolution
1526–1739 Mughal Empire	**1556–1605** Akbar, Mughal emperor **1619** Dutch colonize Indonesia **1641** Dutch capture Malacca from Portuguese
1573–1600 Unification of Japan **1592, 1597** Japanese expeditions to Korea	**1600–1868** Tokugawa Shogunate **1630** Japan closed to foreigners **1638** Russians reach Pacific **1644–1911** Qing dynasty
1607 Jamestown settled **1608** Quebec founded **1609** Henry Hudson explores Hudson River	**1620** Puritans land in Massachusetts **1624** Dutch found New Amsterdam **1636** Harvard College founded **1642** Dutch discover New Zealand

Portuguese caravel, ***ca.*** **1400**

Incan silver figurine, ***ca.*** **1400.**

24 The Age of Discovery and the Greatness of Spain

The Protestant Reformation was only one of three revolutions that brought into being a new epoch in European history around the turn of the sixteenth century. Humanist thought and the Renaissance in the arts had already begun the second of the revolutions, the creation of a new historical consciousness that made Europeans aware of the rise and fall of civilizations. The third great revolution was caused by the discovery of the sea route around Africa to India and East Asia and the discovery of the New World.

For Europeans, the fifteenth and sixteenth centuries were the age of discovery without parallel. Although, like the Reformation and the Renaissance, the expansion of European knowledge and experience of the world had roots in medieval civilization, the new explorations had a revolutionary effect on Europeans' consciousness because the voyages put them for the first time in direct contact with all the inhabited continents on the globe and with all the civilized peoples who inhabited them. By the time the Peace of Augsburg (1555) set the foundation for the settlement of religious strife in Germany, the contact with the non-European world had begun also to have a profound effect on the economy and politics of Europe.

The contact with alien civilizations also forced Europeans to reconsider the ideas they had about their relationships with non-Europeans. Their traditional ideas had been formed in centuries of conflict with the Muslims and interaction with Jews. But these peoples were part of the family of civilizations of the Mediterranean Basin and the conflicts among them were in the nature of family feuds. Now, they faced the challenge of completely unknown and different peoples, and European—particularly Spanish—thinkers tried to develop ethical and legal principles that could guide their compatriots in their dealings with those who had built civilizations without the benefit of Christianity.

THE DEVELOPMENT OF OCEANIC COMMERCE

In 1400 Europeans knew scarcely more about the earth than the Romans had, for during the Middle Ages Europe was mostly the goal rather than the source of explorations and migrations. Only a few Europeans had ventured beyond the Mediterranean Basin. During the eleventh century—at the beginning of the crusading movement—western Europeans became directly acquainted with the whole Mediterranean world, but this first expansion of Europe only reestablished the boundaries of ancient civilization. The crusaders and those who followed them were setting foot in lands already described in their old books.

In Scandinavia there was a true expansion beyond the old world. The sagas recorded traditions of the voyages of Lief Ericsson and other Viking seamen to North America. During the eleventh century, the Icelanders had established settlements on Greenland and around Hudson Bay, and they apparently had explored down the eastern seashore of North America, but these expeditions left little evidence behind to mark their occurrence. The Hudson Bay communities apparently lasted only a short time, but the Greenland settlements throve until the middle of the thirteenth century. At that time, there was a cooling trend—which might also have been responsible for the climatic troubles in European agriculture later in the century—that forced the closing of the Greenland communities in 1258, but there is evidence that English sailors visited them up to the end of the century.

As Greenland was being abandoned, Italians were opening up a trade route to China. Franciscan friars and the Polos of Venice showed that China could be reached by land and that the steppes linked Europe and Asia. Marco Polo (*ca.* 1254–1324) went east with his father and uncle in 1271 and remained in China, at the court of the Mongol emperor Khubilai Khan, for over fifteen years. He returned to Europe in 1295 and wrote an account of the journey that became a widely read book in Europe. It contributed greatly both to the Europeans' geographical knowledge of the East and to their interest in Chinese civilization. But after the collapse of the Mongol Empire in the fourteenth century, the routes across the steppes were no longer safe for missionaries or merchants. The new enthusiasm for Chinese and other Eastern goods was now

Toynbee on the Age of Discovery

Since A.D. 1500 the map of the civilized world has indeed been transformed out of all recognition. Down to that date it was composed of a belt of civilizations girdling the Old World from the Japanese Isles on the north-east to the British Isles on the north-west. . . . The main line of communication was provided by the chain of steppes and deserts that cut across the belt of civilizations from the Sahara to Mongolia. For human purposes, the Steppe was an inland sea. . . . This waterless sea had its dry-shod ships and its quayless ports. The steppe-galleons were camels, the steppe-galleys horses, and the steppe-ports "caravan cities." . . . The great revolution was a technological revolution by which the West made its fortune, got the better of all the other living civilizations, and forcibly united them into a single society of literally world-wide range. The revolutionary Western invention was the substitution of the Ocean for the Steppe as the principal medium of world-communication. This use of the Ocean, first by sailing ships and then by steamships, enabled the West to unify the whole inhabited and habitable world.

From Arnold J. Toynbee, *Civilization on Trial* (New York: Oxford University Press, 1948), pp. 67–70.

satisfied by Arab traders who operated in the Indian Ocean. They brought spices and textiles to Alexandria and Beirut, from which the Venetians distributed them to European markets.

By the end of the sixteenth century, these indirect contacts with the Orient had been replaced by a worldwide trade controlled by the Europeans. The ocean had become the world's highway, and Europeans were in a position to dominate the world by controlling it. The Mongol Empire — the largest in geographical extent ever known up to that time — had rested on mastery of the steppes. The empires of the future would rest on mastery of the seas. When the first ship to circumnavigate the globe completed its journey in 1522, Europe had begun to cast a web of communication and influence around the earth. During the next four centuries that web was to draw all the civilizations of the world under the influence of Europe.

Conditions for Maritime Discovery

The age of exploration could not have occurred without significant advances in both the design of ships and knowledge of navigation. The Vikings had made relatively short voyages across the North Atlantic — Greenland was twelve days journey from Norway — but in their small, open boats, even these trips were daring. What made the western explorations possible at all was a rare climatic condition of the north that occasionally gave Scandinavian boatmen a hazy glimpse of a land beyond the horizon. These occurrences provided would-be explorers with a direction and a confidence that land would be reached just beyond the usual range of sight.

Under rare climatic conditions, men in boats off the western coast of Iceland could "see" Greenland. The phenomenon is a reverse of the mirage familiar to almost everyone in which water appears in the distance on dry ground. This is actually a reflection of the sky on the ground caused by the difference in temperature between the hot ground and the cool air. In the northern seas, this extreme temperature difference occurs in reverse in the winter, when the air is colder than the water. The reverse mirroring effect can occur in which land far out beyond the horizon — over the curvature of the earth — is reflected in the sky. The great Icelandic and Norwegian explorers had confidence that they would find a new land in the West.

Viking ship (*ca.* 1000) unearthed at Oseberg, Sweden. During the pagan period Norse kings were buried in ships prepared for their final journey to the hereafter.

Moreover, on their way to Greenland, Scandinavian sailors could stop off in Iceland and the Faeroe Islands. Their small boats and their lack of navigational skills therefore did not prevent them from making wonderful discoveries. But the Northmen's boats were too small and too unseaworthy for maintaining regular contact — a true oceanic commerce — with North American colonies, so that the small communities that they did establish in Greenland had a precarious, largely independent, existence in a difficult climate. Before Europeans could make a sustained drive to push out across the great Atlantic distances in the temperate zones and before they could establish thriving colonies that were commercially linked with the mother countries, they had to develop better ships, more reliable aids to navigation, and stronger motivation than their Norse predecessors.

The development of oceangoing ships took a long time. Ships of the Mediterranean were oar-propelled galleys that were effective in the coastal waters in which they most often operated. Sailors rarely struck out across the Mediterranean and did so only in those places where it was relatively narrow —as between Sicily and North Africa. By the thirteenth century, Genoese and Venetian galleys were venturing out into the Atlantic to Morocco and Flanders, but they did so by keeping close to the coast. On the open seas, where the distances were vast, mariners needed sails rather than oars, and broad, round hulls rather than the long, narrow ones of the galleys. These needs stemmed from the equation of manpower and provisions that were required for a long journey on the sea. The galleys had fifty or more rowers who expended an enormous number of calories each day and consequently required vast amounts of provisions. But these ships, which were built for a coasting trade or for the brief encounters of war, could not carry such stores. The new sailing ships could operate with small crews whose bodies did not burn thousands of calories a day in strenuous physical labor, and only ships that balanced the needs of their crews with their capacity to carry provisions could make the months-long journeys across the Atlantic.

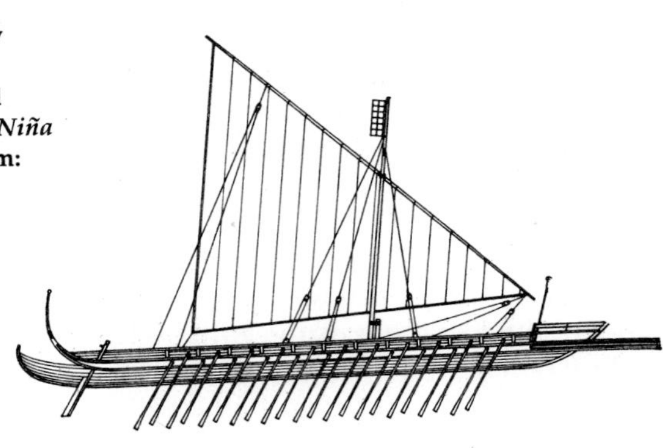

Top: Mediterranean war galley with lateen sail (*ca.* twelfth century); middle: lateen-rigged vessel, much like Columbus's *Niña* (early fifteenth century); bottom: Spanish galleon, the typical long-distance ship for Spanish commerce (sixteenth century).

The Portuguese, who faced the Atlantic directly, were the ones who finally developed a truly oceangoing vessel. By the fifteenth century they had built the squat, three-masted caravel, which combined the shipbuilding techniques of the Europeans and Muslims. The caravel had two masts with square sails in the European mode and one with a triangular lateen sail favored by the Muslims. The square rigs were best for running before the wind, while the lateen rig was better for sailing close to the wind. The new ship was slower and less maneuverable than the galley, but it had more space for cargo and provisions for long voyages.

Before mariners could venture out on the vast open waters of the western ocean, shipmasters had to have some way of determining their direction and position. The compass (used in Europe by the thirteenth century) gave them a sense of direction in dark weather; the astrolabe (used as early as the eleventh century, but perhaps as old as the third century B.C.) enabled them to determine their latitude by measuring the elevation of the sun and stars; and the portulan charts (first developed for the Mediterranean) gave them confidence that they could recognize the approaches to most European ports. (No precise way to determine longitude was discovered until the eighteenth century, when Edmund Halley—

for whom the comet is named—developed a reasonably accurate chronometer.)

Besides technological advances, the exploration of the oceans required political and economic development. City-states were the original bases for long-range shipping. The ancient Phoenicians sent out expeditions to the western Mediterranean—at least as far as Sicily and Sardinia—and the Greeks discovered the Black Sea to the east and also travelled west. The Venetians and Genoese merchants linked the Black Sea and eastern Mediterranean with England and Flanders, and the German merchants of the Hanseatic League (a confederation of trading cities) traded from Russian Novgorod to French Bordeaux. But transoceanic exploration, trade, and colonization required resources far beyond the capacities of city-states. It was only after the western European monarchies had consolidated their power and unified their countries that there existed powers with enough concentration of wealth to man and equip fleets of oceangoing vessels. Thus, after 1400 the western monarchies gradually replaced the city-states as the major centers of commercial enterprise.

It is not easy to determine why, among the seafaring peoples of the world, the Europeans desired so strongly to discover the unknown world. This question is related to the problem of why the Europeans were so inquisitive about nature and so eager to develop new technological devices, while the Muslims and Chinese, who had some instruments for industry and science much earlier than the Europeans, never fully exploited them. Muslim traders had been venturing across the Indian Ocean for centuries, but they never went beyond the familiar coastal routes, into the Pacific or around Africa. The Chinese had also regularly sailed into the Indian Ocean and up and down the coast of East Asia, but they too did not venture much into the unknown. Perhaps the frequent disruptions of migration and war in Europe had prevented the society from settling into comfortable ways in which people had complete confidence. Perhaps the perennial conflict of the different civilizations in the Mediterranean prevented Europeans from developing a complacency about their civilization and its circumscribed world and produced a missionary spirit in them—mobilized in the crusades—that impelled them to convert all peoples to their religion. Perhaps the universalism of Christianity and the belief that the longed-for end of the world

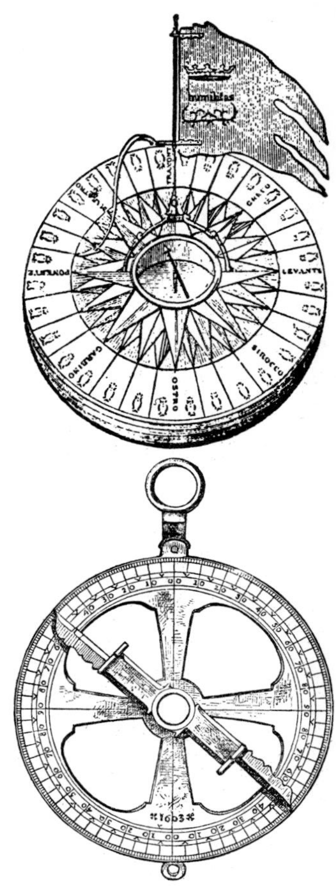

Early compass and astrolabe.

An illustration from a sailing book, *Art de Naviguer* (1583), demonstrating how to determine latitude by observing the sun's height.

would not take place until all were converted to Christianity made Europeans willing to risk their lives in oceanic adventures. The reasons why the Europeans were so extraordinarily venturesome are not clear, but it is clear that religious and worldly motives were inextricably combined in the exploration movement.

One worldly motive for exploration was the need to find new, direct trade routes to the East. In an age without refrigeration, the spices that helped preserve meats and make them palatable — pepper from India, cinnamon from Sri Lanka (Ceylon), ginger from China, nutmeg and cloves from the East Indies — were luxuries that were almost necessities. The Arab-Venetian trade monopoly made these goods — and others such as cotton and silk textiles — extremely expensive, and the newly powerful monarchs of western Europe, particularly those in the Iberian peninsula, were eager to find an independent route for the trade.

A second, and probably the principal, motivation for the exploration movement was the need to find precious metals. The Europeans had a serious trade imbalance with Asia because the Asians did not need the products of the European economy. Furthermore, since most of those products were bulky — such as wood and iron — or both bulky and perishable — such as foodstuffs — they were not suitable for the long-distance trade. Before a credit system became widely used in the seventeenth and eighteenth centuries, the only practical way to provide money for the imports — and for other projects such as industry — was to increase the supply of bullion. European mines of gold and silver had never been especially productive and were nearly exhausted by 1400. Moreover, there was a steady flow of gold and silver out of Europe to East Asia. European monarchs were therefore acutely aware of their need for new sources of gold.

By the late fifteenth century a restless, energetic, and bold seafaring population was scattered along Europe's Atlantic coastline. They had strong religious motivations and ships and navigational instruments good enough to allow them to overcome their fear of the open, unknown sea. They also had enough mistaken information to make success appear to be almost probable. Europeans' knowledge of the earth's size rested on the second-century Greek writer Ptolemy, who had underestimated it. As a result, fifteenth-century geographers were convinced that Japan and China lay only a few thousand miles west of Europe. The size of Africa had also been underestimated, so that an eastern route around it seemed relatively easy. Therefore, both an eastern and a western route seemed possible.

Portuguese Exploration

At the beginning of the age of exploration stands one of its most interesting figures — Prince Henry the Navigator (1394–1460), the younger son of King John I of Portugal. At a remarkable observatory at Sagres on Cape St. Vincent, on the southwestern tip of Portugal, Henry assembled the scientific and seafaring knowledge of his day. He devoted his life to organizing, equipping, and sending out fleets to explore the coast of Africa, with which he was obsessed. He had vague notions of outflanking Islam by reaching lands that the Muslims had never touched, but his main goal was to find gold. When his fleets reached the Gold Coast of Africa in the 1450s, he achieved this objective.

After Henry's death, the Portuguese exploration lost its impetus for a time. Sailors did discover and settle clusters of small islands in the Atlantic — the Madeiras and the Azores — but they were not very profitable. Their discovery was only of importance because it showed that there was land eight hundred miles out in the Atlantic, and this encouraged further exploration.

The interest in the voyages was taken up again by Henry's grandnephew, King John II (r. 1481–95),

The World of the Voyagers 1415–1550

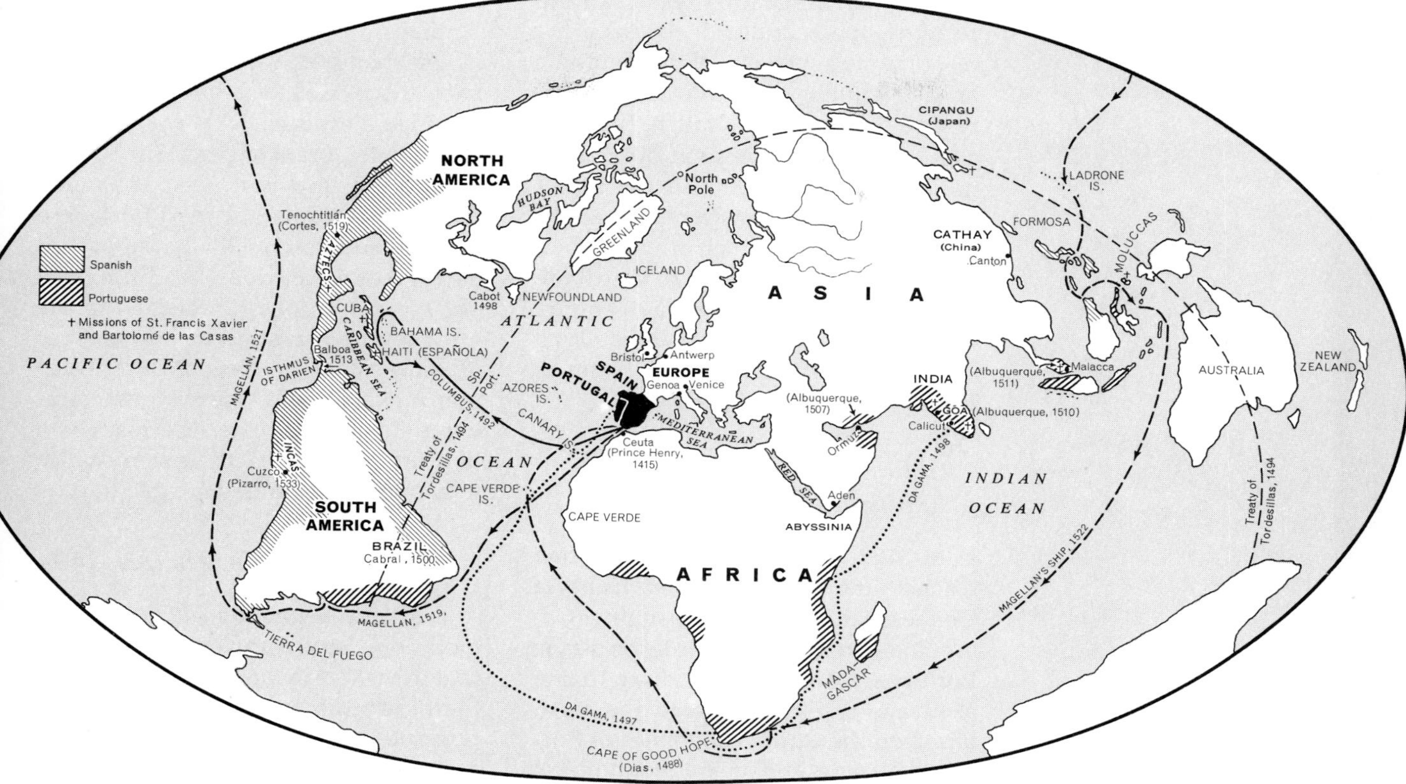

who encouraged the effort to find an all-water route to India that would destroy the Arab-Venetian monopoly. By 1488 Bartholomeu Dias had discovered the Cape of Good Hope, and in 1497 Vasco da Gama rounded the cape with four ships. Da Gama reached Calicut on the Malabar Coast of India in 1498 and was back in Lisbon with two of his ships in 1499. In 1500 Pedro Alvares Cabral led a large fleet to Brazil and then on to India.

Cabral established the first Portuguese trading stations in India, and his work, following da Gama's, had a lasting importance. At first, however, the Portuguese did not find a particularly warm welcome from either the Hindus or the Muslims in India. Da Gama found Indian civilization unimpressive and apparently said so. Cabral had to defend himself against hostile Muslims, who killed many of his men. But during the sixteenth century the Portuguese strove to build a commercial empire in the Indian Ocean. The architect of this new empire was Affonso de Albuquerque, the governor of Portuguese India from 1509 to 1515.

Already before his appointment to the governorship, Albuquerque had been active in the Indian Ocean. He had conquered Goa, which later became his capital, and had established strategic fortresses in East Africa to disrupt Arab trade with India. As governor, he seized Malacca on the Strait of Malacca to control the trade between the Spice Islands and the Indian Ocean, and Hormuz—an island in the Persian Gulf—from which he could raid the coasts of the region and disrupt Arab shipping. He failed to take Aden, which would have given him control of the Red Sea, through which the Arab-Venetian trade passed. At his death, Portugal controlled a large portion of the spice trade and had strategic bases all the way from Africa to the East Indies.

Portugal's success was short-lived. Although the early voyages earned large profits, the country was small and relatively poor and did not have the resources to establish colonies in India or to maintain the navy required to protect its commerce. Italian, German, and Flemish bankers soon dominated the Portuguese trade, and the spices that arrived at Lisbon were sent on directly to Antwerp, which proved to be a better point from which to distribute them to Europe. The burden of empire was already extremely heavy when Portugal fell into the grip of Spain in 1580.

Columbus and Spanish Exploration

In 1484, before the Portuguese had reached the Cape of Good Hope, a Genoese sailor named Christopher Columbus had tried in vain to persuade Portuguese King John II to back him in a voyage of exploration to the west. Based on the earlier experience of Portuguese sailors and on the geographical knowledge derived from Ptolemy, Columbus was convinced that it would be relatively easy to reach Cipangu (Japan) by sailing due west. But for a long time he could not persuade any monarch to back him. Then in January 1492, the combined Spanish monarchies under Ferdinand and Isabella finally conquered the Kingdom of Granada, the last Moorish stronghold on the Iberian peninsula, and the kings were free to turn their attention and resources to other projects. Isabella of Castille agreed to equip Columbus for his famous voyage. It took the Portuguese almost a century of patient effort to develop the eastward route to the Old World; the Spanish reached the New World westward in one brilliant voyage.

Christopher Columbus. This portrait is thought to be the closest existing likeness of him. It is a copy, made in about 1525, of an earlier painting that has been lost.

Columbus touched land in the Bahamas on October 12, 1492, thinking he had struck some small islands in the Japanese archipelago. Throughout four voyages and until his death in 1506, he remained convinced, even after touching the mainland, that he had reached the Old World of Japan and China. It was Columbus who named the natives he found in the newly discovered lands "Indians."

The man who recognized what had been discovered was another Italian, Amerigo Vespucci, who was head of the Medici branch bank in Seville, Spain's principal port. Vespucci sailed on both Spanish and Portuguese voyages and described what he saw in letters that were widely read throughout Europe. In one he referred to the great southern continent in the west as *Mundus novus,* a New World. Later map makers labeled the two new continents "America," after the man who had first recognized their significance to knowledge of the earth's geography.

The Treaty of Tordesillas, 1494

From the beginning of Spanish exploration, Spain and Portugal knew that they were in direct competition for the newly discovered lands. The two countries turned to Pope Alexander VI to draw a line of demarcation between their respective areas of potential empire. Alexander was a Spaniard and his line—a hundred leagues west of the Cape Verde Islands (off the coast of Mauritania in West Africa)—favored the Spanish. In 1494, the Portuguese persuaded the Spanish to negotiate the bilateral Treaty of Tordesillas, which made a division that both could be reasonably happy with and that would avoid unwanted war. This treaty also used the Cape Verde Islands as the point of reference, but it drew a line from pole to pole 370 leagues west of the islands.

Misunderstanding remained, however. The Portuguese assumed that the line applied only to the Atlantic (it gave them Brazil, though they did not know this in 1494), while the Spanish thought the line went clear around the earth. By this interpretation the Spanish could claim the Moluccas, which were the heart of the Spice Islands, and in fact it would also have given them part of what is now Indonesia. But the trouble that these conflicting interpretations of the treaty might have caused did not occur, because Spain became so occupied with its new possessions in the Americas that in 1527 it sold its claims in the East to Portugal.

By 1512 Albuquerque had established the Portuguese in the Moluccas, and a year later the Spaniard Balboa sighted the Pacific Ocean from the Isthmus of Darien (south of Panama) in Central America. The first of these achievements increased the need of the Spaniards to find a route westward to the Spice Islands, and the second made it seem that it would be possible to find a strait through the New World. In 1519, the Portuguese navigator Magellan — with Spanish backing, because his success would benefit Spain under the treaty of 1494 — undertook the third of the great voyages — along with those of Columbus and da Gama. Magellan negotiated the treacherous straits at the southern tip of South America and made it across the Pacific despite incredible hardships, only to be killed by natives in the Philippines. His navigator, Sebastian del Cano, brought back to Lisbon by way of the Cape of Good Hope in 1522 one of the five original ships — the first ship to circumnavigate the world.

THE SPANISH EMPIRE IN THE AMERICAS

About the time Magellan sailed, the Spanish began to carve out an empire in the New World. From 1520 to 1550, Spanish conquistadors conquered wealthy civilizations in Mexico and Peru. The most notable of the conquistadors were Hernando Cortes and Francisco Pizarro. From 1519 to 1521 Cortes conquered the formidable Aztec Empire in Mexico with six hundred men, sixteen horses, and a few cannon, and from 1533 to 1534 Pizarro conquered the Inca Empire in the Andes of Peru with even fewer men.

The American civilizations were wealthy and sophisticated, but they did not have a military technology to match that of the Spaniards. In addition, the small Spanish troops were well disciplined and daring and took advantage of every opportunity. Their initial successes were easy to consolidate later for two basic reasons: First, the political power of both the Aztecs and the Incas had been highly centralized, so that after the collapse of the central authorities, no local leaders could keep up resistance. Second, the Europeans brought diseases (especially smallpox) against which the native populations had no natural defenses, and within a short time, the natives were so reduced in numbers that rebellion was impossible.

The new empire raised conflicts within Spain because different groups wanted to accomplish different ends in the new lands. There were three competing elements — the settlers who went out to the New World, the government in Madrid, and the Franciscan friars. The settlers sent to the new colonies wanted to exploit the land by setting up a manorial system based on the old European model and by using the forced labor of the natives. The colonists also did not want to take orders from or to serve the interests of the Spanish government. The government

Hernando Cortes accepting the surrender of the last emperor of the Aztecs (illustration from an Aztec manuscript).

naturally wanted to centralize all power over the colonies in its own hands, and its principal goal was to find and exploit sources of precious metals. Because the Aztecs and Incas used an enormous amount of gold for ornamentation, the government had great confidence that this policy could be successful. The friars wanted to convert the new populations.

The discovery of civilized heathens raised theological and moral questions about how such people ought to be treated. Spanish scholars dredged up the works of medieval thinkers who had speculated about whether the biblical texts according to which rulers receive their authority from God (such as St. Paul to the Romans) applied to those who did not accept or did not know the sacred text. There were also questions about the marriages of the new converts. Were the "marriages" of the Indians valid? This question arose because the Catholic Church considered marriage to be a sacrament — God joined husband and wife, making an indissoluble union of them — and medieval thinkers, who had asked the question about heathens and Muslims, developed a theory that the marriages of such people were valid, but illicit. According to this conception, God created the union in such marriages — which made them valid — but the Church had not recognized them — which made them illicit or outside the law. The distinction here was basically the one between acts performed in accordance with natural law (which stems from God directly) and human law (which stems from God indirectly, through the medium of human institutions), and sixteenth-century thought about the status and condition of the Indians made much of this basic distinction. The Indians lived not according to canon law, but by natural law alone, and they were therefore God's people who lived without the benefit of the Church. The man who worked out this theory most fully was the Dominican Bartolomé de Las Casas (1474–1566).

Las Casas went to the New World in 1502 to convert the Indians, and he soon was engaged in a struggle to get better treatment for them. He and his fellow missionaries wanted to treat the converts as fellow Christians, and he made several trips back to Spain to plead for this goal. In the early 1520s, he was involved in a project to found free cities of Christianized Indians, but this failed, and Las Casas returned to Spain and retired. In retirement, he wrote many learned works defending his position and completed a great *History of the Indians,* based on what he had learned while in America.

The policy of the Spanish Empire was a compromise among the interests represented by the settlers, the government, and the friars. The settlers were permitted to command the forced labor of the subject Indians, but they were regulated by public authority, which ameliorated some of the worst abuses. Meanwhile the friars were given a wide latitude to evangelize the native popu-

Las Casas on the American Indians in the Sixteenth Century

It has been written that these peoples of the Indies, lacking human governance and ordered nations, did not have the power of reason to govern themselves — which was inferred only from their having been found to be gentle, patient and humble. It has been implied that God became careless in creating so immense a number of rational souls and let human nature, which He so largely determined and provided for, go astray in the almost infinitesimal part of the human lineage which they comprise. From this it follows that they have all proven themselves unsocial and therefore monstrous, contrary to the natural bent of all peoples of the world.

. . . Not only have [the Indians] shown themselves to be very wise peoples and possessed of lively and marked understanding, prudently governing and providing for their nations (as much as they can be nations, without faith in or knowledge of the true God) and making them prosper in justice; but they have equalled many diverse nations of the world, past and present, that have been praised for their governance, politics and customs, and exceed by no small measure the wisest of all these, such as the Greeks and Romans, in adherence to the rules of natural reason.

From Bartolomé de Las Casas, *Apologética historia de las Indias,* in *Introduction to Contemporary Civilization in the West,* 3rd ed. (New York: Columbia University Press, 1960), Vol. I, p. 539.

lation and to bring them into the fold of European civilization, and this process also balanced the tendency of the settlers to exploit and mistreat the Indians. By contemporary standards, Spanish imperial policy was, therefore, quite humane, and the Spanish came close to accomplishing what the Portuguese failed to accomplish in the East and what the English never attempted in North America: the Christianization and Europeanization of a whole native population.

Nonetheless, the primary purpose of the Empire was economic exploitation. After the discovery of enormously rich silver mines in Mexico in 1545, the extraction and shipment of silver became the main business of the Empire as a whole. Every spring after 1564 the plate fleet of twenty to sixty ships gathered at Havana harbor to be convoyed by warships to Seville. And every year the Spanish government waited anxiously until the bullion, which everyone agreed was the key to national strength, was safely in harbor.

The land had agricultural wealth as well, particularly in the wet lowlands of the Caribbean. When sugar became an important crop in these places, the Spanish settlers found that the Indian workers died in droves from disease, and they began to import Negro slaves from Africa. While the Spanish and Indian populations tended to intermarry, so that eventually the mestizos—offspring of mixed marriages—outnumbered the purebred of either race, the Negroes remained outside the society, enslaved.

Contemporary illustration of a priest baptizing four Tlaxcalan chiefs as Cortes watches (from *Lienzo de Tlaxcala*).

IMPERIAL SPAIN: THE REIGN OF PHILIP II

The wealth produced by the colonies made Spain the most powerful nation in Europe at the same time that the accession of the Habsburg Charles (r. 1516–56) gave Spain a new role in European affairs. Charles V, who had inherited Austria and the Netherlands through his mother, Mary of Burgundy, and had been elected Holy Roman Emperor in 1519, used Spanish money and troops to counter the Protestant heretics, to protect Austria from the Turks, and to conquer the New World. These far-flung actions stretched Spanish resources to the maximum, but under Charles and his son Philip II (r. 1556–98), the newly powerful nation was almost equal to the task. The sixteenth and early seventeenth centuries were the golden age of Spain.

Although he was the scion of a "European" family, Philip was thoroughly Spanish in speech, thought, and character. After 1559, when the Habsburgs concluded peace with France, he spent the remaining forty years of his life in Spain. He was a conscientious king, but he was also distrustful of his advisers, unable to delegate even in minor matters, and strongly Catholic in religion (his enemies would have said "bigoted"). He devoted himself to restoring the unity of the Christian world, with the Spanish monarchy as its temporal leader.

Philip II of Spain, by Titian.

Economic Policy

Early in the sixteenth century the bullion imported from the New World in steadily increasing amounts had been mostly gold, but after 1545, it was mostly silver. The value of the treasure rose dramatically during the century. In the early years it amounted to something under $300,000; by about 1550 the value had increased fifteen times; and by 1600 it was about $12,000,000. Then a steady decline set in, until about 1660 when the average value was down to $1,200,000. The crown received about one-quarter of the total as its share. The influx of bullion, together with internal financial problems, contributed to a steep rise of prices. By the middle of the sixteenth century, inflation was rampant and had spread from Spain to the rest of Europe. It has been estimated that prices quadrupled in Spain in the course of the century, an economic disaster.

The rise in prices outstripped the rise in tax revenues, and Philip II was forced to repudiate his government's debts three times — in 1557, 1575, and 1596. (His successors had to do the same in 1607, 1627, and 1647.) In effect, these repudiations were declarations of bankruptcy in which the king announced that he could not repay his debts and would not do so. As might be expected, such events sent shockwaves through Europe's financial institutions, but besides damaging Spain's credit, the inflation ruined its industry, which had looked promising at the beginning of the century. Because prices rose fastest and first in Spain, its producers were at a disadvantage in the international markets, and there was a perennial trade imbalance against Spain. As imports increasingly outstripped exports, Spanish industry withered, and Spanish bullion flowed out of the country. When the sources of bullion in America began to dry up in the mid-seventeenth century, Spanish industry and agriculture were ruined, and the nation quickly declined into a second-rate power.

Religious Policy

Philip II's religious policy was the most narrowly intolerant of his time. He once said that he would rather be king of a desert than of a land of heretics. His grandparents, Ferdinand and Isabella, had already forced the Moors and Jews to convert and had set the Spanish Inquisition to watching that they remained Christian. Nonetheless, it was widely believed that the Moriscos (former Moors) continued to practice their original religion in private, and Philip moved to eradicate such practices. In 1566, he ordered the Moriscos to stop using the Arabic language, to give up their traditional dress, and to stop taking hot baths, as was their custom. Three years later the Moriscos rebelled against this suppression of their cultural heritage, and Philip savagely put down the rebellion and drove them out of Andalusia, the southern region where they chiefly lived. Many left Spain for North Africa depriving Spain of an important segment of its population. The Moriscos were among the leaders of Spanish agriculture and industry, and their loss therefore had an economic effect out of proportion with their actual numbers.

This internal religious policy was coupled with a foreign policy aimed at controlling the Ottoman Turks in the eastern Mediterranean. In 1570 the Turks took Cyprus from the Venetians, and the next year a combined Spanish and Venetian fleet defeated the Turks at Lepanto in the Gulf of Corinth. The victory was hailed throughout Europe, but it had little effect because the Christian forces were unable to take advantage of it. Immediately after Lepanto, Philip was at the height of his power and prestige. But the moment of greatness was brief. During the last quarter of the sixteenth century, his dream of a revived Catholic Europe under his authority was shattered by the revolt of the Netherlands, the rise of English sea power, and the accession of a former Protestant to the throne of France.

THE REVOLT OF THE NETHERLANDS

The three million people in the seventeen provinces of the Netherlands constituted one of the most prosperous populations in Europe. The comfortable houses of Bruges, Ghent, Antwerp, and Amsterdam were built with the profits of a flourishing textile industry and a widespread commercial network. During the fifteenth century, the provinces had been united in a personal union by the dukes of Burgundy, but there was little national consciousness until the reign of Charles V. Charles was the closest thing to a native ruler the united Netherlands had had, but he regularly sacrificed the interests of the cities to his imperial aims. This treatment created the first stirrings of nationalism in the provinces.

Under Philip II, religious conflict added to the people's sense of alienation from Habsburg rule. The Netherlands were a crossroads of ideas as well as of commerce, and the teachings of Luther and Calvin took root early there. By the 1550s, Calvinists constituted tight-knit minorities in most of the cities of the seventeen provinces.

Philip's religious policies were bound to alienate most of his Dutch and Flemish subjects. The urban-commercial culture of the region had already been out of tune with the Catholic Church because of its restrictive attitude toward business practices, and the northern urban populations had evolved a tradition of moderation in religious matters — which had permitted the rise of such groups as the Brethren of the Common Life — that was totally at odds with the king's reli-

Europe about 1560

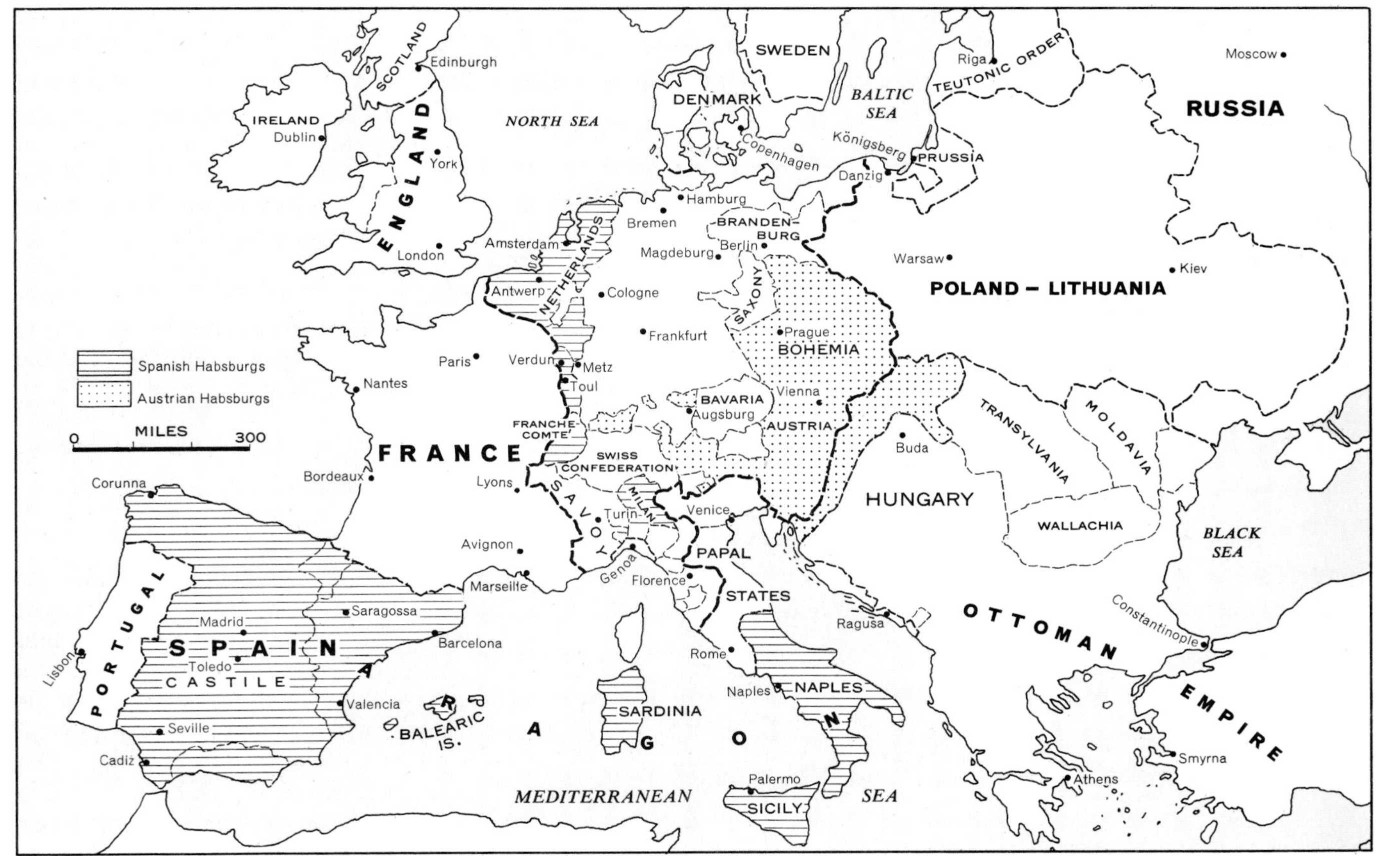

gious fanaticism. But Philip increased his problems in the Netherlands by overstepping the traditional limits of his authority. The cities had won substantial liberties from earlier dukes, but in his effort to stamp out heresy Philip ignored the traditional restraints on his authority as duke of the provinces.

In reaction, Calvinist mobs began to break images of the saints and smash stained-glass windows in Catholic churches throughout the Netherlands in 1566. Philip sent the Duke of Alva with about ten thousand Spanish regulars to suppress the iconoclasts. Alva set up what came to be called the "Council of Blood" and boasted (with some exaggeration) that in his six years' residence in the Netherlands (1567–73), he executed eighteen thousand people. His government also confiscated enormous tracts of land and imposed a ten percent sales tax that seriously injured commerce.

These measures solidified resistance, and by 1572 the Dutch had found a leader in William the Silent, Prince of Orange, the wealthiest landowner in the provinces. William lost almost every battle he fought against the Spanish, but he had political wisdom, integrity, and patience. He also had a deep hatred of religious fanaticism and was thus a foil for Philip II. Dutch nationalism increased under his leadership, helped by the actions of the Spanish themselves. In 1576, the Spanish responded to Calvinist excesses by a frightful sack of Antwerp, which became known as the "Spanish Fury." As a result of this event, the seventeen provinces rushed into an agreement to present a united front against Philip—the so-called Pacification of Ghent.

The Division of the Netherlands
1581

The union did not last long. The religious fanatics on both sides—Calvinist and Catholic—got out of control, and the moderates of both parties lost influence. The almost universal opposition to Alva and his successors gradually gave way to a savage civil war in which the well-organized Calvinists gained the upper hand. The result was that the Catholics fled south to the ten Walloon provinces that were under the protection of the Spanish troops, while the Calvinists migrated north to the Dutch regions. In 1579 the Dutch provinces formed the Union of Utrecht, which ultimately became the foundation of the United Provinces or Dutch Netherlands. These provinces declared their independence from Philip II in 1581. The southern provinces remained under Habsburg rule and eventually (in 1830) became the kingdom of Belgium.

The Rise of the United Netherlands

After the declaration of independence in 1581, the Dutch had to fight for two generations to achieve actual independence. William the Silent was assassinated in 1584, but his descendants carried on his tradition of able and disinterested leadership. The "United Provinces" were never more than the loosest of confederations, but the Dutch fought with stubbornness whenever they had to.

Philip II had countered the union by sending the Duke of Parma—one of the age's best military leaders—in 1578, but he was hampered by his inability to control the sea. The Dutch privateers—called "Sea Beggars"—controlled the English Channel and prevented the resupply of the Spanish troops by sea. The naval problems in the campaign against the Netherlands brought Spain into conflict with England (of which Philip had once been the royal consort) and in trying to deal with the English, the Spanish sent a great flotilla to clear the English Channel. The defeat of this armada ended any chance of a reconquest of the Dutch provinces. Finally, in 1648, the king of Spain formally recognized the independence of the Dutch.

The Dutch emerged from this war the most powerful commercial nation in Europe. By the early seventeenth century they were building more and better ships than anyone else—it was said that they built two thousand per year—and they were capturing more and more of the carrying trade not just of Europe but of the whole world. Antwerp, once the financial capital of Europe, was in the Spanish Netherlands; when the Dutch blocked its access to the sea, Amsterdam took its place.

The geographical extent of Dutch shipping and commercial operations was remarkable. The Dutch handled much of the grain trade of the Baltic and a large part of the carrying trade of England, France, Italy, and Portugal. When Philip II closed Lisbon to the Dutch—after he seized the crown of Portugal in 1580—the Dutch merely went directly to the source of spices in the Moluccas. In 1602 the Dutch East India Company was formed and soon established its headquarters at Batavia on the island of Java. By the middle of the seventeenth century the Dutch were in control of the richest part of the Portuguese empire in the East. In 1652 the Dutch established a colony at the Cape of Good Hope as a way station on the route to the East. A few decades earlier, they had almost ousted the Portuguese from Brazil and had

Amsterdam harbor, center of a worldwide trade (detail from an engraving by Pieter Bast, 1597).

founded a colony, called New Amsterdam, on Manhattan Island in the Hudson River (1624), which became the center for a large Dutch carrying trade in the New World. When the French and English began to develop overseas empires in the seventeenth century, they found the Dutch ahead of them all over the world.

ELIZABETHAN ENGLAND

For a few years in the middle of the sixteenth century (1554–58), England had been brought within the orbit of Habsburg power because Queen Mary of England was married to Philip II of Spain. But the accession of Elizabeth I (r. 1558–1603) to the throne after Mary's death changed everything. Elizabeth was the greatest Tudor monarch of England—the last of the direct descendants of Henry VII Tudor (r. 1485–1509). She was a cautious and moderate ruler, whose instinct was to temporize and compromise. Although she could never allow England to submit to papal authority—which had declared the marriage of her mother Ann Boleyn to Henry VIII invalid—she followed a moderate religious policy and was herself conservative in theological and liturgical matters.

She compromised and temporized in foreign policy also. She tried to avoid committing herself, kept a dozen intrigues afoot at all times to give herself an avenue of escape, and seems to have aimed at avoiding war at any cost. The chief foreign danger to the realm when Elizabeth came to the throne was from French influence in Scotland. Elizabeth's cousin, Mary Stuart, Queen of Scots, was married in 1558 to the heir of the French crown, and the alliance between the French and Scots looked as if it would become truly formidable.

But in 1559 the Scot John Knox returned from Geneva and began preaching Calvinism. His success undermined the influence of Catholicism and the French. In this instance Elizabeth made a rapid decision. She allied herself with the Calvinist party in Scotland and tried to keep the French out. By 1560, Knox, the Kirk (Scottish church), and the pro-English party were in control, and the French had lost all influence in Scotland.

While these things were happening, Mary was in France. She returned to Scotland in 1561, after the death of her husband, and hoped to reestablish Catholicism along with her own authority. But she faced unbending opposition from Knox and the Kirk, and after a second marriage that turned out badly, she was forced to abdicate in 1567. A year later Mary fled to England, where Elizabeth received her coolly, but permitted her to stay. Mary soon became the center of every French and Spanish plot against Elizabeth, who kept a watch on her, but refused to imprison or execute her. Then in 1587 Elizabeth's ministers presented incontrovertible evidence of Mary's complicity in an assassination plot, and the queen reluctantly consented to her execution.

The Indian village of Pomeiock in "Virginia" (actually North Carolina), watercolor by John White, an artist who took part in Raleigh's attempt to establish a colony at Roanoke in 1585. In his text White notes that mats and the bark of trees were used to cover the dwellings; the town was encompassed by poles instead of a wall.

The Anglo-Spanish Conflict

Although there were many causes of conflict, Philip II of Spain and Elizabeth I of England remained on good terms for over twenty years. The quarter-century of peace gave English industry and commerce a chance to expand considerably, and when the Spanish were unable to produce sufficient goods for their colonies, the English were ready to supply the deficiency. In 1562 an aggressive merchant named Sir John Hawkins was the first Englishman to carry both goods and slaves directly to the Spanish settlements in the New World. The Spanish sought to prevent such direct trade because it drew profit from their colonies without giving the mother country its due, and in 1569 Sir John and his cousin Sir Francis Drake were almost destroyed when their ships were attacked by a Spanish fleet. In revenge, Drake seized the silver shipment from Peru.

From 1577 to 1580, Drake followed Magellan's route around the world and demonstrated the vulnerability of the Spanish Empire. Meanwhile other English sailors were probing the coasts of North America in search of a Northwest Passage that would outflank the Portuguese route to the East Indies. By that time, the English were contesting the Spanish-Portuguese monopoly of overseas trade.

It was the revolt of the Netherlands,

however, that finally broke the peace between Spain and England. The English had had close commercial ties with the Low Countries for centuries. Flanders had been the first and remained the best customer for English wool and other goods. Furthermore, Englishmen sympathized with their fellow Protestants in the United Provinces, and English privateers—called "Sea Dogs"—cooperated with their Dutch counterparts against the Duke of Alva. For their part, Philip II's ambassadors in England were deeply involved in successive plots against Elizabeth's life, one of which led to the execution of Mary Stuart.

Then in 1588 Philip decided to make a bold attempt on England. He assembled an enormous fleet, the Invincible Armada, and sent it north to clear the English Channel and prepare the way for an invasion of England by the Duke of Parma. The English met the Armada with smaller, faster ships that could fire at longer range than the Spanish boats, and when the Armada anchored off Calais to await Parma, the English sent fire ships among the Armada and caused panic. The fleet fled north, where the English attacked them off Gravelines. The stormy weather of the North Sea completed what the English sailors had started, and fewer than half of the Armada struggled home by going north and west around the British Isles.

The victory gave a lift to the morale of Englishmen and Protestants everywhere. It ended all further threat of a Spanish conquest of England and also made it impossible for them to reconquer the United Provinces in the Netherlands. When a peace was finally signed in 1604, the English—with the Dutch—were nearly the equals of the Spaniards on the sea.

THE FRENCH WARS OF RELIGION

The rise of Spain and the relative peace in which England lived during Elizabeth's reign certainly had something to

Queen Elizabeth I, by Marc Geerarts. The Armada is shown in the background.

The Armada

When the Spanish Armada challenged the ancient lords of the English on their own grounds, the impending conflict took on the aspect of a judicial duel in which as was expected in such duels, God would defend the right. . . . So when the two fleets approached their appointed battleground, all Europe watched. For the spectators of both parties, the outcome, reinforced, as everyone believed, by an extraordinary tempest, was indeed decisive. The Protestants of France and the Netherlands, Germany and Scandinavia saw with relief that God was, in truth, as they had always supposed, on their side. The Catholics of France and Italy and Germany saw with almost equal relief that Spain was not, after all, God's chosen champion. From that time forward, though Spain's preponderance was to last for more than another generation, the peak of her prestige had passed. . . . So, in spite of the long, indecisive war which followed, the defeat of the Spanish Armada really was decisive. It decided that religious unity was not to be reimposed by force on the heirs of medieval Christendom, and if, in doing so, it only validated what was already by far the most probable outcome, why, perhaps that is all that any of the battles we call decisive has ever done.

From Garrett Mattingly, *The Armada* (Boston: Houghton Mifflin, 1959), pp. 400–401.

do with the weakness of France, which was the most populous and largest nation in Europe. The later sixteenth century was a period of civil and religious strife in France. From 1562 to 1593 the French tore furiously at one another while the monarchy was helpless to restore order and unity.

Although the largest nation in Europe under a single monarchy, France was really not as unified as England or Spain. The aristocracy was still powerful and turbulent, and the provinces had held on to their local customs and privileges. These problems contributed to the divisions that resulted when Calvinism began to spread. Calvin had published a version of his *Institutes* in French, and the work appealed to many Frenchmen. On the eve of the civil wars the French Calvinists—nicknamed the Huguenots—had about 2,500 churches, and, as elsewhere, they formed a small, but well-organized and aggressive minority. They also had support from people in the highest levels of French society. Arrayed against the Huguenots were strongly Catholic noble families, and, more important, the University of Paris and the *parlement* (high court) of Paris. Moreover, the French monarchy had no interest in religious change, because the Concordat of Bologna (1516) had given it control over the appointment of clergy.

Massacre of St. Bartholomew's Day, 1572 (detail from a painting by an eyewitness, François Dubois).

The wars of religion broke out after the death of King Henry II, the husband of Mary Stuart of Scotland, in 1559. Royal authority fell into the hands of the Queen Mother, Catherine de' Medici, who controlled the government during the reigns of Henry's three weak brothers—Francis II (r. 1559–60), Charles IX (r. 1560–74), and Henry III (r. 1574–89). Catherine was an astute ruler, but she lacked formal authority and could not prevent the religious fanatics on both sides from warring. Calvinists sided with discontented nobles and provinces eager to affirm local autonomy. The government and conservative nobility were on the Catholic side. Fanatics on both sides appealed for foreign support—the Huguenots to the English and Dutch, and the Catholics to Spain. England and Spain actually sent troops, mostly at the beginning and at the end of the wars.

The savage fighting devastated large areas of the country. The Catholics won most of the battles, but they could not wipe out the Huguenots. In 1572 Catholic fanatics convinced Catherine that one sharp blow would destroy the Protestants and end the strife. At two o'clock in the morning of St. Bartholomew's Day (August 23), armed bands of Catholics attacked Huguenot leaders who were in Paris for the wedding of the Huguenot Prince Henry of Navarre to the king's sister. The St. Bartholomew's Day Massacre touched off a wave of violence against Protestants that soon spread to other cities. Between late August and October, over ten thousand Protestants—three thousand in Paris alone—were murdered. The event hardened the religious hatred in France and in Europe generally. Pope Gregory XIII and Philip II of Spain hailed the massacre as progress in the fight against Protestantism. Protestants throughout Europe were horrified.

The wars dragged on for twenty years, becoming more and more confused and purposeless, until the Huguenot Henry of Navarre came to the throne as Henry IV (r. 1589–1610). Henry was the nearest male heir to the crown, but his relationship to the previous king was nonetheless quite distant, and he found it difficult to make good his claim. He faced a Catholic League that held Paris and troops of Philip II that intervened from the Netherlands under Parma. After four years of struggle, Henry decided to consolidate his control over the monarchy by renouncing his Protestantism and becoming a Catholic in 1593. He did not, however, turn against his former coreligionists, and five years later he issued the Edict of Nantes (1598), which granted freedom of conscience, freedom of worship in specified places, equal civil rights, and control of some two hundred fortified towns to the Huguenots. The Edict constituted the first official recognition that two religions could coexist without destroying the state.

THE EUROPEAN WORLD IN THE LATER SIXTEENTH CENTURY

The Status and Economic Condition of Peasants

Although much of our discussion has concentrated on cities and urban life, the overwhelming majority of sixteenth-century European society was rural. By the late sixteenth century there had been significant changes in the economic and social conditions of the peasants, but the changes were immensely different from one country to the next. In France and western Germany, the position of the peasants improved. In Spain, eastern Germany, and the eastern European countries, it deteriorated.

In most of western Europe the disastrous plagues of the fourteenth century undermined the old feudal system that had held the peasants in service to their lords. Rural communities and agriculture broke down, and after recovery began in the fifteenth century, the lords gave peasants good terms in order to induce them to cultivate their lands. Some lords had been so seriously damaged by the disasters that they had to sell their lands, and their own peasants were often among the buyers. By the later sixteenth century about 5 percent of the peasants in France and western Germany owned their own land, and about an equal percentage remained bound in serfdom. The great majority of peasants rented lands, but the law increasingly recognized the right of these lease holders to sell or grant their properties.

In 1480, the king of Castile released all peasants in his kingdom from serfdom, and this act also gave them proprietary rights in their lands. But Spanish peasants were not able to take advantage of their new position because the same government that had granted them freedom followed economic policies that undercut them. Within a couple of generations of the act of emancipation the royal government was encouraging the importation of cheap grains, and the peasants could not meet the foreign competition. The peasants of Aragon suffered doubly, since they had not been released from serfdom. By the late sixteenth century the rural populations were in a serious depression; agriculture was one of the weak elements in Philip II's Spain.

Finally, while the economic and social position of western European peasants generally improved, that of their eastern counterparts went lower and lower. The northeastern parts of Germany, which had been conquered from the Slavs in the later Middle Ages, were regions of large estates that used the superb river systems to get crops to the growing urban markets of northern Europe. Consequently, in the later sixteenth century the lords imposed a full serfdom on their peasants in order to exploit their labor. The Russian Tsar Ivan the Dread (r. 1530–84) helped his nobility engage in a similar oppression. He rewarded service to the state by granting large estates with the right to force the peasants into serfdom. Furthermore, the Russian lords had a legal right to punish serfs for wrongdoing.

The Effects of Religious Conflict

The world of Philip II and Elizabeth I was one in which religion strongly affected political and social conflicts. The conflicts themselves stemmed from economic and political changes that predated the Protestant Reformation, but the religious schism embittered every issue and drove out moderation. Some monarchies that had been progressing toward consolidation of their power — like France and Germany — were weakened by the religious strife, while others — like Spain and England — were strengthened. In Spain, embattled Catholicism rallied around Charles V and Philip II. In England, patriotism and Protestantism became associated after Queen Mary (r. 1553 – 58) tried to reverse the reformation begun by her father, Henry VIII.

Just as the troubles of the Great Schism in the Church (1378 – 1417) had stimulated thinkers to create a new constitutional theory of the Church — conciliarism — so the wars of religion spurred important new works on political theory. French theorists first created a doctrine of political obligation that justified rebellion against constituted authority on certain grounds. Protestants in Germany, the Netherlands, and France relied on such theories in arguing that they were justified in rebelling against monarchies that sought to impose a false religion on them. After a generation of religious civil war, French writers like Jean Bodin (1530 – 96) created a new secular theory of political sovereignty that could justify obedience to properly constituted authority without appeal to religious doctrine. This theory became one of the bases of modern political thought.

The religious passion of the age also spawned a terrifying witch-craze in Europe. The craze began in the mid-sixteenth century and lasted until the middle of the next century. Before it ended, thousands of persons — mostly women — had been burned or hanged as witches. The horror seems to have begun when the religious passions created by the Protestant and Counter Reformations mixed with the ancient, pre-Christian superstitions and practices that had survived the Middle Ages. Almost every community had its wizard and cunning woman, to whom neighbors turned when the ministrations of priest or physician did not avail. From time to time during the Middle Ages people like these had been convicted of malevolent witchcraft — that is, of attempting to use occult means to inflict death or disease on others.

During the sixteenth century the number of people accused of witchcraft increased dramatically. In communities throughout Europe accusations of witchcraft triggered chain reactions of arrests. The accused were tortured into confessing the most fantastical acts — of participating in obscene "witches' sabbaths" and of diabolical schemes to harm their neighbors. They were also forced to name their accomplices in these pacts with the Devil, and so one arrest led to others. Often, dozens, even hundreds, of victims in a single community were led to the stake.

By 1660 the witch-panics were subsiding and by 1700 they had all but disappeared. It is hard to say why they ended. Religious warfare ended in the mid-seventeenth century and passions cooled as religious toleration became the normal public policy in Europe. Perhaps more important, the development of a modern scientific outlook — which, among other ways, manifested itself in a dispute over the credibility of miracles — reduced belief in invisible spirits and occult forces among the educated leadership of society. Without the support of these elite elements, the hunt for witches gradually ended. The century-long witch-craze was one of the most tragic episodes in the history of European civilization.

Against the backdrop of religious fanaticism and strife, late sixteenth-century society produced a golden age of art and literature. In painting, the Dutch Frans Hals (*ca.* 1580 – 1666) and

Rembrandt van Rijn (1606–69) and the Spanish El Greco (*ca.* 1548–1614) and Velasquez (1599–1660) brought the Renaissance tradition to a grand fruition. In literature, Shakespeare (*ca.* 1564–1616) and Spencer (*ca.* 1552–99) in England, Cervantes (1547–1616) in Spain, and Vondel (1587–1679) in France created works that to this day remain the jewels of their national literary traditions. During its time of troubles, France produced three writers who have profoundly influenced the French mind: Montaigne (1533–92), Descartes (1596–1650), and Pascal (1623–62). That such genius flourished in the age of the Reformations is an indication that just to tell the story of wars and massacres is to give an incomplete account of the life of the society of the period.

Suggestions for Further Reading

On the geographical discoveries and their technological basis see J. H. Parry, *The Age of Reconnaissance* (1963), and C. Cipolla, *Guns and Sails in the Early Phase of the European Expansion* (1966).

On the effect of the discoveries on Europe, see J. H. Elliott, *The Old World and the New* (1970); H. H. Hart, *The Road to the Indies* (1950); J. B. Brebner, *The Explorers of North America, 1492–1806* (1933); and A. P. Newton, *The European Nations in the West Indies, 1493–1688* (1933). The best account of Columbus is S. E. Morrison, *Admiral of the Ocean Sea,* 2 vols. (1942). For an overall view, see Morrison's *The European Discovery of America* (1971). On the early Spanish colonies, see C. H. Haring, *The Spanish Empire in America* (1947); L. Hanke, *The Spanish Struggle for Justice in the Conquest of America* (1949); and R. Cameron, *Viceroyalties of the West* (1968).

On Spain in the sixteenth century, see J. H. Elliott, *Imperial Spain, 1469–1716* (1964); R. Trevor Davies, *The Golden Century of Spain, 1501–1621* (1937); *Spain in Decline, 1621–1700* (1956); J. H. Parry, *The Spanish Theory of Empire in the Sixteenth Century* (1940); E. J. Hamilton, *American Treasure and the Price Revolution, 1501–1650* (1934); and G. Mattingly, *The Spanish Armada* (1959).

The best history of the Dutch rebellion in P. Geyl, *The Revolt of the Netherlands, 1555–1609* (1932) and *The Netherlands Divided, 1609–1648* (1936). See also C. V. Wedgewood, *William the Silent* (1944), and C. Wilson, *Queen Elizabeth and the Revolt of the Netherlands* (1970).

The wealth of scholarly books on Elizabethan England includes J. Neale, *Queen Elizabeth I* (1952); C. Read's thorough biographies, *Mr. Secretary Walsingham,* 3 vols. (1925) and *Mr. Secretary Cecil* (Lord Burghley), 2 vols. (1955, 1960); A. L. Rowse, *The England of Elizabeth* (1950) and *The Expansion of Elizabethan England* (1955); and J. A. Williamson, *The Age of Drake,* 3rd ed. (1952).

On sixteenth-century France, see J. W. Salmon, *Society in Crisis: France in the Sixteenth Century* (1975); J. E. Neale, *The Age of Catherine de' Medici* (1943); H. Pearson, *Henry of Navarre* (1963); J. W. Thompson, *The Wars of Religion in France, 1559–1576* (1909); F. C. Palm, *Calvinism and the Religious Wars* (1932); A. J. Grant, *The Huguenots* (1934); W. F. Church, *Constitutional Thought in Sixteenth Century France* (1941); and N. Z. Davis's essays in *Society and Culture in Early Modern France* (1975).

	1648			1700		
SOUTHWEST ASIA AND AFRICA	**1652** Dutch found Cape Colony ***ca.* 1700** Rise of Ashanti, West Africa				**1737–47** Nadir Shah, decline of Safavid Empire	
EUROPE	**1660–88** Stuart Restoration **1661–1715** Louis XIV	**1683** Turks besiege Vienna **1685** Edict of Nantes revoked **1685–1750** Johann Sebastian Bach **1687** Newton's Law of Gravitation	**1688** Glorious Revolution **1689–1725** Peter the Great **1690** Locke, *Two Treatises of Civil Government*	**1701–14** War of Spanish Succession **1715–74** Louis XV **1720** South Sea Bubble **1723–42** Robert Walpole	**1740–80** Maria Theresa **1740–86** Frederick the Great **1756–63** Seven Years' War **1756–91** Wolfgang Amadeus Mozart	**1762** Rousseau, *The Social Contract* **1762–96** Catherine the Great **1769** James Watt's first steam engine **1770–1827** Ludwig van Beethoven
SOUTH AND SOUTHEAST ASIA	**1653** Taj Mahal completed **1690** British found Calcutta				**1751** French control Deccan **1757** Battle of Plassey **1773** Regulation Act	
EAST ASIA	**1662–1722** Emperor Kangxi ***ca.* 1675–1725** Golden age of Edo urban culture, Japan			**1736–95** Emperor Qianlong	**1796–1804** White Lotus Rebellion	
THE AMERICAS AND PACIFIC		**1664** British seize New Amsterdam		**1728** Bering explores Alaska **1756–63** French and Indian War	**1765** Stamp Act **1768–80** Cook explores Pacific Ocean **1773** Boston Tea Party **1774** Quebec Act	

Ashanti wood carving.

Napoleon, 1800.

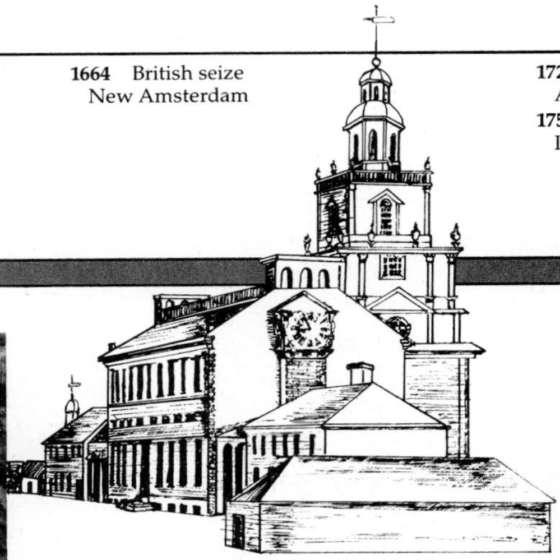

Independence Hall, Philadelphia, 1776.

East India Company merchant, by an Indian artist.

Charles II of England, 1660-85.

Emblem of the Sun King, Louis XIV.

	1815
	1805–48 Mohammed Ali founds dynasty in Egypt **1806** British control Cape Colony **1807** Slavery abolished in British Empire
1776 Smith, *Wealth of Nations* **1789** French Revolution begins	**1798** Malthus, *Essay on the Principle of Population* **1799** Napoleon becomes First Consul **1804–14** Napoleonic Empire
1784 East India Act **1786–93** Cornwallis in Bengal **1796** British conquer Ceylon	
1775–83 American Revolution **1776** US Declaration of Independence **1788** British colonize Australia **1803** Louisiana Purchase	**1807–30** Latin American wars for independence

Chinese fan painting, *ca.* 1700.

***Fuji above Storm,* by Hokusai, 1760-1849.**

25 Three Islamic Empires

During the period when Europeans were embarking on their first great thrust overseas, the world of Islam flourished and expanded. The century that saw the capture of Constantinople (1453) was also marked by the expansion of Islam in Sumatra and Java at the opposite end of Asia, as well as gains in Africa. Most impressive, however, were three great empires—the Safavid (1501–1722), the Ottoman (1453–1918), and the Mughal (1526–1739). They were by far the most powerful Muslim states and even after their demise they left permanent imprints on major regions of Eurasia.

All three empires began as regimes of military conquest and benefited from the introduction of gunpowder. Culturally, Persian literature enjoyed as much prestige in Delhi and Istanbul as it did in Isfahan. All three partook of a common religious heritage. Yet local conditions and local traditions in each area ensured that the differences between these three states would be at least as great as those distinguishing their European contemporaries. Furthermore, Islam was no more monolithic than was Christianity. The Shi'ite empire on the Iranian plateau at the very center of the Islamic world was regarded with hostility by its Sunni neighbors.

THE SAFAVID EMPIRE

The Safavids originated as hereditary leaders of a Sufi order in eastern Azerbaijan, which recruited its members from the pastoral and warlike tribes of the region known as the Turkomans (Persian for "little Turks") to differentiate them from the Ottoman Turks. During the fifteenth century their Sufi mysticism was increasingly blended with Shi'ism, the belief that Ali, Muhammad's cousin and son-in-law, was Muhammad's legitimate successor. The order became increasingly militant, and its leader combined spiritual and secular authority. "Inwardly, following the example of the shaykhs and men of God, he walked the path of spiritual guidance and defence of the faith; outwardly, he was a leader on a throne in the manner of princes." This quote refers to a fifteenth century Safavid who, not uncharacteristically, lost his life in battle.

The fighting qualities of the warriors and the momentum of the movement enabled Ismail I to prevail over rival Turkoman groups and have himself proclaimed Shah in Tabriz in 1501. He then expanded his Empire west to what were to become the furthest reaches of the Safavid Empire. After that he turned east where the Uzbegs expanded their power by having seized Samarkand in 1500. Just as the Safavids persecuted Sunnis many of whom fled east or west, the Uzbegs did not tolerate Shi'ites so that on both sides religious differences reinforced territorial ambitions. In the ensuing war Ismail I defeated the Uzbegs in a major battle (1510), killing their leader whose skull he turned into a drinking cup by pouring liquid gold into it. Then he had the rest of the corpse stuffed with straw and delivered to the Ottoman ruler.

Even without this provocation, the emergence of a militant Shi'ite state in eastern Asia Minor posed a threat to the Ottomans, and war was inevitable. At the battle of Chaldiran (1514) the Ottomans won a decisive victory in good part because the Safavids refused to employ artillery because they considered it cowardly. The Empire survived this disaster largely by adopting a scorched-earth policy which repeatedly protected it against Ottoman invasions as well as Uzbeg attacks. Tabriz as well as Baghdad were lost to the Ottomans, but the state held out until under Shah Abbas I, known as the Great (r. 1588–1629), there was a major resurgence of Safavid power.

The early Safavid state was a theocracy based on Twelver Shi'ism, made the state religion by Ismail I. The belief was that secret teachings had been passed down by Muhammad to Ali and then to twelve successors (imams), the last of whom disappeared in the mid-870s but is expected to reappear one day. In contrast to the Sunnis who depend on the Koran, the traditions, and the holy law as understood by community consensus, Shi'ites have a new source of truth in the twelve imams and those who claim to represent them, thus giving Shi'ism greater flexibility than its rival. They also hold great bitterness towards the supposed murderers of Ali and the imams and express it in the mourning of Hussain (Ali's son and Muhammad's grandson), the observance of which is the

Hodgson on the Sixteenth Century

The sixteenth century undeniably marks the peak of Muslim political power, taken all in all. How the Muslim powers might have fared measured against China we cannot know, but one of the three empires, the Ottoman, could alone defeat any actual alliance of Christian European powers; whereas among themselves the empires treated each other as diplomatic equals and, in such clashes as they had, showed themselves to be not far from each other's equals in power. The Uzbeg state in the Syr and Oxus basins . . . was not far behind them in power; and the Sharifian empire of Morocco was not negligible. Two or three sultanates in southern India and other Muslim powers to the south or to the north, though they sometimes had to admit the superior greatness of one of the major empires, were themselves as strong as most Occidental powers. So far as there was any genuinely "international" law in the world in that period, it was the body of protocol and customs that governed relations among the far-flung Muslim states; and if one had to speak of an "international" language in the world then, it would have been not the relatively parochial French or Latin but Persian, the language of most of their correspondence.

Marshall G. S. Hodgson, *The Venture of Islam: Conscience and History in a World Civilization* (Chicago: The University of Chicago Press, 1974), vol. 3, p. 47.

Three Islamic Empires

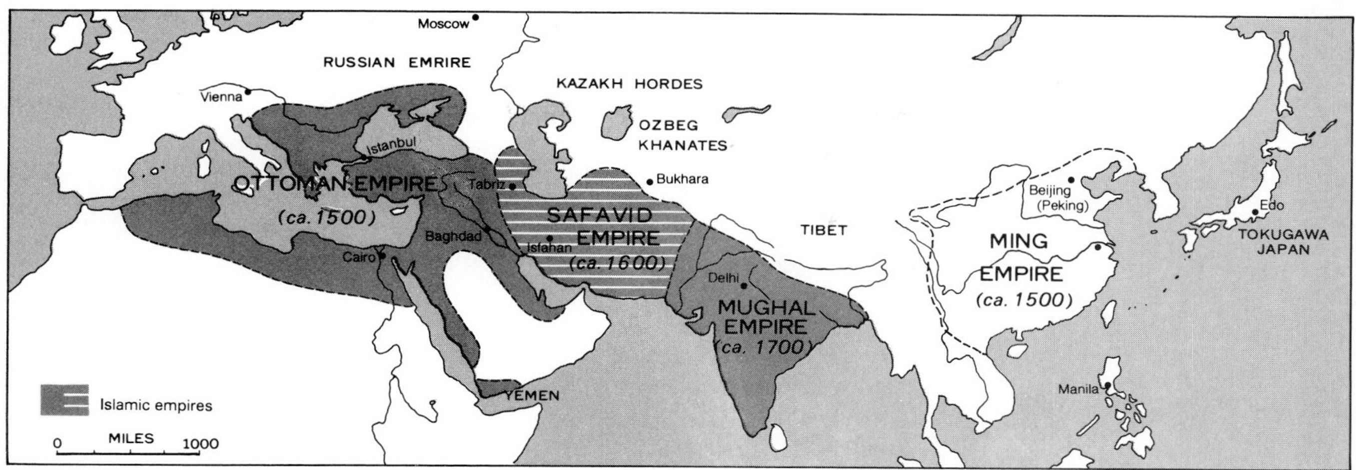

central ceremony of Shi'ism. As part of the ritual performed on the day Hussain died, the Sunnis are formally cursed. The commemoration of Hussain's death is the most important day on the Shi'ite religious calendar.

The religious authority of Shah Ismail I as the head of the Sufi order was immensely strengthened by his claim to be the incarnation of the Twelfth Imam. Furthermore, he also drew on ancient Persian traditions of divine kingship, maintaining that the ruler is God's shadow on earth. This was an imposing theocratic edifice, but it was badly damaged by the defeat at Chaldiran, which brought the Shah's divinity into question.

The efficacy of the Shah's rule depended in large part on his ability to utilize and balance two very disparate groups of men. On the one hand, there were the Turkoman warriors, called Qizilbash, "red heads," because they wore red turbans with twelve folds in honor of the twelve imams. This military elite had little sympathy for civilian Iranian officials, heirs to the classical tradition of Persian learning and administration. Ismail I himself was only partly successful in reconciling these two groups, and upon his death in 1524 the Qizilbash took control for ten years during the minority of Shah Tahmasp (r. 1524–76). To make matters worse, the Turkoman chiefs were themselves torn by rivalries and discord.

Despite internal problems and repeated invasions from east and west, the state survived. Furthermore, during Shah Tahmasp's long reign a beginning was made in strengthening the regime by utilizing the descendants of Georgian, Circassian, and Armenian prisoners captured in campaigns conducted in the Caucasus. Such campaigns provided battle experience and loot for Safavid armies, were justified as holy wars, and resulted in numerous captives—one particular expedition netted thirty thousand. The children, brought up as Muslims and Persianized, had the status of "slaves of the royal household." Neither Turkoman nor Iranian and with ties to neither community, these *ghulams* (a Persian word corresponding to Arabic *mamluk*) were solely dependent on and loyal to the Shah.

The Safavids at Their Height Under Abbas the Great

When Shah Abbas succeeded to the throne in 1588, his first problem was to put an end to the Qizilbash dominance. He accomplished this partly by strength of character but also by realizing the full potential of the *ghulams* as a third force in the state.

The Safavid Empire 1500–1722

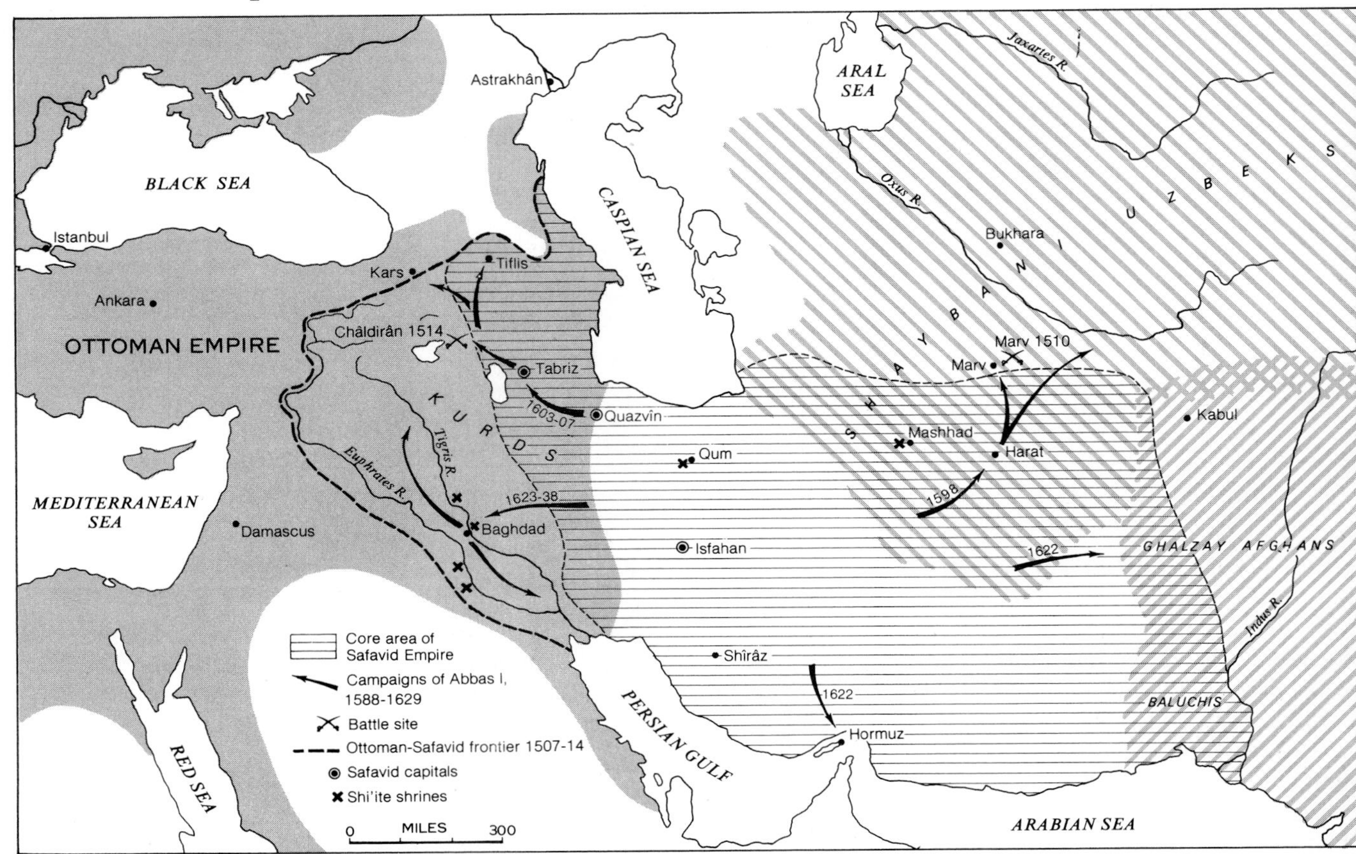

In a significant departure from tradition, Abbas created a standing army always ready to go into action. At its heart were *ghulam* troops organized into cavalry regiments of ten to fifteen thousand men each and supplied with muskets as well as traditional weapons. There were also corps of Iranian musketeers, an artillery corps, and *ghulam* bodyguard of three thousand. Further to keep the Qizilbash in line, he transferred groups belonging to one tribe into the districts of others, placed tribes under officers from other tribes, and also transferred turbulent tribes to frontier areas. The success of his policies was apparent not only in the stability of his internal control but also in victories over both Uzbegs and Ottomans, enabling him to bring back into the Empire much lost territory.

Maintenance of the armies was expensive as was the building program undertaken by the Shah in his new capital of Isfahan. A major source of income, the crown lands were greatly expanded by the addition of territories previously taxed by local chiefs who had been allowed to retain most of the revenue in exchange for fielding armies when called upon. The crown lands were placed under stewards and bailiffs responsible to imperial comptrollers, most frequently *ghulam* without local ties, members of the state bureaucracy in which career advancement was determined by merit, not birth.

The economic mainstays of the Empire were the cattle of the Turkoman tribes and the crops of the Iranian peasants, but Abbas did all he could to encourage trade. He levied a toll on caravans, but built numerous caravansaries (inns to accommodate caravans) where travelers could stay as long as they wished without paying. Since caravans, particularly camel caravans, were slow, many such establishments were necessary. According to European travelers, accommodations as well as the security of travel in the Safavid Empire compared favorably to those offered by the Ottomans.

European traders were welcomed by the Shah. A sizable portion of the royal revenues came from the Shah's lucrative monopoly on silk, a commodity in which Iran remained the leader during the sixteenth and seventeenth centuries. The trade in silk was conducted by Armenian merchants who lived in their own community and benefited from Abbas's policy of religious toleration. Among European merchants residing in Isfahan were members of the English and Dutch East India Companies, and the Shah shrewdly enlisted the English to oust the Portuguese from Hormuz. Commercially more important than the Persian Gulf route, however, was the trade route that crossed the Caspian Sea and then proceeded up the Volga, then west across the Ukraine and on to Europe, thus circumventing the territory of the Safavids' Ottoman enemy.

Shah Abbas's lasting monument was Isfahan, which he turned from an obscure provincial town into one of the world's great cities inhabited by about a million people. It was a city of wide streets, trees so numerous that a French visitor felt he was in a forest, and fine buildings decorated with tiles that still today have not lost their luster. The center of activity was the Maidan, a great square measuring some twenty acres. It was usually filled with booths, tents, and the wares of petty merchants spread along the ground, but it was cleared for special occasions and for polo, a game which the Shah himself played with gusto and skill; whenever he hit the ball, a group of trumpeters responded with a fanfare.

Among the city's amenities were numerous public baths. On the Maidan storytellers, acrobats, and jugglers provided entertainment, and there were many restaurants, taverns (some doubling as brothels), and coffeehouses. Most of the taverns were thick with tobacco smoke, which became so pervasive that the Shah tried to discourage smoking. Hoping to teach by example, he himself gave up smoking. When that had little effect, he tried offering his courtiers a hookah (waterpipe) filled with horse dung. When a courtier politely praised the resulting smoke, the Shah is reported to have replied, "Cursed be the drug that cannot be distinguished from horse dung."

Sixteenth-century Arabic map of the world.

A great general, Abbas himself led his troops on forced marches to surprise the enemy. He was also an astute and ruthless politician: he blinded his brothers so they could never contest the throne, and to avoid the prophecy that the Shah would be assassinated in 1622 (the one thousandth year anniversary of the hegira) he abdicated just long enough to have his hapless substitute killed. He liked to go among the people in mufti to find out for himself what they were saying and on occasion to ferret out misdeeds. He once caught a butcher and a baker cheating on weight. In punishment the Shah had the butcher roasted on a spit and the baker baked in an oven.

Abbas was a generous and enthusiastic patron of the arts. Calligraphy has always had a very special place in the world of Islam, and Abbas too fostered this art, once even holding a candle so that his favorite calligrapher could work. Painting flourished and the art of illustrating manuscripts reached a classic high. A new realistic style of painting also emerged, starting a trend that continued for another two centuries. Carpet weaving reached a new

Palace scene, early Safavid, celebrating a famous fifth-century Persian king.

level of artistic excellence and became organized on a national scale. There were also fine achievements in textiles, metal work, and ceramics. The ceramics industry was spurred on by Abbas's import of three hundred Chinese potters together with their families.

Nor did Abbas neglect literature. He was generous to poets although many of the best Persian poets throughout the Safavid period worked in India, attracted by the munificence of the Mughals. The vigor of intellectual and religious life was reflected in the work of a number of thinkers notably including Mullah Sadra (conventional name for Muhamam ibn-Ibraham Sadr al-Din Shirazi, 1571/72–1640; "mullah" means "teacher") author of over fifty books. Writing in Arabic, the language of theology and philosophy, Mullah Sadra worked out a synthesis of religion and philosophy, a harmonization of revelation, reason, and intuition that was spread to India and prevailed in Persia as the most influential stream of thought for three and a half centuries. Safavid scholars also continued to excel in such traditional fields of excellence as mathematics, music, medicine, alchemy, and astronomy.

Decline of the Safavids

Some of Shah Abbas's measures, while immediately beneficial to the state, were harmful in the long run. For example, the extension of the crown lands at the expense of local chiefs brought in needed revenue but also placed provinces under men whose interest in maximizing tax revenue was not matched by concern for the welfare of the local people. Or again, the measures taken to undermine the power of the Qizilbash also weakened the military strength of the Empire. And, at the very heart of the system, Abbas made a fateful decision concerning the training of princes. Traditionally, the Shah's sons were sent out to govern provinces under the guidance of experienced guardians, thus gaining experience in governing but also posing a danger to smooth succession. To avoid the latter, Abbas had them confined to the harem, but this allowed palace women, eunuchs, and others connected with the harem to have great political influence even as it tended to turn out princes poorly equipped for ruling a great state. After Abbas I's death in 1629 until the end of the dynasty in 1722 there was only one capable ruler, Shah Abbas II (1632–66). After Abbas I, overtaxed people had to support an extravagant, ineffective political establishment.

Along with the deterioration of the Shah's government came an erosion of the state's ideological foundations. Shi'ism remained the state religion, but no longer was the Shah revered as a spiritual leader. In the beginning, the ulama, many of whom were men from Syria or Bahrain sponsored by the Safavids, had been the state's loyal supporters, but after the death of Abbas I they increasingly became its most vehement critics. *Mujtahids,* authorities on Muslim doctrine and law, taught that they, not the Shah, were the legitimate representatives of the imam, and the ordinary people placed their faith in them.

The fragmentation of religious authority was paralleled by the reemergence of local power groups as people focused their loyalty on their own ethnic, tribal, or linguistic community and on local leaders. It was an already debilitated state that fell in 1722 when Afghan tribesmen captured Isfahan while Russians and Ottomans seized the opportunity to expand their own territories at Persia's expense.

Nadir Shah and the Aftermath

The triumph of the Afghans was short-lived, for in 1736 they were defeated by Nadir Shah (r. 1737–47), a Turkoman of one of the Qizilbash tribes, who became the last of the Central Asian conquerors with a reputation for brutality reminiscent of Timur's. Through force of arms, at the height of his power, his rule extended from the Tigris River and the Caucasus Mountains to Delhi, but he did not build a lasting state. After his death, Iran was badly divided and in a state close to anarchy until Agha Muhammad (r. 1779–96, proclaimed Shah in 1796) established the Qajar dynasty with its capital at Tehran. He too was of Qizilbash background and sought, unsuccessfully, to revive Safavid glory. Nevertheless, he at least left Iran sufficiently united and strong enough to survive the imperialistic pressures of the nineteenth century. At the same time, the most abiding legacy of the Safavid period was the identification of Iran with the Shi'ite faith.

The location of the Safavid Empire insured that events there would have repercussions both east and west. For example, Shah Tahmasp gave refuge to the second Mughal emperor, and Nadir Shah's sack of Delhi put an end to effective Mughal power. For the Ottomans, who both preceded and outlasted the Safavids, the presence of a hostile and to them heretical state to their east not only presented a formidable frontier problem but also an impenetrable barrier cutting them off from their fellow Sunnis farther east.

THE OTTOMAN EMPIRE

The Ottoman was the most extensive, diverse, and long lasting of the three Islamic empires. Originating as a small warrior state on the frontier of the Islamic world in western Asia Minor, it grew by military conquest until it encompassed territory on three continents while its navy controlled the Black Sea and, for a time, was paramount in the Mediterranean.

The capture of Constantinople in 1453 signaled the transformation of the Ottoman state into a full-fledged empire, but by that time a century had already passed since the Ottomans first crossed the Dardanelles and entered Europe. Actually, the conquest of Constantinople would most likely have occurred fifty years earlier had the Ottomans not been confronted with Timur to the east.

After Mehemmed II, the Conqueror (r. 1451–81), took Constantinople, he turned its churches, including Hagia Sophia, into mosques, renamed the city Istanbul, and made it his capital. Turning the Black Sea into an Ottoman lake, he forced all the states along its shores to become tributaries and accepted the sultan of the Crimea as a vassal. In the Balkans he reconfirmed Ottoman control over Serbia and Greece, while his naval power extended into the Adriatic. In 1480 the Turks even seized a port in southern Italy. Mehemmed II also fought against the Turkoman tribes of central and eastern Asia Minor and defeated a tribal confederacy.

After the dramatic and strenuous conquests of Mehemmed, the empire enjoyed a thirty years' respite under his successor, but with Selim I, the Inexorable (r. 1512–20), expansion was resumed. Selim ruthlessly enforced Sunni orthodoxy among the Turkish tribesmen and is reported as having killed 40,000 Shi'ites. Alarmed by the growth of the Safavid state, he made war on Ismail I and won the decisive

Mehemmed II, ruler of the Turks when they took Constantinople in 1453.

Sultan Selim II.

victory at Chaldiron (1514). Turning south he then destroyed the Mamluk Sultanate in campaigns during 1515–16, bringing Syria and Egypt into the Empire. At this time he also gained the submission of the shariff of Mecca thus achieving suzerainty over Islam's holiest sites as well as the heartland of the old caliphate. Muslims widely looked to the Ottomans for protection from attack by Christians, and not in vain, for in 1517 a Turkish admiral defeated a Portuguese fleet sent to the Red Sea to attack Jidda and Mecca. In 1519 Selim added Algeria to the Ottoman domains.

Selim I left a great empire, but his son Suleiman I, known as the Lawgiver to the Turks but called the Magnificent in Europe (r. 1520–66), made it even greater. To the southeast he conquered Baghdad, the old capital of the Abbasid caliphate, and annexed Iraq. Further south, along the Red Sea, he added Yemen and Bahrain. In the north he extended the Empire to include most of the old kingdom of Hungary and in 1529 threatened Vienna. Further afield, he subdued the coastal region of North Africa between Algeria and Egypt, thus controlling the southern coast of the Mediterranean with the exception of Morocco. Indeed, the entire Arab world, with the exception only of Morocco and a few desert strongholds, was under the Ottomans.

Meanwhile, the Ottomans clashed with the Portuguese not only on the coast of Africa but even sent a fleet and artillery in 1558 to Southeast Asia where they supported the Muslim Sultanate of Acheh, located on Sumatra, in an unsuccessful attempt to take Malacca from the Portuguese. Much more seriously, the Turks also failed to expel the Portuguese from Hormuz. In the Mediterranean, after capturing Rhodes early in Suleiman's reign, they were unable to capture Malta from the Knights of St. John, who had been expelled from Rhodes. Another development that had serious future implications was Russian expansion along the Volga where Kazan and Astrakhan, which had been under friendly Muslim rule, were lost.

Under Selim II (r. 1566–74), known to his people as the Yellow but to Europeans as the Sot, the Ottomans won a major victory when they conquered Cyprus in 1571, but the Ottoman threat stimulated an alliance between Spain, Venice, and the Papacy that won a major victory in the Battle of Lepanto (October 1571) in which over four hundred ships took part and 59,000 men lost their lives. This great triumph gave an enormous boost to European morale and self-confidence even though the Ottomans quickly rebuilt their navy.

For the remainder of the sixteenth century and the first sixty years of the seventeenth century, the Empire was largely on the defensive. In 1606 the Ottomans even signed a treaty with their traditional antagonist, the Habsburg Emperor, in which the Sultan recognized that monarch as an equal. Then, in the last third of the seventeenth century, came a final reassertion of military expansionism with the seizure of Crete (1669) and the Ukraine (1670s). In 1683 a Turkish army again laid siege to Vienna. However, this attack on Vienna was the last; the Empire never regained the power to go on the offensive.

Sultan Suleiman's Self-Image

Sultan of the Sultans of East and West. Lord born under a fortunate conjunction of the kingdoms of the Romans and Persians and Arabs, hero of all that is, pride of the arena of earth and time: of the Mediterranean and the Black Sea, and the glorified Kaaba and the illumined Medine, the noble Jerusalem and the throne of Egypt, that rarity of the age, and the province of Yemen, and Aden and Sabam and Baghdad the abode of rectitude, and Basra and al-Hasa and the Cities of Nushiravan, and the lands of Algiers and Azerbaijan, the steppes of the Kipchak and the land of the Tartars, and Kurdistan and Luristan, and of the countries of Rumelia and Anatolia and Karaman and Wallachia and Moldavia and Hungary all together, and many more kingdoms and land might of esteem: Sultan and Padishas. . . .

Quoted in Raphaele Lewis, *Everyday Life in Ottoman Turkey* (New York: G. P. Putnam's Sons, 1971), pp. 196–97.

The Ottoman Empire 1512–1718

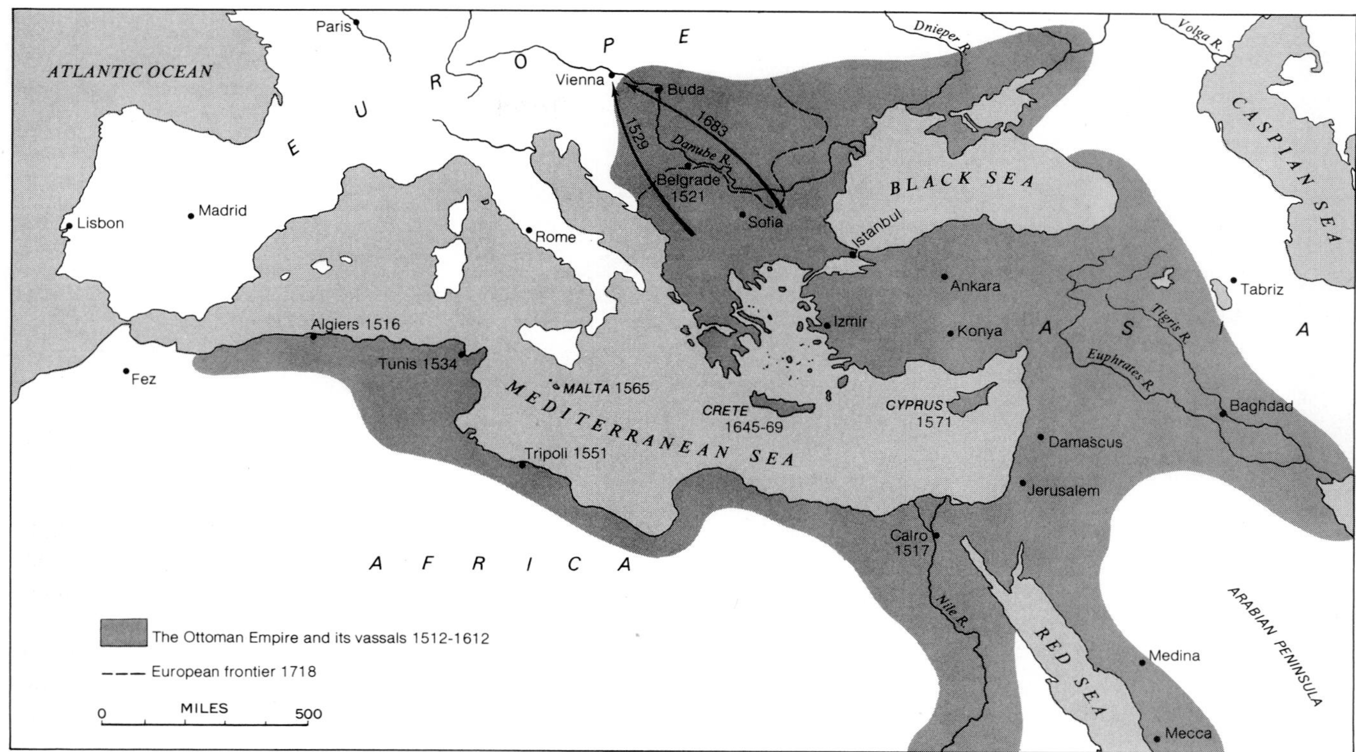

The Ottoman State

At the apex of Ottoman state and society stood the Sultan, in theory the all-powerful, God-designated protector of the people, his "flock"—both Muslims and others. Succession was hereditary, and a single dynasty of sultans continued until the establishment of modern Turkey in 1923. Turkish tradition provided no definite rules concerning which prince should be the heir, holding instead that God's will would be expressed in the outcome of the struggle over the succession. Since the defeated princes often fled to hostile states where they continued to pose a threat, it became customary for the winner to have his brothers killed, a practice legitimized by Mehemmed the Conqueror:

> To whichever of my sons the Sultanate may be vouchsafed, it is proper for him to put his brothers to death, to preserve the order of the world. Most of the ulema allow this. Let them therefore act accordingly.

This fratricide came to an end after Mehemmed III (r. 1595–1603) had nineteen brothers executed when he mounted the throne. Unfortunately, the sultans also abandoned another traditional practice: Up to that time they, like the early Safavids, had sent the princes out to gain experience as governors but now the princes were confined in a two story "cage" on the harem grounds. There they grew up in total isolation from the real world.

Originally the Ottomans were warriors in the holy cause of Islam, and the continued prestige of the military is reflected in the bifurcation of society into a class of subjects and a military class *(askeri)*, which included not only soldiers but also men who served the sultan in civilian capacity. The main military force in the early Empire was the cavalry. While some cavalrymen *(sipahis)* served in a standing force in the capital as part of the sultan's slave household, others were provincial freemen who received grants of land exempt from taxation in order to main-

Fifteenth-century Turkish miniature depicting an Asiatic bowman. Unencumbered by armor he could move swiftly on his small, strong horse.

tain and equip themselves. Those receiving large grants were also responsible for supplying a set number of troops whenever they were called on to join a military expedition. In addition, a supplementary force of irregular cavalry also took part in Ottoman campaigns. In lieu of payment, these men were given the right to pillage enemy lands.

Most feared was the Ottoman infantry, the dreaded Janissaries, highly trained and well-disciplined soldiers equipped with firearms. This was a slave force recruited through the *devshirme,* a system of collecting boys from the rural Christian population of the Balkans. An average of one boy from every forty households was taken, but boys practicing certain trades, only sons, orphans, and the unfit were exempt. These levies took place at intervals of from four to seven years as needed. The boys were usually between eight and eighteen. Once drafted, all ties with their Christian background were severed. Circumsized and converted to Islam, they frequently became fervent Muslims. The great majority, about 90 percent, were hired out to Turkish farmers so that they would grow strong working the land, learn Turkish, and become versed in Islam. When they were physically and mentally ready, they were brought to the capital to join the Janissary force which grew from around 6,000 men during the time of Mehemmed II to 12,000 under Suleiman and reached 37,000 by 1609.

Portrait of a Janissary, by Gentile Bellini (*ca.* 1480).

The most promising boys were selected for palace service and subjected to a long process of training and selection. The most capable and fortunate were educated to read and write Arabic (the language of religion), Persian (the language of literature), and Ottoman Turkish (the language of administration). They were educated in the Koran and the ancillary religious disciplines and taught music, calligraphy, and mathematics. They were also instructed in such martial skills as horsemanship, wrestling, and archery and generally prepared to enter the elite and serve in high administrative office, including that of the grand vizier (wazir in Arabic), the Sultan's deputy. Like the "slaves of the royal household" who served Shah Abbas the Great, the Turkish slaves occupied the highest positions in the military and civil hierarchies. They enjoyed high status, could own property, and had many of the rights of freemen, but their lives and property were for the Sultan to dispose of as he liked. In the early years of the *devshirme* parents tried to bribe officials to release their sons, but as the advantages of this service became apparent others tried to buy their way in.

The grand vizier headed a complex bureaucracy that extended from the capital into the provinces. In Istanbul the Chancellery handled most government business with the exception of matters under the purview of the Finance Division. Important questions were decided in the Imperial Council *(divan)* under the direction of the grand vizier, and the Council also heard personal grievances, for Islamic tradition attached great importance to the ruler's role as upholder of justice. At times over five hundred petitioners waited in the courtyard and were served a midday meal. Although he acted in the name of the sultan, the grand vizier eventually, in the absence of a vigorous sultan, became so important that his residence was regarded as the real center of government.

Provinces were placed under a civilian governor, a high official who conducted his own council, a miniature version of the one in Istanbul.One vital function of provincial government was the collection of taxes for only about one-third of the land was granted tax free to the *sipahis.* Powerful as he was, the governor's authority was far from absolute, for he did not control the military forces in the provinces nor did he have the last word in legal matters. He did not control the provincial *quadis,* judges who could and frequently did appeal to Istanbul to overrule a governor's decision.

The *quadis* belonged to the *ulema,* for in the Ottoman state there was no distinction between religion and law, and they enforced the sultan's edicts as well as Muslim law *(Sharia).* In contrast to the Safavid Empire in which the *ulema* came to oppose the state, in the Ottoman case the religious and political authorities identified with and supported each other. Parallel to the secular political hierarchy was a religious hierarchy headed by the Shaykh al-Islam, the sultan's deputy for spiritual matters who was equal in rank to the grand vizier. Although the *quadis* were appointed by the sultan and served at his pleasure, they were selected according to the advice of the Shaykh al-Islam. Furthermore, he was the ultimate interpreter of Muslim law as codified under Suleiman (hence his appelation as Lawgiver), and as such could decide the gravest issues of state including the legality of a declaration of war, the deposition of a sultan, or the legitimacy of new rules and regulations.

Education and scholarship, like religion and law, were in the hands of the *ulema;* Istanbul's most splendid buildings were its mosques and colleges *(madrasas),* which offered instruction in grammar, logic, metaphysics, geometry, astronomy, and in the case of the higher *madrasas,* law, theology, and exegesis. In this way they trained the next generation of *ulema.* Well-off economically, the religious establishment gave generous endowments to support religious, educational, and charitable institutions. Among the most popular charitable institutions were the free public baths, centers of social life (although the prudent did tip the attendants). Individual men of religion could also be quite wealthy, for they were freemen and could inherit property and pass their possessions on to their descendants.

This established and institutionalized Islam—legalistic, restrained, and aloof—failed to satisfy those Muslims who yearned for a more intense, warm, personal faith. As elsewhere in the Muslim world, this need was met by Sufis, here organized in dervish brotherhoods. In contrast to the austere services conducted in the mosques, dervish religious ceremonies included music, song, and dance. Passionate visionaries, the dervishes were intent on the spirit of religion and tended to neglect or disregard the letter of the law. No wonder the *ulema* questioned their orthodoxy and frequently denounced them. Nor did the dervishes confine their activities to the religious sphere. As early as the thirteenth century there was a major dervish uprising, as well as others in the following four centuries. Yet the dervish orders could not be suppressed because they had the ear of the people. In addition, some were connected to and enjoyed the protection of the Janissaries.

Ottoman Strengths and Weaknesses

For several centuries the Empire's strengths outweighed its weaknesses, and the diverse people living under Ottoman rule enjoyed peace and security. In the Balkans and Eastern Europe prosperity rose as commerce was encouraged through the opening of land and riverine trade routes. At least during Suleiman's reign, conditions for the peasantry were better in the Ottoman Empire than in neighboring and hostile Hungary, and they remained relatively good until late in the sixteenth century when a rapid increase in the population changed the ratio of farmers to the land. Prior to that time, there had been more land than tillers, so that seriously dissatisfied peasants could move elsewhere. Also attractive to its non-Muslim subjects and neighbors was the Ottoman policy of tolerance for "people of the book" protecting Orthodox and other Christians as well as Jews, many of them refugees from persecution in Portugal and Spain. The various Christian communities (Coptic, Greek, Armenian, Syrian) and Jews were free to practice their faiths and were granted a considerable degree of self-government.

The Empire proved remarkably resilient even in the absence of a strong sultan especially after the grand vizier came to dominate the state. A serious problem was often bloody political interference by the Janissaries and the decline of the Janissaries themselves. An ominous development came early in the seventeenth century when the *dveshirme* was stopped. Originally Janissaries had not been allowed to marry, but this ban was lifted with the result that they tried to have their sons succeed them. This, of course, ran directly counter to the original rationale of an army of slaves with no ties to society at large and thus uniquely dependent on the sultan.

In the seventeenth century, the Empire faced with the new and expensive military technology of its European adversaries, found itself short of funds. One solution was to revoke the grants made to the *sipahis* (militarily regarded as outdated) and the assignment of these lands to revenue farmers, a policy which created huge estates often controlled by absentees to the detriment of the peasant cultivators. The financial situation was exacerbated by international developments. One such was the loss of the spice trade, but more serious was the inflow of inexpensive American silver which upset the Ottoman fiscal system and hurt those who were on a fixed, silver-based income, such as government officials. Officials were demoralized, corruption increased, bureaucratic efficiency deteriorated. Vested interests dominated the capital. In the provinces erstwhile tax-farmers became great landholders, and as central government control faded, local despots rose to power.

Another symptom and cause of decline was the Empire's failure to keep

Selim's Mosque, called the Blue Mosque for its colorful tiles, Istanbul (seventeenth century).

up with Europe technologically and intellectually. Confident in the might of their Empire and the perennial truths of their religion, Islamic thinkers concentrated on delving into their own tradition of sacred studies and showed little interest in the ideas being developed by their despised European neighbors.

Despite these problems the Ottomans, unlike the Safavids and Mughals, did not disappear or decline into utter insignificance after the early eighteenth century. There were even attempts at reform, both traditional and those looking to Western models. Thus Selim III, who ascended the throne in 1789 (the first year of the French Revolution), organized a modern Western-style army, but he did not have sufficient backing to escape the wrath of the Janissaries. In the end, his reforms cost him first his throne and then his life. The Empire continued, known as "The Sick Man of Europe." That it survived well into the twentieth century was in part a result of European intervention — but it may also suggest that it was endowed with an unusually strong basic constitution.

When the Ottomans disappeared at last, they left an enduring legacy. Appreciation for Ottoman contributions to scholarship, literature, and the fine arts is increasing, but its architectural achievements have long been acclaimed. It was not without cause that Europeans called Suleiman "the Magnificent." His greatest architect, Sinan (1491 – 1588), served as chief engineer for the Janissaries before being appointed royal architect at the age of forty-seven. Holding that post for half a century, he designed over three hundred buildings. When his Suleiman Mosque was being built, it was said that the workers dug foundations so deep that the sound of their pickaxes was audible to the bull that carries the world at the bottom of the earth. Then, in the dome of the Selim Mosque he outdid the dimensions even of Hagia Sophia and achieved an ultimate expression of the main theme of Ottoman architecture — the integration of the round dome of heaven on the square base of earth:

> The adamantine perfection of the mosque of Sultan Selim has something timeless about it; it evokes the vision of things in pure simultaneity; time stands still; sphere becomes cube; the instant becomes space.

Titus Burkhard, author of these lines, goes on to say, "That is the fundamental theme of Islamic architecture." But history never stands still.

THE MUGHAL EMPIRE

India, divided among a number of states, provided an attractive object for the imperial ambitions of Babur the Tiger (1483 – 1530), a great-grandson of Timur and related through his mother to Chinggis Khan. Before turning south, he had failed at creating a great Central Asian empire in the manner of his ancestors, but at Panipat in 1526 his Turk and Afghan troops and his artillery defeated the Afghan Lodis and thus put an end to the Delhi Sultanate (see pp. 378 – 80). In the following year he followed up this victory by defeating a coalition of the warrior Rajput princes. Babur established Mughal dominance over North India, but the Empire was almost lost by his son who had to turn to the Safavid Shah for succor. It was really Akbar (b. 1542, r. 1556 – 1605) who secured the Empire's future and constructed its institutional foundations.

As Persianized Turko-Mongols and Muslims, the Mughals continued certain policies first introduced under the Delhi Sultanate, including the use of Persian as the official language of law and administration and the patronage of Persian culture. Akbar's true genius, lay in reconciling and accommodating the diverse population of his pluralistic empire. He abolished the practice of enslaving prisoners of war and converting them to Islam, did away with a tax on Hindu pilgrims, and further placated Hindus by remitting the hated *jizya* tax imposed on non-Muslims. He also outlawed the slaughter of cows, which he made a capital offense. His personal life reflected similar tendencies. He was unusual among Mughal emperors in marrying Rajput princesses (most Mughal emperors had Iranian consorts). The official policy of religious tolerance was matched by Akbar's personal inquisitiveness as he presided over religious discussions in which orthodox *ulema,* Sufis, Hindus, Zoroastrians, Jews, Jains, and Jesuits from Goa argued their views. In his personal faith he was influenced by the Sufis. He even went as far as founding his own "Divine Faith" centered on himself, which won very few adherents but did alarm orthodox Muslims who stirred up rebellions that Akbar had to suppress.

Akbar divided the Empire into provinces. Government was conducted by *mansabdars,* that is, holders of a *mansab,* a Persian word for "office." The *mansab* came to designate a military rank defined in terms of the number of troops its holder was obliged to supply and lead when needed. The highest *mansabs* under Akbar were assigned to royal princes and were for five to ten thousand men. Others ranged from five hundred to five thousand while some were even as small as ten.

Akbar inspecting building operations at a royal city in the Ganges Valley (illumination from the Akbar-nama manuscript, *ca.* 1590).

The *mansabdars* were supported by *jagirs,* assignments to collect revenue for the government as well as their salaries and expenses from designated lands. These lands were frequently scattered, subject to reassignment, and not hereditary. One reason for the Mughal success was that the emperors granted *jagirs* to, and thereby made allies of, a diverse elite. There were Rajputs and Afghans, Turkish and Persian immigrants, South Indian Muslims, prominent Hindus, and Muslims from conquered regional states. The system was designed to prevent *mansabdars* from turning into local powerholders, but it was hard on the people who actually worked the land because the holder of a *jagir* had no incentive to invest in land that he would soon lose. His interest was not in the well-being of the peasantry but in garnering the maximum revenue from his *jagir* as rapidly as possible. Under Akbar peasants were taxed one-third of their harvest with a provision that the tax would be remitted in bad years.

A substantial number of town dwellers were Muslims. As elsewhere the *ulema* operated mosques and settled matters of law, but their influence and prestige remained limited. Partly this was because Muslims remained a minority in the Mughal Empire, but even within the Muslim community the *ulema* found it difficult to compete with the established Sufi orders that had originally introduced Islam to the subcontinent. Thus the Mughal Shaykh al-Islam enjoyed less power than his Ottoman counterpart; nor did the *ulema* grow strong at the expense of the state as under the Safavids. Instead they remained dependent on the state.

The great majority of peasants in a land of peasants were Hindus, as were the revenue collectors. Aside from paying their taxes, ordinary villagers had little contact with the state, and Hindus continued to live under Hindu laws. People's lives continued to be structured by their kinship groups, foremost their *jati,* and by their villages. State building remained a matter of horizontal expansion to include as much territory as feasible under the imperial umbrella rather than vertical penetration down to the village and into everyday life.

This was true also in the cities where occupational and religious groups enjoyed considerable traditional autonomy. For example, by Akbar's time the Portuguese were well established as the dominant sea power along India's western coast. The merchants of Gujarat dealt with the Europeans quite independently of their sultan who remained unconcerned as long as his own prerogatives were not involved. When Gujarat was incorporated into the Mughal Empire, little changed. Akbar signed an agreement with the Portuguese in which he promised not to shelter pirates, and the Portuguese agreed to grant his petition for a pass each year exempting one ship from paying duty on its voyage to the Red Sea. Throughout the seventeenth century the proud Mughal emperors continued to petition for the pass thus tacitly accepting Portuguese control of the sea trade as proper and not offending against their own sense of sovereignty. For the Portuguese it was a costly arrangement because Indian merchants habitually transported the most valuable goods on Akbar's ship. But the Portuguese adhered to it because they did not want to offend the powerful emperor.

The major item of commerce, international as well as domestic, was textiles. Cotton from Gujarat was widely used in Africa as well as in Asia and was much appreciated in Europe where Indian weavers did not yet face competition from machines. Calicut (cotton cloth named after Calicut, modern Kozhikode, on India's southwest coast) was especially popular, and "calico" became part of the English language. Cashmere is another example of an Indian textile so prized abroad that the word became a common English noun. The Mughal government did its part to further trade by providing security, building roads, bridges, and caravansaries, and attempting to standardize weights and measures. It also maintained its own workshops for the manufacture of luxury items, invested in commercial ventures, and used the great merchant houses for banking transactions, such as bills of exchange to transfer funds and loans to finance military campaigns. However, little of the wealth of the rich urban commercial establishments trickled down to the mass of ordinary artisans and weavers.

Brilliance and Splendor

Although less able than Akbar, his son Jahangir (r. 1605–27) and, in turn, his son Shah Jahan (r. 1628–57) generally continued a policy of religious tolerance and lavish patronage of the arts. Akbar supported more than a hundred painters giving them *mansabar* rank and, although himself illiterate, left a library of 24,000 illustrated manuscripts, which included such Indian classics as the *Ramayana* and *Mahabharata* alongside traditional Persian literary works. Jahangir was an even more enthusiastic and discriminating connoisseur of painting. Encouraged by his Persian wife, he filled his court with Persian poets and musicians as

A Portrait of Akbar by His Son

My father always associated with the learned of every creed and religion: especially the Pundits and the learned of India, and, although he was illiterate, so much became clear to him through constant intercourse with them, that no one knew him to be illiterate. . . . In his august personal appearance he was of middle height, but inclining to be tall; he was of the hue of wheat; his eyes and eyebrows were black and his complexion rather dark than fair; he was lion-bodied with a broad chest, and his hands and arms long. On the left side of his nose he had a fleshy mold, very agreeable in appearance, of the size of half a pea. . . . His august voice was very loud and in speaking and explaining had a peculiar richness.

Memoirs of Jahangir, trans. Rogers and Beveridge (London, 1909–14), pp. 33–34 as quoted in H. G. Rawlinson, *India: A Short Cultural History* (London: The Cresset Press, revised ed. 1952), pp. 317–18.

Jahangir in audience with subjects and a European (seventeenth-century manuscript illustration).

well as artists and architects. His capital, Agra, prospered and became twice as large as Isfahan. Despite his admiration of Persian culture, he furthered a more naturalistic and Indian style of painting.

The Mughal court acquired a legendary reputation for opulence and extravagance. There are reports of a gigantic imperial establishment complete with a vast harem, overflowing stables stocked with elephants and horses, an enormous staff of servants, cooks, and animal handlers, accounts of vast quantities of sparkling jewels and rare Chinese porcelains that were thought to crack on contact with poison. Shah Jahan was the biggest of the Mughal spenders. Countless sums went into the transformation of Delhi, which he made his capital in 1648. There he built palace walls of marble inlaid with precious stones and ceilings of gold and silver. Most famous was the Peacock Throne. Standing on six legs of solid gold it featured an enameled canopy resting on six pillars inlaid with emeralds. Between the pillars were pairs of peacocks studded with large, brilliant diamonds, rubies, emeralds, and pearls. It took the court jeweler seven years to complete and was valued at ten million rupees. It dazzled those admitted to the Hall of Private Audience, where on one wall was carved the Persian couplet, "If there be Paradise, on earth,/It is Here, It is Here, It is Here!"

Shah Jahan also sponsored and most probably helped to design the magnificent and incomparable Taj Mahal, built as a mausoleum for his beloved wife who died giving birth to their fifteenth child. Originally he planned another mausoleum to be built in black marble for himself across the river from the Taj to contrast with its pure, gleaming white, but this was not to be and ultimately the emperor was interred next to his wife. Although the Taj was built by Persian architects, it represents a fusion of Persian and Indian traditions. Responding to the ever-changing light as day advances from dawn to dusk, it has rightfully been deemed one of the wonders of the world.

There was a dark underside, however, to all this splendor. The emperor might fancy himself in paradise, but his projects, military as well as civil, weighed heavily on the people. When a terrible famine struck in the Deccan, Shah Jahan contributed a mere five thousand rupees a week for relief. Military campaigns, south in the Deccan and also north in Central Asia, required vast expenditures. The government's response to the need for funds was to raise the peasant's tax to half the crop.

Aurangzeb

Shah Jahan's favorite son, Dara Shikoh (1615–59) was a man of wide learning and deep mysticism. His search for a common ground for Islam and Hinduism was in keeping with the syncretic tendencies of his forebears, but it heightened the alarm of those who, ever since the time of Akbar, had feared that a turn to pantheism was undermining the very foundations of Islam. Among those convinced of this

The Taj Mahal.

stricter view was Aurangzeb, the prince who defeated his brothers through his brilliance and ruthlessness in a bloody struggle for the throne.

Aurangzeb (r. 1658–1707) was personally pious and set an example for sobriety and abstention that contrasted markedly with the behavior of his father and grandfather. He also reversed previous religious permissiveness and attempted to turn his empire into a Muslim state. Thus he denied permission for the building of new Hindu temples and the rebuilding of old ones, recast the calendar, reimposed the hated *jizya,* and tried to enforce Muslim laws against drinking, gambling, and prostitution. His personal asceticism and devotion to Islam won him the accolades of fervent fellow believers, but his policies were hardly reassuring to his Hindu subjects.

Hindu resentment was all the more dangerous because the empire was suffering from mounting economic ills. On the one hand, Aurangzeb, who mounted the throne as Alamgir, "World Conqueror," was an indefatigable campaigner but lacked new lands with which to reward his *mansabdars,* and on the other, *mansabdars* often squeezed the peasants beyond tolerable limits. Many, in dire straits, were ready to follow regional leaders in resisting Mughal power.

In the North Aurangzeb faced and triumphed over repeated challenges not only from Rajputs but also from Sikhs, for by then the followers of the faith founded by Nanak (see p. 380) had developed into a militant group. After Aurangzeb had the ninth Sikh guru beheaded, his son, the tenth and last in line, vowed eternal vengeance. The Sikhs became a cohesive, tough body of fighters. At one time they numbered 20,000, a formidable force but not enough to defeat the imperial

The Mughal Empire at Its Height 1700

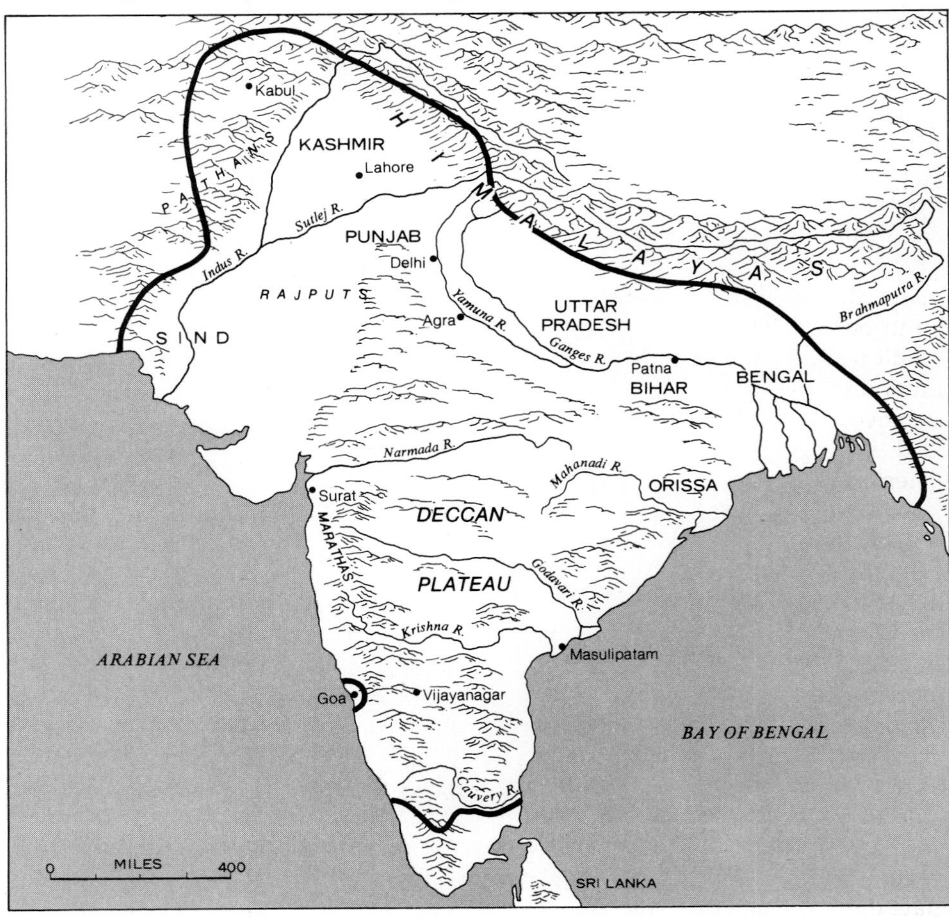

armies. Even more troublesome was opposition in the South. Here the Marathas under the leadership of Shivaji Bhonsle (1627–80) waged a relentless guerrilla war against the emperor, and a war for independence continued after Shivaji's death. One reason why Aurangzeb was victorious was the inability of his Hindu opponents to move beyond regional loyalties to coordinated attack.

The "World Conqueror" did not stop at repressing revolts but extended the Empire to its furthest reaches so that it became even larger than that of Ashoka. But his campaigns in the Deccan, which kept him occupied for the last quarter century of his reign, were extremely costly in lives, money, and resources as the emperor moved through the Deccan with his enormous entourage. What one scholar has termed his "moving capital" covered an area over thirty miles in circumference and included 250 bazaars, half a million civilians, 50,000 camels and 30,000 elephants. The campaigns took a terrible toll, and the Marathas remained hostile and defiant. By 1605 when the aged emperor decided to call a halt and return to Delhi, even he was no longer clear what had been the purpose of this prodigious effort and terrible suffering.

The Demise of the Empire

Aurangzeb's death was followed by the traditional war of succession; fighting consumed half of the five-year reign of his immediate successor. After that, the history of the court was dominated by factional infighting and intrigue while control over the Empire steadily slipped away as the Marathas and then the state of Hyderabad (South India) gained all but titular independence. Administrative inefficiency fostered by Aurangzeb's twenty-year absence from the capital, failure to appreciate sea power or devise means for dealing with the mobile warfare practiced by the Marathas, and especially the economic deterioration all contributed to the Mughal decline. The result was that Nadir Shah was able to enter India with impunity. When he reached Delhi he conducted a massacre and a thorough sack of the capital. Then he returned north laden with booty, including the peacock throne.

This was not the last disaster to befall the capital. It was pillaged again by an Afghan chief in 1757, by Marathas in 1760, and the Afghans returned in 1761. By that time the Marathas were the most powerful of a number of virtually independent states although the fiction of an empire was retained and a titular emperor continued to reside in Delhi until the last of the line formally abdicated in 1858. With no regional power strong enough to dominate the subcontinent, it was left to the British to become the true heirs to the Mughals.

THE EMPIRES COMPARED

During their twilight years, all three empires suffered from centrifugal tendencies that prefigured eventual fragmentation. All three failed to respond creatively to new military and technological challenges. In all three, institutions became disfunctional, and they all shared a sense that the days of glory lay in the past. Yet the differences between them remain at least as important as their similarities. There were no Janissaries nor a silver-induced fiscal crisis in India, nor was there a counterpart to Aurangzeb among the Ottomans; and if they shared an Islamic heritage, the role of the *ulema* differed in each of the three states.

All three empires had dealings with the early European maritime powers and lived in a world that was slowly being drawn closer together. All three used gunpowder and traded extensively. The Ottomans, as an empire straddling Europe and Asia, were drawn early into the European balance of power, but even for them the decisive historical forces remained regional rather than global. By the time a transformed West had developed the strength to challenge all other civilizations on the globe, the three empires were either moribund or dead.

Suggestions for Further Reading

Francis Robinson, *Atlas of the Islamic World since 1500* (1982) is outstanding and its bibliography is very useful. R. M. Savory, *Iran under the Safavids* (1980), is the best book on its subject. Recommended for the Ottoman Empire are Norman Itzkowitz, *Ottoman Empire and Islamic Tradition* (1972); Bernard Lewis, *Istanbul and the Civilization of the Ottoman Empire* (1963); and Raphaele Lewis, *Everyday Life in Ottoman Turkey* (1971). S. Wolpert, *A New History of India* (2nd ed. 1982), is a good place to begin reading about Mughal India. J. Habib, *The Agrarian System of Mughal India* (1963) is an important study. M. N. Pearson, *Merchants and Rulers in Gujarat: The Response to the Portuguese in the Sixteenth Century* (1976), demonstrates the limited reach of government at the time and offers insights further refined in the same author's "Premodern Muslim Political Systems," *Journal of the American Oriental Society*, Vol. 102, No. 1 (1982), pp. 47–58.

	1648			1700		
SOUTHWEST ASIA AND AFRICA	**1652** Dutch found Cape Colony *ca.* **1700** Rise of Ashanti, West Africa				**1737–47** Nadir Shah, decline of Safavid Empire	
EUROPE	**1660–88** Stuart Restoration **1661–1715** Louis XIV	**1683** Turks besiege Vienna **1685** Edict of Nantes revoked **1685–1750** Johann Sebastian Bach **1687** Newton's Law of Gravitation	**1688** Glorious Revolution **1689–1725** Peter the Great **1690** Locke, *Two Treatises of Civil Government*	**1701–14** War of Spanish Succession **1715–74** Louis XV **1720** South Sea Bubble **1723–42** Robert Walpole	**1740–80** Maria Theresa **1740–86** Frederick the Great **1756–63** Seven Years' War **1756–91** Wolfgang Amadeus Mozart	**1762** Rousseau, *The Social Contract* **1762–96** Catherine the Great **1769** James Watt's first steam engine **1770–1827** Ludwig van Beethoven
SOUTH AND SOUTHEAST ASIA	**1653** Taj Mahal completed **1690** British found Calcutta				**1751** French control Deccan **1757** Battle of Plassey **1773** Regulation Act	
EAST ASIA	**1662–1722** Emperor Kangxi *ca.* **1675–1725** Golden age of Edo urban culture, Japan			**1736–95** Emperor Qianlong	**1796–1804** White Lotus Rebellion	
THE AMERICAS AND PACIFIC		**1664** British seize New Amsterdam		**1728** Bering explores Alaska **1756–63** French and Indian War	**1765** Stamp Act **1768–80** Cook explores Pacific Ocean **1773** Boston Tea Party **1774** Quebec Act	

Ashanti wood carving.

Napoleon, 1800.

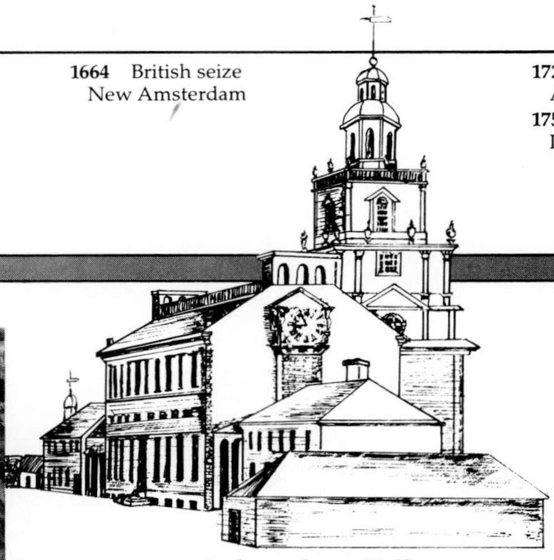

Independence Hall, Philadelphia, 1776.

East India Company merchant, by an Indian artist.

Emblem of the Sun King, Louis XIV.

Charles II of England, 1660-85.

	1815
	1805–48 Mohammed Ali founds dynasty in Egypt **1806** British control Cape Colony **1807** Slavery abolished in British Empire
1776 Smith, *Wealth of Nations* **1789** French Revolution begins	**1798** Malthus, *Essay on the Principle of Population* **1799** Napoleon becomes First Consul **1804–14** Napoleonic Empire
1784 East India Act **1786–93** Cornwallis in Bengal **1796** British conquer Ceylon	
1775–83 American Revolution **1776** US Declaration of Independence **1788** British colonize Australia **1803** Louisiana Purchase	**1807–30** Latin American wars for independence

Chinese fan painting, *ca.* 1700.

***Fuji above Storm,* by Hokusai, 1760-1849.**

26 Qing China and Tokugawa Japan

The Seventeenth and Eighteenth Centuries

During the seventeenth and eighteenth centuries the civilizations of China and Japan remained vigorous and essentially autonomous. Although during these centuries the West was growing in strength, it did not as yet pose a major threat. East Asia was left free to develop according to its own rhythms and patterns. China and Japan continued to differ greatly from each other, but for both this was a period of new achievements as well as new problems. The study of this period is therefore crucial not only for an understanding of what was to follow in modern times but also because it affords a last look at the internal dynamics of Chinese and Japanese history before the intervention of the West.

CHINA

The Founding of the Qing Dynasty

The Qing (Ch'ing) dynasty (1644–1911) was only the second non-Chinese dynasty to rule over all of China and did so far more successfully than the first, the Yüan. One reason for this may well have been that by the time they founded the Qing, the Manchus were quite familiar with Chinese civilization. Nurhachi (1559–1626), the founder of the Manchu state, originally enjoyed the support of China's Ming dynasty and continued to send tribute to Beijing (Peking) until 1609. Basic to his military power was a system of

Temple of Heaven, Qing dynasty, Beijing.

The Coming of Autumn, hanging scroll by Hongren (1610–63).

armies known as banners. In 1621 the first Mongol banner was added to augment Manchu strength. Chinese banners followed. By the time of the conquest there were 278 Manchu, 120 Mongol, and 165 Chinese banners. By that time, there were more Chinese than Manchus living in the Manchu state.

The expansion of Manchu power begun by Nurhachi was continued by his son Abahai (r. 1626–43) who adopted the name Qing for his regime and established the principle that there should be an ethnic balance in the central government under Manchu supervision. Abahai reduced Inner Mongolia to vassalage, defeated and gained the submission of Korea, and, in the North, established control over the Amur River region. The conquest of North China, however, was achieved after his death by Dorgon (1612–50) acting as regent for Abahai's six-year-old son and successor.

The Manchus did not overthrow the Ming. That was accomplished by the rebellion of Li Zicheng (Li Tzu-ch'eng) who gained control of the capital but was unable to establish a viable government (see pp. 488–89). The Qing armies were allowed to enter North China when a Chinese general threw in his lot with them rather than the Chinese rebels. After Dorgon entered Beijing in June 1644, he buried the last Ming emperor and empress with full honors and announced that he had come to punish the rebels.

The conquest of the South took longer and could not have been accomplished without the assistance of Chinese generals and the acquiescence of many Chinese ready to cooperate with the Qing. Three of these generals, however, carved out territories for themselves. It took the costly War of the Three Feudatories (1673–81), undertaken by the fifteen-year-old Emperor Kangxi (K'ang-hsi), to subjugate the South. The last area to submit was the island of Taiwan (Formosa), which was incorporated into the Empire in 1683 and then placed under the administration of Fujian (Fukien) Province.

When it was no longer possible to fight for the old dynasty, some men nevertheless refused to serve the new. Among them were three of China's most notable thinkers. Despite his intellectual range and depth, Wang Fuzhi (Wang Fu-chih, 1619–1704) remained unknown for some two hundred years until he was finally appreciated for his anti-Manchu views. Living in unusually troubled times, all three men were deeply interested in history. Huang Zongxi (Huang Tsung-hsi, 1610–95) authored a compendium of Ming thought that remains a basic scholarly resource, while his *Plan for the Prince* is a wide-ranging study of government noted for its stringent criticism of imperial despotism. The third thinker, Gu Yenwu (Ku Yen-wu, 1613–82) insisted on solid, practical learning that led him to the study of statecraft and philology. Most influential was his insistence on careful textual scholarship which, rejecting Song (Sung) and later commentaries, went back to the original sources to reconstruct their meaning. In these textual studies the dynasty's scholars went on to make their greatest contributions. Contemporary with these three great thinkers were some of China's most individualistic and indeed eccentric painters.

The Reign of Kangxi

Kangxi, one of China's grandest and most illustrious emperors, was on the throne for sixty years, from 1662 to 1722, and actually ruled from 1668 on. After subduing the South and annexing Taiwan, Kangxi turned his attention to China's other borders. In the Amur River region, his army destroyed a Russian Cossack base. This military success was followed by a diplomatic success—the Treaty of Nerchinsk, signed with Russia in 1689, which settled frontier problems between the two great Empires and regularized relations between them. The treaty also removed the threat of a possible alliance between the Russians and a confederation of Western Mongols. Against the latter, Kangxi personally led his troops in 1696–97 and won a great victory. Around the middle of the seventeenth century, Western Mongols had intervened in the politico-religious struggles taking place in Tibet and had remained as conquerors. Under Kangxi, the Qing, too, became deeply involved. In 1720 Qing armies entered Tibet and installed a pro-Chinese Dalai Lama (the spiritual and secular ruler of Tibet).

Kangxi's martial exploits were, in part, a reflection of a conscious sense of identification with his Manchu forebears and his desire to preserve the traditional Manchu way of life, which he saw as essential to maintaining Manchu supremacy. Another expression of this feeling was the organization of great hunting expeditions, in which he took considerable delight. To help preserve Manchu distinctiveness, one of the first acts of Kangxi's reign was the closing of Manchuria to Chinese immigration. Furthermore, during the Qing, Manchus were not allowed to marry

Emperor Kangxi, a nineteenth-century portrait.

Chinese, and Manchu women were not allowed to bind their feet (a painful practice of tightly wrapping the feet from childhood on to produce the tiny feet considered a mark of feminine beauty). On the other hand, even before the conquest, Chinese men were forced by the Manchu rulers to wear their hair in a queue (pigtail) and to shave the rest of their heads in the Manchu fashion.

Kangxi was very much the Manchu, but he was not anti-Chinese. Like previous non-Chinese rulers, however, he felt impelled to take steps to avoid being submerged in the larger Chinese population and more sophisticated Chinese culture. Politically, a strict balance was maintained between Manchus and Chinese in the top government positions in the capital, and in the provinces, generally, a Chinese governor was counterbalanced by a governor-general, usually placed over two provinces, who was a Manchu, a Mon-

The Imperial Palace, Beijing.

gol, or a Chinese bannerman. The hereditary banner forces lived apart from the general population in their own communities and were commanded by a general responsible directly to Beijing. Another group used by the emperor for confidential tasks were his Chinese bondservants, who managed the imperial household. Like eunuchs, they were dependent on imperial favor, but unlike eunuchs, they did not offend Chinese feelings. Bondservants were used by Kangxi to submit secret memorials (reports) on conditions in the provinces and also managed the emperor's personal treasury and the monopolies, including maritime customs.

Kangxi was a very vigorous man. He rose well before dawn each day to go through a great stack of memorials before receiving officials, beginning at 5 A.M. (later changed to 7 A.M.). His tours of personal inspection in the South are famous. To show his benevolence, he reduced taxes and forced Manchu aristocrats to stop seizing Chinese lands. He was also a man of wide intellectual interests, including Western learning. He won the affection and respect of many Chinese scholars by holding a special honorific examination to attract those who had remained loyal to the Ming and by sponsoring the compilation of the official Ming history, a great phrase dictionary, a giant encyclopedia, and an exhaustive dictionary of Chinese characters. The philosophy of Zhu Xi (Chu Hsi) received his special support. The emperor was also a notable patron of the arts.

China in the Eighteenth Century: Yongzheng and Qianlong

Kangxi's reign was of a length unprecedented in Chinese history, and he was one of the most successful Chinese emperors, but he was unable to arrange for a smooth succession. After his death, the throne was seized in a military coup by a prince who became Emperor Yongzheng (Yung-cheng, r. 1723–35). After he became emperor Yongzheng censored the record of his accession to the throne and also suppressed other writings he deemed inimical to his regime, particularly those with an anti-Manchu bias. He was a tough and hard-working ruler bent on effective government at minimum expense. Like his father, he used military force to preserve the dynasty's position in Outer Mongolia, and when Tibet was torn by civil war during 1717–28, he intervened militarily and left a Qing resident backed by a military garrison to pursue the dynasty's interests. His reign was despotic, efficient, vigorous, and brief. By the simple expedient of sealing the name of the heir-apparent in a box kept in the throne room, Yongzheng was able to assure that on his death there would be no struggle over the succession.

Under Emperor Qianlong (Ch'ien–lung, r. 1736–95) the Qing achieved its greatest prosperity and geographic expansion into Central Asia. Chinese Turkestan was incorporated into the Empire and renamed Xinjiang (Sinkiang), while to the west, Ili was conquered. The Qing also dominated Outer Mongolia after inflicting a final defeat on the Western Mongols. Its policy there was to preserve Mongol institutions, but it allowed Chinese merchants to enter and exploit the people, thus reinforcing the anti-Chinese animosities of the animal-herding Mon-

The Qing Empire 1775

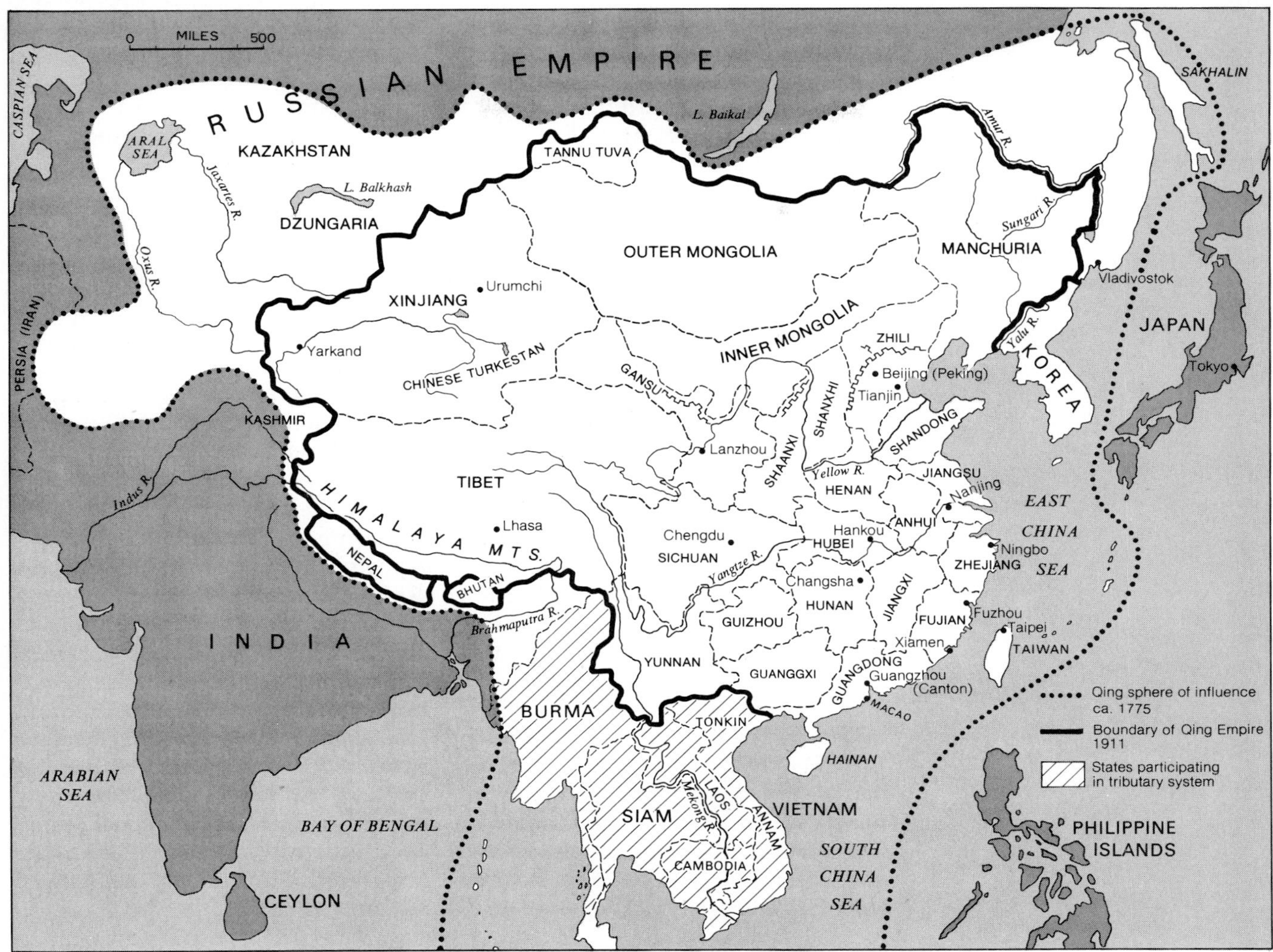

gols. It is no accident that when the Qing fell in the twentieth century, the Mongols promptly declared their independence. Throughout this period there were continued Mongol interventions in Tibet and a reciprocal spread of Tibetan Lamaism in Mongolia. Qianlong again sent armies into Tibet and firmly established the Dalai Lama as ruler, with a Qing resident and garrison to preserve Chinese suzerainty. Other than that, no attempt was made to integrate Tibet into the Empire after the manner of Xinjiang. Further afield, military campaigns against the Annames, Burmese, Nepalese, and Gurkhas forced these peoples to submit and send tribute. Rulers, like the king of England, residing in lands even further removed from the center of the world, were expected to conform to the tribute system while Western traders were confined to the single port of Guangzhou (Canton).

Qing expansion involved millions of square miles and brought into the Empire non-Chinese peoples (such as Uighurs, Kazakhs, Kirghiz, and Mongols) who were at least potentially resentful and hostile. It was also a very expensive enterprise. The dynasty enjoyed unprecedented prosperity and managed in the mid-1780s to accumulate a healthy financial reserve, but its resources were not inexhaustible. Yet the emperor delighted in the glory and wealth. Qianlong built a sumptuous summer residence partly of Western design, and undertook grand tours of the Empire, including six tours of the South.

In his policy toward the literati, Qianlong combined Kangxi's generous patronage of scholarship with Yongjeng's suspiciousness of anti-Manchu writings. The greatest project sponsored by him was the *Complete Library of the Four Treasuries* of 36,000 volumes. It preserved many books but was also a means of ferreting out and suppressing those deemed offensive. This project suggests that scholars of the age were more occupied in preserving and ordering the writings of the past than in embarking on new intellectual quests, a suggestion corroborated by the attention paid to minutiae in much of the philological work. Such textual studies did at times lead to startling and controversial results as when questions were raised concerning the historicity of parts of some of the venerated classics. Moreover, there were also bold and original thinkers such as Dai Zhen (Tai Chen, 1723–77), who disputed Zhu Xi's views on human nature and contributed to linguistics, astronomy, mathematics, and geography as well as philosophy. Dai Zhen shared the contemporary interest in philology, but not so Zhang Xuecheng (Chang Hsüeh-ch'eng, 1738–1801), who sought meaning in the study and writing of history. Zhang once compared a work of history to a living organism: Its facts are like bones, the writing is like the skin, and its meaning corresponds to the organism's vital spirit.

Another man of unconventional ideas was the poet Yuan Mei (1716–97), who rejected the didactic view of poetry and argued that poetry should above all give pleasure. His own verse reflects the life of a talented, refined, and open-minded hedonist unconventional within the bounds of good taste and marginally aware of the exotic West. One of his prized possessions was a large European mirror. The greatest literary achievement of the eighteenth century was, however, not in poetry but in prose. *The Dream of the Red Chamber* (also translated as *Story of the Stone*) by Cao Xuechin (Ts'ao Hsüeh-ch'in, 1715?–63) is generally accepted as China's greatest novel. From the vantage point of a large and eminent family in decline, it offers priceless insights into Qing society. In rich detail it reveals much about how such a family was organized and functioned, the relationships between the generations and the sexes, the life of women, the status of servants, and so on, and does this with fine psychological insight, while the author's Buddhist-Daoist views provide philosophical depth.

Despite its excellence, *The Dream of the Red Chamber* did not gain respectability in scholarly circles; it was not until the twentieth century that the novel was appreciated as a serious literary genre on a level with poetry, essays, and history. During the Qing, it was considered frivolous and low class—something scholars read surreptitiously while they were supposedly engaged in the endless monotony of preparing for the civil service examinations. This study included mastery of a particularly artificial style of literary composition. Meanwhile, the intensity of examination competition made success all the more elusive. One outlet for

The Qianlong Emperor to King George III

Above all, upon you who live in a remote and inaccessible region, far across the space of ocean, but who have shown your submissive loyalty by sending this tribute mission [the Macartney mission of 1793 that failed to achieve an extension of trade or to arrange for diplomatic representation], I have heaped benefits far in excess of those I have accorded to other nations. But the demands presented by your embassy are not only a contravention of dynastic tradition, but would be unproductive of results to yourself, besides being quite impractical. . . . It is your bounden duty reverently to appreciate my feelings and to obey these instructions henceforth for all times, so that you may enjoy the blessings of perpetual peace.

From an imperial decree quoted by Immanuel C. Y. Hsü, *The Rise of Modern China* (New York: Oxford University Press, 1975), p. 231 citing H. F. MacNair, *Modern Chinese History: Selected Readings* (Shanghai, 1913).

those with literary talents was satire. Collections of stories and the novel, *The Scholars,* illustrate the shortcomings of the system and the foibles of those involved in it. Beyond that, they present a disillusioned view of official life and elite mores. *The Scholars,* like *The Dream of the Red Chamber,* is also notable for its sympathy for women.

The satirical and critical literature has little to say about the peasantry. There was a vital popular culture with its own religious beliefs, dramas, and traditions, as well as its folk arts and handicrafts; but the patterns of cultural interchange between various levels of society remain to be worked out. However, scholars studying the rise of the novel in the West have linked it to social changes associated with the development of a money economy and the accompanying social changes. In this respect, China offers striking similarities.

The Economy

The eighteenth century was a period of prosperity. Economic development had been retarded by the destruction and dislocation that accompanied the collapse of the Ming, but once peace and order were restored by the Qing, the economy more than recovered. The central economic fact of this period was an increase in agricultural production, partly the result of the maximum spread of known products and techniques—superior strains of rice, improved irrigation methods, and better fertilizers, such as soybean cakes. However, production was also increased through the introduction of new crops originally native to America—corn, the sweet potato, and the peanut. The sweet potato and the peanut were of special importance because they did not require the same quality of soil or climatic conditions as other crops grown in China and thus could be grown on land not previously cultivated. One result of increased output was tax reduction. Emperor Yongzheng's reform of the tax system was designed particularly to benefit poor peasant farmers. The century saw an increase in life expectancy and an all-around improvement in the standard of living. These in turn contributed to further agricultural production and economic development.

Agriculture provided a foundation for the development of trade and manufacturing. The colorful and highly decorated ceramics produced by China's kilns were world famous and helped to stimulate a craze for "chinoiserie" in eighteenth century Europe. Another flourishing industry was the cotton trade. Silk and hemp, brewing and paper, mining and metal working deserve mention as do the spread of tea and sugar production. Stimulated by vigorous internal trade, market towns prospered and merchant guilds operated on an interprovincial and interregional basis. The salt merchants of Yangzhou (Yangchow) were especially prosperous. Although the total value of internal trade was far greater than that of foreign commerce, both contributed to Chinese prosperity. Throughout the century the balance of overseas trade was in China's favor, and there was a strong inflow of gold and silver.

Agricultural growth and economic prosperity, peace and stability, the strength of China's family ethos—all contributed to a dramatic increase in China's population, an increase comparable to that which took place in Eu-

Printing with moveable type, illustration by Jin Jian (1776).

Yuan Mei

BOOKS

If one opens a book one meets the men of old;
If one goes into the street, one meets the people of today.
The men of old! Their bones are turned to dust;
It can only be with their feelings that one makes friends.
The people of today are of one's own kind,
But to hear their talk is like chewing a candle!
I had far rather live with sticks and stones
Than spend my time with ordinary people.
Fortunately one need not belong to one's own time;
One's real date is the date of the books one reads!

Arthur Waley, *Yuan Mei: Eighteenth Century Poet* (New York: Grove Press, 1956), p. 85.

Porcelain figure of Guanyin (early Qing).

rope during the following century. By the end of the eighteenth century more people lived in China than in Europe; the Chinese population was in the neighborhood of 300 million, about double what it had been two centuries earlier. At the same time per-capita production remained constant during this period of remarkable economic growth. However, without radical technological change production could not forever keep up with expanding population. By the end of the century, population growth was putting new strains on the economy, the state, and society. As in other parts of the world, stresses resulting from population growth helped to undermine the traditional order. The challenge of population growth did not go unnoticed. The Chinese scholar Hong Liangji (Hung Liang-chi, 1746–1809) first wrote about the dangers inherent in this process in 1793. The new population pressures resulted in population shifts: the previously marginal areas in China "filled up," and the emigration of Chinese people into Southeast Asia increased. Subsequently they became important minorities in a number of states.

While the population and the economy expanded, the government did not. There was no increase in the number of posts in the civil service to keep pace with a growing number of candidates, many of them superbly educated. Even in the Song (Sung) there had been cases of men spending a lifetime taking examinations—when the emperor asked his age, one such man replied, "fifty years ago, twenty-three." Now the aged examination graduate became a stock figure in literature. The government even relaxed standards for men over seventy, so that, past retirement age, they could at least enjoy the psychological satisfaction of receiving a degree. In an effort to weed out candidates, new examinations were introduced. In 1788, when the reexamination of provincial and capital graduates was introduced, the total minimum number of examinations required for the highest degree came to eight, not counting a final placement examination given to the successful candidates. By this time the criteria for judging papers had become exceedingly formalistic.

Tension and Decay

The unsatisfactory state of the examination system, and the tendency of the government to tinker and elaborate rather than to reform and innovate, suggests a dangerous hardening of the institutional arteries during the last twenty years of Qianlong's reign. This was particularly ominous because it came at a time of fiscal problems. As the expense of military campaigns far beyond the bounds of China proper mounted, the resources of even the prosperous Qianlong regime were strained to the utmost, while administrative laxity and corruption were making the government less efficient and more expensive. The worst offender was a Manchu favorite of Emperor Qianlong, a man named Heshen (1750–99), who prospered for twenty-three years. Assured of imperial support, he built up a network of corruption and amassed a huge fortune.

Although bitterly detested he could not be removed, for he never lost Qianlong's confidence and affection. An attack on Heshen implied an attack on the aging emperor's own judgment and, furthermore, suggested the disease of factionalism. Perhaps Qianlong was especially sensitive to any signs of factionalism since his father, Emperor Yongzheng, had written a very strong critique on this subject. Like his political authority, the moral and intellectual authority of the emperor was now beyond question. Emperor Qianlong abdicated after his sixtieth year on the throne in order not to rule longer than his illustrious grandfather, but he continued to dominate the government until his death in 1799. Only then was Heshen removed and, in lieu of execution, allowed to take his own life.

As always, the burden of extravagance and corruption was borne by the common people. As a result many of them joined in the White Lotus Rebellion, which broke out in 1796 and was not completely suppressed until 1804. At its height it affected Sichuan, Hubei, Henan, Gansu, and Shanxi. It drew its following by promising the coming of Maitreya, the Buddha of the future, as well as a restoration of the Ming, and the rescue of the people from all suffering. It gained momentum as it attracted the destitute and desperate. It was also encouraged by the ineffectiveness of the dynasty's response; government generals used the occasion to line their own pockets and bannermen proved their total incompetence. Not until after Heshen's fall did the government make real headway. A very capable new commander was appointed, disaffected areas were slowly regained, and military bands organized by the local elite, whose members had the most to lose from radical social change, proved effective in putting down insurgency.

China in 1800

Both Hoshen and the White Lotus Rebellion were destroyed in the end, but corruption in government and misery in the countryside remained. The

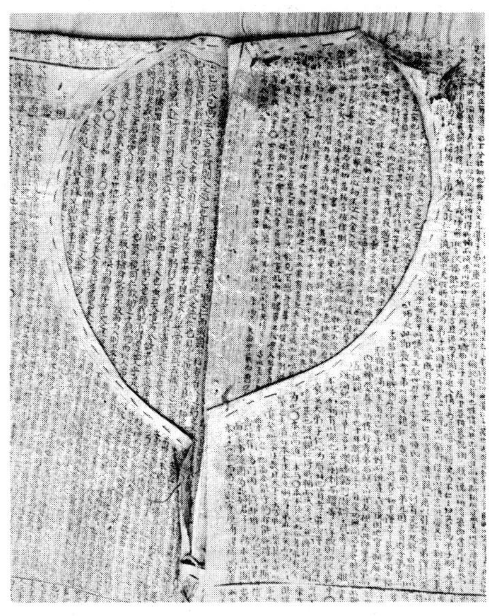

Cheating shirt for use in civil service examinations.

nineteenth century, like the seventeenth, was to be turbulent and traumatic, thus highlighting the placidity and stability of the eighteenth. But the White Lotus Rebellion is just one indication of tensions and dissatisfactions beneath the surface. And even the achievements of the elite sometimes suggest that this was more a time of harvesting the fruits of past efforts rather than one of setting forth on bold ventures.

Internationally, the regime could take great pride since the perennial problem of invasion from Inner Asia had been solved once and for all. Meanwhile, the seaborne Westerners, confined to trading at the single port of Guangzhou hardly seemed to pose a threat (see pp. 832–33). Earlier, serious dialogue between learned Catholic fathers and Chinese scholars had come to an end when the papacy ruled against the Jesuit position that Confucian rites were compatible with Christianity. In 1700 there had been about 300,000 Christians in China; by the end of the century that tiny number had been cut in half. At court, Western things appealed to a taste for the exotic. Thus Qianlong had a portrait painted in the European manner of an imperial concubine playing at being a European peasant girl and dressed accordingly. Just as Louis XV of France sometimes amused himself by having his courtiers and their ladies assume Chinese dress, the Qing emperor enjoyed exotic Western costume on occasion.

China was ill prepared to handle the onslaught that came later when it faced a Europe which, during the last years of Qianlong's reign, was being refashioned by the French and Industrial Revolutions. That despite economic growth and population pressures, political ills and social disaffection, there was no indication of comparable revolution about to erupt in China suggests (for better or worse) the resilience of China's social structure and the continuing compatibility between that structure and the political system.

JAPAN

The Tokugawa Shogunate

The founders of the Tokugawa Shogunate (1600–1868), like those of the Qing, put a premium on stability. They sought political stability through a system designed to preserve Tokugawa supremacy and by excluding potentially destabilizing influences from abroad, and they sought social stability by freezing class lines. Consequently, the Tokugawa has been seen as a conservative, even reactionary, period responsible for suppressing change and retarding Japan's modernization. Tokugawa rigidity has also been cited in explanation of the persistence of traditional elements even in comtemporary Japan. But the remarkable ease of the transition after Japan was reopened in the mid-nineteenth century, and the rapidity of Japan's modernization thereafter, would have been impossible without the foundations laid in the Tokugawa period.

The essential structure of the Tokugawa political system was devised by Ieyasu, the founder of the shogunate, and completed by his two immediate successors, Hidetada (r. 1616–23) and Iemitsu (r. 1623–51). Ieyasu himself rose to supremacy as the leader of a group of lords, or *daimyo,* each of whom was backed by his own vassals and supported by his independent power base. All the *daimyo* were the shogun's vassals, bound to him by solemn oath, and when an heir took the place of a deceased *daimyo,* the new man had to sign a pledge of vassalage to the shogun in blood. Still, some vassals were more reliable than others, and the Tokugawa classified them into three groups. Least trusted and potentially the most dangerous were the "outside" or allied *daimyo (tozama)* who were too powerful to be considered Tokugawa subordinates. Some had come over to the Tokugawa only after Ieyasu's victory at the battle of Sekigahara in 1600 had left them with no other alternative. More reliable were the "house *daimyo*" *(fudai)* most of whom had been Tokugawa family vassals raised to *daimyo* status by the Tokugawa and thus, unlike the outside *daimyo,* indebted to the shogunate for their status and domains. The third group were the "collateral *daimyo*" *(shimpan)* who belonged to Tokugawa branch families. The Tokugawa also held its own land, which supported direct retainers. Some of these held fiefs too small to qualify for *daimyo* status, but many of them received stipends directly from the *bakufu* (the shogun's government).

The *bakufu* itself was located in Edo (modern Tokyo), which was a small village of about a hundred houses at the time Ieyasu selected it for his headquarters but was destined to grow into one of the world's greatest cities. The shogunate also maintained castles at Osaka and Shizuoka as well as a castle in Kyoto where it maintained a deputy responsible for the government of the capital city who also served as the shogun's representative at the imperial court. In theory the shogun was the emperor's deputy as well as the feudal overlord of all the *daimyo.* As during preceding shogunates, the throne remained the prime source of legitimacy.

To secure itself militarily, the Tokugawa placed its house *daimyo* in strategic areas. It dominated the Japanese heartlands while the outside *daimyo* had their territories in the outer areas.

A *daimyo* procession leaving Edo, from *Fifty-three Stages on the Tokaido,* by Hiroshige.

A number of policies prevented the *daimyo* from acquiring too much strength. They were restricted to one castle each and had to secure the *bakufu's* permission before they could repair this castle. They were allowed to maintain only a fixed number of men at arms and forbidden to build large ships. To keep them from political alliances that might threaten the *bakufu,* they were required to obtain *bakufu* assent for their marriage plans.

During the first half of the seventeenth century the shogunate's policy was to increase its own strength at the expense of the *daimyo.* In this period there were 281 cases in which *daimyo* were transferred from one fief to another. Another 213 domains were confiscated outright. This happened sometimes as a disciplinary measure, as when a lord proved incompetent or the domain was torn by a succession dispute, but more often confiscation resulted from failure to produce an heir. Deathbed adoptions of an heir were not recognized. By such means the Tokugawa more than tripled the size of its holdings, until its own domain was calculated as worth 6.8 million *koku* of rice annually (1 *koku* = 4.98 bushels). By way of comparison, in the mid-Tokugawa period collateral *daimyo* held land worth 2.6 million *koku;* house *daimyo,* 6.7 million; and outside *daimyo,* 9.8 million. It is indicative of the decline of their economic and political power that religious institutions held only around 600,000 *koku,* and the emperor and the court nobility could draw on land worth only 187,000 *koku.* The distribution of their holdings also favored the Tokugawa economically, as it did militarily, because they were in possession of many of Japan's mines and most of its important cities, such as Osaka, Kyoto, and Nagasaki. The early *bakufu* also asserted its financial predominance when it reserved for itself the right to issue paper currency.

To see to it that the *daimyo* obeyed *bakufu* orders, the shogunate sent out its own inspectors. It also devised a highly effective system of strengthening itself politically (while at the same time draining the *daimyo* financially) by requiring them to spend alternate years in residence in Edo, where the *bakufu* could keep them under surveillance. When they did go back home to their domains, they had to leave their wives and children behind as hostages. This system of alternate attendance forced the *daimyo* to spend large sums traveling back and forth with their retinues. The maintenance of suitably elaborate residences in Edo was a further strain on *daimyo* resources. The *daimyo* were also called upon to support public projects such as waterworks or the repair of the shogun's castle at Edo, but such exactions were not as burdensome as the constant expense of alternate attendance. The residential requirement had the additional effect of turning Edo into a capital not only of the *bakufu* but of all Japan.

The Bakufu *and the* Han

Despite the shogunate's preeminence as the central power, the *daimyo* remained free to manage their own domains or *han.* The *bakufu* usually interfered only when a *daimyo* was incapable of managing his *han* or when problems involving more than one *han* arose. The *daimyo* themselves were naturally concerned to develop the strength of their own domains while keeping *bakufu* interference to a minimum. Even while tightening the administration of their domains, their self-interest lay in preserving the decentralized aspect of the larger political system, thereby retaining their own feudal autonomy.

Under the fourth shogun, Ietsuna (r. 1651–80), the *daimyo* regained lost ground as *bakufu* policy was reversed. There was a drastic decline in the number of *daimyo* transferred and *han* confiscated. Deathbed adoptions were recognized as legitimate. The shogunate even began permitting *han* to issue their own paper money, a policy which led to the proliferation of local currencies. Anxious to protect their own money, some *han* in the eighteenth century prohibited the use of outside currencies—including the *bakufu's* money!

The vigorous but eccentric fifth shogun, Tsunayoshi (r. 1680–1709) presided over a reassertion of *bakufu* power that earned him the enmity of the *daimyo.* Subsequently, the pendulum continued to swing between the *bakufu* and the *han.* Vigorous shoguns worked with trusted advisers drawn from among the Tokugawa's low-ranking retainers and disregarded the Senior Councillors who were always selected from the house *daimyo (fudai).* But when the shogun was a minor or incompetent, control over the *bakufu* reverted back to the Senior Councillors who, while conscious of their heritage of special obligation toward the shogunate, also had to consider their particular responsibilities and opportunities as *daimyo.* The tensions between the shogunate and the *han* were mirrored in their own person as they faced the demands of *bakufu* and *han,* demands often in conflict with each other. The usual pattern was for them to act more as *daimyo* than as *bakufu* officials, and they were responsible for the relaxation of *bakufu* policies. As it turned out, there were periodic shifts in the balance of power between the *bakufu* and the *han,* but the issue was never resolved completely in favor of one or the other.

The more than 250 *han* varied widely in size, local conditions, and prosperity, and all the lands held by a *daimyo* were not necessarily contiguous. Some domains were more easily organized than others. In general, the *daimyo* tended to centralize the administration of their *han* even while resisting shogunal efforts to centralize the whole system. Operating on a smaller scale than the *bakufu,* the *han* governments were generally more successful in controlling their lord's retainers. Accordingly, the trend toward divorcing samurai from the land and concentrating them in the *han* capitals, already visible in the sixteenth century, continued to be strong under the Tokugawa. By the last decade of the seventeenth century over 80 percent of the *daimyo* were paying stipends to their samurai. Looking at the system in terms of the samurai rather than their lords, it is significant that by the end of the eighteenth century 90 percent of the samurai were entirely dependent on their stipends. Only 10 percent still retained local roots in the country districts.

Assigned to various administrative, financial, and military duties, the samurai staffed the increasingly bureaucratized administrative machinery of the domains and the *bakufu.* Many of them were occupied more with government than with military affairs, and numerous samurai followed the urgings of the Tokugawa that in times of peace samurai should devote themselves to study. The shogunate itself maintained a Confucian Academy. Song Confucianism meshed with the founding shogun's anti-Buddhist proclivities and in Japan, as in China, proved compatible with bureaucratic government. Intellectually as well as professionally, the samurai of 1800 was quite different from his ancestors two centuries earlier. In other ways also, Japan experienced great changes during this period.

Writing box with cranes, designed by Korin (Tokugawa period).

Economic and Social Change

Economic growth was made possible by the Tokugawa peace and was spurred by a rise in demand created by the need to support the samurai and meet the growing expenses of the *daimyo.* Agricultural productivity increased substantially. Cultivated acreage doubled and technological improvements, the practice of multiple cropping, better seeds strains, and improved fertilizers contributed to increased output. Useful information was disseminated through agricultural handbooks. The develpment of a market network was accompanied by regional specialization in cash crops such as cotton, mulberry trees for the rearing of silk worms, indigo, tobacco, sugar cane, and so forth, but grain continued to be grown in all of Japan.

Japan's population rose from about 18 million at the beginning of the Tokugawa to around 30 million by the middle of the period. From then until the end of the shogunate the population fluctuated but did not increase, as hunger and disease took their toll. Historians report three major famines, 1732–33, 1783–87, and 1833–36 as well as many lesser ones. As an agricultural land, Japan remained at the mercy of the elements; too much or too little rain, a cold wave, typhoons, or locusts brought starvation. In desperate times people resorted to infanticide.

With the samurai largely removed from the land, the villages were left virtually autonomous, but were still responsible for the payment of taxes to the political authorities. Within the village, neither the benefits of agricultural growth nor the burdens of taxation were shared equally because of wide gradations in wealth and power in the countryside. Since tax reassessments were infrequent, wealthy peasants who were able to open new lands and otherwise increase their yields found their incomes rising and were able to accumulate funds with which to acquire still more land.

The increased use of money undermined the traditional village social-economic order based on an extended family system. Traditionally the main house of the extended family had claims on the services of the lesser households as well as some obligations to look after the poorer members. Furthermore, the heads of the main houses formed the traditional village leadership. During the Tokugawa, wealthy villagers turned increasingly to hired labor or tenant farmers to work their land. They also put their money to work in rural commerce and industry and engaged in money-lending, the extraction of vegetable oils, the production of soya sauce, and sake brewing. The fact that these wealthy villagers did not necessarily belong to the old main-house families caused considerable tension in the village.

These tensions were heightened by

Shono, from *Fifty-three Stages on the Tokaido,* by Hiroshige.

economic disparities. While some profited from the commercialization of agriculture, the poorer farmers and the landless shared little, if at all, in the prosperity of the countryside. They suffered from the dislocations caused by the economic and social change as contractual relationships replaced those based on family. Mostly they endured in silence, but sometimes peasants expressed their resentment in uprisings. Peasant unrest was on the increase in the late Tokugawa. In contrast to early Tokugawa rural uprisings, which were often led by village headmen, those of the late period were frequently directed against the wealthy and powerful village leaders. However, neither the uprisings nor the changes in agricultural technology seriously threatened the basic stability of the village. Violence was a form of protest, not a means toward revolution. Changes in agriculture increased yield but did not alter the basic pattern of rice farming with its need for intensive labor and community cooperation.

The official Confucian theory recognized only four social classes and thus failed to reflect the more complex stratification of the countryside. Still less in keeping with Confucian theory was the growing wealth of the merchant class, theoretically considered economic parasites and relegated to the bottom of society. The authorities found that they could control the merchants politically and keep them in their place socially, but they were too dependent on their services to do them permanent economic harm as a class. In addition to Edo where a little over half the population consisted of townspeople *(chōnon),* Osaka developed as a prosperous commercial and shipping center while Kyoto also continued as a major city. *Han* capitals, originally founded as political and military centers, also became centers of trade. Privileged merchants, usually operating under license, supplied the link between the cities and the rural hinterlands, and between the local centers and the capital.

Merchants also handled the warehousing of rice and other commodities and were licensed to operate the *han* monopolies. Brokers converted rice into cash or credit for sellers. Important merchants acted as financial and forwarding agents for the *daimyo,* handling shipments to Osaka for exchange or to Edo for consumption. They supplied banking services, dealing in the various *han* currencies, transferring funds, and repeatedly issuing loans to the political authorities and to hard-pressed samurai. The position of individual merchants could be precarious, and in extreme cases a wealthy merchant with heavy loans out to the powerful might suffer confiscation so that the loans could go unpaid, as happened to a great Osaka merchant in 1705. However, these were exceptions, and government measures to force creditors to settle for less than full payment or for the cancellation of loans simply had the effect of raising the cost of new loans, because the authorities never found a way to eliminate the need for such borrowing. The *bakufu*, *daimyo*, and samurai depended on the merchants as fiscal agents, and the merchants prospered. In the second half of the eighteenth century there were over two hundred mercantile houses valued at over 200,000 gold *ryo*, a monetary unit worth roughly a *koku* of rice. Such merchants were fully the economic equals of the *daimyo*. Some of the great modern commercial and financial empires go back to the early Tokugawa, most notably the house of Mitsui, founded in 1620.

As in the villages, also great differences in status and wealth existed among the town dwellers; for every great merchant there were many more humble shopkeepers and artisans. At the very bottom of society were the people who did not belong even theoretically in the four Confucian classes. Beggars, traveling performers, prostitutes, scavengers, and so forth were outcasts by occupation. Still worse off were pariahs (then called *eta*, today known as *burakumin*) whose position beyond the pale of ordinary society was hereditary. Some were butchers and tanners, performing tasks considered unclean. Others were simple artisans or farmers. Considered defiling, they were discriminated against in law and kept in enforced segregation. The total number of occupational outcasts and pariahs is estimated at around 380,000 for the closing years of the Tokugawa.

Samurai and Commoners

Ieyasu, following the example of Hideyoshi, used all the resources of law and ideology to draw a strict line between samurai and commoners. On the surface at least, there was no conflict with the four classes of Confucian theory, for the character read *shi (shih)* in Chinese and designating the scholar (at the top of the Chinese social hierarchy) was in Japanese pronounced *samurai*. The most visible sign of the samurai's privilege was his sole right to wear swords, symbols of the samurai even after they had ceased to be his major tools. In an era of peace, when his duties were largely civil, the samurai was sent to school, to absorb the Confucian ethic of dutiful obedience to superiors and conscientious concern for those below him on the social scale. Ideally, he was supposed to combine the virtues of the Confucian scholar with those of the old-time warrior and thus to serve as both the moral leader and defender of society, totally devoted to his moral duty.

Although it did happen that a masterless samurai *(rōnin)* dropped out of his class or a merchant family formed a marriage alliance with an impoverished samurai family, such exceptions to the rigid maintenance of hereditary class identity were rare. As is to be expected, the world of samurai and merchant did share certain traits and

Saikaku on How to Become a Millionaire

When the three guests had seated themselves the pounding of an earthenware mortar could be heard from the kitchen, and the sound fell with pleasant promise on their ears. They speculated on what was in store for them. One thought it would be miso soup and pickled whale skin. "No," said the second, "as this is our first visit of the New Year it should be miso soup and rice cakes." But the third, after careful reflection, settled firmly for miso soup and noodles. . . . Fujiichi then came into the room and talked to the three of them on the requisites for a successful career. Then he concluded, "You have been talking with me since early in the evening, and you may think it high time the supper was served. But one way to become a millionaire is not to provide supper. The noise of the mortar which you heard when you first arrived was the pounding of starch for the paper covers of the great ledger."

From Donald Keene, *Japanese Literature* (New York: Grove Press, 1955), p. 84.

Irises, sixfold screen by Korin, the last syllable of whose name was used to designate the Rimpa school ("Rin school").

values; the great merchant establishments resembled feudal fiefs not only in their wealth but also in their expectation of lifelong loyal service from their employees, who in turn were entitled to be treated with due paternalistic solicitude. However, the ultimate aim of the merchant houses was to make money, whereas it was the mark of samurai pride to regard consideration of financial gain as beneath contempt.

The Tokugawa period's finest poet, Bashō (1644–94), master of the seventeen-syllable *haiku,* was born a samurai but gave up his rank to live the life of a commoner, earning his living as a poet. Others who contributed notably to the period's cultural life were born commoners. These include the members of Kyoto's remarkable Rimpa School, artists who gave new life to an aristocratic tradition going back to the Heian period and thus rejected the values of the military class that continued to patronize Chinese styles.

Equally Japanese but drawing its nourishment from different roots was the urban culture of Edo, which reached a high point during the last quarter of the seventeenth and first quarter of the eighteenth centuries. Most large cities of the world have "pleasure districts," which are more or less tolerated by the political authorities, that is, sections of town devoted to bohemian life, erotic activities, entertainment, and gambling. But rarely, if ever, have such quarters produced a first-rate aesthetic as they did in Yoshiwara, the home of Edo's "floating world." Here, and in similar quarters in the other large towns, the Japanese tradition of aesthetic discrimination once more led to keen appreciation of stylistic excellence in dress and coiffure, in gesture and perfume, and in life itself. Particularly admired were the spirit and elegant chic of the great courtesans who presided over this world.

Portraits of courtesans are among the masterpieces of the Japanese print, perhaps the last major accomplishment

Itō Jinsai: Homage to the Analects

The *Analects* alone is a book which can serve as the standard and guide for the teaching of the Way in all times. What it says is supremely right and supremely true, penetrating everything from first to last. Add one word to it and it is one word too long; take one word away and it is one word too short. In this book the Way finds its ultimate expression and learning discovers its highest realization. The *Analects* is like the boundless universe which men live in without comprehending its full magnitude. Enduring and immutable throughout the ages; in every part of the world it serves as an infallible guide. Is it not, indeed, great!

Ryusaku Tsunoda, Wm. Theodore de Bary, Donald Keene, *Sources of Japanese Tradition* (New York: Columbia University Press, 1958), p. 419.

Far left: *Girl in Transparent Dress Tying Her Obi,* woodcut print by Okumura Masanobu (1686–1764). Left: *The Actor Otani Oniji III as Edohei,* woodcut by Sharaku (1794).

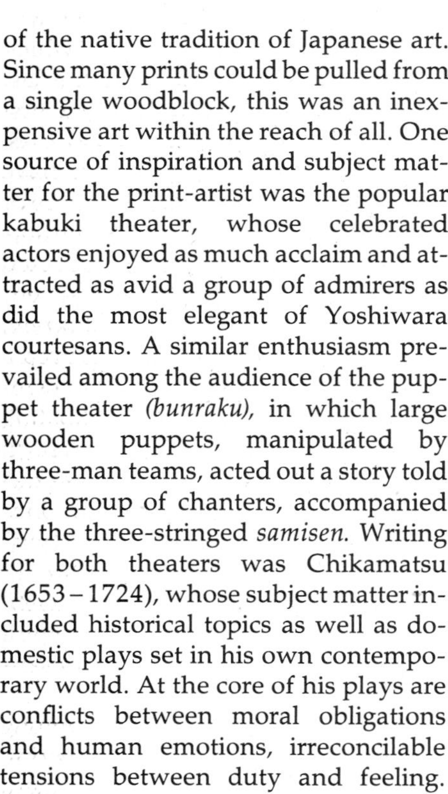

of the native tradition of Japanese art. Since many prints could be pulled from a single woodblock, this was an inexpensive art within the reach of all. One source of inspiration and subject matter for the print-artist was the popular kabuki theater, whose celebrated actors enjoyed as much acclaim and attracted as avid a group of admirers as did the most elegant of Yoshiwara courtesans. A similar enthusiasm prevailed among the audience of the puppet theater *(bunraku),* in which large wooden puppets, manipulated by three-man teams, acted out a story told by a group of chanters, accompanied by the three-stringed *samisen.* Writing for both theaters was Chikamatsu (1653–1724), whose subject matter included historical topics as well as domestic plays set in his own contemporary world. At the core of his plays are conflicts between moral obligations and human emotions, irreconcilable tensions between duty and feeling. Typically a small shopkeeper is torn between his obligations to his family and business, on the one hand, and his love for a lovely courtesan on the other. Such a conflict often ends in suicide. Art imitates life, but life also imitates art; the plays produced such a rash of love suicides that the government finally banned all plays with the words "love suicide" in the title.

Winds of Change

Japan's society and economy by 1800 were quite different from what they had been two hundred years earlier when Ieyasu established the Tokugawa order. This was reflected not only in the arts but also in intellectual life. Inspired by continental Neo-Confucianism Japanese scholars developed their own theories and interpretations that they expounded in official and private academies such as that of Ito Jinsai (1627–1705) in Kyoto. The decentralization of power and patronage helped to sustain a vigorous intellectual diversity. By no means was this confined to Confucian studies: Some scholars found new meaning in Japan's own religious and literary heritage and brought about a Shinto revival. Both Confucians and nativists found much to praise in the Japanese tradition but both also harbored a potential for undercutting the Tokugawa because both emphasized the central importance of the emperor rather than the shogun.

The early contacts with Europe, which seemed to hold so much promise, ended in disillusionment and apprehension on the part of shoguns alarmed by European political ambitions as exemplified by the Spanish seizure of the Philippines. Furthermore, they were also worried about the subversiveness of Christianity in their own country, for the Shimabara Rebellion (1637–38) in Kyushu was fought under banners inscribed with Christian slogans written in Portuguese. After fierce and ruthless persecution, Christianity was almost completely stamped out. For additional security, the *bakufu* expelled all Europeans with the exception only of the non-proselytizing Dutch, who were limited to a small island in Nagasaki Harbor where they were isolated and confined much as though in a prison. The *bakufu* also issued a decree forbidding Japanese from traveling overseas.

The annual Dutch vessel to Nagasaki and some limited commerce with China was all that remained to link Japan to the outside world. Nevertheless, a small but indefatigable group of scholars courageously wrestled with the difficulties of the Dutch language to pursue studies in Western medicine, astronomy, geography, and other sciences. By the end of the eighteenth century these scholars of "Dutch Learning," despite the *bakufu,* no longer confined themselves to science but also turned to political, military, and economic matters. Implicit in the views of the scholars of Dutch Learning was dissatisfaction with the Tokugawa seclusion policy, which stood in the way of their learning more about Western civilization and prevented them from traveling abroad.

The absence of a Chinese equivalent to the school of Dutch Learning is simply one of the many differences between China and Japan in 1800, differences not only in the scale of their territories and populations but also in their social structures, political systems, and to a considerable degree also in the values of their peoples as expressed in their artistic and intellectual creations. They resembled each other in that in both the Qing and the Tokugawa, fissures had begun to appear in the body politic and both regimes had passed their prime. The Qing was to outlast the Tokugawa by forty-four years, but, by coincidence, it also began forty-four years earlier. In any case, no educated person in 1800 in Beijing or Edo expected his regime to last forever, but no one could anticipate how very different the future would be.

Suggestions for Further Reading

Emperor of China: Self Portrait of K'ang-hsi (1974) and *Death of Woman Wang* (1978) by Jonathan Spence provide strikingly different perspectives on Qing China. Ping-ti Ho, *Studies in the Population of China, 1368–1953* (1959) is a basic book on a major subject. Also recommended are John Watt, *The District Magistrate in Late Imperial China* (1972); I. Miyazaki, *China's Examination Hell: The Civil Service Examinations of Imperial China* (1978) trans. by Conrad Schirokauer; Arthur Waley, *Yuan Mei: Eighteenth Century Chinese Poet* (1956); and Paul Ropp, *Dissent in Early Modern China: Ju-lin wai-shih and Ch'ing Social Criticism* (1981). Thomas A. Metzger, *Escape from Predicament: Neo-Confucianism and China's Evolving Political Culture* (1977), is seminal but difficult.

A stimulating interpretation of the Tokugawa political system is provided by Harold Bolitho, *Treasures Among Men: The Fudai Daimyo in Tokugawa Japan* (1974). Also see Conrad Totman, *Politics in the Tokugawa Bakufu, 1600–1843* (1967). On Tokugawa economic history see Thomas C. Smith, *The Agrarian Origins of Modern Japan* (1959). A major work on Tokugawa social history as well as on values is Ronald P. Dore, *Education in Tokugawa Japan* (1965). On the lively culture of the Tokugawa townspeople see Howard Hibbett, *The Floating World in Japanese Fiction* (1959). Also recommended is Richard Lane, *Images from the Floating World: The Japanese Print* (1978). Donald Keene, *World Within Walls: Japanese Literature of the Pre-modern Era, 1600–1867* (1976), is a definitive treatment. Also see Peter Nosco, ed., *Confucianism and Japanese Culture* (1984).

An informative account of the early contacts between modern Europe and Japan is C. R. Boxer, *The Christian Century in Japan* (1951). Also see Michael Cooper, S. J., *They Came to Japan—An Anthology of European Reports on Japan, 1543–1640* (1965), and George Elison, *Deus Destroyed: The Image of Christianity in Early Modern Japan* (1973). Recommended for China are Arnold H. Rowbotham, *Missionary and Mandarin: The Jesuits at the Court of China* (1942) and Jonathan Spence, *The Memory Palace of Matteo Ricci* (1984). European knowledge of and reactions to Asia is the subject of a multi-volume work still in progress: Donald Lach, *Asia in the Making of Europe* (1965–   ).

	1648			1700		
SOUTHWEST ASIA AND AFRICA	**1652** Dutch found Cape Colony ***ca.* 1700** Rise of Ashanti, West Africa				**1737–47** Nadir Shah, decline of Safavid Empire	
EUROPE	**1660–88** Stuart Restoration **1661–1715** Louis XIV	**1683** Turks besiege Vienna **1685** Edict of Nantes revoked **1685–1750** Johann Sebastian Bach **1687** Newton's Law of Gravitation	**1688** Glorious Revolution **1689–1725** Peter the Great **1690** Locke, *Two Treatises of Civil Government*	**1701–14** War of Spanish Succession **1715–74** Louis XV **1720** South Sea Bubble **1723–42** Robert Walpole	**1740–80** Maria Theresa **1740–86** Frederick the Great **1756–63** Seven Years' War **1756–91** Wolfgang Amadeus Mozart	**1762** Rousseau, *The Social Contract* **1762–96** Catherine the Great **1769** James Watt's first steam engine **1770–1827** Ludwig van Beethoven
SOUTH AND SOUTHEAST ASIA	**1653** Taj Mahal completed **1690** British found Calcutta				**1751** French control Deccan **1757** Battle of Plassey **1773** Regulation Act	
EAST ASIA	**1662–1722** Emperor Kangxi ***ca.* 1675–1725** Golden age of Edo urban culture, Japan			**1736–95** Emperor Qianlong	**1796–1804** White Lotus Rebellion	
THE AMERICAS AND PACIFIC		**1664** British seize New Amsterdam		**1728** Bering explores Alaska **1756–63** French and Indian War	**1765** Stamp Act **1768–80** Cook explores Pacific Ocean **1773** Boston Tea Party **1774** Quebec Act	

Ashanti wood carving.

Napoleon, 1800.

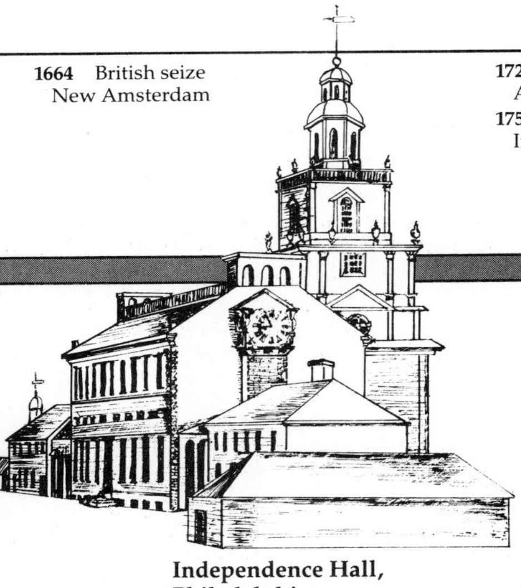

Independence Hall, Philadelphia, 1776.

East India Company merchant, by an Indian artist.

Charles II of England, 1660-85.

Emblem of the Sun King, Louis XIV.

	1815
	1805–48 Mohammed Ali founds dynasty in Egypt **1806** British control Cape Colony **1807** Slavery abolished in British Empire
1776 Smith, *Wealth of Nations* **1789** French Revolution begins	**1798** Malthus, *Essay on the Principle of Population* **1799** Napoleon becomes First Consul **1804–14** Napoleonic Empire
1784 East India Act **1786–93** Cornwallis in Bengal **1796** British conquer Ceylon	
1775–83 American Revolution **1776** US Declaration of Independence **1788** British colonize Australia **1803** Louisiana Purchase	**1807–30** Latin American wars for independence

Chinese fan painting, *ca.* 1700.

***Fuji above Storm,* by Hokusai, 1760-1849.**

27 Europe in the Seventeenth Century
Political and Economic Crises

The seventeenth century, much more than the fifteenth or sixteenth, is the century in which modern European civilization took on recognizable form. It was also a century afflicted by severe political, social, and economic crises, crises at least as dangerous as those that had shaken the medieval civilization of Europe in the fourteenth century. Everywhere the growing power of the state was challenged, and in the 1640s the three strongest European monarchies—Spain, France, and England—were weakened by outright rebellions. War was endemic—the last of the religious wars merged with wars to preserve the balance of power, and these in turn with the first commercial wars. The ravages of war were compounded by famine and plague. Population growth leveled off, and in some areas, notably Germany, population declined. There was also a prolonged economic depression, running through the middle decades of the century. The flow of silver from the New World, which had stimulated the economy, dropped off sharply, and industrial production in Europe increased only slightly, if at all. Only gradually, after 1670, did commerce and industry start again. Meanwhile, poverty exacerbated social unrest, and inadequate revenues limited the capabilities of governments.

Yet out of this unpromising environment a new Europe emerged. Governments, businessmen, and intellectual leaders were determined not to be deprived of the gains they had made in the last two centuries. Every challenge was met, at different dates and by different means in different countries. But the net result was that Europe was richer, controlled more of the world's commerce, and had more effective governments in 1700 than in 1600. And, as an unexpected bonus, there was an intellectual revolution, a sharp change in ways of thinking about man and the universe, that did more to affect the nature of human life than any of the new ideas that had emerged during the Italian Renaissance (see pp. 413–29).

Although the seventeenth-century statesmen and writers recognized the importance of economic problems more clearly than had their predecessors, they still felt that political problems deserved primary consideration. They wanted to complete the process that had begun in the thirteenth century, the building of sovereign territorial states. This process had been interrupted by the troubles of the fourteenth century and the religious conflicts of the seventeenth century; now it was to be pushed to a conclusion. From a theoretical point of view, this meant defining the concept of sovereignty ever more clearly. From a practical point of view, it meant concentrating supreme power in some organ of the state, either in the monarchy (as in France and most other states) or in the representative assembly (as in England).

FRANCE: IN SEARCH OF ORDER AND AUTHORITY, 1598–1661

Seventeenth-century France still felt the effects of the anarchy that had prevailed for almost half a century before the Edict of Nantes in 1598. Three weak kings had tarnished the prestige of the monarchy, and the great nobles had become powerful and unruly. Merchants and manufacturers had been hard hit by the wars, and the peasants had suffered heavily from the ravages of undisciplined soldiers. The mass of the people were weary of disorder, eager for security, but still somewhat suspicious of any authority that might violate local privileges and increase the burden of taxation.

Jean Bodin, the most penetrating political thinker of those tragic years, had seen what was needed. In his book *The Republic* (1576), Bodin argued that in any well-ordered state, supreme power or sovereignty must be clearly lodged somewhere, preferably in the monarchy. Sovereignty he defined as the power of "giving laws to the people as a whole without their consent." Bodin did not think of this power as arbitrary or capricious: the sovereign was still subject to the laws of God and of nature. But he insisted that sovereign power must not be limited by any human agency—that is, it must be "absolute" to be effective. He insisted that it could not be divided—for instance, among king, Estates General, and *parlements.* It must be recognized as legitimately residing in one person or one political institution. Bodin's prescription was fulfilled in the French ab-

Jean Bodin on Sovereignty

Jean Bodin was a sixteenth-century French lawyer who was interested in political and economic problems. The *fact* of sovereignty had been recognized for some time, but Bodin was the first writer to express the *idea* in clear and uncompromising terms.

Sovereignty is supreme power over citizens and subjects unrestrained by laws. . . . A prince is bound by no law of his predecessor, and much less by his own laws. . . . He may repeal, modify, or replace a law made by himself and without the consent of his subjects. . . . The opinion of those who have written that the king is bound by the popular will must be disregarded; such doctrine furnishes seditious men with material for revolutionary plots. No reasonable ground can be found to claim that subjects should control princes or that power should be attributed to popular assemblies. . . . The highest privilege of sovereignty consists in giving laws to the people as a whole without their consent. . . . Under this supreme power of making and repealing laws it is clear that all other functions of sovereignty are included.

From Jean Bodin, *Six Books Concerning the Republic,* from the Latin version of 1586 [the French version of 1576 is less coherent], trans. by F. W. Coker, in *Readings in Political Philosophy* (New York: Macmillan, 1938), pp. 374, 375, 376, 377, 380.

solute monarchy that became the model and envy of most of Europe.

Henry IV and Sully

The first steps toward restoring the power of the monarchy were taken by Henry IV (r. 1589–1610) and his minister, the duke of Sully. Henry, the first of the Bourbon dynasty, was a popular king—courageous, vigorous, humorous, and tolerant. But he spent much of his time hunting and lovemaking and left the routine business of government to Sully and others. Sully was a puritanical Huguenot with a keen sense of economy and a hatred of dishonesty. He improved the financial condition of the monarchy, partly by avoiding expensive wars and partly by patching up the tax-collecting system. The French taxation system was inefficient, corrupt, and inequitable. Many taxes were "farmed"—that is, the right to collect them was granted to private collectors who paid the government a fixed sum and then collected all they could. The burden fell most heavily on the peasants, since the nobles and the upper bourgeoisie were exempt from major taxes. Sully could do nothing to make the system more just, but he could make it work better by discharging dishonest and inefficient tax farmers. Moreover, the reestablishment of internal peace and order, which allowed agriculture and commerce to recover, helped to increase the government's revenues. When Henry IV was assassinated by a Catholic fanatic in 1610 there was a sizable surplus in the treasury.

The Estates General of 1614

Within a few years the work of Henry and Sully was in ruins. Under the regency of Henry's widow, Marie de' Medici, the treasury surplus was squandered by rapacious courtiers, and Spain began once more to intervene in French affairs, sometimes in alliance with the Huguenots. In 1614 the Estates General were summoned to one of their rare meetings, but the deliberations soon turned into a struggle between the First and Second Estates (the clergy and the nobility) and the Third Estate (the bourgeoisie). No group was willing to take responsibility; and no group had the power to demand reform. The assembly dissolved with a strong declaration that "the king is sovereign in France, and holds his crown from God only." It was not to meet again until 1789, on the eve of the Revolution.

Contemporary illustration of the assassination of Henry IV.

Richelieu (1624–42)

In 1614 Henry IV's son, Louis XIII (r. 1610–43), was only fourteen years old. He was soon to be married to Anne of Austria, daughter of Philip III of Spain, as a symbol of Habsburg influence on France. There was not much to be hoped for from the monarch himself — except that he might choose some able first minister. The man was already in sight—a brilliant young bishop named Richelieu—but it took him several years to become a cardinal (in 1622) and head of the king's council (in 1624). From 1624 to his death in 1642 Richelieu was the real ruler of France. More than anyone he established absolute monarchy in France.

Three studies of Richelieu by Philippe de Champaigne.

Richelieu had the clearest and most penetrating mind of any statesman of his generation. His purpose was to enhance the power and prestige of the French monarchy beyond any possibility of challenge. He came to his task with a superb grasp of political and diplomatic possibilities and an inflexible will unhampered by moral scruples. Richelieu admired Machiavelli's writings, and the heart of his political creed was *raison d'état*—the doctrine that the good of the state is the supreme good, and that any means may be used to attain it. He was not irreligious, but the workings of his mind were overwhelmingly this-worldly. His policy was that of an astute secular statesman who put public order before religious zeal.

Richelieu had three concrete objectives. First, he meant to break the political and military power of the Huguenots. Second, he meant to crush the political influence of the great nobles. And finally, he meant to destroy the power of the Habsburgs to intervene in French internal affairs.

The Edict of Nantes had allowed the Huguenots to garrison about two hundred towns, the chief of which was La Rochelle on the west coast. Richelieu persuaded Louis XIII that he would never be master in his own house until he had wiped out this "empire within an empire." Rumors that the government had decided to attack provoked the Huguenots to rebel, and Richelieu proceeded to besiege and capture La Rochelle. At the Peace of Alais in 1629, which settled the dispute, Richelieu was unexpectedly generous in his terms. He allowed the Huguenots the right to worship as they pleased once he had attained his primary objective of eliminating their political and military autonomy. He did not wish to alienate Protestants abroad who could help him in a war with Spain and Austria, and he hoped he could make loyal and useful citizens out of the Huguenots. In this he was successful.

Richelieu's attack on the political power of the nobility was less successful, but it was just as determined. Until the very end of his career, he was constantly threatened by aristocratic intrigues. In response he developed a network of spies, set up a special tribunal to try noble lawbreakers, and sternly forbade dueling, a privilege that marked the freedom of the aristocracy from ordinary restraints. He gradually weakened the power of the great nobles who were provincial governors and gave more local administrative responsibilities to direct representatives of the crown. These representatives, called *intendants,* were usually drawn from the *noblesse de la robe,* ennobled officeholders of middle-class origin, who were more dependent on the monarchy than the older nobility. Richelieu did nothing to lessen the economic and social privileges of the French nobility, but he did curtail its political power.

Richelieu was no financier, nor did he have any interest in bettering the condition of the common people. He spent large sums on rebuilding the armed forces and even more in actual warfare against Spain. He left the government's finances and the nation's peasants in worse condition than he had found them. But through his subtle diplomacy and his well-timed intervention in the Thirty Years' War, he made France, instead of Spain, the leading European power.

Mazarin and the Fronde

Richelieu's death in 1642 (Louis XIII died a few months later, in 1643) put his work to a severe test. Louis XIV was only five when his father died, and so his mother, Anne of Austria, was appointed regent. However, she left the business of government to the man whom Richelieu had picked and trained to succeed himself, an Italian cardinal named Mazarin. Mazarin had the subtlety and political skill of his master but not his inflexible will; he was both more adaptable and, as a foreigner, less popular than Richelieu. His two main objectives were to continue the war against Spain and to maintain the prestige of the monarchy at the level to which Richelieu had raised it. The nobility hated him as a foreign upstart, however, and the bourgeoisie hated him for the high taxes he imposed to carry on the war. The result was the last serious rebellion to take place against the monarchy until the French Revolution—a complicated and uncoordinated movement of resistance known as the Fronde (1648–52).

The word *Fronde* referred to a game of slinging clods at passing coaches, which was played by the urchins of Paris. The rebellion was like the game; it was annoying, but in the end it did not keep the monarchy from driving along the road to absolutism. The leaders did not want to destroy the French monarchy nor did they wish to upset the established social order. They were composed of several groups—the judges of the High Courts, the chief financial officers, and the nobles led by princes of the blood. Each group wanted to modify the structure of government so that it could have more influence. But no group could agree with others on a joint program, with the exception of exiling Mazarin. Thus the *parlements,* which began the struggle, stood for the privileges of the corporations of bureaucrats who controlled the courts and the financial bureaus. They wanted the king to rule with their advice, rather than with that of councillors whom he could make or break as he pleased. They insisted especially that no tax could be imposed without their consent. The nobles, who joined the rebellion later, had no intention of letting the *parlements* become dominant; they wanted to get rid of the *intendants* and regain their old powers as provincial governors. The result might have been different if anyone had dared draw on the deep-seated resentment of the lower classes—a resentment that had been expressed during the first half of the century in many local riots against taxation and misgovernment. But no one was willing to take the chance of unleashing forces that might not be controllable. Unlike the contemporary English rebellion, in which the middle and lower classes accepted radical doctrines and defeated the king (see p. 569), the Fronde remained dominated by the nobility and the upper bourgeoisie. The innate conservatism of these groups, combined with lack of unity among the leaders, led to the disintegration of the rebellion. There was very little hard fighting; by the end of 1652, Mazarin was once more back in control. Most Frenchmen concluded that a strong monarchy was preferable to futile civil war. The young king, Louis XIV, was to profit from this reaction when he came of age. Meanwhile, he remembered with loathing the violence of the Fronde and came to hate Paris, from which he had had to flee in 1648.

A wax medallion of Cardinal Mazarin (*ca.* 1650).

In spite of the Fronde and the tax burden that continued to oppress the common people, Mazarin carried on the war with Spain until the Spaniards were forced to ask for terms in 1659. France gained two Pyrenees counties, and Maria Theresa, daughter of Philip

IV of Spain, was married to Louis XIV. Both the treaty and the marriage symbolized the humiliation of Spain and the triumph of France as the leading power in Europe. Mazarin died in 1661, and Louis XIV announced to his ministers that he would henceforth be his own prime minister. The work of Richelieu had now come to full fruition. The French monarchy no longer had anything to fear from Huguenots and nobles at home or from Habsburgs abroad. It was an absolute monarchy, endowed with a fuller sovereignty than any other yet seen in European history.

ENGLAND: IN SEARCH OF CIVIL AND RELIGIOUS LIBERTY, 1603–60

While Richelieu and Mazarin were laying the foundations of absolute monarchy by divine right, leaders in England were slowly developing a constitutional, parliamentary monarchy. Richelieu could see clearly where he was going, but the goal was never clear to English leaders during their century of conflict with the crown. Englishmen groped their way toward a conception of sovereignty as something rooted in law rather than in personal authority, something to be lodged in the hands of an assembly that represented the community, or at least its more wealthy and influential members. England was not alone in its resistance to absolute monarchy, but the result in other countries, such as Poland, was anarchy and confusion. Only in England was a representative assembly able to increase its power without wrecking the state. When Queen Anne came to the throne in 1702 the English government was both a stronger and more popular government than it had been in 1603 when James I succeeded Elizabeth I. The example of England was to have an enormous influence on Western history throughout the following two centuries.

England, on the periphery of Europe, had always been peculiar in its political development. For instance, although the strong monarchy of the Tudors (1485–1603) was part of a general European trend, the survival and strengthening of Parliament under such a monarchy was without parallel elsewhere. The Tudors continued to use Parliament in legislation and taxation, whereas rulers on the Continent found representative assemblies either useless or obstructive. Parliament, particularly the House of Commons, slowly acquired a corporate feeling and a sense of being an integral part of the national government. The House of Commons represented both the mercantile classes in the towns and the landed gentry (knights and squires) in the country. The gentry had been increasing in numbers, wealth, and political influence since the dissolution of the monasteries. They governed England at the local level as justices of the peace (the English monarchy had no paid bureaucrats like the French *intendants*), and they dominated the lower house of Parliament by sitting as representatives not only of the counties but of many boroughs as well. In any other country they would have been considered members of the lesser nobility; in England they sat in the House of Commons with merchants and lawyers.

The English Parliament in the early seventeenth century thus represented all the politically active classes of the nation in a way no other representative assembly in Europe did. There were no provincial estates or privileges in England as there were in France, and the class lines among peers, gentry, and wealthy burgesses were not so sharply drawn. The rigid English rule of primogeniture meant that younger sons of the nobility, who were commoners, often went into the professions. On the other hand, English merchants were continually buying land and becoming gentry. This meant that if the monarchy should ever fall out with Parliament—and with the social groups it represented—it would not be able to play class against class or district against district.

James I and Parliament

The Stuarts, who ruled from 1603 to 1714, either could not or would not cooperate with Parliament. James I (r. 1603–25, king of Scotland and of England), the son of Mary Queen of Scots, was a well-meaning but pedantic intellectual who never understood the social structure or the political realities of the kingdom he inherited from Elizabeth. He had been raised as a Protestant, but he had not greatly enjoyed his Presbyterian upbringing. His aims were praiseworthy—peace with Spain, toleration of the Catholic minority in England, union of England and Scotland, and a strong but benevolent monarchy—but he did not inspire confidence as a political leader. Moreover, many of his ministers were incompetent. Unlike Elizabeth, who often concealed her imperious will in cloudy and ambiguous language, James liked to have things dangerously clear. He had written a book, *The True Law of Free Monarchies,* in which he insisted that kings were responsible only to God, and in fact were themselves like gods on earth.

His belief in a monarchy free to do as it pleased for the common good did not appeal to the classes represented in Parliament. Some of James's policies might have really helped the poor; others simply transferred wealth from one privileged group to another. In either case, opposition to the king could not endanger the country. The Tudors had long ago ended the threat of aristocratic violence, and peace with Spain in 1604 removed the danger of foreign conquest. Only their own king could now attack the beliefs or interfere with the property rights of the privileged classes. Parliament, fearing royal tyranny, began to criticize James's acts. James, fearing parliamentary intervention, began to scold Parliament. The delicate Tudor balance was destroyed.

Friction rapidly developed over three related issues: religion, finance, and foreign policy. The Puritans and their sympathizers in the House of Commons wished to "purify" the Anglican Church of everything that savored of Catholic practice, from "popish" ritual to the authority of bishops. James was convinced that the Presbyterian system of church government would not only destroy royal control of the Church, but would threaten the monarchy itself. Parliament, annoyed by the extravagance of James's court and dubious about his policies, denied him enough money to meet the rising costs of government. James replied by raising money without parliamentary approval—for example, by increasing the customs duties. When his right to take such actions was contested, the courts ruled in his favor. This seeming subservience of the courts to the royal will further disturbed Parliament.

James I, attributed to Federigo Zuccharo.

Meanwhile James's foreign policy exasperated the Puritan majority in Parliament. He was too friendly with Spain for the Puritan taste, he did little to defend Protestants abroad against the rising tide of Catholicism, and he tried in vain to marry his son Charles to the Spanish Infanta. When James chided the House of Commons in 1621 for even discussing his foreign policy, the House passed a unanimous Protestation defending its right to discuss "the arduous and urgent affairs concerning the King, State, and defence of the realm, and of the Church of England." This was revolutionary talk. James tore the resolution from the Commons' *Journal,* but he could not undo what had been done. The House of Commons, which Queen Elizabeth had kept under the control of her privy councillors, was now taking the initiative under leaders of its own. An aggressive and powerful element among James's subjects was demanding a voice in politics that he was utterly unwilling to grant.

Charles I and the English Revolution

The situation rapidly worsened during the early years of the reign of Charles I (r. 1625–49). Charles tried to

England During the English Revolution 1642–49

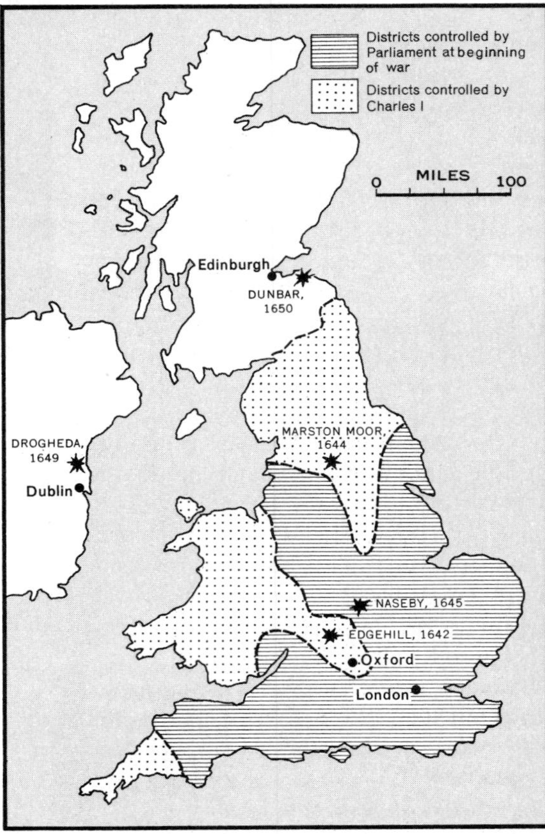

Charles I, by Daniel Mytens (1631).

please Parliament by attacking Catholic countries, but his incompetent favorite, the Duke of Buckingham, failed to capture Cadiz in Spain or to relieve the French Huguenots at La Rochelle. Parliament had urged war but had not granted adequate taxes, so the government tried to pay for the wars by levying a forced loan. Parliament in 1628 drew up a formal protest in the form of a Petition of Right, which they finally compelled Charles to approve. Its two main provisions were that no one should henceforth be forced to pay any tax or loan "without common consent by Act of Parliament," and that no one should be imprisoned without cause shown.

By the next year the House of Commons was roused to fury by Charles's assertions of his full control of Church and state. It declared that anyone who introduced anything savoring of Catholic practices in the Anglican Church was "a capital enemy to this kingdom and commonwealth," and that anyone who advised or submitted to the levying of taxes without parliamentary consent was "a betrayer of the liberties of England." The issue of "sovereignty" had finally been raised, and the word itself was being debated by lawyers and parliamentary orators. Where did the supreme power in England lie—in the king or in Parliament? The older answer, that it lay in the "king-in-Parliament," would no longer do. The royal prerogative and the "liberties of England" were not reconcilable any longer.

Charles I took things into his own hands and ruled without Parliament for eleven years (1629–40). He was less intelligent and more stubborn than his father. James had always yielded before conflict became irreconcilable. Rather than yield, Charles was to resort to duplicity and falsehood in the crises ahead of him, and as a result he ended his life on the block. Trying to duplicate Richelieu's brilliant work, he chose tough-minded advisers: Thomas Wentworth, Earl of Strafford, in political affairs, and William Laud, Archbishop of Canterbury, in ecclesiastical matters. With them and others, Charles devised new methods of nonparliamentary taxation that provided enough money to run the government so long as it stayed out of war. Laud began a movement back toward more ritual in the Anglican service, a movement the Puritans regarded as an attempt to restore Catholicism. All opposition was sternly suppressed by the courts. Everything went well until Laud tried to force the Anglican Book of Common Prayer on stubbornly Presbyterian Scotland. Before long an angry Scottish army was encamped in northern England. Charles and Strafford, finding themselves unable to raise an army to fight the Scots, had to summon Parliament to get the money to buy them off.

The Long Parliament, which met in November 1640 and was not dissolved until 1653, became a workshop of revolution. It sent Strafford and Laud to the block. It passed an act stating that a Parliament must be summoned at least every three years. It outlawed nonparliamentary taxation and abolished the special royal courts (the Court of Star Chamber, which dealt with opposition to the government, and the Court of High Commission, for ecclesiastical affairs), which had been the chief instruments of the "Eleven Years' Tyranny." In other words, in less than a year (1640–41) Parliament had made absolute monarchy impossible in England. This much of its work won unwilling approval from Charles, since sentiment for it was virtually unanimous. But when the more radical Puritans in Parliament went on to abolish bishops in the Anglican Church and seek control of the army, a party began to form around Charles in opposition to the parliamentary majority. The result was a civil war, which lasted from 1642 until 1649.

The English Revolution was primarily a war of ideas, not of classes or of districts or even of interests. Generally the towns, the middle class, and the economically advanced southeastern counties supported Parliament, while many rural areas, aristocrats, and the backward northwest supported Charles. But nobles, squires, and artisans from all parts of England were to be found on both sides. Unlike the Fronde, in which narrow interest groups failed to work out programs with broad appeal, the English Revolution offered a real alternative to the established order: parliamentary monarchy instead of benevolent absolutism, and a Presbyterian Church governed by elected "presbyters," or elders, instead of an Anglican Church governed by bishops appointed by the crown. Unlike the Fronde again, the English Revolution was able to attract and to accept men with really radical ideas—men who wanted neither a monarchy, nor an established church, nor power in the hands of landlords.

As the civil war intensified, Parliament proved to be more successful than the king in raising money and in building a strong army. A brilliant cavalry officer named Oliver Cromwell formed a "New Model Army" largely from among his fellow Independents, or Congregationalists. These Independents were generally of lower economic status than either Anglicans or Presbyterians. They were unsophisticated, Bible-reading Puritans of strict morals who believed in independent congregations democratically organized, with little or no national organization. Cromwell and his army finally defeated the king's forces in 1645, only to fall out with the Presbyterians, who had dominated Parliament since the Anglicans withdrew in 1642 to join Charles. With Parliament and the army at loggerheads about what to do with the king and what sort of government to set up in England (many in the army wanted a truly democratic regime), the king was able to escape and make one last bid for victory before being finally defeated by Cromwell in 1648. Cromwell and the Independents were determined now to get at what they considered the root of the trouble. They "purged" Parliament of its Presbyterian members, executed King Charles I in 1649, abolished the monarchy and the House of Lords, and set up a republic, or "Commonwealth," with the "rump" of the Long Parliament as its government and Cromwell as its moving spirit.

Oliver Cromwell, painting from the original panel by Samuel Cooper.

Cromwell expelling Parliament, 1653.

Oliver Cromwell

Cromwell was a deeply religious man who tried in vain to avoid becoming a dictator. Yet he was ruthless and determined when he felt his policies were threatened. He massacred the Catholic Irish when they rebelled, defeated the Scots when they intervened in favor of the son of Charles I, fought a commercial war with the Dutch (1652–54), and boldly dissolved what was left of the Long Parliament in 1653. In a few short years he had decisively won a civil war, united the British Isles under one government for the first time, made England again the terror of the seas, and apparently wiped the slate clean for any political experiment he wished to try. The rest of his career until his death in 1658, however, was a tragic search for answers to insoluble problems: how to guarantee religious toleration to all kinds of Protestants except determined Anglicans, and at the same time how to develop some constitutional basis for his government. Cromwell tried to rule through a written constitution (the first in the history of any major state) and with the assent of Parliament. He took the title of Lord Protector instead of king, but he quarreled with his Parliaments as bitterly as the Stuarts had quarreled with theirs. At one point Cromwell had to set up an open military dictatorship to keep his Parliament from disbanding his army and persecuting his coreligionists. The plain fact was that most Englishmen were not ready for religious toleration of the radical religious minorities that made up a large part of Cromwell's army.

In addition, it became more and more evident that breaking completely with history was impossible, as was setting up a new sort of government simply by writing a constitution. There was already a "constitution" deeply ingrained in the English political tradition, although it was nowhere written down. Soon after Cromwell's death even his own supporters saw that the only possible alternative to military dictatorship was Parliament, and that the only way to restore Parliament was also to restore the monarchy. In 1660 the monarchy, Parliament, and the Anglican Church were all restored when a "Convention Parliament" invited Charles II to return from France and take up the crown.

The Restoration

At first glance nothing more remained in England after twenty years of civil war and revolutionary experiment than had remained in France after the defeat of the Fronde. To this day Englishmen refer to the events just described as the "Puritan Rebellion." They do not call it a revolution because it was succeeded by the "Restoration." But one thing at least had been decided: There was to be no absolute monarchy in England. All acts of the Long Parliament passed before the outbreak of the civil war were still valid, and these acts put severe limitations on royal power, even if the balance of power between king and Parliament was still uncertain. Strafford and Laud had tried to do for Charles I what Richelieu and Mazarin had done for Louis XIV, but all three Englishmen died on the block, while all three Frenchmen died in their beds. The turmoil of the first half of the seventeenth century left most Englishmen with certain half-expressed convictions whose effects can be traced in English history for generations. Among these convictions were a fear of allowing any one individual to acquire too much political power, a deepened respect for government by law rather than by personal command, a reverence for Parliament as the defender of individual rights against arbitrary despotism, and a distaste for standing armies.

GERMANY: DISINTEGRATION AND DISASTER, 1618–48

While France was building the strongest monarchy in Europe and England was undergoing a constitutional crisis from which it was to emerge with new strength, the German-speaking peoples were caught up in one of the most futile and destructive wars in the history of Europe. The Thirty Years' War (1618–48) was really four successive wars that began in Bohemia, spread to the rest of the Holy Roman Empire, and finally involved most of the major powers on the Continent. It was a savage and demoralizing conflict that left "Germany" poorer and weaker than the western European states.

The Causes of the Thirty Years' War

The war sprang out of a complicated mixture of religious and political grievances. Lutherans and Catholics had not fought each other since the Peace of Augsburg (1555), but the Catholics were disturbed by the fact that, in spite of the provisions of the peace, most of the Catholic bishoprics in northern Germany had fallen into Lutheran or secular hands. This gave some grounds for creating an ultra-Catholic movement headed by the Jesuits and the German Catholic princes, particularly Maximilian, Duke of Bavaria. The spread of Calvinism, furthermore, introduced a new source of friction because Calvinists had been excluded from the Peace of Augsburg. When Maximilian roughly disciplined the Protestant town of Donauwörth, Frederick V, the Calvinist ruler of the Palatinate, a small state on the middle Rhine, took the lead in forming a Protestant Union among the German princes and cities in 1608. In reply, a Catholic League was organized the next year under the leadership of Maximilian. By 1609 two military alliances faced each other within the Empire, each afraid of the other and each determined to keep the rival religion from making any further gains.

Revolt in Bohemia

As these developments show, each part of the Empire was a virtually independent state. The Habsburgs, who held the imperial title, realized that the only way to rebuild and expand imperial authority was to establish firmer control over what had been their old family domains—Austria, Bohemia, and Hungary. Thus the Austrian Habsburg, Ferdinand of Styria, had himself elected king of Bohemia in 1617.

Bohemia was a flourishing kingdom in which two nationalities (Germans and Czechs) and several religions (Catholicism, Lutheranism, Calvinism, and remnants of the Hussite movement of two centuries earlier) lived fairly peaceably together under earlier Habsburg promises of toleration. Ferdinand, a zealous Catholic, began systematically to undermine this toleration and to re-Catholicize the country. This action provoked rebellion by the Bohemian Estates, which were dominated by a strong Protestant majority. In May 1618 two of Ferdinand's councillors were tossed from a castle window in Prague, and civil war broke out between the Habsburg ruler and the Estates. The Estates raised an army, deposed Ferdinand, and offered the crown of Bohemia to Frederick V of the Palatinate. When Frederick unwisely accepted, the Protestant Union became involved in defending the Bohemian Estates, while Maximilian of Bavaria brought the Catholic League to the support of Ferdinand. In 1619 Ferdinand was elected emperor. Thus a war that might have remained a local affair soon spread throughout the Empire.

The Bohemian phase of the war was soon ended. The forces of the emperor and the League won an overwhelming victory in 1620. Frederick fled, and the emperor proceeded to work his will on the prostrate Bohemians. Half the property in the country changed hands through confiscation. The Jesuits, with strong secular backing, set out to reconvert the country to Catholicism. The prosperity of the country was ruined, Protestantism was stamped out, and Czech nationalism was crushed for two centuries to come. The Habsburgs and their Catholic allies had won the first round decisively.

Danish Intervention

The fall of Bohemia terrified German Protestants and elated the Catho-

Gustavus Adolphus.

lics. The Spanish Habsburgs came to the aid of their fellow Catholics, and the armies of the League were everywhere triumphant. In spite of the common danger, the Protestants could not unite. The Lutherans had been more afraid of a Calvinist victory in Bohemia than of an imperial triumph, and so Lutheran Saxony had actually helped Ferdinand put down the revolt. Although Frederick V was the son-in-law of James I, Protestant England gave no help because James and Charles were too involved in difficulties at home.

In 1625 the Protestant king of Denmark intervened, partly to save the cause of his coreligionists but primarily to pick up some territory in northern Germany. Within a year he was beaten by a large army raised by the most inscrutable figure of the war, a wealthy war profiteer and professional soldier named Albrecht von Wallenstein, who had offered the emperor his services. Wallenstein had no serious religious convictions, and his political aims have puzzled historians. His immediate aim seems to have been to build an imperial Habsburg military machine of such strength that it could not only eliminate all Protestant opposition but could operate independently of all other forces in the Empire, including the Catholic League. Before long Wallenstein and the League were as much at loggerheads on one side as Calvinists and Lutherans were on the other. Religion slowly receded in significance as the war became a struggle for the hegemony of Europe.

The siege of Magdeburg in 1631 by Habsburg and Catholic forces. This siege resulted in one of the bloodiest massacres of the Thirty Years' War.

The high-water mark of Habsburg triumph and Catholic recovery was reached in 1629. Denmark withdrew from the war, leaving Wallenstein's army supreme. The Catholic League and Jesuit advisers persuaded Ferdinand to issue the Edict of Restitution, which restored to Catholic hands all ecclesiastical lands lost to Protestantism since 1552. It was evident that this edict could not be carried out without more bloodshed, because it meant that Catholic bishops were to be restored throughout northern Germany. Such an act would destroy the rough balance between Catholicism and Protestantism in Germany and weaken the northern states for the benefit of Austria and Bavaria. This threat finally roused the Lutherans inside and outside Germany to a sense of their peril.

Swedish Intervention: Gustavus Adolphus

In 1631 growing Habsburg power was blocked by the intervention of Sweden, a country that had not appeared before on the stage of international politics. Gustavus II (Gustavus Adolphus, r. 1611–32) was the ablest ruler of his generation. His country was sparse in population and resources, but he had cultivated its iron and timber industries, united the nation behind him, and built the best army of the day. It was not large, but it was well equipped (with the first uniforms and an improved musket), well disciplined, and inspired by high morale. Gustavus had already come close to making the Baltic a Swedish lake in wars with Denmark and Poland. He now stepped into the fray as the sincere champion of Lutheranism, hoping apparently to set up a federation of Protestant states in Germany under Swedish leadership.

Gustavus arrived too late to save Magdeburg from a terrible sack by the Habsburg Imperialists in May 1631, but in the fall of 1631 he overwhelmed the imperial armies at Breitenfeld in Saxony. He then marched triumphantly to the Rhine. Wallenstein, whom the emperor had dismissed under pressure from the Catholic League, was recalled, only to be beaten by Gustavus at Lützen in 1632. Gustavus himself was killed in the battle, however, and by 1634 his army had finally been outnumbered and beaten. Wallenstein had been murdered by one of his staff, and another phase of the war had come to an end. Swedish intervention had saved German Protestantism but had not gained a decision. The most powerful state of all had been watching the course of events closely and was now about to intervene with decisive results.

French Intervention: Richelieu

Since coming to power in 1624, Richelieu had kept in close touch with the progress of the war through his ambassadors and agents. But for ten years he did not feel that the French army was strong enough to intervene in Germany. His major purpose was to crush the Habsburgs, both Austrian and Spanish, and he was ready to ally with anyone, Protestant or Catholic, who was opposed to them. The Dutch, who went back to war with their old enemies the Spanish, were his first allies, and in 1631 he subsidized the invasion by Gustavus Adolphus. When the Swedes were finally defeated, Richelieu saw that he would have to intervene directly if he was to check Habsburg expansion in, and perhaps control of, Europe. And so in May 1635 he declared war on the king of Spain.

The Thirty Years' War had lasted for seventeen years with no decisive result, and it was to continue for thirteen more years while French, Swedish, and Dutch armies fought against the Spanish and Austrian Habsburgs. Spain was weakened by the successful rebellion of Portugal and the almost successful rebellion of Catalonia (1640). In 1643 the French finally destroyed the legend of Spanish invincibility by crushing a Spanish army at Rocroi in the Netherlands. It was the first time in 150 years that a Spanish army had suffered a major defeat. The emperor's allies deserted him, and by 1648 the Swedes were threatening Vienna and storming Prague. The dream of Emperor Ferdinand II (who had died in 1637) of re-Catholicizing Germany and establishing Habsburg control over the Empire lay in ruins.

The Peace of Westphalia, 1648

A peace was finally worked out at the Congress of Westphalia (1643–48), Europe's first great peace conference and the first international gathering of importance since the Council of Constance (1414–18). But it was a far different gathering from that of two centuries earlier. The atmosphere and the business at hand were now entirely secular, and the communities represented were sovereign territorial states that recognized no earthly superior and only the most shadowy common interests. "Christendom" had dissolved, and the word *civilization* would not be coined till the next century to express in secular terms what *Christendom* had once meant to Europeans in religious terms.

The Sack of Magdeburg

1631

Then was there naught but beating and burning, plundering, torture, and murder. Most especially was every one of the enemy bent on securing much booty. When a marauding party entered a house, if its master had anything to give he might thereby purchase respite and protection for himself and his family till the next man, who also wanted something, should come along. It was only when everything had been brought forth and there was nothing left to give that the real trouble commenced. Then, what with blows and threats of shooting, stabbing, and hanging, the poor people were so terrified that if they had had anything left they would have brought it forth if it had been buried in the earth or hidden away in a thousand castles. In this frenzied rage, the great and splendid city that had stood like a fair princess in the land was now, in its hour of direst need and unutterable distress and woe, given over to the flames, and thousands of innocent men, women, and children, in the midst of a horrible din of heartrending shrieks and cries, were tortured and put to death in so cruel and shameful a manner that no words would suffice to describe, nor no tears to bewail it.

From Otto von Guericke, in *Readings in European History*, ed. by James Harvey Robinson (Boston: Ginn, 1906), Vol. II, pp. 211-12.

Europe in 1648

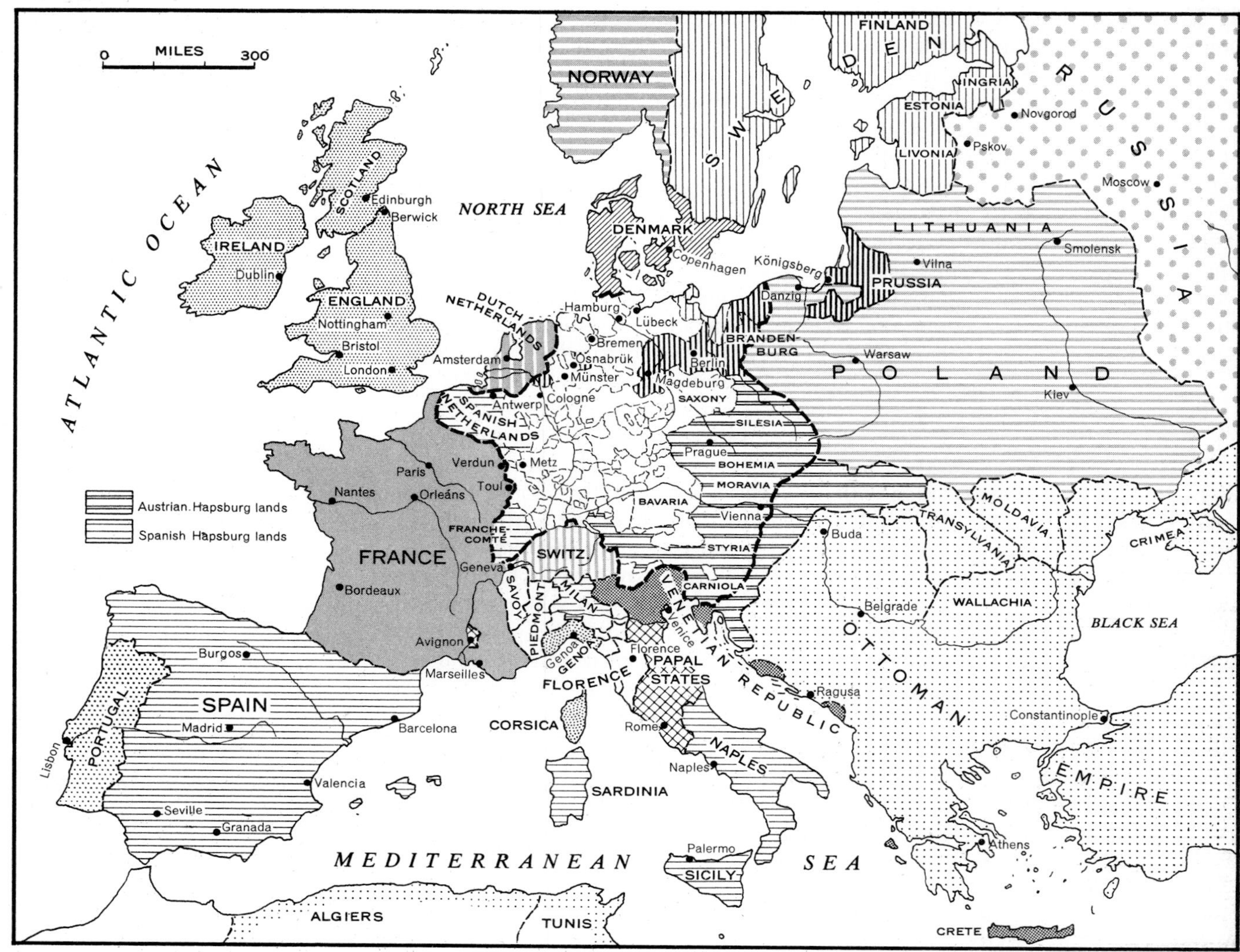

Almost every act of the Congress emphasized the importance of the sovereign state. For example, it recognized the right of each German principality to make alliances and to declare war. This constituted recognition of the disintegration of the Empire into over three hundred separate sovereignties. Switzerland and the Dutch Netherlands were recognized as sovereign states, independent of all ties to the Empire. France acquired some ambiguous rights to Alsace, Sweden acquired strips of German territory along the Baltic and the North Sea, and the two German states of Brandenburg and Bavaria ended up with increased territory and prestige. As for religion, the old principle of *cuius regio, eius religio* was reaffirmed. Calvinism was simply added to Catholicism and Lutheranism as one of the recognized faiths. The ownership of church lands was settled as of 1624, meaning that northern Germany remained predominantly Protestant and southern Germany, Catholic. France and Spain were unable to reach agreement, so their war continued until French victory was finally recognized in the Peace of the Pyrenees in 1659. France received some territory along the Pyrenees and in Flanders, and the Spanish princess, Maria Theresa, married Louis XIV. In general, the peace settlements of the middle of the century left France the strongest power in Europe, Spain prostrate, the Empire shattered, and a kind of power vacuum in the center of Europe.

The Social Results of the War

The Thirty Years' War was one of the most brutal and destructive wars until the twentieth century. Armies robbed, raped, and murdered their way back and forth across Germany. There are gruesome records of towns totally wiped out, cities reduced to a small fraction of their original population, and cultivated land reverting to waste. Starvation and disease killed more than the sword. It is impossible to be sure of the total decline in population, but some historians believe that Germany lost almost a third of its inhabitants. Others insist that the destruction was not so great as contemporary sources would suggest, and that recovery in farming districts was rapid. The social and psychological effects, however, were certainly terrible. A whole generation grew up accepting violence and brutality as normal. The fragmentation of the Empire into practically independent states hampered economic recovery. Cultural and political provincialism were to go hand in hand for the next two centuries in German history. In fact, it is almost impossible to find any good result of the generation of aimless fighting in Germany known as the Thirty Years' War.

DUTCH UNREST AND SPANISH DECLINE

England, France, and Germany were not the only countries to experience political crises in the first half of the seventeenth century. Political upheavals in this era touched every part of Europe. Even far-away Russia underwent an anarchic "Time of Troubles" before settling down uneasily under the rule of the first Romanov tsar in 1613. In the West, there were violent upheavals in the Netherlands and in Spain.

The northern Netherlands had achieved effective independence from Spain by the beginning of the century and were enjoying enormous economic success. Yet the United Provinces were riven by political and religious conflicts. One party, supported by orthodox Calvinists and led by the House of Orange (William the Silent's family), pressed for an aggressive war against Spain in the southern Netherlands. A second party, supported by the religiously tolerant Arminians (who were unwilling to accept the doctrine of predestination) and led by the mercantile class, favored a policy that might open the way to peaceful trading with Spain. As the Thirty Years' War approached, this tolerant "peace party" was overthrown: war with Spain resumed in 1621 and continued until the Peace of Westphalia. Tensions between the House of Orange and a "regent class" of mercantile interests continued throughout the century. For two decades after 1650 the "regents" dominated Dutch affairs. But when invasion again loomed in 1672—this time France, not Spain, was the enemy—the old conflicts surfaced again. The leading regent, Jan de Witt, was torn to pieces by a mob in The Hague, and the head of the House of Orange—the young Prince William III—was summoned to lead the Dutch war effort.

In Spain, problems that had been building up for decades exploded all at once in 1640. The resumption of warfare in the Netherlands, in Germany, and, finally, with France, put intolerable financial burdens on the Spanish state. Efforts by the leading minister, the Count-Duke of Olivares, to impose a more efficient centralized government and a more effective system of tax collection on the different sections of the Spanish kingdom led to two bitter rebellions in 1640. Portugal (which had been united with Spain since 1580) successfully broke away and regained its independence. And in the same year a revolt broke out in the province of Catalonia. Aided by the French, the Catalans held out for over a decade.

Meanwhile unrest also broke out in Spain's Italian provinces.

All of these problems contributed to the decline of Spain and made inevitable its surrender to France in 1659. Yet behind Spain's political troubles lay an even deeper source of trouble: the diminishing strength of Spain's overseas empire. For the decline of Spain was caused largely by changes in the European (and world) economy during the seventeenth century.

THE MERCANTILE ECONOMY OF EARLY MODERN EUROPE

Seventeenth-century kings and ministers were aware that political power depended on economic strength. They sought to increase the wealth of their own countries and to decrease the wealth of rival countries, or at least to prevent its growth. Agriculture, of course, was still the chief occupation in every part of Europe, but very little could be done either to increase home production or to decrease foreign production of food and fibers. Industry was more susceptible to state interference, but none of the major countries was dependent on industry. On the other hand, the volume and value of European trade had increased enormously. Growth between 1500 and 1600 had been so spectacular that some historians have described it as a "Commercial Revolution." And the countries that were assuming political leadership in Europe were becoming the centers of trade. The main routes now led to Amsterdam, London, and Paris rather than to Venice, Lisbon, and Seville. In the Netherlands, England, and France, the merchant was far more important than the industrialist and far more influential than the farmer.

Therefore, a ruler who wanted to use economic controls as a political weapon thought primarily in terms of altering the patterns of international trade. This policy seemed so natural that no one bothered to give it a name. In 1776, however, Adam Smith, looking at the process with some disapproval, coined the phrase "the mercantile system." This phrase, or its equivalent "mercantilism," has been used ever since.

Problems of Economic Organization

By the end of the sixteenth century it was evident that old forms of economic organization were not able to deal with the vast increase in the volume of trade. The guilds, which controlled production in many towns, could not supply the growing demands of merchants and governments. Most guilds were geared only to local markets and insisted on following traditional methods of work. Governments tried to regulate guilds in order to get uniform, nationwide standards of production, but except for a few luxury articles, this policy proved a failure. It was easier to let the merchants deal with the problem of industrial organization.

One method, already used by the end of the Middle Ages, was called the putting-out system. In the textile industry, for example, an entrepreneur might buy wool, pass it out to peasants to be spun into thread, carry the thread to others to be woven into cloth, take the cloth to dyers, and finally sell the finished product. This system had the double advantage of bypassing the guild restrictions in the towns and of tapping new sources of cheap labor in the countryside.

Another type of organization was the gathering-in system. In industries like printing, cannon founding, mining, and shipbuilding, and even in some textile processes such as silk weaving and calico printing, it was more efficient to gather workers together at some central place where their work could be directly supervised and coordinated. In both the putting-out and the gathering-in systems, it was almost invariably a merchant, not the manufacturer, who did the organizing.

The Center of European Economy Early Seventeenth Century

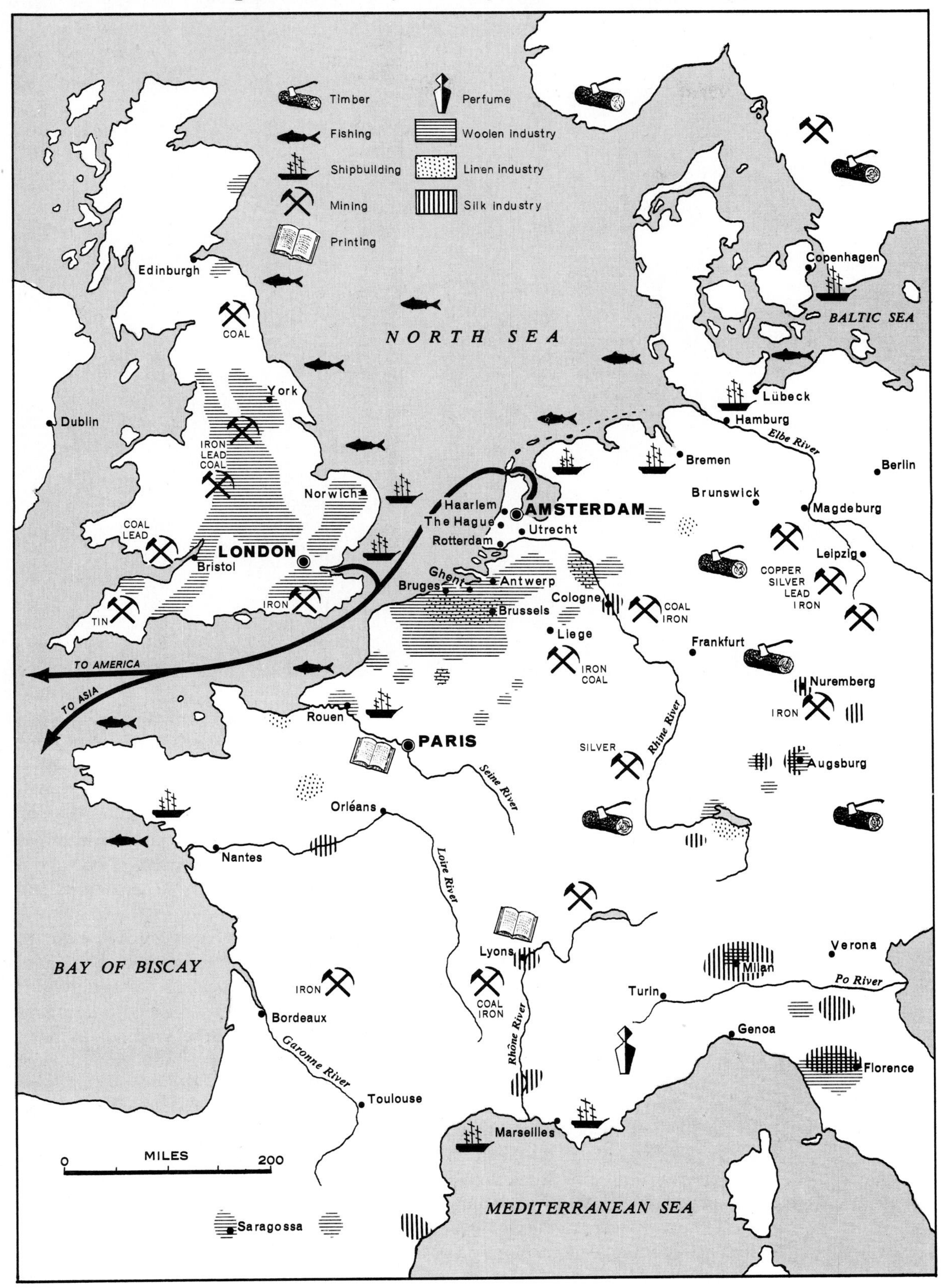

Syndics of the Cloth Guild, **by Rembrandt van Rijn (1662).**

Joint Stock Companies

In commerce an important innovation was the joint stock company. The small partnerships of the Middle Ages (and even the Fugger Bank was small by seventeenth-century standards) could not raise the capital needed for large-scale overseas voyages. So merchants formed associations called "regulated companies." Governments gave such groups a monopoly on trade to a given area, but each member of the group, while helping to meet common expenses, traded on his own account. They were associations of men, not of capital. What was needed, however, was a type of association that would attract investments from outside. The answer was the joint stock company, an amazingly flexible institution that was to be the parent of many other economic and political institutions on both sides of the Atlantic.

The joint stock company began as an association of investors, not of traders. Individuals bought shares in a venture, such as a trading voyage, and shared in the profits in proportion to their investment. When the association continued beyond a single venture, it became a joint stock company. This device had two advantages: It enabled anyone from a modestly wealthy man to Queen Elizabeth to invest in a business enterprise like Drake's voyages, and it associated businessmen with courtiers and statesmen at a time when both business sense and influence at court were necessary to the success of commercial ventures. The joint stock idea originated in southern Europe, but it was first applied to large-scale overseas enterprise in England in the Russia Company of 1553. The English East India Company, the companies that founded Virginia and Massachusetts, and the Bank of England were all joint stock companies. As these examples show, the first joint stock companies were dependent on government support (usually in the form of a trade monopoly) and were not concerned with industry. The joint stock company rapidly became the dominant form of commercial organization.

The cumulative effect of these changes was to make the king, not the town, the chief regulator of economic activity. The unit of economic activity in the Middle Ages, apart from agriculture, had been the town or the city-state. As stronger monarchs appeared at the end of the Middle Ages, urban economy was steadily absorbed into the national economy throughout much of Europe, except in Italy and Germany. The monarch stepped into the shoes of medieval town officials and regulated trade and production much as municipal governments had done, but on a larger scale.

Mercantilism

The original aim of economic regulation was to advance the common good, not to increase the wealth of individuals. But a king's definition of the common good was the strength and security of his realm, not a general rise in consumption or standards of living. During the seventeenth century monarchs began to believe that their goals could be attained by following the economic doctrine of mercantilism. This doctrine assumed that there is only a certain stock of wealth in the world at any given time, and if one country gains wealth another loses it. To prevent loss, home industries and shipping should be encouraged and colonies founded to provide raw materials that would otherwise have to be bought from foreigners. By regulating trade in these ways a country's stock of precious metals might be increased and surely would not decrease. This was not an unreasonable precaution in an age when credit devices were in their infancy and when, in case of war, a country had to have a reserve of gold and silver to pay its suppliers and soldiers.

The obvious way to build such a reserve—short of discovering new mines or capturing a Spanish plate fleet—was for a nation to export more than it imported. At the very least there would be a balance of trade, so that more money would not leave the country than stayed in it. And so mercantilism called for tariffs to discourage imports and various benefits to encourage exports. But it was thought that some exports, such as gold and silver, scarce raw materials, and skilled workmen, would weaken a state and should therefore be forbidden. At the core of mercantilism was the conviction that trade is the most important of all economic activities, that the regulation of trade is the government's most vital economic concern, and that regulation should result in self-sufficiency and readiness for war.

An Englishman on the Importance of Trade

ca. 1630

Although a kingdom may be enriched by gifts received, or by purchase taken from some other nations, yet these are things uncertain and of small consideration when they happen. The ordinary means therefore to increase our wealth and treasure is by foreign trade, wherein we must ever observe this rule; to sell more to strangers yearly than we consume of theirs in value. For suppose that when this kingdom is plentifully served with the cloth, lead, tin, iron, fish and other native commodities, we do yearly export the overplus to foreign countries to the value of twenty-two hundred thousand pounds; by which means we are enabled beyond the seas to buy and bring in foreign wares for our use and consumptions, to the value of twenty hundred thousand pounds; by this order duly kept in our trading, we may rest assured that the kingdom shall be enriched yearly two hundred thousand pounds, which must be brought to us in so much treasure; because that part of our stock which is not returned to us in wares must necessarily be brought home in treasure. . . .

Behold then the true form and worth of foreign trade, which is, the great revenue of the king, the honour of the kingdom, the noble profession of the merchant, the school of our arts, the supply of our wants, the employment of our poor, the improvements of our lands, the nursery of our mariners, the walls of the kingdoms, the means of our treasure, the sinews of our wars, the terror of our enemies.

From Thomas Mun, *England's Treasure by Foreign Trade* (New York: Oxford University Press, 1933), p. 5.

As we shall see, when new colonial policies were developed during the seventeenth century, mercantilists favored tropical colonies that enhanced the strength of the mother country by furnishing products such as sugar and tea and by buying home manufactures. They had no use for colonies that raised crops or produced manufactured goods that competed with the home country's products, nor for colonies that traded directly with other nations. The integration of colonies into the home economy was a cardinal mercantilist principle.

Mercantilism has necessarily been made to seem more clearcut and consistent than it actually was. It differed from one country to another. In France the system was often called *Étatisme,* or state-ism. Government intervention in France was direct and positive; regulation was intense; and relatively little initiative was left to individual enterprise. In England mercantilism also meant regulation of the economy in the government's interest. But even before the Revolution of 1688, and especially afterward, the English government was more responsive to the pressures of businessmen than was the French. It is often very difficult to tell whether English economic policy represented the interest of the state as a whole or the interests of individual entrepreneurs. In the United Provinces, where the government was in effect one of businessmen, the interest of the state and the interests of the business community practically coincided. Dutch mercantilism was not so much the regulation of trade by the state as it was the control of economic policy by organized business. However, in the rest of Europe—in Spain, Portugal, Austria, Prussia, and Sweden—mercantilism represented primarily the interest of the monarchy and so followed the French model more than the Dutch.

Financial Problems

The rise in prices that had marked the sixteenth century slowed down in the seventeenth, and may even have been reversed for a while. It has been estimated that while prices more than quadrupled between 1500 and 1600, they rose no more than 20 percent during the next hundred years, and most of that gain came during the first two or the last two decades of the century. The problems of inflation had been hard enough to handle. With prices rising faster than government income, bankruptcy was always just around the corner. But the problems of deflation were even more serious. Taxes brought in less, while government expenditures (mostly for wars) continued to increase. The optimism that comes with inflation, at least to the classes able to profit from it, decreased. The classes that had profited from the inflation of the sixteenth century—merchants, bankers, men who invested in land (like the English gentry)—found the financial atmosphere of the seventeenth century rather chilling. This is one reason why taxation seemed so oppressive after 1600.

Spain never managed to solve its problems and continued to hang on the edge of bankruptcy until late in the century. France did better, partly because its taxes fell most heavily on the peasants, and agricultural prices remained at a higher level than prices of other commodities. But the French taxation system was antiquated, and trouble was simply postponed. In England

The fashionable shops in the arcades of the Royal Palace in Paris, mid-seventeenth century. Left to right: bookseller, fan and ribbon dealer, and specializers in collars (after a copper engraving by Abraham Bosse, 1602–76).

the Stuarts were never able to build a sound system of government finance because they lost the confidence of Parliament, which controlled the major part of the royal revenue. But after 1688 a government that had gained the confidence of Parliament as well as the business community was able to construct an exceptionally strong system of public finance that included parliamentary taxation, a national bank, and a permanent public debt. In large measure this system was modeled on Dutch governmental finance, the most successful of the age. Since the rulers of the United Provinces were representatives of this business community, they had little difficulty, at least for a century, in raising the money and credit they needed for their overseas empire building and their wars. In an age dominated by trade, a state that had a flourishing commerce and could command the confidence of its merchants could weather any financial storm. A state that had little commerce, or in which commerce was growing slowly while merchants were discouraged, was likely to find itself in financial difficulties.

CONCLUSION

The first half of the seventeenth century was the threshold of what historians have come to call Early Modern Europe. It saw the rise of absolute monarchy in France and laid the foundations for constitutional monarchy in England. It witnessed the decline of Spain, and it shattered the Holy Roman Empire, leaving a virtual power vacuum in the center of Europe. France was now the strongest power in Europe. The role which religion had played in the past was taken over by more worldly concerns. Economic rivalry, within Europe and overseas, henceforth became a dominant theme in international affairs.

Suggestions for Further Reading

Among general surveys, D. Ogg, *Europe in the Seventeenth Century* (1925, 1960), and G. N. Clark, *The Seventeenth Century* (1931), are authoritative studies. G. Parker, *Europe in Crisis* (1979) is a more recent treatment. The fullest discussion of mercantilism is E. F. Heckscher, *Mercantilism*, 2 vols. (1935). C. Cipolla, *Before the Industrial Revolution* (1976), incorporates recent scholarship.

On the background of revolutionary developments in England, see L. Stone, *The Causes of the English Revolution 1529–1642* (1972). On Cromwell, C. H. Firth, *Oliver Cromwell and the Rule of the Puritans in England* (1900, 1925), is still one of the best biographies. See also M. Ashley, *The Greatness of Oliver Cromwell* (1966). P. Laslett, *The World We Have Lost* (2nd ed., 1971), is a vivid introduction to the social history of seventeenth-century England. On events in France, G. R. R. Treasure, *Seventeenth Century France* (1966), presents a detailed survey. C. W. Wedgwood, *Richelieu and the French Monarchy* (1962), and C. J. Burckhardt, *Richelieu: His Rise to Power* (1964), are sound studies. P. Goubert, *The Ancien Regime: French Society, 1600–1750* (1973), deals with France's social structure. Events in central Europe are covered in R. W. J. Evans, *The Making of the Habsburg Monarchy* (1979). C. W. Wedgwood, *The Thirty Years War* (1938), is the best general account in English of that crucial event.

Relations between Europe and the rest of the world are the subject of J. H. Parry, *Europe and a Wider World, 1415–1715* (1949), and C. E. Nowell, *The Great Discoveries and the First Colonial Empires* (1954). J. H. Elliott, *The Old World and the New* (1970), is excellent.

	1648			1700		
SOUTHWEST ASIA AND AFRICA	**1652** Dutch found Cape Colony ***ca.* 1700** Rise of Ashanti, West Africa				**1737–47** Nadir Shah, decline of Safavid Empire	
EUROPE	**1660–88** Stuart Restoration **1661–1715** Louis XIV	**1683** Turks besiege Vienna **1685** Edict of Nantes revoked **1685–1750** Johann Sebastian Bach **1687** Newton's Law of Gravitation	**1688** Glorious Revolution **1689–1725** Peter the Great **1690** Locke, *Two Treatises of Civil Government*	**1701–14** War of Spanish Succession **1715–74** Louis XV **1720** South Sea Bubble **1723–42** Robert Walpole	**1740–80** Maria Theresa **1740–86** Frederick the Great **1756–63** Seven Years' War **1756–91** Wolfgang Amadeus Mozart	**1762** Rousseau, *The Social Contract* **1762–96** Catherine the Great **1769** James Watt's first steam engine **1770–1827** Ludwig van Beethoven
SOUTH AND SOUTHEAST ASIA	**1653** Taj Mahal completed **1690** British found Calcutta				**1751** French control Deccan **1757** Battle of Plassey **1773** Regulation Act	
EAST ASIA	**1662–1722** Emperor Kangxi ***ca.* 1675–1725** Golden age of Edo urban culture, Japan			**1736–95** Emperor Qianlong	**1796–1804** White Lotus Rebellion	
THE AMERICAS AND PACIFIC		**1664** British seize New Amsterdam		**1728** Bering explores Alaska **1756–63** French and Indian War	**1765** Stamp Act **1768–80** Cook explores Pacific Ocean **1773** Boston Tea Party **1774** Quebec Act	

Ashanti wood carving.

Napoleon, 1800.

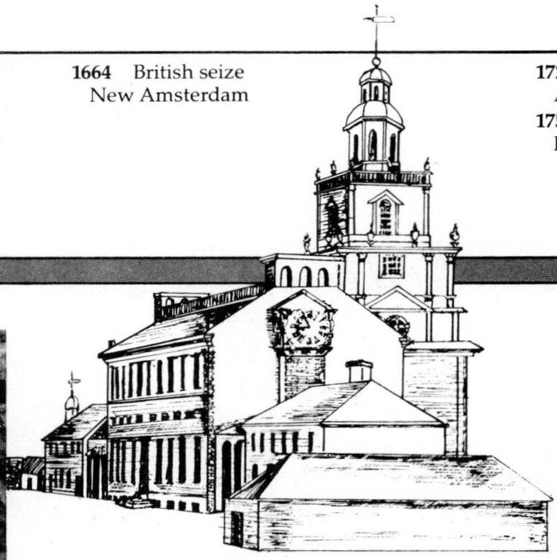

Independence Hall, Philadelphia, 1776.

East India Company merchant, by an Indian artist.

Emblem of the Sun King, Louis XIV.

Charles II of England, 1660-85.

1815	
	1805–48 Mohammed Ali founds dynasty in Egypt **1806** British control Cape Colony **1807** Slavery abolished in British Empire
1776 Smith, *Wealth of Nations* **1789** French Revolution begins	**1798** Malthus, *Essay on the Principle of Population* **1799** Napoleon becomes First Consul **1804–14** Napoleonic Empire
1784 East India Act **1786–93** Cornwallis in Bengal **1796** British conquer Ceylon	
1775–83 American Revolution **1776** US Declaration of Independence **1788** British colonize Australia **1803** Louisiana Purchase	**1807–30** Latin American wars for independence

Chinese fan painting, *ca.* 1700.

***Fuji above Storm*, by Hokusai, 1760-1849.**

28 Europe in the Seventeenth Century

Absolutism and Constitutionalism, 1660–1715

During the latter half of the seventeenth century France was the leading nation of Europe. Its population was twice that of Spain and over four times that of England. Its land was fertile and its commerce and industry were growing.

FRANCE UNDER LOUIS XIV

There were no disturbing arguments over forms of government. Absolute monarchy was accepted by almost all Frenchmen as necessary, reasonable, and right. By the Peace of the Pyrenees (1659) the French army had displaced the Spanish as the strongest force on the Continent. As time went on, it seemed as if not only French generals, French military engineers, and French diplomatists but also French architects, painters, dramatists, and philosophers were the best in Europe. French fashions dominated the Continent; the French language became the language of diplomacy and polite conversation; and the French court with its elaborate ceremonial became the model for courts throughout Europe. As Florence had been the nerve center of the Italian Renaissance and Spain of the Catholic Reformation, so France was the nerve center of late seventeenth-century politics, diplomacy, and culture.

Much of this predominance was due to the long reign of Louis XIV. He was born in 1638, became king in 1643, took the reins of power into his own hands in 1661, and died in 1715 at

Louis XIV, by Hyacinthe Rigaud (1701).

the age of seventy-seven. Louis was the very incarnation of divine-right monarchy—the idea that hereditary monarchy is the only divinely ordained form of government, that kings are responsible to God alone for their conduct, and that subjects should obey their kings as the direct representatives of God on earth. In an age that put its trust in absolute rulers, the achievements of the French people at the peak of their greatness cannot be separated from the personality of Louis XIV, even if many of these achievements were unrelated to him.

Louis is said to have remarked, "I am the state." The words reveal more of the true importance of his reign than anything else he said or wrote. Louis XIV set out early in his reign to personify the concept of sovereignty. He dramatized this aim after Mazarin's death by ordering his ministers thereafter to report to him in person, not to a "first minister." To be the real head of a large and complicated government required long hard work, and Louis paid the price. His education was poor, and he had little imagination, no sense of humor, and only a mediocre intelligence. But he had common sense and a willingness to work steadily at the business of governing. Painstakingly he caught up all the threads of power in his own hands. All major decisions were made in four great councils, which he attended regularly. These decisions were then carried out by professional "secretaries" at the head of organized bureaucracies. In the provinces, the *intendants* more and more represented the direct authority of the central government in justice, finance, and general administration. The old French monarchy imposed its authority through judicial decisions and had frequently consulted local and central assemblies. The new monarchy, begun by Richelieu and perfected by Louis XIV, imposed its authority through executive decisions. Louis reduced the importance of the *parlements,* never summoned the Estates General, and, so far as such a thing was humanly possible, built a government that was himself.

Louis XIV on the Duties of a King

1661

During the early period of his direct rule, Louis XIV prepared notes for the instruction of his son in the art of ruling. He had assistance in this task, and the texts do not necessarily give his exact words. They do express his ideas.

I have often wondered how it could be that love for work being a quality so necessary to sovereigns should yet be one that is so rarely found in them. Most princes, because they have a great many servants and subjects, do not feel obliged to go to any trouble and do not consider that if they have an infinite number of people working under their orders, there are infinitely more who rely on their conduct and that it takes a great deal of watching and a great deal of work merely to insure that those who act do only what they should and that those who rely tolerate only what they must. The deference and the respect that we receive from our subjects are not a free gift from them but payment for the justice and the protection that they expect to receive from us. Just as they must honor us, we must protect and defend them, and our debts toward them are even more binding than theirs to us, for indeed, if one of them lacks the skill or the willingness to execute our orders, a thousand others come in a crowd to fill his post, whereas the position of a sovereign can be properly filled only by the sovereign himself.

. . . of all the functions of sovereignty, the one that a prince must guard most jealously is the handling of the finances. It is the most delicate of all because it is the one that is most capable of seducing the one who performs it, and which makes it easiest for him to spread corruption. The prince alone should have sovereign direction over it because he alone has no fortune to establish but that of the state.

From Louis XIV, *Memoires for the Instruction of the Dauphin,* ed. by Paul Sonnino (New York: Free Press, 1970), pp. 63–64.

Colbert and the Economy

Jean Baptiste Colbert, Louis XIV's Controller General of Finance, systematically ordered the economic life of the country under royal direction. He was an extreme mercantilist; everything he did was consciously or unconsciously meant to strengthen the country for war. He set up high protective tariffs to help home industry, fostered new export industries, encouraged the French colonies in Canada and the West Indies, and did everything he could to develop a powerful navy and a strong merchant marine. Some historians hold that his minute regulation of the economy did more to hinder than to help. But until the burden of foreign wars became heavy in the 1680s, national production and wealth were increasing. Colbert cut down waste and corruption in the collection of taxes, but he was unable to make the burden of taxation more equitable because of the exemptions held by members of the nobility and the bourgeoisie.

The Nobility

The most dangerous potential opponents of royal absolutism were the members of the nobility. Louis excluded the nobles completely from all responsible positions in government and cheapened their status by increasing their numbers. All important positions in Louis XIV's government, such as secretaryships and intendancies, were filled by men of bourgeois or recently ennobled families. Louis did not attack the social privileges of the nobility; he used them to make the nobles utterly dependent on him. In 1683 he moved his court from the Louvre in Paris to Versailles, fifteen miles away. He had hated Paris since the riots of the Fronde, and now in the formal gardens and ornate chateau of Versailles he felt at home. Here the great nobles were also obliged to live. Instead of competing for political power, nobles squandered their fortunes and exhausted their energies in jockeying for social prestige.

The regular rectangular shapes of the gardens, the balanced classical lines of the baroque architecture, the bright glint of mirrors and chandeliers, all these seemed to symbolize the isolation of Versailles from nature, from the French nation, from the real world. Through all this the Sun King, as he came to be called, moved with impassive dignity. Years of self-conscious practice in kingship had given him a kind of public personality—cool, courteous, impersonal, imperturbable—which carried out perfectly the artificiality of the little world at Versailles. At his death he left to his successors a privileged nobility shorn of all political power and responsibility, demoralized by the empty pleasures and petty intrigues of court life and uneasily aware of its uselessness. It was a dangerous legacy.

The palace at Versailles (1668). Louis XIV is shown arriving in a carriage.

Religious Policy

The only other potential opponents of Louis's absolutism were religious groups. The king had his differences with several popes who disliked his Gallican principles, which stressed royal control over the Church in France. These quarrels, however, never led to a real breach. Louis was always a good Catholic in a formal sense. He disliked and persecuted the Jansenists, an austere group of Catholic "puritans" who emphasized the teachings of St. Augustine on original sin, the depravity of man, and the need for divine grace. They felt that the Jesuits were far too optimistic about man's ability to work out his own salvation, and far too ready to compromise with the world. Louis thought the Jansenists subversive (they had been condemned by the pope) and impertinent (they disapproved of his numerous mistresses). After 1680 he seems to have become increasingly concerned about the fate of his own soul. When his queen, Maria Theresa, died in 1683, he gave up his mistresses and secretly married Ma-

Officer and musketeer of the French Guard (late seventeenth century).

dame de Maintenon, a pious Catholic. In 1685 he shocked Protestant Europe by revoking the Edict of Nantes, by which Henry IV had granted religious toleration to the Huguenots.

There were about a million Huguenots out of a total population of perhaps 18 million at the opening of Louis XIV's reign. After Richelieu deprived them of their military and political privileges, they had become good citizens and had remained loyal to the crown during the Fronde. The French Catholic clergy had long tried to persuade Louis XIV that the continued exercise of the Protestant religion in France was an insult to his authority, and as the king became more concerned about his salvation the idea of atoning for his sins of the flesh by crushing heresy became more attractive to him. Finally, aided and abetted by his Jesuit advisers, Louis announced that because all the heretics had finally been reconverted to Catholicism there was no further need for the Edict of Nantes, and it was therefore revoked. Protestant churches and schools were closed, and all Protestant children were baptized as Catholics. The Revocation was enforced by imprisonment, torture, and condemnation to the galleys, but many Huguenots continued to practice their faith in secret. Others fled to England, the Dutch Netherlands, Brandenburg, and the New World. The industry and skill of the 200,000 or so Huguenots who escaped contributed appreciably to the economic life of their new homes. The Revocation of the Edict of Nantes was an anachronistic act of religious intolerance that gained Louis XIV little and lost him much.

Bishop Bossuet on Absolutism

Jacques Bénigne Bossuet was tutor to Louis XIV's son in the 1670s.

The royal power is absolute. With the aim of making this truth hateful and insufferable, many writers have tried to confound absolute government with arbitrary government. But no two things could be more unlike. . . . The prince need render an account of his acts to no one. . . . Without this absolute authority the king could neither do good nor repress evil. . . . God is infinite, God is all. The prince, as prince, is not regarded as a private person: he is a public personage, all the state is in him; the will of all the people is included in his. As all perfection and all strength are united in God, so all the power of individuals is united in the person of the prince. What grandeur that a single man should embody so much! . . . Behold this holy power, paternal and absolute; behold the secret cause which governs the whole body of the state, contained in a single head: you see the image of God in the king, and you have the idea of royal majesty. God is holiness itself, goodness itself, and power itself. In these things lies the majesty of God. In the image of these things lies the majesty of the prince.

From Jacques Bénigne Bossuet, "Politics Drawn from the Very Words of Scripture," in *Readings in European History,* ed. by James Harvey Robinson (Boston: Ginn, 1906), Vol. II, pp. 275–76.

The Wars of Louis XIV

Richelieu and Mazarin had begun the process of strengthening the French army, but French military power reached its peak under Louis XIV. Le Tellier and his son Louvois were the ministers of war for almost fifty years. They subordinated the aristocratic officer class to the royal authority, developed a supply system, coordinated infantry and artillery, and, like Gustavus Adolphus, supplied the soldiers with uniforms. Vauban, one of the great military engineers of history, invented the fixed bayonet and perfected the art of building fortifications. Louvois provided his master with the largest and best-equipped army in Europe. This achievement in turn tempted the king to use his power in foreign wars. War would please the nobles, who had little outlet for their ambitions at home. War would exercise and justify the enormous standing army. Above all, successful war would enhance the glory of the monarch and perhaps make Louis the arbiter of Europe. For half a century Europe was ravaged by wars that were caused by the Sun King's desire to maintain French prestige and increase French territory. As Louis's thirst for power grew, so did his enemies' fear of him.

The aims of Louis's earlier wars were relatively limited and understandable. With Spain's power broken and the Empire in a state of collapse, he wanted to annex the Spanish Netherlands (later Belgium), Franche-Comté, and bits of western German territories. He fought two wars for these objectives, but each time, after early victories, he found himself thwarted by an alliance of other powers. By 1678 he had gained only Franche-Comté and a few border towns in Flanders.

For a time Louis tried legal chicanery in place of bullets to gain more territory. French courts called "Chambers of Reunion" were set up to reunite to France any land that at any time had been a dependency of a French territory. This process gave Louis control of the independent Protestant republic of Strasbourg in 1681. The Revocation of the Edict of Nantes in 1685 was further evidence to European statesmen of Louis's intemperance, and in 1686 the defensive League of Augsburg was formed by the emperor, Spain, Sweden, and several German states. Europe was already at war when William of Orange, ruler of the Dutch Netherlands and Louis's most implacable enemy, became King William III of England in 1689. The circle was closed around France when the English and the Dutch joined the League.

This time France was on the defensive. At the very outset, in 1688, the French united their enemies by perpetrating one of the most senseless atrocities of the century, the systematic devastation of the Palatinate by the occupying French troops before they withdrew. The War of the League of Augsburg was waged in India and America as well as in Europe, so it may be called the first of the modern world wars. After ten years of fighting, France agreed to the Peace of Ryswick (1697), by which Louis XIV managed to retain his gains up to 1678 but was forced to renounce nearly all accessions after that date except Strasbourg. England came out of the war considerably stronger as a naval and military power; France, however, came out of it weaker than it had been a decade earlier.

The Conquests of Louis XIV 1661–1715

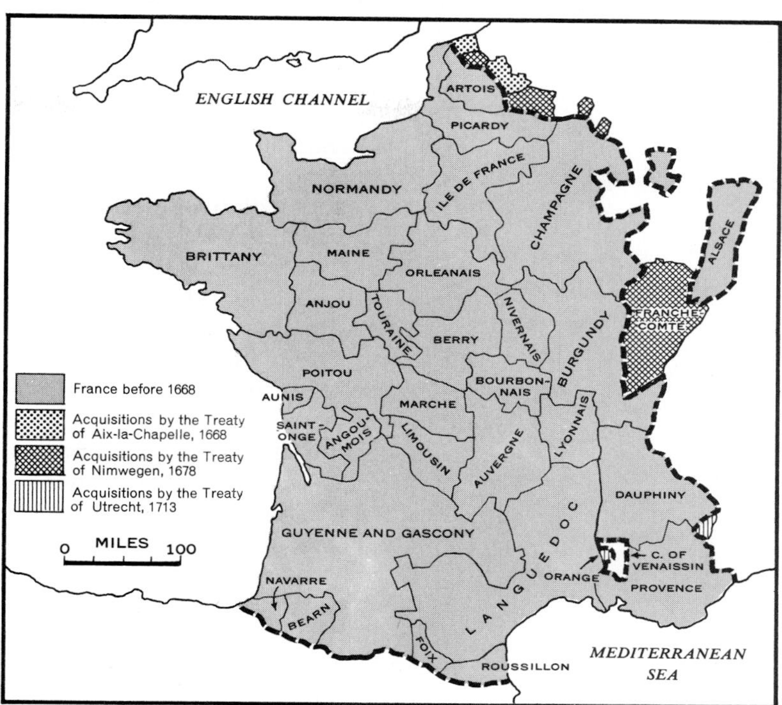

The War of the Spanish Succession, 1701–14

At the turn of the century all the resentments that had built up during a generation of fighting were concentrated in a fourth struggle, the War of the Spanish Succession (1701–14). This war, like that of the League of Augsburg (1688–97), was fought in America and India as well as in Europe. In its origins and its course, the older motives of dynastic ambition and preservation of the balance of power were mixed with the newer motives of commercial advantage and national sentiment. Religion now played no important part.

In 1698 Charles II of Spain, who for thirty years had suffered from half a dozen fatal diseases, was finally dying. He was the last of the Habsburgs who had ruled Spain since 1516, and he had no direct heirs. The question was whether the Spanish Empire would fall to some member of the Austrian Habsburg family or to some member of the French Bourbon dynasty (both Louis XIV's mother and first wife had been Spanish Habsburg princesses) or would be partitioned or dismembered in some way. The English and the Dutch had obvious reasons for keeping France from gaining control of the Spanish colonial trade or of the Spanish Netherlands. Louis seemed willing to compromise and twice concluded secret treaties with the English and the Dutch to partition the Spanish dominions, but when news of the second treaty reached Madrid the dying king lost his temper. In order to preserve the Spanish Empire intact as a bulwark of Catholicism, he made a will leaving all his dominions to a grandson of Louis XIV. This grandson was proclaimed King Philip V of Spain shortly after the death of Charles II in 1700.

Louis XIV recognized the will of Charles II and sent French troops into the Spanish Netherlands. In 1701 William III of England concluded the Grand Alliance of the Hague by which the English, the Dutch, and the Austrian Habsburg emperor bound themselves to fight until they had ended the threat of Bourbon control of Spain and of the Spanish colonies. Louis XIV had made his last and most arrogant bid for the dominance of Europe, but this time he was forced to fight against enemies who proved as unyielding as he. Within a few years the large allied forces under the brilliant command of Prince Eugene of Savoy and the English Duke of Marlborough had beaten the French in four bloody battles (Blenheim, 1704; Ramillies, 1706; Oudenarde, 1708; Malplaquet, 1709). The English navy had trounced the French at sea, and the English had seized Gibraltar. An allied army had even dethroned Philip V in Spain for a time.

Louis XIV, his country exhausted, sued for peace on almost any terms, only to be met by an allied demand that he contribute French troops to expel his own grandson from Madrid. This was too much for even a badly beaten monarch, and he refused, backed by a rising tide of national feeling in France. A similar national reaction in Spain in favor of Philip V resulted in the defeat of English and Austrian troops there. In 1710 a victory of the Tories over the Whigs, who had been the war party in England, brought in a government in London favorable to peace. And finally in 1712 the French won their only important victory of the war. In the end the allies paid the price for having asked too much from Louis.

The Peace of Utrecht, 1713–14

In theory, the Peace of Utrecht gave the French the prize that they had sought at the beginning of the war. Philip V remained on the throne of Spain, but only on condition that the crowns of Spain and France should never be worn by the same monarch. In every other aim, however, the French were thwarted. They gave up all conquests east of the Rhine, failed to win the Spanish Netherlands, and lost their bid for control of the Spanish colonial trade. England was the chief winner, taking Newfoundland, Acadia (modern New Brunswick and Nova Scotia), and Hudson's Bay Territory from France, and Gibraltar and Minorca from Spain. In addition, the English received the *Asiento* — the right to supply black slaves to the Spanish colonies, a privilege that proved very lucrative.

England thus came out of the war rich and powerful, in a position to dominate international commerce and with the strongest navy in Europe. France came out of it still a great nation, but with its people badly exhausted by high taxation and its government bankrupt and unpopular. The Austrian Habsburgs gained the Spanish Netherlands (which now became the Austrian Netherlands), as well as Milan, Naples, and Sicily. Austria thus replaced Spain as the dominant power in Italy. Two new smaller powers, Brandenburg-Prussia and the Duchy of Savoy, came out of the war with increased territories and heightened prestige for having been on the winning side. A century and a half later Prussia was to unify Germany, and Savoy, as the Kingdom of Sardinia, was to take the lead in the unification of Italy. The Dutch kept the Scheldt River closed, thus blocking the trade of Antwerp, the chief port of the Austrian Netherlands. But they were soon to disappear from the ranks of the great powers.

The Peace of Utrecht ended the first attempt by a European state to establish an overwhelming predominance of power since the days of Philip II of Spain. When Louis XIV died in 1715, rulers outside France breathed a sigh of relief. His bid for European hegemony had been defeated by the workings of the balance-of-power principle, but the seeds of future war were unfortunately still deep in the European soil.

ENGLAND: THE EMERGENCE OF A PARLIAMENTARY MONARCHY

While Louis XIV was putting the finishing touches on the institution of absolute monarchy in France, the English, without any very clear idea of where they were headed, were completing the foundation of a constitutional monarchy controlled by Parliament.

The restoration of the king, Parliament, and the Anglican Church in 1660 had established a kind of equilibrium between the crown and Parliament, but it was soon evident that it was a very unstable balance. Who was really to control the government—the king or the wealthy landowners and merchants who dominated Parliament? What was the religious settlement to be, and who was to have the last word in making it? Who was to control foreign policy? These three main questions of the past two generations—the questions of politics, religion, and foreign policy—still awaited final answers. It took two more generations of domestic intrigue and foreign war for the answers to be found.

Charles II

Charles II (r. 1660–85) was quite unlike his father—witty, wordly-wise, attractive, a man of easy morals and shrewd political sense. He had lived long in exile in France, and his cousin Louis XIV was his model. He would have liked to restore England to Catholicism and to set up an absolute monarchy on the French model, but he was too intelligent to ignore the difficulties and was resolved not to risk exile or execution. If his goal was to be reached, it would be by intrigue, manipulation, and compromise, not by force. The result was twenty-five years of complex party politics and secret diplomacy in which the issues were never very clear to the people or to the members of Parliament, or even to the king's ministers.

The Cavalier Parliament, 1661–79

Parliament held a commanding position at the beginning of the reign. The "Cavalier Parliament," which met in 1661 and was not dissolved until 1679, was dominated by the landed nobility and gentry, who were now restored to their ancient influence in both local and national government. Both groups were strongly royalist for the moment, and both determined to stamp out all remnants of religious and political radicalism. But at the same time they were not willing to see the crown recover any real financial independence of Parliament. In place of the old idea that "the king should live of his own," Parliament now granted Charles a regular income. Since Charles found that he could not meet expenses from his own revenues, he had to let Parliament have its way, under the leadership of his father's adviser, Edward Hyde, Earl of Clarendon.

Parliament also had the last word in the religious settlement. The Cavalier Parliament was as strongly pro-Anglican as it was pro-royalist. In a series of statutes passed between 1661 and 1665 and known as the "Clarendon Code," Puritans who dissented from the established Church were excluded from local government and Puritan ministers were rooted out of the Angli-

The House of Commons, on the Great Seal of England (1651).

can clergy. Later legislation made it illegal for a dissenter to sit in Parliament, to serve in the army or navy, or to attend the universities at Oxford or Cambridge. Behind this attempt to discourage dissent was the fear that Puritans were inevitably political radicals. But while the Clarendon Code lowered the social position and narrowed opportunities for dissenters, it did not greatly decrease their numbers. Presbyterians, Congregationalists, Baptists, and Quakers (also Methodists a century later) formed permanent but peaceful minority groups. The dissenters remained antagonistic to the ruling Anglican majority, but they were even more bitterly opposed to Catholicism.

Charles did not like the Clarendon Code. He would have preferred a policy that tolerated both Puritans and Catholics, but Parliament would not stand for this. In 1762 Charles issued a "Declaration of Indulgence," which suspended the operation of the laws against both groups. But the next year Parliament forced him to withdraw the declaration and accept a severe Test Act excluding all but Anglicans from civil and military office. To the Anglican gentry in Parliament, Puritans were still radicals and Catholics still traitors.

Foreign Policy

Two natural calamities, an outbreak of plague in 1665 and a fire that destroyed much of London in 1666, contributed to general unrest. Uneasiness increased as king and Parliament drifted apart over foreign policy. In 1665 Parliament forced Charles into a commercial war with the Dutch but did not give him enough money to win it. When victories failed to develop, Clarendon was unfairly held responsible and was exiled. After Louis XIV began his attacks on the Spanish Netherlands in 1667, Englishmen began to see Catholic France as more of a threat than the Protestant Dutch. But to Charles II, Louis was still the ideal ally —powerful, wealthy, and a personal friend.

In 1670 England once more allied itself with France against the Dutch, and Charles negotiated one of the most notorious deals in the history of English foreign policy, the secret Treaty of Dover. By this agreement Charles promised to reconvert England to Catholicism in return for French money and, if necessary, French troops. Probably Charles himself was not sure how far he meant to go, but at the least he was ready to adopt a pro-French foreign policy. Between 1675 and 1681 four more secret agreements were concluded between Charles and Louis in which Charles promised to thwart Parliament's anti-French moves in return for subsidies from France. The close understanding between Charles and Louis leaked out and gradually built up English fears of Catholicism and French dominance. The landed classes represented in Parliament were suspicious of Charles, increasingly less royalist in sentiment, and ready to give way to panic if any incident should excite their fear of France and popery.

Illustration of the Great Fire of London (1666).

Whigs and Tories

In 1678 these accumulated fears were fanned into flame by a lurid incident known as the Popish Plot. A disreputable character named Titus Oates concocted a story, accepted by almost everyone, that there was a Jesuit plot to murder the king and put his Catholic brother James, the Duke of York, on the throne with French help. A "Country Party," led by the Earl of Shaftesbury campaigned at the polls and supported a bill to exclude the Duke of York from the succession to the throne. An Anglican and royalist "Court Party" rallied to the support of Charles II and his brother. Members of the first group were called Whigs (a name hitherto applied to fanatical Scottish Presbyterians); members of the second group were called Tories (a name for Catholic outlaws in Ireland). The Whigs controlled the three brief Parliaments that followed the dissolution of the Cavalier Parliament in 1679, and innocent men went to their deaths for complicity in the Popish Plot. But the Whig leaders soon overplayed their hand; public opinion swung back in favor of the king, and it was now the turn of innocent Whigs to suffer. By 1681 Shaftesbury had fled abroad, the inventors of the Popish Plot were disgraced or executed, and Charles was stronger than ever before. Until his death four years later he ruled without Parliament, thanks to Louis's subsidies, with his brother James by his side. The origin of political parties in the modern sense—groups organized for the purpose of electioneering and controlling government through a representative assembly—lies in these chaotic years of English history. The eventual outcome was the "two-party system," which came to be characteristic of English and American politics.

James II

The Duke of York, who succeeded Charles II as James II (r. 1685–88), was a very different sort of person from his brother—a bigoted convert to Catholicism without any of Charles's political shrewdness or tendency to compromise. Within three short years James managed to infuriate almost every group of any importance in English political and religious life, and in the end he provoked the revolution that Charles had succeeded in avoiding. Made overconfident by early successes, he introduced Catholics into the high command of both army and navy and camped a standing army a few miles from London. He surrounded himself with Catholic advisers and attacked Anglican control of the universities. James claimed the power to suspend or dispense with acts of Parliament. In a vain attempt to win the support of Puritans as well as Catholics, he issued a Declaration of Indulgence along the lines of his brother's. By revoking borough charters and browbeating sheriffs he tried to ensure the election of a Parliament favorable to his policies. Louis XIV's Revocation of the Edict of Nantes in 1685 had already terrified Protestants in England. They held back as long as James's heir, his oldest daughter, was a Protestant; but their fears became unbearable when the hope of a Protestant succession was destroyed by the unexpected birth of a son to James's Catholic queen.

The Glorious Revolution of 1688

In spite of the intense political tension, civil war did not break out in 1688 as it had in 1642. Englishmen still remembered the horrors of civil war, and this time there was only one side. James had no support of any significance, except for a handful of personal friends. He had alienated both Anglicans and nonconformists, Tories and Whigs, nobles and common people. The result, therefore, was a "bloodless revolution," a thoroughgoing political overturn that answered all the main questions of the century in favor of a limited, or parliamentary, monarchy and established the constitutional pattern of English public life that has persisted to the present time.

James II had two daughters by his first wife (Clarendon's daughter), both of whom remained Protestants. The elder, Mary, was married in 1677 to the *statholder* of the Dutch Republic, William of Orange, who was Louis XIV's outstanding Protestant opponent on the Continent. In June 1688 a group of prominent Englishmen, both Whigs

William and Mary's coronation medal, designed by George Bower, and their signatures.

and Tories, invited William to save the Protestant cause in England. In the following November William landed on the southern coast of England with a Dutch army and marched slowly on London. There was little resistance. James II fled to France, and a Convention Parliament (an irregular assembly of men who had had parliamentary seats) declared that James had "abdicated" the throne. It then invited William and Mary to become joint sovereigns. A "Bill of Rights" was passed and the "Glorious Revolution" was accomplished.

The chief result of the Revolution was the establishment of parliamentary sovereignty over the crown. Parliament had made a king and could regulate the right of succession to the throne. Though William was a strong-willed man, especially in matters of foreign policy, he knew that Parliament had the final say. And though the supporters of James II and his son intrigued and even staged two abortive rebellions, there was no second Restoration. Parliament could criticize, influence, and eventually make the government's policy.

The Bill of Rights emphatically denied the king's right to suspend acts of Parliament or to interfere with the ordinary course of justice. It furnished a base for the steady expansion of civil liberties in the generation after 1688. Religious toleration and freedom from arbitrary arrest were established by law; censorship of the press was dropped. The king had to summon Parliament every year because he could not pay or control his armed forces without parliamentary consent. These regular meetings strengthened the parties and made the king dependent on their support. In 1707 the monarch for the last time vetoed a parliamentary bill.

Struggles were no longer between king and Parliament, but between factions in Parliament. The Revolution did not establish democracy, but it did establish control by the wealthy landed proprietors and merchants over both the central and local organs of English government. Generally speaking, the greater noble landowners, the bankers and the merchants, and most dissenters were Whigs, while the smaller gentry, the Anglican parish clergy, and some great lords were Tories. But parties were still loosely organized, and small factions with selfish interests often held the balance of power. England was governed by shifting alliances among leaders of the propertied classes.

The Cabinet System

It took over a century for parliamentary leaders to work out a smooth and efficient way to run the government. The ultimate answer was to be the "cabinet system"—that is, government by a committee of leaders of the majority party in Parliament, holding the chief executive offices, acting under the leadership of a "prime minister," and acknowledging primary responsibility to Parliament rather than to the crown for their actions. During the reigns of William and Mary (r. 1689–1702) and of Mary's sister, Queen Anne (r. 1702–14), the first fumbling moves were made that led to such a system, though parliamentary leaders had as yet no sense of their goal, and monarchs still considered ministers to be responsible to them rather than to Parliament. The privy council had long been too large and unwieldy for effective action, so that a "cabinet council," or inner circle of important ministers, had developed under Charles II. The members of this "cabinet" slowly found that it was better to discuss major questions among themselves and to present a united front to the monarch on matters of policy. Sometimes a leading member of the "cabinet" was referred to as "prime minister." In order to gain Parliament's indispensable support in war or peace, both William and Anne occasionally found that it was better to choose their ministers not from both parties but from the majority party. By the time Queen Anne died in 1714 it had become evident that the real government of England was slowly falling into the hands of a cabinet of ministers who controlled a parliamentary majority, often by bribery, and felt themselves ultimately responsible to the political interests of this majority.

Religious Toleration

The Revolution had also produced a certain measure of religious toleration. Broad-mindedness was becoming fashionable in educated circles, and both Anglicans and Puritans were now more afraid of Catholic France than they were of each other. Puritans had supported Anglicans against James II, and King William, who came from the most tolerant country in Europe, insisted on a religious truce. The result was the "Toleration Act" of 1689, which allowed dissenters to worship as they pleased and to educate their clergy and laity in schools of their own. Dissenters were still legally excluded from all civil and military offices, however, and there was no repeal of the long series of anti-Catholic statutes, although they were not enforced with any great rigor after 1689. Protestant fear that a Catholic might succeed to the throne was finally quieted by the Act of Settlement of 1701, which provided that the sovereign should always be an Anglican. The act also settled the succession, in case James II's two daughters should die without children, on the descendants of that daughter of James I who had married the ill-fated Elector of the Palatinate before the Thirty Years' War. In this way the elector of Hanover came to the throne in 1714, when Queen Anne died without issue, thus bringing the Stuart dynasty to a close.

Growth of English Power

A third result of the Revolution was to unite crown and Parliament on foreign policy and thus to turn the energies of a generation of Englishmen from domestic affairs to foreign war. Given English fear of Catholicism, King William had no difficulty bringing England into the Grand Alliance against Louis XIV, who was sheltering James II in exile. Parliamentary monarchy soon demonstrated that it was a more formidable foe than the absolute monarchy of the Stuarts had been. The English government was able to raise money to fight its wars in a way that was barred to all other European governments except the Dutch. The founding of the Bank of England in 1694 was an important event in the history of English public finance. Within a few days of its founding, it had raised over a million pounds of investors' money that it promptly lent to the government at 8 percent interest. So long as the government continued to pay the interest, the bank made no demand for repayment of this loan. Thus the present permanent, or "funded," national debt began. The merchants and tradesmen, large and small, who invested their money in the bank obviously had confidence in the government, and their investment bound them still more firmly to support the revolutionary settlement.

Throughout the next century English wealth combined with English sea power was to give the island kingdom a striking power out of all proportion to its area and population. During the reigns of William and Mary and of Anne, trade, which was more and more the foundation of English wealth, increased considerably. The Peace of Utrecht (1713) gave English sea power an almost unrivaled position, making England within the next fifty years the most powerful nation in Europe.

Ireland and Scotland

The Revolution also indirectly furthered the unification of the British Isles. England, Ireland, and Scotland all had the same king from 1603 on, but union went no further than the common crown. The two smaller kingdoms, especially Ireland, suffered greatly during the seventeenth century through involvement in England's religious and political divisions. The native Irish were Catholic, and the Prot-

Medal of Queen Anne and her signature.

estant English both despised and feared them as potential allies of the Catholic Spanish and French. By settling Protestant colonists in Ulster, James I began to create a Protestant majority in the northeastern region of Ireland. But the Ulster Protestants were Presbyterians and soon became anti-Stuart, while the rest of the Irish were generally loyal to the Stuart dynasty, and for that reason suffered cruelly under Cromwell. After the Revolution, James II tried to fight his way back to his throne by way of Ireland. He was defeated at the Battle of the Boyne (1689), an event whose memory still stirs up bitter feelings between Catholics and Protestants in Ulster. James's defeat led to a systematic persecution of the Catholic Irish by English (and Irish) Protestant landlords, comparable only to Louis XIV's brutal treatment of the Huguenots. The Irish were exploited and bled white economically, their priests were persecuted, and their Parliament was reserved for Protestants only.

Locke on Government by Consent
1690

Compare "Bishop Bossuet on Absolutism," p. 586.

Men being, as has been said, by nature all free, equal, and independent, no one can be put out of this estate and subjected to the political power of another without his own consent, which is done by agreeing with other men, to join and unite into a community for their comfortable, safe, and peaceful living, one amongst another, in a secure enjoyment of their properties, and a greater security against any that are not of it. . . . When any number of men have so consented to make one community or government, they are thereby presently incorporated, and make one body politic, wherein the majority have the right to act and conclude the rest. . . . Absolute, arbitrary power, or governing without settled standing laws, can neither of them consist with the ends of society and government, which men would not quit the freedom of the state of Nature for, and tie themselves up under, were it not to preserve their lives, liberties, and fortunes, and by stated rules of right and property to secure their peace and quiet.

From John Locke, *Of Civil Government: Two Treatises* (New York: Everyman's Library, 1924), pp. 164–65, 186.

The Scots fared somewhat better, although they too suffered by being involved in England's troubles through the century. Scotland had gained little by giving a king to England in 1603. It remained a poor but proud neighbor of a larger kingdom, excluded from the benefits of English trade, jealously guarding its own law and its own Parliament, and firmly defending its Presbyterian Church against Anglican attacks. Although the Scots had touched off the revolution against Charles I, there was strong attachment to the native Stuart dynasty in Scotland, especially among Catholic clansmen of the Highlands. After 1649 and again after 1689 Scotland became a base for risings in support of the Stuarts. The Scots accepted the Revolution of 1688, but they did not accept the Act of Settlement of 1701. They threatened to choose a separate king of their own—possibly the exiled pretender James II—in case James's last daughter, Anne, died without issue. This frightened the English into serious negotiations. In 1701 an organic union between the two kingdoms was finally agreed on and was confirmed by an Act of Union. Scotland retained its own law and its established Presbyterian religion, but it surrendered its separate Parliament in return for representation in the English Parliament. Scottish nationalists were (and still are) angry over their loss of independence, but Scotland gained much by becoming an integral part during the eighteenth century in building the British Empire and in furthering the Enlightenment.

John Locke

The Revolution of 1640 and the Glorious Revolution of 1688 together constituted the first of those revolutions in modern western states that ended absolute divine-right monarchy and eventually put the middle classes in control of government. English leaders did their best to insist to the outside world in 1688 and 1689 that they were doing nothing new or revolutionary at all, but they never succeeded in persuading foreigners that they were merely conservative supporters of ancient English liberties. Europe was more interested in the interpretation of the Revolution by John Locke (1632–1704), a friend of the Earl of Shaftesbury, the founder of the Whig Party. In *Of Civil Government: Two Treatises* (1690), Locke set down in plain common-sense fashion the general principles underlying the English struggle for limited monarchy that culminated in the Revolution of 1688. Even if the logic was not always clear, the reasonableness of the discussion had great influence throughout the eighteenth century (see p. 612). Inalienable rights, government by consent, separation of powers, the right of revolution — these were the ideas that Locke implied were at the heart of the Glorious Revolution. These were the ideas that seemed self-evident truths to Americans in 1776 and to Frenchmen in 1789 and that formed a link between the English, the American, and the French revolutions.

John Locke.

CENTRAL AND EASTERN EUROPE, 1648–1721

The economy of early modern Europe was divided into two sharply defined halves by an imaginary line running north from the head of the Adriatic Sea, around the Bohemian mountains, and down the Elbe River to the North Sea. West of this line was an area that was increasingly affected by the growth of towns and trade. The majority of the population still lived on the land, but most peasants were free workers and many of them small landowners. Most serfs in western Europe had become agricultural laborers for pay, and most feudal nobles had become landlords who hired labor for wages (particularly in England) or simply lived on rents. Though still a minority, the bourgeoisie were increasingly influential in society and politics.

East of the line was a society still largely agrarian and feudal, an area of few large towns and an insignificant bourgeoisie. Here in Hungary, Bohemia, Poland, Prussia, and Russia, the landed estates were larger and the landed nobility more powerful than in western Europe. During the sixteenth and seventeenth centuries the nobles of eastern Europe managed to reduce the peasants to a state of serfdom in which they were bound to the land and forced to work from two to five days a week for their lord. One reason for this drive to enslave the peasant was that grain prices were rising in western markets, and eastern landlords had every inducement to increase the production of their estates. Another reason was that the governments of eastern Europe were either dominated by nobles, as in Hungary and Poland, or favorable to the growth of serfdom because it supported the nobles who served the state, as in Prussia and Russia. In western Europe, money was increasingly the key to power and influence; in eastern Europe, ownership of land and command of compulsory services were still the secrets of power.

Warfare was as common in eastern as in western Europe. States with no natural frontiers on the flat plains of central and eastern Europe could easily be wiped out. Modernized armies were needed, but such armies could be created only by strong, centralized administrations and supported only by effective tax systems. Neither centralization nor taxation was easy. Eastern rulers were facing roughly the same obstacles to the growth of centralized government that western rulers had faced two centuries and more earlier: a powerful landed nobility, a church that held itself above dynastic interests and owned a large portion of the land, and an agrarian economy with limited commerce and infant industries, a bourgeoisie still too small to bear the weight of heavy taxation, and an ignorant and exploited peasantry tied to the land and thus incapable of meeting the need of new industries for labor. To build a "modern" state in the face of these difficulties was beyond the capacity of all but the ablest rulers.

The Division of Eastern and Western Europe

The Holy Roman Empire

The one large political organization bridging eastern and western Europe was the Holy Roman Empire. But although there was still an emperor, and a diet, which met "perpetually" at Regensburg after 1663, the Empire was a political fiction. It had no central administration, no system of imperial taxation, no standing army, no common law, no tariff union, not even a common calendar. The Peace of Westphalia had recognized the sovereignty of the individual states, as well as the right of France and Sweden to take part in the deliberations of the diet. In the welter of political units—free cities, ecclesiastical principalities, counties, margravates, and duchies, together with one kingdom (Bohemia)—that made up the Empire, almost every petty princeling fancied himself a Louis XIV and fashioned a court modeled as closely as possible on Versailles. The ruling families of a few of the larger states—Bavaria, Saxony, Hanover, Brandenburg, and Austria—were trying hard to expand their territories by war or marriage and to gain royal titles. Augustus the Strong of Saxony managed to get himself elected king of Poland in 1696. In 1701 the Elector of Brandenburg obtained the emperor's consent to style himself king in Prussia. And in 1714 the Elector of Hanover became king of England. But only two great powers eventually grew out of the wreck of the Empire. These were Austria and Brandenburg-Prussia.

Prince Eugene of Savoy, Habsburg commander, detail from a painting by Kupezky.

The Habsburgs and Austria

The attempt of Emperor Ferdinand II (r. 1619–37) to revive and strengthen the Empire under Habsburg control was defeated in the Thirty Years' War. The Habsburgs thereafter turned to a policy of consolidating and expanding their hereditary lands in Austria and the Danube Valley. Thus a centralized Habsburg monarchy might be developed that could hold its own with the states of the West. The Emperor Leopold I (r. 1658–1705) was the chief architect of this policy, aided, and at times prodded, by some capable civil servants and one remarkable general, Prince Eugene of Savoy.

To weld a centralized monarchy together, Leopold had to reduce three separate areas—Austria, Bohemia, and Hungary—to some semblance of unity. In the Duchy of Austria his lawyers were able to establish his ascendancy over a feudal nobility whose economic position was still strong. Bohemia had been reduced to obedience early in the Thirty Years' War; the real problem was Hungary. Although the Habsburgs had been the elected monarchs of the kingdom since the early sixteenth century, hardly a third of Hungary was actually in Habsburg hands. The rest was either directly or indirectly ruled by the Ottoman Turks. The Ottoman Empire was not the power it had been in the sixteenth century, but since 1656 it had been undergoing a revival under a vigorous line of grand viziers of the Kiuprili family, who in the 1660s began a new thrust up the Danube Valley directed at their old enemies, the Habsburgs. Louis XIV, also an inveterate enemy of the Habsburgs, allied himself with the Turks and Hungarian rebels against his Austrian foes.

The crisis came in 1683. In July of that year a Turkish army laid siege to Vienna, and for two months the fate of Austria seemed to hang in the balance. Volunteers from all over the Continent helped the emperor in his extremity. Pope Innocent XI contributed moral and material aid, and King John Sobieski of Poland arrived with an army that helped rout the Turks. The retreat continued for several years as the impetus of Europe's last crusade carried on down the Danube, until Eugene of Savoy broke Turkish military power at the battle of Zenta (1697). The Peace of Carlowitz in 1699 gave the Habsburgs full control of Hungary. The Hungarian Protestants were crushed. The landowning nobility was left in full control of its serfs and in possession of many of its old privileges, in return for recognizing the ultimate sovereignty of the chancellery in Vienna. The Habsburgs left local administration much as they found it, but they had established a strong monarchy in the Danube Valley where none had existed before.

The Treaties of Ryswick (1697) and Carlowitz (1699) marked the appearance on the European stage of two new great powers: England and Austria. Each had risen in response to Louis XIV's bid to make himself the heir of Habsburg power in Spain and Germany. The two illustrated how diverse great powers could be in the seventeenth century: England, a parliamentary monarchy controlled by a commercial and landed aristocracy, its strength based on commerce and sea power; Austria, a bureaucratic monarchy with agriculture and a standing army its most conspicuous sources of strength. At about the same time two more powers were just beginning to appear, each as distinct and different as England and Austria: Brandenburg-Prussia and Russia.

The Rise of Brandenburg-Prussia

The rise of the Hohenzollerns in northern Germany is somewhat parallel to that of the Habsburgs in the south, except that the Hohenzollerns started with less and had farther to go. They had been margraves (border counts) of Brandenburg since 1417. To this small territory around Berlin they had added two other areas: Cleves and some neighboring lands on the Rhine (1614), and the Duchy of Prussia on the Baltic to the northeast (1618). When the Thirty Years' War broke out there was nothing to suggest that the ruler of these scattered territories had any brighter future than a dozen other German princes. He was an Elector — that is, one of the seven princes who (theoretically) chose the emperor — and thus a member of the highest echelon of German princes. But his lands had no natural boundaries, no traditional ties with one another, few resources, and a sparse population of a million and a half. Furthermore, they were especially hard hit by the Thirty Years' War, when Swedish and Imperialist armies tramped back and forth across Brandenburg and Berlin lost over half its population.

The Great Elector

Frederick William (r. 1640–88), called the Great Elector, was twenty years old when he became Elector. He was a devout Calvinist, but nevertheless respected the Lutheranism of his subjects and was genuinely tolerant in an age of intolerance. The helplessness of Brandenburg during the Thirty Years' War taught him that his first and foremost task must be the development of an army. In 1640 he had a poorly equipped and ineffective army of 2,500 men. By 1688, it had increased to 30,000 and Brandenburg-Prussia had become the strongest military power in Germany except for Austria. If there was an explanation, it was the single-minded devotion of the Great Elector to this goal.

The first thing he had to do was to establish his authority over the Estates of Brandenburg and Prussia, which had almost complete control of taxation. In Brandenburg the Great Elector followed the practice of Louis XIV and simply continued to raise taxes that had once been granted by the Estates, which were never summoned again after 1653. In Prussia the townsmen were more stubborn and the Junkers (or nobles) more unruly, and Frederick William finally had to have the ringleaders of the opposition executed. In the end the Great Elector set up a taxation system for the support of his army that was common to all his territories, administered by civil servants and independent of local control. The nobility were shorn of their power in the Estates and pressed into service as officers in the army. In return, the power of the Junkers over their serfs was left untouched. Military strength, not social betterment, was the General Elector's objective.

Frederick William used his army as a weapon in diplomacy rather than in

Frederick William, the Great Elector, as a young man; painting by his contemporary Mathias Czwiczeic.

war by selling support to one side or another in return for subsidies. The contributions helped to pay for the army, and the alliances seldom required much fighting. By pursuing this policy, the Great Elector and his immediate successors made substantial territorial gains. Frederick William's economic policy was designed to develop his lands so they could support his army without the need for foreign subsidies. He did much to revive and improve agriculture after 1648, and much to encourage industry and commerce. His tolerant policies made Brandenburg a haven for religious refugees, above all French Huguenots after the Revocation of the Edict of Nantes in 1685. The recognition of the Great Elector's son as King Frederick I in 1701 symbolized the appearance of a new power in Europe. Prussia (as the Hohenzollern lands came to be known) had devoted relatively more of its population, its resources, and its energies to military purposes than had any other German state. It has been said that in Prussia the army created the state. But while the needs of the army were especially important in Prussia, they played a significant role in the development of every great power in Europe except England.

The Baltic: A Swedish Lake 1621–1721

Sweden

While Prussia was growing in strength, its neighbors, Sweden and Poland, were declining. Sweden had burst on the European horizon as a military power of first rank during Gustavus Adolphus's invasion of Germany (1631–32). During the latter part of the century the Baltic became a Swedish lake, with a Swedish empire reaching from the Gulf of Finland to the North Sea. Copper, iron ore, and agriculture were the Swedes' chief resources, a technically superior musket their chief military advantage.

Swedish power, however, rested on shaky foundations. The country had a population of less than 2 million—not much larger than Prussia or the Dutch Republic. Its lines of empire were overextended and its enemies—from Russia and Poland to Prussia and Denmark—were hungry for revenge. When young Charles XII (r. 1697–1718) came to the throne, a coalition of Russia, Poland, and Denmark pounced on his Baltic territories. Charles XII proved to be a military genius and crushed his enemies in a series of lightning campaigns. But he became intoxicated by success and engaged in political adventures that far exceeded his country's resources. He marched deep into Russian territory and was totally defeated at Poltava in 1709. He failed to get Turkish support, though he spent some years at the Ottoman court seeking an alliance. Finally, he lost his life in a raid on Norway in 1718. In the peace settlements of 1719 to 1721, the Swedish empire outside Sweden was divided among Hanover, Denmark, Prussia, and Russia. Sweden settled down in the eighteenth century to its earlier role of second-class power.

Poland

The case of Poland was quite different, though the results were similar. Poland, formed in 1386 by the union of Poland and Lithuania, was, after Russia, the largest state in Europe. Poland had reached its peak in the sixteenth century, when the Polish people, linked by Roman Catholicism to western Europe, had felt the effects of the Renaissance, the Protestant revolt, and the Catholic Reformation. By the beginning of the seventeenth century, however, economic and political decline had set in. The Polish monarchy had always been elective. Until about 1572 the nobles had usually elected the legal heirs of the monarch, but after this they began to choose anyone whom they believed they could control. By 1700 the real power in Poland lay in the hands of the nobility. The monarchy was almost powerless. The peasants were the most depressed in Europe, sunk deep in serfdom. There was almost no bourgeoisie, because the towns had not flourished. Political power was concentrated in the diet, which by now represented only the nobility.

The diet was notorious for its futility; one negative vote (the *liberum veto*) could block any action. If legislation did succeed in running the gauntlet of this national assembly, there was still no way of getting it enforced in the provincial assemblies of lesser nobles. John Sobieski (r. 1674–96), who made a serious effort to lead the country out of its weakness, was the last great king of Poland. After him the Polish crown became simply the prize of foreign intrigue, and Poland started down the path that led to extinction at the hands of more powerful neighbors at the end of the eighteenth century.

Russia

Throughout the seventeenth century there was no great power east of Sweden, Poland, and the Ottoman Empire. The Grand Duchy of Moscow (see pp. 432–34) had fallen on evil days after the death of Ivan the Dread in 1584. Disputes about the succession to the tsar's crown led to a "Time of Troubles," and the accession of the Romanovs, who were to rule Russia from 1613 to 1917, at first did little to strengthen the state. In the 1650s a near revolution was provoked by a reforming patriarch of the Orthodox Church, who ordered that the ritual and liturgy be brought closer to the original Greek text of the Bible. The order exasperated the uneducated masses to whom the Slavonic texts were sacrosanct. For many years after, "Old Believers" resisted the official religious policy of the government.

Russia was a victim state through most of the century, often unable to defend its frontiers against invading Swedes, Poles, and Turks, and still cut off from access to either the Baltic or the Black Sea. English merchants had made contact with Moscow in the 1550s through the White Sea, and German merchants were active in the capital. But while Russia absorbed some of the technology of the West, it remained untouched by cultural changes in the rest of Europe. The Renaissance, the Reformation, and the scientific revolution remained almost unknown to the peoples living east of Catholic Poland.

Peter the Great

In 1689 one of the most remarkable rulers ever came to power in Russia. Peter the Great (r. 1689–1725), as he became known to history, was a young man of insatiable curiosity and inexhaustible energy. His great passion in life was to make Russia a great power by rapidly westernizing its technology, its civil and military institutions, and its popular customs. Peter's plans at first developed slowly. Using his old-fashioned army, he failed to capture Azov at the mouth of the Don from the Turks in 1695. Next year, after he had built a river fleet with Dutch help, Azov fell. Peter had learned a lesson: In order to build a navy and to modernize his army, he would have to learn a great deal from the West. From 1696 to 1698,

Peter the Great, by Aert de Gelder.

Russian beard license. Russian nobles who wanted to keep their beards after Tsar Peter outlawed wearing them had to pay a tax and carry this license.

disguised as a private citizen, Peter visited Holland, England, and Germany. Here he learned how an utterly different society built its ships, made its munitions, and conducted its diplomacy. He also hired over seven hundred technicians of various sorts to return with him to Russia.

During his absence, a serious revolt had broken out among the palace guard *(streltsi)*, who, together with the "Old Believers," were the most backward and reactionary element in Russia. Peter hastened back to Moscow and made a fearful example of the rebels, executing over a thousand of them. As a sign of his determination to westernize even the personal habits of his subjects, he forbade the wearing of beards and long robes. To Peter, beards symbolized the old Russia of reaction, rebellion, and religious fanaticism. There was nothing particularly original about what Peter did to reform the military, political, and social institutions of his country. He borrowed his ideas and techniques from what other statesmen were doing at the time. But his methods were more casual and informal, more brutal and ruthless, than were those of western countries.

An overwhelming defeat by the Swedes at Narva in 1700 spurred on Peter's efforts to improve his army. With the help of foreign officers and advisers he had trained a formidable force of over one hundred thousand by 1709, the year he annihilated Charles XII's forces at Poltava. Years of warfare against the Turks were less successful, and even Azov was lost once again. But decisive victories came in the north. In the Great Northern War (1700–21) Peter gained territory on the Gulf of Finland that had once belonged to Sweden. This gave him the "window on the sea," the direct contact with western Europe, that was his primary aim. To man his army, Peter introduced conscription, and to pay for it he taxed anything and everything—births, marriages, caskets, graves, and beards.

Political reforms followed military reforms, though more slowly. Peter's method of governing was informal and haphazard. Toward the end of his reign, some order was brought about: the first provincial governments were set up; "colleges" were established to supervise government projects; and a "senate," or central administrative body, was instituted to interpret the tsar's orders and to carry out his will. A secret police provided a check on all officials. In Russia the imperial government did more and nonofficial groups did less than in any other European country. After 1700 the Orthodox Church was strictly subordinated to the state. When new industries were needed to support the army, government contractors founded them, using forced labor. One of Peter's greatest achievements was to compel the nobility to serve the state. At the same time he enlisted commoners, giving them land and titles of nobility. To support this "service nobility," he allowed them a free hand with their own serfs. A census for tax purposes resulted in greatly increasing the number of serfs in Russia by classifying doubtful cases as servile. And while in central Europe a serf was usually bound to the land, in Russia he could be sold apart from the land, like a slave.

In 1707 Peter moved his government to a new city that he had built at the eastern end of the Gulf of Finland and had named in honor of his patron saint. St. Petersburg was a perfect symbol of his work. Unlike Moscow, it had no roots in the past. The nobles were ordered to build houses, and merchants were ordered to settle there. The nobility and civil servants hated it at first, but in the end it became their capital. As Versailles came to stand for the France of Louis XIV, so St. Petersburg came to stand for the Russia of Peter the Great.

Historians differ in estimating the value of Peter's work, but on some things they agree. Western influences were having their effect in Russia before Peter appeared; he merely hastened changes that would have come in any case. He cannot be blamed for some of the negative results that followed, because many of them, such as the intensification of serfdom, had their roots in the past and owed much to Peter's successors. Two things he did accomplish: He transformed Russia from a victim state into a great power, and he involved it irrevocably with the future development of Europe. Peter's westernizing policy ultimately provoked a strong nationalistic and orthodox reaction, leaving Russia divided to the present day between deep suspicion of everything foreign and eager admiration of western technology and culture.

CONCLUSION

The half-century between 1660 and 1715 thus saw significant changes in the political and social structure of Europe. Absolute divine-right monarchy reached its apogee in the France of Louis XIV and was imitated from Madrid to St. Petersburg. It took the English Revolution to demonstrate that there was a practical alternative to absolute monarchy. So by 1715 the political systems of absolutism and constitutionalism were each embodied in a great power. At the same time there were important shifts within the European state system. The French bid for predominance failed, provoking the rise of England and Austria as great powers. Two great empires of the sixteenth century, the Spanish and the Ottoman, were in decline. Two peoples of limited resources and numbers, the Dutch and the Swedes, had bid strongly for great power status, but by 1715 their strength was spent. Two new powers had appeared in eastern Europe to join the balance, the small military Kingdom of Prussia and the vast semibarbarous Tsardom of Russia. The rivalries of these states — England versus France, France versus Austria, Austria versus Prussia, Austria and Russia versus the Ottoman Empire — were to become the dynamic elements in eighteenth-century war and diplomacy.

Suggestions for Further Reading

Good general accounts of the period are J. Stoye, *Europe Unfolding, 1648–1688* (1969), and J. B. Wolf, *The Emergence of the Great Powers, 1685–1715* (1951). R. Hatton, *Europe in the Age of Louis XIV* (1969), is excellent on social history. C. J. Friedrich and C. Blitzer, *The Age of Power* (1957), deals with the general theme of this chapter. J. B. Wolf, *Louis XIV* (1968), is a good biography. P. Goubert, *Louis XIV and Twenty Million Frenchmen* (1970), relates the career of the king to the social history of France. W. H. Lewis, *The Splendid Century* (1954), is a fascinating popular account of all aspects of Louis' reign. The whole period of revolution in England is treated in C. Hill, *The Century of Revolution, 1603–1714* (1961). G. N. Clark, *The Later Stuarts, 1660–1714* (1934), in the *Oxford History of England* series, is a fine synthesis. C. H. Wilson, *England's Apprenticeship, 1603–1763* (1965), deals with England's emergence as a great power.

The problems of eastern Europe are introduced in S. H. Cross, *Slavic Civilization Through the Ages* (1948), and O. Halecki, *Borderlands of Western Civilization* (1952). For Germany as a whole, see H. Holborn, *A History of Modern Germany, 1648–1840* (1964). R. W. J. Evans, *The Making of the Habsburg Monarchy* (1979), and H. G. Hoenigsberger, *The Habsburgs and Europe* (1971), are useful surveys. On Prussia, S. B. Fay and K. Epstein, *The Rise of Brandenburg-Prussia to 1786* (1937, 1964), is brief but excellent. F. Schevill, *The Great Elector* (1947), is an admiring biography. J. A. R. Marriott, *The Eastern Question* (1917, 1940), deals with the slow disintegration of the Ottoman Empire and its repercussions in Europe. B. H. Sumner, *Peter the Great and the Emergence of Russia* (1950), is a good short account. J. Blum, *Lord and Peasant in Russia from the Ninth to the Nineteenth Century* (1961), deals with the major components of Russian society.

	1648			1700		
SOUTHWEST ASIA AND AFRICA	**1652** Dutch found Cape Colony *ca.* **1700** Rise of Ashanti, West Africa				**1737–47** Nadir Shah, decline of Safavid Empire	
EUROPE	**1660–88** Stuart Restoration **1661–1715** Louis XIV	**1683** Turks besiege Vienna **1685** Edict of Nantes revoked **1685–1750** Johann Sebastian Bach **1687** Newton's Law of Gravitation	**1688** Glorious Revolution **1689–1725** Peter the Great **1690** Locke, *Two Treatises of Civil Government*	**1701–14** War of Spanish Succession **1715–74** Louis XV **1720** South Sea Bubble **1723–42** Robert Walpole	**1740–80** Maria Theresa **1740–86** Frederick the Great **1756–63** Seven Years' War **1756–91** Wolfgang Amadeus Mozart	**1762** Rousseau, *The Social Contract* **1762–96** Catherine the Great **1769** James Watt's first steam engine **1770–1827** Ludwig van Beethoven
SOUTH AND SOUTHEAST ASIA	**1653** Taj Mahal completed **1690** British found Calcutta				**1751** French control Deccan **1757** Battle of Plassey **1773** Regulation Act	
EAST ASIA	**1662–1722** Emperor Kangxi *ca.* **1675–1725** Golden age of Edo urban culture, Japan			**1736–95** Emperor Qianlong	**1796–1804** White Lotus Rebellion	
THE AMERICAS AND PACIFIC		**1664** British seize New Amsterdam		**1728** Bering explores Alaska **1756–63** French and Indian War	**1765** Stamp Act **1768–80** Cook explores Pacific Ocean **1773** Boston Tea Party **1774** Quebec Act	

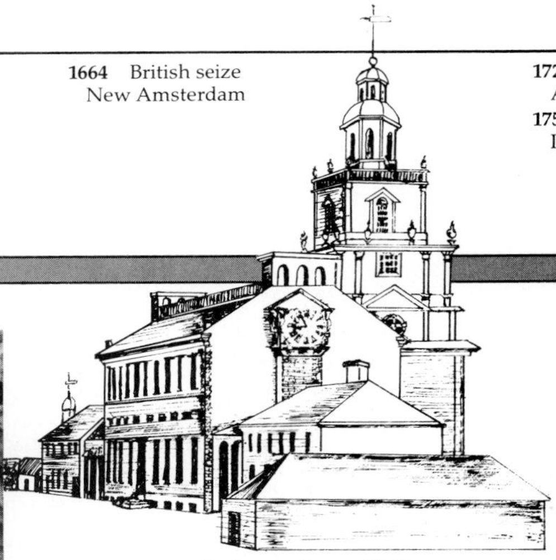

Independence Hall, Philadelphia, 1776.

Napoleon, 1800.

Ashanti wood carving.

East India Company merchant, by an Indian artist.

Emblem of the Sun King, Louis XIV.

Charles II of England, 1660-85.

	1815
	1805–48 Mohammed Ali founds dynasty in Egypt **1806** British control Cape Colony **1807** Slavery abolished in British Empire
1776 Smith, *Wealth of Nations* **1789** French Revolution begins	**1798** Malthus, *Essay on the Principle of Population* **1799** Napoleon becomes First Consul **1804–14** Napoleonic Empire
1784 East India Act **1786–93** Cornwallis in Bengal **1796** British conquer Ceylon	
1775–83 American Revolution **1776** US Declaration of Independence **1788** British colonize Australia **1803** Louisiana Purchase	**1807–30** Latin American wars for independence

Chinese fan painting, *ca.* 1700.

***Fuji above Storm*, by Hokusai, 1760-1849.**

29 The Scientific Revolution and the Enlightenment

The political and economic changes that took place in Europe during the seventeenth century, were paralleled by equally important changes in Europe's intellectual and cultural climate. Until the seventeenth century, knowledge about the natural world had grown slowly and fitfully. There had been many individual observations of natural phenomena, from which some useful generalizations had been derived. But many of these generalizations were poorly stated, and others were entirely erroneous. "Experiments" in the modern sense were all but unheard of. By the eighteenth century a startling change had occurred. A large body of verifiable knowledge about nature had accumulated and continued to accumulate at an increasing rate. Our civilization since then has been a "scientific civilization."

THE SCIENTIFIC REVOLUTION

This quality began to be noticeable in the seventeenth century. A new method of inquiry—the scientific method—had already developed in the late thirteenth and fourteenth centuries and come to fruition in western Europe after 1600. The new method was a combination of two elements: careful observation and experimentation, and rational interpretation of the results of this experimentation, preferably by use of mathematics. Science, hitherto the pursuit of lonely individuals, now became a social enterprise.

The Background of Change

Precisely *why* all this took place when and where it did is still a puzzle. We can only say that ever since the twelfth century the people of western Europe had been interested in scientific problems. But the medieval answers to these problems were based on deep-rooted, traditional assumptions about the nature of the universe. For example, it was generally believed that the universe was a finite sphere with the earth at the center. Between the center and the outermost limits were nine transparent spheres that carried the stars, the planets, the sun, and the moon in their daily revolutions around the earth, which remained motionless.

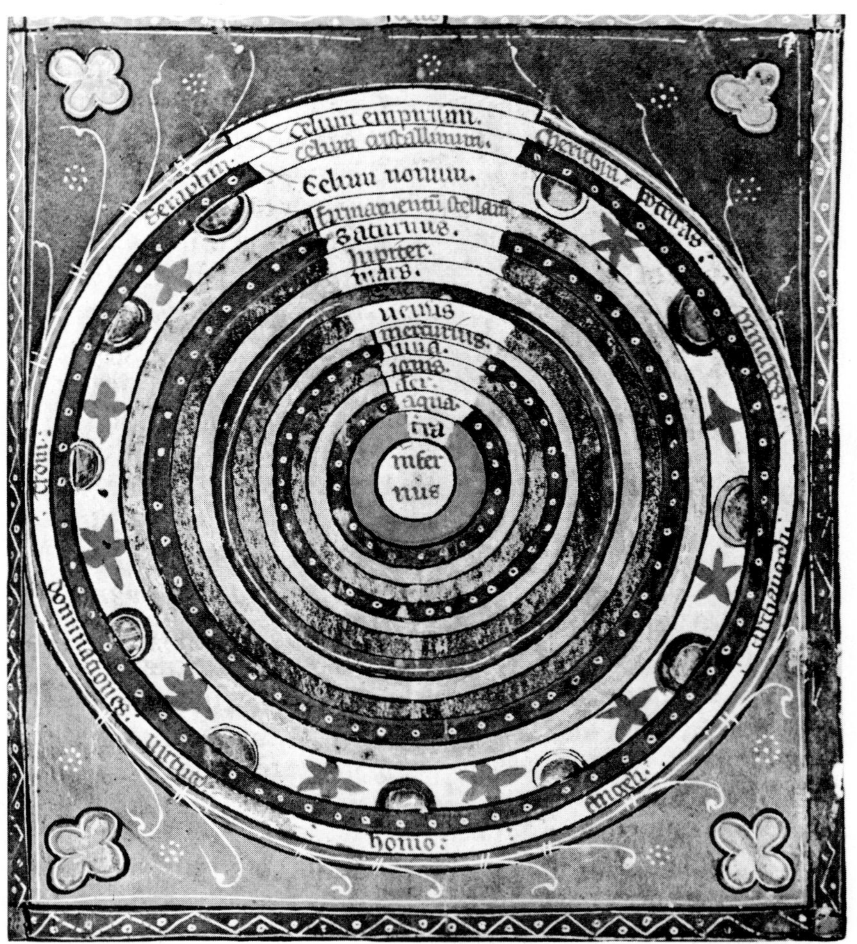

The medieval cosmos based on the earth-centered Ptolemaic conception. Ptolemy's explanation of the universe as a closed and defined system seemed so perfectly put together that it was not criticized for fourteen centuries—until the discoveries of Copernicus and Galileo.

Even in the Middle Ages, however, not all men were satisfied with this relatively simple conception. In the thirteenth and fourteenth centuries a small number of scholars began to question existing explanations. Medieval universities, notably at Oxford, Paris, and Padua, kept interest in science alive. But most Europeans of 1500 did not question the standard Greek authorities. The normal state of everything in the universe was a state of rest: things moved only if they were pushed by a mover—so said Aristotle. Galen, in the second century, had described the anatomy of the human body so convincingly that doctors still saw the human organs through his eyes. Ptolemy in the same century had worked out such an ingenious mathematical explanation of the observed irregularities in the movements of the planets that no one in 1500 thought it could be improved on. All motion in the heavens was circular, Ptolemy assumed, but there were small circles, or "epicycles," whose centers moved around the circumference of larger circles, and on the circumferences of these smaller circles the planets moved. This system worked quite well in explaining the observed phenomena. There seemed to be very little reason at the close of the Middle Ages to try to improve on either the observations or the theories of these ancient writers.

In the fourteenth, fifteenth, and sixteenth centuries, however, certain developments in European society were preparing the way for a change in the general view of nature. The development of the glass industry and the invention of the lens, for example, gave the promise of vastly extending man's powers of observing natural processes. New techniques in shipbuilding, furthermore, led to voyages of discovery, which in turn stimulated people's attention to problems of navigation.

1543: Vesalius and Copernicus

In 1543 two notable scientific works heralded the end of medieval science and the beginnings of a revolution in western man's conception of nature. Andreas Vesalius's *On the Structure of the Human Body* was for its day a marvelously careful description of human anatomy based on direct observation in dissection. Vesalius did not free himself completely from the authority of Galen, but it was an influential example of the power of observation. Nicholas Copernicus's *On the Revolution of the Heavenly Bodies,* a brilliant mathematical treatise, showed that the number of Ptolemy's epicycles could be reduced, if one assumed that the earth turned on its axis once a day and moved around the sun once a year. Unlike Vesalius, Copernicus was no observer. He learned during his study at Padua that there was an ancient opinion that the earth moved, and he found that this assumption made everything simpler to explain mathematically. Because medieval theory decreed that "nature always acts in the simplest ways," the simpler explanation must be the truer. And so with no experimental or observational proof, Copernicus presented a universe in which the earth was no longer the center. The experimental and the theoretical sides of the modern scientific method were perfectly exemplified in Vesalius's and Copernicus's books, but they were not yet conjoined in one man or one work.

In 1600, an Italian monk, Giordano Bruno, was burned at the stake for preaching that the universe was not finite but infinite in extent, that it was filled with numberless suns and planets like our own, and that God was equally in every planet or atom in the cosmos. Bruno had been inspired by Copernicus, although Copernicus himself believed in the finite sphere of the fixed stars and the uniqueness of the earth. The intuition of the infinity of the universe spread only gradually among scientists.

Bacon and Descartes

Two major prophets of the Scientific Revolution were Francis Bacon (1561–1626) and René Descartes (1596–1650). Bacon, an Englishman, waged a vigorous battle in his books against the deductive method of Scholasticism, which started from premises usually taken on authority. This method might help to organize truths already known, but it could never lead to the discovery of new truths. Only inductive reasoning, starting from direct observations and then explaining these observations, can produce new truth. Bacon pictured an imaginary society of scientists whose end was to benefit mankind by conducting experiments to discover useful facts. The founding in 1662 of the Royal Society of London, the first scientific society in England, owed much to Bacon's inspiration.

Sir Francis Bacon.

Descartes, a French mathematician and philosopher, was a more important figure than Bacon, but he lacked Bacon's understanding of the need for careful observations. To Descartes, the excitement of science lay in mathematical analysis and theory. He told in his autobiography how the literature and philosophy he studied as a youth left

The Scientific Revolution

ALFRED NORTH WHITEHEAD

A brief and sufficiently accurate description of the intellectual life of the European races during the succeeding two centuries and a quarter up to our own times is that they have been living upon the accumulated capital of ideas provided for them by the genius of the seventeenth century. . . . It is the one century which consistently, and throughout the whole range of human activities, provided intellectual genius adequate for the greatness of its occasions. . . . The issue of the combined labors of four men [Descartes, Galileo, Huyghens, and Newton] has some right to be considered as the greatest single intellectual success which mankind has achieved.

HERBERT BUTTERFIELD

The so-called "scientific revolution," popularly associated with the sixteenth and seventeenth centuries, but reaching back in an unmistakably continuous line to a period much earlier still . . . outshines everything since the rise of Christianity and reduces the Renaissance and Reformation to the rank of mere episodes, mere internal displacements, within the system of medieval Christendom.

From Alfred North Whitehead, *Science and the Modern World* (New York: Macmillan, 1925), pp. 57–58, 67; from Herbert Butterfield, *The Origins of Modern Science* (London: Bell, 1949), p. vii.

René Descartes.

him unsatisfied because they reached no certain conclusions, how mathematics had charmed him by its precision and certainty, and how he set out to discover a "method of rightly conducting the reason and discovering truth in the sciences." In 1619, in a moment of intuition, he saw the exact correspondence between geometry and algebra: the truth that any equation can be translated into a curve on a graph, and that any regular curve can be translated into an equation. This vision suggested to him a new way of grasping ultimate truth. If only we would systematically doubt all notions based on authority or custom and start with clear and precise ideas we know to be true, the whole universe might be deduced from a few simple principles and thus comprehended as clearly as the coordinate geometry he had discovered.

Descartes was one of the first to believe that science could save humanity. He reduced the universe, including the human body, to a mathematically intelligible mechanism. He took mind out of the world of matter entirely and defined it as a separate substance that comprehended the world of matter but did not exist in it. His generalizations in astronomy, physics, and anatomy were often premature, and his passion for system building went beyond his capacity to check by experiment. But his enthusiasm for scientific "method," his belief that everything could be reduced to mathematical terms, and his insistence on systematic doubt of earlier theories left a profound mark on the thinking of scientists in the next two centuries.

Experiment and Mathematics

Both Bacon and Descartes were overoptimistic. Bacon thought that a generation of experimentation would establish a solid body of knowledge about the universe. Descartes thought that a universal science could be deduced from a few basic mathematical axioms. But experimentation and mathematics were developing slowly and steadily in the hands of a growing host of scientists. William Gilbert used what little was known of the mysterious force of electricity to deduce that the earth itself was a great magnet (1600). William Harvey proved that the blood must circulate from arteries to veins to heart to lungs and back to heart and then arteries again (1628). Later in the century the new microscope revealed the tiny capillaries that actually connect arteries to veins. Torricelli, Pascal, and others investigated the ancient proposition that "nature abhors a vacuum," a proposition that had been firmly believed from Aristotle to Descartes. In order to prove the falseness of the proposition, investigators created vacuums in test tubes, invented the barometer, and discovered the pressure of the atmosphere. All these advances evidenced a growing precision in observation and an increasing sophistication both in controlling experiments and in quantifying their results.

At the same time, mathematics was making rapid strides. The invention of decimals and of logarithms early in the century facilitated calculation. Pascal inaugurated the study of probability. And at the end of the century Newton and Leibniz crowned the work of many others by simultaneously inventing calculus, which provided the first method of analyzing regularly accelerating or decelerating motion.

Kepler

In astronomy and physics observation and mathematics found their most fruitful union. The German astronomer Johannes Kepler (1571–1630) was troubled by discrepancies in Copernicus's theory, which he nevertheless believed to be true. He worked from the observations of his Danish master, Tycho Brahe (1546–1601), which were far more accurate than those available to Copernicus. Copernicus had clung to the old belief that all heavenly bodies moved in circles. But to Kepler it was obvious that this was wrong. The planets' orbits, he announced, are elliptical, with the sun in one of the two focuses of the ellipse. Further, a line from the sun to a planet sweeps out equal areas of the ellipse in equal times, and the cube of the distance of each planet from the sun is proportional to the square of the time of its revolution. Here was astounding proof of the intuition of Descartes and others that nature in some mysterious sense was mathematical. A geometrical figure, the ellipse, studied for centuries as an abstract form, was found to "fit" the facts of nature. The implication was that nature was perhaps really a machine, intelligible to careful observers with the aid of mathematics.

Galileo

The first fruits of Kepler's work appeared in 1609. During that year the Italian Galileo Galilei (1564–1642), professor at Padua and Pisa, turned a newly invented instrument, the telescope, on the heavens. The accepted appearance of the heavenly bodies dissolved before his gaze. The moon had craters and mountains; there were moving spots on the sun; there were rings around Saturn; and Jupiter proved to have four moons of its own. A bright new star had been noted in 1572, and in 1577 a new comet had appeared. The finite, spherical universe of the Middle Ages was shattered, and scientists suspected strongly that they were looking out into boundless space, containing other stars like the sun and possibly other solar systems as well. The old distinction between terrestrial and celestial physics was apparently dissolving. The moon and sun were not perfect globes, and the stars were not changeless. Perhaps the same forces and laws operated both on earth and in the heavens. Nor was the earth any longer the motionless center of the universe. The earth was a planet circling the sun like Jupiter or any other, and round about the solar system were infinite, silent spaces.

This was too much for obscurantists in the Church. The Copernican theory had been denounced in 1616, and in 1632 Galileo himself was condemned by the Roman Inquisition, threatened with torture, and forced to recant. Nevertheless, his brilliantly written dialogues contributed to the overthrow not only of Ptolemy in favor of Copernicus, but also of Aristotle in favor of a new physics.

Galileo's physics was inspired by the speculations of the fourteenth-century Franciscans, but he went much further and was much more accurate in developing mathematical formulas to describe the laws of motion. He worked out the law of falling bodies: The distance covered increases as the square of the time. He saw that the path followed by a projectile is a regular curve, a parabola, produced by two forces—the initial impetus and the pull of the earth. He came close to formulating the key concept of modern mechanics, the law of inertia: that all bodies tend to remain at rest or to continue in motion in straight lines unless acted on by outside forces. From this deceptively simple proposition—so fundamentally different from Aristotle's conception of motion as the result of some mover's action—was to spring the law of gravitation.

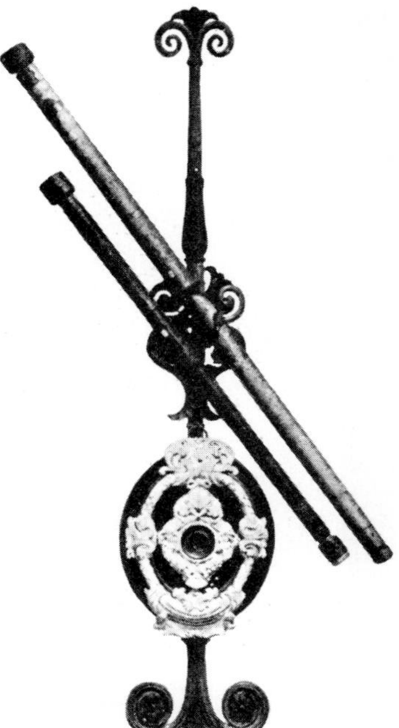

Two of Galileo's telescopes.

Newton

It was the genius of Sir Isaac Newton (1642–1727) that related Kepler's astronomy to Galileo's physics, erased all distinction between celestial and terrestrial physics, and accomplished at least part of Descartes's dream of establishing a "universal science." The basic idea came to Newton while still a student at Cambridge University. It occurred to him that the force that bends the moon into an orbit about the earth must be exactly the same force that pulls an apple from its branch to the ground. There must be a reciprocal force of attraction between every body in the universe, and this force must be calculable. Newton's earliest calculations came close enough to mathematical proof to persuade him that it was in truth the same force that operated on the moon and the apple, and that this force varied "directly as the product of

Sir Isaac Newton.

the masses" involved and "inversely as the square of the distance" separating the bodies. Newton developed the necessary mathematics (the calculus) to prove his theory, and published his conclusions in *The Mathematical Principles of Natural Philosophy* (1687). This proved to be one of the most influential books ever written in the history of science as well as in the history of human thought.

To scientists Newton's law of gravitation provided a simple explanation of a growing mass of data in astronomy and physics and laid the foundations for further research in both these sciences. Newton's support of the experimental, or inductive, approach was aimed at the premature generalizing of Descartes and his followers. But obviously he did not underestimate the value of mathematical theory, as Bacon had. In Newton the slow growing together of empirical observation and rational interpretation reached maturity.

The Newtonian Universe

Newton's new universe was a far cry from the small and finite medieval universe. It was a universe in which bodies or masses were moving about in infinite space in response to regularly operating forces. Mass, force, and motion were key concepts, and mathematics was the means of understanding them. The world of Kepler, Galileo, and Newton was a vast machine, working according to laws that could be mathematically expressed, and were intelligible to anyone who followed the proper experimental and mathematical methods.

SEVENTEENTH-CENTURY THOUGHT ABOUT GOD

What was the place of God in this universe? No serious seventeenth-century scientist thought that he was reading God out of the universe. Descartes considered himself a good Catholic and was not troubled by the dangers inherent in his separation of the world of matter from the world of mind. Newton spent most of his later years in religious speculation. Contradictions between faith and science were not evident to the first modern scientists.

Still, the religious view of life was weakening in the later seventeenth century, and the development of science was in part the result of this decline. The charters of the scientific societies and academies that sprang up throughout Europe usually contained clauses stating that purely theological or political discussion would not be tolerated and that "ultimate" or "final" causes were not part of the group's concern. Science was impartial politically and theologically; it did not stir men's tempers; it would not start religious wars; and above all, it was useful —it could benefit mankind. Scientific truth was an alternative to theological truth. It was more than coincidence that modern science arose in a century that saw Europe's last violent struggles over religion.

Spinoza and Pascal

One sensitive thinker—an obscure Dutch lens grinder, Baruch Spinoza (1632–77)—felt the religious awe implicit in the new mechanistic picture of the universe. To Spinoza the new universe of mass, force, and motion, operating in strict obedience to inexorable laws, was God. There was no need to consider God as above, behind, or beyond nature. God is not a "free cause" apart from natural law. He is not "Creator" or "Redeemer." He is natural law. "God never can decree, nor ever would have decreed, anything but what is; God did not exist before his decrees, and would not exist without them." Nature is "a fixed and immutable order," with "no particular goal in view." Man, like everything else, is part of this order. So Spinoza could write a book called *Ethics Demonstrated in the Geometrical Manner* and say, "I shall consider human activities and desires in exactly the same manner as though I were concerned with lines, planes, and solids." This was Spinoza's religion. Naturally such arguments were called atheistical, and Spinoza was considered a dangerous radical.

For most men, however, the new science did not destroy the traditional religion. Rather it compelled them to consider the religious significance of a greatly expanded and complicated universe. The telescope was revealing the immense size of the universe, displacing the earth and even the sun from its center. The microscope was beginning to reveal the wonders of the world's minutiae—the capillaries, the bacteria, the cells, the foundations of life. No one felt the two infinities—the infinitely great and the infinitesimally small—so keenly or speculated so profoundly about their religious significance as the Frenchman Blaise Pascal (1623–62). "The whole visible world is only an imperceptible atom in the ample bosom of nature," he wrote. The universe is "an infinite sphere, the center of which is everywhere, the circumference nowhere." "The eternal silence of these infinite spaces frightens me." Yet to examine a tiny organism, a mite, is equally astonishing. "What is man in nature? A Nothing in comparison with the Infinite, and All in comparison with the Nothing, a mean between nothing and everything." And yet man is greater than anything in the universe because he comprehends all this, and because Christ died on the cross for him. In this way, Pascal related the new universe to Christianity. Other Christians were not so concerned about the new science, and other scientists were not so concerned to articulate a Christian interpretation.

THE CULTURE OF THE SEVENTEENTH CENTURY

The Baroque Style in Art

The age of the scientific revolution was also the age of the "baroque" style in art—a style that sprang up in the later sixteenth century, reached its climax about the middle of the seventeenth, and came to its end around the middle of the eighteenth. The term *baroque* (French for "odd" or "irregular") was used by eighteenth-century critics who regarded seventeenth-century art as a grotesque corruption of Renaissance art. But modern critics consider the baroque a "high-water mark of European creative effort." As a style it is difficult to define because it reflected all the contrasts and contradictions of seventeenth-century culture in general: its religious ardor and its sensual worldliness, its credulity and its rationalism, its violence and its respect for order. Baroque painters and sculptors were influenced by all these contradictions. They portrayed voluptuous women in repose, military heroes in battle, and saints in ecstasy with equal skill and zest.

The dominant notes of the baroque were a sense of tension and conflict and a liking for the grandiose and dramatic. The conflicts of man and the universe, of man and man, and of man with himself were conceived on a more heroic, and often more tragic, scale than they had been in the Renaissance. Renaissance painters and writers had been interested in the individual. Baroque painters and writers were fascinated by individuals in their environment—torn by conflicting passions, confronted by human and supernatu-

View of the baroque interior of Vierzehnheiligen, a church in Bavaria, Germany.

ral enemies, buffeted by elemental forces beyond their control.

There were instructive parallels between the thought-worlds of the artists and the thought-worlds of the scientists of the period. To Galileo and Newton, bodies or masses moving through space in response to conflicting forces such as gravitation and centrifugal force were the objects to study. To the great French dramatists of the age—Corneille, Racine, and Molière—the objects of study were typical human beings acting and reacting in response to conflicting passions such as love and duty. Baroque painters were intrigued by space and light. The Dutchman Jan Vermeer portrayed figures in a space that was bathed and suffused with light; his countryman Rembrandt spotlighted them in the midst of darkened space; and others pictured them floating through apparently infinite space. The scientists' concern with "mass, force, and motion" seems closely related to the painters' and poets' concern with individuals caught in the tension between elemental forces in their environment. The typical hero of baroque literature, it has been said, is Satan in Milton's *Paradise Lost*—swayed by colossal passions, moving through vast three-dimensional spaces, commanding many of the natural forces in the universe, but ultimately checked and frustrated by God.

Young Woman with a Water Jug, **by Vermeer (*ca.* 1665).**

The most typical product of baroque architecture was the royal palace: Versailles in France, Schönbrunn in Austria, or Blenheim, Marlborough's regal residence in England. The style was fundamentally Renaissance classical, but grander and more ornate. These palaces were designed to be stage settings of worldly greatness. The vast reception rooms, the halls of mirrors, the great sweeping staircases, and the long vistas of formal gardens were designed to enhance the drama of royalty and aristocracy. Even the churches of the period—such as Bernini's colonnades framing St. Peter's in Rome—suggested the majesty of God rather than his mercy.

But the operas that originated in Italy in the seventeenth century were the most original creation of the baroque. The union of dramatic action and a less polyphonic, more direct musical style was a great popular success, and opera continued to grow as a distinct art form down to our own day. The grandiose and palatial stage, the dramatic conflicts of the action, and the emotive power of the music exactly suited the taste of the period. Italian composers—Monteverdi, the father of the opera, Frescobaldi, Scarlatti, and Vivaldi—led the way in the seventeenth century.

SEVENTEENTH-CENTURY THOUGHT ABOUT MAN

The seventeenth century developed conceptions about man that were based on Renaissance views but went beyond them. These conceptions may

Blenheim, the Duke of Marlborough's residence.

be summed up under three heads: individualism, relativism, and rationalism.

Individualism

Advanced thinkers of the seventeenth century took an increasingly individualistic view of man. The most intense Christian piety of the period—whether it was the Catholic devotion preached by St. François de Sales, the stern conscience of Puritans and Jansenists, or the warm inner conviction of German Pietists—was highly individualistic. The trend was equally evident in political theory. The fashion was to start with the individual and then to ask how society and the state could have originated and could be justified. Supporters of the divine right of kings were still numerous, but advanced thinkers were arguing that the state was based on a contrast between the people and the ruler. Some, like Thomas Hobbes (1588–1679), argued that this contract, once made, was irrevocable. Others, like John Locke (1632–1704), insisted that if the ruler broke the terms of the contract, the people might depose him and set up a new ruler. This idea of a "political contract" between ruler and people had some basis in the Old Testament and had been reinforced by feudal "contracts" between lords and vassals.

As time went on, the idea of a "social contract" took its place by the side of the "political contract." This was the idea that society was the result of a voluntary agreement among individuals who had been absolutely independent in their original "state of nature." The two ideas were mixed, somewhat confusedly, in Locke and later theorists. In both contracts, individual rights came first; then came society or the state. In contrast, the Middle Ages had thought of society as an organism or a "body" in which individuals were mere "members." The more radical thinkers of the seventeenth century conceived society as an artificial organization of independent individuals based on voluntary agreement.

Relativism

The great thinkers of the Middle Ages were sure that the people of Christendom were God's chosen and that the truth had been revealed once and for all to Christians. During the sixteenth and seventeenth centuries, humanism, the voyages of discovery, and the development of science greatly weakened this assurance.

Humanism had shaken this assurance by revealing Greco-Roman civilization in clearer historical perspective. Here—in a society long since dead, but still alive in its literature, its art, and its historical records — was an alternative to the medieval Christian view of life. The steady development of the "historical sciences"— history, archeology, philology — slowly impressed on thoughtful Europeans that there had been other societies in other times with values, beliefs, and institutions quite different from those of the present. Thus the idea of relativism in time was born. What had been right behavior for a Roman was perhaps not right behavior in other times.

The idea of relativism in space resulted from the geographical discoveries. The discovery in America of societies far less civilized than Europe and of societies in Asia more civilized in many respects had the effect of shaking European provincialism. Perhaps the "noble savages" of the New World were happier than the more cultured but more corrupt Christians of Europe. Perhaps Christians had something to learn from Persian sages and Chinese philosophers. Each society had different standards; was any set of standards absolutely right?

As the temporal and geographical horizons of the European imagination widened, the vision of man's place in nature was complicated by scientific discovery. European Christians were not unique in time and space, as they had once thought; nor, perhaps, was man himself unique.

The intellectual results of these developments are best seen in the work of Pierre Bayle (1647–1706), the great skeptic of the later seventeenth century. Originally a Huguenot, Bayle was briefly converted to Catholicism, but finally renounced all orthodox beliefs. He took up residence in the more tolerant Dutch Netherlands and devoted the latter part of his life to a crusade against superstition and religious intolerance. In 1697 Bayle published a huge rambling book, a *Historical and Critical Dictionary*, which had enormous influence on eighteenth-century thinkers. Into this book he poured all the relativism and skepticism that he had acquired through his historical study, his amateur knowledge of science, and his personal experience. He argued that atheists might be good citizens and insisted that there is nothing more abominable than to make religious conversions by force. He ridiculed the idea that stars and planets could influence human life and mercilessly attacked superstition on every front. He distrusted all historical authorities, including the writers of the Old Testament, unless he was sure that their account of events was inherently credible. His test of truth was reason — and few if any accounts of miracles met this rigorous test. Bayle was the most thoroughgoing skeptic and the most destructive critic of his generation.

Rationalism and Empiricism

The leading thinkers of the seventeenth century were predominantly rationalistic. Reason was the faculty that distinguished humans from animals, and the triumph of seventeenth-century science proved that reason could be trusted. This optimistic attitude was reflected in the belief in "natural law." The idea of a law of nature that served as a standard of moral behavior for all men at all times originated with the Stoics and was developed by medieval scholars. During the Renaissance and the Reformation this idea went into eclipse, but the discovery of scientific "laws of nature" helped to revive the belief in natural laws of human behavior. Cicero had given the idea its classic formulation: "There is in fact a true law — namely right reason — which is in accordance with nature, applies to all men, and is unchangeable and eternal." This law was implanted in the minds of men by God himself. It was understood to include respect for life and property, good faith and fair dealing, giving each man his due. These principles could always be discovered by reason, just as reason could discover the proof of a geometrical proposition. Hugo Grotius, a Dutch jurist, in his book *On the Law of War and Peace* (1625), turned to the law of nature in an attempt to find some basis for a "law of nations" that would transcend the religious fanaticism of the Thirty Years' War. And in more general terms, if natural law is the same for all men, then it lessens the contradictions caused by the relativism in time and space that was perplexing the seventeenth century.

John Locke

The most influential example of this kind of thinking was John Locke's faith that there are certain "natural rights" vested in every individual in the "state of nature," notably life, liberty, and property. From this it follows logically that societies are formed and governments set up mainly to preserve these rights. Descartes had hoped to be able to deduce the universe from a few central mathematical principles; Locke in his *Second Treatise of Government* (1690) assumed that he could deduce society and government from a few simple axioms about man and natural law.

This enthusiastic rationalism in the study of man and society was qualified by an undercurrent of empiricism, of respect for sense-experience. Here again Locke led the way in his *Essay Concerning Human Understanding.* Many of its readers thought that it did for the study of man what Newton had done for the study of nature. Locke argued that all our ideas come from experience. The mind at birth is a *tabula rasa,* a clean slate, on which our sense-experiences gradually imprint conceptions. There are no "innate ideas." The mind and its ideas can be explained only by the outside forces that act on it.

This was the purest empiricism. Locke hoped that it would provide a weapon for getting rid of all the superstitions and prejudices that cluttered men's minds; but it could destroy many things besides superstitions, including some of Locke's own doctrines. Logically, Locke's theory of the mind did away with original sin (which was held to be born into all humans), with revelation (which did not come through the senses), with mathematical axioms, and with all "natural rights" (which were obviously innate and not based on experience). And so the rationalism of Locke's theory of society clashed with the empiricism of his theory of the mind—as the mathematical tendency clashed with the fact-finding tendency in seventeenth-century study of man in general. The eighteenth century was to inherit both: a strong faith in reason and natural law, together with a firm confidence in the value of sense-experience. Out of these two a new blend was to come in the "Enlightenment."

THE ENLIGHTENMENT

The task that the leading thinkers of the eighteenth century set themselves was to popularize the methods and principles of seventeenth-century natural science and to apply these methods and principles to God, man, and society. Scientific discovery continued, but the work that attracted the most brilliant writers was that of applying the new scientific methods to long-festering human ills—economic, social, political, and ecclesiastical. Their concern was not so much to discover new truth about nature as to use the methods of natural science to reform society.

The eighteenth century's name for this movement was the "Enlightenment." This term suggested the dawn of an age of light after a long night of darkness, ignorance, superstition, and intolerance. There were "enlightened" writers in every country of Europe from Russia to Spain and from England to Italy. Correspondence, exchange of publications, and travel linked these writers together. Even in far-off America, Benjamin Franklin and Thomas Jefferson were in close touch with and accepted by leaders of the Enlightenment. Nevertheless, this international movement was centered in France. After the death of Louis XIV in 1715, the French government became steadily more inept and ineffective, while the social tension between the privileged aristocracy and the less privileged wealthy bourgeoisie became more acute. Many leaders of the Enlightenment were bourgeois, and their writings often reflected bourgeois interests. These men of letters were angered by bureaucratic stupidity and aristocratic arrogance; they wanted to get rid of privilege and obscurantism. They wrote with clarity and wit so that they influenced not only their fellow bourgeois but many members of the nobility as well.

For someone interested in ideas, Paris was the most exciting place in Europe. Here the intellectuals were in close touch with one another, excited by the feeling that they were helping to guide a revolution of ideas, and bound together in a crusade to put an end to the barbarities and absurdities of the old order. Other countries were too small or too backward to become major centers of enlightened thought and agitation. England, which had its own Enlightenment or pre-Enlightenment with Hobbes and Locke, was too complacent to become an intellectual center. But the Scots delighted in stirring up their duller neighbors to the south; David Hume and Adam Smith were major Enlightenment figures, and Edinburgh in the eighteenth century was one of the great European intellectual centers.

An assembly of *philosophes:* Voltaire (1), Adam (2), Abbé Maure (3), d'Alembert (4), Condorcet (5), Diderot (6), and Laharpe (7). Contemporary engraving by Jean Huber.

Voltaire

Voltaire (1694–1778)—his real name was François Marie Arouet—became the central figure and moving spirit of the Enlightenment, in part at least as a result of his visit to England (1726–29). There he read Newton and Locke and enjoyed the relative freedom of English society compared with his own. After his return to France he published his *Philosophical Letters on the English* (1733), in which he passed on Newton's main principles, as well as Locke's theories of human nature and political freedom. Voltaire skillfully contrasted the rationality of Newton's method and the reasonableness of the English way of life with the more unreasonable aspects of church, state, and society in France.

These letters set the tone of "enlightenment" propaganda in France. They were "philosophical"—that is to say, they reflected on the facts of life to discover their meaning, and they searched for general principles that might be useful to mankind. The men of the Enlightenment thus called themselves *philosophes,* observers of the human scene with breadth of view and a sense of the practical. Voltaire was the greatest of them—the most prolific, the wittiest, the most readable, and the angriest. His prime targets were religious bigotry and superstition. The close union in France of religious persecution and theological obscurantism with a capricious monarchical despotism exasperated him.

In an essay on "religion" he described a vision he had of a desert covered with piles of bones, the bones of "Christians slaughtered by each other in metaphysical quarrels." He went on to report a "philosophical" conversation with the shades of Socrates and Jesus, who both deplored the spectacle he had just seen. And he attacked intolerance in his own day as vigorously as the barbarism of the past.

When Voltaire died in 1778, he was the most widely read author in Europe and the first writer to have made a fortune from the sale of his writings. He was buried in Paris in a ceremony worthy of a king.

Montesquieu

Another leading figure of the Enlightenment, the French Baron de Montesquieu (1689–1755), tried to create a "social science" by applying the methods of the natural sciences to the study of society. In *The Spirit of the Laws* (1748) he suggested that forms of government were related to climate and other environmental factors, and he tried to discover what form of government best fitted a given set of conditions. The book was not "scientific" by later standards, but it was the first serious attempt to relate society to its environment. Like Voltaire, Montesquieu was impressed by Locke's theories about the English constitution. He concluded that the ideal form of political organization was a separation and balance of powers within government. This conclusion was to have great influence on the authors of the U.S. Constitution.

Diderot and the Encyclopaedia

A third major figure of the Enlightenment was Denis Diderot (1713–84), coeditor of a huge *Encyclopaedia* designed to sum up human knowledge and provide a handbook of enlightened philosophy. Diderot saw the relationship between science and technology more clearly than most of the *philosophes.* The illustrations showing machinery and industrial processes are among the most remarkable features of the *Encyclopaedia,* which appeared in thirty-five volumes over the course of thirty years (1751–80). Much of the most trenchant writing of Diderot, Voltaire, and other *philosophes* (or Encyclopedists) was done in articles for the *Encyclopaedia.* The book succeeded in becoming a bible of the Enlightenment.

Leading Ideas of the Enlightenment

No intellectual movement is successful unless it has followers as well as leaders, and the Enlightenment, like the Renaissance, produced its full quota of disciples, who used Enlightenment language to attack their enemies. But the silent supporters of the Enlightenment were even more numerous than the writers who jumped aboard the bandwagon. The main ideas of the Enlightenment struck root all over Europe and produced a generation with new ideas about religion and social organization. These ruling ideas may be summed up under five headings: reason, nature, happiness, progress, and liberty.

The eighteenth century believed as passionately in *reason* as the seventeenth, but with a difference. Voltaire's "reason" relied more on experience and less on mathematics than Descartes's. It was a weapon of skeptical inquiry based on observed facts, rather than an instrument of deduction from axioms. Reason could discover the fundamental rationality of the universe, and it could also make human society more sensible. It was a pragmatic in-

The Encyclopaedia *on "Philosopher"*

Other men are carried away by their passions, their actions not being preceded by reflection: these are the men who walk in darkness. On the other hand, the philosopher, even in his passions, acts only after reflection; he walks in the dark, but by a torch.

The philosopher forms his principles from an infinity of particular observations. Most people adopt principles without thinking of the observations that have produced them: they believe that maxims exist, so to speak, by themselves. But the philosopher takes maxims from their source; he examines their origin; he knows their proper value, and he makes use of them only in so far as they suit him.

Truth is not for the philosopher a mistress who corrupts his imagination and whom he believes is to be found everywhere; he contents himself with being able to unravel it where he can perceive it. He does not confound it with probability; he takes for true what is true, for false what is false, for doubtful what is doubtful, and for probable what is only probable. He does more, and here you have a great perfection of the philosopher: when he has no reason by which to judge, he knows how to live in suspension of judgment.

From Denis Diderot, *Encyclopedia,* 1778, trans. by F. L. Baumer, in *Main Currents in Western Thought* (New York: Knopf, 1952), p. 374.

strument, applicable not only to astronomy and physics but to agriculture, government, and social relations as well.

Nature was one of the favorite words of the Enlightenment. It was not always clear just what the *philosophes* meant by it, but it was clear enough that to nearly all of them "nature" or "the natural" were the proper standards for measuring God and man. If a thing was according to "nature," it was reasonable and therefore good. Voltaire and his contemporaries brought the idea of natural law to the peak of its prestige and the beginning of its decline. There are laws, they believed, throughout the universe—laws of economics, of politics, of morality, as well as of physics and astronomy. Men may ignore or defy them, but they do so at their peril. To the enlightened, the way to happiness lay in conforming to nature and nature's laws.

The end in view was *happiness,* not salvation—happiness here in this world, not joy in the next. The Enlightenment was thoroughly secular in its thinking. When Jefferson included "the pursuit of happiness" along with life and liberty as an inalienable human right, he was expressing the general agreement of the enlightened. The tendency of medieval Christianity to ignore misery in this life because it would be compensated for in the next angered the *philosophes,* who insisted that Christian ideals, if they were worth anything at all, must be realized here and now. Voltaire and his fellows were humanitarians. They abominated torture and cruelty, slavery, and the callous treatment of the insane. An Italian, Cesare Beccaria (1738–94), was the first to point out that savage penalties do not stop crime and to demand more humane treatment of criminals. The *philosophes* were also cosmopolitan and pacifist. Some of the bitterest passages ever written about the insanity of war and the absurdity of blind patriotism were penned by Voltaire.

The *philosophes* were also the first sizable group of educated Europeans to believe in *progress.* They took the older Christian idea of the spiritual progression of mankind from the Creation through the Incarnation to the Last Judgement and secularized it. The progress of civilization, they believed, was now out of God's hands and in man's own. Once we had discovered and applied nature's laws to society, progress was sure, inevitable, and swift.

This was a major revolution in western thought. The Middle Ages could not have conceived so purely secular progress unrelated to God. Men of the Renaissance still felt themselves inferior to the heroic Greeks and Romans. But in a literary battle between "ancients" and "moderns" that began in 1687 the idea appeared that the "moderns" were as good as, and probably better than, the "ancients." By 1750 a French *philosophe* and economist, Robert Turgot (1727–81), suggested that the essential element in history was mankind's slow struggle upward to the crucial development of the scientific method. In 1794, a French mathematician, Marie-Jean Condorcet (1743–94), wrote a *Sketch for a Historical Picture of the Progress of the Human Mind,* which summed up all the optimism of his century. He saw "the strongest reasons for believing that nature has set no limit to the realization of our hopes" and foresaw "the abolition of inequality between nations, the progress of equality within nations, and the true perfection of mankind." Progress, he concluded, was now "independent of any power that might wish to halt it" and "will never be reversed."

All *philosophes,* finally, were concerned about *liberty.* They were acutely aware of the restrictions on liberty that prevailed in France—on freedom of speech, freedom of religion, freedom of trade, freedom to choose a profession, and freedom from arbitrary arrest. They envied Englishmen their economic, political, and religious liberty. Their concern about liberty was potentially the most explosive part of their thinking; but almost none of them felt that violence was necessary. Their belief in liberty was tied to their belief in reason. Reason would reveal the true natural laws governing everything from trade and government to religion. The artificiality of French society, government, and religious practices would become evident, and benevolent despotism, enlightened by this knowledge, would set things right.

THE ENLIGHTENMENT AND RELIGION

Deism

These ideas inevitably affected the religious thought of Europe. The fashionable belief among educated persons in the eighteenth century came to be Deism, the belief in God the Creator but not Redeemer. Like a watchmaker, God created the universe as a complicated piece of machinery, started it going, and then stepped aside to let it run according to its natural laws. God does not concern himself with redeeming mankind. The essence of religion is awe and reverence before the rationality and perfection of the universe. To a Deist all talk of revelation or miracle, all belief in the special intervention of God in the natural order, was false. All dogma and ritual were superstition, since man needed only his reason to understand God. The heart of natural religion was the morality common to all mankind.

Obviously, Deism tended to undermine orthodox Christianity and to substitute for it a rational belief in God as First Cause and natural law as man's moral guide. A few of the *philosophes* went further and pushed beyond Deism to atheism. The French Baron Paul d'Holbach (1723–89), for example, argued that there is nothing but matter in the universe, that man is a conglomeration of atoms, and that everything that happens is determined by natural law. But in the end many Protestants were able to find a compromise between Christian beliefs and the Enlightenment's rationalism, humanitarianism, and tolerance.

Pietism and Methodism

Others reacted against Deism in the direction of more intense piety. To the enlightened, religious fervor of any sort savored of the fanaticism that had caused the wars of religion. But Deism was understood only by the educated, and its cold rationality had no appeal to the emotions. Hence the wide popularity of two warmly emotional Protestant movements, Pietism in Germany and Methodism in England and America. Both emphasized the importance of inner religious experience, of individual "conversion." Pietism was a second and milder Protestant Reformation, directed this time not against the pope but against both the dogmatically orthodox and those inclined to Deism. Individualistic, tolerant, and unconcerned about creeds or ceremonies, the Pietists attracted followers among both Catholics and Protestants.

John Wesley (1703–91) was the leader of a somewhat parallel revival of a warm, personal Christian piety in England. Finding his efforts resisted by the Anglican clergy, he took his message directly to the people, addressing huge congregations, teaching them to sing their way to heaven with the hymns of his brother Charles, and sending out streams of pamphlets from his printing presses to the congregations he had established. In the end Wesley was forced to establish a new denomination outside the Anglican Church—the Methodist (originally a term of derision directed at the "methodical" piety of Wesley's followers). Methodism touched thousands of Englishmen at home and in the colonies who cared nothing for the arid intellectualism of many of the Anglican clergy. Some historians have suggested that Methodism kept the English lower classes from turning to revolutionary violence during the first impact of the Industrial Revolution.

Adam Smith.

SOCIAL AND POLITICAL THOUGHT

The *philosophes* were interested in social and political problems, but they were reformers, not revolutionists. Their formula was simple: discover by reason and experience the natural laws that should operate in any given situation, clear away all obstacles to their operation, and the result will be progress toward happiness and freedom. The first "economists" in the modern sense used this formula to launch an attack on mercantilism. In 1758 François Quesnay published his *Economic Survey,* which argued for the existence of natural economic laws that must be allowed to operate freely. In 1776 the Scot Adam Smith published his *Wealth of Nations,* which argued in parallel fashion that all nations would be wealthier if they removed restrictions on trade and let the natural law of supply and demand govern the exchange of commodities. Quesnay was primarily interested in agriculture and Smith in commerce, but both came to the same conclusion: that economic laws, like other natural laws, should be respected; that interference with these laws is dangerous; and that the greatest happiness and freedom come from allowing these laws to operate.

The same line of reasoning in political thought led to the theory of enlightened despotism. The *philosophes* hoped that divine-right monarchy would become benevolent monarchy, that monarchs would gradually become "enlightened" and so govern their people according to natural law rather than their own caprice. To Voltaire and most of his fellows, government should be for the people but not necessarily by the people. A smaller group believed that reason pointed in the direction of constitutional monarchy like that in England, with a separation of powers as a further guarantee of political liberty. Finally, to enlightened despotism and constitutional government there was added a third theory, democracy, still too radical to be of much immediate influence but of enormous importance for the future. This was the theory obscurely but excitingly preached in *The Social Contract* (1762) by Jean Jacques Rousseau (1712–78).

Rousseau

Rousseau, a native of Geneva, turned up in Paris after a troubled and wandering youth, came to know Diderot and others of the *philosophes,* and for a time tried to become one of them. He was never easy in their company, however. He trusted reason, but he relied even more on emotion. He trusted nature, but to him nature was the unspoiled simplicity of precivilized man, the "noble savage." He became convinced that mankind had lost more than it had gained by cultivating the arts and sciences. He felt that he had been corrupted and humiliated by an artificial society to which he did not and could not belong.

To what kind of society or state could he give himself, then? Only to a society in which there were no hereditary rulers, no privileged aristocracy, no one with any right to lord it over others. In *The Social Contract* he developed a theory of liberty as willing obe-

Rousseau on the Social Contract

The problem is to find a form of association . . . in which each, while uniting himself with all, may still obey himself alone, and remain as free as before. This is the fundamental problem of which the Social Contract provides the solution: . . . the total alienation of each associate, together with all his rights, to the whole community. . . . Each man, in giving himself to all, gives himself to nobody. . . . Each of us puts his person and all his power in common under the supreme direction of the general will, and, in our corporate capacity, we receive each member as an indivisible part of the whole. . . . In order that the social compact may not be an empty formula, it tacitly includes the undertaking, which alone can give force to the rest, that whoever refuses to obey the general will shall be compelled to do so by the whole body. This means nothing less than that he will be forced to be free.

From Jean Jacques Rousseau, *The Social Contract* (New York and London: Everyman's Library, 1913), Book I, Chs. 6, 7, pp. 14–18.

dience to laws that the individual himself had helped to make as an active citizen. Locke and Montesquieu had thought that the way to political liberty was to guarantee individual rights and to separate the organs of government so that no one of them could gain unrestricted control. Rousseau thought he would never feel free until he could find a community to which he could give up everything, on condition that all others did the same. In such a community there would be no division between rulers and ruled; the people would rule themselves. If the people really governed themselves, there should be no checks and balances, no separation of powers, no protection of rights.

Rousseau was picturing democracy in its purest and simplest form: a tight-knit community of loyal and active citizens, unhampered by any checks on their collective will because they accepted this "general will" as their own. His book was highly abstract and difficult to understand. But when revolution actually flared up in France after his death, *The Social Contract* came into its own. It was not a work of the Enlightenment; its full force could be felt only in the new age of democratic revolution, nationalism, and Romanticism.

ARTS AND LETTERS IN THE EIGHTEENTH CENTURY

The pervasive faith in the rationality, intelligibility, and order of the universe displayed by the scientists and philosophers of the age was also reflected in the art and literature of the later seventeenth and early eighteenth centuries. Rationalism blended easily with classicism. The regularity and harmony of Newton's universe seemed to accord with the balance and proportion that Greek architects had admired and with the rationality and restraint that Greek and Roman writers had held up as literary ideals. The dictators of literary and artistic taste at the close of the seventeenth century were classicists, and when *philosophes* like Voltaire wrote dramas they accepted the classical standards as unquestioningly as Corneille and Racine had done. Architects accepted classical rules of balance and unity with equal zeal in the "Georgian" buildings of England and the beautifully proportioned Place de la Concorde in Paris. Enthusiasm for classical antiquity reached its post-Renaissance climax in 1748, when the remains of the Roman city of Pompeii were discovered in startlingly well-preserved condition under the lava of Mt. Vesuvius.

An Age of Prose

The age of reason was primarily an age of prose. Essays, satirical tales, novels, letters, and histories were the characteristic literary forms of the eighteenth century. Authors bent their energies to description and narrative rather than to suggestion and imagination. The essays of Joseph Addison and Sir Richard Steele, which began to appear in 1709, sketched a delightful picture of English rural society, while Jonathan Swift's *Gulliver's Travels* (1726) and Voltaire's *Candide* (1759) were more biting and satirical commentaries on human society. As the century progressed, the novel emerged as the favorite form of literary expression; the most mature example was Henry Fielding's *Tom Jones* (1749). Besides

The Morning Walk, **by Thomas Gainsborough (*ca.* 1785).**

Johann Sebastian Bach.

Wolfgang Amadeus Mozart, unfinished painting by Joseph Lange.

fiction, readers studied philosophy, economics and history — of which Edward Gibbon's majestic *History of the Decline and Fall of the Roman Empire,* (1776–88) was the most enduring example. Everything that could be done in prose — argument, satire, realistic description, historical narrative — was tried and done well by some French, British, or German writer.

The elegance and aristocratic flavor of eighteenth-century society can be seen in its painting, and especially in the portraits, which were the most characteristic form of the art. The delicate-featured and exquisitely groomed women who look coolly down on the observer, and the worldly, sometimes arrogant faces of their husbands under their powdered wigs suggest the artificiality of their society and sometimes the haughtiness of their characters. Furniture, tableware, and the great town and country houses of nobles and wealthy merchants reflect the same elegance and aristocratic spirit.

Not all the books, the arts, and the crafts were meant for the enjoyment of the aristocracy, however. The eighteenth century saw the appearance of the first newspapers, written for a wider audience. William Hogarth (1697–1764) made engravings of his satirical sketches of English society and sold them widely. Above all, writers, artists, and musicians began to appeal to a middle-class audience that went beyond the limits of the aristocracy. After the 1770s the plays and operas in Paris were apt to have a keen, satirical edge and to be directed at bourgeois listeners. The heroes and heroines of the novels were more often of middle-class origins than either upper- or lower-class. Music began to move from the aristocratic salon into the public auditorium.

Music

The greatest cultural achievement of the eighteenth century was its music. The musical world of the early century was dominated by two great Germans: Johann Sebastian Bach (1685–1750) and Georg Friedrich Handel (1685–1759), who spent most of his life in England. Together they realized all the dramatic and emotive possibilities of the baroque style — Handel in his oratories, Bach in his works for keyboard instruments, chamber groups, orchestras, and choruses. In the latter part of the century the orchestra, which had originated in the seventeenth century, was expanded and strengthened, the pianoforte invented, and music brought more and more into touch with a wider public. Franz Joseph Haydn (1732–1809) developed the musical forms known as sonatas and symphonies. The other outstanding musical personality of the latter half of the century, Wolfgang Amadeus Mozart (1756–91), was possibly the most gifted musician who ever lived. A child prodigy, he lived only thirty-five years and died in poverty; but within this short span he produced string quartets, concertos, symphonies, and operas that were timeless masterpieces.

THE BEGINNINGS OF ROMANTICISM

Beneath the dominant tendency to admire rational structure and classical balance, however, there were some countercurrents. Evidence of these currents was seen in Pietism and Methodism, and in Rousseau's distrust of an exclusive reliance on reason. More clearly than Rousseau, the Scottish philosopher David Hume (1711–76) criticized reason as a method of knowing truth and defended the validity in human experience of feeling, conscience, and habit. French and English novelists developed sentimentalism to a fine art, putting their heroines through heartrending misfortune and trying at every turn to arouse the reader's anger, pity, or love. The most influential example was Samuel Richardson's two-thousand-page tear-jerker, *Clarissa* (1748), which influenced Rousseau in writing his *Nouvelle Héloise* (1761). The strange, the unusual, and the fantastic began to come into fashion. Gothic architecture began to be appreciated once more, and a collection of poems (1762) ostensibly by a medieval poet named Ossian was very popular, though it turned out to be a forgery.

In Germany, which never came totally under the sway of the French Enlightenment, a "Storm and Stress" *(Sturm und Drang)* movement in literature emphasized the elemental emotions and denied the supremacy of reason. Johann Gottfried von Herder (1744 – 1803) worked out a philosophy of history that emphasized the uniqueness and peculiarity of each nation or people and the individuality of its genius. Johann Wolfgang von Goethe (1749 – 1832) at the start of his long literary career published *The Sorrows of Young Werther* (1774), a morbid tale ending in suicide, which appealed to lovers of sentiment and sensibility. The greatest philosopher of the age, Immanuel Kant (1724 – 1804), launched a powerful attack on rationalism as too narrow and too dogmatic. In his *Critique of Pure Reason* (1781), a very difficult book, Kant distinguished between speculative (or scientific) reason and practical (or moral) reason. The effect of his work was to make a new case for religion and morality based on man's conscience.

Taken together, these various tendencies heralded the beginnings of what was to be called Romanticism. The "Age of Reason" thus contained within itself the seeds of an age that would rely for its artistic, philosophical, and even social insight on emotion and conscience rather than on reason.

CONCLUSION

The two centuries that saw the Scientific Revolution and the Enlightenment might well be called the most revolutionary centuries in western intellectual history. The true watershed between what we call "medieval" and "modern" thought about God, man, and nature runs somewhere through these two centuries. The world of Luther and Loyola, of Charles V and Philip II, was still related to the Middle Ages. The world of Newton and Locke, of Voltaire and Rousseau, unmistakably belonged to our own.

Suggestions for Further Reading

M. Ashley, *The Golden Century* (1968), is a well-written survey of seventeenth-century social and cultural history. A. R. Hall, *The Scientific Revolution 1500 – 1800* (1966), is the best recent account but H. Butterfield, *The Origins of Modern Science 1300 – 1800* (1949), is more readable. C. Brinton, *The Shaping of the Modern Mind* (1953), covers a longer period. T. S. Kuhn, *The Copernican Revolution* (1957), describes the transformation of astronomical thought. On the social background of scientific development, see D. Stimson, *Scientists and Amateurs: A History of the Royal Society* (1948). G. de Santillana, *The Crime of Galileo* (1955), elucidates a famous case in the history of freedom of thought.

The following are reliable treatments of specific subjects: M. F. Bukofzer, *Music in the Baroque Era* (1947); F. Fosca, *The Eighteenth Century* (1953), on painting; M. L. Edwards, *John Wesley and the Eighteenth Century* (1933), and G. R. Craig, *The Church in the Age of Reason* (1961), deal with religious developments. The most significant study of the transition from the Scientific Revolution to the Enlightenment is P. Hazard, *The European Mind: The Critical Years, 1680 – 1715* (1935, 1952). The most searching interpretation of the Enlightenment as a whole is E. Cassirer, *The Philosophy of the Enlightenment* (1932, 1951). P. Gay, *The Enlightenment: An Interpretation,* 2 vols. (1966, 1969), presents an important synthesis. N. Hampson, *A Cultural History of the Enlightenment* (1969), is a useful introduction. C. R. Cragg, *Reason and Authority in the Eighteenth Century* (1964), and D. Mornet, *French Thought in the Eighteenth Century* (1929), deal with England and France respectively. Some of the leading intellectuals of the period are discussed in R. S. Westfall, *Never at Rest: A Biography of Isaac Newton* (1981); T. Bestermann, *Voltaire* (1969); and J. N. Shklar, *Men and Citizens: A study of Rousseau's Social Theory* (1969). L. Krieger, *Kings and Philosophers, 1689 – 1789* (1970), relates thought to politics.

	1648			1700		
SOUTHWEST ASIA AND AFRICA	**1652** Dutch found Cape Colony *ca.* **1700** Rise of Ashanti, West Africa				**1737–47** Nadir Shah, decline of Safavid Empire	
EUROPE	**1660–88** Stuart Restoration **1661–1715** Louis XIV	**1683** Turks besiege Vienna **1685** Edict of Nantes revoked **1685–1750** Johann Sebastian Bach **1687** Newton's Law of Gravitation	**1688** Glorious Revolution **1689–1725** Peter the Great **1690** Locke, *Two Treatises of Civil Government*	**1701–14** War of Spanish Succession **1715–74** Louis XV **1720** South Sea Bubble **1723–42** Robert Walpole	**1740–80** Maria Theresa **1740–86** Frederick the Great **1756–63** Seven Years' War **1756–91** Wolfgang Amadeus Mozart	**1762** Rousseau, *The Social Contract* **1762–96** Catherine the Great **1769** James Watt's first steam engine **1770–1827** Ludwig van Beethoven
SOUTH AND SOUTHEAST ASIA	**1653** Taj Mahal completed **1690** British found Calcutta				**1751** French control Deccan **1757** Battle of Plassey **1773** Regulation Act	
EAST ASIA	**1662–1722** Emperor Kangxi *ca.* **1675–1725** Golden age of Edo urban culture, Japan			**1736–95** Emperor Qianlong	**1796–1804** White Lotus Rebellion	
THE AMERICAS AND PACIFIC		**1664** British seize New Amsterdam		**1728** Bering explores Alaska **1756–63** French and Indian War	**1765** Stamp Act **1768–80** Cook explores Pacific Ocean **1773** Boston Tea Party **1774** Quebec Act	

Ashanti wood carving.

Napoleon, 1800.

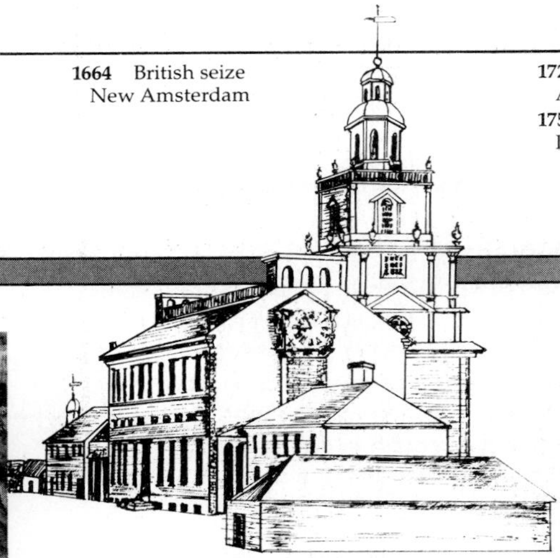

Independence Hall, Philadelphia, 1776.

East India Company merchant, by an Indian artist.

Emblem of the Sun King, Louis XIV.

Charles II of England, 1660-85.

	1815
	1805–48 Mohammed Ali founds dynasty in Egypt **1806** British control Cape Colony **1807** Slavery abolished in British Empire
1776 Smith, *Wealth of Nations* **1789** French Revolution begins	**1798** Malthus, *Essay on the Principle of Population* **1799** Napoleon becomes First Consul **1804–14** Napoleonic Empire
1784 East India Act **1786–93** Cornwallis in Bengal **1796** British conquer Ceylon	
1775–83 American Revolution **1776** US Declaration of Independence **1788** British colonize Australia **1803** Louisiana Purchase	**1807–30** Latin American wars for independence

Chinese fan painting, *ca.* 1700.

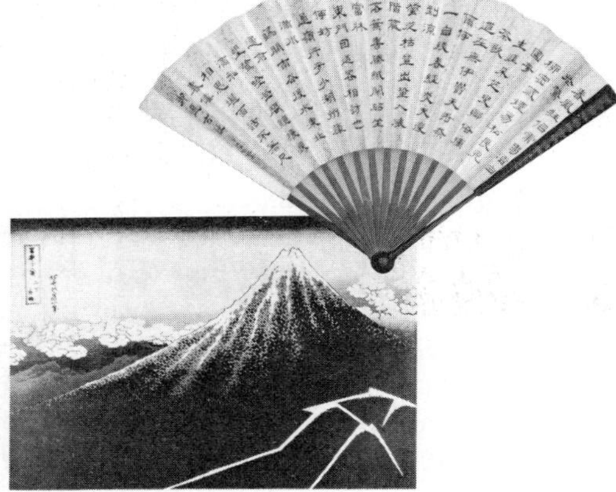

***Fuji above Storm,* by Hokusai, 1760-1849.**

30 Europe in the Eighteenth Century, 1715–89

The "Old Regime"

The seventy-five years between the death of Louis XIV (1715) and the outbreak of the French Revolution (1789) have a character of their own. This was a period of stability and equilibrium. There were no religious wars and no social upheavals (except for an uprising of serfs in far-off Russia), and there was less social mobility than in the seventeenth century. Monarchy was the most prevalent form of government, with divine-right monarchy evolving into "enlightened despotism."

Closely examined, however, the governments of the European states in the eighteenth century, both monarchies and republics, are better described as "aristocracies." Everywhere landed or moneyed minorities controlled or strongly influenced the governments of Europe. The Whig nobles and merchants who dominated the English Parliament, the French nobles and lawyers who dominated the royal councils and the law courts of France after the death of Louis XIV, the Junkers who commanded the Prussian armies, the landed nobles who made a farce of the Polish Diet, the "service nobility" that ceased to serve any but its own interests after the reign of Peter the Great in Russia, the wealthy bourgeois who controlled the governments of the Dutch Republic and the German free cities—all were rich, well-born, and privileged, and thus fitted the eighteenth-century definition of aristocrats. Everywhere "aristocracy" was resurgent against absolute monarchy, and many of the gains of seventeenth-century monarchies were lost or compromised. Only where the monarch or chief minister was of unusual ability was this revival of aristocratic influence turned to the benefit of the central government.

In this contest between monarchs and aristocrats, a compromise was generally reached. Eighteenth-century governments maintained an uneasy balance between centralization and decentralization, between absolute monarchy and aristocratic privilege. This might seem inconsistent, but strict adherence to basic principles had caused the bloody religious and civil wars of the last two centuries. Most people were content to accept the structure of society and government as they found it. It was a glorious age to be alive during the "old regime" (as it later came to be called)—if you were well-to-do. There was abject poverty and injustice in European society; but these could be forgotten if one centered one's attention on the brilliant "civilization" (the word first appeared in the 1770s) of the Paris salons or the London coffeehouses. To men who remembered the devastation of the Thirty Years' War or the fanaticism of Cromwell's "saints," social stability and political equilibrium were worth many injustices.

Aristocracy

[By the 1760s] the world had become more aristocratic. Aristocracy in the eighteenth century may even be thought of as a new and recent development, if it be distinguished from the older institution of nobility. In one way it was more exclusive than mere nobility. A king could create nobles, but, as the saying went, it took four generations to make a gentleman. In another way aristocracy was broader than nobility. Countries that had no nobles, like Switzerland or British America, or countries that had few nobles of importance, like the Dutch provinces, might have aristocracies that even nobles recognized as such. . . . Aristocracy was nobility civilized, polished by that "refinement of manners" of which people talked, enjoying not only superiority of birth but a superior mode of life. It was a way of life as pleasing as any that mankind has ever developed, and which the middle classes were to imitate as much and as long as they could, a way of life characterized by dignified homes and by gardens and well-kept lawns, by private tutors and grand tours and sojourns at watering places, by annual migration between town and country and an abundance of respectful and unobtrusive servants.

From R. R. Palmer, *The Age of the Democratic Revolution* (Princeton, N.J.: Princeton University Press, 1959), pp. 29–30.

INTERNATIONAL RELATIONS

Equilibrium was also the rule in international relations. The defeat of Louis XIV's bid for preponderance in Europe had been bloody and costly, and European statesmen were tacitly agreed that all attempts at hegemony should be stopped at the outset. The balancing of power among the "great powers" of Europe—France, Britain, Austria, Prussia, and Russia (Spain, Holland, Sweden, Poland, and the Ottoman Empire could no longer qualify)—became the chief concern of diplomats.

The balance, of course, seldom remained steady for very long. Every country was constantly on the lookout for additional territory or for new colonies and trading opportunities abroad. In order to avoid large-scale wars like those needed to curb Louis XIV's ambitions, it became the custom for the great powers to expect "compensation" whenever one of them was fortunate or daring enough to acquire new territory. This was hard on the weaker states, which were carved up to provide such compensation, but it admittedly preserved the balance and often maintained the peace.

There were frequent wars, but they were not so bloody or exhausting as those of the seventeenth century. Generally they were "limited wars," limited in the numbers of persons who took part in them or were affected by them. Eighteenth-century armies were professional armies, often recruited or kidnapped from the dregs of society or composed of foreign mercenaries. Except in Russia, where serfs made up most of the army, there was no general conscription, and civilians were usually little affected by wars. Warfare

Europe in 1715

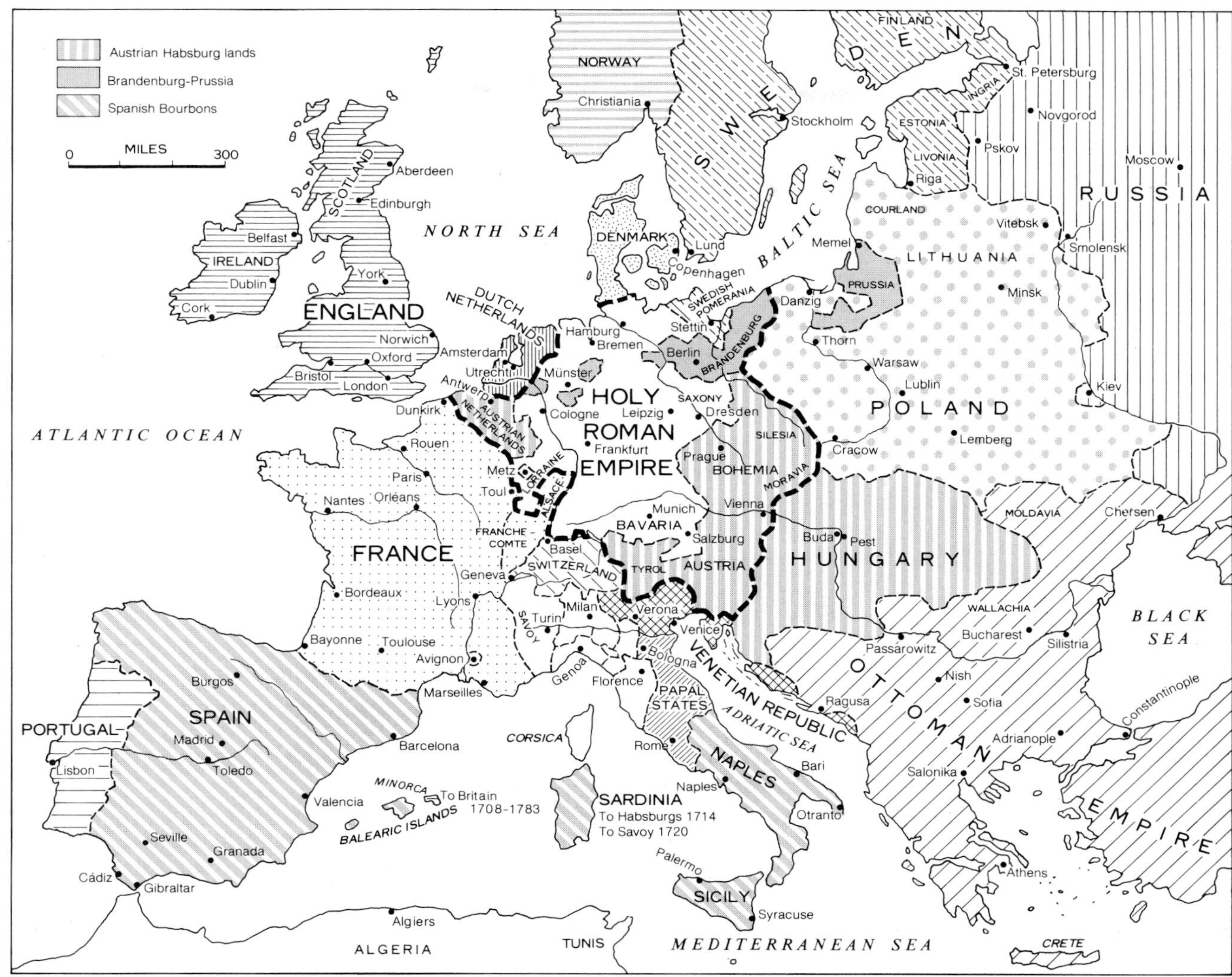

consisted of elaborate maneuvering by highly disciplined professional units rather than bloody mass combat. There was little pillaging, even in enemy territory, because it was bad business to devastate a territory that might be annexed.

Wars were limited also in their objectives. There were no wars of annihilation. The enemy of today might be the ally of tomorrow, and to defeat any power too thoroughly would disturb the balance. The religious hatreds of the seventeenth century had cooled, and the passions of revolutionary liberalism and nationalism had not yet sprung up. The statesmen and generals fought for definite political and economic objectives, not for ideologies. When the objectives were obtained— or when it became clear that they could not be attained—the statesmen made peace or arranged a truce. There was no need to fight for unconditional surrender. In spite of cutthroat competition for "empire"—in the form of land, population, colonies, or trade—the monarchs, bureaucrats, and aristocrats of the eighteenth century felt themselves part of a common civilization. The competition was a jockeying for power among cousins rather than a fight for survival against deadly enemies.

The picture of a stable, well-balanced eighteenth-century society sketched here can be compared to Newton's picture of the universe—a stable order of perfectly balanced gravitational pushes and pulls in which every mass moved along discoverable lines of force. But this picture must not be exaggerated. The eighteenth century was also a dynamic age. Its precarious equilibrium was an equilibrium among rapidly expanding forces. Wealth and trade were increasing; something like a revolution in agriculture was in the making; and a revolution in industry had begun. European economy and diplomacy were rapidly becoming global rather than continental, and the struggle for empire was reaching the farthest corners of the earth. For the first time, battles fought in America, Africa, and Asia began to tip the balance of power in Europe. And in trying to keep the balance, each country accentuated its own particular sources of strength. England relied more and more on naval power and commerce, Prussia on its army and bureaucracy. Russia intensified its reliance on serfdom, while Austria made up for weakness in Germany by increasing its power in southeastern Europe. France found itself coming out second-best in most fields—naval power, military power, and industrial growth; but its intellectual and cultural leadership masked these weaknesses. In short, differences in the bases of power among European nations increased rather than decreased during the period and made it harder to keep the balance. With growing political rivalry added to rapid social change, the eighteenth century was not all order and stability. It was pregnant with revolution as well.

The years from 1715 to 1789 may conveniently be divided into three periods of about twenty-five years each: (1) a generation of peace and prosperity, 1715–40; (2) a period of worldwide warfare, 1740–63; and (3) an interval of enlightened despotism, aristocratic resurgence, and revolutionary stirrings, 1763–89.

PEACE AND PROSPERITY, 1715–40

After the peace settlements of 1713 in western Europe and of 1719 to 1721 in eastern Europe, governments and peoples were weary of war. The age that followed was unheroic, unexciting, and corrupt, like many other postwar periods. But peace restored law and order, and order stimulated an enormous expansion of trade, particularly in western Europe.

Increase of Commerce and Wealth

Seaborne commerce was the key to wealth in the eighteenth century. Thanks to the enterprise of their merchants and the technical skill of their mariners, the foreign trade of Britain and France increased about five times during the eighteenth century. In the case of Britain the sharpest increase was in colonial trade. This meant that Britain needed a larger merchant marine than its rivals and forced the British to build the strongest navy to protect its overseas trade. In the case of France the greatest increase was in trade with other European nations. In both cases the accumulation of wealth among the upper classes was spectacular. For the first time the wealth of Europe began to eclipse the wealth of Asia. The two preceding centuries of exploration and establishment of overseas trading connections had begun to pay off handsomely in material benefits. The dinner table of a merchant of Liverpool, for instance, was graced by sugar from the West Indies, wine from Portugal, and tobacco from Virginia. His wife might wear calico from India in summer and furs from Canada in winter. Their daughter might be married to a nobleman whose capacious Georgian house had been built on the combined profits from his land and his mercantile investments.

But many of the commodities on which this thriving trade was based were derived from the labor of slaves or

Custom House, Dublin, Ireland. This stately building suggests the importance of trade and its regulation in the eighteenth century.

serfs. Only African slaves could be forced to do the kind of work required on the sugar plantations of the West Indies. There was an almost insatiable demand for black slaves in the sugar islands, a demand that was met largely by English slave traders. The serfs who toiled without recompense for their noble landlords in the grain-producing regions of eastern Europe were in much the same position in the economic order as the slaves of the West Indies. In short, a large part of the European economy was still based, as the economy of Greece and Rome had been, on servile labor.

There were signs in England, however, of the beginnings of revolutionary changes in both farming and industry. Eventually these changes were to result in an unprecedented expansion in the amount and variety of food, clothing, shelter, and luxuries that Europeans could produce. Historians speak of these changes as the "Agricultural Revolution" and the "Industrial Revolution," but these two revolutions picked up speed very slowly. Since the results of the Agricultural and Industrial Revolutions were seen most clearly in the nineteenth century, they will be discussed later (see pp. 715–21).

Mississippi and South Sea "Bubbles"

European commercial capitalism was still expanding its field of operations in the early eighteenth century. The period of peace after 1713 encouraged both private financial speculation and wildcat commercial ventures. The years 1719 and 1720 saw the first large-scale example of a typically modern phenomenon, a cycle of boom-and-bust, or, as contemporaries called it, a "bubble."

The wars of Louis XIV had burdened both the French and the English governments with large debts. When a Scottish promoter named John Law showed up at the French court after the death of Louis XIV and offered to solve the government's financial troubles, he was given *carte blanche* to manage the French economy as he saw fit. He set up a bank to issue paper currency and organized a Mississippi Company to trade with France's colony in Louisiana. The company boldly took over the government's debt, accepting government bonds in payment for shares of its own stock. Then it promoted a boom in the price of its stock by spreading tall tales of its commercial prospects. When the price finally

"Bubble Card," a satirical view showing the frenzied investors climbing aboard and eventually plunging into the water.

reached forty times its original value, investors began to sell in order to cash in on the profits. Before long, the price had plummeted, the bubble had burst, and Law fled the country.

A similar episode occurred across the Channel. A South Sea Company had been organized in London, to exploit the trade with the Spanish colonies provided for by the Peace of Utrecht. It too took over much of the government's debt, and it too promoted a boom in its own stock. In 1720, a few months after Law's failure, the South Sea bubble also burst.

The collapse of the Mississippi and South Sea companies hampered the development of joint stock ventures and ruined a good many individual investors. But the two companies had shown how to mobilize vast amounts of capital and how to find new sources of support for the public debt. Deliberate encouragement of speculation had tarnished both objectives, but the underlying commercial purposes of the two companies were essentially sound. When they were reorganized, both continued to make money for their investors for many years. French trade, particularly, was stimulated, although investors lost confidence in the French government. In contrast, the English government came to acknowledge the national debt as a public obligation and never again permitted private interests to assume responsibility for it. The government thus gained the confidence of investors.

England under Walpole

During the generation of peace that followed the death of Louis XIV, the English worked out some of their internal political problems. As had been determined by the Act of Settlement, the Elector of Hanover succeeded Queen Anne as ruler of England in 1714. Compared with the Stuarts, the first two Hanoverian monarchs, George I (r. 1714–27) and George II (r. 1727–60), were colorless figures. Both were unintelligent and spoke little or no English. They interfered in minor details of government, but neither was capable of grasping the larger issues. As a result, an "inner cabinet" of ministers became more and more responsible for policy decisions. Legally, the king was still free to choose his own ministers. Actually, he had to select men who could influence elections and control a majority in Parliament. These leading ministers began to meet to concert policy. They forced out of office colleagues who disagreed with the group's majority, and they usually accepted the leadership of the ablest or most powerful among them in presenting their policy to the king. These informal practices vaguely foreshadowed the "cabinet system" and "prime minister" of the nineteenth century.

Robert Walpole (1676–1745), a country squire who had family connections with both the landed and the commercial aristocracies, is generally considered the first prime minister in English history, although he would not have acknowledged the title. For some twenty years, from 1721 to 1742, he was the manager of the Whig faction in Parliament and the leading minister in the government. The first two Hanoverians by necessity chose their ministers from Whigs, because the Tories were tainted by affection for the Stuarts and had little strength in Parliament.

Walpole was a good-natured, hard-headed politician who understood the landed and financial interests represented in Parliament and knew how to hold a parliamentary majority together by tact, persuasion, and, if necessary, bribery and corruption. The fact that he liked to drink and tell off-color stories helped rather than hurt him in managing the Whig merchants and landed gentry who controlled Parliament and ran local government as justices of the peace. Walpole took care never to stir up any issue, at home or abroad, that might arouse passion and conflict. In 1733, for instance, he proposed a sensible scheme for raising more revenue from excise taxes and less from customs duties in order to discourage smuggling and encourage legitimate trade. But when his scheme was met by a storm of irrational abuse, he dropped it. So far as the colonies were concerned, he followed a policy of "salutary neglect," leaving them to grow in population and wealth by their own efforts. In foreign affairs he preserved the peace until 1739, when the London merchants and their spokesmen in Parliament forced him into a commercial war with Spain. Even then he tried to keep the war as limited as possible.

On the whole, Walpole's ministry was a fruitful time for England. Both the mother country and the colonies prospered; the credit of the government was never better; and the ruling landed and commercial aristocracy governed with a loose rein. When Voltaire visited England (1726–29) he may have idealized English society and government. But there was without question more equality before the law in England, more personal freedom, more sense of public obligation in the ruling class, more security of property, and more widespread prosperity than anywhere else in Europe.

Louis XV and Cardinal Fleury

The generation of peace that brought strength to Britain brought weakness to France. Louis XIV's great-grandson, Louis XV (r. 1715–74), was a child of five when he came to the throne. The Regency that governed in his name for eight years had to make concessions to all the powerful elements in French society that had been kept in leash by the Sun King. The result was an aristocratic reaction in French government. Nobles began to reappear as policymakers on the royal councils, and the *Parlement* of Paris boldly reasserted its ancient claim to register and enforce royal legislation or not, as it saw fit. The French monarchy remained as absolute as ever in theory, but after Louis XIV there was no strong hand to make the theory work. French government became inefficient and inconstant. Aristocratic privilege exasperated the middle classes and in the long run made it impossible for the government to avoid financial insolvency.

For a time the decline was arrested by Cardinal Fleury, the leading minister from 1726 to 1743. Fleury had ability, but he was no Richelieu. He was past seventy when he came to power, and his policy, much like Walpole's, was to preserve the peace, make cautious compromises, and avoid direct confrontation with the holders of power—in this case the nobility. Fleury dissociated himself from the statesmanlike attempt of another minister to tax the nobility like everyone else, but he stabilized the currency, encouraged trade, and did all he could to make the old system of tax-farming work. His monarch was too debauched and incapable to set a more constructive course.

Fleury lost power in his last years, and when he died at the age of ninety, Louis XV decided that he would govern by himself. This simply meant that France now had a king who was incapable of governing or of letting anyone else govern for him. Louis XV's best-known remark, "After me, the deluge," perfectly expressed his attitude. The aristocracy naturally took advantage of this situation and greatly increased its influence. France remained the largest and potentially most powerful nation in Europe. French trade and

George R

George I of England, and his signature. Medal by John Croker.

Madame de Pompadour (1721–64), the first official mistress of Louis XV, by Francois Boucher.

industry were growing at a rapid rate, but the government was run by royal mistresses and favorites (Mme. de Pompadour was the most prominent), and the French state could not make full use of its resources.

Declining Monarchies and Empires

Elsewhere in Europe, with few exceptions, monarchical institutions were in decline as they were in France during the generation after the Peace of Utrecht.

In Spain the Bourbon whom Louis XIV established on the throne, Philip V (r. 1700–46), managed to curb the nobility somewhat and to encourage trade and industry. But the dry rot had eaten too deeply into Spanish society and government to allow a real revival of the nation's greatness. Neither the Spanish economy, nor the army and navy, nor the colonies made any significant gains.

Austria was an imperfectly united empire composed of three separate kingdoms (Austria, Bohemia, and Hungary) and two dependencies of quite different cultures and traditions (northern Italy and the Netherlands). The Habsburg Emperor Charles VI (r. 1711–40) had to spend years in persuading his own subjects and foreign governments to accept a "Pragmatic Sanction" that provided for his daughter, Maria Theresa (Charles had no sons), to succeed him as ruler of all his various lands. By the time of his death he had the agreement of everyone concerned, but no one was sure just how long the agreement would be respected by greedy neighboring monarchs or restless Hungarian nobles.

Farther east, the Polish and Ottoman empires continued to decline. A desultory and trivial war over the succession to the Polish crown was fought between 1733 and 1738 by France and Spain against Austria and Russia. The Russian candidate for the throne won out, and all the losers were "compensated" by being given scraps of territory elsewhere—Spain in Naples and Sicily, for instance. At the same time Austria and Russia were once more at war with the Ottoman Turks. The Turks were never completely dominated by their neighbors, as were the Poles, but it was evident that neither state counted for much in the European power structure.

In the generation after Peter the Great's death in 1725 a series of palace revolutions placed the Russian crown successively on the heads of half a dozen children or incompetent women. German, particularly Prussian, influence was very strong at the court. As in France, the nobles managed to free themselves from many of the restrictions placed on them by earlier and stronger monarchs. The Russian nobles extended the power that Peter had given them over their own serfs but tried to renounce the obligation to serve the state that he had imposed on them in return. In Russia, as in Hungary and Prussia, the peasants sank deeper and deeper into serfdom, while the governments made one concession after another to the nobles in order to gain their favor. Until the accession of Catherine the Great in 1762 there was no strong hand at the helm of the Russian state; but Peter's work in raising his country to the position of a great power in European war and diplomacy proved to be permanent.

Frederick William I of Prussia

The most successful ruler of his generation apart from Walpole was King Frederick William I of Brandenburg-Prussia (r. 1713–40). While absolute monarchy seemed to be in decline elsewhere, this strange, uncouth, and choleric man continued the work of transforming one of the smallest and poorest states of Europe into a great military power. Following in the footsteps of the Great Elector (1640–88), he centralized the administration in a so-called General Directory, pared civil expenditures to the bone, and worked his subordinates remorselessly, all with the object of building the best-disciplined and most formidable army in Europe. "Salvation cames from the Lord," he remarked, "but everything else is my affair." When he was through he had increased his army to over 80,000 men, twice what it had been under his father. But while Frederick William built the fourth largest and the most efficient army on the Continent, he drew back when it came to using it. He left his son a full treasury, an efficient civil bureaucracy, and a highly trained army—one that had not fought a battle in over a generation.

He despised his son, Frederick, for his unmilitary habits and his taste for reading Voltaire and playing the flute. When Frederick tried to flee the country with a friend, his father had the friend beheaded before his son's eyes and put Frederick to work in the bureaucracy. The shock treatment worked. Without losing his taste for literature and music, Frederick grew interested in administration and the army. He succeeded his father as Frederick II (r. 1740–86), better known to history as Frederick the Great.

Frederick William I, by Antoine Pesne.

WORLDWIDE WARFARE, 1740–63

The peaceful generation just described was followed by a generation dominated by two wars, the War of the Austrian Succession (1740–48) and the Seven Years' War (1756–63), separated by a few years of intensive diplomacy. These wars grew out of two irreconcilable rivalries for power. One was the rivalry between the rising Hohenzollerns of Prussia and the more established Habsburgs of Austria for territory in central Europe. The other was the rivalry between Great Britain and France for trade and colonial empire in North America, the West Indies, Africa, and India. Twice these two rivalries became entangled with each other, although the partnerships changed between the wars. And by the final peace of 1763 England and Prussia had gained at the expense of France and Austria.

The British Navy and the Prussian Army

These wars were to demonstrate that the most efficient fighting units in eighteenth-century Europe were the British navy and the Prussian army. The most obvious explanation of superiority in each case was the unrivaled excellence of the officers corps. But behind the two arms were two sharply different societies and political systems, each well adapted to the particular sort of competition in which the nation found itself.

Great Britain had many advantages in the race for sea power. It was an island, safe from invasion by land, and therefore able to pour into ships the men and money that continental states had to pour into armies. Maritime enterprise was both profitable and patriotic; a seafaring career attracted enterprising younger sons of the nobility and gentry as well as yeomen and artisans. The reservoir of experienced sailors was larger in England than in France, its nearest rival, because the British had the largest merchant marine in the world. Finally, the government and the ruling classes recognized the importance of trade and sea power, and in spite of periods of neglect they supported naval construction and encouraged British shipping.

Britain's rival, France, had almost all the advantages England had—experienced sailors, a large merchant marine, warships superior in design even to the British, and colonial bases overseas. But France had long land frontiers and a tradition of intervening in the affairs of central Europe. This situation created an impossible dilemma. France could not be both the greatest land power and the greatest sea power, and if the army was favored, then the navy suffered.

The Prussian army was the creation of the Hohenzollerns, who had shaped a society and designed a state to support it. The Prussian bureaucracy and fiscal system had grown out of institutions devised to provide direct support to the army. The Junkers had been taught that their calling was to serve the king, in the army and in the civil service. In return they were given wide powers over the serfs who supported them. Enterprising members of the small middle class were also enlisted into the civil service, and serfs were conscripted when needed into the army. The proverbial discipline of the Prussian army pervaded to some degree both the society and the government. In England, central government by Parliament, local government by amateurs, and a considerable amount of freedom proved to be a good formula for producing sea power. In Prussia, centralized professional administration with an absolute monarch leading a disciplined aristocracy proved to be a successful formula for producing land power.

The War of the Austrian Succession, 1740–48

In 1740 Maria Theresa, a comely but inexperienced young woman, succeeded her father in the Habsburg dominions, to which her right of succession had been guaranteed by the Pragmatic Sanction. Frederick II of Prussia almost immediately threw his army into Silesia, one of Austria's richest provinces, on the northeastern frontier of Bohemia. Frederick had published an anonymous little book against the immorality of Machiavelli, but he had learned some of the Florentine's precepts as well. Silesia, with its million inhabitants, its linen industry, and its mineral resources, would finally make Brandenburg-Prussia a great power. Both Maria Theresa and the European powers were caught off guard. Frederick seized what he needed and spent the next twenty years defending his gain.

For a time this was not too difficult. Frederick's bold-faced aggression encouraged every enemy of the Habsburgs to join in the attack—Bavaria, Spain, and finally France. Strangely enough, Hungary, which resented Habsburg rule, proved to be Maria Theresa's salvation. When she went to Budapest with her infant son to make an emotional appeal to the Hungarian Parliament, the chivalrous nobility rose to her support. During the wars that followed, an able minister, Count Friedrich Wilhelm Haugwitz (1700–65), centralized the Habsburg administration and reorganized the army. Austria, a helpless victim state in 1740, was able to revive and become a formidable antagonist to the king of Prussia. Frederick's armies fought brilliantly, however, and the combined pressure of France, Bavaria, and Prussia — shaky though the alliance was — proved to be too much for Maria Theresa. In 1748, at Aix-la-Chapelle, she agreed to a peace treaty that left Silesia in Frederick's hands.

Meanwhile the Anglo-French rivalry had also broken out into war. When war began between England and Spain in 1739, it was only a question of time before France would be drawn in. France and Spain cooperated closely in the eighteenth century. Both had Bourbon rulers, and France had a large economic stake in the Spanish Empire because France supplied the Spanish colonies with most of their manufactured goods. English and French interests clashed in America and India. In North America the English felt threatened by the French military hold on Canada and Louisiana, while the French felt threatened by the pressure of the English colonies expanding northward and westward. In the West Indies there was rivalry over the sugar islands. In India the death of the last strong Mughal emperor in 1707 had led to the collapse of all central administration. Both the French and the British East India companies were trying to influence native principalities, particularly around Madras and Pondicherry. From Canada to the Carnatic Coast of India uneasy Frenchmen and Englishmen were ready to fly to arms.

In 1744 France declared war on Great Britain, and immediately the war in Europe and the war overseas merged into one. In 1745 the American colonists captured Louisbourg in Canada, and in 1746 the French seized Madras. Nothing decisive came of the conflict, however, because the English could not yet make up their minds whether to concentrate their efforts on a land war on the Continent against France or on the war overseas. The former policy was denounced by the "Patriots" in Parliament as "Hanoverianism" — that is, pandering to the interests of the Monarch, George II, who was also Elector of Hanover in Germany. The English navy defeated the French; the French army defeated the English on the Continent; but neither side pressed its successes very far, either on sea or on land. A typical "limited" war, the War of the Austrian Succession ended in a stalemate so far as Britain and France were concerned. The French gave up their conquest of Madras, and the English government, much to the disgust of the American colonists, gave back Louisbourg. The French came out of the war with no gains over either Austria or England. The English came out of it with a clearer sense of how they should fight their next war with France.

Maria Theresa of Austria with her husband, Emperor Francis I, and eleven of their children. The future Emperor Joseph II stands in the right center. Painting by Meytens.

The Diplomatic Revolution

England had fought in the War of the Austrian Succession in loose agreement with its old ally, Austria. France had fought in a still looser alliance with Prussia (Frederick deserted his ally twice to make truces with Austria). During the years between 1748 and 1756, a "diplomatic revolution" took place in which the chief antagonists in the first general war of mid-century changed partners in preparation for the second. This "revolution" illustrates nicely the main characteristics of eighteenth-century diplomacy.

The chief instigator of the revolution was Count Wenzel Kaunitz (1711–94), the Austrian state chancellor. Burning with desire to crush Frederick and recover Silesia, he decided that the only practical way was to heal the old antagonism between Bourbons and Habsburgs and to gain the support of France—and if possible of Russia as well—in a new war against Prussia. Prussia, he was sure, could not last long against the three strongest powers on the Continent. Kaunitz worked carefully to bring the mistress of Louis XV, Mme. de Pompadour, around to his side, but it was a chain of calculations and miscalculations by other statesmen that finally persuaded France to agree to the alliance. The English ministry became worried about whether Austria had the will and ability to help England defend Hanover against France. Prussia was obviously better placed to defend Hanover, but when Frederick agreed to do so in return for British subsidies, the French were irritated. Since Frederick had made an agreement with France's ancient enemy, England, the French were now ready to reach an agreement with Frederick's enemy, Austria. Soon a coalition of France, Austria, and Russia was arranged, and it looked as if Prussia's situation was hopeless. Frederick saw that his only chance was to catch his enemies off guard, and, characteristically, he started the war with an offensive in 1756, almost a year earlier than his opponents had planned.

William Pitt the Elder, by Richard Brompton.

Conflict Overseas

War had already broken out between the British and the French overseas. In India, Joseph Dupleix (1697–1763) had been trying since 1749 to make the French East India Company a political as well as a commercial power. The English East India Company soon became alarmed, and there were some armed clashes in which Dupleix's forces were defeated. In 1754 the French company's directors, afraid that Dupleix was leading them into serious conflict with the British, recalled him to France. Ironically, his idea of increasing the company's revenue through domination of native states was adopted by the British East India Company under its brilliant local leader, Robert Clive (1725–74). His victory over the French at Plassey (1757) firmly established British control and became the foundation of British territorial rule in India.

The situation in America was even more tense than in India. The French in Canada had used the interval of peace to build a chain of forts from the St. Lawrence down the Ohio River to the Mississippi River, and the British government had countered by sending ships and troops to the American colonies. There were now about a million and a half British subjects (including slaves) in North America and only about sixty thousand French. British troops and colonists began to strike at the French forts, and in 1755, England and France were at war.

So in 1756 Europe was once more deep in conflict—this time France, Austria, and Russia against England and Prussia. The largest navy in the world had little to fear, but the odds were against the Prussian army in Europe. If Prussia were defeated and partitioned, any British gains overseas might well be wiped out. The Anglo-French and the Austro-Prussian rivalries had become inextricably mingled.

The Seven Years' War, 1756–63

England made no headway in the war until the summer of 1757, when William Pitt, later Earl of Chatham (1708–78), became virtual prime minister. Pitt, one of Britain's greatest war ministers, shrewdly focused the nation's war efforts on conquests overseas. His policy represented the commercial aims of the London business community, but it also appealed to the pride of the ordinary Englishman in the navy and the growing colonial empire. Pitt concentrated power in his own hands, and his energy and his enthusiasm stimulated his subordinates to unheard-of efforts. The "year of miracles" (1759) demonstrated Pitt's remarkable ability to direct a complex series of operations and to choose first-rate commanders. In this one year Quebec fell, Guadaloupe was taken, French military power in India was broken, and the French fleet was crushed off Quiberon Bay in Brittany. England's control of the seas enabled it to hold Canada and India, a classic example of the strategic importance of sea power.

While Britain was destroying the French Empire abroad, Prussia was fighting for its life on the Continent. England's "year of miracles" was a year of near disaster for Prussia. Its army was badly defeated by the Russians at Kunersdorf in 1759; the Prussians now needed a miracle to survive. Only the divisions among his enemies allowed Frederick to prolong the war. Kaunitz had not promised enough of the spoils to France and Russia to stimulate an all-out effort from either country. Pitt's subsidies to German forces were just enough to pin the French down in bloody fighting in Westphalia. The war was unpopular in France and was putting a heavy strain on the already shaky French financial system. Austrian armies were poorly led, and the Austrian government was almost as afraid of the Russian army as it was of the Prussian. So Frederick held on, though his resources were almost exhausted, until the "Hohenzollern miracle" occurred. Empress Elizabeth of Russia died in 1762 and was succeeded by her nephew, Peter III, a warm admirer of the king of Prussia. Peter promptly withdrew from the war, and Austria now had only a crippled and sulky France as a major ally. With no hope of winning a decisive victory, Maria Theresa decided to end the war. Peace was made in 1763, leaving Frederick in permanent possession of Silesia. Prussia had clearly established itself as one of the great powers.

The death of an empress saved Frederick the Great from possible defeat. The death of a king indirectly robbed Britain of some of the fruits of victory. When George III succeeded his grandfather in 1760 he wished to prove himself thoroughly English, unlike the first two Georges. This meant withdrawing from all involvement in German affairs, contrary to Pitt's advice. By October 1761, Pitt had been forced out of office. Lord Bute, George's Scottish favorite, deserted Frederick II and set himself to get peace with France at almost any price.

George III of England.

The Peace of Paris, 1763

The peace finally signed at Paris in January 1763 was overwhelmingly favorable to Great Britain, but it was not so severe on the French as Pitt would have wished. France received back most of its purely economic stakes around the world: trading posts in India, slave stations in West Africa, the rich sugar islands in the West Indies, and fishing rights off Canada, together with two tiny islands off Newfoundland, St. Pierre and Miquelon. But in India and in North America the new colonial system required control of large territories to supply the trading posts. The sugar islands could produce great wealth in a few square miles, and the French were happy to retain their possessions in the Caribbean. But in the long run the continents counted most. With the collapse of its political and military power in India and on the North American continent, the first French colonial empire was permanently broken. France agreed to maintain no more troops in India and ceded the whole of Canada and everything east of the Mississippi to Britain and Louisiana west of the Mississippi to Spain. Henceforth the British had no serious competitors in North America.

"ENLIGHTENED" DESPOTISM, 1763–89

During the twenty-five years that followed the Peace of Paris, the "enlightened" ideas and practices of a number of European monarchs fired the imagination of educated men. The ancient institution of monarchy seemed to take a new lease on life. It looked as if the major ideals of the Enlightenment—reason, natural law, liberty, and progress—were motivating the rulers. The later *philosophes* had questioned aristocratic and ecclesiastical privileges, unequal taxation, and the unfair treatment of certain social classes. In addition, the mid-century wars had left almost every European state in need of reform and reconstruction. Law and order had to be restored, trade revived, and government treasuries refilled. So the practical needs of a postwar era, added to the ferment of new ideas, produced what was known as "enlightened despotism."

Russia's Growth in Europe 1462–1796

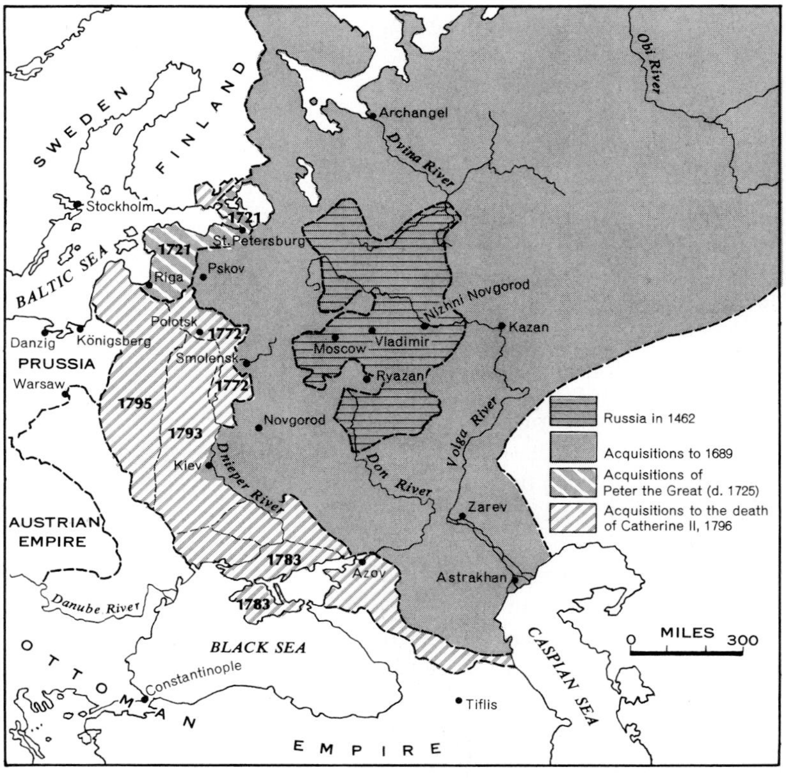

Russia in 1462
Acquisitions to 1689
Acquisitions of Peter the Great (d. 1725)
Acquisitions to the death of Catherine II, 1796

This apparently new kind of monarchy was in many ways a revival of older monarchical ideas, and a reaction against the power that the aristocracy had gained in the eighteenth century. In rooting out irrational customs and vested interests, enlightened despots could curb the power of the nobility and the clergy and attack local and provincial privileges just as monarchs before them had been doing for several centuries. The difference was in the way the enlightened despots justified what they did. They talked little about divine right or hereditary title and a great deal about following reason and serving the public. Frederick the Great called himself "merely the first servant of the state," liable at any moment to render an account of his service to his subjects. But this did not mean that he or any other monarch felt he was really responsible to his people. Monarchs might be "enlightened," but they were still "despots."

Not all the rulers who dominated the political horizon of the later eighteenth century could actually be called "enlightened." George III of England (r. 1760–1820) and Louis XV of France (r. 1715–74) were hardly enlightened, although some of their policies were. Among the minor monarchs, Gustavus III of Sweden (r. 1771–92) and Charles III of Spain (r. 1759–88) had good claims to the title, but the three rulers whom the *philosophes* cited most often as enlightened despots were Catherine the Great of Russia, Frederick the Great of Prussia, and Joseph II of Austria.

Catherine the Great of Russia

Catherine II (r. 1762–96) was a German princess who became empress of Russia through a conspiracy of her friends that led to the assassination of her husband, Tsar Peter III (1762). Uneasy about being a usurper, she tried to make Russia great in an effort to endear herself to her people. She had to make concessions to preserve the support of the nobility, including lavish gifts to a long succession of lovers whom she used as her chief officers of state. She read the books of the French *philosophes,* corresponded with Voltaire, persuaded Diderot to visit her court, and made much of her "enlightenment" for publicity purposes. In 1767 she excited her admirers by summoning a legislative commission to codify the laws of Russia and to give the nation a sort of constitution. The representatives were elected by every class in the land except the serfs, and they came armed with statements of grievances. Very little came out of their deliberations, however: some slight religious toleration and some limitation of torture in legal proceedings. The members went home in 1768, and the Russian government was to make no further attempt to summon a representative assembly until the twentieth century.

The net result, in fact, of Catherine's reign was not enlightened government but the strengthening of the nobility and the extension of serfdom. From 1773 to 1775 a vast uprising of serfs broke out in the Volga valley, led by a Cossack named Pugachev. The revolt was directed at the local landlords and officials; and after it was broken and Pugachev had been brought to Moscow to be executed, these landlords and officials profited by the reaction. Peter the Great's idea of service nobility had long been weakening. In 1785 Catherine freed the nobles from both military service and taxation and gave them absolute control over the serfs on their estates. Further, she gave away large tracts of crown land to noble favorites, thus subjecting hordes of relatively free peasants on these estates to serfdom. At the end of her reign it has been estimated that 34 million out of a population of 36 million Russians were in a state of serfdom or virtual slavery.

Catherine was called "the Great" not because of her enlightenment—if she had any—but because of her conquests. Peter the Great had pushed his possessions to the Baltic in the northwest at the expense of Sweden. Catherine expanded the frontiers of her state many hundreds of miles to the west and south at the expense of Poland and the Ottoman Empire. Russians were concerned about the large Orthodox minority in Catholic Poland. Furthermore, during a large part of the seventeenth century, the Poles had threatened Moscow, and the Polish frontier was still only about two hundred miles from the old Russian capital. The ancient Russian thirst for vengeance on the Poles was to be richly satisfied after 1763 when Catherine put one of her favorites, Stanislaus Poniatowski (1732–98), on the Polish throne. From that time on, Russia and Prussia made it their business to see that the anarchy and confusion of Polish politics continued and that any suggestion of constitutional reform or revival of the national spirit was snuffed out.

Catherine the Great, on a gold medal struck to celebrate her accession as empress of Russia.

The Partitions of Poland

In 1772 Catherine and Frederick the Great arranged the first partition of Poland. Frederick took West Prussia and so joined Prussia to Brandenburg. Catherine took a generous slice of northeastern Poland. To preserve the balance of power they thought it wise to give Maria Theresa a share of the loot (Galicia). This first partition shocked the Poles into a nationalist revival. King Stanislaus himself was

French engraving satirizing the first partition of Poland (1772). Catherine of Russia, Joseph of Austria, and Frederick of Prussia point to their respective shares, while King Stanislaus of Poland tries to keep his crown.

The Partitions of Poland

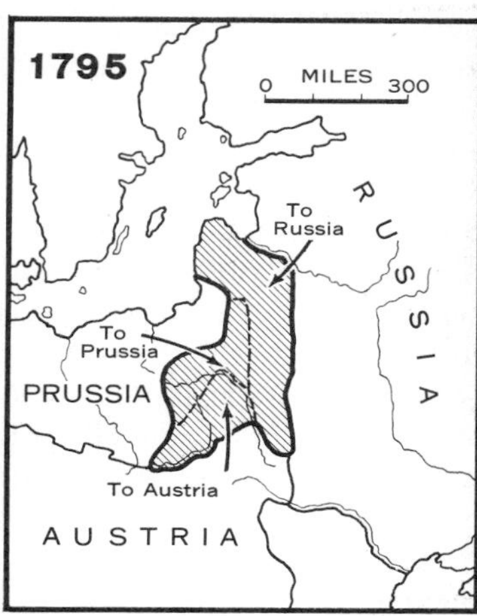

swept along by the patriotic fervor and forgot that he owed his throne to Catherine. In 1791 after the outbreak of the French Revolution, a reform constitution was instituted setting up a strong monarchy and abolishing the *liberum veto.* Catherine's answer was swift and ruthless. Early in 1792 she called off the war she was fighting against the Turks, rushed an army into Poland, abolished the new constitution, restored the old anarchy, and arranged a second partition of Polish territory in 1793, this time with Prussia alone.

These events were followed by a genuinely popular uprising in what was left of Poland, led by a Pole who had fought for the Americans in their revolution, Thaddeus Kosciuszko (1746–1817). The end was inevitable. Kosciuszko was captured by the Russians, the revolt collapsed, and Stanislaus was forced to abdicate. The Kingdom of Poland was wiped off the map in a third partition in 1795 among Russia, Prussia, and Austria. In the three partitions, Russia took almost two-thirds of the original Polish territory, and Prussia and Austria divided the remainder.

Catherine's successes against the crumbling Ottoman Empire were almost as decisive. In a series of wars running from 1768 to 1792 Catherine gained the Crimea and most of the northern shore of the Black Sea. The Treaty of Kuchuk Kainardji (1774) also gave Russia vague rights to protect Orthodox Christians in the Ottoman Empire—rights that were to be used later as excuses for Russian intervention in Turkish affairs. The Ottoman Empire escaped the fate of Poland because it was stronger internally and because its two chief enemies, Austria and Russia, were jealous of each other. But when Catherine died in 1796 there seemed to be little obstacle to a Russian advance to Constantinople and the Mediterranean.

Frederick the Great, King of Prussia. This portrait by Ziesenig is the only one painted from life.

Frederick the Great of Prussia

Frederick II of Prussia (r. 1740–86) had a somewhat better claim than Catherine to be considered "enlightened." He had a first-rate mind and a real grasp of what the *philosophes* were talking about. He invited Voltaire to Potsdam, and although they soon fell to quarreling over the merits of Frederick's French poetry, they both agreed that it was the job of a king to combat ignorance and superstition among his people, to enhance their welfare, and to promote religious toleration. Frederick welcomed religious exiles of all sorts—even Jesuits expelled from France and Spain. He treated the Jews badly, but his general tolerance in religion was the best evidence of his enlightenment. He was a mercantilist in

The Growth of Brandenburg-Prussia 1640–1795

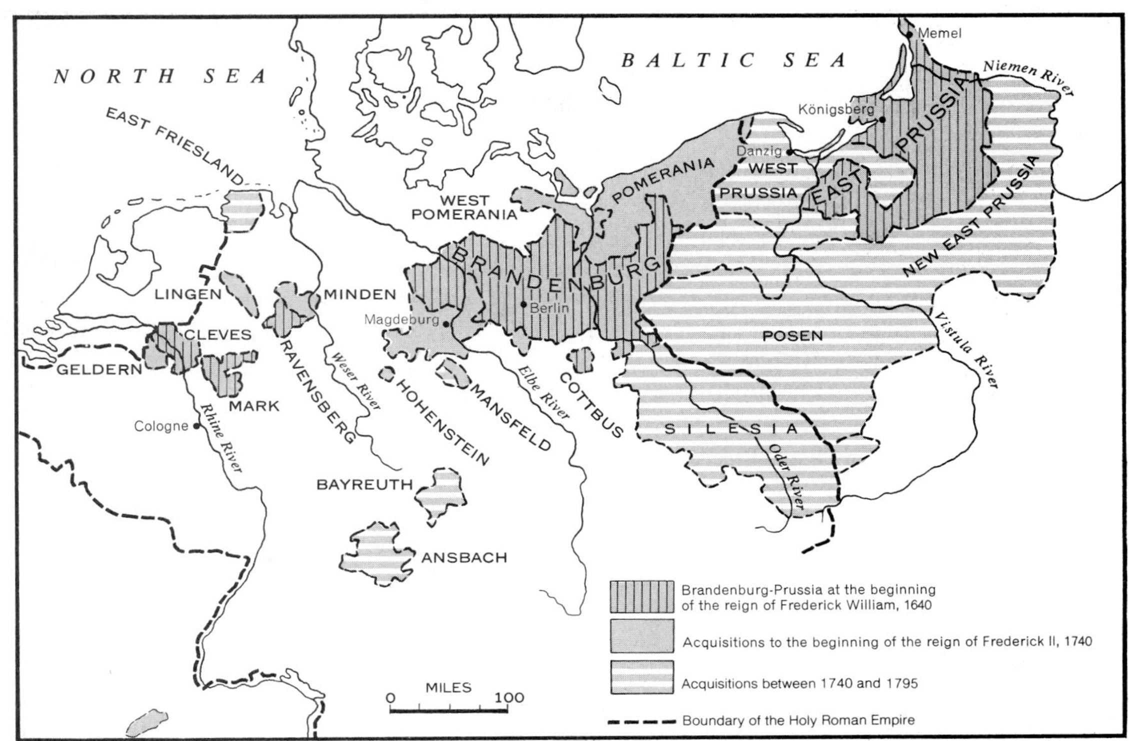

his economic policies; he sought national self-sufficiency and used protective tariffs to foster infant industries. Interested in the new scientific agriculture, he tried to encourage new methods by bringing foreign farmers to his kingdom. Some three hundred thousand immigrants entered Prussia during his reign. Finally, he rationalized and simplified the Prussian laws and court procedures—another typical objective of enlightened despotism.

In some respects, however, Frederick was not at all enlightened. He believed firmly in social rank and privilege. The Junkers served him well as officers in his army, and the army was the most important organ of the state. In return for their services, he allowed the nobles to keep full control over the peasants on their estates. He strictly defined the ranks of noble, bourgeois, and peasant and made it difficult if not impossible for anyone to move from one class to another. Prussian serfs were not so badly off as Russian and Polish serfs, but those who lived on private estates were almost as much at their lord's mercy. Frederick did something to improve the lot of serfs on his own estates, but otherwise he showed no taste for social reform.

In some respects the discipline, the machinelike efficiency, and the strict centralization of power in the Prussian monarchy were the results of a long Hohenzollern tradition, quite unrelated to the influence of the Enlightenment. The powerful state that Frederick II erected in twenty-three years of war (1740–63) and consolidated in twenty-three years of peace (1763–86) was the most striking political achievement of his time. But twenty years after the strong hand of the despot was removed, Prussia proved to be an easy victim for Napoleon. The weakness of enlightened despotism, as well as its strength, lay in the fact that everything depended on the monarch.

Joseph II of Austria

The monarch with the best claim to be called an enlightened despot was

Joseph II of Austria (1741–90). Although he professed contempt for the *philosophes,* he was more thoroughly converted to the main tenets of the Enlightenment than any of his fellow monarchs. And he was probably more sincerely devoted to his people's welfare than any of the others.

Frederick II's seizure of Silesia in 1740 was the signal for a reorganization of the Habsburg Empire. During Maria Theresa's long reign (1740–80) an imperial bureaucracy was developed that was able to centralize in Vienna the administration of all the divisions of the Empire except Hungary. All parts but Hungary were brought into a tariff union in 1775. The nobles were compelled to assume at least some of the burden of taxation. Maria Theresa did more for the serfs in her kingdom than any other ruler of her time by limiting the amount of labor they owed their lords and by curbing the lords' power to abuse them. In much of this she was aided and abetted by her son, Joseph, who became emperor and coregent after the death of her husband in 1765. But Joseph wished to move much further and faster than his mother. Until her death in 1780 he chafed under the compromises and conservatism that characterized Maria Theresa's policies, especially in the field of religion.

In the ten years of Joseph II's own rule (1780–90), literally thousands of decrees poured out from the imperial chancellery in Vienna. He proclaimed religious toleration for all Christians and Jews. He dissolved monasteries devoted solely to contemplation and turned their revenues over to the hospitals that in time made Vienna the medical center of Europe. He applied a system of equal taxation in proportion to income to everyone in the Habsburg dominions, regardless of rank or nationality. He imposed one language, German, for official business. Most significant of all, Joseph abolished serfdom. Early in his reign he issued a number of decrees that gave all serfs in the Habsburg dominions personal freedom—freedom to leave the land, to marry whom they pleased, to choose any job they liked. This much of Joseph's work was permanent. In later years he tried to relieve peasants who stayed on the land of all forced labor and to turn them into property-owners, but these decrees were repealed by his successors.

Joseph II made many enemies by his policy of centralization and reform: the clergy, the landed nobility, non-German parts of his empire, even peasants who failed to understand his intentions. In 1789, when revolution broke out in France, peasants in the Austrian Empire began to plunder and to murder landlords to gain the rights Joseph had held out to them. In 1790 both Belgium and Hungary were in re-

Joseph II, an Enlightened Despot

The following two extracts show both sides of enlightened despotism. Joseph wanted to reform the state, but he could do so only by autocratic methods.

I have not confined myself simply to issuing orders; I have expounded and explained them. With enlightenment I have sought to weaken and with arguments I have sought to overcome the abuses which had arisen out of prejudice and deeply rooted customs. I have sought to imbue every official of the state with the love I myself feel for the wellbeing of the whole. . . .

The good of the state can be understood only in general terms, only in terms of the greatest number. Similarly, all the provinces of the monarchy constitute one whole and therefore can have only one aim. It is necessary therefore that there should be an end to all the prejudices and all the jealousies between provinces [and] all races which have caused so much fruitless bickering. [Circular letter of Joseph II, 1783.]

Unity and the end of prejudices, however, were to be achieved by dictates of the monarch. A common language was needed; Joseph II determined what it should be.

The German language is the universal tongue of my empire. I am the emperor of Germany. The states which I possess are provinces that form only one body—the state of which I am the head. If the kingdom of Hungary were the most important of my possessions, I would not hesitate to impose its language on the other countries. [Letter to a Hungarian noble, 1783.]

From T. C. W. Blanning, *Joseph II and Enlightened Despotism* (London: Longman Group, 1970), pp. 131–32; from Louis Léger, *Histoire de l'Autriche Hongrie* (Paris, 1879), p. 373.

Emperor Joseph II putting his hands to the plow in 1769 to dramatize the dignity of farming.

volt against his rule. The Church was bitterly hostile to him. Joseph felt lonely and deserted. Worn out, he died in 1790, choosing as his own epitaph: "Here lies Joseph II, who was unfortunate in everything that he undertook."

It is clear why Joseph II has been called "the revolutionary Emperor." Like Peter the Great he had shown what a single determined will could accomplish in the face of stubborn private interests. Unlike Peter, he had been guided by the principles of reason, tolerance, and humanitarianism. But Joseph was a revolutionary without a party. He had to depend on an unimaginative bureaucracy and on the secret police that he found it necessary to set up. Enlightened despotism in his hands might have formed a bridge between divine-right monarchy and democratic revolution. But it also suggested that successful revolution demanded a broader base of popular understanding and support than he had been able to command.

FRANCE, ENGLAND, AND THE AMERICAN REVOLUTION, 1763–89

France and Great Britain were the centers of the Enlightenment, but neither had an enlightened despot as monarch. Perhaps as a result (such large generalizations are very difficult to prove), each suffered a revolution from below. The American colonists won their independence from England in the name of reason and natural rights, and the French bourgeoisie, fired by the same ideals, destroyed aristocratic privilege in France.

Abortive Revolution from Above in France

When the Seven Years' War ended in 1763, both the French and the British governments needed more revenue to carry the burden of their war debts and to meet the rising costs of administration. Louis XV proposed to continue a war tax that fell on nobles and commoners alike and to institute a new tax on officeholders. It was a statesmanlike proposal, but Louis's program was greeted by a storm of opposition from nobles and wealthy bourgeois alike. It looked like a minor "enlightened" revolution, but it did not last. Louis XV died in 1774, and his son, Louis XVI, was neither strong enough nor determined enough to continue the fight against privilege. In the end, Louis XV's abortive reforms resulted in a further aristocratic reaction, ultimately leading to revolution.

Europe and the American Revolution

The political and social situation was different in England, but the course of events was somewhat similar. A reasonable attempt by the government to raise new revenue was met by a storm of opposition in the American colonies. As a result, the attitude of the English governing classes stiffened. Concessions either to the colonists abroad or to reformers at home became impossible, and an irreconcilable conflict broke out that ultimately split the British Empire.

William Pitt Addresses Parliament on the Revolt of the American Colonies

JANUARY 20, 1775

This resistance to your arbitrary system of taxation might have been foreseen; it was obvious from the nature of things and of mankind, and, above all, from the Whiggish spirit flourishing in that country. The spirit which now resists your taxation in America is the same which formerly opposed loans, benevolences, and ship money in England; the same spirit which called all England on its legs, and by the Bill of Rights vindicated the English constitution; the same spirit which established the great, fundamental, essential maxim of our liberties, that no subject of England shall be taxed but by his own consent.

This glorious spirit of Whiggism animates three millions in America, who prefer poverty with liberty to gilded chains and sordid affluence, and who will die in the defense of their rights as men, as free men. What shall oppose this spirit, aided by the congenial flame glowing in the breast of every Whig in England, to the amount, I hope, of double the American numbers? Ireland they have to a man. In that country, joined as it is with the cause of the colonies, and placed at their head, the distinction I contend for is and must be observed. This country superintends and controls their trade and navigation, but they tax themselves. And this distinction between external and internal control is sacred and insurmountable; it is involved in the abstract nature of things. . . . Let this distinction then remain forever ascertained: taxation is theirs, commercial regulation is ours. As an American, I would recognize to England her supreme right of regulating commerce and navigation; as an Englishman by birth and principle, I recognize to the Americans their supreme unalienable right in their property,—a right which they are justified in the defense to the last extremity.

From James Harvey Robinson, *Readings in European History* (Boston: Ginn & Company, 1906), Vol. II, pp. 354–55.

The causes, outbreak, and course of the American Revolution will be discussed in the next chapter. We are here mainly concerned with its effects upon Europe. The American War of Independence (1775–83) was in a certain sense a civil war within the British Empire on both sides of the Atlantic. The colonists had friends in England, and the Irish sympathized with American grievances. The Whig faction to which Edmund Burke belonged tried in vain to induce George III and his prime minister, Lord North (1770–82), to follow a more moderate policy. A group of true "radicals," inspired by John Wilkes (1727–97), attacked the king's influence in Parliament, urged the publication of Parliamentary debates, and agitated for more democracy in the election of members. The radicals were too small a minority to carry any weight, but their political faith was that of the American Declaration of Independence: that government must be by consent of the governed. Conversely, there were "Tories" in the colonies who agreed with Parliament and deplored the breach with England.

The War of Independence was won by the American colonists with French help. Following the principles of balance of power, France wanted compensation for the loss of Canada by depriving Britain of its American colonies. French supplies and French troops and ships were of inestimable help to General Washington in his struggle to wear down the British forces in the colonies. In the peace treaty of 1783 the thirteen colonies gained their independence and won title to all the land east of the Mississippi, north of Florida, and south of the Great Lakes.

The Significance of the American Revolution

The success of the American Revolution had profound effects on Europe and eventually on other parts of the world. As opponents of the old regime in Europe saw it, a people had taken its destiny into its own hands, had revolted against its established rulers, and had set up a government of its own choosing. It had gained its liberty without falling into license. John Locke's ideas—natural equality, inalienable rights, government by consent of the governed, and the ultimate right of revolution—had been vindicated. Montesquieu's theory of a separation of powers had been written into both state and federal constitutions across the Atlantic. The Declaration of Independence (July 4, 1776) rang like a tocsin summoning people to rebellion throughout the Old World.

Furthermore, events in America seemed to demonstrate that smaller political units could be federated into a larger union without recourse to despotism. In sum, the American Revolution dramatized and passed on to the western world two political ideas of great importance for the future: the idea of limited, or constitutional, government (which had a long history reaching far back into the ancient and medieval worlds), and the idea of popular sovereignty, or democracy (which was relatively new in an age still strongly aristocratic in its thinking).

The quarter-century between the Peace of Paris and the outbreak of revolution in France opened to the western world three possible roads for future development: enlightened despotism, aristocratic domination, or democratic revolution.

Suggestions for Further Reading

The best general accounts of the century in English are in the relevant volumes of the *Rise of Modern Europe* series: P. Roberts, *The Quest for Security, 1715–1740* (1947); W. L. Dorn, *Competition for Empire, 1740–1763* (1940); and L. Gershoy, *From Despotism to Revolution, 1763–1789* (1944). M. S. Anderson, *Europe in the Eighteenth Century* (1961), is a good survey. G. Rudé, *Europe in the Eighteenth Century* (1972), emphasizes social history. A. Goodwin, ed., *The European Nobility in the Eighteenth Century* (1953), contains essays on various countries. O. H. Hufton, *The Poor of Eighteenth-Century France, 1750–1789* (1975), and L. Stone, *The Family, Sex and Marriage in England 1500–1800* (1977), are pioneering studies. F. Braudel, *Capitalism and Material Life, 1400–1800* (1974), and his *The Structures of Everyday Life: The Limits of the Possible* (1982), are by a leading social historian. On European expansion overseas, see J. H. Parry, *Trade and Dominion: The European Overseas Empires in the Eighteenth Century* (1971); C. G. Robertson, *Chatham and the British Empire* (1948); and L. B. Wright, *The Atlantic Frontier: Colonial American Civilization, 1607–1763* (1947).

Developments in major countries are covered in J. Lough, *Introduction to Eighteenth-Century France* (1960); J. H. Plumb, *England in the Eighteenth Century* (1951); W. H. Bruford, *Germany in the Eighteenth Century* (1952); and H. Rosenberg, *Bureaucracy and Autocracy, the Prussian Experience* (1958). For biographies of leading figures, see J. H. Plumb, *The First Four Georges* (1957); G. Ritter, *Frederick the Great* (trans. 1968); C. L. Morris, *Maria Theresa: The Last Conservative* (1937); and G. S. Thomson, *Catherine the Great and the Expansion of Russia* (1950). On the American Revolution, E. S. Morgan, *The Birth of the Republic, 1763–1789* (1956); P. Maier, *From Resistance to Revolution* (1972); and R. M. Calhoon, *Revolutionary America: An Interpretive Overview* (1976), are stimulating works.

	1648			1700		
SOUTHWEST ASIA AND AFRICA	**1652** Dutch found Cape Colony *ca.* **1700** Rise of Ashanti, West Africa				**1737–47** Nadir Shah, decline of Safavid Empire	
EUROPE	**1660–88** Stuart Restoration **1661–1715** Louis XIV	**1683** Turks besiege Vienna **1685** Edict of Nantes revoked **1685–1750** Johann Sebastian Bach **1687** Newton's Law of Gravitation	**1688** Glorious Revolution **1689–1725** Peter the Great **1690** Locke, *Two Treatises of Civil Government*	**1701–14** War of Spanish Succession **1715–74** Louis XV **1720** South Sea Bubble **1723–42** Robert Walpole	**1740–80** Maria Theresa **1740–86** Frederick the Great **1756–63** Seven Years' War **1756–91** Wolfgang Amadeus Mozart	**1762** Rousseau, *The Social Contract* **1762–96** Catherine the Great **1769** James Watt's first steam engine **1770–1827** Ludwig van Beethoven
SOUTH AND SOUTHEAST ASIA	**1653** Taj Mahal completed **1690** British found Calcutta				**1751** French control Deccan **1757** Battle of Plassey **1773** Regulation Act	
EAST ASIA	**1662–1722** Emperor Kangxi *ca.* **1675–1725** Golden age of Edo urban culture, Japan			**1736–95** Emperor Qianlong	**1796–1804** White Lotus Rebellion	
THE AMERICAS AND PACIFIC		**1664** British seize New Amsterdam		**1728** Bering explores Alaska **1756–63** French and Indian War	**1765** Stamp Act **1768–80** Cook explores Pacific Ocean **1773** Boston Tea Party **1774** Quebec Act	

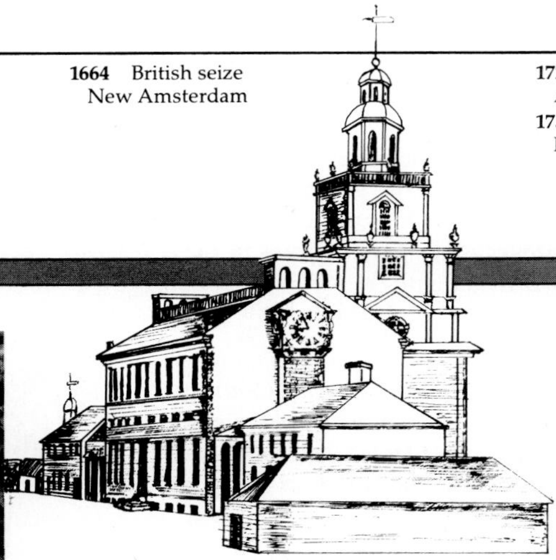

Independence Hall, Philadelphia, 1776.

Napoleon, 1800.

Ashanti wood carving.

East India Company merchant, by an Indian artist.

Emblem of the Sun King, Louis XIV.

Charles II of England, 1660-85.

	1815
	1805–48 Mohammed Ali founds dynasty in Egypt **1806** British control Cape Colony **1807** Slavery abolished in British Empire
1776 Smith, *Wealth of Nations* **1789** French Revolution begins	**1798** Malthus, *Essay on the Principle of Population* **1799** Napoleon becomes First Consul **1804–14** Napoleonic Empire
1784 East India Act **1786–93** Cornwallis in Bengal **1796** British conquer Ceylon	
1775–83 American Revolution **1776** US Declaration of Independence **1788** British colonize Australia **1803** Louisiana Purchase	**1807–30** Latin American wars for independence

Chinese fan painting, *ca.* 1700.

***Fuji above Storm,* by Hokusai, 1760-1849.**

31 European Colonies
The Seventeenth and Eighteenth Centuries

The European colonization movement began in the sixteenth century and continued in the seventeenth. The earlier part of the European expansion overseas had been supported by Portugal and Spain, two countries in which the commercial and industrial economy was growing at the end of the fifteenth century and the religious controversy started by Martin Luther had relatively little effect. During the sixteenth century—as Spain in particular was drawn into the religious struggle and became involved in the politics of all Europe—colonies supported Spanish power by providing an increasing supply of gold and silver bullion. By 1600 Portugal had fallen under the protection of the Spanish crown, and the Portuguese were no longer in a position to hold their widely spread colonies.

After 1600 Spanish power declined steadily, and the northern European states—the Netherlands, England, and France—joined the colonization movement. The new participants made great progress in building colonial empires despite the continuation of the religious wars, civil wars in England and France (and Spain), the renewal of plague and famine, and a prolonged economic depression in the middle of the century. Despite all these problems, the European economy expanded during the seventeenth century and European military and commercial power was felt throughout the world. By 1700 Europe was richer, controlled more of the world's commerce, and had more effective governments than it had had in 1600.

During the seventeenth century, the Europeans developed a theory of colonial exploitation that changed the way they used their foreign holdings. The new set of ideas—mercantilism—replaced the old notion that the colonies were most valuable as sources of bullion for the treasuries of the monarchies and the elite classes. In fact, the theory of mercantilism (see pp. 576–81) revealed a new economic value in the colonies just as the flow of bullion from the New World diminished, so that all the nation-states of Europe competed for foreign lands. The seventeenth and eighteenth centuries thus became the period when Europe gained control of the world.

The earliest and easiest type of colonization was the establishment of fortified trading posts, to which natives from the surrounding areas brought goods to trade. This was the Portuguese pattern, and the Dutch followed it too when they ousted the Portuguese from the East Indies. But this system worked only where the natives were politically organized and had readily tradable goods to bring in. Thus it remained the pattern in Africa, where the coastal kingdoms supplied gold and slaves to the European traders. Elsewhere the chief value of the colonies—such as precious metals and agricultural products—could only be had through the labor of the native populations, and colonial powers had to take administrative charge of the natives. The Spaniards recognized very early that they would not be able to exploit their New World territories unless they took over the Aztec and Inca Empires, which had organized the exploitation of the lands before Columbus.

Further, mercantilist theory provided a stimulus to the development of

European Colonization Seventeenth Century

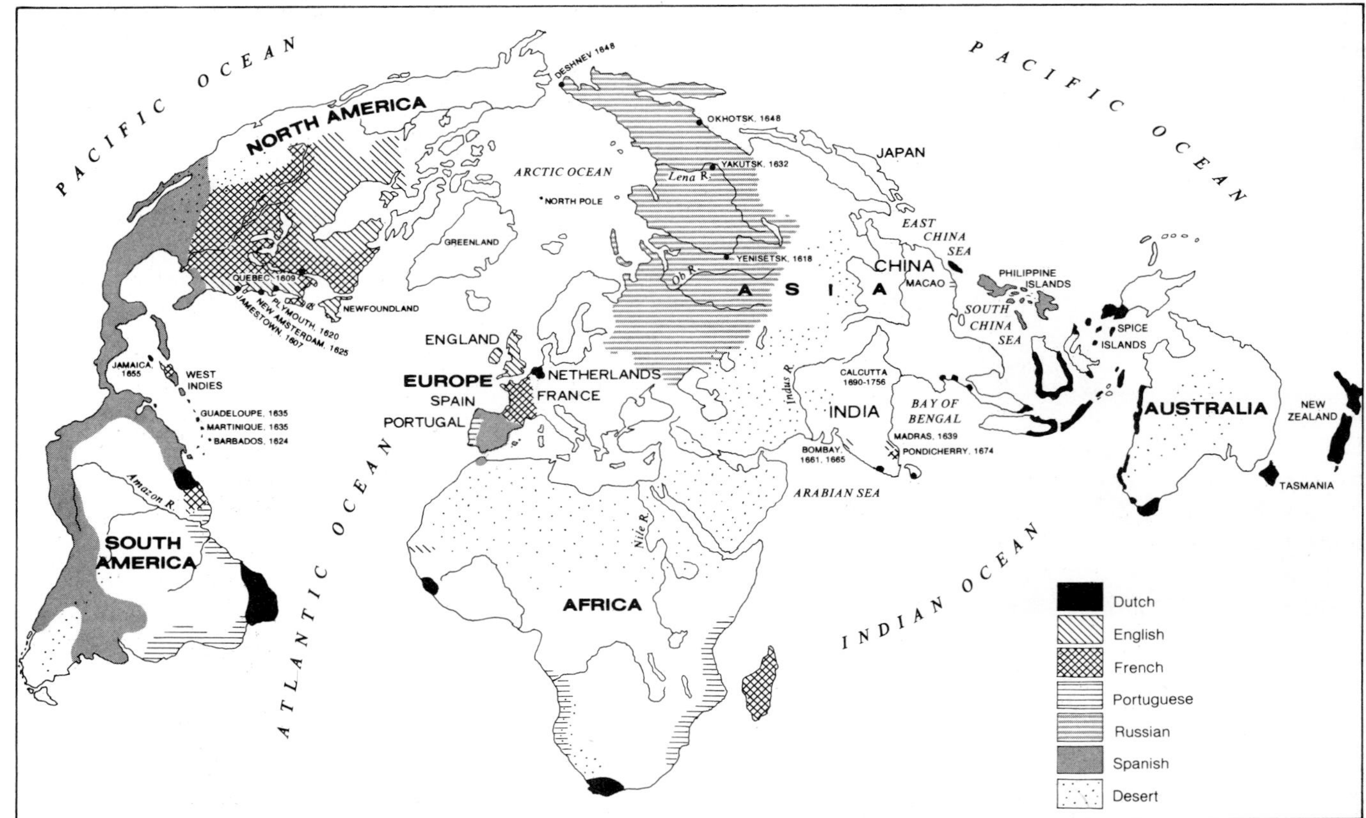

a new type of colony — the colony settled by Europeans that was like an economic and social extension of the mother country. Like the colonies whose economic worth depended on the labor of the natives, these colonies of Europeans were intended to produce raw materials needed by the home economy. The first colonies of the new type were the sugar islands of the Caribbean; later came the tobacco, tea, and coffee colonies.

Engraving from a seventeenth-century history of the West Indies showing the workings of a sugar plantation.

THE SPANISH COLONIES

The Viceroyalties

When she agreed to support Christopher Columbus in 1492, Queen Isabella of Castile expected him to establish colonies under her government in whatever lands he discovered. She commissioned him as viceroy, governor, captain-general (a military office), and admiral. In these capacities, Columbus went out to America three times, in 1492, 1493, and 1497, and ruled the first colony, the island of Hispaniola (now divided between Haiti and the Dominican Republic) until 1500, when he was removed from office. Successful as he was as an explorer, he was unable to manage the affairs of the new settlement.

The exploration and colonization of the New World was controlled by the Castilian monarchy. At first, only Castilians were permitted to emigrate to the colonies. Ferdinand and Isabella represented the union of the two principal kingdoms of the Spanish peninsula, but their kingdoms and governments remained distinct. After Isabella's death in 1504, Ferdinand ruled the growing colonies as regent of the crown of Castile, and colonial institutions and laws were modelled on those of Castile, not Aragon. Both monarchs had viewed the "freedoms" of Aragon, which limited the rights of the king and gave significant authority to the *cortes,* the estates of the realm, as contrary to the royal dignity, and they wanted to organize the colonies in accord with the absolutist constitution of Castile.

The work of exploring, conquering, and colonizing the mainland was carried out by private individuals who had permission of the Castilian monarchy and a contract that specified royal rights in the new lands. Juan Ponce de Leon in Florida (1512), Pedro de Alvarado in Guatemala (1523), and Pedro de Mendoza in Argentina (1536) were all explorers and colonists of this type, and they apparently hoped to exploit the new lands far from the government in Castile. Control of the distant colonists became a preoccupation of the Spanish crown.

The great age of the independent *conquistadores* ended with the subjection of the Aztecs and Incas in the 1520s and 1530s. Thereafter, the Spanish government sought to organize the New World colonies under a regular government. This organization was based on the idea that the colonies were part of the crown of Castile. The king ruled the colonies in the same way as he ruled his own country, and all arrangements for governance of the New World were fashioned in the royal court.

After the mainland surpassed Hispaniola in population and economic value, the Spaniards created two large viceroyalties, New Spain centered in Mexico City (1529) and Peru centered in Lima (1544). The territories governed from these political centers were vast. Mexico City ruled all of Spanish America north of Panama, while

Lima's territory stretched from Panama to Cape Horn. As new colonial centers were established in Argentina, Bogota, and Santiago, governments were formed in them, formally subject to the viceroyalty but effectively independent. Their independence rested not only on their distance from the capital, but also on their status as kingdoms; they were among the kingdoms ruled by the house of Castile.

The viceroyalties remained virtually unchanged for the sixteenth and seventeenth centuries. The viceroys had great authority as governors and captains-general of the central parts of the kingdoms of New Spain and Peru, and they supervised the other kingdoms in their viceroyalties. Each viceroy shared his great authority with an *audiencia,* a panel of judges that functioned both as a high court and as an administrative body. Eventually, the viceroy became president of the *audiencia,* but its members still often stood against him and constituted a check on his authority. The government in Spain also occasionally sent visitors to investigate conditions in the colonies, men who superseded the authority of the viceroy.

Within the kingdoms, the local districts were under *audiencias,* each with a president. Hence, the districts were called presidencies. In the seventeenth century, the presidents were given additional power as governors and, where necessary, captains-general, but as in the capitals, the *audiencias* constituted a check on the absolute power of the presidents.

The whole colonial administration was controlled from Spain by the Council of the Indies, created in 1524. The council—ever fearful of colonial independence—issued exceptionally detailed instructions to the viceroys, and these documents provide a great deal of information about the organization of the colonial territories. The council was second in stature only to the Council of Castile, the principal royal council. Service on the Council of the Indies was a high rung on the ladder to the chief offices of state, and by the seventeenth century it had a large, expensive staff that drained the royal treasury.

The voluminous regulations of the council in Spain and the myriad laws and administrative rules issued by the viceroys and *audiencias* produced a confusing mass of colonial laws. In the 1630s the government in Spain commissioned a new code to clear up confusions and contradictions. The *Recapitulation* was completed in 1636, but the government was penniless, and the code was not printed until 1680.

The stable, but rigid, colonial organization established in the sixteenth century by the Habsburg kings was reformed by the Bourbons after the War of the Spanish Succession (1701–14). The Bourbon kings, especially Charles III (r. 1759–88), wanted to model colonial administration exactly on the government in Madrid, so that men from the capital in Spain would not have to learn a new system when they went out to the New World. In the 1780s, one of the Bourbon reforms reorganized the provincial administration into *intendencias. Intendentes,* the new royal governors, were modeled on the French intendant and had broad financial and administrative authority.

Society and Economy in Spanish America

The Spaniards took a long tradition of colonization to the New World. From the eleventh to the late fifteenth century, the Spanish kingdoms had been engaged in a reconquest of the Iberian Peninsula, and as they conquered parts of Moorish Spain, they took them over as colonies. In region after region, the Spanish conquerors resettled agricultural districts, established new towns, and reconstructed the secular and ecclesiastical institutions of Christian society. The well-tried mechanisms of this old "internal" colonization were carried to the New World, where military men, settlers, and churchmen created the new society in concert.

The economy of the Spanish colonies was based on exploitation. The crown, hoping to find gold and silver in the New World, was not disappointed. Private individuals received the right to mine precious metals in return for payment of a "royalty." Many of the wealthiest families in the colonies made their fortunes in mining.

The agricultural system rested on the *encomienda,* a royal grant that entrusted the care and governance of a certain number of Indians to its holder. The holder of the *encomienda* could exact labor services and tribute from his charges. Although the government strictly limited these exactions, abuse was widespread. In fact, much of the activity of the colonial government was devoted to enforcing the regulations on *encomiendas,* but, in most places, the Indians were reduced to virtual servitude.

Some settlers, particularly ecclesiastical landlords, treated the Indians well by the standards of the day. In the sixteenth century, Bishop Vasco de Quiroga of Michoacan in New Spain, an enthusiast of Thomas More's *Utopia* (see p. 442), created Indian communities modeled on More's literary ideal. The members of these villages owned the land in common, although each family had a cottage and garden. The villagers cooperated in the cultivation of the land and in herding, organized by a few friars. Quiroga's communities became the model for those set up by missionary orders. He also set up schools for the Indians and inspired the foundation of like institutions elsewhere in the colonies.

Colonial society was divided into castes. At the top were the native Spaniards, then came the creoles, those born in America of Spanish parents. For both of these groups, it was important to maintain purity of blood. Beneath the whites came the mestizos, mixed Spanish and Indian blood, who were considered a problem. So many of them were illegitimate that the words mestizo and bastard were often used interchangeably. Still further down the social ladder were the mulattos, mixed Spanish and Negro (Africans were brought to America as slaves early in

Silver mines at Potosi, Bolivia, opened in 1545. The mines were a source of wealth for both the Spanish crown and the colonists.

the sixteenth century). Pureblood Indians stood apart from the rest of the population. They were treated as an inferior nation, at first governed by their own chiefs.

The society was dominated by peninsular Spaniards. The royal government was always nervous about rebellion in the distant provinces and considered the climate there to be conducive to indolence. It therefore insisted that all high offices be held by men sent out from Spain. Of the viceroys who served in the New World between 1492 and 1813, only four were born in America, and all four were sons of Spanish officials, rather than of private citizens. Only 14 of 602 captains-general, governors, and presidents and only 105 of 706 bishops were creoles. The crown also limited the commercial opportunities of those born in the colonies. Nonetheless, the law did not in general recognize the distinction between Spaniards and creoles; the distinction, strong as it was, was purely social.

The lower classes in Spanish America were composed of mestizos and a bewildering variety of other mixed elements. The Negro slaves came from a wide variety of tribes in West Africa and varied in language, culture, and color. Slaves also intermarried with Indians producing a racial group that the Spaniards called *zambaigos.* The laws governing the colonies recognized many of these groups by giving them names, and of course the population recognized even finer distinctions, with a profusion of names—many of them derogatory. This racial and ethnic nomenclature reveals a characteristic of the colonial society: It was baroque—as one historian has called it—in its complex appearance and in the intricate and complex interrelationships of its many groupings.

The Indian population in Mexico and Central and South America declined drastically for over a century, but the decline stopped about 1650 (perhaps because the Indians acquired immunity to the diseases that had been brought from Europe and Africa during the sixteenth century) and began to rise again. Mexico City—on the site of the old capital of the Aztec Empire—reached about 100,000 inhabitants by the end of the eighteenth century; in Europe only London and Paris were larger. In the 1770s the commercial prosperity of the Spanish colonies increased dramatically because the Spanish government finally permitted direct coastal trade among them. Before 1774 the government, following mercantilist theory, had required all trade to be shipped to the port of Cadiz in Spain and only then to other parts of the colonies. The health of Spanish colonial society was undermined, however, by its reliance on the labor of the Indians, who were hardly integrated into colonial society, and by the power of the Church. But these weaknesses were not yet apparent in the eighteenth century.

A Description of Mexican Society

Madame Calderon de la Barca, wife of the first Spanish ambassador to Mexico after independence (1821), wrote a series of brilliant letters describing the society she found in the new nation. This society had changed little since the eighteenth century.

By daylight we find our house very pretty, with a large garden adjoining, full of flowers and rose bushes in the courtyard, but being all on the ground floor it is somewhat damp and the weather though beautiful is so cool in the morning that carpets, and I sometimes think even a soupçon of a fire would not be amiss. There are neither chimneys nor grates, and I have no doubt a fire would be disagreeable for more than an hour or so in the morning.

We at length found two [male servants] . . . who only got tipsy alternately, so that we considered ourselves very well off. . . . [O]ne of the most disagreeable customs of the women servants is that of wearing their long hair hanging down at its full length, matted, uncombed, and always in the way. . . . Flowing hair sounds very picturesque but when it is very dirty, and suspended over the soup, it is not a pretty picture.

The house [a large hacienda] is merely used as an occasional retreat during the summer months and is generally a large empty building, with innumerable lofty rooms, communicating with each other and containing the scantiest possible supply of furniture—a deal table and a few chairs; a complete absence of the luxurious furniture which in Mexico seems entirely confined to the town houses.

From R. Cameron, *Viceroyalties of the West* (Boston: Weidenfeld, 1968), pp. 93–95.

The Church in Spanish America

From the earliest days of the colonization, the Church was an agent of royal power in America. King Ferdinand received the right of patronage in the New World by a papal decree of 1508, and thereafter the crown controlled all appointments to the bishoprics founded there. In fact, any cleric who wanted to go to America needed a royal license. Caught up in the Counter Reformation, the Spanish kings attempted to ensure that no one tainted with Protestantism entered the colonies.

Bishoprics were set up at a rapid rate as Spanish colonists took over the new land. Until 1545, all bishops were subordinate to the archbishop of Seville in Spain, but then three independent archdioceses were erected in the New World—in Mexico City, Lima, and Santo Domingo (Hispaniola). By the end of the colonial era, there were 38 bishoprics in Spanish America.

The crown wanted to convert the Indians and to teach them European culture. The agents sent to carry out this great work were the friars—Franciscans and Dominicans. Soon, other orders joined them, particularly the Jesuits, who became most important in the viceroyalty of Peru. One result of this influx of missionaries was the foundation of monasteries. By 1574, there were over 200 of them, mostly independent of episcopal control because of papal privileges. Furthermore, because there was an insufficient secular clergy, the friars performed parish duties and occupied church benefices. By the seventeenth century, the bishops were complaining about the usurpations of the friars, and people were saying that there were too many monasteries. Nonetheless, the king did not prohibit monks from occupying parishes until 1757.

Most of the monasteries had only two or three inhabitants, in contradiction to Church law, and in 1611, Pope Paul V suppressed all houses that did not have at least eight members. By that time, the Franciscans alone had 166 houses in the New World, and it was estimated that 10 percent of the population of Lima was made up of clerics, monks, and nuns. In the eighteenth century, the crown and colonists found that this extensive clerical establishment had undermined the economy. Through pious gifts and especially through wills the churches had accumulated an amazing amount of land. Once in the hands of the Church, land was permanently out of circulation and its value and usefulness declined. In some districts 80 percent of the land belonged to the Church, and everywhere land was mortgaged to the Church. The fantastically well-endowed ecclesiastical institutions built up capital that it could lend to upper-class farmers; for decades the Church acted as the principal banker for the colonies.

During the eighteenth century, the kings tried to halt the accumulation of property by the Church. In 1734, they prohibited anyone in New Spain from becoming a monk or friar. In 1754, they prohibited clerics from helping people make their wills and, in 1775, prohibited a confessor and his church from being legatees. None of these measures worked, and the Church steadily increased its economic power until the colonial independence movement stopped it.

Aside from setting up missions for the Indians and monasteries, the Church ran virtually all the charitable institutions and schools in the New World. Every city had several hospitals for the poor and sick; in most cases, the various hospitals were restricted to certain races. In Paraguay, the Jesuits established Indian communities that were rigidly organized and economically successful, a form of communal charitable institution. These foundations collapsed suddenly after the Jesuits were ejected from the colonies (and from Spain) in 1767, demonstrating that the priests had failed to educate their charges in self-governance.

The Inquisition was also brought to America very early, in 1569. Although it was set up to ensure the doctrinal purity of the colonists, it served many other functions. It had purview over all crimes against morality, public and private, and censored the books brought into the colonies. In particular, the inquisitors were intent on keeping out the works of Enlightenment writers, although enterprising readers found ways to bring the books in. Although the colonial Inquisition was tainted with the same vices as the one in Spain, it was not so harsh as the peninsular institution. Much of the attention of the colonial inquisitors was spent on maintaining charities, and in 250 years, very few people were burned as heretics.

THE FRENCH COLONIES IN NORTH AMERICA

Notwithstanding the early success of the French colonies, and the early failures of the English, the English soon overtook the French. French settlements grew slowly because the monarchy, which so thoroughly regulated commerce and industry at home, was equally paternalistic in North America.

After 1663, the government organized and controlled the colonization movement and left little room for individual initiative. As a result, the colony grew significantly only when the government actively encouraged emigration, as it did under the mercantilist finance minister Colbert in the 1660s and 1670s.

The French had been searching for a northwest passage since the early sixteenth century. Cartier discovered the St. Lawrence River in 1535, and throughout the next century and a half French explorers were active in the American continent. There were French settlers in Acadia in 1605, but New France only began to develop after Samuel de Champlain founded Quebec in 1608.

Although Champlain was appointed commandant of the new colony by the king, the French at first relied on private joint stock companies to develop New France. For example, the Company of One Hundred Associates, the largest of these companies, received a royal charter under which it was to transport 4,000 settlers to New France between 1627 and 1642. But most of the companies had failed by 1663, when the government, under the great Colbert, took over the effort. The failures resulted from the incompatibility of the companies' and the government's aims. The companies wanted to create economically viable plantations, while the government aimed at the building of a rigidly centralized social and economic system that would serve the interests of the crown.

Seventeenth-century engraving of Quebec, the capital of New France, by Thomas Johnston.

Like the Spanish, the French brought their political and social system to the New World. The period of French colonization coincided with the reign of Louis XIV (r. 1643–1715), the Sun King, and the centralization and absolutism that was developing rapidly in France was transplanted to New France. The government tried to recreate feudalism in the New World by granting large tracts of land, or *seigneuries,* to a few proprietors. The landlords owed feudal dues to the king, took an oath of fealty and did homage to him, just as their medieval predecessors had. The peasants who were induced to emigrate to these estates paid feudal incidents patterned on those that were already ceasing to be paid in France. Naturally, peasants had little incentive to leave home, which in part accounts for the slow growth of the colony.

The French government intended to create a true New France in North America. Everything in the colony was to be regulated in the interests of the king—whose interests were assumed to be identical to those of France itself. The government thought that it would be able to create an orderly society subject to the divine king. The colony was to be governed by a royal governor and an intendant. The governor was invariably a French nobleman, while the intendant, responsible for financial affairs, was a member of the bourgeois civil service. The aim was to reproduce French society and government in an ideal form.

The holders of the seigneuries were expected to develop their "fiefs" in the interests of the crown. The seigneurs of New France had most of the rights their counterparts in France had—judicial rights, the labor services of their tenants, rents and fines, and a monopoly of milling—but the king set limits on the value of these rights. He was intent on controlling the tendency of feudal lords to become independent and troublesome by regulating the seigneurs, and his ministers in New France watched them closely. The seigneurial rights, so profitable in France, were burdensome in the New World.

The government tried to induce peasants to go to New France to cultivate the seigneuries. Peasants were told that they would have more and better land and lighter burdens in New France than they had at home. In some cases, they were promised subsidies to get started. But the government's agents found it difficult to overcome what one of them described as the peasants' unwillingness to lose sight of the village steeple. The settlers were to remain peasants—tenant farmers on the great estates—and there were few willing to resettle in the unknown continent under those conditions.

Throughout the history of New France, therefore, seigneurs and officials of the government complained about the inadequacy of the labor force. In the early eighteenth century, the governor wrote to his superiors in Paris that there was not enough labor to clear and cultivate even half of the seigneuries. Many seigneuries had only one or two settlers on them, so that the profits both to the seigneurs and the government in Paris were small.

In this situation, the colonial and royal government experimented to increase the influx of new settlers. One governor studied the fertility of Indian women because he thought intermarriage would help increase the population. He reported that their fertility was limited by their long nursing, a problem he thought could be solved by government regulation. This view was typical of the attitude that the French took to the affairs of the new colony. Another governor suggested that those convicted of smuggling salt in the home country be sent as indentured servants to the colony. Yet others issued regulations penalizing single men and rewarding those with many children. Unmarried men over twenty were prohibited from hunting, fishing, and trading with the Indians. A father was summoned to explain himself every six months if he had an unmarried son of twenty or daughter of sixteen. Those with ten or more living children received subsidies from the government.

These measures worked reasonably well. Between 1698 and 1755 (just before the colony was lost to Britain), New France had the highest fertility rate ever recorded. With very little immigration, the population of the colony increased from under 14,000 at the beginning of this period to 55,000 at the end. Nonetheless, New France continued to suffer from a labor shortage and to lag far behind the British colonies in population growth.

The Catholic Church played a large role in New France. Even though its efforts to convert the Indians failed, it became one of the agents of royal control in the colony. It controlled all the schools, and the king relied on it to produce a docile and obedient population. New France was to have an orthodox religious community that would have none of the unfortunate divisions that plagued French society. The government strictly prohibited the emigration of Huguenots to Canada, and even those few who were permitted to go there for trade or other purposes were forbidden to winter there. Huguenots who wanted to emigrate to the New World went to the English colonies instead. Meanwhile, the Church in New France was vigilant against the rise of Protestantism among the colonists and persecuted those who strayed from the Roman fold.

The task of setting up a completely regulated society in the vast wilderness of Canada was formidable. For a time, the French thought that they would be able to convert the Indians and integrate them into the new society, but this goal soon proved unachievable. Although the tribes were willing to trade furs to the French, they resisted both their missionaries and their regulation. By the time the government took direct control of the colony, it was clear that New France would be a purely European settlement.

Furthermore, the fur traders did not fit into the absolutist model centered in Quebec. They formed a fringe society that went native and over which the colonial government never had much control. The government licensed the traders and tried to keep them apart from other colonists. The traders were viewed as irreligious, disorderly, and immoral—an altogether bad influence on the common settlers. Nonetheless, adventurous peasants could escape the strict regulation of the seigneuries by escaping to the woods and the fur trade, and French governors often ignored the home government's admonitions to control the fur traders.

The woodsmen established themselves deep in the American interior. Louis Jolliet led the Jesuit Father Marquette to Arkansas in 1673, and Robert Cavelier de la Salle reached the mouth of the Mississippi in 1682. In 1699, the French built a settlement at Biloxi and took control of Louisiana. In 1702, they founded Mobile. Between their Canadian and Mississippi Valley settlements, they built forts to protect their lines of communication.

The seigneurs were in competition for peasant-settlers and offered good terms to attract them. In fact, the feudal system of New France was so mild that it survived the British conquest and the development of modern society. Feudal incidents were not abolished until 1854, and the last seigneuries were not bought out until 1935. (The buy-out plan set up by the provincial legislature provided such a gradual transition that the last vestiges of the system were not gone until about 1970.)

The competition of the seigneurs meant that they earned even less from their estates than they had anticipated and that the government's hope for a perfectly ordered society in which every member of each class lived under common conditions was frustrated. In myriad ways, the wilderness continent made it impossible for the French government to realize its utopian dreams.

THE ENGLISH COLONIES IN NORTH AMERICA

Virginia

While the French created a carefully wrought society in Canada, the English colonies to the south expanded rapidly and in helter-skelter fashion. There were many reasons for this kind of development. The idea that colonization yielded wealth had been skillfully sold to Englishmen of all classes before the death of Elizabeth I (1603). London and Bristol merchants were ready for colonizing and could organize ventures by means of joint stock companies. The constitutional and religious conflicts that troubled England through most of the seventeenth century provided many people with both material and idealistic motives for wishing to emigrate. Finally the English government — both the Stuart monarchy and its revolutionary opponents—encouraged but did not interfere with colonizing projects. In particular, it put no bar in the way of religious minorities that wished to emigrate.

The English began their colonizing efforts thirty years before the French, but they planted their first successful colony only the year before the foundation of Quebec. In 1576, a group of noble investors in England had formed the Cathay Company (Cathay was another name for China) to support exploration of a western route to China. On behalf of the company Martin Frobisher explored the north, found Baffin Island, Frobisher's Bay, and gold. When the gold turned out to be iron pyrite (fool's gold), the company went under.

About the same time, Humphrey Gilbert recognized the value of actual colonization in North America. In 1578, he received permission to explore the continent and to establish a colony, which he thought could serve as a base for preying on Spanish shipping and for the search for the passage to the East. He made two unsuccessful voyages (1578 and 1583) and went down in a storm during the second one, but he bequeathed his vision to his half-brother Sir Walter Raleigh. Raleigh received a royal charter in 1584 and sent a colonizing expedition to Roanoke Island on the North Carolina coast in 1585. The settlers returned to England in 1586, when Sir Francis Drake visited them on his way back to the mother country from operations in the Caribbean. Raleigh sent a new expedition in 1587, but war with Spain and the attack of the Spanish Armada (1588) prevented him from resupplying the colony. When he sent provisions in 1590, the colonists had disappeared. No one ever found out what happened to them.

Depiction of Roanoke Island from Theodore deBry's *America* (1590).

At the beginning of the seventeenth century, the English tried again. They were still convinced that North American colonies could serve as bases of operations, but now also thought about what products the American continent could provide to the home economy. The development of the sugar plantations in the West Indies had shown that the new land could be profitably exploited. In 1606, King James I (r. 1603–25) authorized the formation of two joint stock companies, the Virginia Company of Plymouth and the Virginia Company of London. In the next year, both companies sent out expeditions. The Plymouth Company planted a colony in southern Maine, but the colonists lasted only one winter there. This failure made colonization of the north appear doomed, and the company went through several reorganizations as its principals sought ways to save their investments.

The London Company achieved a success. Its 1607 expedition established Jamestown, along a river in the southern part of the Chesapeake Bay. The settlers had a difficult time until 1612, when they discovered that tobacco, a native American plant that the Spanish had begun cultivating in the West Indies and had gained a good market in Europe, grew well on their lands. Thus, the Virginia colony and its successors established a single-crop economy very early. This development led to the creation of plantations, manned by laborers brought from England. The company offered free passage to the colony in return for seven years' service, after which the servant was free to work for himself. Because tobacco prices were very high in the 1620s, the company was able to ship out many poor men, who thought that seven years' labor as indentured servants was a good exchange for the future opportunity to make their fortunes in the new land. The lay of the land permitted the planters to cultivate a wide area. The coastal lands were flat and wet, with deep bays and many rivers that could accommodate oceangoing vessels. Plantations established far inland therefore had access to the European market. Even when tobacco prices fell drastically in the 1630s, the plantations were able to make a profit.

But the exploitation of the Virginia colony created very harsh conditions. Although the company relaxed its government of the colony and guaranteed that the colonists would live under English law, there were numerous complaints that the indentured servants were being horribly abused. Between 1618 and 1624, the company sent out over 4,000 men, but in 1624 the population of the colony was only 1,210. The high death rate appears to have resulted from malnutrition and dis-

Early tobacco label, from the Imperial Tobacco Company in Bristol.

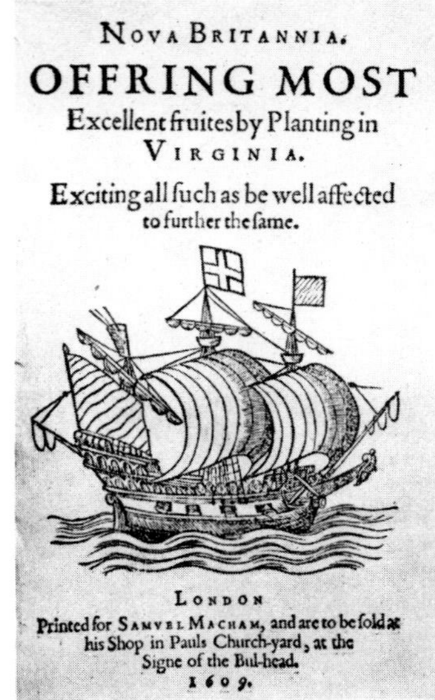

NOVA BRITANNIA.
OFFRING MOST
Excellent fruites by Planting in
VIRGINIA.
Exciting all such as be well affected
to further the same.

LONDON
Printed for SAMVEL MACHAM, and are to be sold at
his Shop in Pauls Church-yard, at the
Signe of the Bul-head.
1609.

Page from a pamphlet put out by the London Company in 1609 to persuade investors to support its enterprise in Virginia.

ease. In 1624, the king commissioned an investigation that led to the dissolution of the company and the conversion of Virginia into a royal colony. Already, the Virginians had asserted a right of self-governance by meeting in a representative assembly in 1619 and after 1629, the assembly met annually to make laws. The kings, particularly Charles I (r. 1625 – 49), resisted this development, but royal governors found that the colony was ungovernable without the support of the local assembly.

The plantation society of Virginia was a male society. Women were not used in the fields, so few of them were sent to the colony. In addition, the death rate declined after the middle of the century, so that increasing numbers of men survived their service. The effects of these developments lasted the entire seventeenth century. The lack of women meant a lack of families, and Virgina soon had a social problem created by the release of indentured servants. Once the tidewater districts had been fully settled, these men moved west, out of range of the tobacco market, where the wilderness could provide only a subsistence living. The royal governors rightly viewed this rabble as dangerous to the peace. In 1676 Nathaniel Bacon led a large army of them into rebellion. The rebels burned Jamestown before the death of Bacon (from disease) deprived them of the leadership necessary to maintain their momentum. The governor and assembly were soon in control again.

The experience of the rebellion may have been a turning point in the development of slavery in Virginia. Although African slaves had first been brought into the colony early in the century, slavery did not immediately become the dominant form of labor. The high death rate made it less economical to buy slaves than to bring in indentured servants. Once the death rate declined the economics slowly changed, but the impetus for a rapid increase in the use of slaves was fear of the poor former servants rather than rational economic analysis. By the end of the colonial era, 20 percent of Virginia's population was made up of slaves.

New England

To the north, in New England, a completely different sort of colonial activity developed. The origins of successful colonization in this area stemmed from religious controversy in England. During the sixteenth century, Calvinism had attracted a certain following within the English Church that had created division. The Puritans, as the Calvinists were called, sought to reform the Anglican Church in conformity with more radical ideas than those held by the queen or her principal churchmen. They wanted the government and Church to regulate be-

Slaves in South Carolina harvesting indigo, one of the colony's three major crops.

havior according to God's laws. They wanted to do away with the liturgy and bishops, which they associated with Roman Catholicism. The Church persecuted the more radical among the Puritans, but many moderate Puritans gained prominent positions in both the economy and Parliament.

In 1607 a small, radical, Puritan community from Scrooby in Nottinghamshire migrated to Holland to escape persecution, but its members soon found that life among the Dutch did not suit them. They therefore turned to English merchants, proposing to found a plantation in their behalf, dividing the profits with their backers for the first seven years and then paying rent to them. In 1620, arrangements were complete and 102 persons embarked on the *Mayflower* for the New World. They landed on Cape Cod and established the colony of Plymouth.

This community eventually succeeded in building a stable and self-supporting colony, but Plymouth never grew to be very large. The development of New England resulted from the activities of the Massachusetts Bay Company, formed in 1628 by a group of wealthy Puritans. In the next year, the company transferred its operations to New England, where its royal charter gave it complete control over the new colony.

In 1630 the Company transported nine hundred settlers to the colony in a well-planned operation and soon it was authorizing new settlements around Massachusetts Bay. The ideal of the colonists was to establish in America the kind of society they had sought unsuccessfully to establish in England. In their communities, the church owned no property and exercised no political power. Nonetheless, the church community was the basis of the new towns. Men gathered in a church sought permission from the Company to found towns that could support their spiritual community. The members of the church received houses in town and plots distributed through the land belonging to the town. The church met in the town meeting hall, which also served as the center of society and government. The town was ruled by a town meeting open to all members of the church.

Massachusetts grew as a Puritan haven, and the laws established by the Company recognized only Puritanism. When people arrived who had religious ideas that differed from the accepted ones, the colony expelled them. In 1636, it banished Roger Williams, who moved with his supporters to Rhode Island and established a colony there based on religious toleration. But religious dispute was not the only reason for migration out of Massachusetts. In the same year that Williams left, Thomas Hooker led a group looking for more land into the Connecticut River Valley. By about 1650 there were about twenty thousand people in New England as a whole.

This society was wholly different from the one being founded in Virginia. The Puritans came in family groupings and founded stable town communities. They found the land and

Articles of Agreement

When the Puritans arrived in Massachusetts, they formed towns based on religious communities. Here are selections from the "Articles of Agreement" by which Springfield, Massachusetts, was founded in May 1636.

1. We intend . . . as soon as we can . . . to procure some Godly and faithful minister with whom we purpose to join in church covenant. . . .

2. We intend that our town shall be composed of forty families, or, . . . not to exceed the number of fifty families, rich and poor.

3. That every inhabitant shall have . . . a house lot. . . .

4. That everyone that hath a house lot shall have a proportion of the cow pasture to the north of End Brook. . . .

6. That the long meadow . . . shall be distributed to every man as we shall think meet. . . .

8. That all rates [taxes] that shall arise upon the town shall be laid upon lands according to everyone's proportion. . . .

From *Remarkable Providences*, ed. by J. Demos (New York: Braziller, 1972), pp. 53–56.

climate unsuited for plantations and built small farms. Later settlements were not so centralized as those around Massachusetts Bay. The farmers lived "out" on the farm, and the towns functioned only as meeting places for governmental and church services.

Because New England could not supply highly valued products for England, its settlers developed a self-sufficient and balanced economy based on individual farms and commerce. The deep woods provided ample supplies for shipbuilding, and by the later part of the seventeenth century, New England had become a major center of shipping. Thus, the northern colonies developed economic interests that were completely different from those of the Virginians and came into direct competition with the merchants of the mother country.

A Guide for New Settlers

In 1650, Cornelius van Tienhoven, secretary of the province of New Netherland, wrote a guide for new settlers. After describing the land he provides advice on establishing oneself in the colony.

All, then, who arrive in New Netherland must immediately set about preparing the soil, so as to be able, if possible, to plant some winter grain, and to proceed the next winter to cut and clear the timber. . . . The farmer, having thus begun, must endeavor every year to clear as much new land as he possibly can. . . . Those in New Netherland and especially in New England, who have no means to build farm houses at first according to their wishes, dig a square pit in the ground, cellar fashion, six or seven feet deep [and] as long and as broad as they think proper. [They] case the earth inside with wood all around the wall, . . . floor this cellar with plank and wainscot it overhead for a ceiling, raise a roof of spars, [and] clear up and cover the spars with bark or green sods—so that they can live dry and warm . . . with their entire families for two, three, and four years, it being understood that partitions are run through those cellars which are adapted to the size of the family. . . . [H]ogs, after having picked up their food for some months in the woods, are crammed with corn in the fall. When fat they are killed and furnish a very hard and clean pork—a good article for the husbandman, who gradually and in time begins to purchase horses and cows with the produce of his grain and the increase of his hogs, and, instead of a cellar as aforesaid, builds good farm houses and barns.

From *Remarkable Providences*, ed. by J. Demos (New York: Braziller, 1972) pp. 47–49.

Proprietary Colonies

After the restoration of the monarchy in England in 1660 (see pp. 570 and 589), the royal government took up the cause of colonization on the basis of mercantilist theory so popular in Europe at that time. During the second half of the century new colonies were founded by royal grants to proprietors. Already in 1632, Charles I had granted 10 million acres north of Virginia to Lord Calvert of Baltimore, who wanted to construct a feudal seigniory in the New World. The Calverts were Catholics and hoped to establish a haven for their coreligionists. The new colony was named Maryland, after Charles I's Catholic wife. Maryland became a second center of religious toleration in the colonies.

In 1663, Charles II granted the Carolinas to a group of proprietors who wanted to develop a new region of plantations using the surplus colonists from Virginia and Barbados. The philosopher John Locke, secretary to one of the proprietors, wrote a constitution for the new colony, which was settled in two regions, around Charleston (South Carolina) and Albemarle Sound (North Carolina). These settlements developed an economy based on growing rice, which was apparently imported from Barbados.

In 1664, Charles sent an expedition to conquer the Dutch colony that had been founded forty years earlier on Manhattan Island at the mouth of the Hudson River. To everyone's surprise, the Dutch colonists put up no resistance, and New Netherlands, with its capital city of New Amsterdam, became an English colony. The king granted it as a proprietary colony to his brother James, Duke of York, and when James became king in 1685, New York became a royal colony.

The last proprietary colony founded was Pennsylvania. By the middle of the seventeenth century, Swedish and Dutch settlers had migrated into the eastern parts of the territory, which became English after the taking of New Netherland in 1664. In 1681, Charles granted a charter for the land to William Penn in payment of a debt the king owed his father. The new colony was named Pennsylvania (sylvania = woodlands). Penn was a Quaker, and he established a law of religious toleration in the colony. By the time he died in 1718, Pennsylvania had become a culturally varied and prosperous society. Its people had founded Philadelphia and begun pushing out over the Appalachians into the French territories to the west and north.

By 1700, there were twelve English colonies altogether, and, an estimated two hundred thousand English settlers lived in North America, as compared with about ten thousand French. The cultural dominance of the English was already established.

Colonial Society and Economy

The English colonies were more divided and less well controlled by the home government than New France. The English settlers lived under twelve separate governments. Each of the twelve colonies eventually won the right to elect a representative assembly to control local affairs, and although the royal governors were not responsible to these assemblies, they did receive their salaries from them. During the 1660s the English Parliament did its best to limit the tendency of the colonies to direct their own affairs and to make them behave as strict mercantilist theory said they should. The principal elements of this policy were the Navigation Acts, requiring that certain exports be sent directly to England in English or colonial ships. The colonists complained vigorously about these measures, and after the Revolution of 1688 the English government became less insistent on asserting its authority. The colonists accepted Parliamentary regulation so long as it was not strictly enforced, and they became increasingly accustomed to running their own affairs.

The society of English America was egalitarian and free, except for the slaves. By 1723, the slaves made up about 23 percent of the population, but they were concentrated in the coastal districts of the southern colonies. In many counties of those regions, slaves outnumbered whites during the eighteenth century.

This was a society without an aristocracy and with a relatively even distribution of wealth, especially when compared with European society. It had a small professional class—ministers, lawyers, and physicians—who perpetuated themselves by sending their sons to universities. Harvard was founded in 1636, William and Mary in 1693, and Yale in 1701. In Massachusetts, towns of fifty families were required to hire a schoolmaster. Overall, colonial society was more literate than that of Europe, and by the end of the seventeenth century there were active printing presses in all the colonies.

The English in the seventeenth century had unconsciously created a new type of colonial empire. The Portuguese and, for the most part, the Dutch empires were based on armed trade. The Spanish Empire rested on the efforts of the ruling class of soldiers, planters, and missionaries to convert the natives and exploit their labor. The Protestant English (and the Protestant Dutch) were never interested in converting the natives. They felt no responsibility for the Indians, perhaps because they did not need to exploit their labor. They therefore simply displaced the native populations with Eu-

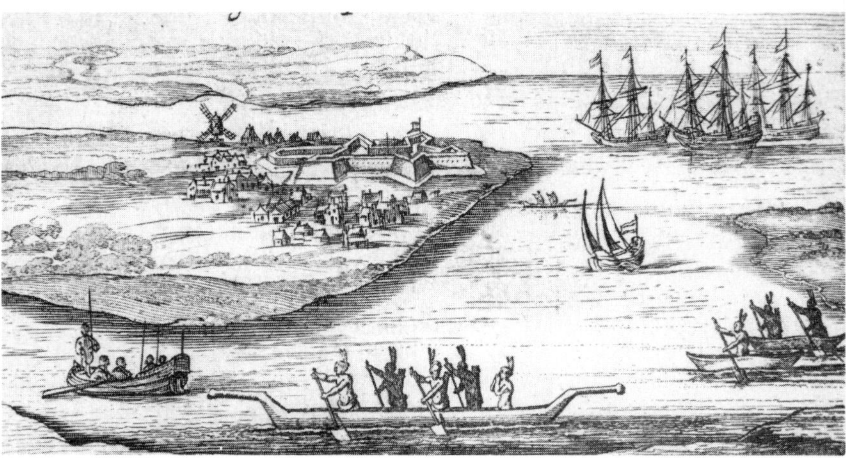

The earliest engraving (1651) of New Amsterdam on lower Manhattan Island. The town was an emporium for the fur trade with the Indians.

ropean immigrants. The English transported a whole population to the New World colonies and permitted it to blend the traditional European institutions with innovations and improvisations evoked by the new environment. Not surprisingly, English colonial society was experimental in many respects, and tended strongly to the exercise of economic, political, and religious freedom.

From the time when Sir Robert Walpole (1721–42) controlled the English government until the 1760s the English followed a policy of "salutary neglect" in the American colonies. In the middle of the century, the government continued the policy because it had to concentrate on the wars and diplomacy in Europe and on establishing its worldwide colonial empire.

In the meantime, the American colonies grew rapidly and prospered. New York became a great port and a substantial city. Boston also grew to a large size and became the port for the timber and furs exported from New England. The whaling industry grew in southern New England, producing oil and other products of the giant mammals. In the South, the plantation economy developed based on tobacco and cotton, which became the second and eventually the dominant crop of the southern colonies.

By the mid-1760s the policy of "salutary neglect" had been in effect for nearly a half century, and the American colonists had become used to self-governance. A thirteenth colony—Georgia—had been founded in 1732, and all thirteen had popularly elected assemblies. Before 1763, the English Parliament did not try to raise tax revenues in the colonies; the customs duties it did levy were designed to force trade to flow toward the mother country, in conformance with mercantilist ideas.

The Colonies After 1763

The Seven Years' War (1756–63; see pp. 635–36) changed all this. On

North America After the Seven Years' War 1763

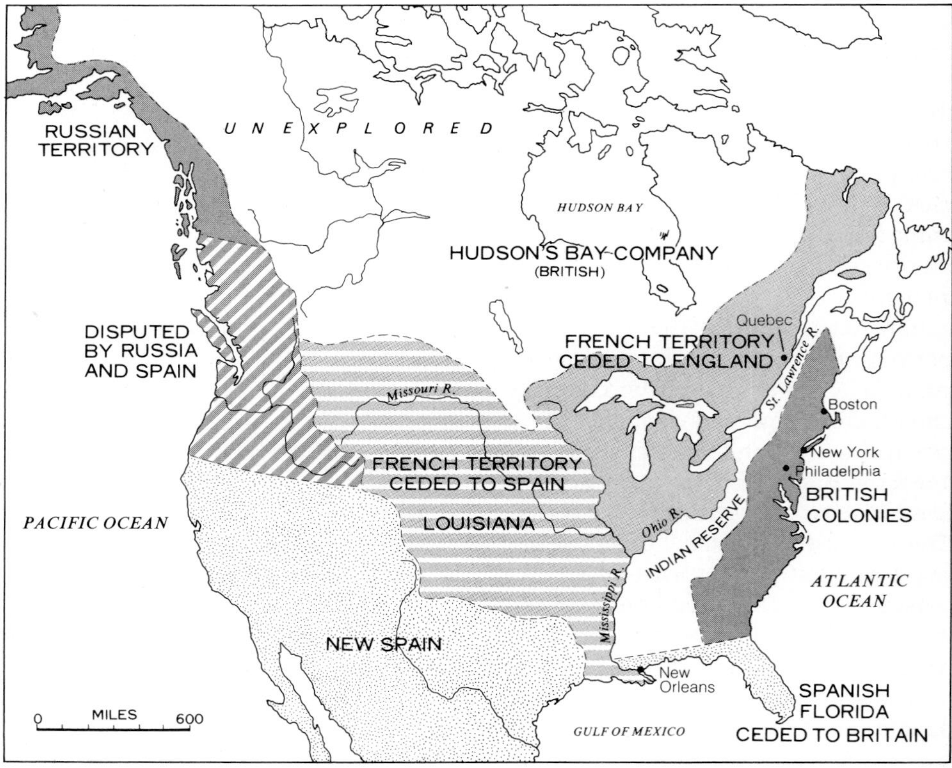

one side, the colonists were freed from the fear of French military action and thought they could do without British military protection. On the other, the war had led the British to establish a system of defense for the colonies, and Parliament now tried to tax the colonies in order that they might carry a fair share of the burden of this system. Furthermore, the average American colonist paid less than one-twenty-fifth of the taxes paid by the average Englishman, and Parliament therefore did not think the colonists were overburdened.

In March 1765 Parliament imposed a stamp tax on paper of all kinds, including legal documents, commercial agreements, and newspapers. Europeans were familiar with such taxes, but the Americans found it oppressive and raised a furious opposition. The leaders of this uproar were the leaders of colonial society — the lawyers, merchants, and editors — who organized a congress at which representatives of nine of the colonies urged "that no taxes be imposed on them but with their own consent." A year later Parliament repealed the act, but proclaimed that the crown and Parliament had a right to impose taxes on the colonies. In 1767 the English government tried again. It passed statutes imposing duties on imports into the colonies of tea, paper, paint, lead, and glass. This new set of taxes was met by a determined colonial boycott, and in 1770 all the duties but those on tea were repealed.

Until 1773 the two sides consistently misunderstood one another and got along badly, but there was no irrevocable break in relations. Parliament based its actions on its appreciation of the needs of the Empire, and the colonists based their objections on their status as British subjects. In 1773, events in far-off India changed the relationship between the British and Americans. In that year, the Regulation Act established governmental control of India, wresting lucrative privileges from the East India Company. In order to compensate the company for the loss of its political power, the government permitted it to sell tea directly — rather than through British dealers — to American retailers. This move would presumably lower prices, increase sales, and thus increase the revenue that the government received from the duty on tea. Whatever the reaction of the colonists, who were sensitive to the impositions of Parliament, might have been, a radical minority in Massachusetts intervened to block the new arrangement. This group was infuriated that the British government would gain more taxes from the colonists without obtaining their consent, and a party of Bostonians disguised as Indians boarded three ships of the East India Company in Boston harbor and dumped thousands of pounds worth of tea into the bay.

The British, for their part, had become sensitive to what they believed was the colonists' unreasonable attitude toward responsible imperial policy, and Parliament overreacted to this incident. It passed laws closing the port of Boston until the company was indemnified for the loss of the tea and depriving the Massachusetts assembly of much of its authority. These actions induced the other twelve colonies to rally behind Massachusetts out of fear that their own charters would similarly be abrogated or arbitrarily revised.

To make matters worse, the controversy over the tea coincided with a

The Boston Tea Party (1773), designed to infuriate the British government. Notice the substantial warehouses in the background.

The British American Colonies 1770

statesmanlike measure designed to ensure the quietude of the French settlers in Canada. The Quebec Act of 1774 guaranteed the preservation of the French language and the Catholic religion in the French districts and defined Canada as including all territory north of the Ohio River and west of the Allegheny Mountains. The act further prohibited settlement beyond the mountains. The definition of Canada's boundaries conformed to the lands claimed and fortified by France before the Seven Years' War, but the English colonists, particularly the Pennsylvanians, who had meanwhile begun to push out across the mountains to settle the virgin forest, viewed the act as a furthur attack on their rights and opportunities. It looked as if Parliament was out to oppress the Americans again. The conflict led to fighting in 1775, when British troops in Boston tried to seize suspected caches of arms at Lexington and Concord. The colonial leaders summoned a continental congress to meet in Philadelphia and on July 4, 1776, this congress formally declared the independence of the colonies.

THE AMERICAN WAR OF INDEPENDENCE

In the first months of the war, the Americans fared rather well. George Washington, who had been named commander-in-chief by the Continental Congress in May 1775, organized the militia around Boston and forced the British to escape by sea to Halifax in Nova Scotia in March 1776. The Americans successfully defended Charles Town (Charleston, South Carolina) against a strong British attack in June. But Washington could not stand long against British attack, and he retreated south to New York where the British attacked him with a large army. After suffering a serious defeat Washington crossed the Delaware River into Pennsylvania to gain time. But by September 1777, the British had won Philadelphia as well, and Washington was forced to winter at Valley Forge in very difficult conditions.

With New York and Philadelphia in their hands, the British thought that they could split the colonies in two. They ordered an army to march from Canada along Lake Champlain to join up with the forces along the coast, but American forces under Generals Horatio Gates and Benedict Arnold harried this invading army and finally forced it to surrender at Saratoga in October 1777, less than a month after the taking of Philadelphia.

After the failure of their grand strategy, the British played it safe, maintaining their control of New York and Philadelphia. In 1778, the French, hoping to gain from a British defeat, sent reinforcements and supplies, but these proved of little worth, partly because of bad luck and partly because the French were really interested in their own welfare rather than that of the American colonists. In 1779, the British decided to attack the southern colonies and left New England. They finally took Charles Town in 1780, but soon found themselves constantly harried by a mobile American force under General Nathaniel Greene. The main British force under Lord Cornwallis then marched north to Yorktown on the Chesapeake Bay.

In August 1781, a French naval force reappeared, and Washington was able to make a concerted attack on the British army at Yorktown. The French ships would protect him from the sea and a French force of seven thousand joined his own troops. Cornwallis surrendered on October 19, 1781, and British military activity in the colonies ended.

A New Nation

It took two years more to bring about an official peace. In the peace treaty of 1783, signed in Paris, the thirteen colonies gained recognition of their independence and won title to all the land east of the Mississippi, north of Florida, and south of the Great Lakes. The generosity of the British was based not on the severity of their defeat, but on a desire to cut their losses, so that France would not gain too much by the conclusion of the war. In fact, the Americans who negotiated the Treaty of Paris—Benjamin Franklin, John Jay, and John Adams—made the agreement in secrecy because they recognized that it would deprive the French of all the benefits they had hoped to get from the war and were consequently afraid of French interference. By the terms of the treaty, the former colonists received back the right to trade in England, but by the end of 1783 the British had closed their West Indian colonies to American traders.

Between 1783 and 1787, the Continental Congress continued to exist, but the balance of power shifted to the individual colonies. This arrangement weakened the union that had won the war and was seen by many as threatening the prosperity of the former colonies. The result was a push to form an effective union that would preserve the gains of 1783 while also preserving the status and local autonomy of the individual states. In 1787 a constitutional congress worked out a compromise of the competing interests in a new Constitution based on federalism.

This Constitution incorporated many of the ideas of the Enlightenment, which emphasized the rational activity of man. This faith in reason had led thinkers like John Locke (1632–1704) to propound the theory that civil government was based on an agreement of rational individuals to end the state of nature into which they had been born in order to provide all with the opportunity to pursue their natural rights in peace and safety. The failure of the British government to protect these rights had been the stated basis of the rebellion of 1776, for a government that failed of its fundamental purpose could be justly overthrown.

The constitution set up a government organized on rational principles to provide for an orderly society. It recognized the sovereignty of the people who gave power to the government by their social compact. It was based on a compact among the independent states and incorporated the idea of a balance of power within the government that had been suggested by Montesquieu. It recognized the need to preserve local customs and law against the tendency toward centralization that was so prevalent in Europe. And it did not recognize political power based on birth.

In the same year that the new constitution was approved, the Congress passed the momentous Northwest Ordinance, which extended the principles for which they had fought to the still unsettled territories in the interior of the continent. This meant that as they were settled the new territories would become constituent members of the union, not colonies or dependent territories.

THE DUTCH IN INDONESIA

The Dutch explored the Hudson River in 1609 and founded New Amsterdam on Manhattan Island at its mouth in 1624. They apparently intended the town to become a trading post for commerce in furs and other raw materials, but Dutch settlers were soon establishing large landed estates both on Long Island and up the Hudson.

In the meantime, the Dutch were engaged in challenging the Portuguese and Spanish for empire. They were taking over the route to the Spice Islands and searching for footholds in the Caribbean. In the 1620s, they tried unsuccessfully to seize Brazil from the Portuguese. Soon afterwards, they gained control of Curacao, which became a base from which to raid Spanish commerce. After 1623, when the English withdrew, the Dutch controlled the Spice Islands. In Europe, the Dutch dominated the shipping industry, carrying the goods of all countries (even of Britain). The seventeenth century was the Dutch century.

Colonization of the East Indies was carried out by the Dutch East India Company (founded 1602). The Indonesian archipelago (the Spice Islands) had a long imperial history, and its people had for centuries carried on a prosperous trade with China and India. It was a wealthy, literate society subject

George Washington at Princeton, **portrait by Charles Willson Peale.**

The Javanese port of Batavia, from a Dutch engraving of 1682. Notice the Dutch architecture, entirely inappropriate for the climate.

to many foreign influences and subdivided into many kingdoms under god-kings. Islam reached the islands in the eleventh century — probably from India — but the great spread of the religion only took place from the thirteenth century on. When the Portuguese arrived in the sixteenth century, they played little role in Indonesian history. They were merely foreign traders like so many others before them.

At first, the Dutch also existed on the fringes of Indonesian society and political life, but soon they were drawn into the politics of the islands and, in the interest of their trade, began to dominate the native kingdoms. By playing royal rivals off against one another, the Dutch gradually gained control over more and more territory, until by 1704, they governed most of Java. At the same time, they gained territory on Sumatra, but complete domination of that island was not achieved until the nineteenth century.

The Company administered its territories through the local aristocracy. Having overthrown the kings, it merely substituted itself for them, collecting tribute as they had. Gradually, the native system was transformed into an administrative bureaucracy. But the main purpose of the Company was trade, not government. It set up trading posts, where the native rulers under its control delivered their produce. The Company had undertaken governmental activities to force Indonesian communities and kingdoms to trade exclusively with its posts. The locals received little from the trade. It stimulated no significant changes in the life of the islands; the Dutch garnered all the profit.

During the eighteenth century, Dutch domination of the East Indies was again challenged by the British. But the Company had other difficulties as well. Smugglers created serious problems; the transformation of colonial government into a regular bureaucracy raised costs; the people working for the Company became corrupt. The Treaty of Paris, which ended the American War of Independence in 1783, also affected the Dutch colonies in Southeast Asia. The treaty gave the British the right to trade in the Indies and thereby increased competition for the Company. Finally, the Dutch government dissolved the Company in 1799.

THE BRITISH IN INDIA

While the Dutch gained a monopoly in the East Indies, the British achieved the same in India. By 1612, the British East India Company (founded in 1600) had defeated the Portuguese, and during the next few years it won concessions from the Mughal ruler in Delhi. The Mughals granted trading privileges to British trading posts, and the Company provided naval support for the inland Empire.

Throughout the seventeenth century, the British traded successfully with the Indian states of the interior. This was mostly a trade in bulky goods — cotton, saltpeter (for gunpowder), indigo, silk, and sugar — and the trade did not go only to England. Opium was traded with East Asia and later became the basis of the tea trade. The British also did not have a monopoly, as the Dutch had in Indonesia. Dutch, French, and Portuguese competed for the profits. The English maintained themselves by diplomacy, rather than force.

During the eighteenth century, the French emerged as the chief rivals of the English. The French government had established an East India Company in 1664 — at the same time that it was taking over the colonization of Canada — but little progress was made before 1720. After this, the Company expanded its trade, until the War of the Austrian Succession in Europe (1740–48) made England and France enemies. From the early 1740s, the English made a concerted effort to oust the French from India, but the French prevailed at first. By 1750, they were dominant in the South. Then, there was a dramatic turnaround, and by 1752 the British began to win significant victories, including the Battle of Plassey. By 1763, the struggle was over, and Britain was in control of the Indian trading posts and exercised the overriding influence in the politics of the Indian states.

The architect of the British victory was Robert Clive, an agent of the East India Company. After he had defeated the French militarily, he established a new system of government in the Indian states under his control. The Company controlled the collection of taxes and the treasury, while the native rulers ran the administration and judiciary. Thus, the natives no longer had the resources to field armies. In the later part of the century, Warren Hastings, the Company's governor in Bengal, began an Anglicization of the financial administration, substituting British for Indian civil servants. He also set up a system of courts under British law and judges.

The Company had been transformed into a governing body, and the British government stepped in in 1773 to regulate its activities. By the Regulation Act, Parliament reorganized the colonial government in India, making the governor of Bengal (still Hastings at that time) responsible for Madras and Bombay. At the same time, the government regulated the Company's activities in England. After Hastings returned to England, he was prosecuted by his enemies for alleged misgovernment and corruption, and although he was acquitted, the trial (1787–95) made it clear that the royal government expected the Company to be responsible to the governed in India.

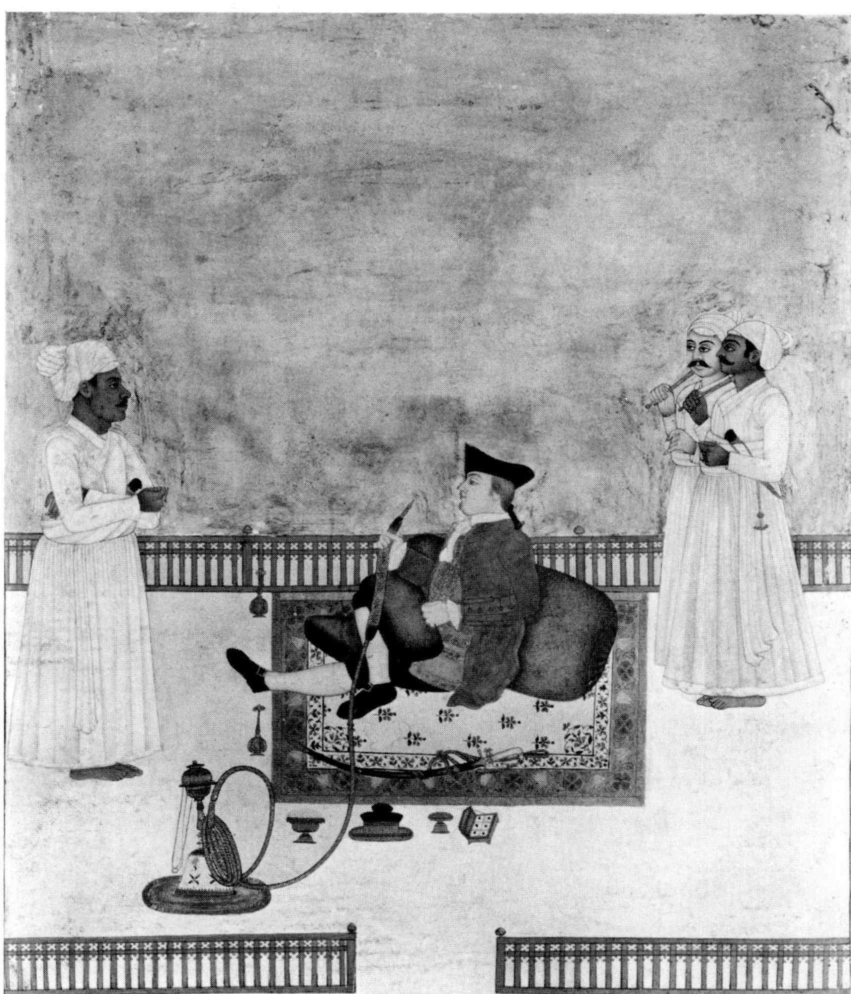

Bengal miniature of about 1760 showing a British East India Company employee adapting to his Indian environment.

Finally, the East India Act of 1784 limited the Company to commercial activities and put the government of the Indian colonies under a Board of Control made up of seven commissioners. The Company continued to carry out the functions of government under the direction of the Board. This was another dual system of government. Under the Act, the government was to make a full inquiry into Indian affairs every twenty years, when the Company's privileges were to be renewed. From this point on, the Company was more and more subordinated to the government, until by the mid-nineteenth century, it had lost virtually all of its authority and even its monopoly on trade.

A Cossack warrior.

THE RUSSIANS IN SIBERIA

The picture of seventeenth-century colonialism would not be complete without taking into account the Russians' move into Siberia and beyond to the western coast of North America. This movement was strikingly like the English and French movements in the Atlantic coastal districts of the newly discovered continent. In 1581 groups of Cossacks—"pioneers" or "frontiersmen," who had earlier pushed back the Turks and Tartars and had settled in the lower valleys of the Dnieper, the Don, and the Volga rivers—began to move eastward from the Urals under a leader, Ermak, who became famed in song and story. The Cossacks, like the French in America, were primarily interested in furs, and they followed the pine forests across northern Asia. This region was crisscrossed by large river systems, which permitted the Cossacks to move across the continent mostly by water.

The Cossacks' movement was not organized or planned. Groups moved through sparsely settled territory east of the Urals and set up small communities. The string of scattered settlements reached the Pacific in the 1640s, just two generations after the movement began. The distance covered by the Cossack settlers was greater than that traversed by the western Europeans who migrated to America, but there were no ocean or mountain barriers to cross, and no resistance from natives until they reached the Amur Valley. There the Russians were stopped by the superior power of the Chinese, and in 1689 the first Russo-Chinese treaty required that the Russians withdraw from the Amur basin.

The early settlements of the Cossacks were not subject to any central government and were often wild and lawless, like the later towns of the American "wild west." But the tsar's government soon pushed out to gain control of the region, which produced a rich trade in furs. The result was the establishment of a colonial regime more like the French than the English one in North America. But unlike the French, the tsarist government encouraged emigration and settlement. By 1700 there were about one and a half times as many Russians in Siberia as French and English in North America.

The Russian colonization of eastern Asia continued to expand in the eighteenth century. Between 1728 and 1740, the Russian naval commander Vitus Bering discovered the strait between Asia and Alaska that is named for him and explored Alaska itself. Within a short time, the Russians had established a small settlement in the Aleutian Islands and began to venture down the North American coast in search of seals. The English and Spaniards responded by pushing out from their colonial bases in eastern Canada and California. The English Hudson Bay Company sent explorers out into the vast Canadian continent and laid claim to all of the land east of the Rocky Mountains. The Spanish extended their line of missions to Nootka on Vancouver Island. By the middle of the century the North American map was divided among the English, French, Spanish, and Russians, even though the actual colonies were separated by huge, unknown territories.

Suggestions for Further Reading

The classic work on the Spanish Empire is R. B. Merriman, *The Rise of the Spanish Empire in the Old World and the New,* 4 vols. (1918–34). For a brief, up-to-date survey, see J. H. Parry, *The Spanish Seaborne Empire* (1973). On the Spanish colonies, see C. H. Haring, *The Spanish Empire in America* (1947); R. Cameron, *Viceroyalties of the West* (1968); L. B. Simpson, *The Encomienda System in New Spain* (1950); I. A. Leonard, *Baroque Times in Old Mexico* (1959); F. Chevalier, *Land and Society in Colonial Mexico* (1963); C. Gibson, *The Aztecs under Spanish*

Rule, 1519–1821 (1964); F. Tannenbaum, *Slave and Citizen: The Negro in the Americas* (1947); and J. L. Mecham, *Church and State in Latin America* (1934).

On French Canada see F. Parkman, *Count Frontenac and New France under Louis XIV,* rev. ed. (1922) and *The Old Regime in Canada* (1874). More modern and scholarly works include W. B. Munro, *Crusaders of New France* (1918); G. M. Wrong, *The Rise and Fall of New France* (1928); G. Lanctot, *The History of Canada,* 3 vols. (1963–65), the best recent work; W. B. Munro, *The Seignorial System in Canada* (1927); H. A. Innis, *The Fur Trade in Canada* (1956); S. D. Clark, *The Social Development of Canada* (1942); M. Wade, *The French Canadians 1760–1945* (1955); and J. H. Kennedy, *Jesuit and Savage in New France* (1950).

The enormous literature on the English colonies in North America includes W. Notestein, *The English People on the Eve of Colonization, 1603–1630* (1954); P. Laslett, *The World We Have Lost,* 2nd ed. (1971); A. L. Rowse, *The Elizabethans and America* (1959); C. M. Andrews, *The Colonial Period of American History,* 4 vols. (1934–38). On colonial government and economy, see L. W. Larabee, *Royal Government in America* (1930), and B. Bailyn, *New England Merchants in the Seventeenth Century* (1955). For social history see D. Boorstin, *The Americans: The Colonial Experience* (1958); J. Henretta, *The Evolution of American Society, 1700–1815* (1973); and C. Bridenbaugh, *Cities in Revolt: Urban Life in America, 1743–1776* (1955). On the revolution, see L. H. Gibson, *The Coming of the Revolution, 1763–1775* (1954), and J. R. Alden, *The American Revolution, 1775–1783* (1954). On the formation of the new nation, see E. S. Morgan, *The Birth of the Republic, 1763–1789* (1956). On the development of slavery, see H. A. Wyndham, *The Atlantic and Slavery* (1935).

For the Dutch in the East Indies, see C. R. Boxer, *The Dutch Seaborne Empire* (1973), and B. H. M. Vlekke, *The Story of the Dutch East Indies* (1945). On the British in India, see E. Thompson and G. T. Garratt, *The Rise and Fulfillment of British Rule in India* (1934); H. Furber, *John Company at Work: A Study of European Expansion in India in the Late Eighteenth Century* (1948). For an account of the Russian expansion into Siberia, see R. J. Kerner, *The Urge to the Sea: The Course of Russian History* (1942).

	1648			1700		
SOUTHWEST ASIA AND AFRICA	**1652** Dutch found Cape Colony *ca.* **1700** Rise of Ashanti, West Africa				**1737–47** Nadir Shah, decline of Safavid Empire	
EUROPE	**1660–88** Stuart Restoration **1661–1715** Louis XIV	**1683** Turks besiege Vienna **1685** Edict of Nantes revoked **1685–1750** Johann Sebastian Bach **1687** Newton's Law of Gravitation	**1688** Glorious Revolution **1689–1725** Peter the Great **1690** Locke, *Two Treatises of Civil Government*	**1701–14** War of Spanish Succession **1715–74** Louis XV **1720** South Sea Bubble **1723–42** Robert Walpole	**1740–80** Maria Theresa **1740–86** Frederick the Great **1756–63** Seven Years' War **1756–91** Wolfgang Amadeus Mozart	**1762** Rousseau, *The Social Contract* **1762–96** Catherine the Great **1769** James Watt's first steam engine **1770–1827** Ludwig van Beethoven
SOUTH AND SOUTHEAST ASIA	**1653** Taj Mahal completed **1690** British found Calcutta				**1751** French control Deccan **1757** Battle of Plassey **1773** Regulation Act	
EAST ASIA	**1662–1722** Emperor Kangxi *ca.* **1675–1725** Golden age of Edo urban culture, Japan			**1736–95** Emperor Qianlong	**1796–1804** White Lotus Rebellion	
THE AMERICAS AND PACIFIC		**1664** British seize New Amsterdam		**1728** Bering explores Alaska **1756–63** French and Indian War	**1765** Stamp Act **1768–80** Cook explores Pacific Ocean **1773** Boston Tea Party **1774** Quebec Act	

East India Company merchant, by an Indian artist.

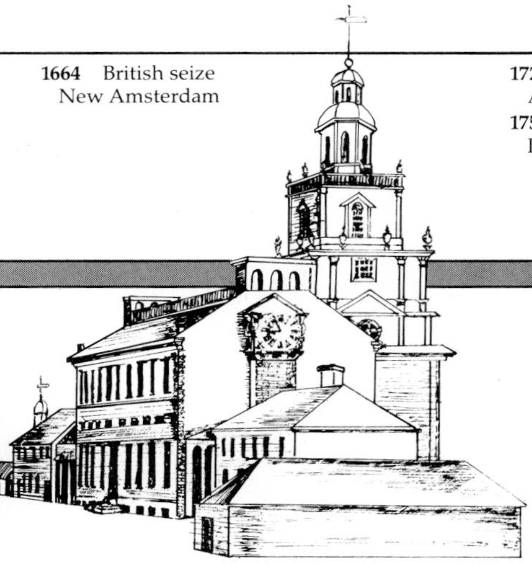

Independence Hall, Philadelphia, 1776.

Napoleon, 1800.

Ashanti wood carving.

Emblem of the Sun King, Louis XIV.

Charles II of England, 1660-85.

	1815
	1805–48 Mohammed Ali founds dynasty in Egypt **1806** British control Cape Colony **1807** Slavery abolished in British Empire
1776 Smith, *Wealth of Nations* **1789** French Revolution begins	**1798** Malthus, *Essay on the Principle of Population* **1799** Napoleon becomes First Consul **1804–14** Napoleonic Empire
1784 East India Act **1786–93** Cornwallis in Bengal **1796** British conquer Ceylon	
1775–83 American Revolution **1776** US Declaration of Independence **1788** British colonize Australia **1803** Louisiana Purchase	**1807–30** Latin American wars for independence

Chinese fan painting, ***ca.*** **1700.**

Fuji above Storm, **by Hokusai, 1760-1849.**

32 The French Revolution and Napoleon

The French Revolution marked a turning point in European history. The events that began in 1787 and ended with the fall of Napoleon Bonaparte in 1815 unleashed forces that altered not only the political and social structure of states but the map of Europe. Many attempts were made in France and elsewhere to undo the work of the Revolution and to repress the ideas of liberty, equality, and nationalism that the Revolution had inspired. But the Old Regime was dead, in France at least, and a Europe dominated by monarchy and aristocracy and by a hierarchical social order could never be fully restored. With the coming of the French Revolution, then, we enter a more modern world—a world of class conflict, middle-class ascendancy, acute national consciousness, and popular democracy. Together with industrialization, the Revolution reshaped the institutions, the societies, and even the mentalities of Europeans.

THE ORIGINS OF THE FRENCH REVOLUTION

By the last half of the eighteenth century, France appeared to have overcome the dismal cycle of famine, plague, and high mortality that in the preceding century had inhibited both demographic and economic growth. The majority of Frenchmen who lived in the villages and tilled the fields were better off than their counterparts in most of Europe. French peasants, for example, owned some 40 percent of the country's farmlands. The mild inflationary trend that characterized much of the eighteenth century increased the wealth of large landowners and surplus wealth in agriculture served to stimulate the expansion of the French economy as a whole. Modest advances in the textile and metallurgical industries, the construction of new roads and canals, and urban growth were other indications of economic development.

Yet despite signs of prosperity, there was much discontent and restlessness in France in the 1780s. French institutions were obsolete, inefficient, and uncoordinated. They were controlled by the nobility and by self-perpetuating corporations of hereditary officeholders. To anyone touched by the ideas of the Enlightenment they seemed irrational and unjust. The middle classes especially were offended by the legal and social distinctions that kept them from attaining high office or exerting political influence. Every bishop in France was of noble birth; only nobles could receive commissions in the army; bourgeois plans for economic reform were constantly thwarted by the privileged classes. The economy, particularly in agriculture, remained unstable and subject to fluctuations that could drive the peasants and urban poor to starvation. An inefficient and inequitable tax system yielded too small an income to support the state, discouraged economic growth, and fell most heavily on the poor. On the eve of the Revolution, France faced a conjuncture of crises. Three of these crises—agrarian distress, financial chaos, and aristocratic reaction—were particularly acute.

Agrarian Distress

Wretched weather and poor harvests in 1787 and 1788 weakened the agricultural economy. The poorer peasants lived at a subsistence level at best, and the purchasing power of well-to-do peasants declined. Grain shortages led to sharp increases in the cost of bread. Moreover, from the late 1770s the long-term growth of the French economy had been interrupted in several important areas such as the wine trade, and between 1776 and 1787 agricultural profits generally declined, though not to the low levels of the first part of the century. Nevertheless, noblemen and other large landowners who had become accustomed to high profits sought to save their declining fortunes by demanding from their tenant farmers dues and obligations that had long been neglected. The countryside was ready for a change.

Financial Chaos

The finances of Louis XVI's government were a shambles. By 1787 one-half of the nation's tax revenues went to service the massive public debt that Louis XIV had left behind. France's involvement in the Seven Years' War and in the American War for Independence had driven the government further along the road to bankruptcy. Without a reform of the tax system the king could not meet his obligations. But such a reform would mean an attack on the privileges of the upper classes, and this Louis could never quite summon the courage to do.

Three ministers in succession struggled with the problem. The first, the Swiss banker Jacques Necker, was dismissed by the king in 1781 after he had proposed some modest reforms. Necker's successor, Charles de Calonne, thought he could carry on without much change. But as the deficit mounted he grew alarmed, and in 1786 he proposed a much more radical reform program than Necker's, including a direct tax on all landowners. To oversee the assessment of the new tax, Calonne suggested that the king create local and provincial assemblies in which all men of property would be represented regardless of social status. In addition, older taxes, such as the *taille,* which weighed on the lower orders, were to be reduced. These reforms struck at the very heart of the system of privilege and the social hierarchy. Calonne, aware that there would be bitter opposition to his plans, persuaded Louis XVI to call a conference of notables in the hope that they could be induced to back his program. But the members of this assembly, which met in February 1787, refused their support.

The king now dismissed Calonne and put in his place one of Calonne's chief opponents, Lomenie de Brienne, Archbishop of Toulouse. This prelate, though a member of both the higher nobility and the higher clergy, soon came to the same conclusion as Calonne. He tried to enact a similar reform program, but the *Parlement* of Paris, the most privileged of all the corporations of officeholders, refused to register the royal edicts. It declared that only the Estates General could approve such measures. When Brienne tried to break the opposition by exiling the magistrates of the *Parlement* and by abolishing the high courts, he touched off furious protests by many members of the upper bourgeoisie and the nobility. In the face of these attacks, the government backed away from its reform program. In July 1788 the king yielded to the opposition and ordered a meeting of the Estates General for May 1789.

Aristocratic Reaction

During the 1780s, then, aristocratic demands on the peasantry were aggravating the distress of the countryside, and aristocratic resistance to tax reform was hampering the government its attempts to revamp the nation's financial structure. These were two facets of the aristocratic reaction that was directly responsible for the coming of the French Revolution.

The tremendous strength of the French privileged classes had been built up steadily during the reigns of Louis XV and Louis XVI. At every turn the poor and the aspiring middle class confronted the fact of privilege. Some men of the Enlightenment, in particular Voltaire, and such royal ministers as Turgot and Calonne encouraged the king to bring a measure of justice to French society at the expense of the privileged groups. But by the 1780s it appeared that the French king was the prisoner of the nobility and that he would do nothing to displease them.

Moreover, the nobles were particularly skillful in confusing the issue. Certain privileges, such as those that protected the provinces from encroachments by the central government, limited the arbitrary power of the king. These privileges, or liberties, were compared with the restrictions on royal power in England, and the English were regarded as the freest people in Europe. Thus the nobles could resist royal attacks on privilege by asserting that the king was simply trying to get rid of all restrictions on his power. Through this device, the nobility and the *parlements* were able to gain wide support and considerable sympathy when they resisted the arbitrary orders of the king, even when those orders were directed toward desirable ends.

There were those, however, who were not deceived by the rhetoric of the privileged orders. The hesitations of the king and the intransigence of the aristocracy increased the bitterness of large sections of the population. They wanted to put an end to privilege, and they felt that the unreformed monarchy would not help them in this struggle. The attack on privilege and the demand for equality before the law were the driving forces in the Revolution from beginning to end. Privilege, it seemed, could be destroyed only by attacking aristocracy and monarchy.

THE FRENCH REVOLUTION AND THE KING

The Estates General, which had not met since 1614, was convened by the king at Versailles on May 5, 1789. The process by which deputies were selected was a relatively generous one: All adult males had the right to vote, indirectly, for representatives to the Third Estate, which served the interests of the commoners. Moreover, following some recent examples in provincial assemblies, the Third Estate was given twice as many representatives as the other two Estates. The First and Second Estates (the clergy and the nobility, respectively) represented the privileged orders. The king had asked that all local electoral assemblies draw up *cahiers de doléances*—lists of grievances—to submit to the Estates General when it met. Thus in the months preceding the convening of the Estates General, much political debate occurred. Almost all politically minded men agreed that the monarchy should yield some of its powers to an assembly and seek consent to taxation and legislation. By 1788 some noblemen were willing to go part way in abolishing privileges and in equalizing taxation. But the early debates in the Estates General revealed that the lawyers and bourgeois who represented the Third Estate were bent on a much more drastic reform.

The Estates General and the National Assembly

The mood of the Third Estate was best expressed by one of its deputies, the Abbé Sieyès. In a famous pamphlet, *What Is the Third Estate?*, Sieyès argued that the real French nation was made up of people who were neither clergymen nor noblemen, and that this majority should have the decisive voice in all political matters. This idea was translated into action during the opening debate on voting procedures in the Estates General. Since the Third Estate had as many representatives as the other two combined, it wanted the three Estates to meet and vote together. A few liberal nobles and a number of the lower clergy were sure to support the Third Estate. The king and the privileged orders, on the other hand, demanded that the Estates vote separately. This was traditional procedure and it assured that the first two Estates would retain control.

The Third Estate not only rejected the king's plan for separate meetings; on June 17 it declared itself the National Assembly of France and invited the other Estates to sit with it. The National Assembly then assumed the right to approve and withhold all taxation if its political demands were not met. In the face of this bold initiative, the king resorted to a show of force. On June 20 Louis XVI had the Third Estate barred from its usual meeting place. The deputies then convened in a nearby indoor tennis court and took an oath not to disband until they had drafted a constitution. This Tennis Court Oath was the first great act of the bourgeois revolution in France.

In a repetition of the political ineptitude he had shown in previous crises, Louis missed his chance to act as mediator between the hostile Estates. On June 23 he went before the Estates General and offered a program of reform that only partly satisfied the demands of the Third Estate for tax reform and did nothing to abolish the privileges of the nobility. At about the same time, the king began to concentrate troops around Versailles and Paris. By now, however, neither partial reform nor brute force was a sufficient answer to the political crisis. The revolution had become a battle between those who demanded a more equal and open society and those who wanted to preserve the privileges of the aristocracy.

The Oath at the Jeu de Paume, **by Jacques Louis David. The deputies of the Third Estate, joined by some of the clergy and nobility, swear not to disband until they have drafted a constitution.**

The Popular Revolt

Most of the deputies in the Third Estate were lawyers, professional men, and lesser officeholders. Their aspirations were those of the French bourgeoisie. In the urban centers and the countryside resided yet another element of the Third Estate—the mass of artisans, shopkeepers, and peasants who lived in poverty or on the edge of it. Their aspirations and needs were not identical with those of the deputies at Versailles. But in the summer of 1789 a series of spontaneous popular disturbances and revolts linked, for the moment at least, the bourgeoisie and the common people in an uneasy alliance against the aristocracy.

Notable among these uprisings was an attack on July 14 (still France's national holiday) on the Bastille, a royal fortress in Paris. By the end of June the city of Paris had grown tense. The economic depression had reduced the urban poor to misery, and to misery now was added the fear that the king and the aristocrats were conspiring to dissolve the Estates General. When the king's troops appeared, the immediate reaction of the citizens was to arm themselves. Their search for arms brought the leaders of the Parisian electoral assembly and a crowd of journeymen and workers to the Bastille. The commandant at first fired on the attackers but then lost his nerve, opened the gates, and the crowd stormed in and slaughtered the garrison.

The fall of the Bastille was an event of small consequence in itself, but its implications were immense. The attack was regarded as a blow against royal despotism. It demonstrated that the Revolution was not simply a debate over a constitution. Of greatest importance, it brought the city of Paris and the political leaders of Paris to the forefront. A new revolutionary municipal government was formed; henceforth Paris would shape the direction of the Revolution. Finally, the events in Paris set off revolts in the provinces.

The French peasants, also disappointed with the slow pace of reform, now began to take action of their own. Like the poor in the cities, the peasants had been heartened by the political promise of the winter of 1788/89. They had patiently drawn up their *cahiers* and they had chosen their electoral committees; then they had waited confidently for relief to follow. The Estates General met in May. Spring passed and summer came, but the peasants were still poor; they were still not allowed to till the unused land of the nobles; and they still had to pay their customary dues.

Then, during July 1789, the month of the storming of the Bastille, rumors spread through rural France that there would be no reforms and that the aristocrats were coming with troops to impose reaction on the countryside. The result was panic and rioting throughout the country. During the "Great Fear," as it is called, frightened peasants gathered to defend themselves against the unnamed and unseen enemy. Once assembled and armed, however, they turned against the enemy they knew—the local lord. Though the lords themselves were rarely in residence, peasants burned their châteaux, often tossing the first brand into the countinghouse, where the hated records of their payments were kept.

The attack on the Bastille (July 14, 1789).

The Destruction of Privilege

The popular revolts and riots had a profound impact on the king, the aristocracy, and the deputies of the Third Estate alike. Already in June, before the storming of the Bastille, Louis XVI had recognized the National Assembly and ordered the clergy and the nobles to sit with the Third Estate. He also recognized the revolutionary government of Paris and authorized the formation of a national guard composed largely of members of the bourgeoisie. But the king received no credit for his concessions from the revolutionary leaders, who felt, quite rightly, that his sympathies were still with the nobles. At the same time, Louis's indecision had discouraged many supporters of the Old Regime. The most reactionary noblemen, headed by the king's brother, the Count of Artois, began to leave the country.

Other members of the aristocracy sought to preserve their property by making dramatic concessions. On the night of August 4, one nobleman, the Viscount de Moailles, stood before the Assembly and proposed that all feudal levies and obligations be abolished. In a performance at once impressive and bizarre, nobles, clerics, and provincial notables arose to renounce noble privileges, clerical tithes, and provincial liberties. In effect, the Old Regime was dismantled in one night, and the way seemed clear for the Assembly's main business—to draft a constitution. The implementation of the concessions of August 4, however, was halfhearted. The structure of aristocratic privilege was indeed abolished, along with tax exemptions and hereditary officeholding. But peasants were to continue paying customary dues to their lords until they had redeemed them. Only when the Revolution reached a more radical stage was this obligation abolished.

The Declaration of the Rights of Man

On the whole, the National Assembly had succeeded in wiping out the privileges of the upper classes, the corporations of officeholders, and the provinces. Now it faced the task of creating new political, legal, and administrative structures. The ideological framework for this task was set forth by the constitution-makers in the Declaration of the Rights of Man, which they adopted on August 27, 1789.

In this preamble to a constitution, the members of the National Constituent Assembly (that is, the National Assembly acting in its constitution-making role) established a set of principles idealistic enough to sustain the enthusiasm of the mass of Frenchmen for the Revolution and sweeping enough to include all humanity. The basic ideas of this document were personal freedom, equality under the law, the sanctity of property rights, and national sovereignty. The first article declared that "men are born and remain free and

The Declaration of the Rights of Man

August 27, 1789

1. **Men are born and remain free and equal in rights; social distinctions may be based only upon general usefulness.**
2. **The aim of every political association is the preservation of the natural and inalienable rights of man; these rights are liberty, property, security, and resistance to oppression.**
3. **The source of all sovereignty resides essentially in the nation; no group, no individual may exercise authority not emanating expressly therefrom.**
6. **Law is the expression of the general will; all citizens have the right to concur personally or through their representatives in its formation; it must be the same for all, whether it protects or punishes. All citizens, being equal before it, are equally admissible to all public offices, positions, and employments, according to their capacity, and without other distinction than that of virtues and talents.**
10. **No one is to be disquieted because of his opinions; even religious, provided their manifestation does not disturb the public order established by law.**
11. **Free communication of ideas and opinions is one of the most precious of the rights of man. Consequently every citizen may speak, write, and print freely, subject to responsibility for the abuse of such liberty in the cases determined by law. . . .**

From *A Documentary Survey of the French Revolution,* ed. by John Hall Stewart (New York: Macmillan, 1951), p. 114.

equal in rights." There were to be no class privileges and no interference with freedom of thought and religion. Liberty, property, and resistance to oppression were declared inalienable and natural rights. Laws could be made and taxes levied only by the citizens or their representatives. The nation, not the king, was sovereign. Thus was established the framework for a system of liberty under law. The Declaration was a landmark in the fight against privilege and despotism, and it had a great appeal to revolutionary and democratic factions throughout Europe.

The October Days

The Declaration of the Rights of Man was not simply a page lifted from John Locke, the *philosophes,* and the Americans. It was a highly political document hammered out in an Assembly that was showing itself to be increasingly divided. There were those among the moderate leaders of the Assembly who found the Declaration too radical and sweeping. These men desired to construct a constitutional system on the English model with a monarch guided by an assembly controlled by the rich and well-born. The issues that divided the crown and the country could not, however, be compromised. Louis simply refused to give formal approval to the Declaration and the decrees that followed the night of August 4.

The king's recalcitrance, the divisions in the Assembly, and the food shortages combined to produce yet another popular explosion. On October 5, 1789, a crowd of some twenty thousand armed Parisians, including many women, marched on Versailles, demanding bread and insisting that the royal family return to Paris. The king was persuaded by Necker, who had been recalled, and by Lafayette, leader of the National Guard, to appease the crowd and leave Versailles. On October 6 the royal family drove into Paris, surrounded by shouting crowds, and established themselves at the Tuileries palace. A few days later, the National Constituent Assembly followed. Henceforth the deliberations of the Assembly were to take place in the heated atmosphere of Paris. Here in the capital many political clubs were formed to debate the issues and settle on policy. Here too were political agitators, journalists of all opinions, and above all, crowds that could be mobilized to bring pressure on the Assembly. From the autumn of 1789 on, the Revolution became more and more a Parisian affair.

The Achievements of the National Constituent Assembly, 1789–91

It took two years to make the constitution. By the end of that time the government had been reorganized, the Church had been dispossessed of its lands, and the rights of Frenchmen had been more clearly defined.

The Monarchy By acts passed in September 1789, Louis XVI was reduced from a king by divine right to the role of a constitutional monarch. He was given a suspensive veto over legislation that allowed him to delay the passage of laws for two years. The monarchy remained hereditary, and the king retained control of military and foreign affairs.

The Legislature The Constitution of 1791 provided for a unicameral Legislative Assembly, elected for two years. The Assembly had the power to initiate and enact legislation and to control the budget. It also had the exclusive right to declare war. Members of the Constituent Assembly were forbidden to serve in the new legislature, an unfortunate decision that barred experienced men from a body that had few precedents to guide it.

The Electorate The Constitution did not introduce universal manhood suffrage. It divided Frenchmen into active and passive citizens. Only the former, who met a property qualification, had the right to vote. This active category comprised some four million men in a total population of about

French Women Become Free. **Print from the General Collection of Caricatures about the Revolution (1789).**

twenty-five million men and women. Active citizens voted for electors, who in turn elected the Legislative Assembly. These electors were drawn from some fifty thousand of the country's wealthiest men. Even with these restrictions, a far larger percentage of the population could vote and hold office than in England.

The Administration The elimination of aristocratic privilege invalidated most of France's local administration, which had been controlled by the nobility or small oligarchies of officeholders and rich bourgeois. The Assembly completed the process of dismantling the administrative apparatus of the Old Regime by abolishing all former provinces, intendancies, and tax farms. On a clean administrative map they drew eighty-three departments, roughly equal in size, with uniform administrative and judicial systems. Administration was decentralized and put in the hands of some forty thousand local and departmental councils, elected by their constituents.

The Church The reorganization of the French Church was decreed by the Civil Constitution of the Clergy, promulgated in August 1790. It was one of the most important and fateful acts of the Revolution. The Assembly confiscated the lands of the Church and, to relieve the financial distress of the country, issued notes on the security of the confiscated lands. These notes, or *assignats,* circulated as money and temporarily relieved the financial crisis. Clergymen, henceforth, became paid officials of the state, and priests and bishops were to be elected by property-owning citizens.

The Constitution of 1791, together with the Declaration of the Rights of Man, summed up the principles and politics of the men of 1789. In its emphasis on property rights, its restrictive franchise, and its fiscal policy, the Constitution had a distinctly bourgeois bias. To look upon the documents simply as a product of selfish interest, however, would be to underestimate its achievements. A new class of peasant proprietors had been created. The framework for a society open to talent had been established. Administrative decentralization, it was thought, would overcome the fear of despotism. Equality before the law, if not political equality, had been made a fact. These were impressive and revolutionary achievements. But to succeed and mature, the new order needed peace, social stability, and the cooperation of the king. None of these was forthcoming. Within a year the Constitution of 1791 became a dead letter, and the Revolution had entered a new phase.

The Failure of Constitutional Monarchy

The Constitution of 1791 was most certainly an imperfect instrument. The Civil Constitution of the Clergy, for example, offended the pope. Many bishops and priests refused to accept it, and they found broad support in the country. Schism in the Church became a major factor in the eventual failure of the Assembly to create a stable government. Moreover, the restrictive franchise opened the constitution-makers to the charge that they wanted to substitute a wealthy oligarchy for an aristocracy. Such obvious defects, however, were not alone responsible for the failure of constitutional monarchy. The principal culprit was the monarch himself.

At the head of the government stood a king who was thoroughly discredited. In June 1791, Louis XVI tried to escape from France in order to join the forces of counterrevolution abroad. He very nearly succeeded but was caught near the eastern frontier, at Varennes, and was brought back to Paris. This humiliating episode destroyed what little authority Louis still possessed. He now swore to obey the new constitution; but he was only a figurehead.

At this point the situation was complicated by outside pressures. Louis's fellow monarchs were unhappy over the way in which their royal colleague was being treated. The privileged orders in other countries feared that the leveling principles of the Revolution would spread. The English, many of whom had sympathized with the Revolution while it seemed to be following an English model, began to denounce the radicalism and violence of the French. Edmund Burke, in particular, saw clearly the radical nature of the Revolution. In his *Reflections on the Revolution in France* (1790) he insisted on the importance of tradition in preserving an orderly society and declared that it was folly to abandon time-tested institutions in favor of new ones based on abstract principles. He did not convince radical writers, but he convinced almost everyone in power in England. Hostility to France was an old tradition; Burke gave new reasons for continuing it. And everywhere French refugees spread counterrevolutionary propaganda urging Europe's monarchs to intervene.

The Legislative Assembly, September 1791–September 1792

The Legislative Assembly met in an atmosphere of intrigue, fear, and factional strife. There were two issues on which it was almost impossible to find a solid majority. The first was the position of the king. He could not be trusted, and he would not commit himself to the principle of equality, on which everyone did agree. Was it worth compromising with the king in order to preserve the constitution and the unity of the country? If not, how far should the Assembly go in restraining or in punishing the king?

The second problem, which caused even sharper divisions, was that of defining "equality." Was the emphasis to be on equality before the law, or on equality of opportunity, or on political equality, or on economic equality, or on a mixture of these ideals? Here there was not only no clear majority, but no consistency within groups and even within individuals.

There were no parties in the Assembly, but there were the "clubs," loosely organized associations with affiliates in the provinces. One of the largest and best-organized groups was the Jacobin Club, with 136 members out of the 745 representatives. The Jacobins were republicans and wanted to get rid of the king. But they were also well-to-do bourgeois. They were far from agreement on political and economic equality, or on the pace at which change should take place. They were divided into at least two factions. One faction was led by Brissot de Warville, the ablest politician in the Assembly. The other, composed mainly of Parisians, eventually found a leader in Maximilien Robespierre.

As it turned out, the issue that temporarily united the Assembly was that of declaring war on Austria. Inept diplomacy by European monarchs, even more inept politics in the French royal court, and a very real threat of counterrevolution convinced millions of patriotic Frenchmen that the forces of reaction were about to destroy all that had been gained since 1789 and that war was the only way to save their country and their freedom. The emperor of Austria and the king of Prussia in the Declaration of Pillnitz (August 1791) proclaimed that European monarchs must unite to restore order and monarchy in France. This was largely bluff, but it sounded ominous. Some con-

Anonymous contemporary portrait of Robespierre.

servative ministers thought that a victorious war against Austria would strengthen the king and allow him to end the Revolution. However, Louis XVI and his Austrian queen, Marie Antoinette, apparently hoped for a French defeat that would lead to restoration of royal authority.

External threats and court plots played into the hands of Brissot's republican faction. Brissot believed that a crusade to unseat the monarchs of Europe would rekindle the revolutionary fervor of the French people and rally them around his plan to establish a republic. He was opposed in the Jacobin Club by Robespierre, who feared that a war would strengthen the conservatives and lead to dictatorship. But Brissot proved the stronger, and the powerful Jacobin Club passed a resolution advocating a declaration of war. Brissot took the issue before the Assembly, and in April 1792 all but seven deputies voted for war with Austria.

The First War of the Revolution

The declaration of war transformed the Revolution. With war came the end of the monarchy and the constitution. With it also came terror and dictatorship. France became not simply the home of the Revolution but the exporter of revolutionary ideals. Finally, under the stress and emotions of war, France became a unified nation-state.

The war began badly. The French army lacked leadership and discipline. The government was short of money and hampered by factional disputes. The royal family and their supporters encouraged the enemy. It is not surprising that the Austrians and their allies, the Prussians, were soon able to advance along the road to Paris.

Two things saved the Revolution. The Austrian and Prussian generals, who were at least as incompetent as the French, delayed and divided their forces. And there was a genuine outburst of patriotic enthusiasm in France. It was during this crisis that the *Marseillaise* was composed, a stirring appeal to save the country from tyranny. The French kept on fighting despite their failures. As a result, when the Austro-Prussian army was checked at Valmy, one hundred miles from Paris, in September 1792, its cautious commander decided to call off the invasion. The allies had lost their best chance to crush the Revolution before it gathered strength.

Portrait of Louis XVI during his imprisonment at the time of the Revolution, by Joseph Ducreux.

THE FRENCH REPUBLIC

During these gloomy months, when everything seemed to be going wrong, the radical politicians of Paris gained a commanding position in the government. These Jacobins—Robespierre and Georges-Jacques Danton were the most important—based their power on national guards summoned to protect the capital, on the Parisian crowds, and, from August 10, 1792, on an insurrectionary Paris Commune that replaced the legal municipal government. The poorer classes were suffering from economic depression and political uncertainty, and they were afraid that the Old Regime might be revived. The bourgeois radicals in the Assembly never fully sympathized with the desire of Parisian artisans and workers for economic equality, but they could agree with them on the need for drastic political changes. In August the Jacobins touched off an uprising in Paris that forced the Legislative Assembly to suspend the king from office and to issue a call for a revision of the constitution. A National Convention, elected by universal manhood suffrage, was to determine the new form of the French government. The events of August triggered what is often called the Second French Revolution. This revolution began with the deposition of Louis XVI; it ended in a bloody terror that consumed its own leaders. In many ways it confirmed Edmund Burke's most dire prophecies. And yet the Second French Revolution did not follow inexorably upon the first. War created its own necessities, survival being the most pressing.

The Convention and the Jacobins

The National Convention met in Paris on September 21, 1792, in the wake of a fierce bloodletting earlier in the month — the so-called September massacres. These massacres, which took the lives of some thirteen hundred prisoners in Paris, were part of a pattern of fear, terror, and revolutionary justice that persisted throughout much of the Convention's three-year rule.

The delegates to the Convention were elected by a minority of Frenchmen, despite universal manhood suffrage. Many citizens were repelled by the deposition of the king and the violence of the summer of 1792. Others were intimidated. Some were excluded from the electorate by governmental decree. Thus the most radical elements of the French population had disproportionate strength in the elections. Not surprisingly, many of the delegates were Jacobins.

The Jacobins, however, were divided. The followers of Brissot, now called the Girondists, made up one faction. They dominated the Convention in its early months. In general, the Girondists represented the interests of provincial republicans, and they were bitterly opposed to the Paris Commune. Their foreign policy was aggressive and expansionistic. They issued a manifesto in November 1792 offering France's aid to all revolutionaries throughout Europe. In domestic affairs, the Girondists were relatively moderate — at least when compared with their Parisian enemies. On the prime issue of 1792, the fate of the king, the Girondists urged that Louis XVI be imprisoned for the duration of the war. There was little doubt then — and less now — that Louis was guilty of treason. But the resolution condemning him to death passed only by a single vote. He was guillotined on January 21, 1793. This victory for the so-called Mountain — Robespierre and Danton's faction — was followed by a purge of the Girondists in June 1793. The architects of France's war policy were among the first victims of that policy.

Marie Antoinette, Queen of France. She was the daughter of Empress Maria Theresa of Austria.

The Jacobins and the War

The Girondists fell before their Jacobin opponents in the wake of crushing French defeats by an overwhelming new coalition of European powers. The execution of Louis XVI, France's designs on the Netherlands, and its annexation of Savoy and Nice prompted England, Spain, Portugal, and several lesser states to join Austria and Prussia in the war against France. In the face of

Marie Antoinette on the way to her execution, sketched from life by Jacques Louis David.

such a formidable combination, the French armies suffered a series of reversals. The victor of Valmy, General Charles Dumouriez, was badly defeated in Belgium, and in the spring of 1793, he defected to the enemy.

Now the government, under the direction of a Committee of General Defense (later the Committee of Public Safety), undertook to organize the entire nation for war. It applied conscription on a nationwide scale for the first time in modern European history. It raised huge armies, far larger than those that could be called up by the old-fashioned monarchies against which France was fighting. And it supported those armies by confiscation and heavy taxes. The armies were organized by a military genius, Lazare Carnot.

The monarchies of Europe, which were used to fighting limited wars with limited resources for limited gains, were overcome by a French nation organized for war. They could not afford to arm all their people, and much as they despised the Revolution, they were still not prepared to sacrifice all their resources to put it down. Other problems distracted the crowned heads of Europe. England was seeking colonial conquests, and the eastern powers were still concerned with the Polish problem. So the French recovered from the blows of 1793 and by the late spring of 1794 had broken through into the Low Countries. When the Convention ended its work in 1795, France was stronger and held more territory than it had under Louis XIV at the height of his power.

The Instruments of Jacobin Rule

Military success was achieved only through the intensive and often brutal organization of the French people. The Constituent Assembly's program of administrative decentralization had left France without any effective chain of command linking the National Convention in Paris to the provinces. Moreover, the Convention was an ungainly body, incapable of swift action. Into this void moved the radical Jacobins. In the provinces, Jacobin clubs replaced local governing bodies and through their committees of surveillance controlled public life. At the center, executive power was entrusted to two committees — the Committee of Public Safety and the Committee for General Security. The former wielded almost dictatorial power over France from July 1793 until July 1794. It had twelve members, of whom Robespierre was the most prominent.

The genuine achievement of the Committee of Public Safety, in coping with internal unrest and external war, is often overlooked because of the "Reign of Terror" it imposed on France. The Terror must be put into the context of the problems that confronted Robespierre, Carnot, and their colleagues. From early 1793 there had been a series of internal rebellions against the government. Conservative peasants in the Vendée, a region in western France, had revolted against national conscription and in favor of their priests who opposed the Civil Constitution. Later in the year, the Girondists, who opposed what they thought was excessive centralization, stimulated local uprisings in some large provincial towns. In the heat of war, such rebellions appeared treasonable, and the Terror was used as a political weapon to impose order. Also, during much of the Committee's tenure, Parisian politicians, both to the left and to the right of Robespierre, maneuvered to secure power. Terror, against Danton among others, was a weapon in these internecine conflicts. There was an economic terror directed against war profiteers and hoarders. Finally, there were local terrors, uncontrolled from the center, in which Jacobins and undisciplined representatives of the government took revenge on their enemies. In the end, the Terror gained a momentum of its own, and the list of suspects grew. Among the factors in Robespierre's fall was the fear of the Convention that its remaining members would soon become victims of revolutionary justice.

In all, some forty thousand people were killed by the government and its agents. The largest number of victims were peasants; next came rebellious citizens of provincial towns, and politicians. Some hundreds of thousands of suspects were imprisoned. Even the Committee of Public Safety finally divided over the excesses of the Terror. When military successes restored a measure of stability to France, the National Convention reasserted its authority. Among its first acts was the arrest and execution of Robespierre in July 1794.

Jacobinism and French Society

The militant phase of Jacobinism was relatively short. The Committee of Public Safety ruled for a year, and Robespierre had complete authority for only four months. Thus, beyond the brilliant organization of national defense, the Jacobins made few permanent contributions. Certain of their acts, however, remained of symbolic significance to the French Left. Among these were the guarantees of the right to a public education for all and the right of public welfare for the poor; these guarantees were set forth in an abortive constitution drawn up in 1793. In addition, the Jacobins were responsible for price controls and for the division of confiscated property among the poor. These decrees, however, were not the product of a conscious social philosophy; they were opportunistic acts designed to win over the disaffected crowds in the cities and the landless peasants in the countryside. The Jacobins were radical democrats who believed deeply in political equality; they were not socialists. With their fall in the summer of 1794, the Revolution fell back into the hands of the propertied bourgeoisie. It was this class that in the end gained most from the Revolution.

The Thermidorian Reaction and the Directory, 1795–99

The demise of Robespierre and the Jacobins touched off a wave of reaction against the excesses of the Terror. This "Thermidorian reaction," named after the month in the revolutionary calendar when Robespierre was executed (Thermidor/July), turned against the austerity of Jacobin rule and at times took the form of a "white terror" against the radicals in Paris and the provinces.

In 1795 the Convention finally presented France with a constitution, the third since 1789. It provided for a five-man executive board, the Directory, and a two-house legislature. Even the republican-oriented Convention had been sufficiently sobered by the Terror to abandon its promise of universal suffrage, and the franchise was weighted in favor of the propertied classes. Once in office, the Directory proved both incompetent and corrupt.

The Thermidorian Reaction

In two days after the execution of Robespierre, the whole Commune of Paris, consisting of about sixty persons, were guillotined in less than one hour and a half, in the Place de la Révolution; and though I was standing above a hundred paces from the place of execution, the blood of the victims streamed under my feet. What surprised me was, as each head fell into the basket, the cry of the people was no other than a repetition of *"A bas le Maximum!" which was caused by the privations imposed on the populace by the vigorous exaction of that law which set certain prices upon all sorts of provisions, and which was attributed to Robespierre. The persons who now suffered were all of different trades; and many of them, indeed, had taken advantage of that law, and had abused it, by forcing the farmers and others who supplied the Paris market, to sell at the maximum price, and they retailed at an enormous advance to those who could afford to pay. I did not see Robespierre going to the guillotine; but have been informed that the crowd which attended the wagon in which he passed on that occasion, went so far as to thrust their umbrellas into the wagon against his body. . . . It now became a measure of personal safety, to be able to declare that one had been imprisoned during Robespierre's tyranny. It was dangerous even to appear like a Jacobin, as several persons were murdered in the streets, by *La Jeunesse Parisienne,*† merely because they wore long coats and short hair.**

* "Down with price controls!"

† "The (gilded, aristocratic) Paris youth."

From *English Witnesses of the French Revolution,* ed. by J. M. Thompson (Oxford: Basil Blackwell, 1938), pp. 248–49.

The interior of the Great Pyramid, as depicted in the *Description of Egypt* (1809–26), published by the scholars who accompanied Napoleon on his campaign in Egypt. They explored ancient monuments and provided the first modern survey of Egypt.

It maintained a militantly aggressive foreign policy and allowed the French economy to deteriorate disastrously. A more or less communistic movement led by "Gracchus" Babeuf received some support from the poor, but was easily suppressed. The French poor were still largely artisans and peasants —property owners and not wage-earners. More dangerous was a royalist revival. Elections in 1797 demonstrated such an upsurge in royalist sentiment that the results had to be cancelled. The Directory's single source of strength was the army. With the economy foundering and popular unrest increasing, the Directory was ripe for the coup d'etat that in 1799 brought one of its most successful generals, Napoleon Bonaparte, to power.

NAPOLEON'S RISE TO POWER

Napoleon Bonaparte was born on the island of Corsica in 1769, shortly after the island had been annexed by France. The Bonapartes were members of the minor nobility, and at the age of nine Napoleon was admitted to a military school in France. From that time on, he knew no other life than the army. When most of the aristocratic officer corps left France after the fall of the monarchy, Napoleon stayed on to serve the Republic. He rose to become a brigadier general in 1793 at the age of twenty-four. He helped to reconquer Toulon—one of the towns that rebelled against the Convention in 1793—and he suppressed a royalist riot in 1795. By 1797, when the Directory felt its power slipping, Paul Barras, one of the Directors, realized that Napoleon's support could be valuable. He sought Napoleon's friendship first by introducing the young general to one of his cast-off mistresses, Josephine Beauharnais (whom Napoleon married), and then by giving him command of an army that was preparing for an invasion of Lombardy, a province in northern Italy, under the control of Austria.

The Italian campaign of 1797 removed Austria from the war, gave France control of northern Italy, and established Napoleon's reputation as an outstanding general. After the defeat of the Austrians only England was still at war with France. In 1798 Bonaparte took an army by sea to Egypt, where he hoped to sever England's lifeline to India. He easily defeated the Egyptians, but the English admiral Horatio Nelson sank the French fleet near the mouth of the Nile. Napoleon's army, trapped in Egypt, was soon decimated by disease. In the midst of this crisis, Napoleon heard that the Directory was in danger of falling and that some of the Directors wanted to create a military dictatorship. Leaving his army in Egypt, he made his way back to France to offer his services to the conspirators.

The most important Director was the Abbé Sieyès, and it was with this former leader of the First French Revolution that Napoleon conspired. On November 9, 1799, he used military force to compel the legislators to abolish the Directory and substitute a new government in which a board of three consuls would have almost absolute power. The conspirators asked Napoleon to serve as one of the consuls. They hoped he would provide the personal popularity and military power needed to support a regime that would be dominated by the other two consuls. But when the new constitution was written—at Napoleon's orders—the general emerged as First Consul and virtual dictator. When the French people were invited to endorse the constitution in a plebiscite, they voted overwhelmingly to accept it. To Frenchmen exhausted by years of revolution, war, terror, and economic instability, Napoleon seemed to be the guarantor both of the gains of the Revolution and of order.

NAPOLEON AND DOMESTIC REFORM

Bonaparte was, above all, a soldier, and his fortunes always hinged on military success or failure. Yet his domestic reforms were profound and enduring. If the French Revolution gave the country an ideology that, henceforth, would both inspire and divide Frenchmen, Napoleon gave France many of its characteristic institutions. Better than any eighteenth-century monarch, Bonaparte fulfilled the *philosophes'* dream of an enlightened despot.

Between 1799 and 1801 Napoleon led a series of successful campaigns against the coalition that England, Austria, and Russia had formed to defeat him. He wanted to win a favorable peace so that he could devote himself to consolidating his position in France. Hostilities ended in 1801 and did not break out again on any major scale until 1805. Napoleon used those four years to restore domestic concord and economic stability and to establish a network of administrative institutions that gave coherence and uniformity to his government.

Perhaps Napoleon's most characteristic contribution was the *Code Napoléon.* From the laws left by the several legal systems of the Old Regime and the succession of revolutionary governments, Napoleon's advisers compiled a uniform legal code that is still the basis of French law. The *Code* maintained in theory the revolutionary concept of equality before the law, but it was in fact less egalitarian than the laws of the revolutionary era. It emphasized, for instance, the authority of the government over its citizens, of business corporations over their employees, and of male heads of families over their wives and children. Property rights received particularly strong protection.

Other Napoleonic reforms followed a similar pattern. They upheld in principle the ideals of the Enlightenment and the Revolution but served in practice to strengthen France's new authoritarian state. Napoleon retained the divisions of France into eighty-three departments. He used the departmental system, however, not to foster local responsibility, as had been intended, but to create a highly centralized administration controlled directly by the First Consul through administrators called prefects. He also instituted a nationwide system of public schools that not only educated the young—an ideal of the *philosophes*—but imbued them with an exaggerated patriotism and devotion to their ruler.

In reforming France's finances Napoleon followed the British and American examples by chartering a privately owned national bank as a depository for governmental funds and a source of credit for French businessmen. With government deposits as security, the bank issued paper money as legal tender. Increased currency, a stable franc, and improved credit helped to strengthen France's shaky economy. Napoleon also resolved that perennial problem of the Old Regime—taxation—by developing uniform taxes collected by paid officials.

Although Napoleon was far from devout, he understood better than his republican predecessors that domestic peace could not be achieved until the religious question had been settled. Accordingly he signed the Concordat of 1801 with Pope Pius VII, which regularized the situation created by the Revolution. Although the document recognized that the majority of the French were Roman Catholics, the Catholic Church was not to be the established church in France. Church properties confiscated during the Revolution were not restored. Moreover, the First Consul retained the right to appoint bishops. Through the Concordat of 1801, Napoleon regained the loyalty of French Catholics and at the same time won the gratitude of owners of former church properties.

Although Napoleon brought a form of enlightened despotism to France, he did so at the expense of much of the individual liberty that had been the first principle of the Enlightenment. The legislative institutions created by the Constitution of 1799 were a sham. Political opposition was punished and the press was strictly censored. Napoleon's training was military, and too often his solutions to political and social problems was force. Nevertheless, his government in its early years was

Napoleon, **unfinished painting by David.**

Formal portrait of Napoleon as emperor, by Ingres.

popular. He preserved the property of those who had gained from the Revolution. He satisfied the social ideal of the Revolution by maintaining legal equality, equality in taxation, and careers open to talent. In his administration, he incorporated royalists, constitutionalists, and Jacobins. With such accomplishments, he easily won popular approval when he declared himself First Consul for life in 1802. And two years later, on December 2, 1804, the nation rejoiced when, in the presence of the pope, he crowned himself Emperor of the French.

THE NAPOLEONIC EMPIRE

Napoleon did not create French imperialism; he inherited and had been the agent of the aggressive expansion undertaken by the Convention and the Directory. A satellite republic had already been established in Holland in 1795, and during the campaigns against Austria toward the end of the decade, French armies had extended French power to Switzerland and parts of Italy. This burst of French expansion had come to an end when Napoleon signed separate peace treaties with Austria in 1801, and England in 1802. Large-scale hostilities were resumed only in 1805, and from that time until Napoleon's ultimate defeat ten years later, France was almost constantly at war.

If Napoleon could have avoided war he might have consolidated his European empire. But his ambition and the continuing enmity of England made war almost inevitable. England was determined to keep France from becoming the dominant power in Europe. French control of the Low Countries had already violated a basic rule of English foreign policy—namely, to keep these invasion bases and commercial centers out of the hands of a strong power. The British and their ablest statesman of the period, William Pitt the Younger, furthermore, were convinced that Napoleon was using the peace to ready France for yet another war. Pitt soon was able to persuade other continental states that they must join England to restore the balance of power and resist the spread of French influence in central Europe.

Napoleon was just as ready for war as was England. He felt that his empire could never be secure until England had been defeated. The two states drifted into war in 1803, and other continental powers—Austria, Russia, and finally Prussia—joined England. It was a difficult war for the two major contestants. Napoleon could not gain control of the sea, and without it he could not subdue England. He made his greatest effort in 1805 when he concentrated his army at Boulogne and tried to entice the British fleet out of the Channel to facilitate invasion. But the British were not deceived. While one fleet guarded England, another, under Nelson, caught the French off Cape Trafalgar and annihilated them. Napoleon was never again able to threaten England with invasion.

The English, on the other hand, could not defeat the French on the Continent and were dependent on the armies of their allies. By the fall of 1805, the Russian and Austrian armies assembled for a combined assault. Instead of waiting for the attack, Napoleon marched an army deep into central Europe and took the Austrian and Russian generals by surprise. He defeated the Austrian and Russian forces first at Ulm, and then again in the most spectacular of all his victories, at Austerlitz, in December 1805.

With Austria defeated and Russia in retreat, Napoleon followed up his victory with a complete reorganization of the German states. He helped end the Holy Roman Empire and eliminated most of the small German principalities. Out of these petty states he created a satellite system composed of fourteen larger states that were united in a Confederation of the Rhine, with Napoleon as protector.

Prussia, which had not at first joined the coalition against Napoleon, entered the fray in 1806 and was soundly defeated at Jena in October of that year.

King Frederick William III was forced to accept a humiliating peace and to become an ally of France. The following spring, Emperor Alexander I of Russia again sent an army against Napoleon, only to have it defeated at Friedland in June 1807. In three campaigns in three successive years, Napoleon had defeated the three strongest powers on the Continent and established his position as master of Europe. Russia was too large to occupy, but Napoleon had taught Tsar Alexander the futility of opposition. A few weeks after Friedland, Napoleon and Alexander met near Tilsit in eastern Prussia. Alexander recognized Napoleon's supremacy in the West, and Napoleon agreed not to prevent Alexander from extending Russian influence into the Ottoman-controlled Balkans.

Napoleonic Europe and the Continental System

Napoleon had reached the summit of his power. All of Europe, save England, was under his control. France, Belgium, Germany west of the Rhine, and parts of Italy and Illyria constituted a French Empire ruled directly by Napoleon. Holland, Westphalia (a Napoleonic creation in Germany), and southern Italy were nominally independent kingdoms, over which Napoleon placed three of his brothers as kings. Northern Italy was also a kingdom, with Napoleon himself as king. The Grand Duchy of Warsaw was carved out of Prussia's Polish territories and given to France's ally, the king of Saxony. In 1808, the Bourbon monarch of Spain was overthrown and replaced by Napoleon's brother Joseph.

England alone resisted the tide of French expansion. From 1806 on, Napoleon tried to weaken England by wrecking British trade with the Continent. This so-called Continental System imposed heavy penalties on anyone trading with England and put a heavy strain on the economies of the continental countries. England made matters worse by blockading all countries that subscribed to the French system. The English blockade drove Denmark into a close alliance with France and helped cause the War of 1812 with the United States. But the blockade caused less ill will than Napoleon's decrees. It was impossible for the European economy to function properly without English trade. Smuggling became a highly organized and profitable business, and attempts to enforce French regulations strengthened the opposition to Napoleon everywhere. Most important of all, the blockade led to a quarrel between Napoleon and Alexander of Russia.

Tsar Alexander had not been happy with the results of his alliance with Napoleon. France had gained vast territories; Russia had acquired only Finland and Bessarabia. Napoleon's creation of the Grand Duchy of Warsaw menaced Russia's control of the Polish lands it had seized in the 1790s. But the greatest grievance of the Russians was the Continental System. Russia needed English markets for its grain, and Alexander would not and could not enforce the rules against trade with England. Napoleon, bent on the destruction of England, could not tolerate this breach in his system. He requested Alexander to stop the trade; when Alexander refused, Napoleon prepared to invade Russia.

The Weaknesses of the Napoleonic Empire

When Napoleon undertook his Russian campaign in 1812, his hold on Europe and even on the French had begun to weaken. French expansion had at first been greeted with enthusiasm by many of the inhabitants of the Low Countries, Germany, and Italy. Enlightenment ideas were strong in these regions, and their governments were unpopular. In the northern Netherlands there was opposition to the domination of the House of Orange and the urban oligarchy. In the Austrian Netherlands (Belgium), nationalist feelings had led to a revolt against Austrian rule as early as 1789. Italy was

Napoleonic Europe 1812

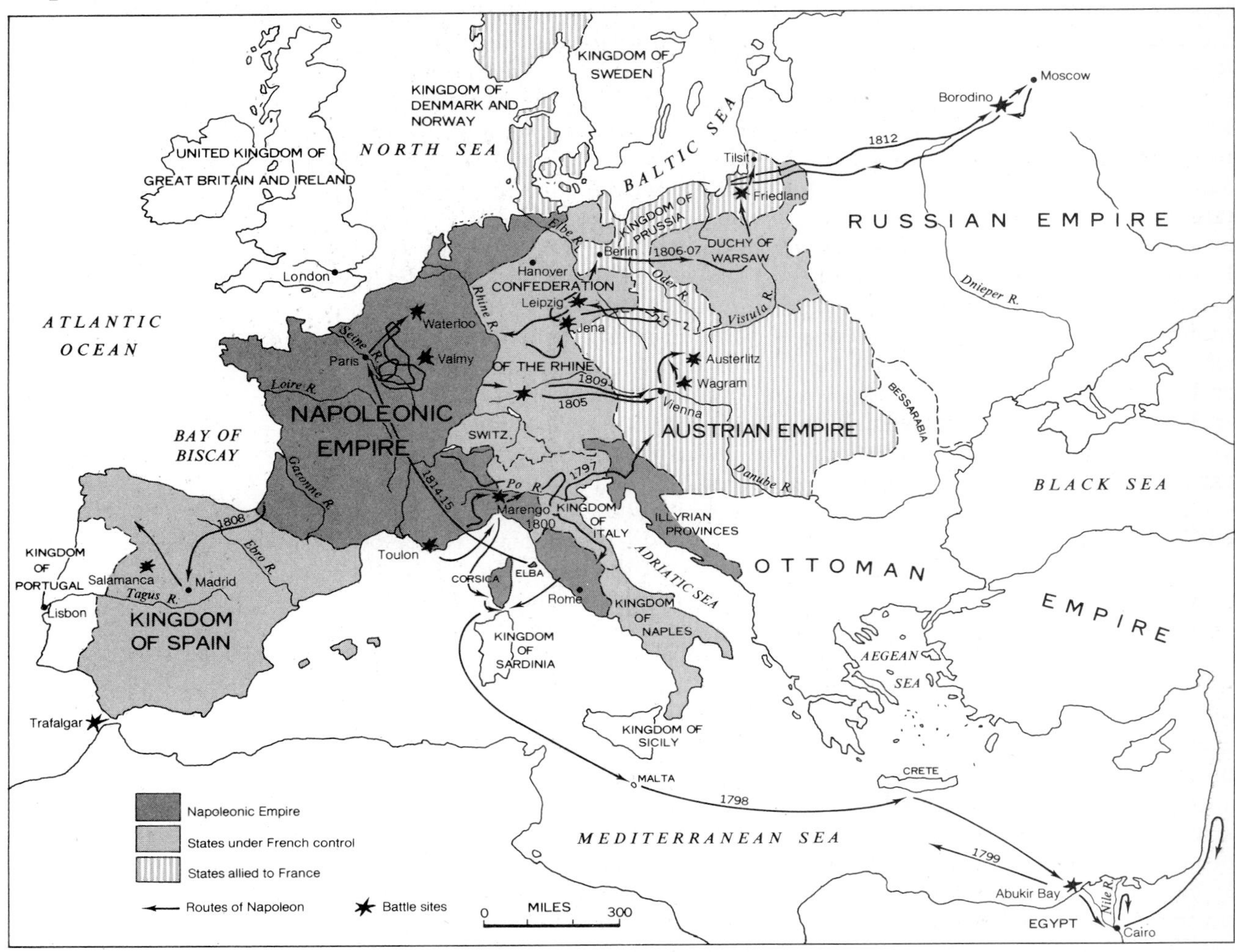

dominated by Spain and Austria, and growing nationalism and spread of the Enlightenment made the ideas of the French Revolution attractive to many Italians. In Germany the writings of the *philosophes* had been eagerly read, and there was general disgust with the archaic structure of the Holy Roman Empire and the stodgy governments of the petty principalities. In short, there had been serious political unrest in much of Europe in the 1780s and 1790s, and the invading French armies had often been hailed as liberators. Napoleon took full advantage of this feeling. He was able to break the archaic political and social structures of many states. Within the Empire, the *Code Napoléon* was established, the privileges of the Church and aristocracies were abolished, and fetters on local industry and commerce were removed. Napoleon saw himself as the "revolution on horseback" and sought to impose a new order on Europe—a new order that was enlightened, rational, and French.

This vision of Napoleon's was, at best, only partially achieved, and even those who had enthusiastically welcomed the invading French armies soon perceived that imperialism was a more important component of Napoleonic rule than was liberation. The Continental System contributed to a general economic crisis that alienated the commercial and industrial interests. High taxes and conscription were imposed on the tributary states. And the

French system was enforced by tight police surveillance. Napoleonic tutelage, even at its most benevolent, appeared incompatible with the libertarian and ·nationalistic ideals of the French Revolution.

Increasingly, Napoleon was beset by the growth of nationalistic feelings and national resistance to his rule. In Germany, Italy, and Spain, national awakening was intimately linked to opposition to French hegemony. This opposition took different forms. In Italy and Germany cultural movements gained momentum that emphasized the common history, language, and literature shared by these fragmented peoples. In Spain resistance was expressed more violently when rebellions broke out in 1808 against the regime of Joseph Bonaparte. There Napoleon first confronted guerrilla warfare and encountered serious failure. A Spanish victory at Baylen in 1808 was the initial break in the emperor's record of invincibility. By 1813, the Spanish rebels, with the help of an English army under Wellington, had driven the French from Madrid and had organized a constitutional government that controlled more than half the country.

The appearance of a well-organized English army on the Continent was one indication that the balance of power in Europe was shifting against Napoleon. There were other signs, the most important of which was the recovery of France's nominal ally and potential enemy, Prussia. After the humiliating defeat at Jena, the process of reconstructing the kingdom was begun. Under Generals Gneisenau and Scharnhorst, the Prussian army was modernized and universal military training was introduced. To revitalize the country, another reformer, Baron vom Stein, persuaded the king to abolish serfdom and to grant a large measure of liberty to Prussian municipalities. Stein's social reforms were limited in their effects, but the military reforms allowed Prussia to play a significant role in the final defeat of Napoleon.

As his enemies were strengthening themselves and challenging the French monopoly of force, Napoleon began to lose his grip at home. Economic domination of Europe, the goal of the Continental System, failed to materialize, and France, like the rest of the Continent, suffered from the economic crisis that marked the last years of Napoleon's rule. Internally, the regime grew more repressive, and Napoleon became increasingly intolerant of criticism. After his divorce from Josephine

Retreat of Napoleon's army across the Beresina River (1812), by an anonymous painter.

Arthur Wellesley, the duke of Wellington, by Goya.

and his marriage to Marie Louise of Austria, Napoleon more and more took on the airs of an Old Regime monarch. Those Frenchmen who had provided him with his magnificent and spirited army were now exhausted by the burdens of empire.

The Invasion of Russia and the Fall of Napoleon

In June 1812 Napoleon marched into Russia with six hundred thousand men, the largest army ever assembled up to then. Most had been recruited in the German states or in other dependencies. Napoleon expected to deliver a fast and decisive blow, but the Russians, greatly outnumbered, did not give battle. Instead they retreated, drawing Napoleon behind them. After one costly but inconclusive engagement at Borodino, Napoleon occupied Moscow in September and waited for Alexander to offer peace terms. But no message came.

After five weeks Napoleon realized that he could not keep so large a force in Russia through the winter, and in October he began the long march westward. Since the land through which he passed had already been devastated, he lost thousands of men to disease and starvation. When the cold came, the weakened soldiers were no match for the elements. When Napoleon reached the German border in December, he could not muster one hundred thousand men. If Austria or Prussia had chosen to launch an attack at this time, the war would have been ended. But the allies did not know the extent of Napoleon's disaster.

Once in German territory, Napoleon hurried to Paris and organized a new army that he marched eastward in the spring of 1813. But defeat had deflated Napoleon's glory, and he was badly beaten by the combined armies of Austria, Prussia, and Russia at Leipzig in October. Napoleon lost two-fifths of his men and retreated back across the Rhine. Meanwhile, Britain's general Wellington defeated another French army in Spain and crossed the border into southern France. On March 31, 1814, the allied armies entered Paris, and one week later Napoleon abdicated. After some debate, the allies restored the Bourbons to the throne of France and then called a conference in Vienna to settle the fate of the rest of Europe.

Napoleon was exiled to the island of Elba, off the Italian coast. But he still had one battle to fight. In March 1815 he escaped and landed in the south of France. The army proved loyal to the deposed leader, and Napoleon was soon in control of France once again. But the allies were prepared. Napoleon was conclusively defeated at Waterloo on June 18, 1815, and three days later he abdicated for the second time. The allies now exiled him to St. Helena, a remote island off the Atlantic coast of Africa. The era of the Revolution and Napoleon had ended.

Napoleon I: A Self-Assessment

1817

In spite of all the libels, I have no fear whatever about my fame. Posterity will do me justice. The truth will be known; and the good I have done will be compared with the faults I have committed. I am not uneasy as to the result. Had I succeeded, I would have died with the reputation of the greatest man that ever existed. As it is, although I have failed, I shall be considered as an extraordinary man: my elevation was unparalleled, because unaccompanied by crime. I have fought fifty pitched battles, almost all of which I have won. I have framed and carried into effect a code of laws that will bear my name to the most distant posterity. I raised myself from nothing to be the most powerful monarch in the world. Europe was at my feet. I have always been of opinion that the sovereignty lay in the people. In fact, the imperial government was a kind of republic. Called to the head of it by the voice of the nation, my maxim was, *la carrière est ouverte aux talents* without distinction of birth or fortune. . . .

From *The Corsican,* ed. by R. M. Johnston (Boston: Houghton Mifflin, 1910), p. 492.

The Legacy of an Era

The era had ended, but it could not be effaced. The allies could restore a Bourbon to the throne of France, but the new king, Louis XVIII, could not restore the Old Regime. He had to accept both the revolutionary principle of equality under the law and the revolutionary land settlement. He also had to grant a constitution to his people. Throughout Europe the great ideas of the Revolution — liberty, equality, and nationalism — lived on, and with them the dangerous concept of revolution as a means of attaining social and political goals. These ideas were only partially recognized in some countries and totally suppressed in others; but they persisted everywhere — smoldering coals that were to burst into flame again and again.

The political balance of power in Europe had been permanently altered. No one could restore the petty states of Germany. No one could ignore the claims of Russia to have, for the first time, a voice in the affairs of western Europe. No one could fail to recognize the tremendous strides that England had made in industry and commerce during the wars. Conversely, for the first time in two centuries, France was no longer the richest and strongest European state. These were some of the new political facts with which the diplomats at Vienna had to deal.

Suggestions for Further Reading

The best general work on the French Revolution is G. Lefebvre's *The French Revolution* (1962–64). C. Brinton, *A Decade of Revolution, 1789–1799* (1934), is still a fine introductory summary. See also A. Soboul, *The French Revolution: 1787–1799* (1975), and M. J. Sydenham, *The French Revolution* (1966). R. R. Palmer, *The World of the French Revolution* (1971), places the revolution in its broader European perspective. The same is done in N. Hampson, *The First European Revolution: 1776–1815* (1969), and, with a neo-Marxian approach, in E. J. Hobsbawm, *The Age of Revolution: 1789–1848* (1962).

An excellent brief introduction to the social history of the revolution is N. Hampson, *Social History of the French Revolution* (1962). A. Cobban, *The Social Interpretation of the French Revolution* (1964), is an important revisionary statement. On the role of the masses, see G. F. E. Rudé, *The Crowd in the French Revolution* (1959). On various phases of the revolution, the following stand out: J. M. Thompson, *Robespierre and the French Revolution* (1953); R. R. Palmer, *Twelve Who Ruled* (1941); A. Soboul, *The Parisian Sans-Culottes and the French Revolution* (1964); Ch. Tilly, *The Vendée* (1964); M. Lyons, *France under the Directory* (1975); and A. Forrest, *The French Revolution and the Poor* (1981).

On Napoleon, G. Bruun, *Europe and the French Imperium, 1799–1814* (1938), is still a good introduction. The best treatment is the two volumes by G. Lefebvre, *Napoléon* (trans. 1969). P. Geyl, *Napoleon: For and Against* (1949), is an excellent guide to interpretations of the period. On Napoleon's domestic policy, see R. Holtman, *The Napoleonic Revolution* (1967), and on his foreign policy, S. T. Ross, *European Diplomatic History 1789–1815: France Against Europe* (1969). Napoleon's relations with the two peripheral powers of Europe are treated in C. Oman, *Britain Against Napoleon* (1944), and in A. Palmer, *Napoleon in Russia* (1967). The best recent treatment of Napoleon's military career is D. Chandler, *The Campaigns of Napoleon* (1966).

	1815				1870	
SOUTHWEST ASIA AND AFRICA	**1818–28** King Shaka, apex of Zulu kingdom	**1836** Boers' Great Trek begins		**1860** French expansion in West Africa **1869** Suez Canal opens		
EUROPE	**1815** Congress of Vienna **1815–83** Karl Marx **1825** Decembrist Revolt, Russia **1825** First commercial railroad	**1829** Treaty of Adrianople **1830** France's "July Monarchy" **1832** Britain's Great Reform Bill **1848** *Communist Manifesto*	**1848–49** Europe in Revolt **1848–61** Unification of Italy **1848–70** Napolean III **1851** Crystal Palace Exhibition, London	**1859** Darwin, *Origin of Species* **1854–56** Crimean War **1861–71** Unification of Germany **1867** Austro-Hungarian *Ausgleich*	**1870–71** Franco-Prussian War **1876** First internal combustion engine **1878** Congress of Berlin	**1882** Triple Alliance **1894** Russo-French Alliance
SOUTH AND SOUTHEAST ASIA	**1819** British found Singapore		**1857–58** Indian Mutiny **1859** French seize Saigon			
EAST ASIA	**1825–30** Java War **1839–42** Opium War		**1850–64** Taiping Rebellion **1854** Perry opens US trade with Japan **1868** Meiji Restoration, Japan			**1893–1976** Mao Zedong **1894–95** Sino-Japanese War
THE AMERICAS AND PACIFIC	**1823** Monroe Doctrine	**1835–40** Alexis de Tocqueville, *Democracy in America* **1840** Britain annexes New Zealand **1846–48** Mexican War	**1849** Gold discovered in California	**1861–65** American Civil War **1867** Russia sells Alaska to US **1867** British North America Act	**1869** Opening of Transcontinental railroad	

***Empire State Express* No. 999, *ca.* 1890.**

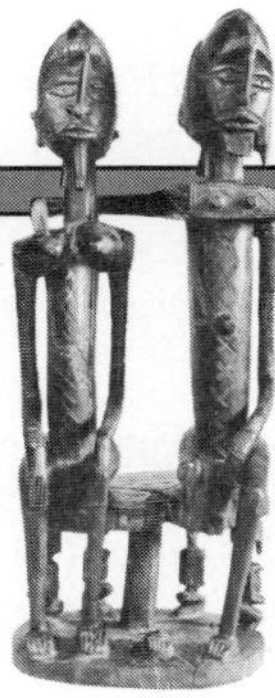

Wood sculpture, Dogon tribe, Mali, West Africa.

Eiffel Tower Paris, 1889.

British suffragette, *ca.* 1910.

Commodore Matthew Perry, a Japanese view, 1853.

Private Edwin Francis Jennison, Confederate Army.

1914	
1886 Gold discovered in Southern Africa **1889** Rhodesia colonized **1899–1902** Boer War **1910** Union of South Africa formed	
1894–1905 Dreyfus Affair **1905** Russian Revolution begins **1905** Einstein's Theory of Relativity **1907** Triple Entente **1912–13** Balkan Wars	
1885 Indian National Congress founded **1906** Muslim League founded	
1900 Boxer Rebellion **1904–05** Russo-Japanese War **1911** Chinese Revolution **1912–49** Chinese Republic	
1889 First Pan-American Conference **1898** Spanish-American War **1910** Mexican Revolution begins	**1914** Panama Canal opens

The Prince of Wales in Bangalore, India, *ca.* 1900.

Gold prospector, California, *ca.* 1850.

33 The Trials of the Vienna System, 1815–50

The unrest that had prevailed in Europe since the French Revolution did not end with the defeat of Napoleon. Many of Europe's troubles stemmed from the long and costly series of recent wars. But there were other causes of unrest. Politically, Europe continued to feel the effects of the issues first raised by the French Revolution—notably liberalism and nationalism. Intellectually, the years after Napoleon saw the flowering of the Age of Romanticism, with its protest against the rationalism of the Enlightenment. Economically and socially, the Continent in the first half of the nineteenth century began to feel in earnest the effects of the "Industrial Revolution," which had already begun in England in the eighteenth century (see pp. 715–35). This chapter concentrates on political and intellectual developments. But we must keep in mind that political tension was often the manifestation of underlying economic and social unrest. The rapid increase of Europe's population alone—from 192 million in 1800 to 272 million in 1850—could not help but have unsettling economic and political effects. And the fact that more and more people now lived in cities did much to change the everyday lives of many Europeans.

Europe's search for stability after 1815 was marked by a contest between the forces of the past and the forces of the future. For a while it seemed as though the traditional agencies of power—the monarchs, the aristocracy, and the Church—might once again resume full control. But potent new forces were ready to oppose this relapse into the past. With the quickening of industrialization, there was now not only a growing middle class, but a wholly new class, the urban workers. Each class came to have its own political and economic philosophy—liberalism and socialism, respectively—which stood opposed to each other as well as to the traditional conservatism of the old order. It was inevitable that these rival classes and ideologies should clash. The resulting revolutions did not end until 1850. By that time the forces of the past were still not defeated, but they were everywhere on the defensive.

Economic growth and ideological unrest were not the only causes of revolution in the early nineteenth century. There was also the force of nationalism, which made itself increasingly felt among Europeans everywhere. Nationalism as an awareness of belonging to a particular nationality was nothing new. What was new was the intensity that this awareness now assumed. There were still signs of eighteenth-century cosmopolitanism, especially among the aristocracy. But for the mass

Europe in 1815

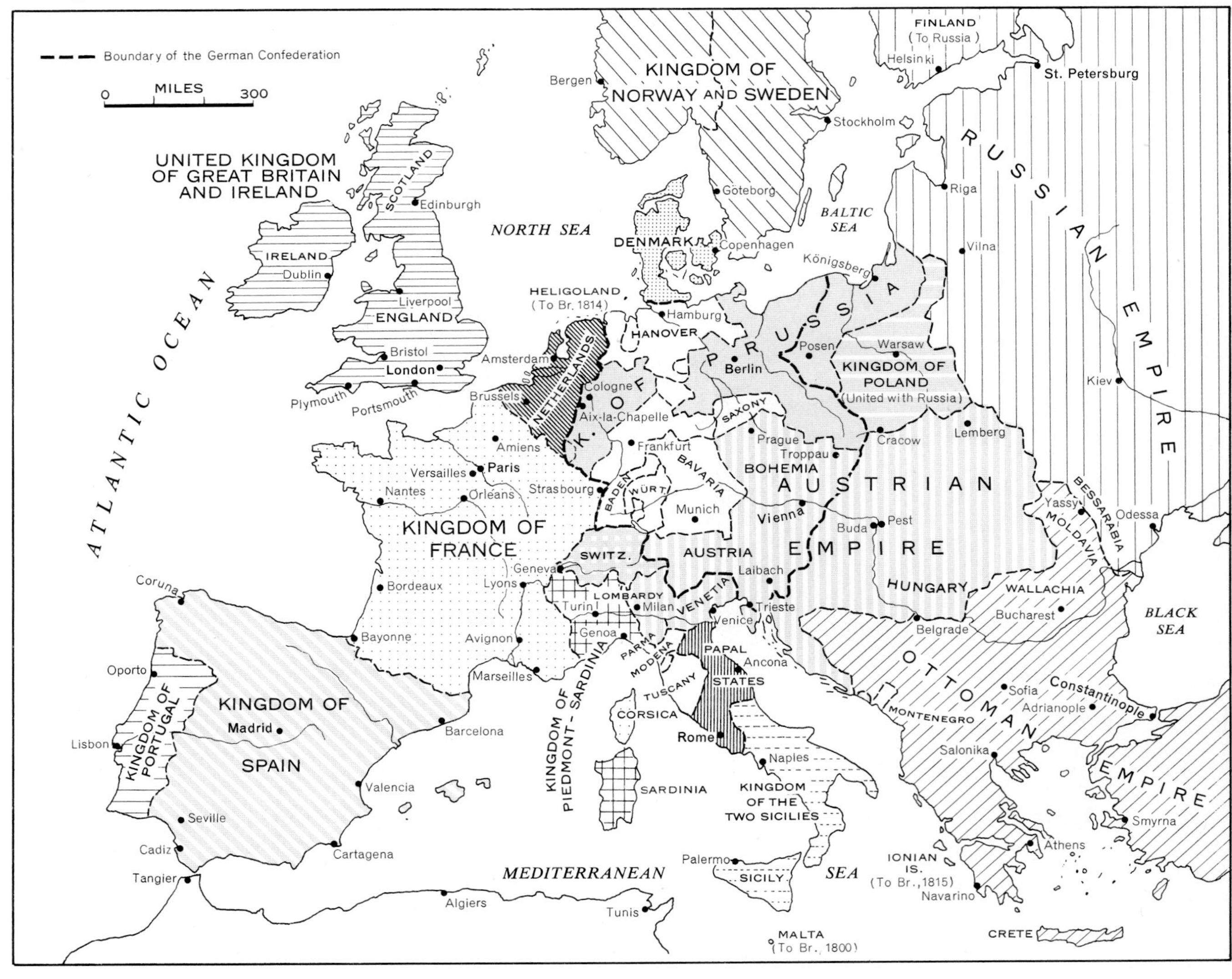

of the people, nationalism became their most ardent emotion, and national unification or independence their most cherished aim.

Generally speaking, the early nineteenth century was a major phase in the slow change from an essentially hierarchical and agrarian order into an increasingly democratic and industrial society. The problem faced by leaders everywhere was to give political expression to the economic and social changes resulting from the industrial transformation of Europe. In trying to do this, they hoped to bring stability to their deeply unsettled world.

The Congress of Vienna, after a painting by Isabey. Prince Metternich stands at left introducing the Duke of Wellington. Talleyrand is seated with his arm on the table at right.

THE RESTORATION OF THE OLD ORDER

The first task facing the allies after defeating Napoleon was to bring order to a continent that had been deeply disrupted by two decades of war. Europe's statesmen in the main tried to restore conditions as they had been before the French Revolution. In domestic affairs they adopted the principle of "legitimacy"—that is, they brought back the dynasties that had been ousted by revolution or war. In international affairs they tried to reconstruct the balance of power that had been upset by France. In retrospect this preoccupation with the past may seem shortsighted. But history shows that most peace settlements are made with a view to the past rather than a vision of the future.

The Congress of Vienna

Peace conferences are usually dominated by a few leading statesmen. In 1814 and 1815 the decisive figures were Austria's chancellor, Prince Metternich; Britain's foreign secretary, Lord Castlereagh; Tsar Alexander I of Russia; the Prussian King Frederick William III; and France's foreign minister, Prince Talleyrand. The fact that the vanquished French were able to make their voice heard shows the moderation and common sense of the victors.

The final peace with France was concluded at Paris in November 1815. France was the first to experience the principle of legitimacy. The new French king, Louis XVIII, was the brother of Louis XVI and the uncle of the deceased dauphin, Louis XVII. Considering the many hardships the French had inflicted on Europe, the peace settlement was remarkably lenient. France was reduced to its frontiers of 1790; it had to pay an indemnity; and it had to submit to an allied army of occupation.

The settlement with France, however, was only part of the work of restoration. A far more difficult task was to reorder the affairs of the rest of Europe. This was done at a separate conference in Vienna. The Congress of Vienna aroused high hopes among those Europeans who desired a stronger voice in government or who, like the Germans and the Italians, longed for national unification. Their hopes were disappointed. The statesmen at Vienna had been deeply disturbed by the excesses of revolution and war and thus were firmly opposed to the forces of liberalism and nationalism in whose name these excesses had been committed.

Considering the conflicting aims of the powers, it is surprising how much was actually achieved. Following the principle of legitimacy, the Bourbons were restored in Spain and Naples, and

Prince Metternich, by Sir Thomas Lawrence.

other rulers were returned to their thrones in the smaller Italian states. Yet legitimacy was frequently ignored, as in the case of republics like Genoa and Venice, neither of which regained its independence. To maintain the balance of power and to keep France from avenging its defeat, the countries along its eastern frontier were either enlarged or otherwise strengthened. The Republic of Holland was joined with the former Austrian Netherlands (Belgium). In place of the defunct Holy Roman Empire, a loosely joined federation of thirty-nine states was set up in Germany. To provide an effective barrier to French expansion in the southeast, Switzerland was reestablished as an independent confederation and was declared perpetually neutral. The containment of France was completed by strengthening the Kingdom of Piedmont in northern Italy. In compensation for relinquishing Belgium, Austria received the Italian provinces of Lombardy and Venetia as well as the Illyrian provinces and the Tyrol (some of which Austria had ruled before 1789). This made Austria the dominant power in Italy and the leading obstacle to Italian unification.

Most of these changes caused no major difficulties, because the great powers saw eye to eye on them. One issue, however, caused much disagreement and at one point threatened to plunge the powers into war: Poland. A favorite scheme of Tsar Alexander I was to pose as the "liberator" of Poland by setting up a Polish kingdom under Russian tutelage. The other powers objected to this: Prussia and Austria because they expected the return of those parts of Poland they had held before Napoleon, and England because it had no desire to see Russia grow too powerful. To gain his end, Alexander promised the Prussians compensations elsewhere if they would support his Polish scheme. The result was a deadlock at Vienna, with England and Austria facing Russia and Prussia. An armed confrontation was avoided when Talleyrand threw the weight of France behind England and Austria. The compromise that was reached was more advantageous to Prussia than to Russia. Russia received less of Poland than hoped for, while Prussia got compensations in northern and western Germany, making it a powerful contender for leadership within the newly formed German Confederation.

While most of the decisions reached at Vienna were on specific territorial issues, the Congress also addressed itself to some general questions. Among them was the slave trade. There had been agitation against this scandalous practice since the late eighteenth century, and it had been outlawed by Britain in 1808. At Vienna, Lord Castlereagh succeeded in having the traffic in slaves condemned, but France, Spain, and Portugal did not comply until 1820. Even then it was only the trade, not slavery itself, that was outlawed. The British Empire abolished slavery in 1833, the United States only a generation later.

The Congress of Vienna had accomplished a great deal, even though it had not lived up to everyone's hopes. In particular, the Vienna settlement ignored the stirrings of nationalism and the hopes for more popular government that the French Revolution had awakened. But more widespread than the middle-class dreams of nationalism and liberalism in 1815 was the hope for peace and order. There was no war among the great powers for forty years, and no war of worldwide dimensions for a whole century.

The "Holy Alliance" and the "Concert of Europe"

An indication of how sincerely the framers of the Vienna settlement sought peace may be seen in the arrangements they made to maintain it. The most famous of these was the "Holy Alliance" of Alexander I. The tsar had long looked upon himself as a kind of world savior. In this role he now proposed that his fellow monarchs should conduct their relations with one another and with their subjects in a spirit of Christian love. To humor the tsar, most European rulers signed his "Holy Alliance"; but it never achieved any significance, except as a symbol of reaction.

Of far greater importance was the Quadruple Alliance signed by England, Austria, Russia, and Prussia at the time of the final treaty with France in 1815. Its primary purpose was to prevent any future French violation of the peace settlement. But the powers also agreed to hold periodic conferences (ultimately to include France as well) to discuss matters of general European concern. This was an important innovation. For the first time statesmen seemed to realize that peace might be preserved by dealing with crises before they led to general war. The "Concert of Europe" was thus born.

As it turned out, however, this congress system was not a great success. At the very first meeting, at Aix-la-Chapelle in 1818, it became clear that the powers did not really agree on the fundamental purpose of their system of international government. To Castlereagh, the Quadruple Alliance was mainly an instrument for containing France and for maintaining international peace. To Alexander I, on the other hand, the Alliance seemed a means of maintaining domestic peace as well. This difference was clearly revealed when Alexander proposed a new alliance that would guarantee not only the territorial status quo but also the existing form of government in every European country. This latter proposal met with determined opposition from Castlereagh, who did not want to extend the alliance "to include all objects, present and future."

The problem of whether to aid legitimate governments against revolution became acute shortly after Aix-la-Chapelle when a whole series of revolutions suddenly broke out in southern Europe. Here was a welcome opportunity for Alexander to repeat his plea for joint intervention. To underline his determination not to meddle in the affairs of other nations, Castlereagh refused to attend the Congress of Troppau (1820), at which such intervention was to be discussed.

With England absent, the other powers were able to adopt the "Troppau Protocol," which promised military aid to any government threatened by revolution. The effects of the Protocol became clear in 1821. In that year a third congress, at Laibach, commissioned Austria to send its forces into the Italian peninsula to put down the insurrections there. Britain protested, but in vain. Similar action was taken at the next and last congress, which met at Verona in 1822. Again the continental powers, against England's objections, sanctioned the dispatch of a French force to put down a Spanish revolution in 1823.

Diplomacy by congress, so promising at first, had thus failed. It had failed because of a fundamental divergence among the victors over the issue of political change, with Britain opposing and the rest of the powers supporting intervention in the domestic affairs of other states to prevent liberal* or national uprisings. There were other efforts to hold congresses, but England refused to attend.

A Wave of Reaction

The revolutions of the early 1820s were caused by the wave of reaction that followed the peace settlements of 1815. Wherever a legitimate monarch returned, he attempted to restore conditions exactly as they had been before he was ousted. In Spain and Naples the returning Bourbons abolished the liberal reforms that had been granted in 1812. In the Papal States, Pope Pius VII abolished French legal reforms, reestablished the Jesuits, revived the Inquisition, and put the Jews back into ghettos. In Piedmont, Victor Emmanuel I had the French botanical gardens torn up and the French furniture

* The term "liberal," as shown in the next chapter, has a variety of meanings. It is used here in the general sense of advocating political and economic reforms, primarily to benefit the middle class.

thrown out of the windows of his palace.

Elsewhere in Italy and over much of Europe the picture was the same. Both Frederick William III of Prussia and Francis I of Austria favored rigorous measures of repression in their respective countries. By tradition as well as actual power, Austria dominated the diet of the new German Confederation at Frankfurt. Here it was Metternich who used his influence to suppress liberal or national stirrings wherever they appeared in Germany. As protests against this repressive "Metternich System" grew more vociferous, Austria and Prussia in 1819 pressured the Frankfurt Diet into adopting the so-called Carlsbad Decrees, which strictly limited intellectual freedom, especially at the universities.

There were very few exceptions to this general rule of reaction. It was felt even in England, whose foreign policy at least was more enlightened than that of the continental powers. Much unrest in postwar Britain was chiefly due to economic causes. Overproduction during the war caused prices to fall, which in turn led to lower wages and growing unemployment. To remedy Britain's ills, a number of middle-class radicals advocated that the government be liberalized through parliamentary reform. But any agitation for reform was met by stern repression. In 1819, after the so-called Peterloo Massacre—when the constabulary of Manchester charged into a peaceful public meeting on parliamentary reform, causing many casualties—Parliament passed the repressive "Six Acts," which was England's version of the Carlsbad Decrees.

THE AGE OF ROMANTICISM

Before considering the several waves of revolution that swept over Europe between 1820 and 1850, we must examine the intellectual climate in which these events took place. Much of the political turmoil of the generation after Napoleon had its counterpart and its cause in the spiritual ferment associated with the Age of Romanticism.

The Main Characteristics of Romanticism

The term *Romanticism* defies clear definition. It differed not only from country to country but from Romanticist to Romanticist. It inspired reactionaries as well as revolutionaries. It made conservatives look longingly to the past and liberals look hopefully to the future. It meant escapism for some and a call to action for others. But with all these contradictions, most Romanticists shared certain characteristics. Most prominent among these was their protest against the rationalism of the eighteenth century. The Enlightenment, with its emphasis on the rational nature of man and the rational order of the universe, had ignored irrational forces. We have already seen some earlier reactions to this narrow rationalism. The French Revolution and the age of Napoleon had given further impetus to this protest. Reason, it seemed, was not the solution to man's problems that the *philosophes* had promised it to be. If reason had failed, what was there to turn to but its opposite—faith or intuition? The typical Romantic followed his heart rather than his head. He was an individualist. The Enlightenment had spoken of man as though he were the same everywhere. The Romanticist stressed differences among men and felt that each should be a law unto himself. Much of Romantic writing was devoted to the strong personality, the hero, both in history and in fiction. One manifestation of Romanticism's interest in the individual was the growing vogue of autobiographies. One of the most revealing of these was Rousseau's famous *Confessions.* Rousseau also regarded education as a means of realizing a person's individuality. The Enlightenment, with its belief in the essential sameness of human minds, had been interested in formal rather than individualized education. Rousseau held that children should be left to de-

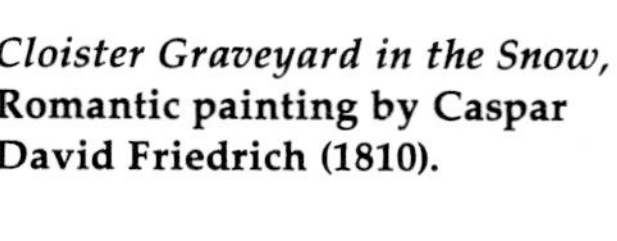

Cloister Graveyard in the Snow, **Romantic painting by Caspar David Friedrich (1810).**

velop their own abilities and potentialities.

While many Romanticists took a lively interest in the world about them, others used their imagination as a means of escape. To the eighteenth-century *philosophe* the world had appeared as a well-ordered mechanism; to the Romanticist, on the other hand, nature was a mysterious organism, whose moods mirrored his innermost feelings. The Enlightenment had liked landscapes that showed the civilizing hand of man; Romanticism, by contrast, preferred its nature wild or dreamlike, as in the paintings of Constable and Turner in England or Caspar David Friedrich in Germany.

This Romantic love of the unusual or unreal in nature was frankly escapist. As factories began to encroach on their surrounding countryside, the Romanticists longed to return to an unspoiled and simple life. They extolled the virtues of country folk, whose customs, tales, and songs they hoped to preserve. The escapism of the Romanticists took various forms. Some Romantic writers let their imagination roam in faraway, exotic places; others preferred to dwell in the realm of the supernatural. Still others escaped into the realm of religious emotion.

Romanticism and Religion

The close relationship between Romanticism and religion, especially Catholicism, is obvious, since both stressed the irrational side of man. The mystery of Catholic theology and the splendor of its ritual provided just the kind of emotional experience the Romanticist craved. As a result, many Romanticists turned to Catholicism, and the Catholic Church, which had been on the defensive since the French Revolution, was able to reassert itself. In 1814, the Jesuit Order was officially restored. In 1816, divorce in France was once again abolished. In Spain and parts of Italy, the Inquisition returned. And almost everywhere on the Continent, education once again became a monopoly of the clergy.

Veneration of the Past

The revival of religious interest was closely allied to the general Romantic veneration for the past. The Enlightenment had derived much of its inspiration from the ancient Greeks and Romans, whose civilizations had appeared both reasonable and attractive. The period from about 400 to 1300 A.D. had been merely "Dark Ages" of ignorance and superstition. The Romanticists now turned to these hitherto neglected centuries attracted by the glamor and grandeur that had survived in medieval castles and Gothic cathedrals.

The Romantic interest in the Middle Ages, by arousing an interest in the past, also awakened a general interest in the study of history. To the Romanticist, the world was an organism that had grown slowly, changed constantly, and was still growing and changing. In an effort to retrace this gradual change, historians in the early nineteenth century developed a careful method of inquiry, using historical sources — documents and other remains — to gain a truer understanding of the past. Modern historical scholarship originated in the Age of Romanticism.

Nationalism and Conservatism

One of the things a study of the past teaches us is that mankind has gradually come to be divided into separate groups, defined by geographic area, language, and historic experience. In time these elements together create a common "national consciousness." Some such feeling had existed in England, France, and even Germany since medieval or early modern times. To transform this national consciousness into nationalism, however, something more was needed — a sense of being not only different from, but superior to, other national groups. The first modern manifestations of nationalism may be seen in the French Revolution and the Napoleonic wars. With its appeal to the emotions, this new nationalism fitted quite naturally into the climate of Romanticism. To the Romanticist, nationalism, like religion, provided something in which he could believe, and for which he could sacrifice himself.

Nationalism in the early nineteenth century was a revolutionary creed. Since it aimed at the liberation of peoples or their unification into a common state, it posed a threat to the established order. In defense of that order, a new political philosophy had already appeared during the French Revolution, the philosophy of conservatism. Its leading proponent was Edmund Burke. We have seen how Burke, in his *Reflections on the Revolution in France,* had warned against the ultimate consequences of that upheaval. He had attacked the revolutionaries for their eighteenth-century belief that man was innately good and endowed with certain natural rights. Far from having any natural rights, man, according to Burke, merely inherited the rights and duties that existed within his society. Since these rights and duties had developed through the ages, they constituted an inheritance that no single generation had the right to destroy. Burke also opposed the eighteenth-century idea that government was the result of a contract among its citizens. Instead, he held that the state was an organism, a mystic community, to which the individual must submit.

Burke's conservatism, with its veneration for the past, its organic view of society, and its prediction of many of the dire consequences of the French Revolution, appealed to the generation

What is Nationalism?

Nationalities are the products of the living forces of history and [are] therefore fluctuating and never rigid. They are groups of the utmost complexity and defy exact definition. Most of them possess certain objective factors distinguishing them from other nationalities, like common descent, language, territory, political entity, customs and traditions, or religion. But it is clear that none of these factors is essential to the existence or definition of nationality. Thus the people of the United States do not claim common descent to form a nationality, and the people of Switzerland speak three or four languages and yet form one well-defined nationality. Although objective factors are of great importance for the formation of nationalities, the most essential element is a living and active corporate will. It is this will which we call nationalism, a state of mind inspiring the large majority of a people and claiming to inspire all its members. It asserts that the nation state is the ideal and the only legitimate form of political organization and that the nationality is the source of all cultural creative energy and of economic well-being.

From Hans Kohn, *Nationalism: Its Meaning and History* (Princeton: Van Nostrand, 1955), pp. 9–10.

after 1815. Like nationalism, conservatism greatly attracted the Romanticists, and Burke found ardent adherents and imitators on the Continent. Initially, conservatism and nationalism often conflicted. Nationalism, to achieve its ends, advocated revolution, which conservatives abhorred. Conservatism, on the other hand, often was indistinguishable from reaction, which opposed change of any kind. In the course of time, however, nationalism, once it had reached its goals, tended to become conservative in order to defend its gains.

There was one point, moreover, on which conservatives and nationalists agreed from the beginning, and that was their admiration of the state as the highest social organism. The leading advocate of the supreme importance of the state was the German philosopher Georg Wilhelm Friedrich Hegel (1770–1831). Like the conservatives, Hegel viewed the state as an organism that had evolved historically. Only in submission to a powerful state, Hegel held, could the individual achieve his true freedom. To be strong, a state must be unified, preferably under the authority of a monarch. Each state, according to Hegel, had its own particular spirit, and by developing that spirit it contributed to the World-Spirit. "The State," Hegel wrote, "is the Divine Idea as it exists on earth." As such it is not bound by the usual laws of morality; its only judge is history. The course of history had evolved in three stages: the Oriental, in which only a despot was free; the Greek and the Roman, in which a few were free; and finally the Germanic, in which all would be free. It was this stress on the unique position of Germany and of Prussia that endeared Hegel to German nationalists.

The Impact of Romanticism

Romanticism, as this brief synopsis shows, was a bundle of contradictions. It helps us understand the conservatives who made the Vienna settlement, as well as the liberals who tried to overthrow it. It was a movement affecting all aspects of human life and thought. It was particularly strong in the arts, not only in literature but also in painting and music. The influence of Romanticism was deep and widespread. All the nations of Europe contributed to it, and it also was a vital force in the United States. The Romantic protest, or at least the Romantic attitude, did not, of course, end with the Romantic era. Its influence is felt to the present day.

Romanticism has been criticized as a rebellion against reason and as a surrender to the murky passions and emotions of the human heart. The German poet Johann Wolfgang von Goethe (1749–1832), himself a Romantic in his youth, looked back with nostalgia to the reasonableness and clarity of eighteenth-century classicism. "Classic," he said "is healthy; Romantic is sick." Romanticism, it is true, did destroy the clear simplicity and unity of thought that had prevailed during the Enlightenment. No longer did one dominant philosophy express the aims and ideals of western civilization as rationalism had done during the eighteenth century. But rationalism had provided a one-sided view of the world, ignoring whole provinces of human experience. Romanticism did much to correct that unbalance. By insisting that the world was not the simple machine it had seemed since Newton and that man was not a mere cog in that machine, Romanticism provided a more complex but also a truer view of the world. With its emphasis on evolution throughout the universe, and its stress on the creativity and uniqueness of the individual, Romanticism came as a breath of fresh air after the formalism of the Enlightenment. This was its major and lasting contribution.

THE FIRST WAVE OF REVOLUTIONS, 1820–29

The restoration of the old order saved Europe from major international wars, but it was also responsible for the almost unbroken series of revolutions that lasted for more than a generation.

We have already noted the unrest in Germany and England shortly after 1815. In France, the assassination of the Duke of Berry, in line to be Louis XVIII's successor, was the signal for abandoning the moderate course Louis had tried to steer. More serious, however, than these sporadic acts of violence was the whole wave of revolutions that swept through southern Europe in the 1820s.

Revolt in Southern Europe

The first of these revolutions broke out in 1820 in Spain, where the army rebelled against being sent to South America to put down the revolutions in the Spanish colonies. From Spain revolution spread to Portugal and somewhat later to Italy. In every case the army took the initiative, forcing reactionary monarchs to grant liberal constitutions. The situation in Italy was particularly complicated. The Italian peninsula was still divided into a number of states of varying size, the most important being the southern Kingdom of the Two Sicilies, the central Papal States, and the northern Kingdom of Piedmont. In addition, Austria ruled directly over the northern provinces of Lombardy and Venetia and exerted influence over the rest of Italy through Austrian or pro-Austrian rulers in many of the smaller states. The revolutions in Italy, therefore, were directed not merely against the reactionary policy of the various local rulers but against the alien influence of Austria.

As a result of these upheavals, the old order in much of southern Italy seemed to be crumbling. But the initial success of the revolutions did not last. The revolutionaries everywhere constituted only a small minority, finding little support among the apathetic mass of illiterate peasants. In addition, there was much disagreement among the leaders when it came to establishing more liberal regimes. More harmful than lack of popular following and differences among the revolutionaries was the intervention of outside forces. Austria, with the blessing of Prussia and Russia, intervened in Italy in 1821, and France intervened in Spain in 1823. Only in Portugal was a semblance of parliamentary government maintained, thanks to the support of Great Britain.

The Monroe Doctrine

With reaction triumphant, there was now a possibility that the powers might try to help Spain recover its colonies in Latin America. Largely under the impact of the French Revolution and the Napoleonic conquest of their mother country, the Spanish colonies, beginning in 1810, had followed the example of the United States and declared their independence. In this they had the sympathy of both the United States and Great Britain, whose commercial interests were eager to gain access to the South American market. In 1822, Britain's new foreign secretary, George Canning, proposed a joint declaration by England and the United States to oppose any European intervention against the Spanish colonies.

The Monroe Doctrine

In the wars of the European powers in matters relating to themselves we have never taken any part, nor does it comport with our policy so to do. It is only when our rights are invaded or seriously menaced that we resent injuries or make preparation for our defense. With the movements in this hemisphere we are of necessity more immediately connected, and by causes which must be obvious to all enlightened and impartial observers. The political system of the allied powers is essentially different in this respect from that of America. . . . We owe it, therefore, to candor and to the amicable relations existing between the United States and those powers to declare that we should consider any attempt on their part to extend their system to any portion of this hemisphere as dangerous to our peace and safety. With the existing colonies or dependencies of any European power we have not interfered and shall not interfere. But with the governments who have declared their independence and maintained it, and whose independence we have, on great consideration and on just principles, acknowledged, we could not view any interposition for the purpose of oppressing them, or controlling in any other manner their destiny, by any European power in any other light than as the manifestation of an unfriendly disposition toward the United States.

From President James Monroe, message to Congress, December 2, 1823.

But the United States was concerned not only about South America but also about the possible extension of Russian influence southward from Alaska and about England's designs on Cuba. President James Monroe, therefore, decided to act on his own. In a message to Congress in December 1823, he warned that any attempt by the powers of Europe to extend their influence over the Western Hemisphere would be considered a "manifestation of an unfriendly disposition toward the United States." The immediate effectiveness of the Monroe Doctrine, of course, depended on the backing of the British navy. For that reason, Canning was justified in his famous boast that he "called the New World into existence to redress the balance of the Old."

The Greek War of Independence

The revolutions in the Iberian and Italian peninsulas, in their aims as well as their failures, had been quite similar. The most important revolution of the 1820s, the Greek War of Independence, was a different matter. That war was almost entirely motivated by nationalism. And while the other revolutions failed largely because of outside intervention, the Greek revolt succeeded because the powers helped rather than hindered it. The Greek revolt against the Ottoman Empire was merely the latest chapter in the slow disintegration of that sprawling state. The Serbs had already staged a successful revolt by 1815. Greek nationalism had been gathering force for some time, especially among the "Island" Greeks, whose far-flung commercial contacts had put them in touch with western ideas. The Island Greeks had founded a secret revolutionary society, and it was this society that inspired an uprising in early 1821, leading to the war against Turkey.

The Greeks, however, were no match for the Turks, especially after Sultan Mahmud II (r. 1808–39) called in his Egyptian vassal, Muhammad Ali, to help him. The great powers watched events in Greece closely, but were kept from intervention through mutual jealousies. Only when the very existence of the Greeks seemed at stake did they realize that something had to be done.

The Greek War of Independence, by an unknown painter.

Public opinion in the West had favored the Greek cause all along, and the pressure of this "philhellenism" was partly responsible for the intervention of the powers. In 1827, British, French, and Russian squadrons destroyed the combined Turkish and Egyptian navies in the battle of Navarino. The following year, Russia declared war on Turkey. After brief fighting, the Turks had to submit to the Treaty of Adrianople (1829). Its terms were moderate, except that Russia was given a protectorate over the Danubian principalities of Moldavia and Wallachia, the later Rumania. After some further negotiations, Greece was set up as an independent kingdom.

The Decembrist Revolt in Russia

While the Greek uprising was still going on, there had been one other attempt at revolution, this time against the most powerful stronghold of reaction, the tsarist regime in Russia. Like the Spanish and Italian revolts, it failed. The enigmatic Alexander I, who liked to pose as a liberal while actually becoming more and more reactionary, left the direction of Russian affairs largely in the hands of his efficient but equally reactionary adviser, Alexis Arakcheiev, who used Alexander's fear of revolution to build a regime of ruthless political oppression.

This policy of repression aroused the opposition of the few liberal elements in Russia. Many members of the army had come in contact with western ideas during the wars against Napoleon and the subsequent allied occupation of France. These officers founded several secret societies. An opportunity for the conspirators to act came in December 1825, when Alexander died and there was some doubt about which of his brothers would succeed him. The revolt failed, however, because it was mostly confined to the army, and its leaders were disunited and lacked popular following. Even so, this so-called Decembrist Revolt was significant. Earlier uprisings in Russia had been entirely spontaneous. Here, for the first time, was a revolt that had been planned by a small minority with a definite program. The Decembrist uprising served as an inspiration to all later revolutionary movements in Russia. Meanwhile, the Decembrist events inspired in Alexander's successor, Nicholas I, an almost pathological fear of revolution. For thirty years he remained the leading proponent of reaction abroad and repression at home.

The February Days in Paris

I spent the whole afternoon in walking about Paris. Two things in particular struck me: the first was, I will not say the mainly, but the uniquely and exclusively popular character of the revolution that had just taken place; the omnipotence it had given to the people properly so-called—that is to say, the classes who work with their hands—over all others. . . . Although the working classes had often played the leading part in the events of the First Revolution, they had never been the sole leaders and masters of the State. . . . The Revolution of July [1830] was effected by the people, but the middle class had stirred it up and led it, and secured the principal fruits of it. The Revolution of February, on the contrary, seemed to be made entirely outside the bourgeoisie and against it. . . .

Throughout this day, I did not see in Paris a single one of the former agents of the public authority; not a soldier, not a gendarme, not a policeman; the National Guard itself had disappeared. The people alone bore arms, guarded the public buildings, watched, gave orders, punished; it was an extraordinary and terrible thing to see in the sole hands of those who possessed nothing, all this immense town, so full of riches, or rather this great nation: for, thanks to centralization, he who reigns in Paris governs France. Hence the terror of all the other classes was extreme. . . .

From *The Recollections of Alexis de Tocqueville,* trans. by Alexander Teixeira de Mattos, ed. by J. P. Mayer (New York: Columbia University Press, 1949), pp. 72–75.

THE SECOND WAVE OF REVOLUTIONS, 1830–33

The first wave of revolution after 1815, far from upsetting the old order, merely seemed to have strengthened its hold. The uprisings had been too sporadic, the work of small army cliques with no following among the mass of the people. The second wave of revolutions was different. It started among the people of Paris, and from there it spread over most of Europe, leaving behind some important political changes.

The French Revolution of 1830

The first years of the restored Bourbon monarchy in France had been peaceful. Louis XVIII had tried sincerely to rally his deeply divided country. But he found it increasingly difficult to do so. To the liberals, led by Lafayette, the new constitution, the Charter, with its limited franchise did not go far enough. To the royalists, or "Ultras," led by the king's brother, the Count of Artois, the Charter was the source of all France's ills. Up to 1820, Louis had been able to maintain a moderate, middle-of-the-road course. But after the assassination of the Duke of Berry, the royalist faction gained the upper hand and moderation came to an end.

Louis XVIII died in 1824 and was succeeded by the Count of Artois, as Charles X. Reaction now went into full force. While liberal opposition became more outspoken, the government's policy became more repressive. In 1829 Charles appointed as his first minister one of the most notorious reactionaries, the Prince de Polignac. In the past the king had always been careful to enlist parliamentary backing, but this situation now changed. In the spring of 1830, when the Chamber turned against the government, Charles dismissed it. And when new elections resulted in another liberal majority, Polignac had the king promulgate the July Ordinances, which dissolved the Chamber, imposed strict censorship, and changed the electoral law to give the government a favorable majority.

Discontent with this arbitrary policy came to a head in the July revolution of 1830. The hope of the men who fought on the barricades — artisans, workers, students, some members of the middle class — was for a republic. But this was not what the more moderate liberals wanted. Much as they hated the high-handed manner of Charles X, they were equally opposed to a republic, which recalled the violent phase of the earlier French Revolution. It was due to the careful machinations of these moderates that France emerged from its July revolution as a constitutional monarchy rather than a republic

The new king was Louis Philippe, Duke of Orléans. Though related to the Bourbons, he had stayed clear of the royalists and had affected a thoroughly bourgeois image. Events in France, of course, violated the status quo established in 1815. But the powers had been taken too much by surprise and were too little united to take any action. Their attention, furthermore, was soon caught by events elsewhere, as the French example set off a whole series of revolutions in other countries.

Revolution in Belgium

The first to follow the lead of France was Belgium. Its union with Holland at Vienna had not proved very successful. The only area in which the two countries got along was in economic matters, and even there the Belgians in time developed grievances. The main differences were administrative and religious. In August 1830, in part inspired by events in Paris, rioting broke out in Brussels. King William I tried to save the situation by granting a separate administration for Belgium, but he was too late. The Dutch troops sent to quell the uprising were quickly defeated; but the ultimate fate of Belgium depended on the attitude of the great powers. France and England looked favorably upon the new state, but the three eastern powers were hostile. Since Austria and Russia were preoccupied with disturbances in Italy and Poland, however, any aid to Holland was out of the question. In December 1830 the five powers agreed to recognize the independence of Belgium. The new state was to remain perpetually neutral.

Liberty Leading the People, **by Delacroix. This painting captures the spirit of the Revolution of 1830.**

Europe in Revolt

France and Belgium were the only nations in which the revolutions of 1830 achieved any lasting success. Yet there was hardly a country that did not feel the tremors of revolution. Across the Rhine the events in Paris caused much excitement among German intellectuals, though there was little echo among the people. Some of the smaller states rid themselves of rulers who were particularly obnoxious, and others won moderately liberal constitutions.

Southern Europe, the scene of revolution a decade earlier, was also aroused by the news from Paris. Struggles among rival claimants to the thrones in Spain and Portugal, together with disturbances fostered by liberals, created widespread confusion. Both nations finally emerged, at least nominally, as constitutional monarchies. In Italy, where secret societies such as the *Carbonari*, or "charcoal burners," were flourishing, revolutions broke out in several states. The revolutionaries hoped to receive aid from France, and had they succeeded they might have won. But Louis Philippe could not afford to antagonize Austria, and Metternich had a free hand. Again Austrian troops restored the legitimate rulers, who then took revenge against the insurgents.

The Polish Insurrection of 1830

The bloodiest struggle of all in 1830 took place in Poland. The Kingdom of Poland already had been a source of trouble to Alexander I. Under Nicholas I tension mounted further. Like revolutionaries elsewhere, the Polish insurgents had founded a number of secret societies to propagate nationalism and to prepare for revolution. When rumors reached Poland in 1830 that Nicholas was planning to use Polish forces to help put down the revolutions in France and Belgium, the conspirators decided to act. Had the Polish people stood united, the revolt might have succeeded. But the revolutionaries were split into moderates and radicals, with neither faction having much following among the mass of the peasants. The hope, furthermore, that England and France would come to their aid proved vain. Even so, it took almost a year before Russia was able to subdue the rebellious Poles and impose a regime of severe repression. For the next generation Russian Poland remained a sad and silent land.

Reform in Great Britain

There was one other country besides France and Belgium where unrest in 1830 and after led to major political changes. More than any other nation, Great Britain had been feeling the effects of rapid industrialization. The change from an agrarian to an industrial society could not help but have political repercussions. That England was able to make this adjustment without a revolution was due to its long parliamentary tradition and able political leadership. Britain did share in the initial wave of reaction after 1815. With the incapable George IV succeeding George III in 1820, and with the Tories in control of Parliament, little relief was in sight.

Beginning in 1822, however, a new and more enlightened element within the Tory Party became aware of the political implications of economic change. The first sign that some improvement was imminent came with the reform of Britain's criminal code after 1822, which drastically reduced the number of capital crimes. In 1824 the Combination Acts, forbidding workers to organize, were repealed. In 1828 a new Corn Law modified the duties on foreign grain, thus lowering the price of bread. The most important reform, however, was the establishment of religious equality. In 1828 the Test and Corporations Acts, which barred Protestant dissenters from holding state offices, were repealed; and in 1829 the Emancipation Bill permitted Catholics to sit in Parliament.

In most of these reforms the moderate element among the Tories had the support of the Whigs. The leaders of the Whig Party differed little from their Tory rivals in social background and outlook. But while the main backing of the Tory Party continued to come from the landed gentry and the established Church, the Whigs were supported by the rising merchant and manufacturing class. For that reason they became the main advocates of parliamentary reform. To the Whigs, parliamentary reform meant giving a fairer share of representation in Parliament to the well-to-do middle class. This they were finally able to achieve in 1832.

The Great Reform Bill of 1832 was passed only after domestic unrest had at times brought England to the verge of revolution. Under the new bill, the franchise was extended to about half again as many voters, and proper representation was given to the new industrial towns. As a result, one in five adult males was now able to vote. The workers, the poor, and all women were still left without a vote; but this was not different from the situation elsewhere in Europe. Even though there was no change in Britain's form of government, the Reform Bill was every bit as much a revolution as the overthrow of Charles X had been in France. Both were significant stages in the rise to power of the middle class.

East and West

Because the revolutions in the early 1830s were successful only in western Europe, they helped widen the already existing gap between the powers of the East and West. France and England, constitutional monarchies both, had seen to it that the revolution in Belgium succeeded. Austria, Russia, and Prussia, still essentially autocratic, had suppressed the uprisings in Germany, Italy, and Poland. The main reason for the success of revolutions in the West had been their popular backing. Industrialization, which had bolstered the ranks of the middle and lower classes in the West, had as yet made little headway in the East. But while the revolutions in western Europe had been successful, they had chiefly benefited the middle class. The artisans and workers, who had done much of the fighting, were left with empty hands. In the West as in the East, therefore, the revolutions of 1830 left much unfinished. Here is the main cause for the third and largest wave of revolutions, which swept across Europe.

THE REFORM BILL.

The Great Reform Bill of 1832 is the subject of this contemporary cartoon. Political corruption is put through the "reform mill" to emerge as a triumphant Britannia.

THE THIRD WAVE OF REVOLUTIONS, 1848–49

The third wave of revolutions lasted for over a year and affected most of Europe. Among the major powers, only England and Russia were spared, though England came close to revolt. There were countless differences among the various upheavals, but there were also some notable similarities. Generally speaking, the revolutions of 1848 were a further attempt to undo the settlement of 1815. In Italy, Germany, Austria, and Hungary the fundamental grievance was still the lack of national freedom and unity. There was also the desire for more representative governments and for the abolition of the remaining vestiges of feudalism. But these were secondary aims. Nationalism was the dominant concern of the revolutionaries in central Europe. In western Europe, neither nationalism nor feudalism was any longer an issue. There the chief aim of revolution was the extension of political power beyond the upper middle class. The revolutionaries did not always agree on how far this liberalization should go. The middle class wanted merely to widen the franchise to include the more substantial citizens, whereas the working class wanted political democracy for everyone and some measure of social and economic democracy as well. With the revolutions of 1848, socialism for the first time became an issue in European politics.

Aside from these political causes, there were also economic reasons for the outbreak of revolutions. Despite, or because of, the unprecedented economic growth of Europe since 1815, there had been several severe economic crises, the latest in 1846 and 1847. These upsets particularly affected the lower classes. The small artisan was fighting against the competition of large-scale industry. At the same time, the industrial workers in the new factories were eking out a marginal existence on a minimum wage. There were also periodic crises in agriculture. Economic hardship in many cases preceded and helped precipitate political action.

There were other common features among the revolutions of 1848. They were all essentially urban. The leaders came from the middle class. Much of the actual fighting was done by the urban lower classes, by artisans and workers. Students also played an important part. None of the revolutions had any agrarian program beyond the abolition of feudal dues and services. Once these had been abolished, the conservative peasants withdrew what initial support they had provided the revolutions.

Europe, in the spring of 1848, was discontented and restless. The causes of discontent differed from middle class to workers to peasants. But so long as these three groups stood united, it was easy for them to overthrow the old order. When it came to building something new, however, all the differences among the revolutionaries asserted themselves. The history of the revolutions of 1848 is a frustrating tale of missed opportunities.

Slum street scene, Manchester, England.

The "July Monarchy" in France

The key nation in the events of 1848 was again France. The reasons for the failure of Louis Philippe's government are not too obvious. France under the "July Monarchy" was prosperous and progressive, with a liberal constitution, a free press, and a competent king. Louis Philippe had all the bourgeois virtues—he was thrifty, kindly, and industrious. He was served by capable ministers, and until about 1846 trade and industry flourished. France, which had fallen behind England economically as a result of the French Revolution, had regained some lost ground. Yet with all these advantages, the July Monarchy was far from popular. Most Frenchmen still smarted from the defeat of Napoleon. Only a glorious foreign policy could wipe out that humiliation. But no sooner was there an opportunity for such a policy than the genuine pacifism of Louis Philippe spoiled it.

In time the opposition against Louis Philippe became crystallized in three factions: the Liberals, the Bonapartists, and the Republicans. The Liberals wanted a further extension of the franchise. The Bonapartists hoped to overthrow Louis Philippe in favor of Prince Louis Napoleon, the emperor's nephew, who promised to restore to France some of the glories associated with his uncle's name. As for Republicanism, it had its roots in the failure of the radicals to assert themselves in 1830. As the number of workers increased, Republican feeling became more widespread. And since the workers also began making economic demands, Republicanism gradually became tinged with socialism.

Discontent in France mounted after 1846, primarily for economic reasons.

In the fall of that year, Europe was hit by a severe depression. In France, as elsewhere, rising prices and growing unemployment particularly affected the workers. To ease tension, Liberals and Republicans joined forces to hold a series of political meetings to discuss parliamentary reform. In February 1848 the government's ban against such meetings brought on a popular demonstration. As a precaution, the king called out the army, and in the ensuing confrontation several of the demonstrators were killed. Blood had been spilled, and the revolution was on. Major casualties were avoided by Louis Philippe's decision to abdicate. On February 25 a republic was proclaimed.

A French cartoon showing Louis Philippe courting the public; it was captioned, "Well, good people, do you want some? Here it is."

The Second French Republic

In a very short time and with little loss of life, a tremendous change had been brought about. The people who had been cheated out of the fruits of revolution in 1830 now had reached their goal; the days of upper-middle-class predominance appeared to be over. But this radical phase of the revolution did not last. The new provisional government was faced with tremendous difficulties. Paris was in a constant state of turmoil, with several political factions jockeying for position. Some wanted to concentrate on domestic reforms; others were more concerned with carrying the revolution abroad. The socialists in the government proclaimed the right to work and introduced a system of "national workshops," advocated by the socialist Louis Blanc (see p. 729).

In this period of confusion, the elections to the new National Assembly came as a severe shock to the radicals. Of some nine hundred delegates elected, fewer than one hundred supported the radical Republicans. The main reason for this sudden shift lay with the French peasantry, whose aims had been met by the first French Revolution and who subsequently had turned conservative.

But the radical element did not give up without a fight. There now followed a series of clashes between the radicals in the provisional government and the moderate National Assembly. Tension came to a head in the bloody "June Days," when the Assembly dissolved the workshops, considered breeding-grounds of discontent. The workers again took to the barricades, and the resulting street fighting caused thousands of casualties. By the end of June 1848 the back of lower-class resistance had been broken, and the middle class once again could make itself prevail. The Constitution of the Second French Republic set up a single Chamber of Representatives, to be elected by universal male suffrage. Executive power was vested in a powerful president, elected by the people.

The first presidential election was in December 1848. The French middle class and the French peasants wanted a strong man, who would banish the "red peril" of socialism. Such a man, they felt, was Louis Napoleon. The first Napoleon had taken over the reins of government after an earlier revolution fifty years ago, and he had brought order at home and glory abroad. Why should history not repeat itself? The victory of Louis Napoleon by an overwhelming majority was thus due chiefly to the glamor of his name. A

Giuseppe Mazzini, Italian nationalist.

sign that he was ready to live up to that name came four years later, in 1852, when he proclaimed himself Emperor Napoleon III.*

The Italian Revolution of 1848

In Italy, revolution had started in Sicily as early as January 1848. From there it had spread north. By the middle of March, most of the Italian states except Lombardy and Venetia had won liberal constitutions.

The origins of the Italian *Risorgimento* ("resurrection") go back to the eighteenth century. The agitation for national liberation and unification had gained momentum during the Napoleonic period. But the hopes of Italian patriots and reformers had been dashed repeatedly since 1815. Despite the failure of the uprisings of 1830, however, Italian intellectuals had continued making plans for the future. Out of the maze of their projects, three main schemes had emerged: Giuseppe Mazzini, a noted Liberal and an ardent Italian nationalist, advocated the formation of a free, united, and republican Italy. Vincenzo Gioberti, a priest, objected to the republican and centralizing tendencies of Mazzini and instead proposed a federated monarchy with a liberal constitution, headed by the pope. The election of the reputedly liberal Pius IX in 1846 gave special emphasis to Gioberti's proposals. A third scheme for the future of Italy looked to Italian unification under the leadership of the house of Piedmont-Sardinia. Here, then, were three different schemes for the liberation and unification of Italy. Each was tried, and each failed.

With Austria the main obstacle to Italian unification, the outbreak of revolution in Vienna naturally aided the Italian cause. As insurrections broke out in the Austrian provinces of Lombardy and Venetia, Charles Albert of Piedmont, in March 1848, gave way to popular pressure and declared war on Austria. Contingents from other Italian states joined the Piedmontese. Pius IX, however, could ill afford to support a war against the leading Catholic power of Europe. His neutrality and subsequent flight from Rome dashed the hopes of those who had looked to the pope as the leader of Italian liberation.

The war of Piedmont against Austria ended in failure. The forces of Charles Albert were no match for the seasoned troops of the Austrian general Radetzky, especially after the Austrian government had succeeded in putting down its revolution at home. The final defeat of Charles Albert at Novara in March 1849 ended, for the time being, the chance of uniting Italy under the leadership of Piedmont-Sardinia.

Mazzini's alternative for the unification of Italy, the creation of a republic, also was given a brief chance. With Pius IX away from Rome, radicalism had a free hand. In February 1849 a constituent assembly proclaimed the Roman Republic, under the leadership of Mazzini, and with an army led by another hero of Italian unification, Giuseppe Garibaldi. But as Austria regained its position in northern Italy and as the troops of the ousted King Ferdinand II regained control of the Kingdom of the Two Sicilies, the Roman Republic became a liberal island in a sea of reaction. To make matters worse, Louis Napoleon, newly elected president of France, to ingratiate himself with his Catholic subjects, sent an expeditionary force to Rome. It defeated the forces of Garibaldi and thus ended the dream of a republican Italy.

The revolution in Italy had failed. It had done so chiefly because the Austrians had once again proved too strong and because the Italians had proved too little united. Piedmont, having been the only state to put up any fight, earned the leadership in Italian affairs. To rally the rest of Italy behind the national cause, Italians had to be promised not only unification but political reforms as well. This the government of Piedmont, now under Victor Em-

* Napoleon II, Napoleon I's son, had never assumed the throne and had died in 1832.

manuel II, realized. Alone among Italian states, Piedmont kept the liberal constitution that had been adopted during the revolution. It thus became the hope of Italian nationalists and liberals alike.

Revolutions in the Habsburg Empire

In Italy, revolution had erupted before it did in France. The outbreaks in Austria were directly touched off by the events in Paris. The Habsburg Empire had long been ripe for revolution. Its government was cumbersome and corrupt, and Metternich's efforts at reform had been of no avail. The main problem facing the Austrian Empire was its conglomeration of nationalities. Besides the Germans in Austria proper, there were the Magyars in Hungary, the Czechs and Slovaks in Bohemia and Moravia, the Poles in Galicia, and the Italians in Lombardy and Venetia. Almost everywhere these peoples, together with Slovenes, Croats, Serbs, Ruthenians, and Rumanians, created a situation of utmost ethnic confusion. With the advent of nationalism, this situation endangered the very existence of the Habsburg Empire.

In addition to the demands of these subject peoples for some measure of autonomy, there was also a growing demand for governmental reforms. Industrial progress had increased the ranks of the middle class and had created an urban proletariat, both of which now added their voices to the liberal protests of university professors and other intellectuals.

The news of the revolution in Paris caused more excitement among the

Nationalities of the Habsburg Empire

Engraving of a barricade in Vienna (1848).

subject nationalities than it did in Austria. There were some student demonstrations in Vienna, and a deputation of citizens asked for the resignation of Metternich. With Metternich gone, events moved swiftly. The citizens of Vienna elected a National Assembly to draft a constitution. One of its first acts was to lift the last feudal burdens from Austria's peasants, completing a process begun by Joseph II two generations earlier.

From Vienna, revolution spread to other parts of the Empire. The uprisings in Lombardy and Venetia have already been discussed. Bohemia, except for some local unrest, remained quiet until early in June of 1848. At that time, disturbances broke out in connection with the first Pan-Slav Congress in Prague, which proclaimed the solidarity of the Slavic peoples against the Germans. Popular demonstrations were quelled when Austria's military governor ordered the bombardment of Prague. This was a significant event, for it was the first major setback of revolution anywhere in Europe. In Hungary, meanwhile, the Austrian government had agreed to the March Laws, which guaranteed self-government. Hungary also followed the Austrian example in abolishing the remains of feudalism. But while the Hungarians thus secured freedom for themselves, they refused to grant the same freedom to the Croats within their own borders. Austria could thus play one nationality against the other. In September 1848, Croatian forces with Austrian backing invaded Hungary.

With imperial armies scoring successes against the revolutionaries in Bohemia, Hungary, and Lombardy, the tide of revolution in the Austrian Empire was definitely turning. A second, more radical outbreak in Vienna in October 1848 was soon put down. The Austrian government was now entrusted to Prince Felix Schwarzenberg, a strong-willed reactionary who urged the emperor, Ferdinand I, to resign in favor of his nephew, Francis Joseph. In March 1849 Schwarzenberg dissolved the National Assembly and imposed his own centralized constitution on the whole Empire.

By early spring of 1849 the Austrian government was again in control everywhere except in Hungary. In April 1849 Hungary proclaimed itself a republic, with Louis Kossuth as president. At this point Francis Joseph accepted the offer of Nicholas I to help put down the Hungarians. The tsar was motivated by feelings of monarchical solidarity and by the fear that revolution might spread to the Danubian principalities and Poland. Hungarian resistance was finally crushed by the joint invasion of Russian and Austrian forces and by simultaneous uprisings among the Slavic people of southern Hungary. By mid-August of 1849 Austria was once again in control of its own house.

The "Germanies" in Revolt

The victory of reaction in Austria, as we have seen, affected the fate of revolution in Italy. It had a similar effect in Germany. There the chances for the success of revolution seemed most favorable. Unlike Austria, Germany did not suffer from ethnic disunity, nor was there any need to expel a foreign power, as there was in Italy. The failure of the revolution was due to many causes, most important among them the division of the country into many separate states and the general apathy of the population. The majority of Germans seemed content to lead a life of modest comfort and to pursue cultural rather than political interests.

Still, there was enough ferment among German intellectuals to keep alive the agitation for a united and liberal state. These aims found support among the growing industrial middle class. The formation of a German customs union, or *Zollverein,* had eased the movement of goods throughout Germany and thus aided industrial development. But industrialization had also brought many hardships, especially to the artisans. Another discontented group were the peasants in eastern Germany. Since their liberation from serfdom, they were often unable to make a living on their small holdings and instead had to become agricultural or industrial laborers. This economic discontent, which became especially strong during the 1840s, added a new dimension to the liberal and national aims of the German intellectuals. Had the revolutionary leaders understood and utilized this discontent, the results of the revolutions might have been different.

The first German uprising occurred in Bavaria before the events in France. With the news from Paris, the revolutions became general. Because Prussia, next to Austria, played the leading role in the German Confederation, events in Berlin were watched with particular interest. Prussia, since 1840, had been ruled by the brilliant but unstable Frederick William IV. The new king started out with a series of liberal reforms, but his liberalism was largely a pose. When the revolution came to Berlin in March 1848, Frederick William was easily frightened into appointing a liberal ministry and agreeing to a constituent assembly. But the old regime in Prussia was not really beaten, especially since the army had remained intact. While middle-class delegates were drawing up a constitution, the lower classes were agitating for more drastic changes—including universal manhood suffrage, socialism, and even a republic. These radical demands drove the middle class, including well-to-do peasants, back into the arms of reaction. When Austria successfully moved against its revolution in the fall of 1848, Frederick William dissolved the Constituent Assembly and later imposed his own constitution. By the end of 1848, the revolution in Prussia had been defeated.

But German liberals did not give up hope. Since spring, another assembly had been in session in Frankfurt to draft a constitution for all of Germany, including Austria, rather than for Prussia alone. Its delegates had been elected by the people. The majority were professional people, including many professors. Deliberations dragged on for almost a year. The main argument developed over the question of whether or not the new German state should be under the leadership of Austria or Prussia. The issue resolved itself when the victory of reaction in Vienna disqualified Austria in the eyes of German liberals.

The Frankfurt Constitution, which was finally adopted in March 1849, called for a constitutional monarchy with a parliament elected by universal male suffrage. The Frankfurt Parliament elected Frederick William IV as "Emperor of the Germans." But the king of Prussia refused a crown offered him by the people. He would accept it only from his fellow princes. With reaction everywhere triumphant, Frederick William's refusal all but finished the revolution in Germany. There were some last flashes of violence in the smaller states, but Prussian troops soon restored order. The attempt of the German people to build a unified nation under a government of their own choosing had failed.

England in the Age of Reform

The one country in western Europe where many people had expected revolution to strike first was Great Britain. And yet, except for a brief flare-up in Ireland, the British Isles proved the major exception to the rule of revolution. The Reform Bill of 1832 had been merely the most prominent of a large series of reforms. Most important among these was the establishment of free trade. Britain's merchants and industrialists had long agitated against import duties, but tariffs had been defended on the grounds that the government needed the income. With the reintroduction of the income tax in 1842, however, that argument lost ground, and protective tariffs were gradually abolished. Only in agriculture did they survive. To fight for the abolition of agricultural tariffs, the Anti-Corn Law League had been formed in 1839. In 1846 its relentless pressure succeeded, and the Corn Laws were repealed.

Along with this agitation for economic freedom, there also arose during the 1830s a movement for greater political freedom. The Reform Bill of 1832 had been a disappointment to the lower classes, among whom the so-called Chartist Movement gained its major support. The movement took its name from the "People's Charter" of 1838, drawn up by a group of radical reformers and calling for a further democratization of Parliament. But Parliament repeatedly turned down petitions based on the Charter. By 1848 discontent had mounted to such a pitch that there seemed to be a real threat of revolution. The Chartists prepared a "monster petition" demanding universal manhood suffrage and other political reforms and started a demonstration to present it to Parliament. When it began to rain, however, the demonstrators let themselves be dispersed peacefully. The truth of the matter was that a good deal of the discontent in the Chartist Movement was economic, and had disappeared with the repeal of the Corn Laws and a general increase in prosperity. Henceforth workers were turning more and more to trade unionism as a means of improving their status. England thus remained a quiet haven of refuge in the upheavals of 1848, giving asylum to refugees from revolution and reaction alike, including Metternich as well as Marx. Many of the revolutionaries, however, preferred to leave Europe altogether, chiefly for the United States.

Chartist rally, Kennington Common, April 10, 1848.

Why Did the Revolutions of 1848 Fail?

The revolutions of 1848 thus had failed everywhere. They had done so because of weaknesses in the revolutionary camp, because of the continued strength of the forces of reaction, and because the economic conditions that helped bring on the revolutions did not last.

The weakness of the revolutionaries was due partly to the lack of well-defined programs or the existence of too many different programs and to the indecision of their leaders. This indecision lost valuable time, which the reactionaries used to prepare for counterrevolution. But the primary weakness of the revolutionaries was lack of widespread popular support. The middle class, in most countries, did not really want a revolution. It preferred to achieve its aims through reform, as in England. But once revolution came, the middle class tried to reap its benefits. Much of the actual fighting was done by artisans and workers, who wanted more than limited democracy for the well-to-do. They wanted complete democracy, political and, in some cases, economic as well. To the middle class, these demands, especially the socialist ones, not only threatened its political predominance but its very existence. This bourgeois fear of a "red peril" was exaggerated. Despite the incendiary language of *The Communist Manifesto* (which appeared in 1848), the majority of the lower class were perfectly ready to follow the leadership of the middle class if that would improve their condition. But the middle class did not live up to these expectations; as a result the lower class more and more came to distrust the men it had helped gain power.

Not only was there disunity among the revolutionaries, there was no attempt to coordinate the revolutions in different countries. While the forces of reaction worked together, there was little collaboration among the revolutionaries. On the contrary, almost everywhere their programs showed traces of a selfish nationalism. There was nationalism behind France's talk of spreading the blessings of revolution. The Germans wanted to unite all German-speaking peoples, but they also wanted to lord it over the Poles, and they actually carried on a brief war against the Danes. The Poles wanted to be liberated and united, but they did not want to see the Ukrainians win the same benefits. And the Hungarians behaved every bit as selfishly toward the Croats as the Austrians did toward the Hungarians.

Yet though reaction won a full victory in 1849, the revolutions of 1848 had not been entirely in vain. Some changes for the better were preserved. In France political power had been somewhat broadened. In Italy, some leaders had learned useful lessons of how to go about achieving unification. In Austria the abolition of serfdom could not be undone, and Metternich did not return to power. Even in Germany, where the failure of revolution had more tragic long-range consequences than anywhere else, a few lasting gains were made.

The mid-century revolutions came at a turning point in European history. Up to this time, the economy of the Continent had still been largely agrarian. From now on, industrialization really took hold. Metternich, the dominant figure after 1815, had been a relic of the eighteenth century. The future was to belong to more modern politicians. Two forces were henceforth to dominate the history of Europe and the world—nationalism and socialism. Neither was new, but both had lost much of their earlier idealism and utopianism. Henceforth nationalism and socialism respectively became the main issues in the struggle of nation against nation and class against class.

Suggestions for Further Reading

A very good introduction to the period following the French Revolution is E. J. Hobsbawm, *The Age of Revolution, 1789–1848* (1962). Detailed histories are F. A. Artz, *Reaction and Revolution, 1814–1832* (1934), and W. L. Langer, *Political and Social Upheaval, 1832–1852* (1969). J. Droz, *Europe between Revolutions, 1815–1848* (1968), is by a noted French social historian.

Among national histories, the following are recommended: A. Briggs, *The Making of Modern England* (1959); A. Cobban, *A History of Modern France,* vol. II (1957); T. S. Hamerow, *Restoration, Revolution, Reaction: Economics and Politics in Germany, 1815–1871* (1958); A. J. P. Taylor, *The Hapsburg Monarchy, 1809–1918* (1948); A. J. Whyte, *The Evolution of Modern Italy, 1715–1920* (1944); and R. Pipes, *Russia under the Old Regime* (1975). Standard works on liberalism and nationalism are H. J. Laski, *The Rise of European Liberalism* (1936), and H. Kohn, *The Idea of Nationalism* (1944).

On the Congress of Vienna, see H. Nicolson, *The Congress of Vienna: A Study in Allied Unity, 1812–1822* (1946). Good biographies of the leading figures at Vienna are: G. de Bertier de Sauvigny, *Metternich and His Times* (1962); C. Brinton, *The Lives of Talleyrand* (1936); A. Palmer, *Alexander I, Tsar of War and Peace* (1974); and J. C. Bartlett, *Castlereagh* (1967). The diplomatic events after Vienna are treated in H. G. Schenk, *The Aftermath of the Napoleonic Wars: The Concert of Europe* (1947).

A good introduction to the complexities of Romanticism is J. B. Halsted, ed., *Romanticism* (1965). More recent works are J. Clay, *Romanticism* (1980), and M. Le Bris, *Romantics and Romanticism* (1980). On the numerous upheavals in the 1820s and 1830s, see J. Plamenatz, *The Revolutionary Movement in France, 1815–1871* (1952); D. Dakin, *The Struggle for Greek Independence* (1973); M. Raeff, *The Decembrist Movement* (1966); and J. A. Betley, *Belgium and Poland in International Relations, 1830–1831* (1960). The most successful attempts to present an overview of the revolutions of 1848 are P. Robertson, *Revolutions of 1848: A Social History* (1952), and P. Stearns, *1848: The Revolutionary Tide in Europe* (1974).

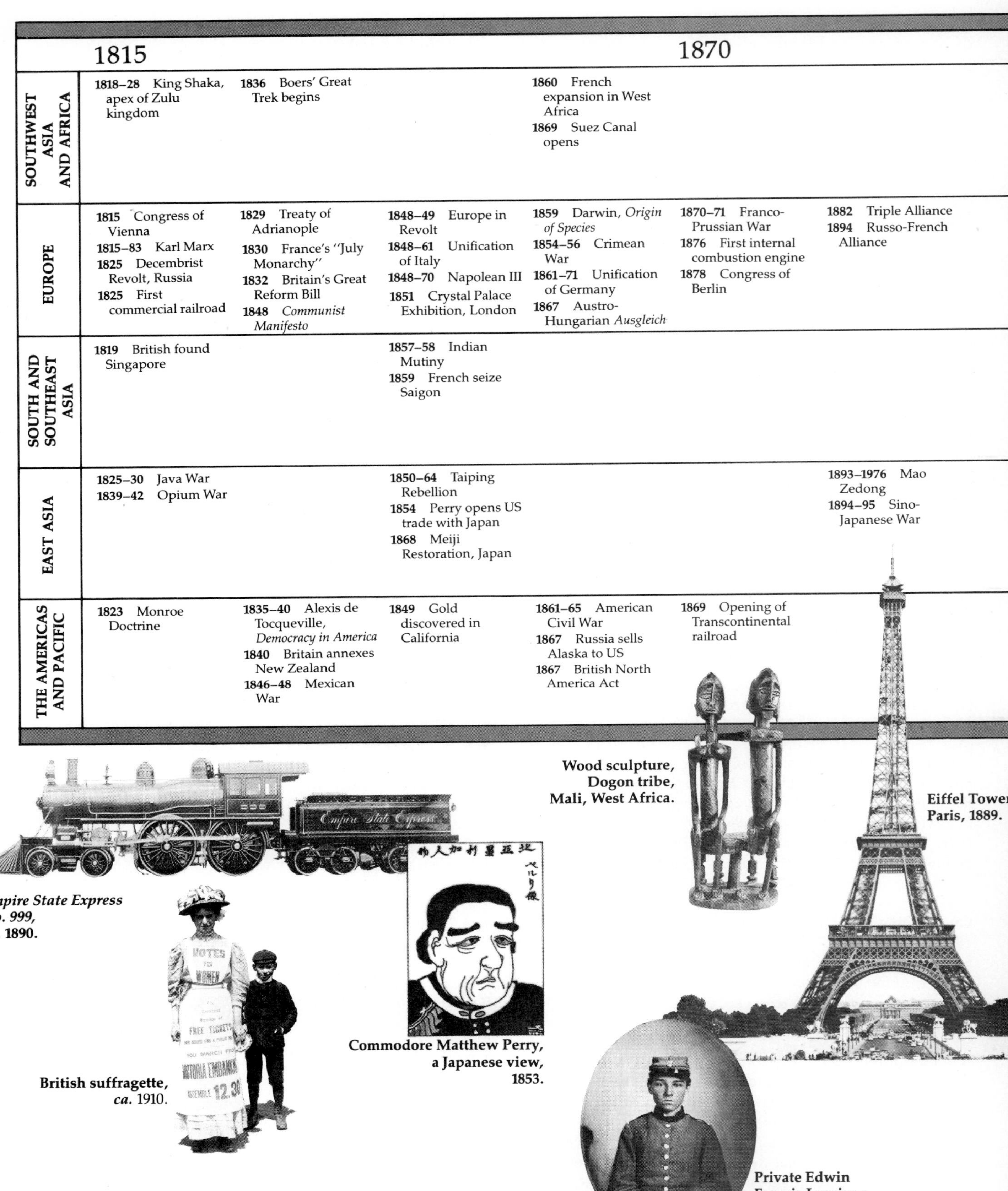

	1815				1870	
SOUTHWEST ASIA AND AFRICA	**1818–28** King Shaka, apex of Zulu kingdom	**1836** Boers' Great Trek begins		**1860** French expansion in West Africa **1869** Suez Canal opens		
EUROPE	**1815** Congress of Vienna **1815–83** Karl Marx **1825** Decembrist Revolt, Russia **1825** First commercial railroad	**1829** Treaty of Adrianople **1830** France's "July Monarchy" **1832** Britain's Great Reform Bill **1848** *Communist Manifesto*	**1848–49** Europe in Revolt **1848–61** Unification of Italy **1848–70** Napolean III **1851** Crystal Palace Exhibition, London	**1859** Darwin, *Origin of Species* **1854–56** Crimean War **1861–71** Unification of Germany **1867** Austro-Hungarian *Ausgleich*	**1870–71** Franco-Prussian War **1876** First internal combustion engine **1878** Congress of Berlin	**1882** Triple Alliance **1894** Russo-French Alliance
SOUTH AND SOUTHEAST ASIA	**1819** British found Singapore		**1857–58** Indian Mutiny **1859** French seize Saigon			
EAST ASIA	**1825–30** Java War **1839–42** Opium War		**1850–64** Taiping Rebellion **1854** Perry opens US trade with Japan **1868** Meiji Restoration, Japan			**1893–1976** Mao Zedong **1894–95** Sino-Japanese War
THE AMERICAS AND PACIFIC	**1823** Monroe Doctrine	**1835–40** Alexis de Tocqueville, *Democracy in America* **1840** Britain annexes New Zealand **1846–48** Mexican War	**1849** Gold discovered in California	**1861–65** American Civil War **1867** Russia sells Alaska to US **1867** British North America Act	**1869** Opening of Transcontinental railroad	

***Empire State Express No. 999, ca.* 1890.**

British suffragette, *ca.* 1910.

Commodore Matthew Perry, a Japanese view, 1853.

Wood sculpture, Dogon tribe, Mali, West Africa.

Eiffel Tower, Paris, 1889.

Private Edwin Francis Jennison, Confederate Army.

1914	
1886 Gold discovered in Southern Africa **1889** Rhodesia colonized **1899–1902** Boer War **1910** Union of South Africa formed	
1894–1905 Dreyfus Affair **1905** Russian Revolution begins **1905** Einstein's Theory of Relativity **1907** Triple Entente **1912–13** Balkan Wars	
1885 Indian National Congress founded **1906** Muslim League founded	
1900 Boxer Rebellion **1904–05** Russo-Japanese War **1911** Chinese Revolution **1912–49** Chinese Republic	
1889 First Pan-American Conference **1898** Spanish-American War **1910** Mexican Revolution begins	**1914** Panama Canal opens

The Prince of Wales in Bangalore, India, *ca.* 1900.

Gold prospector, California, *ca.* 1850.

34 From Agriculture to Industry

The Industrial Revolution

Much of the political tension in Europe during the first half of the nineteenth century was due to underlying economic unrest caused by the gradual transformation of Europe's economy from agriculture to industry. This change began around the middle of the eighteenth century, but it did not become pronounced until after 1815. From then on it gathered momentum, first in England and later on the Continent, until by the end of the nineteenth century most of western Europe had become industrialized.

The term "Industrial Revolution," often used to describe this industrialization, has come in for some criticism. The change from agriculture to industry, it seems, was a gradual process. Only when considering the total effect of this change does the term *revolution* seem justified. By vastly improving the means of communication, industrialization made the world seem much smaller; by enabling more people to make a living, it made the world much more crowded; and by raising the standard of living, it made life more agreeable. Industrialization has elevated nations that heretofore were insignificant and has demoted others that do not have the manpower or raw materials that industry requires. Industrialization has dissolved a rigid and hierarchical social order and has substituted a fluid and egalitarian mass society.

Not all these changes have necessarily been for the better. While industry created wealth for some, it emphasized the poverty of others. While it made nations and individuals more dependent on one another, it also increased their rivalry for a share of the world's riches. The preoccupation of modern society with material well-being has diverted mankind from more elevated concerns. But while we may wonder how beneficial the change from agriculture to industry has been, about the magnitude of that change there can be no doubt.

THE ROOTS OF MODERN INDUSTRIALISM

By modern industrialism we mean the mass production of goods by machines driven by generated power and set up in factories. There had been few machines before the eighteenth century. During the Middle Ages, goods had been produced by hand for local consumption. With the Age of Discovery and the "Commercial Revolution" in the sixteenth century, the demand for goods and their production had increased. Because the small artisan did not have the capital to buy large quantities of raw materials, to produce a large stock, and to sell it in a distant market, a class of wealthy capitalists and merchants began to join in the production process. They supplied the artisan with raw materials and sometimes tools, and they took over the finished product to sell at a profit. This "domestic" or "putting-out" system had become quite common by the seventeenth century. There were even a few simple machines, but they still had to be operated by humans or animals, or by wind or water power. During the eighteenth century the trend toward larger-scale production was accelerated by numerous new machines. The most important step came with the application of steam power to these inventions. From here on the domestic system gradually declined, as production shifted from home to factory.

It was no accident that modern industrialism should have its start in the eighteenth century. The intellectual climate of the Enlightenment, its interest in science, and its emphasis on progress were favorable to such a development. The beginnings of modern industrialism fall into the period after 1760, and the growth of industrialism was most pronounced in England. England was a wealthy country with large overseas holdings; its parliamentary system gave some influence to the rising industrial middle class; it had sufficient surplus capital; and it had an ample supply of basic raw materials and manpower. Early industrialization in England was also aided by drastic changes in British agriculture—an "Agricultural Revolution"—which increased Britain's food supply and provided some additional manpower for industry.

THE AGRICULTURAL REVOLUTION

Before the eighteenth century, most of Britain's land was still worked under the open-field system. The holdings of individual owners were scattered about in strips, separated from those of other landholders by a double furrow. Each landholder also shared in the common pastures and woodlands of his community. This arrangement was of particular advantage to the small farmers and cottagers, who shared in the rights of the "commons." But the open-field system was both inefficient and wasteful. The prevailing mode of cultivation was still by traditional three-field rotation, under which one-third of the land remained fallow each year. Any attempt to change this routine by experimenting with new crops was impossible, because all strips in a given field had to be cultivated at the same time and planted with identical crops.

The "Enclosure Movement"

Beginning at the time of the Tudors in the sixteenth century, an "enclosure movement" had started in England, under which the scattered strips of individual owners were consolidated into compact holdings surrounded by fences. Enclosure meant a gain of usable land because it did away with the double furrows, and it made cultivation easier. But since enclosure also entailed a division of the commons, it worked to the detriment of the small farmer, who thereby lost part of his livelihood. As the population of England increased, agricultural production for the distant market rather than for local consumption became more profitable. The trend toward large-scale farming and especially sheep raising through enclosures therefore gained momentum. Between 1702 and 1797, Parliament passed some 1,776 enclosure acts affecting three million acres. In each case the larger landowner profited at the expense of the smaller farmer. Left with too little land and deprived of his share in the commons, the small farmer had to become a tenant farmer or move to the cities. Many took the latter course, providing some of the manpower without which the rapid growth of Britain's industry could not have taken place.

The enclosure movement brought hardships to many, but it also brought a dramatic improvement in agriculture and animal husbandry. Freed from the restrictions of collective cultivation, landowners now could try new methods and new crops. The result was more food from the same amount of land. The improvement was such as to justify the term "Agricultural Revolution." Like its industrial counterpart, the Agricultural Revolution at first was almost entirely restricted to Britain. Only with the advent of industrialization did larger landholders on the Continent begin to experiment with British methods. The small peasants, on the other hand, continued in their backward ways. As new industrial centers developed, new markets for agricultural produce opened up. Improvements in transportation facilitated marketing; and new scientific discoveries and the use of chemical fertilizers brought larger crop yields. These developments brought renewed hope for western Europe's farmers, who were gradually being overtaken by the industrialists and were also beginning to feel the competition of the vast agrarian lands of eastern Europe and America.

THE BEGINNINGS OF INDUSTRIALIZATION

Inventions and the Rise of the Factory System

The early history of industrialization is closely tied to the rise of mechanical inventions. Their numbers accelerated as one discovery created the need for another. When John Kay invented the flying shuttle in 1733, enabling one weaver to do the work of two, the need arose for some new device to speed up spinning. This demand was met in 1764 by James Hargreaves and his spinning jenny, which permitted the simultaneous spinning of sixteen or more threads. Some years later, Richard Arkwright devised the water frame, and in 1779 Samuel Crompton perfected the "mule," a hybrid that combined features of both Hargreaves's and Arkwright's inventions. This acceleration in spinning in turn called for further improvements in weaving. In 1787 Edmund Cartwright patented a new power loom. Once it was perfected, the demand for cotton increased. Cotton production received a boost when an American, Eli Whitney, in 1793 developed the cotton "gin," which speeded up removing the cotton fiber from its boll. Most inventions were made in the cotton industry: It was new, it had a large overseas market, and cotton lent itself particularly well to mechanical treatment.

Because most of these earlier devices were small, inexpensive, and hand-operated, they could be used as part of the domestic system in the workers' cottages. Arkwright's water frame, however, was large, expensive, and it needed water power to operate. Arkwright therefore, moved into the heart of the English textile region, where he operated the first spinning mill in 1771. By 1779 he was employing some three hundred workers operating several thousand spindles. Arkwright's example was gradually followed by other manufacturers and ultimately led to the establishment of the factory system.

The Steam Engine

Of all the inventions in the early years of industrialism, the steam engine was the most important. Until the advent of electricity it remained the chief source of artificial power. The development of the steam engine is closely related to the two basic commodities of modern industrialization—coal and iron. In the early eighteenth century the smelting of iron was still done with charcoal. The depletion of Britain's wood supply, however, and the discovery of a process for smelting iron with coke, shifted the emphasis to coal. The mining of coal was made easier by a simple steam engine, developed by Thomas Newcomen, to pump water from the coal mines. This early eighteenth-century engine was a long way from the steam engine that could be used to run other machines. The credit for developing such an engine belongs to the Scotsman James Watt, who patented his first steam engine in 1769. By 1800 some three hundred steam engines were at work in England, mostly in the cotton industry. The use of steam engines further increased the need for coal and iron. Improvements in iron production, on the other hand, in turn led to improvements in the making of steam engines. The interaction of one discovery with another thus continued to be a major feature of industrial development.

James Watt's plan of the first steam engine powered by steam pressure.

Early Industry on the Continent

Prior to 1815 the Industrial Revolution was chiefly a British phenomenon. An economic revival in France after 1763, helping to make up for the loss of the French colonies to Britain, had been interrupted by the French Revolution. However, the Continental System of Napoleon, which excluded British goods from the Continent, had proved most beneficial to French industry.

Elsewhere in Europe there were few signs of industrialization. Economic development in Germany was retarded by political disunity. The rich coal fields of the Ruhr, Saar, and Silesia were hardly worked before 1815, and what little industry there was, especially in textiles, still operated under the "putting-out" system. Russia, Italy, and Austria were almost wholly agrarian. After 1815, continental industries remained far behind those of Britain. It was only after the advent of the railroad in the 1830s that the situation began to improve.

THE RAILWAY AGE

Transportation in the Eighteenth Century

Industrial development was closely related to improvements in transportation. England again had special advantages in being able to use coastal shipping for the movement of bulky goods. Like other countries, however, it depended on roads and canals for inland transportation. As industrialization increased the need for transport, toll roads and canals became a profitable business. England added thousands of miles to its system of roads and canals during the eighteenth century, and France before the Revolution had the finest highway system in Europe. Napoleon improved matters further by pushing highways far into the Netherlands and Germany. In eastern Europe, however, paved roads were rare. Prussia constructed canals and improved riverways, but the movement of goods was hampered by innumerable tolls and tariffs. Farther east, dirt roads that turned to mud and rivers that ran shallow in summer and froze during the winter were the only arteries of communication.

The Advent of the Railroad

The railroad, which was to change all this, again had its start in England. Well before 1800, horse-drawn carts, moving first on wooden and later on iron rails, had been used to haul coal and iron. During the 1820s there were several hundred miles of such "rail ways." The problem of providing a faster means of locomotion was solved by putting the steam engine on wheels. The first commercial steam railroad was opened between Stockton and Darlington in 1825. By 1840 Britain had some eight hundred miles of track, and by 1850 it had more than six thousand. On the Continent, the railroad was slower in taking hold. The first railroad in France was opened in 1837, and by the middle of the century there were two thousand miles of track. Germany then had three thousand miles, Austria had one thousand, and Italy and Russia had merely a few fragmentary lines.

The economic impact of the railroad was overwhelming. Here was a wholly new industry, answering a universal need, employing thousands of people, offering unprecedented opportunities for investment, and introducing greater speed into all commercial transactions. England, already far ahead of the Continent in economic development, took the Railway Age pretty much in stride. Britain had been the workshop of the world for some time, and there was no indication that it would cease to be so. Railroad building vastly increased the demand for coal and iron, and England continued to lead the world in the production of both.

Britain also maintained its naval lead. The shipping industry was slow to feel the impact of steam. Even though Robert Fulton's steamboat had made its first successful run on the Hudson River in 1807, it was not until 1840 that Samuel Cunard established the first transatlantic steamer line. Even then the inefficiency of marine engines and the large amounts of coal needed for long voyages retarded the development of steamship service. Well into the second half of the nineteenth century the fast clipper ship re-

Early trains on the Liverpool and Manchester Railway.

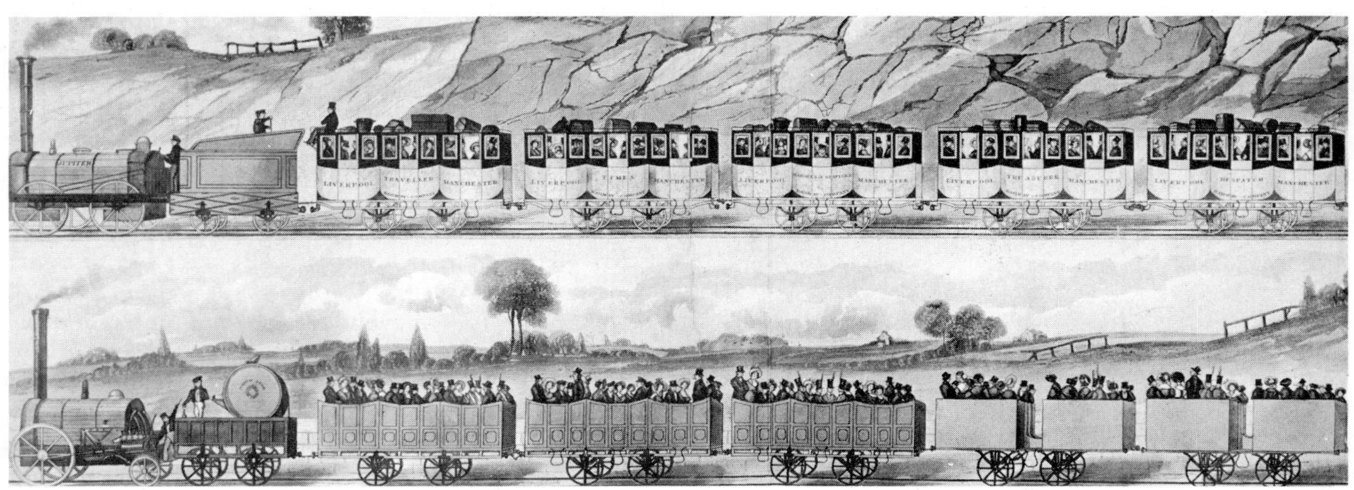

mained the chief means of ocean transport.

There were other important innovations and inventions in the early nineteenth century, with England again leading the way. The introduction of the penny post in 1840 helped business and private correspondence alike. The telegraph, invented by the American Samuel Morse, was first used extensively by Julius Reuter's news agency, established in 1851, the same year in which the first submarine cable crossed the English Channel. A reduction in the stamp tax in 1836 substantially lowered the price of newspapers, and by the middle of the century the circulation of the British press had risen more than threefold. The communication of news and ideas kept pace with the faster movements of goods and persons.

The Railway Age on the Continent

In May 1851 the "Great Exhibition of the Works of Industry of All Nations" opened in London's "Crystal Palace." This first "world's fair" was dramatic proof of Britain's industrial world leadership, but it also showed that other nations were beginning to catch up. The country in which industrialization made the most rapid progress was Belgium. An ample supply of coal and a skilled labor force were the chief reasons, but technical aid by British engineers and investment of British capital also helped.

The "Crystal Palace" in London, which housed the Great Exhibition of 1851.

In France, economic development was much slower. The French had lost some of their best coal mines to Belgium in 1815; and while European populations were increasing, the French birth rate had actually begun to decline. Still, with the encouragement given to commerce and industry by the July Monarchy, the middle class could not help but prosper. Pig-iron production, generally considered an index of industrial growth, increased fourfold in France during the thirty years after 1825; but it was still only one-quarter that of Great Britain. While England's population by the middle of the century was more than half urban, France remained predominantly rural. Imports of food were thus unnecessary and the domestic market was virtually self-contained.

In both Italy and Germany political disunity hampered economic growth. Industry in northern Italy remained insignificant until later in the century. In Germany, the *Zollverein* (see p. 710) did much to aid industrial development. Machines, imported from England, were used more and more. With the sinking of the first deep pit in the Ruhr in 1841, coal production began in earnest. But France, despite much slimmer resources, still produced more coal than Germany. As for pig iron, the total German output in 1855 was only half that of France. Railroad construction in Germany made rapid progress during the 1840s. The absence of natural obstacles kept construction costs low. The progress in railroad building gave some inkling of the economic vitality of the German people, which was merely awaiting political unification to assert itself.

Beyond western and central Europe, industrialization had made hardly any headway by 1850. Austria and Russia were still predominantly agrarian. Industry depended on an abundant supply of free labor. This supply did not exist in Austria until after the last feudal restrictions were abolished in 1849, and in Russia until the abolition of serfdom in 1861. Outside Europe only the United States was showing signs of industrialization. By 1850 New England had become largely industrialized, but the total output of American industry was still behind that of France and far behind that of Britain. Like Germany, America was to become a leading industrial power only toward the end of the century.

THE SOCIAL EFFECTS OF INDUSTRIALIZATION

The beginnings of modern industrialization in the eighteenth century seemed to bear out the claim of the Enlightenment that human reason and ingenuity could perfect the world. The invention of labor-saving machines promised to transform man from a beast of burden into a creature of leisure. But that promise soon began to fade. The "Industrial Revolution," in the beginning at least, benefited only a minority, the middle class, while it brought utmost misery and destitution to the growing working class. Only after industrialization had outgrown its infancy did its blessings come to be shared by the majority of people.

Population Growth

Many of the early hardships of industralization were due to an unprecedented population growth. Between 1815 and 1914, the population of Europe increased from 100 million to 460 million. Another 40 million Europeans migrated to other parts of the world, especially the United States. The rate of growth differed from country to country. It was largest in Russia, less in England and Germany, and least in France. Population growth was due both to an increase in the birth rate and a drop in the death rate. This drop had many causes: improvements in medicine and public hygiene, absence of major wars, greater efficiency in government and administration, the changes in agriculture leading to better diets and more ample food supplies, and, most important, the acceleration of industrial development. Industry provided the means whereby more people could live, and the increase of population, in turn, supplied the necessary labor force and swelled the ranks of consumers. The growth of population and industry thus interacted upon each other.

Urbanization and Working-Class Misery

With the increase in population and the growth of industry there came a further important demographic change—the movement of people from the country to the city. Large-scale urbanization had been virtually unknown before the early nineteenth century. But as workers began to flock to the mills, small villages grew into crowded towns and quiet towns into

Life in the Slums

It is impossible to give a proper representation of the wretched state of many of the inhabitants of the indigent class, situated in the confined streets . . . where each small, ill ventilated apartment of the house contained a family with lodgers in number from seven to nine, and seldom more than two beds for the whole. The want of convenient offices in the neighborhood is attended with many very unpleasant circumstances, as it induces the lazy inmates to make use of chamber utensils, which are suffered to remain in the most offensive state for several days, and are then emptied out of the windows. The writer had occasion a short time ago to visit a person ill of the cholera; his lodgings were in a room of a miserable house situated in the very filthiest part of Pipewellgate, divided into six apartments, and occupied by different families to the number of 26 persons in all. The room contained three wretched beds with two persons sleeping in each; it measured about 12 feet in length and 7 in breadth, and its greatest height would not admit of a person's standing erect; it received light from a small window, the sash of which was fixed. Two of the number lay ill of the cholera, and the rest appeared afraid of the admission of pure air, having carefully closed up the broken panes with plugs of old linen.

From "Report . . . from the Poor Law Commissioners on . . . the Sanitary Conditions of the Labouring Population of Great Britain," 1842, pp. 21–22.

Close, No. 118 High Street, Glasgow (*ca.* 1868–77).

noisy cities. This sudden influx of people brought on wretched housing conditions. Teeming slums turned into breeding places of disease, vice, and crime. There was no effective municipal administration to cope with these novel problems, and the workers themselves were too poor to improve their condition.

Poor housing was not the only hardship afflicting the early workers. Since mechanized industry required few skills, there was always an abundance of manpower, and wages remained at a minimum. The average working day was between twelve and sixteen hours. Since even this rarely yielded sufficient pay to support a worker's family, women and children had to work as well. Being more easily controlled and receiving less pay, they were much in demand. But women and children also suffered more than men did from the harsh conditions in factories and mines. No provisions were made for the workers' safety, and mishaps resulting from strange machines were frequent. There was no insurance against accidents, sickness, or old age. Furthermore, as more efficient machines were invented, unemployment added to the workers' hardships. As industrialization spread to the Continent, so did the abuses that accompanied it. Conditions in Belgium and France were almost as bad as those in England.

Middle-Class Indifference

The attitude of much of the bourgeois middle classes toward the misery of the working class was one of indifference. The new "captains of industry" had to be tough and ruthless men if they wanted to survive. Competition was keen and risks were great. The path of early industrialism was lined with bankruptcies. Economic booms burst; wars closed markets; machinery broke down or became obsolete; and the agrarian supporters of the old order fought stubbornly against middle-class efforts to gain economic and political influence.

In order to understand the seemingly callous attitude of the bourgeoisie toward the hardships of the workers, we must consider the middle-class philosophy of liberalism, which helped justify such selfish behavior. It was the belief in economic liberalism that prevented any drastic social reforms in the early part of the nineteenth century. The absence of such reforms, in turn, led to various protests on behalf of the workers, of which Marxian socialism became the most effective.

MIDDLE-CLASS LIBERALISM

The term *liberalism* has assumed so many different meanings that it defies clear definition. In the early nineteenth century, however, liberalism had definite meaning and aims. A liberal was a person who believed in freedom—freedom of thought, freedom of religion, freedom from economic restrictions, freedom of trade, and freedom from the political injustices of the old regime. Most of these freedoms had already been demanded by the Enlightenment. The *philosophes* held that every man had certain natural rights—life, liberty, and property. These rights the middle class had demanded before and during the French Revolution, and it continued to demand them. But as time went on, its claims were based not on natural law, as they had been during the eighteenth century, but on the grounds of utility, as the best way to bring about the "greatest happiness of the greatest number."

A Victorian family at home (*ca.* 1860).

"Utilitarianism"

The key figure in the transformation of liberal thought from the Enlightenment to the nineteenth century was the English philosopher and reformer Jeremy Bentham (1748–1832). To Bentham, the reasonableness of an institution depended on its utility. How was this utility to be determined? Bentham wrote: "For everyone, his own pleasure and his own freedom from pain is the sole good, his own pain and his own unfreedom the sole evil. Man's happiness and welfare consist exclusively of pleasurable feelings and of freedom from pain." Translated into politics, this meant that the best government was the one that ensured the most pleasure and gave the least pain to the largest number of people. The type of government most likely to produce that effect, according to Bentham, was a democracy.

Bentham's philosophy found numerous disciples, especially in England. Many of the British reforms in the 1820s and 1830s were due to the agitation of the "Utilitarians," or "Philosophical Radicals." The most influential follower of Bentham was John Stuart Mill (1806–73). Mill was an active public servant, a leading reformer, and a prolific writer on a wide range of subjects. Among his most famous writings was the essay *On Liberty* (1859). Its purpose was to set forth the basic principle according to which relations between the individual and society, between the citizen and his government, should be regulated. That principle, Mill said, is "that the sole end for which mankind may interfere with the liberty of action of the individual is self-protection. The only purpose for which power can be rightfully exercised over any member of a civilized community, against his will, is to prevent harm to others." Mill based his plea for individual liberty not on natural law, as earlier advocates of individual freedom had done, but on utility. "I regard utility," he said, "as the ultimate appeal on all ethical questions."

Mill's emphasis on the right of everyone to do as he saw fit as long as his actions did not conflict with society had tremendous appeal to the middle-class industrialist and businessman of the nineteenth century. Here was a philosophy that opposed any but the most necessary interference by the government in the affairs of the individual. "That government is best that governs least." In another essay, *Considerations on Representative Government* (1861), Mill discussed the purpose of government in terms that appealed to businessmen. "Government," he said, "is a problem to be worked like

John Stuart Mill.

any other question of business. The first step is to define the purpose which governments are required to promote. The next is to inquire what form of government is best fitted to fulfill these purposes." In answer to the first question, Mill held that it was the purpose of good government "to promote the virtue and intelligence of its people"; and in answer to the second question, what form of government is best, Mill, like Bentham, decided in favor of democracy.

Mill's belief in democracy was not shared by most members of the middle class. Nor were his proposals that the government should intervene to protect working children and improve housing and working conditions. Mill was especially concerned about the inequality that women still suffered in Victorian England. His essay *The Subjection of Women* (1869) was a ringing indictment of male chauvinism, and it became the bible of the women's suffrage movement. It remains as meaningful today as it was more than a century ago. There were already in Mill signs of a new type of liberalism that was ultimately to replace the dogmatic liberalism of the early nineteenth century (see p. 765). But even though Mill showed compassion for the underprivileged, his demand that the government leave the individual alone as much as possible clearly expressed the sentiments held by the majority of the bourgeoisie throughout the nineteenth century.

John Stuart Mill on the "Subjection of Women"

1869

Men do not want solely the obedience of women, they want their sentiments. . . . They have therefore put everything in practice to enslave their minds. . . . The masters of women wanted more than simple obedience, and they turned the whole force of education to effect their purpose. All women are brought up from the very earliest years in the belief that their ideal character is the very opposite to that of men; not self-will, and government by self-control, but submission, and yielding to the control of others. All the moralities tell them that it is the duty of women, and all the current sentimentalities that it is their nature, to live for others; to make complete abnegation of themselves, and to have no life but in their affections. And by their affections are meant the only ones they are allowed to have—those to the men with whom they are connected, or to the children who constitute an additional and indefeasible tie between them and a man. When we put together three things—first, the natural attraction between opposite sexes; secondly, the wife's entire dependence on the husband, every privilege or pleasure she has being either his gift, or depending on his will; and lastly, that the principal object of human pursuit, consideration, and all objects of social ambition, can in general be sought or obtained by her only through him—it would be a miracle if the object of being attractive to men had not become the polar star of feminine education and formation of character. And, this great means of influence over the minds of women having been acquired, an instinct of selfishness made men avail themselves of it to the utmost as a means of holding women in subjection, by representing to them meekness, submissiveness, and resignation of all individual will into the hands of a man, as an essential part of sexual attractiveness.

From John Stuart Mill, *On Liberty, Representative Government, The Subjection of Women* (London: Oxford University Press, 1960), pp. 443–4.

Liberalism in Politics

The middle class was primarily concerned with economic matters, and liberalism developed its own economic doctrine. But the bourgeoisie also realized that economic freedom was of no value unless it was complemented by political rights. The main guarantee of such rights was seen in a written constitution, like that of the United States or the French Constitution of 1791. There were many others between 1812 and 1849. Most of these constitutions favored constitutional monarchy rather than democracy. To ensure the predominance of the middle class, property qualifications for voting and for holding office were part of all liberal constitutions. Anyone who found this restriction unjust needed only to work hard and improve his economic status in order to gain a share in the government. Only in their guarantee of individual liberty did these constitutions advocate equality for everyone. Freedom of the press, freedom of conscience, freedom of association, and freedom from arbitrary arrest—these were shared by rich and poor alike, at least theoretically. Workers who tried to improve their condition through collective bargaining, however, or socialists who used the press to attack existing injustices, would soon find out that the individual liberties guaranteed in the constitutions did not apply to them.

The political ideal of early nineteenth-century liberalism was limited democracy. It has been aptly characterized as government of the wealthy, for the wealthy, by the wealthy. It was this ideal that motivated the bourgeoisie in the various revolutions discussed previously and that accounted for the widening rift between the middle and lower classes in these revolutions.

The "Classical Economists"

As for the economic philosophy of liberalism, its roots, too, went back to the eighteenth century. Its basic elements were already contained in the writings of Adam Smith (1723–90). This Glasgow professor, in his *Wealth of Nations* (1776), had advocated a policy of individual self-interest, free from any government interference, as the surest road to economic prosperity for society as a whole. Smith had proposed this policy of laissez-faire, of leaving things alone, in order to liberate the individual from the many governmental restrictions that had hampered economic progress under mercantilism. He was the first of several writers who are usually called the classical economists. These men, for the first time, formulated certain general economic laws that, they claimed, applied at all times and in all societies. The most prominent members of the group were Smith, Thomas Robert Malthus (1766–1823), and David Ricardo (1772–1823).

Malthus wrote his famous *Essay on the Principle of Population* in 1798 to criticize the Enlightenment's belief in unlimited human progress. To him the rapidly increasing population of western Europe was an insurmountable obstacle to progress. "The power of population," he wrote, "is indefinitely greater than the power in earth to produce subsistence for man. Population, when unchecked, increases in a geometrical ratio. Subsistence only increases in an arithmetical ratio." Here was the basic hypothesis of Malthusianism: People increased more rapidly than the food that was needed to keep them alive. Human misery, it seemed, was unavoidable. Poverty rather than progess was the normal state of human affairs.

Thomas Robert Malthus.

Many objections can be raised to the dire prophecies of Malthus. Even in his own day, improvements in agriculture and the opening to cultivation of vast new regions in America and elsewhere were increasing the world's food supply. Since then there have been further changes, especially with scientific farming and the development of birth control, to help maintain the balance between people and food. Still, the threat of overpopulation is with us today and shows no sign of abating.

To the majority of people in the early nineteenth century, the warnings of Malthus came as a shock. The future, which only recently held such promise, now suddenly looked bleak; no wonder the new science of political economy was soon called the "dismal science." Yet it was not dismal to everyone. As industrialists were growing rich while workers were sinking into misery, some voices now favored a more equitable distribution of profits. Such proposals, however, could not stand up against Malthus's assertion that poverty was inevitable. The poor were already increasing much faster than the rich. Giving them more wages or charity, the middle class could argue, would only result in their having more children. The best solution was to keep the poor as poor as possible. Adam Smith had asked government to keep its hands off business; Malthus advocated a similar attitude of laissez-faire in regard to social reform.

The pessimistic note that characterizes the teachings of Malthus is also found in the writings of David Ricardo. His basic work, *On the Principles of Political Economy and Taxation* (1817), was the first real textbook on economics. One of Ricardo's major contributions to the economic theory of early nineteenth-century liberalism was what his disciples called the "iron law of wages." Labor, to Ricardo, was like any other commodity. When it was plentiful, it was cheap; when it was scarce, it was expensive. As long as there is an ample supply of workers, wages will inevitably sink to the lowest possible level, just above starvation. To remedy this situation by lowering profits and raising wages would be futile, since it would merely increase the number of workers' children and, by limiting the supply of capital, cut down production. "Like all other contracts," Ricardo said, "wages should be left to the fair and free competition of the market, and should never be controlled by the interference of the legislature."

Here was another economic law as dismal in its prospects for the lower classes as Malthus's predictions. If people lived on the verge of starvation, if wages were low and children had to work sixteen hours a day, that was unfortunate; but it was also, as Malthus and Ricardo had shown, unavoidable. Attempts to change the situation through charity or legislation were opposed by middle-class liberals as interference with the beneficent principle of laissez-faire.

Liberalism on the Continent

All the intellectual figures mentioned so far in this discussion of liberalism were British. Since England had a larger and more influential middle class than most continental countries, this is not surprising. But the writings of these men had a deep effect on continental liberalism as well. Adam Smith's *Wealth of Nations,* in particular, supplied most of the ammunition for the attacks of continental liberals on the economic restrictions and regulations of their governments. There were some differences in the direction or emphasis of these attacks. French liberalism, for instance, was more concerned with economic matters than was liberalism in Germany, where the problems of political reform and national unification overshadowed all other issues. Outside England, France, and Germany, the philosophy of liberalism had few contributors. Liberalism, after all, was the credo of a class that had as yet made little headway outside western Europe.

SOCIAL REFORM

Given the laissez-faire attitude of liberalism, it is not surprising that efforts to solve social problems through government action found little support among the middle class. What social reforms were introduced owed much to the agitation of a few individuals, who were motivated either by humanitarianism or, as in the case of Britain's "Philosophical Radicals," by a desire to be utilitarian and efficient.

Factory Acts

Some of the most effective opposition to early nineteenth-century liberalism came from representatives of the old order. For political and economic but also humanitarian reasons, some Tories attacked the new industrial system in its most vulnerable spot, the terrible conditions in the mines and factories. As far back as 1802, Parliament had lowered the working hours of apprentices. The first real factory act, passed in 1819, forbade the employment in cotton mills of children under nine years old and limited the daily labor of children over nine to twelve hours. In 1831 night work was abolished for persons under twenty-one. In 1847 the maximum working day for women and children was set at ten hours. Two acts in 1842 and 1855 made it illegal to employ women and children in the mining industry.

Despite the best intentions on the part of their sponsors, however, these early factory acts were not very effective. They were not strictly enforced, and they applied chiefly to the cotton industry. Not until 1833 was their scope extended to include other industries, and only then was some system of inspection set up to enforce the new provisions.

Social Legislation

There were other reforms in England besides factory acts. The Municipal Corporations Act of 1835 enabled municipalities to cope more effectively with problems of rapid urbanization. To ensure uniformity in matters of public health, Parliament in 1848 set up a system of local boards of health. One of the most pressing social problems was the care of the poor. The New Poor Law of 1834 for the first time brought some order into the complicated system of poor relief. It was, however, a mixed blessing. The law abolished the traditional practice of "outdoor relief," under which the wages of the poorest workers had been supplemented from public funds. Henceforth, to be eligible for relief the poor had to report to workhouses; and by making conditions in these establishments as unpleasant as possible, all but those who could not possibly make a living otherwise were discouraged from going on relief. Here was a measure, clearly utilitarian, that delighted the middle class. It discouraged idleness and cut the expense of poor relief.

On the Continent, little was done to reform the abuses of early industrialism. A French Law in 1803 prohibited work in factories before 3:00 A.M. Under the reign of Louis Philippe, the employment of children under eight was prohibited, and the work of children under twelve was limited to eight hours a day. But enforcement of these laws, in France as in England, was very lax. In Belgium, nothing at all was being done to improve the lot of the workers. The only German state with any industry was Prussia, and here the government, in 1839, introduced a factory law that forbade the employment of children under nine and limited the working hours of older children to ten hours.

Liberalism and Education

The only field of social reform in which the Continent was ahead of Great Britain was education. Here, for once, liberalism was a great help. Like the *philosophe* of the eighteenth century, the nineteenth-century liberal was a firm believer in education as a means of improving the world. Any governmental measure in favor of education, therefore, had liberal support. Both France and Prussia had long traditions of public education, which they maintained during the nineteenth century. There was a brief reaction in favor of religious education under the Bourbons, but the Education Act passed under Louis Philippe again asserted the state's role. Britain's first provision of public funds for education was not until 1833. It was increased in subsequent years, but the amount set aside for education in 1839 was still only half of what it cost to maintain Queen Victoria's horses. Not until 1870 was the first general education act adopted in England. In the meantime, education depended on private initiative, in which the middle class played a beneficial role.

As this discussion has shown, some genuine attempts were made in the first half of the nineteenth century to cope with the ills of early industrialism through social reform. But such attempts ran counter to the laissez-faire philosophy of liberalism. Economic liberalism, to some extent, was a mere rationalization of selfish interests by the middle class. But there was also in it much of the eighteenth-century belief that the world operated according to certain basic laws that could not be altered and that ultimately made for the greater happiness of the greatest number.

This passive acquiescence in things as they were, however, could not possibly satisfy the workers. They refused to believe that the only solution to their troubles was to do nothing, to let matters take their course. They demanded that remedial action be taken on their behalf, else they were prepared to act for themselves.

WORKING-CLASS PROTEST

The protest of the working class took various forms. Some of the discontent expressed itself in political action, as in the revolutions of 1830 and 1848. In another form of protest, workers vented their anger and frustration on the very instruments that to them seemed primarily responsible for their plight—the machines. Sporadic instances of such "machine-breaking" occurred during the early phase of industrialization, both in England and on the Continent. But these acts of despair could not halt the advance of the machine age. Instead of waging war against mechanization, workers increasingly tried to escape industrialization altogether by emigrating to the United States, where virgin lands offered an opportunity of starting a new and better life.

Early Labor Unions

There was another way in which the working class tried to fight the injustices of industrialism. As the number of workers increased, they became aware that they constituted a separate class whose interests conflicted with those of their employers. This growing class consciousness among workers led them to organize, in an effort to gain better treatment.

The first country in which labor unions made any headway again was Great Britain. The British government, impressed by the radicalism of the French Revolution, had watched with apprehension labor's early efforts to organize. In 1799 and 1800 Parliament passed the Combination Acts, which prohibited workers from organizing to improve their condition. Labor's continued activities, however, together with the agitation of some middle-class reformers, finally made the government relent. In 1824 and 1825, the Combination Acts were repealed. Henceforth, trade unions in England were no longer illegal, though it was still prohibited to engage in strikes and other forms of protest. Even so, local unions now arose throughout Britain. The next step was the formation of a labor organization. This stage happened in 1834, and more successfully in 1845, with the organization of the "National Association for the Protection of Labour." In 1859 the Association pressured Parliament to allow peaceful picketing. In 1868 a Trades Union Congress representing more than one hundred thousand members met in Manchester. By 1875, trade unions in Britain had won full legal status, including the right to strike and to picket peacefully. The British labor movement had at last come into its own.

On the Continent, labor's efforts at self-help were much less successful. Labor unions were forbidden in Belgium until 1866, and there was no labor movement in Germany to speak of until after 1870. In France, the right of workers to organize had been forbidden even during the Revolution. This ban was reiterated in the *Code Napoléon* of 1803. Some French workers organized secret societies that fomented strikes and local uprisings; but these only made the government more repressive. Still, some people in France, the early socialists, took a more sympathetic view of the workers' fate. If England was prominent in defining the middle-class philosophy of liberalism, France was equally prominent in launching its counterpart, the working-class philosophy of socialism.

THE BEGINNINGS OF MODERN SOCIALISM

Socialism as a mode of life is nothing new. It always existed, and still does, in primitive communities where people work together and share the proceeds of their common labor. Socialism as an economic and social philosophy, on the other hand, is a recent development, closely connected with the rise of industrialism. The term *socialism* did not come into use until the 1830s. Like liberalism, it has assumed a wide variety of meanings. Today almost any kind of government interference with the free play of economic forces is called socialism, be it the communist system of Russia or the welfare state of America.

While there are many varieties of socialism, all share certain basic principles. All socialists claim that the existing distribution of wealth is unjust—giving a few people far more than they need and leaving large numbers of people with barely enough to exist. To close this gap between haves and have-nots, socialists advocate common ownership of society's resources and means of production. The fruits of production—that is, the profits of human labor—socialists propose to distribute in such a way that everyone receives an equal or at least equitable share. All schools of socialism agree that there should be far-reaching changes in the direction of economic and social as well as political equality.

The Utopian Socialists

Historically, modern socialism is divided into pre-Marxian and post-Marxian socialism or, in Marxist terms, into "Utopian" and "scientific" socialism. The Utopian socialists earned their epithet because of the unrealistic nature of their schemes. Most of the Utopians were French, and they all came from the middle or upper classes. Given the workers' poverty and lack of education, this is hardly surprising.

The first Utopian socialist to achieve any prominence was a French nobleman, Count Henri de Saint-Simon (1760–1825). Concerned by the social and economic injustices of a laissez-faire economy, Saint-Simon suggested that the state take a hand in organizing society in such a way that people, instead of exploiting one another, join forces to exploit nature. "The whole society," he held, "ought to strive toward the amelioration of the moral and physical existence of the most numerous and poorest class." Saint-Simon defined the principle according to which this amelioration should operate as: "From each according to his capacity, to each according to his work." This became one of the basic slogans of socialism.

Another prominent Utopian was Charles Fourier (1772–1837). Most of society's ills, Fourier held, were due to the improper environment in which most people lived. To provide more favorable surroundings, Fourier proposed the creation of so-called phalanxes. These were to be pleasant communities of some eighteen hundred people, living on five thousand acres of land, and forming a self-sufficient economic unit. Fourier's plans never materialized in Europe, but in the United States, where land was cheap and pioneering more common, a number of cooperative establishments were tried. None of them, however, became a lasting success.

Charles Fourier.

The only one among the French Utopians to play an active political role was Louis Blanc (1811–82). Blanc realized that economic reform, to be effective, must be preceded by political reform. Once true democracy had been achieved, the state could initiate the new type of industrial organizations that Blanc proposed. These consisted of social or national workshops—that is, self-supporting units of production, owned and operated by the workers. Workshops of this kind were given a brief try by the revolutionary government of 1848, of which Louis Blanc was a member. The experiment failed, however, largely because the original purpose of the workshops was subordinated to the needs of the moment, the temporary relief of unemployment.

The most prominent Utopian socialist outside France was the British industrialist Robert Owen (1771–1858). Appalled by conditions he found when he took over the cotton mills at New Lanark in Scotland, Owen gave his workers decent housing, increased their pay, and shortened their hours. In the model community he created, both productivity and profits increased, thus bearing out Owen's contention that satisfied workers were also better workers. Owen was less fortunate with a project he attempted on this side of the Atlantic. The community of New Harmony in Indiana, conceived along the lines of Fourier's phalanxes, turned out to be a fiasco.

Utopian socialism, in fact, had little to show for its manifold efforts. Like

Robert Owen's vision for New Harmony, his model socialist community in the wilderness of Indiana.

the *philosophes,* the Utopians believed in the natural goodness of man and the perfectibility of the world. They soon discovered that men were not naturally good and reasonable. But the failure of the Utopians contained a useful lesson. It showed that idealism and the best intentions are not sufficient to reform society. A more realistic and more militant type of socialism was needed that would use the workers' potential economic and political power to wrest concessions from the middle class. This new kind of socialism was first presented in the writings of Karl Marx (1818–83) and Friedrich Engels (1820–95).

MARXIAN SOCIALISM

One of the reasons for the failure of the Utopians was that they never sparked any substantial movement among the workers. There were some working-class organizations during the 1830s and 1840s, but they were secret conspiracies rather than open political parties. In France, Auguste Blanqui founded the "Society of Families" and the "Society of Seasons," both of them socialistic or communistic. Another such society, founded by German exiles, was the "League of the Just." Its program was supplied by Wilhelm Weitling, a German tailor who in 1842 published his *Guarantee of Harmony and Freedom.* These various underground organizations were influenced by the writings of the Utopian socialists, but in their demands for complete economic equality, or communism, they went considerably beyond the demands of the Utopians.

Communism — that is, the abolition of all private property — ultimately became the basis of most socialist programs. A century ago, the term *communism* did not have the connotations it has assumed since the Bolshevik Revolution. The number of communist socialists in the first half of the nineteenth century was very small, and few people realized the ultimate implications of their aims. In 1844 two young Germans, Karl Marx and Friedrich Engels, made contact with the "League of the Just." Soon thereafter its name was changed to "Communist League," and from secret revolutionary conspiracy it now shifted to open propaganda. In 1847, Marx and Engels supplied the League with its new program, *The Communist Manifesto.*

Karl Marx and Friedrich Engels

Both Marx and Engels came from the middle class that they spent most of their lives attacking. As a university student in Germany, Marx had shown a lively interest in social issues. His early writings got him into trouble and in 1843 led to his first exile in Paris. There he met Engels, the son of a wealthy German industrialist with industrial holdings in England. Engels was already a communist, and a close intellectual partnership developed between the two men. Engels through most of his life also supported Marx financially.

The first result of their collaboration was *The Communist Manifesto,* which appeared during the revolutions of 1848. Marx welcomed the revolutions, and he was present during the upheavals in Paris. When the revolutions failed, he went to England, where he remained until his death in 1883. While in England Marx wrote most of his basic works, notably *Das Kapital,* the first volume of which appeared in 1867.

The Communist Manifesto

The basic elements in Marx's social philosophy were contained in the brief and persuasive *Communist Manifesto.* Its fundamental proposition, as restated by Engels in his introduction to a later edition of the *Manifesto,* was

> that in every historical epoch the prevailing mode of economic production and exchange, and the social organization necessarily following from it, form the basis upon which is built up, and from which alone can be explained, the political and intellectual history of that epoch; that consequently the whole history of mankind (since the dissolution of primitive tribal society, holding land in common ownership) has been a history of class struggles, contests between exploiting and exploited, ruling and oppressed classes; that the history of these struggles forms a series of evolutions in which, nowadays, a stage has been reached where the exploited and oppressed class — the proletariat — cannot attain its emancipation from the sway of the exploiting and ruling class — the bourgeoisie — without, at the same time and once and for all, emancipating society at large from all exploitation, oppression, class distinctions, and class struggles.

Here are the two basic tenets for which Marx is most famous: his economic, or materialistic, interpretation of history, and his theory of the class struggle. Others before Marx had recognized the influence of external factors upon history. But Marx focused his attention on one particular aspect of environment that he considered fundamental: the means of production, the way in which people make a living. The economic structure of society, according to Marx, determines its social, political, legal, and even cultural aspects. Historians before Marx, especially since the eighteenth century, had viewed history as an intellectually determined process. Marx took a diametrically opposite view, recognizing material, nonintellectual forces as the sole determining factors.

To illustrate his economic interpretation of history as well as his theory of the class struggle, Marx, in *The Communist Manifesto,* gave a brief survey of the history of western civilization as he saw it:

Family photograph of Karl Marx (right), his wife, and two daughters in the 1860s. Friedrich Engels is at left.

The history of all hitherto existing society is the history of class struggles. Freeman and slave, patrician and plebeian, lord and serf, guildmaster and journeyman, in a word, oppressor and oppressed, stood in constant opposition to one another, carried on an uninterrupted, now hidden, now open fight, a fight that each time ended either in a revolutionary reconstitution of society at large, or in the common ruin of the contending classes.

Marx then examined the history of western society beginning with the Middle Ages. At that time, the economy of Europe was predominantly agrarian, with a large class of serfs supporting a small class of feudal nobles. Upon this society, material changes began to work: money, trade, the beginnings of a commercial, capitalist economy. As these changes took hold, a new trading or bourgeois class was formed. And between the old feudal nobility and the new middle class a struggle arose, which led to some preliminary victories of the bourgeoisie in England and Holland and culminated in the American War of Independence and the French Revolution.

The final victory of the middle class came in the nineteenth century. But this did not end the struggle. Because now a new struggle began, this time between the bourgeoisie and the proletariat. It was brought about by another change in the mode of production, the introduction of the factory system and the rise of industrial capitalism. The workers in this new struggle, which Marx saw going on around him, were held down by the iron laws of capitalist economics to a bare subsistence level. But there was one thing these workers could do, according to Marx: they could organize, they could become class conscious.

Marx felt certain that the bourgeoisie and the workers were already locked in their death struggle. And the victory of the proletariat in this struggle, Marx held, could be predicted with scientific certainty—hence the term *scientific socialism.* By the laws of capitalist competition there were bound to be periodic crises, caused by "epidemics of overproduction." As a result of these crises, the poor would get poorer and the rich would get richer. And there would come a time when

it becomes evident, that the bourgeoisie is unfit any longer to be the ruling class in society. . . . because it is incompetent to assure an existence to its slave within his slavery. . . . Society can no longer live under this bourgeoisie. . . . Its fall and the victory of the proletariat are equally inevitable.

So much for the collapse of capitalism. What then? What will the world be like after the proletariat has won? On that subject Marx was not too clear. At one point he envisaged a transition period—the "dictatorship of the proletariat"—in which the proletariat by revolution will destroy the existing machinery of the state, will convert the means of production into public property, and will gradually bring about a classless society. The state, as Engels put it, will gradually "wither away." Then what? "In place of the old bourgeois society, with its classes and class antagonisms," Marx concludes, "we shall have an association in which the free development of each is the condition for the free development of all." This is an idyllic, but rather vague picture, not very different from the kind of society certain eighteenth-century writers had envisaged. There was, in fact, a good deal of the eighteenth century in Marxism. It shared the *philosophes'* belief in progress, in the good life on earth, and in the natural goodness of man.

The Errors and Contributions of Marx

What about Marx's concept of classes, and of history as a series of class struggles? The concept of class certainly was a useful contribution; and if Marx did not make us class conscious, he helped our understanding of past and present society by making us aware of classes. But his definition of classes entirely in economic terms is far too narrow; and by denying the role of the individual, it runs counter to the liberal belief in individualism. As for Marx's view of the past as a series of class struggles, it does not really fit the facts of history, nor does his emphasis on merely two opposing classes. Marx recognized the existence of other classes, but he believed that they would ultimately be absorbed by either the bourgeoisie or the proletariat. This prediction, like so many others Marx made, thus far has failed to materialize.

There were, then, a good many blind spots in Marx's socialist theories. While the rich were getting richer, the poor did not necessarily get poorer. The general standard of living in the world's industrial nations was to reach heights undreamed of by Marx. Man, furthermore, does not seem to be motivated exclusively, or even primarily, by economic concerns. Despite Marx's attacks on religion, the established churches continued to play an important part even in the lives of the lower classes. Another force that increasingly came to command the allegiance of rich and poor alike was nationalism. The great wars of the last century were fought not between workers and capitalists, but between the citizens of different countries for the defense or the greater glory of their nation.

Despite errors and shortcomings, however, Marx's contributions to modern thought have been immeasurable. By bridging the gap between politics and economics, he enriched our understanding of the past. We may not accept the dominant role he assigned to economic factors, but we have come to realize the importance of these factors. Prior to Marx, the division of society into rich and poor was accepted as a natural, unchangeable fact. It was chiefly due to Marx that society was jolted out of such complacent acceptance of the status quo. By predicting far-reaching changes, he made people aware that changes were possible. The threat of revolutionary change conjured up in Marx's writings did much to hasten the peaceful evolution that has so markedly improved the condition of the lower orders in industrial societies. Marxian socialism offered its followers a seemingly logical, scientifically certain answer to the many perplexities of modern society. This explains its appeal to workers and intellectuals alike. The ultimate appeal of Marxism lay in the almost religious fervor it inspired among its disciples.

OTHER FORMS OF SOCIAL CRITICISM

Marxian socialism, in its ultimate effects on society, turned out to be the most important attack on the capitalist philosophy of laissez-faire. Other critics of this philosophy, however, tried in different ways to awaken their contemporaries to the social problems created by the industrialization of society.

Humanitarianism

Novelists like Victor Hugo and Honoré de Balzac in France and

Engels's Funeral Oration for Marx

(1883)

Karl Marx was one of those outstanding men few of whom are produced in any century. Charles Darwin discovered the laws of evolution of organic nature on our planet. Marx is the discoverer of the fundamental law that determines the course and development of human history. . . .

Above all, he saw in science a great lever of history, a revolutionary force in the best sense of the term. And in this sense, he applied his immense knowledge, especially of history, to all the fields he mastered.

For he was truly a revolutionary, as he called himself. The struggle for the emancipation of the wage-earning class from the fetters of the modern capitalist system of exploitation was his true mission. . . .

Nobody can fight for a cause without making enemies. And he had many of them. Throughout the greatest part of his political life he was the most hated and most calumniated man in Europe. But he hardly paid attention to the calumnies. . . . At the end of his life, he could proudly glimpse millions of followers in the mines of Siberia as well as in the workshops of Europe and America. He saw his economic theories becoming the indisputable basis of socialism throughout the whole world.

From Saul K. Padover, *Karl Marx: An Intimate Biography* (New York: McGraw-Hill, 1978), p. 591.

Charles Dickens at age forty-seven.

Mikhail Bakunin.

Charles Dickens in England, by dwelling on the more sordid aspects of the new industrialism, played on human sympathy in the hope of creating a climate favorable to reform. The historian Thomas Carlyle, in his *Past and Present* (1843), showed deep concern over the growing division between the working classes on the one hand and the wealthy on the other. He turned against the "mammonism" and the "mechanism" of his times and admonished the new captains of industry to be aware of their responsibilities as successors to the old aristocracy. Benjamin Disraeli, one of the rising young Tories, in his social novel *Sybil* (1845), deplored the wide gap that industrialization had opened between the rich and the poor. It was, he said, as though England had split into two nations "between whom there was no intercourse and no sympathy."

Christian Socialism

Another body of social criticism arose within the Christian churches, first in England and later on the Continent. For centuries past, organized Christianity had been the chief dispenser of charity. The beginnings of modern Christian Socialism go back to a small group of British clergymen who felt that the best way to attack the evils of industrialism was to reaffirm the gospel of charity and brotherly love. The leader of the Christian Socialist movement was the Anglican theologian Frederick Denison Maurice. Its best-known propagandist was the clergyman and novelist Charles Kingsley. In his famous tract, *Cheap Clothes and Nasty* (1850), Kingsley attacked the condition of "ever-increasing darkness and despair" in the British clothing industry, whose sweatshops were "rank with human blood." To remedy a situation in which men were like "beasts of prey, eating one another up by competition, as in some confined pike-pond, where the great pike, having dispatched the little ones, begin to devour each other," Kingsley proposed the formation of cooperative enterprises in which everyone would be "working together for common profit in the spirit of mutual self-sacrifice." Christian Socialism, in appealing to social consciousness, helped to modify the belief in laissez-faire and to prepare the soil for the movement of social reform that gained momentum in the second half of the nineteenth century.

Anarchism

One other form of social protest of quite a different nature deserves mention here, even though its effects were not felt until later in the century. Anarchism, like socialism, was intended to overthrow capitalism. But while the socialists were ready to use the state as a stepping-stone for their aims, the anarchists were deeply opposed to any kind of governmental authority. One of the earliest theorists of anarchism was the French publicist Pierre-Joseph Proudhon (1809–65). In his pamphlet *First Memoir on Property* (1840), he asked "What is property?" and replied with the well-known slogan, "Property is theft!" This opposition to private property appeared to align Proudhon with Marx. The latter's admiration cooled, however, when he discovered that Proudhon was less interested in overthrowing the middle class than in raising the worker to the level of that class. Proudhon was against any kind of government, be it by an individual or party. "Society," he wrote, "finds its highest perfection in the union of order with anarchy."

The most famous proponent of anarchism was a Russian nobleman, Mikhail Bakunin (1814–76). A theorist of anarchism, he also practiced what he preached. Bakunin was involved in several revolutions, was three times condemned to death, and spent long years in prison and exile. Bakunin attributed most of the evils of his day to two agencies—the state and the Church—both enemies of human freedom. His ideal society was a loose federation of local communities, each with maximum autonomy. In each of these communities the means of production were to be held in common. The way to achieve this governmentless condition, Bakunin held, was not by waiting patiently for the state to wither away, as Marx held, but by helping matters along, if necessary by means of terrorism, assassination, and insurrection. The last decade of the nineteenth century, as we shall see, witnessed a whole series of assassinations attributed to anarchists. But anarchism never developed into a well-defined movement, partly because of Bakunin's death in 1876, partly because of the impracticable nature of its doctrine. Traces of it, however, survived into the twentieth century and contributed to another type of social protest, syndicalism (see p. 764).

By the middle of the nineteenth century, the coming of the Industrial Age, with its revolutionary political, social, and economic effects, had made itself felt over most of Europe. For the next two decades, people's attention becameabsorbed by momentous political developments. A series of wars radically changed the existing international order and overshadowed economic developments. Once the political situation had become stabilized, however, after 1870, a second wave of economic development swept over Europe and the world, a wave of sufficient magnitude to justify the term "Second Industrial Revolution" (see pp. 762–63).

Suggestions for Further Reading

Changing views of the Industrial Revolution are discussed in D. Landes, *The Unbound Prometheus: Technological Change and Industrial Development in Western Europe from 1750 to the Present* (1969). A good account of early industrialization is P. Deane, *The First Industrial Revolution* (1965). T. S. Ashton, *The Industrial Revolution 1760–1830* (1948), corrects many misconceptions. Besides England, only France experienced any noticeable early industrial development; see A. L. Dunham, *The Industrial Revolution in France, 1815–1848* (1955). The spread of industrialization is stressed in W. O. Henderson, *The Industrial Revolution on the Continent* (1961). The traditional emphasis on the negative social effects of early industrialism is confirmed in E. P. Thompson, *The Making of the English Working Class* (1963). S. G. Checkland, *The Rise of Industrial Society in England, 1815–1885* (1964), presents a more neutral picture. On urban growth, see E. Gauldie, *Cruel Habitation: A History of Working-Class Housing, 1780–1918* (1974). The situation in France is described in L. Chevalier, *Working Classes and Dangerous Classes in Paris During the First Part of the Nineteenth Century* (1971).

The best way to study the utilitarians and classical economists is through their writings, available in many editions. Among secondary treatments, E. Halévy, *The Growth of Philosophic Radicalism* (1955), is a standard work. More recent treatments are J. Hamburger, *Intellectuals in Politics: John Stuart Mill and the Philosophic Radicals* (1965), and S. H. Letwin, *The Pursuit of Certainty: David Hume; Jeremy Bentham; John Stuart Mill; Beatrice Webb* (1965). On social reform, see W. M. Thomas, *The Early Factory Legislation* (1948), and more generally, E. L. Woodward, *The Age of Reform, 1815–1870* (1938).

On socialism, G. Lichtheim, *The Origins of Socialism* (1969), is brilliant. F. Manuel, *The Prophets of Paris* (1962), deals with the French Utopian socialists. The literature on Marxian socialism is staggering. The following are good to excellent: G. Lichtheim, *Marxism* (1961); S. Avineri, *The Social and Political Thought of Karl Marx* (1969); J. Seigel, *Marx's Fate: The Shape of a Life* (1978); and I. Berlin, *Karl Marx: His Life and Environment* (1963).

	1815				1870	
SOUTHWEST ASIA AND AFRICA	**1818–28** King Shaka, apex of Zulu kingdom	**1836** Boers' Great Trek begins		**1860** French expansion in West Africa **1869** Suez Canal opens		
EUROPE	**1815** Congress of Vienna **1815–83** Karl Marx **1825** Decembrist Revolt, Russia **1825** First commercial railroad	**1829** Treaty of Adrianople **1830** France's "July Monarchy" **1832** Britain's Great Reform Bill **1848** *Communist Manifesto*	**1848–49** Europe in Revolt **1848–61** Unification of Italy **1848–70** Napolean III **1851** Crystal Palace Exhibition, London	**1859** Darwin, *Origin of Species* **1854–56** Crimean War **1861–71** Unification of Germany **1867** Austro-Hungarian *Ausgleich*	**1870–71** Franco-Prussian War **1876** First internal combustion engine **1878** Congress of Berlin	**1882** Triple Alliance **1894** Russo-French Alliance
SOUTH AND SOUTHEAST ASIA	**1819** British found Singapore		**1857–58** Indian Mutiny **1859** French seize Saigon			
EAST ASIA	**1825–30** Java War **1839–42** Opium War		**1850–64** Taiping Rebellion **1854** Perry opens US trade with Japan **1868** Meiji Restoration, Japan			**1893–1976** Mao Zedong **1894–95** Sino-Japanese War
THE AMERICAS AND PACIFIC	**1823** Monroe Doctrine	**1835–40** Alexis de Tocqueville, *Democracy in America* **1840** Britain annexes New Zealand **1846–48** Mexican War	**1849** Gold discovered in California	**1861–65** American Civil War **1867** Russia sells Alaska to US **1867** British North America Act	**1869** Opening of Transcontinental railroad	

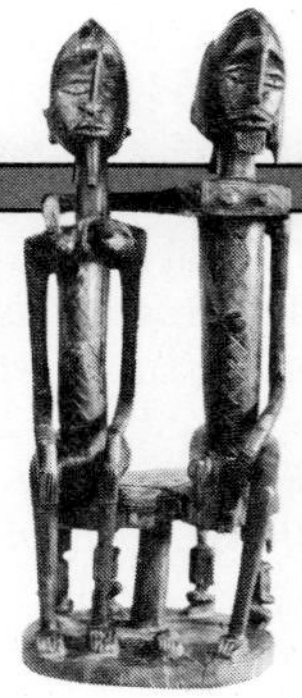

Wood sculpture, Dogon tribe, Mali, West Africa.

Eiffel Tower, Paris, 1889.

***Empire State Express* *No. 999,* *ca.* 1890.**

Commodore Matthew Perry, a Japanese view, 1853.

British suffragette, ***ca.*** **1910.**

Private Edwin Francis Jennison, Confederate Army.

1914	
1886 Gold discovered in Southern Africa **1889** Rhodesia colonized **1899–1902** Boer War **1910** Union of South Africa formed	
1894–1905 Dreyfus Affair **1905** Russian Revolution begins **1905** Einstein's Theory of Relativity **1907** Triple Entente **1912–13** Balkan Wars	
1885 Indian National Congress founded **1906** Muslim League founded	
1900 Boxer Rebellion **1904–05** Russo-Japanese War **1911** Chinese Revolution **1912–49** Chinese Republic	
1889 First Pan-American Conference **1898** Spanish-American War **1910** Mexican Revolution begins	**1914** Panama Canal opens

The Prince of Wales in Bangalore, India, *ca.* 1900.

Gold prospector, California, *ca.* 1850.

35 The End of the Vienna System, 1850–71

The main concern of European statesmen in the first half of the nineteenth century had been to reconcile the traditional claims of the old monarchical and aristocratic order with the democratic demands of the rising middle and lower classes. By 1850 the middle class had won some notable victories in western Europe, but east of the Rhine, the old regime had stood its ground. In the past, the defenders of the old order and the advocates of the new had been divided along ideological lines, with conservatives trying to maintain the status quo, and liberals hoping to change it. The men who rose to leadership after 1850 were more flexible. They were realists, ready to forgo some of their principles to achieve some of their aims. Demands for political reform continued. But the unprecedented economic growth of Europe helped divert the attention of the middle class from politics to economics.

Besides economics, there was nationalism to absorb people's attention. Before 1850, domestic upheavals and international peace had been the order of the day; after 1850, the reverse was true. Five wars involving great powers were fought between 1854 and 1871, all of them prompted by nationalism. In the past, whenever the Vienna System had been threatened, the "Concert of Europe" had collaborated to see that peace was restored and the balance of power maintained. With the rise of nationalism, however, the European concert became more tenuous. Even before

1850 the powers had failed to agree on certain international issues. But the first major showdown did not occur until after 1850. The Crimean War (1854–55) was the first in a whole series of conflicts that put at least a temporary end to the Concert of Europe. By 1871, the Vienna System had collapsed, and a new balance of power had emerged on the Continent.

THE EASTERN QUESTION

The Crimean War was the latest phase in the slow disintegration of the Ottoman Empire. The "Eastern Question" had already caused one brief war between Russia and Turkey in 1828–29. To ensure ice-free navigation, Russia needed free access to the Black Sea through the Turkish Straits. This it had gained for its merchant ships in 1774, and again in 1829. Attempts to gain exclusive passage for Russian warships, however, had run into opposition from the rest of the powers, because that would have ensured Russian predominance in the Black Sea. Instead the Straits Convention of 1841 maintained the closure of the Straits to *all* foreign warships.

The Straits were not the only issue behind the Eastern Question. Both France and Great Britain had considerable commercial interests in Southwest Asia, and the British regarded the eastern Mediterranean as the chief approach to India. These interests were threatened by Russia's gradual encroachment on Turkey, as in its occupation of the Danubian principalities after 1829. While Russia was thus threatening to change the status quo in the Ottoman Empire, France and England hoped to maintain it.

Florence Nightingale.

Another source of friction, which was the immediate cause for the Crimean War, concerned the so-called Holy Places in Jerusalem and Palestine that were closely associated with the life of Christ. Christians within the Ottoman Empire had long been guaranteed certain rights, and pilgrims had been granted access to the Holy Land. The interests of Catholics were traditionally championed by France, while Russia was the guardian of eastern, Greek Orthodox rights. Shortly after 1850, when conflicts between the two religious groups led to a number of incidents, the tsar tried to pressure Turkey into officially recognizing Russia's role as protector of Greek Orthodox rights. In order to emphasize their own interests, Britain and France sent naval contingents to the entrance of the Straits. Russia replied by reoccupying the Danubian principalities that it had evacuated two years earlier. The Concert of Europe, acting on Austrian initiative, vainly tried to keep tension from mounting. In October 1853 Turkey, trusting in British and French support, declared war on Russia. Pressure of public opinion and concern over the expansion of Russian influence later brought the western powers into the war on Turkey's side. For the first time in forty years, the great powers had become involved in war with each other.

The Crimean War and the Peace of Paris

The major action of the Crimean War was a year-long siege of Sebastopol on the Crimean Peninsula. It was one of history's costliest operations, with most of the casualties caused by disease. One of its effects was the creation of the first modern nursing and medical services under the direction of Florence Nightingale, from which ultimately arose the International Red Cross.

The Crimean War lined up most of Europe against Russia. As the war progressed, Austria drew closer to the western powers. The Austrians never did any actual fighting, but Nicholas I resented their "ingratitude" for his aid during the Hungarian uprisings in 1849. Prussia outwardly followed Austria's lead but secretly aided the Russian cause. The small kingdom of Piedmont-Sardinia also entered the war on the side of the western powers, hoping to gain their support for Italian unification.

Sebastopol fell in September 1855. Nicholas I had died in March, and his successor, Alexander II, was now ready to talk peace. The Paris Peace Conference met in the spring of 1856. To curtail Russian influence over the Ottoman Empire, the Black Sea was neutralized, which meant that Russia could not have any warships or fortifications there. In addition, navigation on the Danube River was declared open to all powers, and Russia had to surrender part of Bessarabia at the mouth of the Danube to the Turkish principality of Moldavia. Both Moldavia and Wallachia were placed under the temporary supervision of the great powers and were given separate governments. In 1858, however, both principalities elected the same man, Prince Alexander Cuza, as their ruler, and in 1862 they were recognized by the great powers as the autonomous state of Rumania. The principle of nationality had triumphed once again.

Among the other decisions of the Paris Conference was the formal admission of Turkey to the family of powers, upon promise that it would introduce much-needed reforms. The Conference also issued a declaration against privateering and specified that a blockade, to be effective, had to be backed by force. This principle of the "freedom of the seas" was intended to safeguard the rights of neutrals in time of war. Finally, the Conference took notice of the "Italian Question" by permitting Cavour, the prime minister of Piedmont, to plead the cause of Italian unification before the assembled dignitaries.

The Peace of Paris, like the Vienna settlement forty years earlier, was an effort by the great powers to remove the sources of tension that had led to war and to restore the balance of power that had been threatened by one of them. But while the Vienna settlement had succeeded in restoring international stability, the Paris settlement left a legacy of discontent. The Russians, in particular, felt humiliated, and henceforth would try to recoup the losses they had suffered. The French took pride in the fact that their emperor had emerged as the leading figure at the Paris Peace Conference. But Napoleon III's role as arbiter of Europe merely whetted his appetite for further foreign ventures, and he was soon to come up with new plans for revising the map of Europe. Furthermore, the fact that Cavour had been permitted to raise the question of Italy's future, gave fresh hope to Italian nationalists, whose aspirations could be fulfilled only by war against Austria.

Other than Russia, the country most seriously affected by the Crimean War was Austria. It had been seriously weakened not only by estrangement from Russia, but from Prussia as well. Prussia, already restive under the domination that Austria had resumed in German affairs after 1850, was further

Crimean Casualties

In assessing the Crimean War and the armies that fought there, the public mind has been greatly influenced by the highly dramatized accounts of the sufferings that took place. Much of the criticism has been focused on the medical services, which were quite unable to cope with the strain put on them. . . . The 'hospital' in the Scutari, an old Turkish barracks, was of course appalling. Whether the smell there was worse than from the Thames at the same time might be debatable. . . . Although bad smells—with the exception of that from farmyard manure—were thought to be unhealthy there was no understanding why this might be so. Only after the Crimean War was over did Pasteur and Lister prove that microbes and bacteria existed. . . . Surgery, as far as the battlefield was concerned, consisted mainly of amputation. . . . There were, of course, no facilities for anything, no proper anaesthetics, antiseptics, dressings, bandages, nor any means even for sharpening the few and inadequate instruments. . . . Surgeon-General Longmore, who conducted an inquiry into the medical service in the Crimea, produced some surprising information. His, and other reports, showed that many of the deaths could have been prevented had the administration been better. The total number of British deaths in the Crimea was 18,058. Of these 1,761 died from enemy action, the remaining 16,297 from disease. . . . As the average strength of the British forces in the first nine months was thirty one thousand the mortality rate in the Crimea during this period was therefore sixty per cent. This was greater than the mortality rate had been in England during the great plagues.

From Philip Warner, *The Crimean War: A Reappraisal* (New York: Taplinger, 1973), pp. 211–13.

Participants in the Paris Peace Conference (1856). Seated: Baron Hübner (Austria), Ali Pasha (Turkey), Lord Clarendon (Britain), Count Walewski (France), Count Orlov (Russia), Baron de Bourqueney (France), and Lord Cowley (Britain). Standing: Count Cavour (Sardinia), De Villamarina (Sardinia), Count Hatzfeldt (Prussia), Count Vincent Benedetti (France), Mohammed Jemil Bey (Turkey), Baron Brunnov (Russia), Baron Manteuffel (Prussia), and Count Buol (Austria).

alienated by Austria's attempts to involve the two German powers in the Crimean War. This isolation of Austria from its traditional friends, Russia and Prussia, was perhaps the most significant result of the war. It was the more ominous because England, having learned a bitter lesson at Sebastopol, once more withdrew from continental affairs. Austria was thus left alone at the mercy of Italian and German nationalism. The stage had been set for one of the most dramatic periods in European history. The tragic hero of this drama was the French Emperor, Napoleon III.

THE SECOND FRENCH EMPIRE

Napoleon III remains very much an enigma. After his fall from power in 1870, there was little doubt in anyone's mind that he was a fraud and a failure. More recently, however, historians have become somewhat more charitable in their judgment. In his domestic policy, Napoleon III gave France some of the best years in its history. And if in his foreign policy he showed an unerring instinct for doing the wrong thing, his motives were idealistic, and many of his reverses were due to forces over which he had no control.

Louis Napoleon became emperor by a coup d'etat. Like most countries after 1848, the Second French Republic experienced a wave of reaction. Socialists were ejected from the legislature, the right to vote was curtailed, public meetings were restricted, and the press was curbed. France's new president, Louis Napoleon, was eager to gain the support of the French masses. In December 1851, he dissolved the Assembly and called for new presidential elections. The French people once again endorsed the name Napoleon by a vast majority. A year later, the president finished his overthrow of the Republic by proclaiming himself Emperor of the French, thus pursuing further the historical parallel between himself and his uncle.

The analogy was carried still further in the Empire's political institutions, which closely followed those of the first Napoleon. There were two parliamentary bodies — an appointed senate and a legislature elected by universal male suffrage—both of which could merely discuss what the emperor put before them. Furthermore, by carefully managing elections, Napoleon was always in a position to command a parliamentary majority. Most major decisions were reached by the emperor himself in consultation with a Council of State with purely advisory functions. The Second Empire, at least during its first ten years, was little more than a thinly disguised dictatorship.

The "Authoritarian Empire"

The authoritarian phase of Napoleon's rule was a period of relative content. The emperor gave his countrymen what they wanted most—prosperity at home and glory abroad. Like most dictators, Napoleon III tried to do something for everyone. The peasants, who had voted him into office and who continued to endorse his policy in numerous plebiscites, were helped by large-scale public works and improved credit facilities. The workers, who remained cool to the new regime, were aided by social legislation and public housing. But the class with which Napoleon's relations were most harmonious, at least in time of prosperity, was the industrial and commercial middle class. More than any other statesman of his time, the Emperor of the French realized the importance and implications of modern industrialization, and he did his best to create conditions favorable to industrial growth. French railway mileage during the 1850s alone increased more than fivefold. A French law of 1863 permitted the formation of "limited liability" companies, which made investment less risky and thus attracted the savings of the proverbially thrifty Frenchman. In a series of commercial treaties, notably the Cobden-Chevalier agreement (1860) with England, Napoleon abandoned the traditional protectionism of France in favor of moderate free trade. As a result, French exports soon exceeded imports. France in 1870 was still the chief industrial competitor of Great Britain. French industrial expansion had some negative aspects. There was an air of gaudiness and vulgarity about the newly enriched middle class. Speculation and overexpansion led to periodic economic crises. But on the whole the new prosperity was sound and was shared by all classes.

As a symbol of the Empire's prosperity and splendor, Napoleon had the city of Paris transformed into the beautiful work of art it remains to the present day. The center of the city was completely rebuilt, with wide boulevards, stately squares, and lovely parks. Like so many of Napoleon's projects, this "urban renewal program" served a dual purpose. By providing employment and eradicating ugly slums, it aided the workers; but at the same time it did away with the breeding-grounds of radicalism and revolution. The wide avenues of the new city were unsuitable for building barricades, and they permitted the use of cavalry and artillery in case there should be another popular uprising.

Napoleon III and his wife Eugenie.

Napoleon III

Napoleon III was, to borrow Gamaliel Bradford's phrase, a "damaged soul"; and, after 1860, a damaged soul imprisoned in a damaged body. Grave, thoughtful, kind, devoted to noble causes, determined withal, fearless, and surprisingly practical, he had in him also the tortuousness of the eternal plotter, the vagueness of the Utopian, the weakened fiber of the sensualist, the fatalism of the gambler. Some characters in history are obvious in their greatness, mediocrity, or turpitude: even though our sympathies may widely differ, we feel we can focus Washington, Victoria, Gladstone, and even Napoleon I. Napoleon III is not one of these. His elusive physiognomy changes altogether with the light that is turned upon it. At one moment, he appears impressive: the only political leader in the nineteenth century whose thought could still be a guide for us today. At other times, the caricature drawn by Kinglake and Victor Hugo seems almost convincing: the middle-aged rake in imperial trappings, sinister even in his futility. The most searching, the most persistent light of all, the one in which he was seen by every one who approached him, reveals him as gentle, not merely in speech and smile, but to the very depths of his being.

From Albert Guérard, *Napoleon III* (Cambridge, Mass.: Harvard University Press, 1943), p. 290.

A Paris boulevard (1860). Detail of one part of a stereographic pair on glass, showing the results of Napoleon III's "urban renewal" program.

The Second Empire came to an end on the battlefield in 1870. Before that time, however, domestic discontent had already forced Napoleon to abandon many of the authoritarian practices of his earlier years. Most of this discontent was provoked by his blundering foreign policy. The French people were not opposed to war, so long as they won. France's involvement in the Crimean War had been popular, and the same was true of a number of small colonial ventures. The occupation of Algeria was completed; new French settlements were established in West Africa; New Caledonia was occupied in 1853; and during the 1860s protectorates were secured over Cambodia and the region later called French Indochina. The French participation in the wars of Italian unification, on the other hand, while it brought some military glory and new territory, was resented by French Catholics, because it deprived the papacy of its territorial holdings. Still more disastrous in French eyes were Napoleon's futile efforts, between 1862 and 1867, to establish a French protectorate over Mexico (see p. 855). The crowning blow to Napoleon's prestige, however, came when he failed to secure territorial compensations for France during Prussia's unification of Germany (see pp. 750–51).

The "Liberal Empire"

To pacify the growing domestic opposition during the 1860s, Napoleon attempted a gradual liberalization of French political life. The "Liberal Empire" was initiated in 1860, when restrictions on the legislative body were lifted and parliamentary proceedings were made public. Subsequent decrees extended the powers of the legislature and relaxed the restrictions on public meetings and the press that had existed since 1852. But these concessions only helped to swell the ranks of the opposition. By 1869 the government had so lost its grip that the parliamentary elections of that year returned ninety-three opposition candidates, thirty of whom were republicans. With labor unrest causing a growing epidemic of strikes, and with the republican program of Léon Gambetta gaining more and more adherents, the government made some sweeping last-minute efforts to save its life. In their totality, these reforms amounted to the establishment of a parliamentary regime. In May 1870 the French electorate endorsed these constitutional changes with a rousing majority. Two months later the war with Prussia broke out, sweeping away the Empire and bringing in the Third Republic.

THE UNIFICATION OF ITALY

The domestic events in France must be viewed against the background of Napoleon's foreign policy. He had two main motives: to gain glory and to win freedom for suppressed nationalities. The conflict between the selfishness and the altruism inherent in these aims accounts for much of the fateful vacillation in Napoleon's policy. The vacillation first manifested itself in his dealings with Italy.

Italy after 1848

As a result of the abortive revolutions of 1848, unification under the kingdom of Piedmont-Sardinia had emerged as the most feasible course for Italy. Victor Emmanuel II had been unique in not revoking the liberal constitution granted his state during the revolution. He did not relent, furthermore, in his hostile policy toward Austria. Turin, the capital of Piedmont, soon became a haven for Italian patriots from all over the peninsula trying to escape the persecution of their reactionary, pro-Austrian rulers.

The man who realized the unique position of Piedmont and used it to bring about the unification of Italy was Count Camillo di Cavour. In 1850 Cavour was appointed minister of agriculture and commerce, and in 1852 he became prime minister. Cavour at first was not so much interested in uniting the whole of Italy as he was in extending the power of Piedmont. This, he realized, could only be done against the opposition of Austria. To prepare for a showdown with Austria thus became one of his major concerns.

Before Austria could be tackled, several things were needed. The first was to create sympathy for the "Italian Question" outside Italy. This was done by having Piedmontese troops participate in the Crimean War. A second prerequisite for a successful war against Austria was the military and economic strengthening of Piedmont. Cavour did his best to improve the armed forces and to further the building of railroads, of whose strategic importance he was much aware. In a number of commercial treaties, Cavour integrated the economy of Piedmont with that of western Europe. He also improved the structure of business corporations, credit institutions, and cooperative societies. These economic measures alone entitle Cavour to a high place in his country's history.

Cavour and Napoleon III

The third requirement to move against Austria was outside military aid. To get such aid, Cavour looked to Napoleon III. The French emperor had always held a lingering affection for Italy. To aid Italian unification not only appealed to his idealism, but it also would strengthen the prestige of France and of himself. Considerations like these led to a super-secret meeting at Plombières in 1858 at which Napoleon promised Cavour his aid in a war between Piedmont and Austria. If victorious, Piedmont would form an enlarged kingdom of Upper Italy, and the whole peninsula was then to be loosely federated under the pope. France was to be rewarded for its help with the Piedmontese regions of Nice and Savoy. The Plombières agreement did not call for an Italy united under Piedmont.

While trying to find a pretext for war with Austria, the two conspirators continued their preparations. As rumors of an impending war in Italy grew, the other powers became concerned. The Austrians were the least worried. They were used to recurrent rumors of an Italian war and refused to take them seriously. England and Prussia, on the other hand, were less confident. In the spring of 1859, England proposed the evacuation of Austrian troops from the peninsula and the creation of an Italian federation. This was an appealing scheme and Napoleon began to show signs of trying to back out of his agreement with Piedmont. At this point, when Cavour's carefully laid plans seemed about to fail, the Austrian Emperor, Francis Joseph, forced a showdown by demanding that Piedmont demobilize its forces. When Piedmont turned down this ultimatum, Austrian troops invaded Piedmont on April 29, 1859. France thereupon joined its ally in the war against Austria.

The Unification of Italy 1859–70

The War of 1859

After six weeks of fighting, the French and Italian armies had won two bloody but indecisive victories at Magenta and Solferino and had driven the Austrians out of Lombardy. The next obvious step was the liberation of Venetia. But at this point, in July 1859, Napoleon surprised his ally and the world by concluding an armistice with Francis Joseph at Villafranca. There were several reasons for Napoleon's sudden defection: He apparently had been shocked by the bloodshed at Magenta and Solferino; the Austrian army was by no means beaten; there was dissatisfaction among many Frenchmen with a war against another Catholic power; and there was apprehension that Prussia might come to Austria's aid. Under the terms of the Villafranca agreement, Napoleon broke his promise that Piedmont should get both Lombardy and Venetia. Austria merely surrendered Lombardy, which Napoleon then offered to Victor Emmanuel. The king, much to Cavour's consternation, accepted.

The First Phase of Italian Unification

Villafranca turned out to be a blessing in disguise for the Italians. Up to this point the war had been chiefly for the enlargement of Piedmont. Now suddenly it became a national war for Italian unification. At the start of the war, some of the small states in northern Italy had revolted and driven out their rulers. The prospect of their return now led these regions to raise an army and to proclaim their union with Piedmont. Cavour, in January 1860, asked Napoleon's consent to Piedmont's annexation of the central Italian states. Napoleon agreed, in return for the surrender of Nice and Savoy, which he had forfeited at Villafranca. In March 1860 plebiscites in Parma, Modena, Romagna, and Tuscany confirmed the union of central Italy with Piedmont.

The next act in the drama of unification was dominated not by Cavour but by a man who was his opposite in all respects — a romantic, a republican, an effective leader of men, but a complete political amateur — Giuseppe Garibaldi. In May 1860 Garibaldi assembled an expeditionary force at Genoa. Its task was to help complete the liberation of the Kingdom of the Two Sicilies, where an uprising against the reactionary Bourbon regime was under way. Aided by the local population, Garibaldi's small force of "Redshirts" defeated an army twenty times its size. By August Sicily was in Garibaldi's hands.

Garibaldi's success and his growing popularity now threatened to displace Victor Emmanuel as the leader of a unified Italy. Garibaldi might give in to the urgings of Mazzini and surrender the southern half of the peninsula to republicanism; or else he might move against Rome, to complete the unification of Italy. Such a move might lead to a conflict with France, still considered the protector of the papacy. To avert such a crisis, Cavour convinced Napoleon that the only way to stop Garibaldi was for Victor Emmanuel to meet him on the way. The Piedmontese army now invaded the Papal States, defeated the papal forces, and after bypassing Rome came face to face with Garibaldi's band not far from Naples. The situation was tense. But Garibaldi was too much of a patriot to let selfish ambition interfere with his hope for a united Italy. Instead, he voluntarily submitted to Victor Emmanuel, thus completing the first phase of Italian unification.

The Kingdom of Italy

The Kingdom of Italy was proclaimed in March 1861. Two months later Cavour died, just as his country needed him most. The unification of Italy was by no means completed. Venetia did not become part of the kingdom until after another Austrian defeat in 1866; and Rome remained in papal hands until 1870. Other difficulties beset the new state. Not all Italians were happy with the results of unification. The followers of Mazzini would have preferred a republic, and even many monarchists would rather have seen a loose federation than a centralized monarchy. Regionalism and particularism also interfered with the integration of the eight or more separate states. Tensions between the prosperous north and the poverty-ridden south were especially marked. The illiteracy of the Italian masses, furthermore, hampered popular rule and Italy's parliamentary regime soon became known for its corruption. The wars of unification imposed staggering financial burdens, and taxes were higher than ever before. At the same time, lack of coal and iron prevented large-scale industrialization that might have relieved Italy's economic plight. Yet despite these shortcomings, the new Italy considered itself a great power and tried to imitate the wealthier nations by maintaining an army and navy far beyond its means.

Much of the discontent and disillusionment in Italy after unification was blamed on Cavour. But we must remember that the unification of Italy had not really been his goal at the start. Much of his policy was determined by the other two makers of Italy, Napoleon III and Garibaldi, and by the force of nationalism, which he could not control. Where we might find fault with Cavour was in the devious methods he employed to achieve his aims. But such *Realpolitik*, as it came to be called, was not considered out of place by an age that gloried in nationalism and worshipped success. Much the same spirit that animated Cavour was to guide Bismarck in his German policy. And just as Cavour had started out in the hope of enlarging Piedmont but ended by creating the Kingdom of Italy, so Bismarck began by working for a greater Prussia and wound up with a German Reich.

AUSTRO-PRUSSIAN RIVALRY

The most striking similarity between the unification of Italy and that of Ger-

Giuseppe Garibaldi.

many was Austria's involvement in both. Austria's defeats in 1859 and 1866 were due in large measure to internal weakness caused by political disunity. Nationalism, which proved a boon to Cavour and Bismarck, was a source of infinite trouble to Francis Joseph and the many capable Austrian ministers who tried to find some way of keeping their empire from falling to pieces.

Nationalism in the Austrian Empire

Prince Schwarzenberg, who had succeeded Metternich in 1848, had given Austria a constitution early in 1849. While calling for a high degree of centralization, it had recognized at least some local and provincial privileges. These mild concessions to the spirit of nationalism, however, were only temporary. Beginning in 1850, all but the centralizing tendencies of the constitution were ignored. Petty officials, most of them German, directed the affairs of provinces whose language they did not speak and whose customs they ignored. Yet instead of counteracting the centrifugal tendencies of nationalism, this system merely increased the tension between the German ruling caste and the subject peoples.

Francis Joseph I, emperor of Austria and king of Hungary.

Austria's defeat at the hands of France and Piedmont in 1859 once again brought home the need for reform. As a result, the excessive centralization of the preceding decade now gave way to some degree of provincial autonomy. In 1861 a new constitution established a central legislature, the *Reichsrat,* made up of delegates from the various regional diets. But the new system, like all earlier ones, had serious flaws. Because the German element was still guaranteed a majority, some of the other nationalities, especially the Hungarians (or Magyars), refused to attend the meetings of the *Reichsrat.* It soon became clear that another effort at solving the nationalities problem had failed. In 1865 Francis Joseph suspended the constitution.

At this point the war with Prussia intervened, leaving Austria still weaker and less able to resist the demands of the Hungarian nationalists. As a result of long negotiations between Austrian and Hungarian leaders, a compromise, or *Ausgleich,* was finally reached in 1867. Under the new arrangement a Dual Monarchy was established, with Francis Joseph serving both as emperor of Austria and king of Hungary. Except in finance, foreign affairs, and war, where joint ministries were set up, the two parts of the monarchy now were entirely autonomous. Yet the *Ausgleich* did not solve the nationalities problem. Subsequent efforts to recognize the Slavic regions by establishing a Triple Monarchy were defeated by opposition from Germans and Hungarians alike. This continued oppression of Slavic nationalism constituted a major threat to the existence of Austria-Hungary and to the peace of Europe.

Prussia After 1850

In administrative efficiency, financial soundness, and military strength, Prussia after 1850 was far superior to its Austrian rival. Except for a small Polish minority, its population was homogeneous. And while in Austria industrialization had hardly begun, Prussia during the 1850s began to take its place among the leading industrial powers of the Continent.

Like Austria, Prussia had been granted a constitution in 1849. By dividing the electorate into three classes according to the taxes each voter paid, the Prussian constitution made certain that the wealthiest citizens controlled a majority in the lower house of the *Landtag.* With this arrangement it was not surprising that Prussia continued to be one of the most reactionary states in Germany. In 1857 King Frederick William IV was succeeded by his brother, Prince William, first as regent and in 1861 as king. William was sixty-two years old and an archconservative. Having spent most of his life in the army, he had little experience in government. It was due to William's concern over the shortcomings of Prussia's military establishment that Prussia, in 1860, entered upon one of the most serious crises in its history.

Despite a considerable increase in population, Prussia's armed forces in 1860 were still essentially what they had been in 1814. When William tried to correct this situation, he ran into opposition from the liberal majority in the *Landtag,* which had to authorize the necessary funds. By 1862 king and parliament had become deadlocked. At this point William decided to recall his ambassador to Paris, Otto von Bismarck, and charge him with carrying on the fight with the *Landtag.*

Bismarck and the Constitutional Conflict

The man who was soon to direct the affairs of Germany as first chancellor of the German Reich was then forty-seven years old. He came from an old Prussian family of noble landowners, or Junkers. During the revolution of 1848 he had proved himself a devoted royalist. As a reward he had been appointed Prussia's delegate to the Frankfurt Diet during the 1850s and later ambassador to St. Petersburg and Paris. In these various assignments he had shown outstanding ability as a diplomat. He was also known as a fighter. This combination had recommended him to William I.

Bismarck first tried to mediate the conflict between king and parliament. When this proved impossible, he carried out the proposed army reforms without parliamentary approval. The conflict was never resolved but was ultimately overshadowed by more spectacular events. Two wars, in 1864 and 1866, not only gave proof of the excellence of Prussia's reformed army but so aroused the patriotism of the *Landtag* delegates that they were ready to forget their liberal principles. During the war with Austria in 1866, when Bismarck asked parliament for retroactive assent to the unauthorized expenditure of the previous years, the majority of delegates supported him.

The Prussian constitutional conflict had thus been "resolved." But in the process, Prussian and German liberalism had suffered a serious defeat. Liberals in Germany henceforth were split in two factions — a larger one that continued to support Bismarck, putting nationalism above liberalism, and a smaller faction that stuck to its liberal principles. This split within German liberalism was never healed. It was the most fateful legacy of the period of German unification.

Rivalry Between Austria and Prussia

Bismarck did not really plan the unification of Germany; it developed more or less accidentally out of Prussia's desire to assert itself against Austria's claims for supremacy in German affairs. The rivalry between Austria and Prussia was of long standing, going back at least to the days of Frederick the Great and Maria Theresa in the eighteenth century (see p. 632). During most of the intervening period, Prussia had been quite ready to recognize Austria's traditional leadership. The most recent manifestation of Prussia's subjection to Austria had occurred in 1850 at Olmütz, when Austria had prevented a scheme advanced by Frederick William IV for a union of German princes under Prussian leadership.

Bismarck, as Prussia's delegate to the Frankfurt Diet, did not object to Austria's leadership in German affairs so long as Austria, in return, recognized Prussia's preeminence in northern Germany. Only after Bismarck realized Austria's unwillingness to cooperate did he decide that the interest of Prussia demanded that Austria be excluded from Germany. Before Prussia could assume leadership in Germany, however, it had to make sure of the good will, or at least the acquiescence, of the great powers. The Italian national movement had enjoyed the sympathy of almost everyone outside Austria, but few people in western Europe wanted to see a Germany united under Prussian auspices. During the

Prussian soldier. The Prussian army was considered the best in Europe.

Crimean War, Austria had tried to induce Prussia to join in aiding the western powers, but Prussia had remained friendly toward Russia. This was the basis for a close friendship between Prussia and Russia that was to last for the next few decades.

The first outward sign of Prussia's emancipation from Austrian tutelage came during the Italian war of 1859. Austria at the time fully expected Prussia's help against Piedmont and France. Prussia was ready, but asked to be put in charge of its own and whatever other German forces might be raised. Austria, still filled with its own importance, refused this understandable request. Prussia's neutrality during the war won the gratitude of both France and Italy. Austria's defeat, on the other hand, clearly showed how much its claim to leadership was based on past prestige rather than present power.

By the end of the 1850s most German liberals were expecting Prussia to take the lead in unifying Germany. The constitutional struggle over the reform of the Prussian army, however, put a temporary damper on their enthusiasm. At the same time, the Austrian constitution of 1861 seemed to indicate more liberal tendencies in the Habsburg Empire. It thus encouraged the Catholic and traditionalist circles in southern Germany, who hoped for a united Germany under Austrian leadership. To take advantage of this shift, Austria convened a congress in 1863 to consider the reform of the German Confederation in the direction of greater national unity. But Bismarck urged his king to boycott the congress. Without Prussia, the Frankfurt meeting was doomed to failure.

The Schleswig-Holstein Question and the War with Denmark

The final showdown between Austria and Prussia grew out of their involvement with the two northern German duchies of Schleswig and Holstein. These duchies, largely German but partly Danish, had long been held in personal union by the king of Denmark. In an age of rising nationalism, this indeterminate status became increasingly difficult. The issue had already led to a brief war between Danes and Germans in 1848, in which Denmark had been defeated. The problem became acute again in 1863, when Denmark tried to annex Schleswig. This time both Austria and Prussia rushed to the defense. Both wanted to pose as defenders of German unity, but Prussia also wanted to expand its power in northern Germany.

The war itself was brief, and the Danes suffered a crushing defeat. Under the Peace of Vienna in 1864 Denmark surrendered Schleswig and Holstein to Austria and Prussia. In this joint possession of the duchies lay the seeds of the war between Austria and Prussia two years later. Austria and most of the German states wanted the duchies to go to a German claimant, the Duke of Augustenburg, but Bismarck wanted the duchies for Prussia. In 1865 the victors reached a temporary compromise in the Convention of Gastein, under which Prussia was to administer Schleswig and Austria Holstein, while the future of the duchies was to remain a joint responsibility. But as Austria continued to encourage the aspirations of the Duke of Augustenburg, and as Prussia proceeded to make itself at home in Schleswig, it became clear that compromise was impossible.

The War of 1866

In the fall of 1865, Bismarck met Napoleon III at Biarritz to sound him out on France's attitude toward a possible war between Prussia and Austria. The meeting suggests a parallel to the Plombières meeting of Cavour and Napoleon, except that Bismarck was not asking for French aid; all he wanted was a promise of neutrality. This Napoleon gave, hinting at some unspecified compensations for France. In the spring of 1866, Prussia concluded an alliance with Italy, to which Napoleon also gave his blessing. The remaining great powers did not present much of a problem. Since England had stood by while Denmark was defeated, Bismarck felt that it would not intervene to save Austria. And Russia's friendship for Prussia and its antagonism toward Austria left little doubt where it would stand.

With the diplomatic spadework done, Bismarck's next task was to find a cause for war with Austria that would rally the rest of Germany to Prussia's side. This was not easy, since most of the German princes sided with Austria on the future of Schleswig-Holstein. When Bismarck finally used Prussia's differences with Austria over the duchies as an excuse to order Prussian troops into Holstein, the remaining members of the German Confederation joined the Austrian side. The war of 1866 was thus not only a war of Prussia against Austria but against most of the rest of Germany as well.

There was little enthusiasm on either side at the start. Austria was deeply divided and poorly prepared, and was handicapped by having to fight on two fronts, Italy and Germany. The Prussians, however, were in excellent military form, equipped with the latest weapons and led by a master-strategist, Count Helmuth von Moltke. The war was over in a few weeks. It was decided almost entirely by one major battle, near Königgrätz and Sadowa, in Bohemia, in which the Austrians were defeated, though not annihilated.

The final peace treaty was signed at Prague in August 1866. The settlement was remarkably lenient. Bismarck realized that the rest of the powers, especially France, would not stand for a punitive peace. Austria consented to the dissolution of the German Confederation and recognized the various territorial gains Prussia had made in the north, including Schleswig-Holstein. In a separate settlement Austria surrendered Venetia, which went to Italy. As for Austria's German allies, most of the northern ones were annexed by Prussia, while the southern ones had to pay indemnities and conclude military alliances with Prussia. Prussia thus consolidated its northern holdings and assumed indirect control over the rest of Germany.

THE UNIFICATION OF GERMANY

The war of 1866 had been waged for the aggrandizement of Prussia. But in the minds of most Germans it soon appeared as a deliberate stage in the unification of Germany. During the winter of 1866/67, delegates from the states that were left in northern Germany after the peace settlement met in Berlin to form a North German Confederation. The plan had originated with Bismarck, whose aim was to establish Prussia's preponderance over the whole region north of the Main River.

The North German Confederation

The constitution of the North German Confederation established a federal system under which the central government controlled foreign and military affairs. The executive was vested in the king of Prussia as president, assisted by a chancellor—Bismarck. An upper house, or *Bundesrat,* consisted of delegates from the various member states. The lower house, or *Reichstag,* was made up of deputies elected by universal manhood suffrage. Most of the power was vested in the upper house, in which Prussian influence prevailed. There was no ministerial responsibility, because the only minister was the chancellor, and he was responsible only to the president, or king.

The main significance of the North German Confederation's constitution was that it served as a basis for the constitution of the German Empire after 1871. Just as it assured the domination of Prussia in northern Germany after 1867, so after 1871 it perpetuated Prussia's domination over the rest of Germany. How far Bismarck actually foresaw developments beyond 1867 is

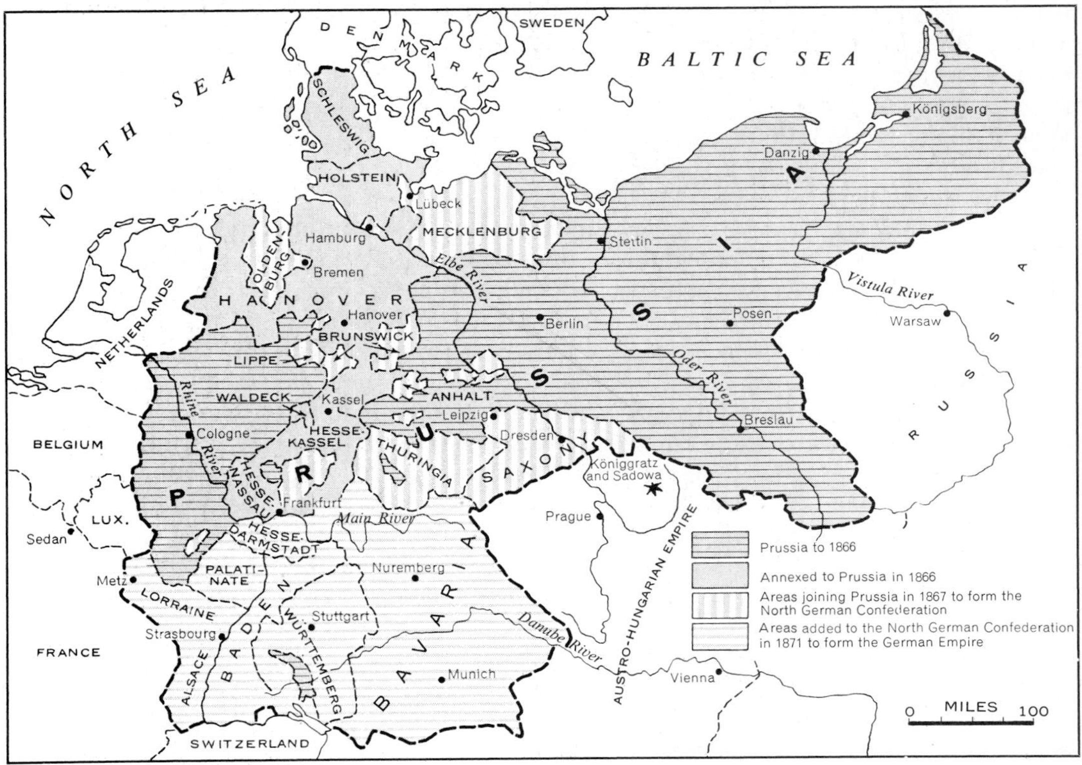

The Unification of Germany 1866–71

hard to say. He was never a German nationalist—his major concern was with the power and security of Prussia. Nor was there much desire among the rulers of southern Germany to submit to the king of Prussia. The state of affairs that existed in 1867, therefore, could have lasted for a long time had it not been for the unfortunate machinations of Napoleon III. Like his uncle, Napoleon served as the involuntary agent of German nationalism.

Bismarck and Napoleon III

Napoleon's readiness at Biarritz to let Prussia settle accounts with Austria had been due to his underestimation of Prussian strength. Thinking Prussia and Austria evenly matched, he had expected to throw French power into the balance at the crucial moment. Austria's defeat at Sadowa, therefore, had come as a shock. Together with France's fiasco in Mexico, the defeat of Austria was seen by Napoleon's opponents as a major French defeat. The only way to save face was through some kind of territorial compensations such as France had gained during the unification of Italy.

Napoleon should have pressed his demands for compensations while the fate of Austria still hung in the balance. Once Prussia had won, Bismarck was no longer ready to make concessions. On the contrary, Napoleon's demands served Bismarck to good effect in furthering his own policy. He used Napoleon's bid for territories in the west or south of Germany to cement ties with the southern German states as the best possible protection against French designs; and he later tried to use Napoleon's request for Prussian support in acquiring Belgium to incriminate France in the eyes of Great Britain. In a third attempt to gain compensation, Napoleon tried to buy the Duchy of Luxembourg. Bismarck at first approved but later changed his mind.

Napoleon III, faced with mounting criticism at home and frustrated in his efforts to gather laurels abroad, gradually realized that an armed showdown with Prussia might be inevitable. To prepare himself, he began casting about for allies. But neither Austria nor Italy had any desire to become involved in a war between France and Prussia. Even so, Napoleon assumed that in case of such a war he could count on the aid of one or both of the Catholic powers.

The War of 1870

The immediate cause of the war between France and Prussia was the offer of the Spanish throne, temporarily vacated by revolution, to a Hohenzollern prince, distantly related to the king of Prussia. Bismarck was instrumental in having the prince accept the offer; yet when France protested the Spanish candidacy, the Prussian government urged the prince to abandon the project. But this did not satisfy the French, who demanded an apology from King William and a promise that the candidacy would not be renewed. This demand the king refused, in an interview with the Fench ambassador at the watering place of Ems. When news of the incident reached Berlin, Bismarck edited the report in such a way to make it look as though France had suffered a major diplomatic defeat. It was this edited "Ems dispatch" that led France to declare war on Prussia. In this case Bismarck had foreseen the results, and to that extent he may be held responsible for the war of 1870. Yet this was merely the latest in a whole series of mutual recriminations, and most historians now agree that responsibility for the war must be shared by both sides.

Events in the early summer of 1870 had moved so fast that all of Europe was taken by surprise. France's precipitate action lost whatever sympathy it had enjoyed. England maintained the aloofness it had shown ever since the Crimean War. Russia continued its policy of benevolent neutrality toward Prussia. Italy was preoccupied with completing its unification by taking the city of Rome. And Austria would be dangerous only if Prussia ran into difficulties. But there was little chance of

Animated French map of Europe in 1870. A caption with it explains: "England, isolated, swears with rage and almost forgets Ireland, whom she holds on a leash. Spain frets, propped up by Portugal. France repulses the invasion of Prussia, who reaches with one hand for Holland and the other for Austria. Italy, also, says to Bismarck: 'Take your feet away from there.' Corsica and Sardinia . . . a regular urchin who laughs at it all. Denmark, who has lost his legs in Holstein, hopes to regain them. European Turkey yawns and wakes up. Asiatic Turkey inhales the smoke of her water pipe. Sweden leaps like a panther, and Russia resembles a bugbear out to fill his basket."

French battery in front of Belfort (Alsace), which capitulated to the Germans on February 13, 1871, after a siege of 108 days.

that. In numbers, leadership, and morale, Prussia's forces were far superior to those of France. The participation of southern German contingents made this a national German war. The French army fought valiantly, but the quality of its leadership was low. The fact that Napoleon III, worn out by a lingering illness, assumed personal command did not help matters.

The war was decided in a series of bloody battles. The climax came on September 2, with Napoleon's capitulation at Sedan. But the fighting continued for several more months, and the city of Paris, where a republic had been proclaimed, did not surrender until the end of January 1871. A temporary armistice was concluded on January 28, pending the election of a National Assembly. The assembly chose the liberal monarchist Adolphe Thiers as chief executive, to negotiate a final settlement with Bismarck.

The Results of the War

The peace signed at Frankfurt in May 1871 was a harsh one. France had to pay an indemnity of 5 billion francs and was to remain occupied until it had been paid. In addition, France had to cede Alsace-Lorraine, which, for the most part, it had taken from the Holy Roman Empire in the seventeenth century. The inhabitants of Alsace spoke German, but they were pro-French in feeling. To take so large a territory in an age of ardent nationalism was a dangerous move. The issue of the "lost provinces" remained an insuperable obstacle to Franco-German rapprochement.

The signing of the peace did not end France's troubles. The new National Assembly had a majority of monarchists, and the survival of the republic depended on the continued split among the three monarchist factions—Bourbon, Orléanist, and Bonapartist. The republican minority had its main support in the city of Paris. Here, in March 1871, fear of a monarchist revival, indignation over a humiliating peace, and general misery resulting from the recent siege led to a violent uprising. The Paris Commune, as the government of the insurgents was called, lasted until the end of May. Its aims, on the whole, were moderate. But the Commune also included some socialists. This fact, plus some of the excesses committed in street fighting, did much to reawaken middle-class fears of a "red peril," of which the Commune remained the symbol. After their defeat in the "Bloody Week" of May, thousands of Communards were executed. The issue of republic against monarchy continued to hang in the balance for some time.

While the siege of Paris was still under way, another important event had taken place. On January 18, 1871, in the Hall of Mirrors in the palace at Versailles, King William of Prussia was proclaimed German Emperor. This ceremony was the climax of long negotiations between Bismarck and the rulers of southern Germany. There had been much hesitation among these Catholic and more liberal states to submit to a confederation dominated by Protestant and reactionary Prussia. Bismarck, the architect of unification, was not motivated by national enthusiasm. But by fulfilling the German people's dream for unity, he hoped to increase the power and prestige of his beloved Prussia.

The Franco-German War not only completed the unification of Germany; it also ended the long struggle for Italian unity. In October 1870, Rome was annexed to Italy and became its capital. A subsequent effort to mollify the papacy by a generous Law of Papal Guarantees was turned down by the pope, who henceforth considered himself "the prisoner of the Vatican."

The year 1871, like the year 1815, was a landmark in European history. Both years saw the end of a major war, and both initiated a long period of peace among the major powers. But this is about as far as the parallel goes. Relations among states in 1815 and after had still been conducted according to certain general rules. But the cynical diplomacy of Cavour, Napoleon III, and Bismarck had changed this. From now on, suspicion rather than trust characterized international dealings, and though there was to be

Europe in 1871

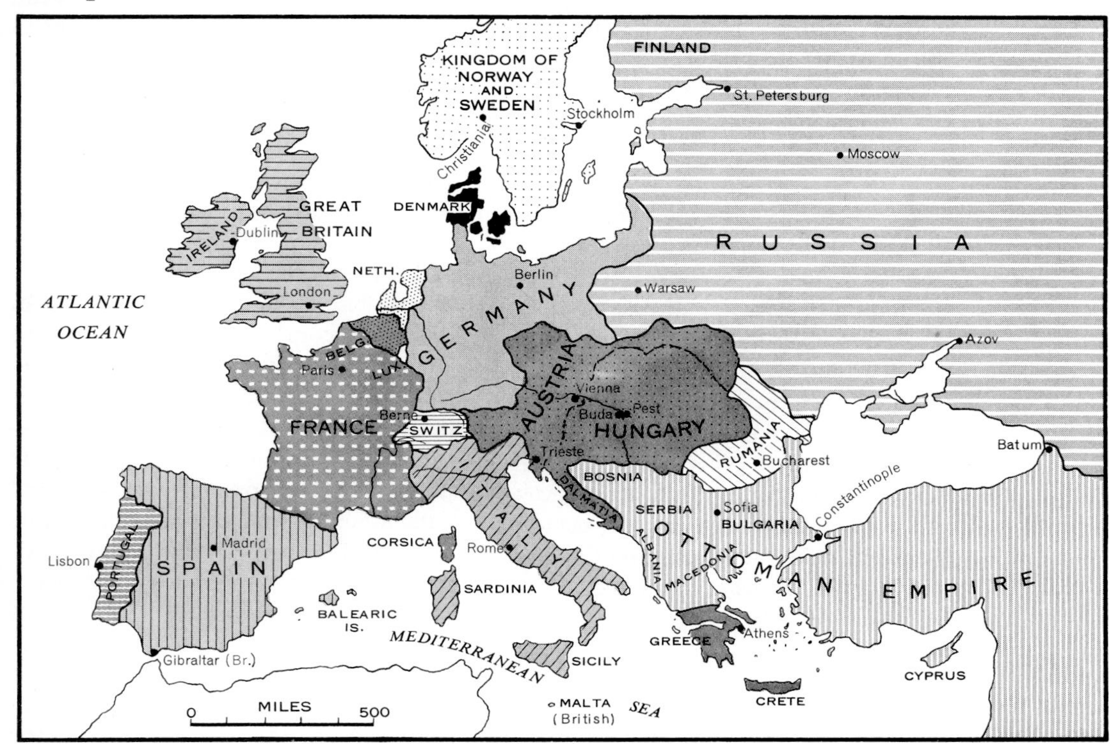

no major war for forty-three years, the threat of war was always present.

In 1815 the balance of power had been revived along traditional lines, but by 1871 an entirely new balance had emerged. Austria, Russia, Great Britain, and France had been the leading powers at Vienna, with Prussia lagging behind and with Italy a mere "geographical expression." By 1871 that order had been thoroughly revised. Both Austria and France now were overshadowed by a Prussianized Germany, and even Italy demanded recognition as a great power. England and Russia continued in their former status; but while at Vienna they had taken an active part in shaping the affairs of the Continent, the balance of 1871 had been brought about without their participation. Here, perhaps, lies the major difference between 1815 and 1871. When Napoleon I had upset the balance of power, the Concert of Europe met at the Congress of Vienna to restore it. There was no such congress in 1871. The Concert of Europe had gone to pieces over the Crimean War. Both Great Britain and Russia had kept out of the subsequent wars of Italian and German unification. The passivity of these peripheral powers, as much as the activities of Cavour, Bismarck, and Napoleon III, brought about the end of the Vienna System.

ENGLAND'S "VICTORIAN COMPROMISE"

England had always maintained a certain isolation from the Continent, and it had added reason to do so after the middle of the nineteenth century. The Crimean War had brought home the futility of military involvement. And besides, it had brought defeat to Russia, whose advances in the eastern Mediterranean had presented the only real threat to British commerce.

The "Workshop of the World"

The twenty years after 1850 were the most prosperous in British history. While wars elsewhere helped retard economic development, Britain's industry and commerce experienced an unprecedented boom. This was the heyday of free trade, from which Britain, as the most advanced industrial nation, profited most. The change in shipbuilding from wood to iron, furthermore, opened up a wholly new field for expansion. By 1870, Britain's carrying trade enjoyed a virtual monopoly. While British engineers were building railroads the world over, Britain's surplus capital sought outlets for investment on the Continent and overseas. Between 1854 and 1870, England's foreign holdings more than doubled.

Though Britain was reluctant to become involved in European politics, it showed no such hesitation overseas. While in some parts of the British Empire, such as Canada and Australia, the basis for self-government was being laid, elsewhere, notably in India, Britain tightened its reins. In 1859 the rule of the East India Company was taken over by the British government. Commercial expansion in China, begun in the 1840s, made rapid advances in the late 1850s. The new Suez Canal, built by French interests, soon became a major artery for British commerce.

The Second Reform Bill

Britain's prosperity did not do away with political discontent. There had been no major political reforms since 1832. The Tories, now called Conservatives, had reluctantly acquiesced in the new conditions created by the Great Reform Bill; and the Whigs, now called Liberals, while favoring reforms in other fields, also considered the Reform Bill final. The aims of the two parties had thus become almost undistinguishable. Neither the aristocracy nor the middle class was dominant. Government proceeded by compromise.

Meanwhile Britain's middle and working classes were growing rapidly. This fact could not help but create a demand for further extension of the franchise. By the 1860s the need for reform could no longer be ignored. Both parties at the time had leaders ready to take charge of the contest over parliamentary reform. Since 1852 the Conservative Benjamin Disraeli and the Liberal William Gladstone had played important roles in cabinets of their respective parties. In 1866 Gladstone introduced a moderate reform bill that was promptly defeated by the Conservatives. A more radical bill introduced the next year by Disraeli was passed, largely with Liberal support. The Second Reform Bill of 1867, by giving the vote to urban workers, doubled the number of voters. It did not introduce universal suffrage, but it did provide the majority of adult British males with a voice in their government.

Gladstone giving a "whistle-stop" speech (1885). His practice of making political speeches from trains was said to have horrified Queen Victoria.

Gladstone's First "Great Ministry"

The agitation surrounding the Second Reform Bill ended the Victorian Compromise. Both Conservatives and Liberals now tightened their organizations and became parties in the modern sense. When the elections of 1868 returned a Liberal majority, Gladstone formed his first "great ministry." Just as the Bill of 1832 had been followed by a long series of domestic reforms, so the years after 1867 saw many overdue measures enacted. Notable among them was the Education Act of 1870, which at long last relieved a situation in which almost half of Britain's children had received no schooling.

The problem that concerned Gladstone above all others was Ireland. That unhappy country, vastly overpopulated, had long been on the verge of starvation. Migration to America relieved some of the pressure but also added to unrest. The Fenian Brotherhood, founded in New York in 1858, was responsible for many acts of violence in England and Ireland. Gladstone considered the solution of the Irish problem his major mission. Its roots were partly religious, partly economic. To solve Ireland's religious grievances, the Disestablishment Act of 1869 freed Irish Catholics from having to support the Anglican Church. To improve land tenure, the Land Act of 1870 curtailed the power of absentee landlords to evict their tenants without compensation. But since the Land Act did not heed Ireland's demands for the "three F's"—fair rent, fixed tenure, and free sale—it was only a half-measure.

Like most of Gladstone's reforms, his Irish policy violated many vested interests and contributed to his defeat in 1874. There were other causes of discontent. Though elected by working-class votes, Gladstone had done little to improve the status of the laborer. Prosperity, meanwhile, had begun to level off, and from 1873 on depression elsewhere made itself felt in Britain as well. Finally, Gladstone's foreign policy—peaceful, sensible, but unexciting—lacked popular support. With Disraeli, who succeeded him in 1874 and who combined social legislation at home with an active imperial policy abroad, a new chapter in British history began.

RUSSIA: REACTION AND REFORM

The second great power on the periphery of Europe, tsarist Russia, pursued its own peculiar course through most of the nineteenth century. The westernization that had begun during the eighteenth century continued, though slowly. Because of its vast size and the multiplicity of its backward peoples, Russia faced a number of problems not shared by any of the other powers. To maintain political control in the face of such obstacles required a regime of strict autocracy. The will of the tsar was law. His decrees were translated into action by a huge bureaucracy whose openness to bribery helped somewhat to soften the harshness of tsarist rule. Russia's government has been aptly described as "despotism tempered by corruption."

Aside from autocracy, there were other institutions peculiar to Russia. While in western Europe the nobility had lost much of its power, Russia's aristocracy continued to enjoy its traditional privileges. Besides owning almost all the land, the nobles were exempt from taxation and from military service. There was as yet no middle class to speak of, except in the few larger towns. The majority of the tsar's subjects, more than 95 percent, were peasants, and most of them were still serfs. Serfdom in Russia was much more burdensome than it had been in western Europe. Even the legally free peasants, who by 1833 constituted about a third of the population, were kept in a decidedly inferior position. Occasionally, when the misery of the Russian masses became too much to bear, they sought relief in local uprisings. There had been more than five hundred such mutinies during the rule of Nicholas I (1825–55). Nicholas actually had introduced some measures aimed at alleviating the worst abuses of serfdom, but to go the root of the evil and to liberate the serfs would have meant taking land away from the nobility; even the autocratic tsars did not dare do that. Instead, Nicholas continued to preach the principles dearest to his reactionary heart—obedience to autocracy, adherence to the traditional Orthodox religion, and patriotic faith in the virtues of Russian nationality.

French satirical drawing of 1854 criticizing the harsh treatment of Russian serfs by their landlords. Russian landlords use bundles of their serfs as stakes in a card game.

"Westerners" versus "Slavophils"

The obstacles that the tsarist government put in the way of education and the restriction it imposed on western ideas helped to keep down the numbers of the Russian "intelligentsia"—that is, those few people whose intellectual interests set them apart from the majority of the people. Still, by the middle of the nineteenth century this group had grown numerous enough to make its influence felt. There were two clearly defined factions among Russian intellectuals—the "Westerners" and the "Slavophils." The Westerners saw their country as essentially a part of western civilization, lagging behind but able eventually to catch up. The Slavophils, on the other hand, held that the difference between Russia and the West was not one of degree but of kind. They pointed to the peculiar foundations of Russian civilization—Byzantine, Slavic, and Greek-Orthodox as compared with the Roman, Germanic, and Catholic roots of western civilization. And they believed that each nation should live according to its own traditions rather than try to imitate the institutions and practices of other countries. These theoretical differences between Westerners and Slavophils also determined their attitude toward current problems. While the Westerners favored constitutional government, rationalism, and industrial progress, the Slavophils saw the salvation of Russia in benevolent autocracy, Orthodox Christianity, and the reform of Russia's predominantly agrarian society. This eastern-versus-western orientation henceforth remained a permanent characteristic of Russian political and social philosophy.

The most important political developments during the regime of Nicholas I were in foreign affairs. One of the main aims of Russian policy continued to be the domination, direct or indirect, over the disintegrating Ottoman Empire. Western opposition to Russia's Turkish aspirations had finally led to the Crimean War. More than any previous event, this conflict had shown the inefficiency, corruption, and poor leadership of the tsarist regime. Nicholas had died during the war. His successor, Alexander II (1855–81), was less reactionary. Though he had little understanding of social and economic problems, he was impressed by the clamor for reform that had set in after the Crimean defeat. The most widespread demand of the reformers was for the emancipation of the serfs.

The Emancipation of the Serfs

Alexander II realized that the alternative to abolishing serfdom from above might ultimately be revolution from below. He therefore initiated a careful study of the situation that finally, in March 1861, led to the Emancipation Edict. Its immediate effects, however, were far from happy. It was of little use for the Russian serf to gain his freedom without at the same time obtaining sufficient land to make a living. Yet to deprive the nobility of its labor force and most of its land would have placed the burden of emancipation entirely on that class. The solution finally arrived at was a compromise that satisfied no one. The peasants were given almost half the land, not in direct ownership but in large holdings administered by the village community, the *mir*. The *mir* in turn apportioned the land among the village households. The landowners were compensated by the government; but the redemption money that the government paid to the nobles had to be repaid over a period of forty-nine years by each village community.

Emancipation thus freed the individual peasant from servitude to his noble master but subjected him to the communal control of his village. To be freed from the redemption payments and the tutelage of the *mir*, and to get hold of the land still in the hands of the nobility—these remained burning issues for the Russian peasantry into the twentieth century.

Alexander II (*ca*. 1876).

Reform, Radicalism, and Reaction

The liberation of the serfs was not the only effort Alexander made to strengthen his regime through timely reforms. In 1863 he granted universities a greater degree of academic freedom. In 1864 he reformed the Russian

Serfdom

Few realize what serfdom was in reality. There is a dim conception that the conditions which it created were very bad; but those conditions, as they affected human beings bodily and mentally, are not generally understood. It is amazing, indeed, to see how quickly an institution and its social consequences are forgotten when the institution has ceased to exist, and with what rapidity men and things change. I will try to recall the conditions of serfdom by telling, not what I heard but what I saw . . . :

> **Father . . . calls in Makár, the piano-tuner and sub-butler, and reminds him of all his recent sins. . . . Of a sudden there is a lull in the storm. My father takes a seat at the table and writes a note. "Take Makár with this note to the police station, and let a hundred lashes with the birch rod be given him."**
>
> **Terror and absolute muteness reign in the house. The clock strikes four, and we all go down to dinner. . . . "Where is Makár?" our stepmother asks. "Call him in." Makár does not appear, and the order is repeated. He enters at last, pale, with a distorted face, ashamed, his eyes cast down. . . . Tears suffocate me, and immediately after dinner is over I run out, catch Makár in the dark passage, and try to kiss his hand; but he tears it away, and says, either as a reproach or as a question, "Let me alone; you, too, when you are grown up, will you not be just the same?"**

From Prince Peter Kropotkin, *Memoirs of a Revolutionist* (Boston: Houghton Mifflin, 1899), pp. 49–51.

judicial system along western lines. The same year Alexander introduced a measure of local and regional self-government through elected assemblies, or *zemstvos*. The hope of the reformers that this development might eventually culminate in a national assembly was disappointed. But even so, the *zemstvos* provided some opportunity for public discussion and the development of civic responsibility, both hitherto unknown in Russia.

The more changes Alexander introduced, the more hopes he aroused. One of the results of his policy had been to give an impetus to various reform movements among the intelligentsia, whose aims and agitation became ever more radical. Western socialism had been slow to gain a hold in Russia, where industry was still in its infancy. Consequently, Russian socialists like Alexander Herzen (1812–70) tried to appeal to the Russian peasant, whose village community already exhibited many of the collective features cherished by socialists. In the 1860s it became the fashion for members of the intelligentsia to go and live among the peasants in the hope of arousing them from their apathy and urging them into starting a revolution. The "go-to-the-people" movement *(Narodniki)*, however, failed because the peasants were too backward and the authorities too vigilant. In their opposition to everything their government stood for, the younger members of the intelligentsia now began to refer to themselves as "nihilists," believers in nothing. Most of them vented their anger over the existing system merely by expounding radical ideas and by disregarding conventional manners and mores. During the 1870s, however, some of the nihilists fell under the influence of Mikhail Bakunin and his philosophy of anarchism (see p. 734). In 1879 this terrorist faction formed a secret society, "The Will of the People," whose aim was to overthrow the government by direct action and assassination.

Frightened by these manifestations of radicalism, Alexander II reverted to a policy of renewed reaction. Yet by resorting to repression, he merely helped to strengthen the revolutionary forces he hoped to combat. The fact was brought home to him in several attempts on his life, and in 1880 he tried once again to return to his initial policy of reform. But by then it was too late. Alexander II was killed by a terrorist bomb in 1881.

THE PRIMACY OF FOREIGN POLICY

During the two decades after 1850 foreign policy in most of Europe overshadowed domestic policy. There were few discernible trends in domestic affairs. Industrialization continued, but its progress was still uneven. Democracy made gains in some countries (notably England), but it suffered reversals in others (notably Germany). Some important reforms helped ease tension — the Emancipation Edict in Russia, the *Ausgleich* between Austria and Hungary, the Second Reform Bill in England. But for each issue resolved, others arose elsewhere — the conflict between monarchism and republicanism in France, the defeat of liberalism in Germany, the tension between North and South in Italy.

The most significant event in the "era of unification" was the emergence of Germany as a great power. From 1871 to 1945 the influence of that belatedly unified nation made itself felt in every major international crisis and in the history of every country. Compared with German unification, the unification of Italy today seems of minor importance, though it did not appear so at the time. Of much greater consequence was the tragic fate of the Second French Empire. Its defeat at the hands of Prussia sowed some of the seeds that brought forth the great wars of our century. But these events were far off in 1871. At the time it seemed as though the Continent at long last had found the stability that statesmen before 1850 had tried so hard to achieve. The future was to show the precariousness of the new balance of power.

Suggestions for Further Reading

Both R. C. Binkley, *Realism and Nationalism, 1852–1871* (1935), and E. J. Hobsbawm, *The Age of Capitalism, 1848–1875* (1976), are comprehensive surveys. The international affairs of Europe are covered in A. J. P. Taylor, *The Struggle for Mastery in Europe, 1848–1918* (1954). The disintegration of the Ottoman Empire is treated in M. S. Anderson, *The Eastern Question* (1966). On the Crimean War and its aftermath, see P. W. Schröder, *Austria, Great Britain, and the Crimean War: The Destruction of the European Concert* (1973), and W. E. Mosse, *The Rise and Fall of the Crimean System, 1855–1871* (1967).

Good histories of the second French Empire are J. M. Thompson, *Louis Napoleon and the Second Empire* (1955), and T. Zeldin, *The Political System of Napoleon III* (1958). A Guérard, *Napoleon III* (1943), is a sympathetic biography. R. L. Williams, *Gaslight and Shadow: The World of Napoleon III* (1957), conveys the atmosphere of the period. The unification of Italy is told in two authoritative studies by D. Mack Smith, *Cavour and Garibaldi, 1860: A Study in Political Conflict* (1954), and *Victor Emmanuel, Cavour, and the Risorgimento* (1971). D. Beales, *The Risorgimento and the Unification of Italy* (1971), is a good brief account.

On the unification of Germany, O. Pflanze, *Bismarck and the Development of Germany: The Period of Unification, 1815–1871* (1963), presents a comprehensive account; T. S. Hamerow, *The Social Foundation of German Unification, 1858–1871* (1969), supplies the domestic background. The most recent and most readable biography of Bismarck in English is A. Palmer, *Bismarck* (1976). Developments in Great Britain are covered in A. Briggs, *The Age of Improvement, 1783–1867* (1959), and G. Kitson-Clark, *The Making of Victorian England* (1962). E. Longford, *Victoria R. I.* (1964), is a charming biography. The history of Russia is covered in R. Pipes, *Russia under the Old Regime* (1975), and H. Seton-Watson, *The Russian Empire, 1801–1917* (1967). On serfdom, see G. T. Robinson, *Rural Russia under the Old Regime* (1949).

	1815				1870	
SOUTHWEST ASIA AND AFRICA	**1818–28** King Shaka, apex of Zulu kingdom	**1836** Boers' Great Trek begins		**1860** French expansion in West Africa **1869** Suez Canal opens		
EUROPE	**1815** Congress of Vienna **1815–83** Karl Marx **1825** Decembrist Revolt, Russia **1825** First commercial railroad	**1829** Treaty of Adrianople **1830** France's "July Monarchy" **1832** Britain's Great Reform Bill **1848** *Communist Manifesto*	**1848–49** Europe in Revolt **1848–61** Unification of Italy **1848–70** Napolean III **1851** Crystal Palace Exhibition, London	**1859** Darwin, *Origin of Species* **1854–56** Crimean War **1861–71** Unification of Germany **1867** Austro-Hungarian *Ausgleich*	**1870–71** Franco-Prussian War **1876** First internal combustion engine **1878** Congress of Berlin	**1882** Triple Alliance **1894** Russo-French Alliance
SOUTH AND SOUTHEAST ASIA	**1819** British found Singapore		**1857–58** Indian Mutiny **1859** French seize Saigon			
EAST ASIA	**1825–30** Java War **1839–42** Opium War		**1850–64** Taiping Rebellion **1854** Perry opens US trade with Japan **1868** Meiji Restoration, Japan			**1893–1976** Mao Zedong **1894–95** Sino-Japanese War
THE AMERICAS AND PACIFIC	**1823** Monroe Doctrine	**1835–40** Alexis de Tocqueville, *Democracy in America* **1840** Britain annexes New Zealand **1846–48** Mexican War	**1849** Gold discovered in California	**1861–65** American Civil War **1867** Russia sells Alaska to US **1867** British North America Act	**1869** Opening of Transcontinental railroad	

***Empire State Express* *No. 999,* *ca.* 1890.**

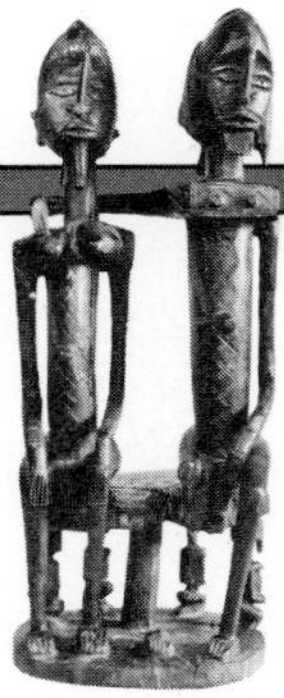

Wood sculpture, Dogon tribe, Mali, West Africa.

Eiffel Tower, Paris, 1889.

Commodore Matthew Perry, a Japanese view, 1853.

British suffragette, *ca.* 1910.

Private Edwin Francis Jennison, Confederate Army.

1914	
1886 Gold discovered in Southern Africa **1889** Rhodesia colonized **1899–1902** Boer War **1910** Union of South Africa formed	
1894–1905 Dreyfus Affair **1905** Russian Revolution begins **1905** Einstein's Theory of Relativity **1907** Triple Entente **1912–13** Balkan Wars	
1885 Indian National Congress founded **1906** Muslim League founded	
1900 Boxer Rebellion **1904–05** Russo-Japanese War **1911** Chinese Revolution **1912–49** Chinese Republic	
1889 First Pan-American Conference **1898** Spanish-American War **1910** Mexican Revolution begins	**1914** Panama Canal opens

The Prince of Wales in Bangalore, India, *ca.* 1900.

Gold prospector, California, *ca.* 1850.

36 Europe 1870–1914
Promise and Pessimism

The last decades of the nineteenth century in Europe were puzzling years. On the one hand, with economic prosperity at home, with peace abroad, and with rapid advances in all fields of scientific research, the belief in progress that had prevailed since the Enlightenment seemed happily confirmed. But on the other hand, from a later vantage point and with the knowledge of what happened in 1914, the period looks different. Despite rising prosperity, several periods of depression occurred, and many Europeans continued to live in poverty. Peace on the European continent was bought at the price of subjugating colonial peoples overseas and suppressing national minorities at home. The preeminence of science, with its stress on material values, makes the pre-1914 period appear in retrospect as a crass and materialistic age. An air of optimism and apprehension, therefore, of promise and pessimism prevailed during the half-century before the First World War.

This chapter is primarily concerned with domestic affairs. Developments in various parts of Europe differed, but certain political, economic, and social trends were common to most countries. In politics, Europe after 1870 witnessed the further spread of constitutional and democratic government; in economics, most countries shared in a "Second Industrial Revolution"; and in the social sphere, the labor movement and socialism came to play an increasingly important role in the affairs of almost all nations.

THE GROWTH OF DEMOCRACY

By 1914 most countries in Europe had universal manhood suffrage and several had parliamentary governments. But the degree and effectiveness of democracy varied. In England some 20 percent of adult males still could not vote. In France and Italy universal manhood suffrage existed, but parliamentary government functioned poorly. Germany, too, had universal manhood suffrage but only limited parliamentary government. In Austria-Hungary the main obstacle to democratic government was the perennial problem of nationalities. In Russia the franchise in 1914 was still limited, and the National Assembly, or *Duma,* had merely advisory functions.

Women's Rights

The only places in 1914 where women were allowed to vote were Norway, New Zealand, Australia, and some parts of the American West. In Europe, agitation for women's rights centered in England and to a lesser extent in Germany. By the end of the century, various women's suffrage societies had grown up in England and on the Continent. The efforts of these determined "suffragettes" to gain political rights for women were met by staunch male and also some female opposition. Outside the political arena, women were gradually being freed from the legal restrictions that had kept them the virtual wards of their husbands or fathers. As more and more women started careers of their own, they also gained economic independence. But most of the professions were still closed to women. Despite some progress toward women's rights, the old cliché that "woman's place is in the home" still prevailed.

Mrs. Emmeline Pankhurst being carried off to jail in 1911 after leading a demonstration of British suffragettes in support of voting rights for women.

Democracy and Education

One profession in which women gained considerable influence was elementary education. The success of democracy depended to no small extent on an informed electorate. In England the Education Act of 1870 made instruction free and compulsory. In Germany, secondary education continued to be a privilege of the well-to-do. French education finally became compulsory and nonsectarian in the 1880s. The need for education was especially acute in countries with high illiteracy rates. The Italian government introduced universal education in 1877, but it was slow to take effect. While all other countries made deliberate efforts to stamp out ignorance, the Russian government discouraged lower-class education on the grounds that it would cause popular unrest.

THE "SECOND INDUSTRIAL REVOLUTION"

The second general trend shared by most of Europe in the late nineteenth century was unparalleled industrial growth. This "Second Industrial Revolution" had certain unique characteristics. New sources of power—electricity and oil—competed with steam and coal in driving more intricate machinery. Improved steel production made that basic commodity available in greater quantities and at a lower price. Synthetic products, notably dyes produced from coal tars, became the foundation of the new chemical industry. New means of communication and transportation helped to speed up business transactions. New methods of promotion boosted sales. And a vast increase in the supply of liquid capital aided economic growth. All these innovations helped to increase industrial output beyond anything ever known. Between 1870 and 1914 the total production of the western world, including the United States, more than tripled.

Social Effects

This increased industrialization accentuated earlier trends in society. The population of Europe, except in France, continued to grow dramatically, and the shift from rural to urban life accelerated. By 1900 between one-third and one-half of the population in the more highly industrialized countries lived in large cities. As industrialization expanded, agriculture declined. Had it not been for the growing agrarian economies of Russia, the Americas, and Australia, Europe would have gone hungry.

Industrialization continued to affect people's lives in other ways. The mass production of consumer goods helped to make life easier and more comfortable. Central heating, the use of gas and electricity, ready-made clothing, and the perfection of canning and refrigeration were only a few of the conveniences now enjoyed by almost everyone.

But mechanization and mass production also had their negative sides. Some critics began to worry that the influence of machines over man might in time make him the slave rather than the master of his inventions. Mass production tended to standardize and cheapen public taste; it also led to overproduction. To stimulate sales, advertising made people buy goods they did not really need or want. Industrialization at best was a mixed blessing.

"Big Business"

One of the characteristics of industrial development after 1870 was the substitution of "big business" for the smaller factories that had prevailed earlier. As enterprises became fewer, larger, and more competitive, producers formed combinations to control production, distribution, and prices. The "trusts" of the United States, the "amalgamations" of Great Britain, and the "cartels" of Germany were alike in their efforts to establish some control over the production and distribution of goods. Opponents of industrial concentration claimed that it created monopolies that kept prices artificially high. But the United States was the only major country to prohibit trusts.

The period of "monopolistic capitalism," as the decades after 1870 are called, was the heyday of the great industrialists — the Carnegies, Rockefellers, Krupps, Nobels, and others. The economic power of these "tycoons" could not help but give them political influence as well. But business leaders did not use their wealth only for their own ends. The ruthlessness of the early days of industrialization was gradually mitigated by signs of social consciousness. An example of this humanitarian attitude was the steel magnate Andrew Carnegie, who laid down his philosophy in *The Gospel of Wealth* (1900) and gave more than $300 million to worthy causes. The Nobel Prizes and the Rhodes Scholarships both commemorate two highly successful humanitarian businessmen.

THE RISE OF THE WORKING CLASS

A third general trend during the period after 1870 was the increasing influence of the working class and its socialist philosophy. Much of the improvement in the worker's condition was due to the political power of the various so-

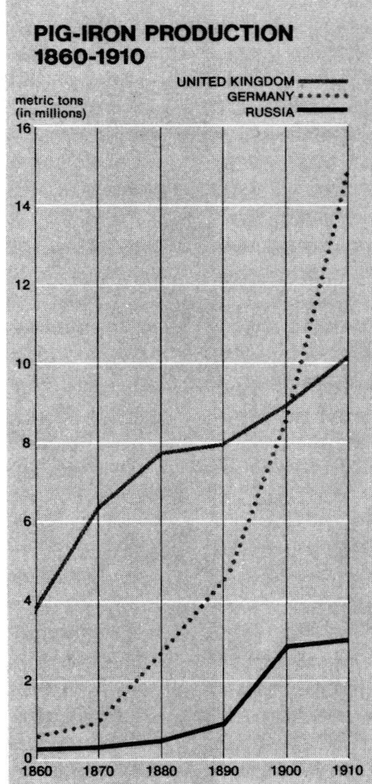

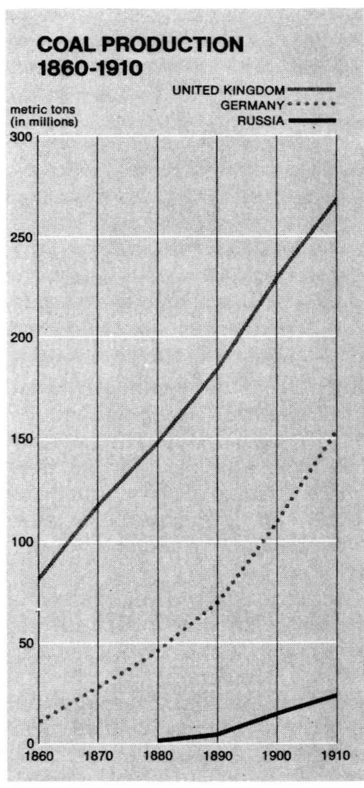

cialist parties and to the economic power of the labor unions. As a result, the status of the European worker by 1914 had been raised far above what it had been in 1870.

New Varieties of Socialism

Events during the late nineteenth century failed to bear out Marx's prediction of the imminent collapse of capitalism. While much capital was concentrated in a few hands, still more of it was diffused through joint stock companies. And while workers still suffered from some of the hardships of the First Industrial Revolution, their condition steadily improved. By the end of the century it became clear that Marx's teachings had to be adjusted to changed circumstances. The result of this adjustment was called "revisionist," or "evolutionary," socialism.

The leading theorist of revisionism was the German socialist Eduard Bernstein. Bernstein had spent some time in England, where he came in contact with the non-Marxian socialism of a group of intellectuals, among them Sidney and Beatrice Webb, H. G. Wells, and George Bernard Shaw. Their socialism was called "Fabianism" after the Roman general Fabius, who preferred to defeat his enemies by gradually exhausting rather than directly attacking them. The Fabian Socialists opposed violent revolution and sought instead to achieve socialization by way of gradual reform. On his return to Germany in the 1890s, Bernstein began to expound his own revised version of Marxian socialism. In his *Evolutionary Socialism* (1899), Bernstein advocated that instead of waging revolution against the middle class, the working class should collaborate with any group, proletarian or bourgeois, that would help improve the workers' condition.

The revisionist ideas of Bernstein caused a major stir in Marxist circles. Orthodox Marxists denounced revisionism and reaffirmed their faith in the validity of Marx's teachings. One of the most determined defenders of pure Marxism, the Russian Vladimir Ilyich Ulyanov, better known by his pseudonym, N. Lenin, held that only a revolution could overthrow the capitalist system, and that it was up to a radical minority within the proletariat to prepare the way for revolution by keeping alive the idea of class struggle. Except in eastern Europe, "Leninism" found few followers before the First World War.

Another form of violent protest arising at the turn of the century was syndicalism. Its main exponent was the Frenchman Georges Sorel, whose *Reflections on Violence* (1908) popularized his philosophy. Like anarchism (see p. 734), syndicalism saw the state as an instrument of oppression and advocated its abolition. Instead, the trade unions (*syndicat* is the French word for "union") should seize control of a socialist society. To achieve their aim, the syndicalists advocated various means of industrial sabotage, culminating in a general strike. Syndicalism flourished most in Italy, Spain, and France; it also influenced the Industrial Workers of the World (IWW) in the United States.

Leninism

1902

I assert: [(1)] That no movement can be durable without a stable organization of leaders to maintain continuity; (2) that the more widely the masses are spontaneously drawn into the struggle and form the basis of the movement, the more necessary it is to have such an organization and the more stable must it be (for it is much easier then for demagogues to sidetrack the more backward sections of the masses); (3) that the organization must consist chiefly of persons engaged in revolutionary activities as a profession; (4) that in a country with an autocratic government, the more we *restrict* the membership of this organization to persons who are engaged in revolution as a profession and who have been professionally trained in the art of combating the political police, the more difficult will it be to catch the organization; and (5) the *wider* will be the circle of men and women of the working class or of other classes of society able to join the movement and perform active work in it.

From N. Lenin, "What Is to Be Done?" in *Selected Works* (London: Lawrence and Wishart, 1936), Vol. II, pp. 138–39.

International Socialism

Marxism was envisaged by its founder as an international movement, and Marx had been instrumental in founding the International Workingmen's Association in 1864. But this First International was not very successful. Marx's domineering manner, his controversy with Bakunin, who was among the leaders of the International, and the excesses of the Paris Commune, which were blamed on the socialists, combined to bring about the demise of the First International in 1876.

With the rise of socialist parties in most major countries during the next decade, however, a Second International was formed in 1889. From the start it was beset by internal differences, especially on the issue of revisionism. As time went on, moreover, it became obvious that the national loyalties of most socialists were stronger than their feelings of international solidarity. When the test came in 1914 the ideals of international socialism quickly gave way to the stronger appeal of national patriotism.

The Growth of Labor Unions

In addition to forming their own political parties, workers tried to improve their lot by organizing labor unions. In the early nineteenth century, unions had made little headway. This situation improved markedly after 1870. In England, in a series of parliamentary acts in 1874 and 1875, unions were given permission to strike and to picket peacefully. As a result of the famous dock strike of 1889, union activity was extended to unskilled labor. On the Continent the labor movement was slower in gaining momentum. In France, the bloody events of the Paris Commune cast a shadow on any kind of labor activity, and it was not until 1884 that the Waldeck-Rousseau Law granted full legal status to unions. In 1895, the General Confederation of Labor (CGT) was organized along syndicalist lines.

In Germany, where the labor movement was closely allied with socialism, it was adversely affected by the antisocialist measures of Bismarck. It thus did not really get under way until after 1890. Under the Imperial Industrial Code, German workers were permitted to strike, but hostile courts restricted their activities wherever possible. In the less industrialized countries of Italy, Austria-Hungary, and Russia, trade unionism played a minor role. In Italy, the socialist General Italian Federation of Labor, the largest union, was founded in 1907. Socialist unions also predominated in Austria, though there was hardly any organized labor in agrarian Hungary. Russia had no real labor unions until after 1905, and even then they did not wield much influence.

The "Welfare State"

The agitation of European workers for political, economic, and social reforms made their governments adopt programs of social legislation designed to help the lower classes. Such intervention by the state was a radical departure from the laissez-faire philosophy of early nineteenth-century liberalism. The idea that the state should become a "welfare state" found acceptance among politicians both in England and on the Continent. The social legislation resulting from this new attitude was so far-reaching that it has been called "state socialism." Its chief purpose was to satisfy the grievances of the workers, and by so doing, preserve the capitalist system.

Similar motives were behind various appeals of the Christian churches for collaboration between employers and workers. Christian Socialism was nothing new, but it gained significance as the teachings of Marx began to compete with and to undermine the influence of Christianity. The leading pronouncement on Christian social policy was made by Pope Leo XIII in his encyclical *Rerum novarum* in 1891, in which he condemned socialist attacks on private property and the Marxian concept of class struggle and suggested that the state aid its poorer citizens and that employers and workers settle their differences in a spirit of Christian brotherhood.

So much for some of the general trends that prevailed in Europe between 1870 and 1914. As we now turn to a discussion of the domestic affairs in the major countries, we shall find these developments much in evidence.

ENGLAND: "MOTHER OF DEMOCRACY"

England after 1870 continued along its road of gradual political and social reform. Gladstone's "great ministry" came to an end in 1874. For the next six years Disraeli, Earl of Beaconsfield after 1876, conducted a policy noted chiefly for its successes abroad. Between 1880 and 1895, Liberal and Conservative governments alternated, with Gladstone heading three more ministries and Lord Salisbury serving as his Conservative counterpart. The last two decades before 1914 were equally divided between the two major parties, the Conservatives remaining in power until 1905 and the Liberals leading thereafter. Generally speaking, the Liberals were more active in domestic affairs, where Gladstone's reforming zeal found its successor after the turn of the century in the dynamic David Lloyd George. The Conservatives, on the other hand, were more concerned with foreign affairs, especially England's overseas interests. Lord Salisbury personally assumed the post of foreign secretary in his three cabinets.

Queen Victoria (center) and some of her royal relatives. Among them included here are her daughters Victoria, wife of the German Emperor Frederick III, and Alexandra, wife of Tsar Nicholas II, and her son the Prince of Wales and future King Edward VII of England.

The problem that overshadowed all others was still Ireland. Gladstone sought once again to remedy some of the worst abuses of Irish land tenure in the Land Act of 1881. He ran into resistance, however, from Ireland's Nationalists, under the leadership of Charles Parnell. The Nationalists demanded political rather than economic reforms. Gladstone hoped to satisfy Irish demands by two Home Rule Bills, but he was defeated both times. Subsequent Land Purchase Acts aimed at helping Irish tenants buy their land, somewhat counteracted the agitation of Irish nationalism. The Irish question became acute once more in 1912, when the Liberals introduced a third Home Rule Bill. Before it became law, however, war had broken out, and home rule had to be postponed.

England's ability to resist serious crises except in Ireland was largely due to the peaceful adjustments it continued to make to the demands for democratic reforms. The franchise that had been granted to urban workers in 1867 was extended to rural laborers under the Franchise Act of 1884. A Redistribution Bill in 1885 established uniform electoral districts, and the Parliament Bill of 1911 abolished the veto power of the House of Lords over money bills. Democracy—for men only—had made considerable progress in Britain by 1914.

Economic Developments

Economically, the picture in England looked somewhat less bright. Before 1870, British industry had enjoyed undisputed leadership, and British agriculture had held its own. This situation gradually changed as Germany and the United States became England's chief industrial rivals, and as the influx of cheap agricultural products from overseas caused a rapid decline in British farming. Germany and America had overtaken England in the basic iron and steel industries by 1914, and England's share of world trade fell from 23 percent in 1876 to 15 percent in 1913.

Much of this relative decline in England's leadership was inevitable, as nations that had once been Britain's customers began to supply their own needs and claim their own share of the world market, but there were other causes also. Scientific and technical education lagged behind that of other nations, notably Germany. England was slow in modernizing its industrial plants and production methods, and it failed to realize the importance of salesmanship. Furthermore, while tariff walls were rising everywhere else, Britain clung to its policy of free trade, despite efforts, notably by Joseph Chamberlain at the turn of the century, to change to protectionism.

Labor and Social Reform

Even though its economic leadership was declining, Britain was still the most prosperous nation in the world. The British worker was far better off than the workers in most continental countries. Great Britain was the only major European country in which Marxian socialism did not gain any large following. The Fabian Society (1883) appealed chiefly to middle-class intellectuals. What political influence the British working class exerted before 1914 came chiefly from the Labour party. Its origins went back to the early 1890s, but its official beginning dates from 1900, when several groups joined forces behind the Labour Representation Committee. In the general election of 1906, the Labour party won twenty-nine seats in Parliament. Its program called for gradual socialization of key industries and utilities along Fabian lines.

Another avenue through which British labor improved its status was union activity. There were occasional reverses, such as the Taff Vale decision of 1901 which made unions liable for damages resulting from strikes, and the Osborne Judgment of 1909, which prohibited unions from paying stipends to Labour members of Parliament. Both restrictions were finally removed under pressure from the Labour party.

While the worker was helping himself, the government also did its share through welfare legislation. Earlier factory legislation was extended by further acts—in 1878, 1901, and 1908—and a minimum-wage law was passed in 1912. Social insurance was initiated, first against accidents (1880), then against old age (1909), and finally against sickness and unemployment (1911). To finance these costly measures, the Liberal government of Lloyd George in 1909 introduced a "People's Budget," which shifted the main tax burden to the rich.

As the result of an enlightened policy at home and a strong position abroad, England in 1914 appeared contented and confident. Yet there were some danger signals, especially in Ireland and India; Britain's economy was going "soft"; and its political system needed further reforms. Some pessimists even wondered if the country would be able to cope with these issues in the future, as it had always been able to in the past.

FRANCE: REPUBLIC IN CRISIS

Britain's steady progress toward political and social democracy had no parallel on the Continent. The French Third Republic, after stormy beginnings, developed a system of government that, while more democratic, was far less stable than that of Britain. The French presidency was largely a ceremonial office. The cabinet was responsible to a bicameral legislature, the lower body of which, the Chamber of Deputies, was elected by universal male suffrage. Instead of clearly defined political parties, France had a large number of loosely organized factions, usually headed by some prominent political figure. This arrangement made the formation of workable majorities extremely difficult. There were more than fifty coalition cabinets during the forty years before the First World War.

Republicans versus Monarchists

One of the main reasons for the erratic course of French politics after 1870 was antirepublicanism. On several occasions in the early years of the Republic, the various royalist factions had come dangerously close to resurrecting the monarchy. Not until 1879 did the French government become wholly republican in its legislative and executive branches.

But the republican elements were no more united than their enemies. A radical faction, led after Gambetta's death in 1882 by Georges Clemenceau, was held together by anticlericalism and hatred of Germany. The moderate republicans, on the other hand, were willing to compromise on domestic and foreign issues. Their chief figure, Jules Ferry, emerged as France's leading statesman in the last decades of the century. During most of the 1880s, radicals and moderates managed to cooperate. Despite their achievements, however, widespread opposition persisted. Beginning in 1886 this opposition rallied around the recently appointed minister of war, General Georges Boulanger. By early 1889 the dashing general might easily have led a successful coup against the Republic, had not his courage failed him at the crucial moment.

As it turned out, the Boulanger affair helped to strengthen the Republic by drawing the radical and moderate republicans more closely together. But this gain was soon lost again in the so-called Panama Scandal, in which a number of radical deputies were found to have accepted large bribes from the corrupt and bankrupt Panama Canal Company. The dust of this affair had still not settled when the Third Republic was shaken by an even more serious crisis, the Dreyfus case.

In the fall of 1894, Captain Alfred Dreyfus, a Jew, was accused of having betrayed military secrets to the Germans and was exiled to Devil's Island. Despite clear evidence of his inno-

Captain Alfred Dreyfus in 1899 passing between a "guard of dishonor," soldiers whose backs are turned to him. The reactionary military faction arranged for this practice in order to discredit and humiliate Dreyfus.

cence, it took five years before he was fully vindicated. During this time, the reactionary right—monarchists, Catholics, and the army, together with a handful of anti-Semites—denounced any attempt to clear Dreyfus as an attack on the honor of the nation and the discipline of the army. The radical left, in defending Dreyfus, cleared its reputation of the blemish incurred in the Panama Scandal. At the same time, the Dreyfus case testified to the continued strength of the forces of reaction.

The most immediate result of the Dreyfus affair was a shift from moderate to radical republicanism. After winning the elections of 1902, the Radicals at long last were able to carry out their own program. Their most drastic measures were against the Catholic Church. A bill for the separation of church and state brought to an end the Concordat of 1801, whereby the state had paid the salaries of the clergy and had participated in the selection of priests. In social reform the Radicals were less successful. With the emergence of socialism in France at the turn of the century, radicalism found a powerful rival with far more sweeping social and economic aims.

Economic Developments

France was set back by the Franco-Prussian War and was slow to profit from the Second Industrial Revolution. The losses in manpower, Germany's demand for a heavy indemnity, and especially the surrender of the valuable industrial region of Alsace-Lorraine, severely slowed French industrial growth. The majority of the French, moreover, were still engaged in agriculture, and protective tariffs mainly aided the farmers. What industry there was consisted largely of small establishments. French foreign trade almost doubled between 1870 and 1914; but because the commerce of its competitors increased at a much greater rate, France found itself demoted from second to fourth place in world trade. In one activity France led the rest of the world: The amount of French money invested abroad during the thirty years before 1914 rose from 13 to 44 billion francs. These foreign loans were a valuable source of national income, and they were used as an effective instrument to facilitate French foreign policy.

Socialism and Social Reform

Because France's working class was still small, French socialism never gained the influence it did in Germany. Socialism in France, furthermore, had received a serious setback in the Paris Commune, from which it did not recover until the late 1870s. Like socialists in most other countries, the French were split into moderates and radicals. The revolutionary group, led by Jules Guesde, and the moderates, led by Jean Jaurès, did not join forces until 1905, when they formed the United Socialist party. Again like most other socialist parties, the French socialist party was revolutionary in theory but evolutionary in practice. Between 1906 and 1914, its membership in the Chamber of Deputies nearly doubled.

In the realm of social reform, France lagged behind England. A factory law of 1874, amended by subsequent acts, fixed the minimum working age at thirteen, restricted working hours for adults to twelve hours, and introduced various other health and sanitation measures. Social insurance did not begin until the end of the century. Accident insurance was introduced in 1898, and old-age pensions were started in 1910. There was no protection against unemployment, and health insurance was left to private initiative.

Even though the French working class was not as numerous as its counterparts in England and Germany, the government's failure to solve some of its economic and social problems caused constant domestic unrest during the years just before 1914. At the same time, the Third Republic continued to be attacked from the right. Royalism and an intense brand of nationalism were kept alive by a few wealthy reactionaries in the *Action Française,* a right-wing pressure group, led by

Charles Maurras and Léon Daudet. Yet the majority of the French seemed to approve the programs of reform at home and peace abroad, which brought resounding victory for the Radicals and Socialists in the elections of 1914. French pacifism, while admirable, came at a most inopportune time, just when Europe was getting ready for a major war. France, on the eve of the First World War, was still a nation divided on many vital issues.

GERMANY: EMPIRE TRIUMPHANT

The new German *Reich* presented a spectacle of success and supreme self-confidence. Had its industrial growth been paralleled by political reforms, Germany might easily have rivaled England as the most progressive nation in Europe. But repeated demands of liberals and socialists for the reform of the Prussian three-class franchise and for the introduction of parliamentary government in the Empire were of no avail. The main direction of policy continued to rest with the chancellor (who was appointed by and responsible to the emperor) and the Federal Council, or *Bundesrat,* in which Prussia held a controlling position. The German electorate, furthermore, was split into five or six major parties, none of which ever won a majority.

Repression at Home — Aggression Abroad

During its first twenty years, the German Empire was ruled by the strong hand of Bismarck. The "iron chancellor's" claim to fame rests on his foreign rather than his domestic policy. During the 1870s Bismarck antagonized large sections of the German people by his fierce struggle against the Catholic Church. The so-called *Kulturkampf* (conflict of cultures), while appealing to liberal anticlericalism, failed in its major objective — to prevent the rise of political Catholicism. The Catholic Center party emerged from its persecution as a potent factor in German politics. During the 1880s, Bismarck's attempt to prevent the rise of a strong Socialist party was equally unsuccessful. By enlisting liberal supporters in his fight against Catholics and socialists, Bismarck perpetuated the political disunity of the German people and contributed further to the decline of German liberalism.

Bismarck had no worthy successor. The unceremonious manner in which he was dismissed by William II in 1890 was indicative of the young emperor's desire to be his own chancellor. But William was unsuited for such a role. Erratic and unstable, the kaiser launched Germany on an expansionist *Weltpolitik* (world policy) that soon lost it the international trust it had gained under Bismarck. The army, long pow-

Kaiser Wilhelm II

Every society, it is sometimes said, gets the ruler it deserves. This is true in part, but only in part, for Wilhelmine Germany. Kaiser Wilhelm II was certainly more representative of his age than Bismarck or Hitler were of theirs. And yet the Second Reich was unlucky in the man fate chose to rule it. He was deformed from birth, his left arm hanging six inches shorter than his right and incapable of movement. . . . His upbringing at the hands of the Calvinist Hinzpeter was severe. He hated his English Liberal mother, and despised his father for permitting her to dominate him. Although inwardly he may have been plagued by a sense of insecurity, his public utterances and actions stressed his own importance to a disturbing degree. He intervened in ship-design, archaeology, music, painting and theatre production with the same self-assurance that characterized his military and political moves. Much of his thinking was tinged with a brutal racialism which most people would now associate with a later period in German history. . . . He warned new recruits that they would have to shoot down their own fathers and brothers if he ordered them to. . . . His strongest language he reserved for the deputies of the Reichstag. They were "scoundrels without a fatherland" who were behaving "more and more like pigs.". . . It is no exaggeration to say that contending with the Kaiser was a major preoccupation of Germany's leading statesmen from Bismarck's fall until the outbreak of the First World War.

From J. C. G. Röhl, *Germany Without Bismarck: The Crisis of Government in the Second Reich, 1890–1900* (London: Batsford, 1967), pp. 27–29.

erful in Prussian affairs, remained one of the cornerstones of the Empire. Except for its budget, which the *Reichstag* had to grant for several years in advance, it remained entirely free from civilian control.

Within the *Reichstag* there was very little chance for any effective opposition. The alliance between prominent industrialists and landowners, instituted under Bismarck, assured the government of a workable parliamentary majority. Both groups profited from tariff protectionism, and both were opposed to lower-class demands for political and social democracy. Against this coalition between the industrialist National Liberals and the agrarian Conservatives, the Socialist opposition and the occasionally critical Center and Progressive parties could do very little. On a few occasions, notably during the "Daily Telegraph Affair" in 1908, when William II made some irresponsible statements on Anglo-German relations, it seemed as though public indignation might check the kaiser's erratic rule. But the discipline so deeply instilled in every German, and the economic prosperity the nation enjoyed, kept the public from taking any drastic steps.

Economic Developments

The immediate effect of Germany's unification in 1871 had been a short-lived economic boom, which had come to a sudden halt in the worldwide depression of 1873. Only during the last two decades of the century did Germany begin to show its great economic power. Much of Germany's economic success can be attributed to the protective policy that Bismarck initiated in 1879. Germany was not the first nation to abandon free trade, but it was Germany's step that ushered in a period of tariff rivalry among the major powers.

Germany's rapid economic growth was due in large measure to the development of its domestic market—its population increased from 41 million to 67 million between 1871 and 1914—but German competition was also felt abroad. The main pillars of German prosperity were coal and iron, concentrated in Alsace-Lorraine, the Saar, Upper Silesia, and particularly the Ruhr area, where the firms of

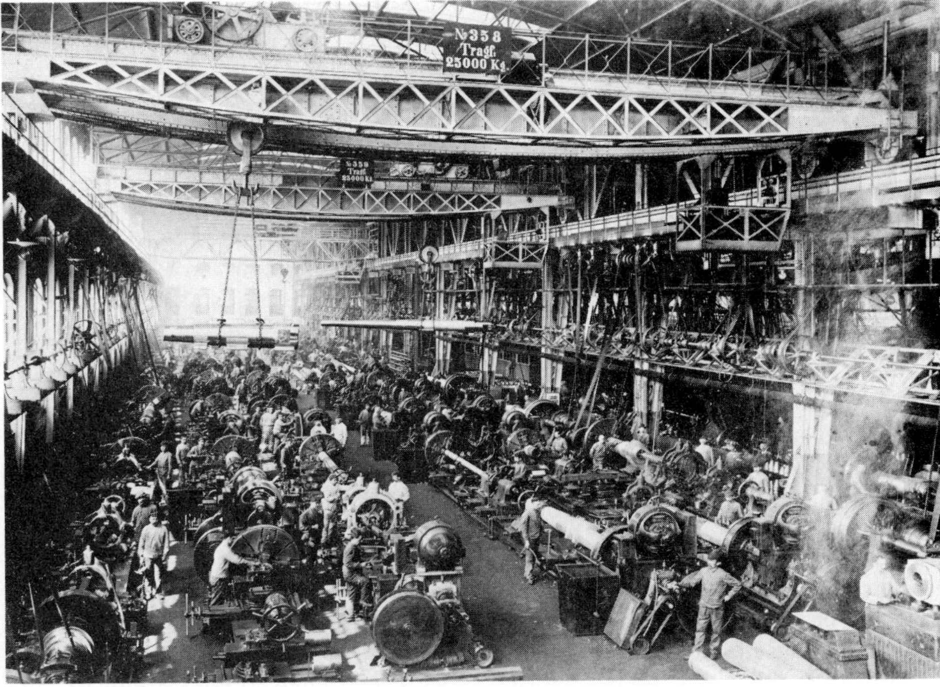

The gun shop at the Krupp works, Essen, Germany, one of the largest military manufacturing plants in Europe.

Krupp, Thyssen, and Stinnes built their huge industrial empires. Germans took the lead in other pursuits as well, especially the electrical and chemical industries. By 1914 Germany's merchant marine was second only to that of Great Britain.

Socialism and Social Reform

The main critics of German domestic and foreign policy were the Social Democrats, the largest and most influential socialist party in Europe. With its origins in the 1860s, it did not become a political force until the formation of the Social Democratic party (SPD) by Wilhelm Liebknecht and August Bebel in 1875. Despite persecution by Bismarck, the numbers of the SPD steadily increased, until by 1912 it had become the largest party in the *Reichstag*. Its program, first formulated at Gotha in 1875 and revised at Erfurt in 1891, while strictly "orthodox" in tone, nevertheless included a number of "revisionist" demands for specific reforms.

The phenomenal economic growth of Germany could not help but be reflected in a rising standard of living for the workers. The German government, through extensive programs of social reform, tried to alleviate the hardships inherent in massive industrialization. In 1878 factory inspection was made compulsory, and in 1891 an Imperial Industrial Code introduced sanitary and safety provisions and regulated working hours for women and children. Germany's pioneering efforts were in the field of social legislation. In a calculated effort to divert German workers from socialism, between 1883 and 1889, Bismarck introduced far-reaching measures for health, accident, and old-age insurance. These served as models for similar legislation in other countries.

The German Empire in 1914 was an anomaly among European powers—economically one of the most advanced, yet politically one of the most backward. The majority of Germans, though unhappy about their political impotence, took comfort in their economic achievements. They might criticize their government's domestic policy, but they saw little wrong with a foreign policy that demanded for Germany the "place in the sun" it deserved.

AUSTRIA-HUNGARY: THE RAMSHACKLE EMPIRE

The Austro-Hungarian Empire, since the *Ausgleich* of 1867, had been virtually divided into two separate states. Both Austria and Hungary were constitutional monarchies, but their governments were far from democratic. Various attempts before 1914 to improve this situation were complicated by the problem of nationalities. After 1873 the Austrian lower house, or *Reichsrat,* was elected by a complicated four-class franchise, which gave disproportionate influence to the upper classes and the German minority among the population. This system, with some minor changes, lasted until 1907. By that time agitation among the subject nationalities could no longer be ignored. The electoral law of 1907 at long last granted universal manhood suffrage. But the return of a large majority of non-German delegates led to such constant wrangling in the *Reichsrat* that rule by decree remained the order of the day. In Hungary the situation was still more hopeless. Here the upper crust of Magyar landowners completely dominated both houses of parliament. Hungary in 1914 remained essentially a feudal state.

Conflict of Nationalities

Among the nationalities of Austria, the Czechs in Bohemia were the main problem. They were closely intermingled with Germans, and attempts to introduce Czech, together with German, as the official languages were met by German opposition. German nationalism found a mouthpiece in the German *Schulverein,* an organization to further the study of German, of Georg von Schönerer. Meanwhile, the "Young Czechs," led by Thomas Masaryk, fought for the rights of their own people.

While Austria made at least some concessions to its minorities, Hungary followed a strict policy of Magyarization. The major problem in Hungary was the Croats, who looked to Serbia for the lead in forming a Yugoslav—that is, South Slav—federation. The situation was complicated by the fact that the region of Bosnia-Herzegovina, since 1878 under Austrian administration, was also inhabited by Southern Slavs. The heir to the Austro-Hungarian crowns, Archduke Francis Ferdinand, was known to favor reforms that would give the Slavic element within the Dual Monarchy equal rights with Germans and Magyars. Neither Hungary nor Serbia liked such schemes. The Hungarians wanted to continue lording it over their Slavs, and the Serbs hoped to attract the Southern Slavs away from Austria-Hungary.

Economic Developments

Even though the Austrian half of the Empire was notably industrialized, the country as a whole remained predominantly agrarian. As such it suffered increasingly from the competition of the larger agrarian economies of Russia, the United States, and Australia. A high tariff policy protecting agriculture kept living costs high, making for high wages and preventing Austrian industries from successfully competing abroad. Even so, there was some economic progress. It would have been greater had the economic interdependence between Austria and Hungary been better utilized. As it was, industrial Austria and agrarian Hungary pursued separate and often contradictory economic policies.

Socialism and Social Reform

Socialism in Austria did not become a political factor until the end of the century. In 1889, Victor Adler, the most prominent Austrian socialist, unified various socialist factions behind the Austrian Social Democratic party. Socialist agitation, in part, was responsible for the introduction of universal suffrage in Austria in 1907. The program of Austrian socialists was revisionist, and their main support came from the working-class population of Vienna. Their major weakness was national diversity: By 1911 the party had split into German, Czech, and Polish factions. There was no socialist movement to speak of in Hungary.

The Austrian government also took a hand in improving the workers' lot. A system of factory inspection was set up in 1883, and an Industrial Code in 1907 set the minimum working age at twelve, provided for an eleven-hour working day, and introduced safety and sanitation standards for factories.

The economic and social problems of the Austro-Hungarian Empire in 1914 were still overshadowed by its nationalities problem. Every possible solution to this problem had been proposed, and a few had been tried. Because each proposal left one or another of the many nationality groups dissatisfied, a policy of repression always prevailed. The result of this negative policy was the assassination of Francis Ferdinand at Sarajevo on June 28, 1914.

Emperor Francis Joseph (center) relaxing with guests at the wedding party of his grandnephew and eventual successor, Archduke Karl Franz Joseph (1911).

ITALY: GREAT POWER BY COURTESY

In Italy, economic backwardness and widespread illiteracy retarded the growth of democracy. The Italian constitution, the *Statuto*, which Piedmont had adopted in 1848, still limited the franchise in 1870 to a mere 2.5 percent of the population. Property qualifications and the voting age were gradually lowered, and virtually all adult males were permitted to vote by 1914. But this extension of the franchise, giving the vote to the illiterate poor, enabled a handful of politicians to manipulate elections. The practice of "transformism"—that is, of avoiding parliamentary opposition by giving the most powerful critics a share in the government—proved a further obstacle to the growth of democracy in Italy.

Political Instability

A great power by courtesy more than through actual strength, Italy's frantic efforts to live up to a glorious past led it into military ventures it could ill afford. The conservative forces that had brought about the country's unification remained in power until 1876. Regional opposition to centralization and widespread discontent with heavy taxation then shifted the power to the more liberal factions. From 1887 to 1891 and from 1893 to 1896, the experienced Francesco Crispi as prime minister provided firm leadership. His attempts to divert attention from discontent at home through colonial ventures abroad suffered a dismal defeat at the hands of Ethiopia in the battle of Adua (1896). The end of the century saw a rising tide of labor unrest. In 1900 King Humbert fell victim to an anarchist assassin and was succeeded by the more liberal Victor Emmanuel III. During the last ten years before the war, Italy, under the capable but unprincipled Giovanni Giolitti at long last made some headway in the solution of its worst economic difficulties. Giolitti also managed to effect a partial reconciliation between the Italian government and the Catholic Church.

Giovanni Giolitti. Five times prime minister of Italy (1892–93, 1903–05, 1906–09, 1911–14, 1920–21).

Economic Developments

Most of Italy's troubles were due to poverty. Italy was still primarily an agrarian nation, yet its soil was too poor and its methods too backward to support its rapidly growing population. The mounting pressure could be relieved only through emigration and industrialization. Industry was hampered by lack of raw materials and shortage of capital. Attempts at protectionism, furthermore, affected Italy's exports, and only with the conclusion of a series of commercial treaties in the 1890s did the economy pick up. With the aid of hydroelectric power, Italy gradually developed its own textile industry and gained world leadership in the production of silk. But despite these improvements, and despite almost a doubling of its foreign commerce between 1900 and 1910, Italy's balance of trade continued to be unfavorable.

Socialism and Social Reform

As almost everywhere else in Europe, industrialization in Italy brought in its wake the rise of socialism. The first socialist party was organized in 1891. It, too, had its difficulties with revisionism, and finally in 1911 the radical, orthodox element gained the upper hand. The Italian socialist party did not gain any mass following until after 1900. Many Italian workers were attracted by the more violent programs of anarchism and syndicalism. The first major general strike took place in 1904 but failed for lack of popular support.

The Italian government tried to cope with the social effects of industrialization by factory acts and social legislation. Accident and old-age insurance were introduced in 1898. But the basic problems—poverty and illiteracy—could not be erased overnight. Meanwhile the Italian people, inexperienced in the ways of democracy, fell more and more under the influence of extremists of the right—calling for glorious ventures abroad—or the left—opposing war and demanding reforms at home. Thus divided, Italy was in no condition to go to war in 1914.

RUSSIA: STRONGHOLD OF AUTOCRACY

Tsarist Russia, to the bitter end, remained the most autocratic among European states. The brief flurry of reforms under Alexander II (r. 1855–81) during the 1860s had soon given way again to Russia's traditional policy of repression. Alexander III (r. 1881–94), was a reactionary and a Slavophile, not unlike Nicholas I. For well over a quarter-century Alexander III and his son and successor, Nicholas II (r. 1894–1917), followed a policy of darkest reaction. Aided by Vyacheslav Plehve, director of the state police and later minister of the interior, and by Constantine Pobedonostsev, who as "Procurator of the Holy Synod" was the highest official in the Russian Orthodox Church and one of the most powerful men in Russia, the principles of orthodoxy, autocracy, and nationality once again became the watchwords of Russian policy. Catholics in Poland and Protestants in the Baltic provinces were persecuted; the powers of local and provincial *zemstvos* (councils), established under Alexander II, were curtailed; and nationalism in Finland, Poland, and the Ukraine was suppressed. A particularly shocking feature of Russian policy was its persecution of the Jews. There were hardly any positive achievements during this period of unrelieved repression, except the economic reforms of Count Witte.

Economic Developments

Russia was the last major European power to feel the impact of industrialization. The government's main concern prior to 1890 had been the improvement of farming methods and the cultivation of new lands. Russia's agricultural exports between 1860 and 1900 increased almost fourfold, despite rising tariff barriers. Beginning in the 1890s, Russia also embarked on a program of industrialization, chiefly under the direction of its minister of finance and commerce, Count Sergei Witte (1849–1915). By introducing the gold standard in 1897, Witte made investment in Russian industry more attractive to outsiders. The construction of the Trans-Siberian Railway, begun in 1891, helped open up the country's rich mineral resources. As a result Russia by 1900 held fourth place among the world's iron producers and second place in the production of oil. The opposition of agrarian interests to Witte's industrial policy, however, led to his retirement in 1903. Together with an economic depression and the Russian defeat in the war with Japan (1904–05), Witte's departure helped to slow down Russia's industrial development. Lack of capital, the educational backwardness of the Russian worker, and his continued subjection to the village community were chiefly responsible for Russia's failure to realize its tremendous economic potential.

Socialism and Social Reform

Because of the government's vigilance toward social and political protest, socialism in Russia was slow to take hold. Only in 1891 was the first Marxian socialist party organized by Georgi V. Plekhanov. The activity of the Social Democratic party was largely clandestine. At a party congress in London in 1903, Russia's socialists split into two groups. The Mensheviks under Julius Martov, advocated a gradual evolution to democracy and socialism, while the Bolsheviks under Lenin followed the more radical, "Leninist" line. Besides Marxian socialism there was also an organization of agrarian socialists in Russia, the Socialist Revolutionaries. Their program harked back to the ideas of Alexander Herzen and to the populist "go-to-the-people" movement. To achieve their goals, the Socialist Revolutionaries advocated terrorism and assassination.

Increased industrialization in Russia brought the usual hardships. With an ample supply of manpower from landless peasants, wages remained low and the Russian worker had to slave long hours to eke out a meager existence. The government did regulate the employment of women and children and introduced maximum working hours. But without a corresponding increase in wages, these restrictions merely lowered the income of workers' families. Moreover, to voice discontent through labor unions was prohibited by law. Even so, unrest among the workers caused frequent strikes of increasing violence.

The Revolution of 1905

The workers were not the only class that was restless. The masses of peasants were landless; opposition among national minorities against the official policy of Russification was increasing; and growing agitation among liberal members of the middle class favored constitutional government. As economic depression worsened the lot of the workers, the Russo-Japanese War upset the rural economy by drafting peasants. With the tide of war turning against Russia, tension finally erupted in revolution on "Bloody Sunday," January 22, 1905. A general strike soon crippled the major industrial centers, peasants rose against their landlords, and mutinies broke out in the army and navy. In October the Social Democrats and the Socialist Revolutionaries set up a Soviet (or Council) of Workers' Delegates in St. Petersburg.

By that time, however, the revolution had run its course. Tsar Nicholas finally gave in and made a number of concessions. The "October Manifesto" guaranteed individual freedoms and called for the election of a National Assembly, or *Duma.* But the promises made by Nicholas under duress were soon forgotten. Three elections were held before a *Duma* was finally elected that satisfied the tsar's wish for an advisory rather than a legislative body. Meanwhile the government had taken savage reprisals, executing an estimated fifteen thousand people. Even so, Russia for the first time in its history now had an elected national assembly that could serve as a training ground in parliamentary procedures.

Repression and Reform

The outstanding figure of the last decade before the war was Peter Stoly-

"Bloody Sunday" (January 22, 1905). A procession of workers on its way to the Winter Palace is fired on by tsarist troops; 70 people were killed and 240 wounded.

pin, chief minister until 1911. A conservative, he nevertheless believed in a limited degree of representative government. He worked harmoniously with the moderate faction within the *Duma,* the "Octobrists," who in contrast to the more liberal "Cadets" (constitutional democrats) were satisfied with a mere consultative role. Stolypin bore down hard on all revolutionary activities by Social Democrats and Socialist Revolutionaries. But he also introduced farsighted reforms. Most important among these was the division of the communal holdings of the villages. This was a slow undertaking, and by 1917 only about one-tenth of Russia's peasants had become independent farmers. If land reform had been completed in time, it might have saved the tsarist regime.

Stolypin's reformist policy was opposed by the advocates of revolution, for whom it did not go far enough, and by the forces of reaction who gained the upper hand when Stolypin was assassinated in 1911. Nicholas II was a weak and vacillating monarch, firmly committed to the autocratic beliefs of his father and deeply under the influence of his German wife. The Tsarina Alexandra had fallen under the spell of an evil and ignorant "holy man," Gregori Rasputin. This power-hungry Siberian peasant gained such influence over the imperial family that he became the real power in Russia. Reaction coupled with corruption and inefficiency led to a gradual paralysis of Russia's government, making it doubly vulnerable to any major crisis, such as arose in 1914.

THE "CULT OF SCIENCE"

Having surveyed the political, economic, and social events in the major powers between 1870 and 1914, we must consider the intellectual and cultural trends of these years. Their outstanding characteristic may be seen as an overriding interest and belief in science. Interest in science was nothing new, but in the second half of the nineteenth century a veritable "cult of science" developed. Scientific research, in the past the domain of a few scientists and gentleman scholars, became the concern of large numbers of people, especially as the application of science to industry gave an incentive for new inventions. "Applied" science took precedence in the minds of most people over "pure" science. A virtually endless series of scientific inventions seemed to be proof of man's ability to unlock the secrets of nature. If support was needed for the optimistic belief in unlimited progress, science provided it.

Rasputin (1915).

Materialism and Positivism

The growing concern with the material aspects of civilization was also reflected in late nineteenth-century thought. A few basic scientific discoveries served as the foundation for an essentially materialistic philosophy that appealed to the educated middle class. An early exponent of this philosophy was the German philosopher Ludwig Feuerbach (1804–72). More influential was the German physician Ludwig Büchner (1824–99), whose book *Force and Matter* (1855), proclaiming the eternity of these two quantities, went through twenty-one editions and was translated into all major languages. Another influential figure was the German biologist Ernest Haeckel (1834–1919), whose *The Riddles of the Universe at the Close of the Nineteenth Century* (1899) became an international best-seller. Haeckel's "monistic philosophy" was entirely concerned with the material world, insisting that even the human mind and soul had their material substance. As for the riddles of the universe, Haeckel declared that all but one of them had been solved; and that one, "what the pious believer called Creator or God," was not worth troubling with, because there was no means of investigating it.

More lasting in its effect than materialism was another philosophy concerned with the impact of science on society—positivism. It had been

Charles Darwin.

worked out in the first half of the century by the Frenchman Auguste Comte (1798–1857), but its influence was not felt until later. According to Comte, man had passed through two phases, the theological and the metaphysical, and had now entered a third phase, the scientific, or positive. In this last phase man no longer concerned himself with ultimate causes, as he had during the metaphysical stage, but was satisfied with the material world and with whatever he might learn from observing it. Here was a philosophy that accepted science as its only guide and authority, and for that reason was eminently suited to the late nineteenth century.

THE DARWINIAN REVOLUTION

The development that had the most revolutionary impact on western thought and society in the nineteenth century occurred in biology. It concerns the theory of evolution set forth by the British scientist Charles Darwin (1809–82). The idea of evolution was nothing new. Both in the general sense of a gradual development of human society from simple to more complex institutions, and in the more narrow biological sense that all organisms had evolved out of more elementary forms, the concept of evolution had earlier roots. Darwin's major contribution was to provide a scientific basis for what had previously been a mere hypothesis.

Darwinism

Darwin was influenced by the geologist Charles Lyell (1797–1875) who, in his *Principles of Geology* (1830), had restated an earlier thesis that the earth's physical appearance was the result of the same geological processes still active today. Darwin applied this idea of gradual changes brought about by natural causes to organisms.

In searching for an explanation of organic evolution, Darwin was impressed by Malthus's account of the intense competition among mankind for the means of subsistence. The essence of Darwinism is stated in the full title of his basic work: *On the Origin of Species by Means of Natural Selection, or the Preservation of Favoured Races in the Struggle for Life* (1859). His theory was subsequently applied to the human species in *The Descent of Man* (1871). According to Darwin, life is a constant "struggle for existence," in which only the fittest survive. This survival of the fittest was due to certain favorable variations within the given organism that aided in its struggle with other organisms. These variations in time would evolve an entirely new species. This "natural selection," Darwin suggested, was further aided by "sexual selection"—the mutual attraction and mating of the fittest members of a species to bring forth the fittest offspring.

Darwin's main idea—that all existing forms of life have evolved from earlier and simpler forms—remains valid to this day. Only his explanation of the actual process of evolution has been challenged. Darwin's concept of evolution as a cumulative result of many minute changes has given way to the view that evolution proceeds by way of larger and more sudden "mutations." But these modifications came later and thus could not affect the revolutionary impact of Darwin's theories when they were first announced.

The Impact of Darwinism

To an age that worshiped science, the thought that man was just as much subject to the logic of science as was everything else in nature held a great fascination. The gentle and retiring scientist himself took little part in the excitement and controversy stirred up by the doctrine that bore his name. The popularization of Darwin's thought was chiefly due to the efforts of other men, especially his friend Thomas Huxley (1825–95). Of all Darwin's new ideas, the concept of a struggle for existence had particular appeal. Darwinism seemed to give scientific sanction to the belief in competition and laissez-faire. But not only the capitalists derived great comfort from Darwinism. Darwin's emphasis on the environment for the improvement of man also gave hope to the socialists in their demands for social and economic reform. To the majority of people the struggle for existence assumed the validity of a natural law, a law, moreover, that applied not just to relations among individuals but to relations among groups.

"Social Darwinism"

Karl Marx, the "Darwin of the social sciences," had already sketched the evolution of society through a series of class struggles. The first to apply Darwinism to groups and states was one of Darwin's admirers, the British philosopher Herbert Spencer (1820–1903). The classical statement of what came to be called "Social Darwinism" was made by the English political scientist Walter Bagehot (1826–77) in his book *Physics and Politics* (1872). According to Bagehot, in the struggle for existence among groups "the majority of the groups which win and conquer are better than the majority of those which fail and perish." In other words, among nations as among individuals the strongest and best survive. Needless to say, this restatement of the maxim that "might makes right" had little to do with Darwin's original theory.

To a generation that had recently experienced several major wars and that was actively engaged in numerous expeditions against colonial peoples overseas, Social Darwinism, with its glorification of war, came as a welcome rationalization. The influence of Social Darwinism may also be seen in the injection of racialism into politics. If being victorious meant being better, what was more natural than to view the triumph of one nation or race over another as a sign of the victor's inherent superiority? Among the earliest writers on racialism was the French count Arthur de Gobineau (1816–82). His *Essay on the Inequality of the Human Races* (1853–55) proclaimed the superiority of the white race and distinguished within that race between the superior Germanic "Aryans" and the inferior Slavs and Jews. Gobineau's doctrine found its main echo in Germany, but the idea of white, specifically Anglo-Saxon, superiority was also popular in England and America.

The "Warfare of Science with Theology"

The most violent impact of Darwinism was felt in the religious field. It was part of a larger conflict, the "warfare of science with theology." The religious revival during the Age of Romanticism had soon given way to a noticeable decline in religious interest. As the state took over the functions of social welfare and education, and as the material benefits of industrialization spread among the lower classes, the need for the churches declined. The reactionary tendencies of the churches, furthermore, antagonized many liberals, and

Spencer on the Survival of the Fittest

1850

Pervading all nature we may see at work a stern discipline, which is a little cruel that it may be very kind. That state of universal warfare maintained throughout the lower creation, to the perplexity of many worthy people, is at bottom the most merciful provision which the circumstances admit of. . . . The poverty of the incapable, the distresses that come upon the imprudent, the starvation of the idle, and those shoulderings aside of the weak by the strong, which leaves so many "in shallows and in miseries," are the decrees of a large, far-seeing benevolence. It seems hard that an unskillfulness which with all his efforts he cannot overcome, should entail hunger upon the artisan. It seems hard that a labourer incapacitated by sickness from competing with his stronger fellows, should have to bear the resulting privations. It seems hard that widows and orphans should be left to struggle for life or death. Nevertheless, when regarded not separately, but in connection with the interests of universal humanity, these harsh fatalities are seen to be full of the highest beneficence—the same beneficence which brings to early graves the children of diseased parents, and singles out the low-spirited, the intemperate, and the debilitated as the victims of an epidemic.

From Herbert Spencer, *Social Statics* (New York: Appleton, 1873), pp. 352–54.

political anticlericalism became an important issue. Finally, the competing appeals of nationalism, socialism, and materialism detracted from the appeal of religion.

The most important reason for the decline in religious interest was the effect of modern science on Christianity. Many scientific discoveries contradicted Christian beliefs, and scientific inquiry, when applied to Christianity itself, produced some disturbing results. Scholars studying the origins of the Bible, for instance, discovered that most of its books were written long after the events, and that few biblical writings existed as they had originally been written. Historians of comparative religion, furthermore, detected striking similarities between Christianity and some of the many mystery cults that had flourished in the eastern Mediterranean at the time of Christ. Christianity, it seemed, was merely the one among many similar religions that had survived.

These discoveries became more widely known when they were used in modern accounts of the life of Christ. A German scholar, David Friedrich Strauss (1808–74), as early as 1835 had written a *Life of Jesus* that denied the divinity of Christ. Less scholarly and more popular was the *Life of Jesus* (1863) by the French writer Ernest Renan (1823–92). Both works recognized Christ as a superior human being, but they denied that he had performed miracles or had risen from the dead.

Darwinism and Religion

Still more drastic in their effect on the faithful were the findings of Darwin. Not only did he and Lyell challenge the biblical view of creation, but by making humans a part of general evolution, Darwin deprived them of the unique position they had hitherto occupied. Why, one might ask, should man alone of all creatures possess an immortal soul?

The Catholic Church, because it was more tightly organized, was able to take a firmer and more consistent stand in this controversy than the various Protestant churches. In 1864 Pope Pius IX issued "A Syllabus of the Principal Errors of Our Times," which condemned most of the new political, economic, and scientific tendencies. Six years later a general Church council, to strengthen the pope's position, proclaimed the dogma of papal infallibility. Henceforth the pope was to be infallible in all statements he made officially *(ex cathedra)* on matters of faith and morals. The succession of the more conciliatory Leo XIII to the papacy in 1878 eased matters. Leo did not oppose discoveries that did not affect Catholic doctrine. Only on the subject of evolution did the papacy persist in its rigid opposition. Some Catholics had begun to reconcile the contradictions between science and theology. But this "modernism" was considered a heresy by the Catholic Church.

In contrast to Catholicism, Protestant (and to some extent Jewish) doctrine and ritual were almost entirely based on the Bible. The effect of scientific discoveries at variance with biblical teachings, therefore, was felt more deeply. The fact that Protestantism was split among some three hundred sects made any uniform stand in the warfare between science and theology very difficult. Protestant emphasis on the freedom of the individual to work out his own relations with God made it possible for many Protestants to reach their own compromise between faith and reason. A minority of Protestants, called "Fundamentalists," continued to cling to a literal interpretation of the Bible and insisted on the validity of the account of creation as given in the Book of Genesis.

Despite the confusion it caused not only among Christians but among Jews, the conflict between science and theology did not seriously interfere with the progress of science. The world in 1914 was still viewed as an intricate mechanism, whose secrets would gradually yield to scientific research. Only a handful of scientists realized that new developments—the discovery of X rays (1895), the isolation of radium (1898), and, most important, the formulation of the theory of relativity (1905)—had opened up an infinite number of new mysteries and had brought the world to the threshold of another scientific revolution.

ART IN THE AGE OF SCIENCE

The cult of science that dominated the intellectual climate at the end of the nineteenth century also had its devotees in art and literature. It is difficult for any period, especially one as diverse as the one discussed in this chapter, to single out those artistic trends that most clearly reflect the spirit of the age. To call the early nineteenth century an Age of Romanticism and the late century an Age of Realism is very much an oversimplification. But there were obvious differences between the two periods.

The Romantic artist had preferred an ideal world of his imagination to the real world in which he lived. He had set his concept of natural beauty against the ugliness of early industrialism. And he had escaped from a harsh present to a more rosy past. Before the middle of the nineteenth century, however, some artists had already begun to be interested in the world as it was, not as they felt it should be. This shift from Romanticism to Realism was most evident in literature; it was less pronounced in painting; and there were hardly any signs in music.

Realism and Naturalism

The novel now became the favorite literary medium. Most of the great novels of the nineteenth century—from Dickens and Thackeray in England to Balzac and Flaubert in France, Fontane in Germany, and Turgenev and Tolstoy in Russia—fall into the category of social novels. Not only did these authors describe the society in which they lived; they dwelled on the problems of that society. Literature was becoming increasingly a form of social criticism.

The shift toward Realism reached its climax in the late nineteenth century in a literary movement called Naturalism. Naturalism represented the conscious effort of some writers to apply scientific principles to art. Naturalistic writers like Émile Zola in France, Henrik Ibsen in Norway, and Gerhart Hauptmann in Germany were not interested so much in beauty as they were in truth. To get at truth they discarded subjective intu-

The Stonebreakers, **by Gustave Courbet, pioneer of the Realist movement.**

ition and strove to describe objectively what they had learned from study and observation. The Naturalist was much impressed with the modern discoveries in biology and such new fields as sociology and psychology. He felt it was one of his chief functions to call attention to existing evils and abuses. If this meant focusing his efforts on the seamy side of life, he did so, hoping that by serving as diagnostician of society's illness he might help cure it.

Impressionism

The change from Romanticism to Realism was less pronounced in painting than in literature, although some new trends did appear. In the past artists had been concerned with the unusual and beautiful, but now they turned more to ordinary and often ugly everyday subjects — farmers, laborers, and urban scenes.

The real innovation in nineteenth-century painting, however, was not so much in subject matter as in technique. As Naturalism did to literature, so Impressionism applied scientific principles to painting. Influenced by discoveries about the composition of light, painters like Camille Pissaro, Claude Monet, and Auguste Renoir used short strokes of pure color to depict nature in its ever-changing moods, not as it appeared to the logical mind but as it "impressed" the eye in viewing a whole scene rather than a series of specific objects. An Impressionist painting, examined at close range, thus appears as a maze of colored dabs that, viewed from a distance, merge into recognizable objects with the vibrant quality imparted by light.

In trying to find the scientific temper of the late nineteenth century reflected in literature and art, however, we must guard against oversimplification. A relationship between art and science certainly existed. But it would be wrong to assume that the majority of people at the time were aware of this relationship. The average person had little use for Naturalist novels or plays or Impressionist paintings. He liked pictures that "told a story," preferably a sentimental one. And he liked second-rate novels of love and adventure by authors long since forgotten.

Symbolism

If these cultural interests of the average man expressed an unconscious desire to escape the realities of the present, a similar tendency may be noted among a few highly sensitive writers. They deplored their generation's preoccupation with material values, and far from singing the praises of the industrial age, they spoke out against its vulgarity. Earlier in the century, the Englishmen Matthew Arnold and John Ruskin had lamented the materialism and loss of esthetic values resulting from industrialization. Their complaints were echoed later by their compatriot William Morris, who would have preferred to withdraw from the machine age and return to the simplicity and dignity of the Middle Ages.

There was a note of romanticism and escapism in this longing for beauty in an age of slums and soot. Naturalism had little use for beauty; art had to serve a purpose. In protest against this arid view, a group of French writers at the end of the century proclaimed that art was sufficient unto itself — "art for art's sake." To these neo-Romantic, or Symbolist, poets — Stéphane Mallarmé, Paul Verlaine, and others — art was not for everyone but only for the select few to whom it spoke in "symbols," using words not so much for their meaning but for the images and analogies they conveyed, often by sound alone. Symbolism is significant as an indication that some people before 1914 did not find all things perfect in a society that gloried in materialism and accepted the struggle for wealth as a sign of progress.

The Symbolists were not alone in their criticism. The most outspoken critic of the generation before 1914 was the German philosopher Friedrich Nietzsche. In a series of beautifully written, epigrammatic books in the 1880s, Nietzsche attacked everything his age held sacred—democracy, socialism, nationalism, racialism, intellectualism, imperialism, militarism, materialism, and especially Christianity. Little understood by his contemporaries and much misunderstood since, Nietzsche's influence was felt more after than before the First World War. Few people today would agree with his wholesale condemnation of his age. Yet in striking out blindly, Nietzsche could not help but hit on many of the weaknesses we have since come to recognize in an age characterized above all by smugness and misplaced self-confidence.

Suggestions for Further Reading

Two broadly conceived works that treat European civilization as an entity are C. J. H. Hayes, *A Generation of Materialism, 1871–1900* (1941), and O. J. Hale, *The Great Illusion, 1900–1914* (1971). Important works on significant developments in the major countries are: G. Dangerfield, *The Strange Death of Liberal England* (1961); E. Weber, *Peasants into Frenchmen: The Modernization of Rural France, 1870–1914* (1976); G. Roth, *Social Democrats in Imperial Germany* (1963); A. J. May, *The Hapsburg Monarchy, 1867–1914* (1951); J. A. Thayer, *Italy and the Great War: Politics and Culture, 1890–1915* (1964); and for Russia, A. Yarmolinsky, *Road to Revolution* (1957).

The progress of political and social democracy is treated in A. Rosenberg, *Democracy and Socialism* (1939). On social thought, see G. Mazur, *Prophets of Yesterday: Studies in European Culture, 1890–1914* (1961), and H. S. Hughes, *Consciousness and Society: The Reorientation of Social Thought, 1850–1930* (1958). Women's efforts for equal rights are the subject of W. L. O'Neill, *Woman Movement: Feminism in the United States and England* (1969). M. Joll, *The Second International, 1889–1914* (1955), surveys international socialism; and P. Gay, *The Dilemma of Democratic Socialism: Eduard Bernstein's Challenge to Marx* (1952), deals with evolutionary socialism. On the growth of organized labor, see W. A. McConagha, *The Development of Labor Movement in Great Britain, France, and Germany* (1942).

The literature on intellectual history is vast. O. Chadwick, *The Secularization of the European Mind in the Nineteenth Century* (1976), and C. Brinton, *Ideas and Men* (1950), are good introductions. Good studies of key intellectual figures are: J. Barzun, *Darwin, Marx, Wagner* (1958); P. J. Sears, *Charles Darwin: The Naturalist as a Cultural Force* (1950); R. Hayman, *Nietzsche: A Critical Life* (1980); and G. Costigan, *Sigmund Freud: A Short Biography* (1965). E. Wilson, *Axel's Castle: A Study in the Imaginative Literature of 1870–1930* (1958), and T. Shapiro, *Painters and Politics: The European Avant-Garde and Society, 1900–1925* (1976), are pioneering works.

	1815				1870	
SOUTHWEST ASIA AND AFRICA	**1818–28** King Shaka, apex of Zulu kingdom	**1836** Boers' Great Trek begins		**1860** French expansion in West Africa **1869** Suez Canal opens		
EUROPE	**1815** Congress of Vienna **1815–83** Karl Marx **1825** Decembrist Revolt, Russia **1825** First commercial railroad	**1829** Treaty of Adrianople **1830** France's "July Monarchy" **1832** Britain's Great Reform Bill **1848** *Communist Manifesto*	**1848–49** Europe in Revolt **1848–61** Unification of Italy **1848–70** Napolean III **1851** Crystal Palace Exhibition, London	**1859** Darwin, *Origin of Species* **1854–56** Crimean War **1861–71** Unification of Germany **1867** Austro-Hungarian *Ausgleich*	**1870–71** Franco-Prussian War **1876** First internal combustion engine **1878** Congress of Berlin	**1882** Triple Alliance **1894** Russo-French Alliance
SOUTH AND SOUTHEAST ASIA	**1819** British found Singapore		**1857–58** Indian Mutiny **1859** French seize Saigon			
EAST ASIA	**1825–30** Java War **1839–42** Opium War		**1850–64** Taiping Rebellion **1854** Perry opens US trade with Japan **1868** Meiji Restoration, Japan			**1893–1976** Mao Zedong **1894–95** Sino-Japanese War
THE AMERICAS AND PACIFIC	**1823** Monroe Doctrine	**1835–40** Alexis de Tocqueville, *Democracy in America* **1840** Britain annexes New Zealand **1846–48** Mexican War	**1849** Gold discovered in California	**1861–65** American Civil War **1867** Russia sells Alaska to US **1867** British North America Act	**1869** Opening of Transcontinental railroad	

Wood sculpture, Dogon tribe, Mali, West Africa.

Eiffel Towe Paris, 1889.

***Empire State Express* No. 999, *ca.* 1890.**

Commodore Matthew Perry, a Japanese view, 1853.

British suffragette, *ca.* 1910.

Private Edwin Francis Jennison, Confederate Army.

1914	
1886 Gold discovered in Southern Africa **1889** Rhodesia colonized **1899–1902** Boer War **1910** Union of South Africa formed	
1894–1905 Dreyfus Affair **1905** Russian Revolution begins **1905** Einstein's Theory of Relativity **1907** Triple Entente **1912–13** Balkan Wars	
1885 Indian National Congress founded **1906** Muslim League founded	
1900 Boxer Rebellion **1904–05** Russo-Japanese War **1911** Chinese Revolution **1912–49** Chinese Republic	
1889 First Pan-American Conference **1898** Spanish-American War **1910** Mexican Revolution begins	**1914** Panama Canal opens

The Prince of Wales in Bangalore, India, *ca.* 1900.

Gold prospector, California, *ca.* 1850.

37 Efforts to Maintain a European Equilibrium, 1871 – 1914

The diplomatic history of Europe and the world between 1871 and 1914 must be viewed in the context of the political, economic, and cultural trends noted in the preceding chapter. The spirit of competition that pervaded relations among individuals and classes had its parallel in the political and economic rivalry among nations. Many international crises arose directly out of domestic tensions. Had the internal affairs of the powers before 1914 been more harmonious, international affairs might possibly have been more peaceful.

Our view of international relations after 1870 is conditioned by knowledge of what happened in 1914. Most historians agree that, while some of the immediate causes that brought about war in 1914 could have been avoided, its real causes were deeply rooted. To understand how deeply, we must remember the far-reaching effects that the unification of Italy and Germany had had on the European balance of power. Two regions that heretofore had been mere pawns in international affairs suddenly emerged as great powers. The political and territorial framework of the Continent thus lost much of its former elasticity. The only region in Europe where major changes were still possible was the Balkan Peninsula. Austria-Hungary, now excluded from German and Italian affairs, claimed the Balkans as its natural sphere of influence. Because Russia and, less strongly, Italy made the same

Prince Otto von Bismarck.

claim, the Balkans became the scene of recurrent international crises.

Another source of international tension was the growing colonial rivalry among the powers. With opportunities for territorial expansion on the Continent restricted, and with expanding economies clamoring for markets and raw materials, colonial conflicts injected an element of perennial friction into international affairs. An added cause for tension was nationalism. As long as members of one nationality were subjected to domination by another, as was the case in Austria-Hungary, Turkey, Russia, and, to a lesser extent, Germany and Great Britain, the peace of Europe remained precarious at best.

THE AGE OF BISMARCK, 1871–90

Despite the unsettling effects of Italian and German unification, Europe at first managed to adjust peacefully to the changed situation. The chief credit for the relative stability that prevailed for the two decades after 1871 belongs to Prince Bismarck. The fundamental aim of the German chancellor was the consolidation of the new German *Reich.* For this he needed peace. Bismarck considered Germany a "satiated" power, with no further territorial ambitions. The main threat to its security was France's desire for revenge. To keep France isolated, therefore, became the guiding principle of Bismarck's foreign policy.

The basic moderation of the German chancellor's aims and the consummate skill of his diplomacy rightly command respect. They show that *Realpolitik* need not necessarily rely on "blood and iron" but can use with equal effect peaceful pressure and persuasion. Yet in merely trying to maintain existing conditions and ignoring those forces that were straining against the status quo—notably nationalism and imperialism—Bismarck showed the same blindness that had characterized Metternich before him. Admirable as the Bismarckian system was, it was to fall to pieces as soon as the masterful guidance of its creator was removed.

The "Three Emperors' League"

The first of Bismarck's many international agreements was concluded in 1872 among Germany, Austria, and Russia. The *Dreikaiserbund* tried to revive the collaboration that had existed in the days of the "Holy Alliance." But the feeling of solidarity that had animated the three conservative powers in the days of Metternich had since given way to mutual rivalries. Russia, in particular, had never forgiven Austria its "ingratitude" during the Crimean War, and it now resented the leadership that Germany assumed within the new Three Emperors' League. A first sign of disagreement between Germany and Russia appeared during the so-called "war-in-sight" crisis of 1875, when rumors that Germany was planning a preventive war against France brought

Bismarck

PRO

Bismarck is generally described in the textbooks as the first *Realpolitiker;* but unfortunately so much has been written about *Realpolitik* that its meaning has become obscure and mixed up with blood and iron and incitement to war by the malicious revision of royal telegrams. . . . It may be permissible to suggest that the essence of Bismarck's realism was his recognition of the limitations of his craft, and that it was this, coupled with the passion and the responsibility that he brought to his vocation, that made him a great statesman.

CON

Himself always plotting combinations against others, Bismarck was convinced that all the world was plotting combinations against him and lived in a half-mad imaginary world in which every statesman was as subtle and calculating, as ruthless and assiduous as he was himself. . . . At bottom he was a barbarian of genius, mastering in the highest degree the mechanical and intellectual side of civilization, altogether untouched by its spirit.

From Gordon A. Craig, *From Bismarck to Adenauer: Aspects of German Statecraft* (Baltimore: Johns Hopkins University Press, 1958), p. 28; from A. J. P. Taylor, *The Course of German History* (New York: Coward-McCann, 1946), pp. 95–96.

protests from England and Russia. Bismarck's role in fomenting the crisis is not quite clear, though there is no evidence that he was seriously considering war against France. Russia's action, therefore, seemed unnecessarily meddlesome, especially in view of its traditional friendship with Prussia. The monarchical front had shown itself far from solid.

The Russo-Turkish War and the Congress of Berlin

A far more serious rift within the Three Emperors' League developed out of Russia's ambitions in the Balkans. The inefficiency and corruption of the disintegrating Ottoman Empire had invited intervention several times before, most recently during the Crimean War. In 1875 new revolts against Turkish misrule broke out in the Balkans. The Turks acted with their usual ferocity in putting down these nationalist uprisings and would have held the upper hand if Russia had not joined the insurgents in the spring of 1877. It did so after making sure of Austrian neutrality and recognizing in return Austria's right to occupy the Turkish provinces of Bosnia and Herzegovina. In addition, Russia promised not to support the formation of any large Balkan state.

The Russo-Turkish War, after some reversals, ended in Russian victory. In a treaty signed at San Stefano in March 1878, several of Turkey's subject nationalities were granted independence. Among them was to be a large Bulgarian state, which Russia was to occupy for several years. In addition, Russia was to get some territorial compensations. This startling increase of Russian influence in the Balkans deeply alarmed the other great powers. Their pressure induced Russia finally to agree to submit the settlement to an international conference at Berlin in June 1878.

Most of the important decisions of the Congress of Berlin were actually reached in preliminary agreements, which the Congress then confirmed. The proposed Greater Bulgaria was divided into three parts, leaving only a small Bulgarian state; Serbia, Montenegro, and Rumania were granted full independence; Austria was given the right to occupy and administer Bosnia and Herzegovina; and England was given control over the island of Cyprus. Russia rightly felt that it had been cheated out of its victory. While England and Austria made substantial gains, Russia had to be satisfied with a small addition to Bessarabia and some

The Treaty of San Stefano 1878

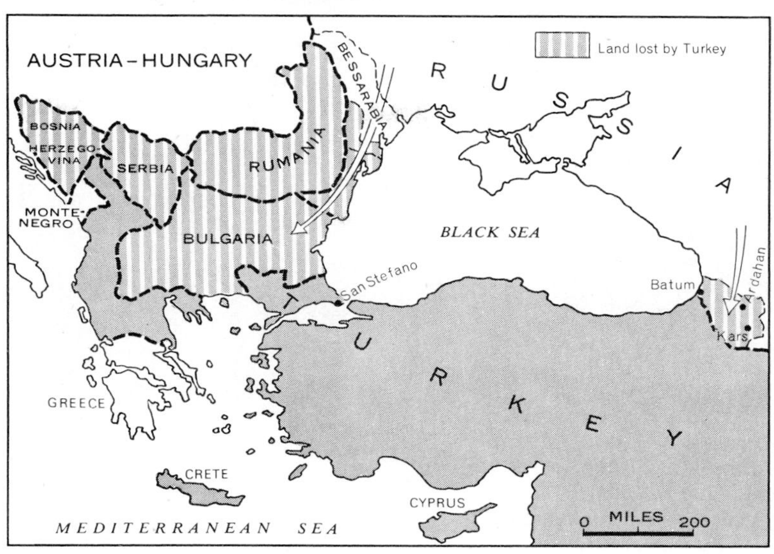

The Congress of Berlin 1878

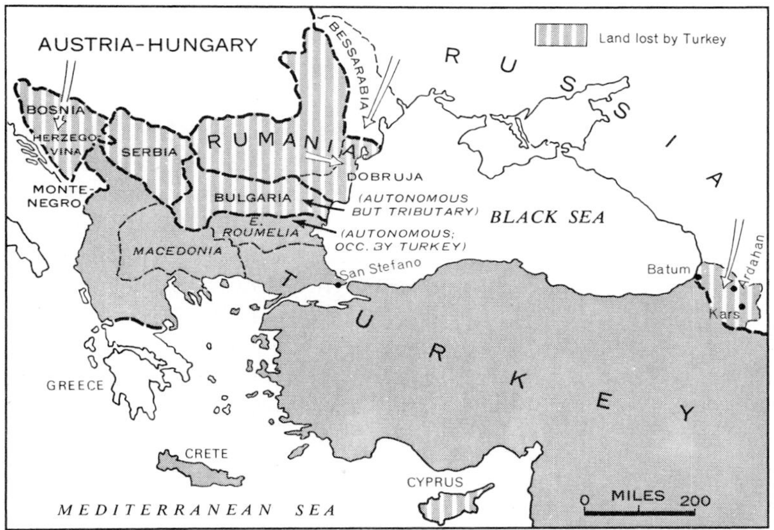

The Congress of Berlin (1878). Russia's Prince Gorchakov (seated at left) is talking to Britain's Disraeli while Bismarck is shaking hands with Russia's second delegate, Count Shuvalov.

gains in the Caucasus. The Russians blamed their defeat on Bismarck, who, they held, had violated his self-styled role as "honest broker" by favoring the interests of Russia's adversaries. The Congress of Berlin provoked a serious crisis in the relations between Germany and Russia and ended the Three Emperors' League.

The Austro-German Alliance

The breakup of the Three Emperors' League forced Bismarck to find a substitute. This he did in a secret alliance with Austria. The Dual Alliance of 1879 was the climax of Germany's rapprochement with Austria that had been Bismarck's concern since 1866. The alliance was renewed periodically and remained in force until 1918. Its provisions were purely defensive, calling for mutual aid if either member was attacked by Russia. Bismarck has been criticized for tying Germany's fate to the ramshackle Dual Monarchy. But he did not necessarily envisage the alliance as permanent, and he thought Germany strong enough to keep Austria's ambitions in the Balkans in check so as to avoid a showdown with Russia. Nor did the union with Austria mean that Germany was ready to sever relations with Russia altogether. Bismarck expected that Russia, unable for ideological reasons to draw closer to republican France, and separated from England by rivalries in Asia, would feel sufficiently isolated to desire a renewal of its former ties with Germany. Bismarck's assumption proved correct.

The Second "Three Emperors' League"

Russia would have preferred a treaty with Germany alone, but Bismarck insisted that Austria be included as well. A new Three Emperors' League was finally concluded in 1881. It provided that in case one of the members became involved in war with a fourth power, the other two would remain neutral. In this way Bismarck relieved his fear that Russia might join France in a war against Germany. The most important provisions of the treaty dealt with the Balkans: any territorial changes in that region henceforth were to require the consent of all three powers; Austria reserved its right to annex Bosnia and Herzegovina at a time of its own choosing; and Russia's wish for the eventual union of Bulgaria and Eastern Roumelia (one of the regions separated from Greater Bulgaria at Berlin) was recognized. By dividing the Balkans into spheres of influence, the three powers seemed finally to have brought the Balkan problem under control. The new arrangement, however, overlooked the national aspirations of the Balkan peoples themselves.

The Triple Alliance

Before the Balkan question became acute once more in 1885, Bismarck had further extended his diplomatic network with the Triple Alliance of Germany, Austria, and Italy in 1882. The initiative this time came from the Italians. Italy for some time had hoped to enhance its status as a great power by occupying the Turkish region of Tunis in North Africa. It was deeply distressed, therefore, when the French took Tunis in 1881. To strengthen its diplomatic position for the future, Italy sought closer ties with Austria and Germany. Like the rest of Bismarck's treaties, the Triple Alliance was primarily defensive. Bismarck never took it very seriously, except for the fact that it contributed to the diplomatic isolation of France.

The years immediately after 1882 mark the high point of Bismarck's influence in Europe. French nationalism appeared to have been successfully diverted into colonial channels in North Africa; the situation in the Balkans appeared under control; and Austria's position had been strengthened by a secret treaty with Serbia in 1881 that made Austria the protector of its small neighbor. In 1883 Rumania concluded an alliance with Austria, to which Germany adhered later. The treaty was chiefly directed against Russian ambitions in the Balkans, where a new crisis flared up in 1885.

The Reinsurance Treaty

This latest Balkan crisis was touched off by an upsurge of Bulgarian nationalism in Eastern Roumelia, leading to the reunion of that region with Bulgaria. During the ensuing wrangle the Three Emperors' League met its final fate. For some time Russian nationalists, resenting German support of Austria in the Balkans, had demanded that Russia seek the friendship of France. Bismarck's worst fears seemed about to come true. But the tsarist government was reluctant to cut its connections with Berlin. Russia, therefore, proposed to the Germans that they enter into an agreement without Austria. The upshot was the so-called Reinsurance Treaty of 1887, which provided for benevolent neutrality in case either partner became involved in war, unless Germany attacked France or Russia attacked Austria. The Reinsurance Treaty also recognized Russia's interests in Bulgaria and the Turkish Straits.

This last of Bismarck's major treaties has been both hailed as a diplomatic masterpiece and condemned as an act of duplicity. It certainly did run counter to the spirit, if not the letter, of the Dual Alliance. But while Bismarck encouraged Russia's Balkan ambitions, he at the same time put an obstacle in the way of these ambitions by sponsoring the so-called Mediterranean Agreements between England, Italy, and Austria. Signed also in 1887, these agreements called for the maintenance of the status quo in the Mediterranean, including the Balkans. Any assurances Bismarck had given to Russia about Bulgaria and the Straits were thus successfully neutralized.

In making a fair appraisal of Bismarck's diplomacy, it is necessary to go beyond a mere comparison of treaty texts and consider the motives behind his treaties. These invariably were to maintain peace. Bismarck hoped to achieve this aim by isolating France and balancing the rest of the powers so that any unilateral disturbance of the peace would automatically result in a hostile coalition against the aggressor. Seen in this light, Bismarck's policy was less crafty than it appeared when the world first learned about the Reinsurance Treaty after the chancellor's retirement. A valid criticism of Bismarck's policy is that it was far too complicated to be successful in the long run and that it rested more on the attitudes of Europe's statesmen than on the sentiments of their peoples. Such disregard of public opinion became increasingly difficult in an age of democracy and nationalism.

FROM EUROPEAN TO WORLD POLITICS

One of the most important trends in international affairs after Bismarck was the growing involvement of Europe in world affairs. This development had started much earlier, of course; but only at the end of the nineteenth century did events in Europe and overseas become so intricately interwoven that the histories of Europe and the rest of the world could no longer be treated separately.

The "New Imperialism"

The expansion of European influence in the late nineteenth century is often called the "new imperialism," to distinguish it from earlier phases of overseas expansion. Its motives were similar to those found earlier in the century, although they now operated with far greater intensity. Imperialism in the past had been chiefly limited in its appeal to the upper classes. Now suddenly it became of vital concern to everyone. More than any other movement, the new imperialism expressed the general climate of the period before 1914. In an age of ardent nationalism, it was considered a point of honor for any great power to raise its flag over as large an area of the globe as possible. At a time, furthermore, when unprecedented industrial growth created an urgent need for raw materials, markets, and outlets for surplus capital and population, colonies and foreign concessions seemed to provide a ready solution to economic problems. Finally, a civilization that considered itself superior to all others could easily convince itself that its members had a civilizing mission and should assume what Rudyard Kipling called "the white man's burden."

Evaluation of Western Imperialism

The new imperialism has come in for a good deal of criticism. There can be no doubt about the sincerity with which most western imperialists believed in the advantages that the spread of their civilization would bring to the rest of the world. Only after the bitter experience of the twentieth century, when the cause of western imperialism suffered one reversal after another, was this belief shaken. Politically, western domination of colonial regions merely seemed to awaken among the subjected peoples a consciousness of their own national interests and a desire for independence. While this in itself may be a positive achievement, it certainly was not what the imperialists of the last century had envisaged. Economically, the advantages derived from imperialism were limited to small groups within the mother countries. As time went on it became clear that the most advantageous policy in the long run was the economic development rather than the exploitation of backward areas. Such development, however, was slow and expensive, and its ultimate effect was to emancipate rather than subdue colonial areas.

About the civilizing effects of western imperialism, there are divided opinions. We need not point out the many advantages that have come to the rest of the world from its contacts with the West. In the field of medicine alone, the lives of millions of people have been saved by western scientists, and the slow but steady rise in the living standards of even the most backward regions would have been impossible without western aid and examples. The fault that has been found with the westernization of the world has been chiefly in the methods employed by western imperialists. Until quite recently the advantages that western civilization brought to many parts of the world were largely incidental to the primarily selfish aims and ambitions of the more advanced nations. The white man's burden, it has been said, has rested heavily on the shoulders of the black, brown, and yellow people who were subjugated by him. Only in our own day have we come to recognize and to correct some of the mistakes made by western imperialism in the past.

COLONIAL RIVALRIES AMONG THE GREAT POWERS

England continued to lead in the new imperialism as it had in the old. After a period of declining interest in overseas expansion, Britain resumed its imperialist course after 1870. By 1914 it controlled one-fifth of the world's land and one-fourth of its population. The second largest colonial empire in 1914, that of France, had been acquired almost entirely during the nineteenth century, beginning with the acquisition of Algiers in 1830. Germany, prior to 1880, had no overseas possessions, and Bismarck was slow to enter the colonial race. When he finally did, in 1884, it was in part to enhance Germany's bargaining position in Europe. It was William II who launched Germany on a course of *Weltpolitik,* in pursuit of which it provoked several international crises. Similar friction was caused by Italy's belated claims to colonies. Russia, as in the past, confined its expansion to adjacent areas in Asia. The only major power refraining from colonial expansion was Austria-Hungary.

We shall deal in the next three chapters with the major developments in Asia, Africa, and the Americas during the nineteenth century. We shall here concentrate on the effects which the colonial rivalries had upon the international relations of Europe.

North Africa

The most spectacular expansion of European influence took place in Africa. Prior to 1870, the interior of the "dark continent" had been largely unexplored, and there were only a few colonial footholds along its coast. By 1914, all of the continent had been divided up, with Britain obtaining the lion's share. The scramble for African territories could not help but lead to confrontations, some of which might have led to war among the major contenders.

In North Africa, the main rivalries were between France on the one hand, and Italy, Britain, and Germany on the other. The region was still nominally part of the Ottoman Empire, but the declining power of the sultan posed no obstacle to the encroachment of the powers. The main issue between France and Italy was Tunis, which Italy wanted, but which France took in 1881. In 1912 the Italians obtained the last unclaimed stretch of land along the Mediterranean—the region of Tripoli (renamed Libya). Meanwhile Italy's desire for Tunis remained a major obstacle to closer relations between the two countries.

The rivalry between France and Britain centered on Egypt and the neighboring Sudan. Egypt's gradual subjugation to foreign control was due to its defaulting on interest payments for foreign loans, chiefly from France and Great Britain. Initially the two countries had exercised joint control over Egypt's finances. But when Britain occupied Egypt in 1882 to counteract a rising tide of Egyptian nationalism, France's influence declined. Tension between the two powers was aggravated by their rivalry over the Sudan. This Egyptian dependency had won temporary independence in 1885. But when France and Belgium began advancing toward the Sudan from Central Africa, British and Egyptian forces in 1896 started to retake the region. The climax of their expedition came in 1898, when British and French forces met at Fashoda on the Upper Nile. As both Britain and France laid claim to the Sudan, war seemed imminent. But the French government, troubled by the Dreyfus affair at home and inferior in naval strength, finally gave in and left England in control. The aftereffects of the Fashoda crisis were finally resolved by the Entente Cordiale of 1904 (see p. 797).

The most serious of the great-power rivalries in North Africa grew out of the

The Sphinx is neck-high in sand and British soldiers in this photograph taken in 1882, after the bombardment of Alexandria.

Protestant missionary baptizing converts in the Belgian Congo (1904).

conflicting interests of France and Germany in the sultanate of Morocco. Since the two Moroccan crises of 1905 and 1911 were part of the escalating tensions during the decade before 1914, and since they involved the rest of the powers as well, they are better discussed later (see pp. 797–801). Coming after France had resolved its rivalries with Italy and Great Britain, they materially contributed to Germany's growing isolation.

Central Africa

In the central part of Africa, the rivalry of the powers, while intense, did not cause any major confrontations. Beginning in 1884 the German government took over the rights that various German merchants and explorers had staked out over parts of Southwest, Central, and East Africa. The British tried to discourage these German moves, but when this attempt proved fruitless, they moved quickly to stake out their own claims. France, meanwhile, extended its holdings in Central and West Africa. Italy acquired Eritrea and Somaliland at the southern end of the Red Sea in 1890. Italy's attempts to extend its holdings inland into Abyssinia, however, were stopped by Ethiopian forces in the battle of Adua (1896).

The most valuable region in Central Africa, the Congo basin, in time became the virtual private domain of King Leopold II of Belgium. The Congo Free State was recognized by an international conference at Berlin in 1885. At that meeting, sponsored by France and Germany, Great Britain found itself outvoted on several important issues, pointing up its rivalry with the continental powers. Leopold's various personal enterprises in the Congo exploited the region in the most ruthless manner. These brutal methods finally led to the transfer of the Congo to the Belgian state in 1908. The Congo was not the only region controlled by a small power. Portugal, Spain, and the Netherlands (in Southeast Asia) also held sizeable colonial areas. Imperialism was not a practice restricted to the great powers.

Southern Africa

Some of the most valuable colonial prizes were to be found in the southern part of the African continent. Britain had acquired the Dutch Cape Colony there in 1806. Conflicts between the original Dutch settlers, or Boers, and the new British immigrants led to the founding of two separate Boer republics in the 1830s—the Orange Free State and the Transvaal. As diamonds and gold were discovered in these regions, the Cape Colony tried to extend British sovereignty over the Boer republics.

The leading advocate of Britain's South African interests in the late nineteenth century was Cecil Rhodes. A typical "empire builder," Rhodes owned extensive interests in South Africa's diamond and gold fields. He became prime minister of the Cape Colony in 1890. Meanwhile a new discovery of gold in the Transvaal in 1886 had touched off a veritable British invasion into the region. To discourage this foreign influx, the president of the Transvaal, Paul Krüger, placed heavy restrictions on British immigrants. One of the more spectacular incidents in the growing tension between Britons and

Boers was the abortive Jameson Raid at the turn of the year 1895/96, an attempt by one of Rhodes's associates to start a revolution among the British minority in the Transvaal. An ill-advised and well-publicized telegram from the German kaiser congratulating Krüger on his defeat of the plot cast a deep shadow on Anglo-German relations at the time.

Finally, in 1899, tension between the Boers and the British led to war. It took Britain two and a half years to defeat the tenacious Boers and incorporate their republics in what ultimately became the Union of South Africa (1910). The Boer War (1899–1902) was a major crisis for the British, who once again found themselves isolated and in fear of a continental league against them. Germany's neutrality on this occasion helped to undo some of the harm done by the kaiser's earlier "Krüger telegram" (1896).

Imperialist Rivalries in East Asia

In contrast to Africa, large parts of Asia had been under European domination for some time. And while in Africa there had been no Russian involvement in the scramble for colonies, the tsarist empire was one of the chief contenders for expansion in Asia. Foremost among Russia's aims in East Asia as in Southwest Asia was to find outlets to the sea and ice-free harbors that would enable it to escape its landlocked position. The main area for Russian expansion was China, where Russia had already acquired a coastal section along the Sea of Japan and founded the port of Vladivostok in 1860.

The main rival in Russia's encroachment upon China was Japan. The region most desired by Japan was Korea, a tributary of China. In 1894–95, the gradual infiltration of Japan into Korea led to the Sino-Japanese War, from which Japan emerged victorious. But the Japanese were prevented from gaining a foothold on the Chinese mainland by the intercession of Russia, supported by France and Germany. Russo-Japanese rivalry remained a dominant factor in East Asian affairs for the next decade.

China's defeat by Japan came at a time when the rivalry among the great powers for overseas territory was at its height. The weakness of China now served as the occasion for an imperialist feast the likes of which the world had rarely seen. Between 1896 and 1898, all the major European powers imposed upon China spheres of influence, trading rights, railway concessions, naval stations, mining rights, and whatever other forms of direct and indirect control western imperialists could devise (see pp. 836–38). This scramble for concessions, far from resolving international tensions, merely increased them. Great Britain, preoccupied with the crisis in the Sudan and faced with war in Southern Africa, found itself frequently at odds with the continental powers in China, of which Russia posed the main threat to British interests. In 1902 Britain and Japan

Cecil Rhodes, prime minister of Cape Colony and founder of Rhodesia (now Zimbabwe), encamped during the Matabele rebellion of 1896.

The Boer War. Half of a stereographic print showing British forces after the capture of Bradfort from the Boers.

Harbor at Vladivostok, Russia's important East Asian port and terminus of the Trans-Siberian Railway.

concluded an alliance, which was clearly directed against Russia.

The rivalry between Japan and Russia came to a head in the Russo-Japanese War (1904–05). The Japanese had definite strategic advantages, but even so the world was little prepared for the resounding defeat they inflicted on the Russians. Japan's victory marked a turning point in relations between Europe and Asia. For the first time in modern history, one of the so-called backward nations had defeated one of the major European powers. As a result of the Russo-Japanese War, Russia's territorial position in East Asia in 1905 was substantially what it had been fifty years earlier. Its failures in the region help explain Russia's renewed interest in the affairs of Europe and Southwest Asia during the last decade before the First World War.

Anglo-Russian Rivalry in Southwest Asia

In Southwest and Central Asia, Russian expansion had made considerable progress during the nineteenth century. By 1880 the whole region north of Iran (Persia) and Afghanistan had become Russian. This extension of Russian power was watched with growing apprehension by Great Britain, which feared that Russia's advance was ultimately directed at India. The mountainous country of Afghanistan served as a buffer against possible invasion of India from the northwest. In 1879 England had overthrown the pro-Russian ruler of Afghanistan and had occupied most of the country. But British-Russian rivalry continued. It was not resolved until 1907, when Russia finally recognized England's predominant position in Afghanistan.

Another scene of Anglo-Russian rivalry was Iran. The contest here was primarily economic, with both Russian and British interests seeking concessions. But England also feared that Iran might serve as another approach to India. Differences in Iran, as in Afghanistan, were negotiated by the Anglo-Russian Entente in 1907 (see p. 797).

Anglo-Russian rivalries throughout Asia—from the Turkish Straits through Iran and Afghanistan to China—constituted one of the seemingly unalterable factors in European international relations, in the same category as the rivalries between England and France in Africa and elsewhere.

Germany's belief in the permanency of these rivalries accounts for many of the miscalculations in German foreign policy before 1914.

The Pacific

The most valuable islands of the Pacific were taken long before 1870. The rivalry of the powers over the few remaining small islands was a sign of how intense the imperialist urge had become. The main contestants in the Pacific were England and Germany, with the United States and France intervening occasionally. It is unnecessary to enumerate all the bits and pieces of land picked up by these powers. The most important, besides America's annexation of the Philippines, was the acquisition of eastern New Guinea by England and Germany in 1884. The most serious crisis arose over the Samoan Islands, which were claimed by Britain, Germany, and the United States. After ten years of intermittent dispute, the islands were divided in 1899 between the United States and Germany, with England receiving compensations in the Solomons.

THE FORMATION OF THE TRIPLE ENTENTE, 1890–1907

The events outside Europe discussed in the preceding pages provide the background for the diplomatic realignment of Europe after 1890 and the succession of international crises that culminated in the First World War.

The Franco-Russian Alliance

When Bismarck was dismissed in 1890, his complicated diplomatic system did not long survive. To start with, William II followed the advice of some of Bismarck's more timid underlings and refused to renew the Reinsurance Treaty with Russia. The cutting of Bismarck's "wire to St. Petersburg" did not by itself make the subsequent rapprochement between Russia and France inevitable. Only when Germany continued to show deliberate coolness toward its former friend while drawing closer to England did Russia begin to listen to French suggestions for a better understanding. The Anglo-German Heligoland-Zanzibar Agreement of 1890, by which Germany surrendered large claims in East Africa to England in return for the small strategic island of Heligoland in the North Sea, was generally interpreted as a sign of German eagerness to oblige England. At the same time, a tariff war was impairing Russo-German commercial relations, and an increase in Germany's armed forces was seen as preparation for a possible war on two fronts. Germany's policy toward Russia, it seemed, was undergoing a complete reorientation.

Even so, Russia was slow to respond to France's overtures. The main obstacle was the differences between their autocratic and republican systems of government. It took four years of deliberations before a final agreement was reached. On January 4, 1894, France and Russia signed a secret military convention that amounted to an alliance. It was designed as a counterpart to the Triple Alliance between Germany, Austria, and Italy. Like the latter, the Franco-Russian alliance was defensive. It protected France against an attack by Germany, or by Italy supported by Germany; and it protected Russia against an attack by Germany, or by Austria supported by Germany.

By the middle of the 1890s, therefore, two sets of European alliances existed. This did not mean, however, that the Continent had been split in two. There were many subsequent occasions when Russia cooperated with Germany and Austria, or when Germany cooperated with Russia and France. International rivalries for the next decade shifted almost entirely to regions outside Europe. Both French and Russian interests in many parts of the world conflicted with those of Great Britain; and Germany, unable to tie England as closely to its side as it wished, now frequently joined the two in opposing British aims. Faced by the discomforting possibility of a continental alliance against it, Britain, rather than Germany, had cause to be alarmed by the new alignment of powers.

Britain's Colonial Rivalries

The regions over which Britain came into conflict with one or several of the continental powers during the 1890s were chiefly Southwest and East Asia, the Sudan, and Southern Africa. In Asia Minor the source of trouble, as usual, was the disintegrating Ottoman Empire. Beginning in 1894 a series of Armenian uprisings against Turkish repression were put down with the massacre of thousands of Armenians. England tried repeatedly to intervene, and Lord Salisbury on two occasions suggested plans for partitioning the Ottoman Empire. But rival interests among the powers and suspicion of British motives prevented what might have been a final settlement of the region's troubles. The situation was further complicated in 1897 by an insurrection against Turkey on Crete in favor of union with Greece. In the resulting war between Greece and Turkey, the British supported Greece, but the rest of the powers prevented any aid from reaching Greece. The Turks were victorious, although the powers succeeded in obtaining autonomy for Crete.

While Britain thus found itself at cross-purposes with the rest of Europe in Southwest Asia, Germany took advantage of the various crises in that region to advance its own economic interests. The main instrument of its push to the southeast was to be a Berlin-to-Baghdad railway, for which the sultan granted a concession in 1899. In 1898, Emperor William, on a visit to Damascus, proclaimed himself the friend of the world's 300 million Muslims. Germany appeared well on the way toward replacing England as the protector of Turkey.

In East Asia the first serious differences between England and the three continental powers came as a result of the Sino-Japanese War in 1895 (see pp. 793–94). When Russia, Germany, and France asked British participation in forcing Japan to give up most of the territory it had taken from China, Britain refused. In the subsequent scramble for concessions from China, France, Germany, and especially Russia gained at the expense of England's hitherto unchallenged dominance there.

All the time that Britain was losing ground in Southwest and East Asia, its situation in Africa was even more serious. First there was the trouble with Germany over the kaiser's "Krüger telegram" (see p. 793); then came the showdown with France over the Sudan; and finally, in 1899 the Boer War broke out. During that war Britain was without a single friend, and it is surprising that Russian proposals for a continental coalition in favor of the Boers did not materialize. The plan failed because of Germany's insistence that the three powers first guarantee one another's own territories in Europe. This would have meant French renunciation of Alsace-Lorraine.

In view of England's many predicaments, it is understandable that it should look for some way out of its no longer splendid isolation. The obvious choice for a possible ally, considering Britain's many points of friction with France and Russia, was Germany. So in 1898 England began to sound out Germany on a closer understanding.

Britain Abandons Isolation

The Anglo-German negotiations failed. And the main reason for the failure was the reluctance of the Germans to abandon what they considered an unusually favorable position between the Franco-Russian and British camps. Overestimating Britain's eagerness to come to an understanding and underestimating Britain's ability to find friends elsewhere, Germany's foreign secretary, Bernhard von Bülow, and his chief adviser, Baron Friedrich von Holstein, made demands on England that it was unwilling to meet. Britain was primarily interested in enlisting German support against further Russian encroachment in East Asia. Germany, on the other hand, was chiefly worried about a war between Russia and Austria in which Germany might become involved and for which it wanted British aid. Britain, however, refused to extend its commitments to eastern Europe, where, as a naval power, it could not be of much use.

When Anglo-German negotiations finally broke down in 1901, England turned elsewhere. In 1902 it concluded an alliance with Japan. This did nothing to end England's isolation in Europe, but it fulfilled a main purpose—to stop Russia's advance in East Asia. Two years later Japan took advantage of this situation and in the Russo-Japanese War destroyed Russian sea power in the Pacific (see p. 794). In this way Japan emerged as the dominant power in the East.

Before the showdown between Russia and Japan, England had already taken a step in Europe to escape its isolation—rapprochement with France. England had long been irked by its dependence on Germany, which the latter used on every possible occasion to wring concessions from the British. By settling its long-standing differences with France, Britain not only hoped to find support against Germany but also to allay once and for all its fear of a continental alliance against it. France also felt a need for new friends. Its alliance with Russia had proved disappointing, especially during the Fashoda crisis, when the Russians had refused to back up their ally (see p. 791). After Fashoda, France had turned its attention once more to the Continent. The aim of its nationalistic foreign minister, Théophile Delcassé, was to strengthen France's position by improving its relations with powers other than Germany. He had taken a first step in this direction in 1902 by concluding a secret agreement with Italy. In return for French support of Italian ambitions in North Africa, the Italians promised to support French aims in Morocco, and to remain neutral in case France became involved in a defensive war, even if France "as the result of a direct provocation" should find it necessary to declare such a war itself.

Pre-First World War Alliances and Alignments

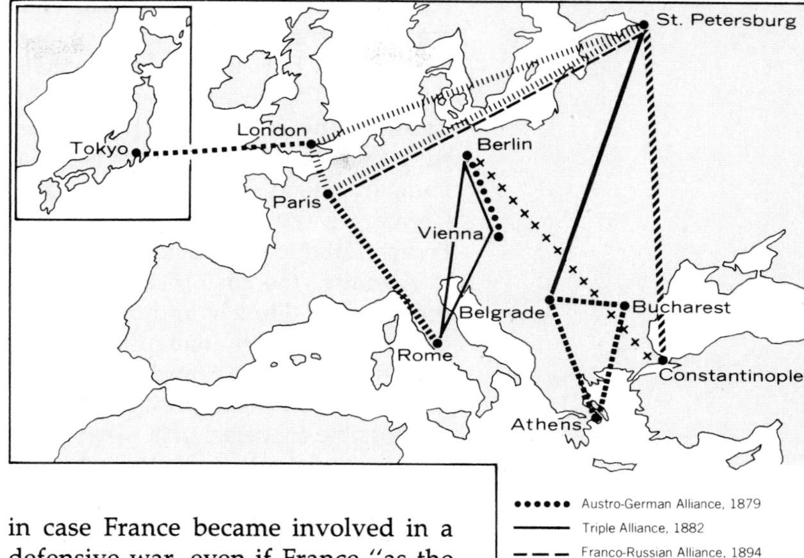

A far greater achievement of Delcassé, however, was the Entente Cordiale between France and England. The Anglo-French agreement of 1904 settled the main colonial differences that had disturbed relations between the two countries, especially in Africa. Most important was France's recognition of British interests in Egypt and Britain's recognition of French interests in Morocco. The agreement was merely a "friendly understanding." It was not an alliance, and it need never have assumed the character of one had it not been for the careless actions of Germany.

The First Moroccan Crisis

Germany, which was understandably alarmed by the agreement between France and Britain, decided to test the strength of the Entente. In March 1905 William II, on a visit to Tangier in Spanish Morocco, proclaimed Germany's continued support of Moroccan independence and served notice that Germany, too, had an interest in Morocco. The ensuing crisis forced the resignation of Delcassé, and Germany seemed ready to go to war.

Franco-German differences were finally brought before an international conference at Algeciras (1906). Here the independence of Morocco was reaffirmed; but in settling specific questions of Moroccan internal administration, the majority of the powers supported the French. Only Austria-Hungary stood by its German ally. Germany's attempt to split the Anglo-French Entente had backfired.

Actually, the first Moroccan crisis brought the French and British still closer together by inaugurating conversations between French and British military and naval authorities concerning possible cooperation in case of war. These conversations continued intermittently until 1914. Beginning in 1912, furthermore, the British navy concentrated its forces in the North Sea, permitting the French to shift their own warships to the Mediterranean. England thus assumed at least a moral obligation for protecting France's northern coast in case of war. The Entente Cordiale, in spirit if not in fact, had been transformed into a virtual alliance.

The Triple Entente

England's close affiliation with France quite naturally raised the question of its relations with France's ally Russia. As a result of Russia's war with Japan, the threat of Russian predominance in China had been removed, and there was now no reason why England should not try to settle its colonial differences with Russia as it had with France. This was done in the Anglo-Russian Entente of 1907, which settled the long-standing rivalries of the two powers in Afghanistan, Iran, and Tibet.

The formation of the Triple Entente, as the agreements of 1904 and 1907 together are called, amounted to a diplomatic revolution. A situation that only a few years earlier Germany had considered impossible had now come to pass: England had settled its differences with France and Russia, and the Triple Alliance had found its match in the Triple Entente. The latter was no more aggressive in its initial intent than the Triple Alliance had originally been. But as areas for compromise outside Europe became fewer with the annexation of the remaining colonial spoils, the scene of international rivalries once more shifted to Europe and especially to the Balkans. In the past, Russia's ambitions in this area had been held in check by the rest of the powers. Now it could count on French and British support against Germany and Austria. Germany, on the other hand, left with only Austria as a reliable friend, could no longer restrain Austria's Balkan policy as it had in the past. Any change in the status quo of the Balkans, therefore, was sure to lead to a major crisis.

THE MOUNTING CRISIS, 1908-13

This brings us to the last fateful years before 1914, when growing international tension, at least in retrospect, appears as a fitting prelude to an inevitable showdown.

Revolution in Turkey and the Bosnian Crisis

The Balkans once again became the scene of international complications in 1908 when a revolution broke out in the Ottoman Empire. Turkey's ruler since 1876, Abdul-Hamid II, had never lived up to his repeated promises of reform. Opposition to the sultan's corrupt and decadent regime centered in a group of liberal patriots, the "Young Turks." Their aim was to reform Turkey along the lines of a liberal constitution that had been granted in 1876 but had been completely disregarded afterward. The revolutionaries had a large following among the Turkish army, and the government's resistance to the uprising in 1908 soon collapsed. The Young Turks, however, though liberal in some respects, were extremely nationalistic in their dealings with Turkey's many national and religious minorities. Persecution of Greek Orthodox Christians and efforts to as-

The Dissolution of the Ottoman Empire to 1914

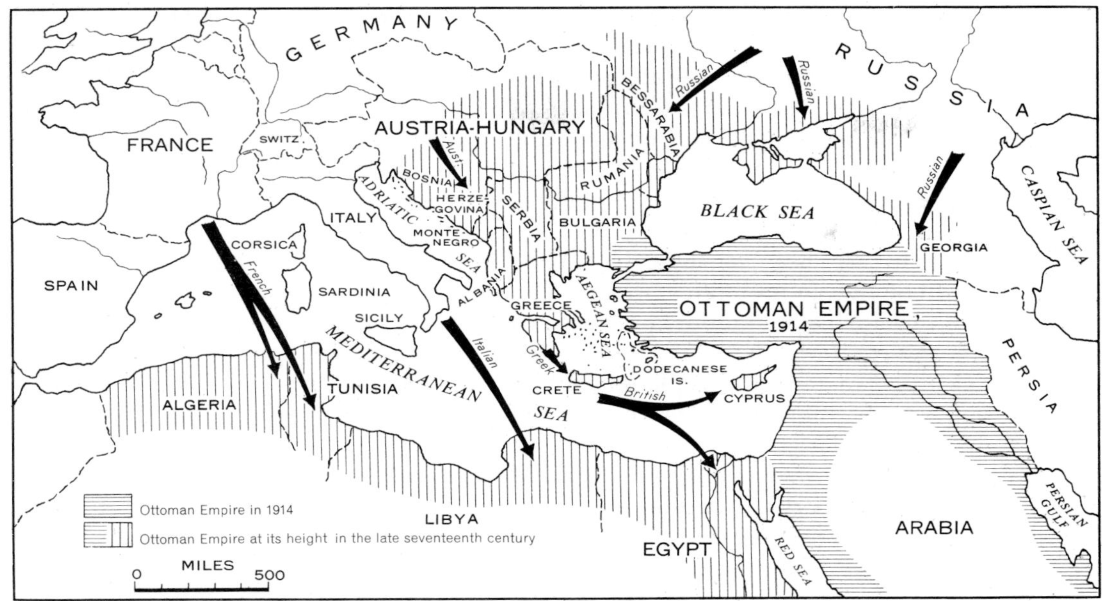

similate Turkey's subject peoples soon led to further disruption of the empire: Bulgaria proclaimed its independence in 1908; Crete completed its union with Greece in 1912; and Albania, after a series of bloody uprisings, finally gained its independence from the Ottoman Empire in 1913.

The most important event connected with the Turkish revolution, in its effects on relations among the great powers, was Austria's annexation of Bosnia and Herzegovina in 1908. There had been no serious tension between Austria and Russia over the Balkans for some twenty years. But this peaceful situation changed after 1905, as Russia once again turned its attention from the East to the Balkans. Russia's foreign minister, Alexander Izvolsky, was an unusually ambitious man, and he found a kindred spirit in his Austrian colleague, Count Alois Aehrenthal. Russia had long hoped to lift the closure of the Turkish Straits to Russian warships; Austria, for its part, had been looking forward to annexing Bosnia and Herzegovina, which it had been administering since 1878. Encouraged by the Turkish revolution, Izvolsky and Aehrenthal met at the latter's castle of Buchlau in September 1908 and there pledged mutual support for their respective aims.

The Bosnian crisis was precipitated when shortly after the Buchlau Agreement Austria went ahead and proclaimed the annexation of Bosnia and Herzegovina without waiting for Russia to act in the Straits. Russia, thereupon, backed by France and England, demanded that Austria's action be brought before an international conference. Germany, on the other hand, supported Austria in opposing a conference unless the annexation of Bosnia-Herzegovina was recognized beforehand. The situation was made more serious because Serbia also had hoped one day to take Bosnia-Herzegovina. Encouraged by Pan-Slav propaganda emanating from Russia, Serbia now demanded compensation from Austria. Since Russia, however, was in no position to fight a war at this time, it had to bring pressure on Serbia to recognize the *fait accompli* in Bosnia and Herzegovina. This the Serbs did under protest.

The Bosnian crisis left a legacy of tension that lasted until the First World War. Both Russia and Serbia had been humiliated. To prevent the recurrence of such a defeat, Russia now began to prepare in earnest for the showdown that seemed inevitable, while Serbia stepped up its agitation among Austria's southern Slavs. Austria had been the real culprit in the affair. But it would have had to back down if it had not had the support of Germany. The fact that such support had been given only reluctantly was not known to the rest of the world. Italy, finally, was hurt not to have been consulted by Austria about the annexation of Bosnia and Herzegovina and not to have received compensations, both of which it felt entitled to under the Triple Alliance. In October 1909 Italy entered into a secret understanding with Russia, the Racconigi Agreement, in which it promised to support Russia's interests in the Straits, while Russia agreed to back Italy's designs in Tripoli. Italy thus had taken another step away from the Triple Alliance.

The Second Moroccan Crisis

Europe had barely recovered from the Bosnian affair when another crisis arose, this time in North Africa. Despite the Act of Algeciras of 1906, friction in Morocco between French and German interests had continued. When native disturbances in Morocco in 1911 led to the intervention of French troops, Germany protested against what it considered a violation of Moroccan independence. To make up for France's increased influence in Morocco, Germany now claimed compensations elsewhere. And to give weight to its demands, it sent a German gunboat, the *Panther,* to the Moroccan port of Agadir, ostensibly to protect German lives and interests. For the most part it was British intervention that finally forced Germany to modify its claims and settle the crisis. But meanwhile Europe had once again been brought to the brink of war.

Anglo-German Naval Rivalry

England, throughout the crisis, suspected that Germany's real aim was to secure a naval base in Morocco, which would have posed a threat to Britain's base at Gibraltar. Anglo-German naval rivalry had by now become a matter of deep concern to the British. Naval expansion was closely related to imperialism. A powerful fleet was considered necessary to protect overseas possessions, and overseas possessions in turn were needed as naval bases and coaling stations. The most influential exponent of this new "navalism" was an American, Captain Alfred T. Mahan, whose writings, especially *The Influence of Sea Power upon History* (1890), were carefully studied in England and Germany.

As a precaution against the naval increases of the rest of the world, England in 1889 had adopted a "two-power standard," which called for a British fleet 10 percent stronger than the combined naval forces of the two next-strongest powers. The most serious challenge to Britain's naval power came from Germany. Beginning in 1898, Germany entered on a course of naval expansion that, by 1914, had made it the second-strongest naval power in the world. Germany's secretary of the navy, Admiral Alfred von Tirpitz, knew that he could not possibly expect to catch up with the British. He tried to build a navy strong enough that no other country would dare risk getting into a fight with Germany. The German navy was built not so much for a possible showdown with England as for reasons of prestige.

It was difficult for England to see matters in quite the same light. The British felt that Germany, primarily a land power, did not really need a navy, especially since it already had a powerful army. If the Germans went to the great expense of building a navy, this could only mean that they expected some day to challenge Britain's naval supremacy. Again and again, notably in 1908 and 1912, Great Britain urged Germany to slow down its naval construction, offering in return to support German colonial aspirations. But William II and Tirpitz saw these efforts merely as a confirmation of their "risk theory" and looked forward to the day when England would be forced to seek an agreement on Germany's terms. More than any other issue, this naval race was responsible for the growing tension between Germany and England during the last decade before the war.

The Balkan Wars

The Moroccan crisis of 1911—besides further strengthening the Anglo-French Entente—also helped to start a series of small wars aimed at the further disruption of the Ottoman Empire. The first of these broke out in the fall of 1911, when Italy, encouraged by France's success in Morocco, decided to embark on the annexation of Tripoli. Since Italy had carefully secured the prior consent of all the great powers, its war with Turkey of 1911 to 1912 did not by itself cause any major crisis. As we have seen, it brought Italy its long-coveted North African colony. The Tripolitanian War, however, encouraged several small Balkan states to move against Turkey and thus to reopen the Balkan question.

The chief motive behind the First Balkan War (1912) was the desire of Bulgaria, Serbia, and Greece to gain further concessions at the expense of Turkey. Together with Montenegro, these countries had formed a Balkan League in early 1912. Taking advantage of the war over Tripoli, they invaded the Ottoman Empire in October. Turkey was decisively defeated, and under the Treaty of London (May 1913) it lost all its European possessions except the region adjacent to the Straits.

The peace was less than a month old when a Second Balkan War broke out, this time among the victors over the distribution of the spoils. Under arrangements made before the first war, Serbia was to receive an outlet to the Adriatic in Albania. This met with Austrian and Italian protests, however. As compensation for its loss, Serbia now demanded some of the territory that Bulgaria had received in Macedonia; and when the Bulgarians refused, war ensued between Bulgaria on the one hand and Serbia, Greece, Montenegro, Rumania, and Turkey on the other. Against such an overwhelming coalition, the Bulgarians proved powerless. In the Treaty of Bucharest (August 1913), Bulgaria kept only a small part of Macedonia, the Greeks and Serbs taking the rest.

Turkish infantry during the First Balkan War (1912).

The Balkan Wars caused deep anxiety among the great powers. A Conference of Ambassadors was convened in London to deal with the Balkan problem, notably the controversy between Austria and Serbia over the latter's aspirations in Albania. As in the past, Russia backed Serbia. Germany, on the other hand, served as a brake on Austria's desire to intervene against Serbia. Since England and Italy also favored the independence of Albania, Russia finally withdrew its support from Serbia and peace was preserved. In the course of events, however, Austria and Russia, together with their allies, had again come close to war. Serbia had suffered another defeat, for which it blamed Austria and for which even its gains in Macedonia could not be consolation enough. Serbia's outraged nationalism sought revenge a year later in the assassination of the Austrian Archduke Francis Ferdinand at Sarajevo.

THE OUTBREAK OF THE GREAT WAR

In discussing the origins of the First World War, historians distinguish between underlying and immediate causes. In the first category belong all those factors that contributed to the acute state of international tension before 1914: nationalism, territorial disputes, economic competition, and imperialist rivalries. Some of the tension has also been blamed on the secret diplomacy of the powers, which led to secret alliances that involved nations in conflicts not of their making. But it has also been held that there was not enough secret diplomacy, that a "summit" meeting of Europe's leading statesmen in the summer of 1914, away from the clamor of their nationalistic press, might have resolved the differences that instead led to war. There had been many instances in the past when such joint action on the part of the Concert of Europe had proved effective. By 1914, however, the feeling of European solidarity that had animated the great powers in the days of Metternich and even Bismarck had everywhere given way to the powerful and divisive force of nationalism. The absence of any effective international agency to preserve peace did much to bring about the catastrophe of 1914.

The story of why and how the war came about has been told many times and in great detail. But to this day there are still wide differences among historians in the evaluation of the available evidence. It is quite possible that a different action by one or another of the statesmen in the summer of 1914 might have once more prevented a general war. Yet it seems unlikely that such a war could have been postponed much longer. If ever there was a time that seemed ripe for war, it was the summer of 1914.

The Causes of Wars

It is true, and it is important to bear in mind in examining the problems of that period, that before 1914 war was almost universally considered an acceptable, perhaps an inevitable and for many people a desirable way of settling international differences, and that the war generally foreseen was expected to be, if not exactly *frisch und fröhlich,* then certainly brief; no longer, certainly, than the war of 1870 that was consciously or unconsciously taken by that generation as a model. Had it not been so generally felt that war was an acceptable and tolerable way of solving international disputes, statesmen and soldiers would no doubt have approached the crisis of 1914 in a very different fashion.

But there was nothing new about this attitude to war. Statesmen had always been able to assume that war would be acceptable at least to those sections of their populations whose opinion mattered to them, and in this respect the decision to go to war in 1914—for Continental statesmen at least—in no way differed from those taken by their predecessors of earlier generations. The causes of the Great War are thus in essence no more complex or profound than those of any previous European war, or indeed than those described by Thucydides as underlying the Peloponnesian War: 'What made war inevitable was the growth of Athenian power and the fear this caused in Sparta.' In Central Europe there was the German fear that the disintegration of the Habsburg Empire would result in an enormous enhancement of Russian power—power already becoming formidable as French-financed industries and railways put Russian manpower at the service of her military machine. In Western Europe there was the traditional British fear that Germany might establish a hegemony over Europe which, even more than that of Napoleon, would place at risk the security of Britain and her own possessions; a fear fuelled by the knowledge that there was within Germany a widespread determination to achieve a world status comparable with her latent power. Consideration of this kind had caused wars in Europe often enough before. Was there really anything different about 1914?

From Michael Howard, *The Causes of Wars and Other Essays* (Cambridge, Mass,: Harvard U. Press, 1983), pp. 9–10.

Sarajevo

As we turn from the underlying to the immediate causes of the war, the most important was the assassination of Austrian Archduke Francis Ferdinand at the Bosnian capital of Sarajevo, on June 28, 1914.

The assassination of the archduke and his wife was carried out by an Austro-Bosnian citizen of Serb nationality, Gavrilo Princip. The crime had been planned and its execution aided by a secret society of Serb nationalists, the

"Black Hand." The archduke had been chosen as victim because he was known to favor reconciling the southern Slav element in the Dual Monarchy, a policy that interfered with the aspirations of Serb nationalism, which hoped for the ultimate union of all southern Slavs under Serbian rule. There is no evidence that the Serbian government had any hand in the plot itself; but Serbia's prime minister, Nicholas Pashitch, had general knowledge of it. Austria, taking for granted that the Serbian government was involved, decided once and for all to settle accounts with Serbia. This it hoped to do in a localized war. But Austria's foreign minister, Count Leopold von Berchtold, did not seem averse to a larger war if it was necessary to achieve Austria's aim.

European reaction to the assassination at first was one of deep shock and genuine sympathy for Austria. In indignation over the horrible crime, Germany gave Austria that fateful promise to "stand behind it as an ally and friend" in anything the Austrian government should decide to do. As it became clear, however, that Austria intended to use the Sarajevo incident to punish Serbia, the powers became alarmed. Russia warned the Austrians that it "would not be indifferent to any effort to humiliate Serbia." At the same time, France's president, Raymond Poincaré, assured the Russians of French support in any action they took on behalf of Serbia, By the middle of July, it was clear that Austria, backed by Germany, was ready to move against Serbia, and that Russia, backed by France, was equally ready to protect Serbia.

The Eve of War

The situation thus far was serious, but it was not as yet critical. It became so when Austria, on July 23, presented a stiff ultimatum to Serbia. The latter's reply, while not wholly complying, nevertheless was favorable enough to justify further negotiations. Instead, Austria broke off diplomatic relations and on July 28 declared war on Serbia. Germany had little choice but to live up to its earlier "blank check" and to support Austria. By doing so, the Germans hoped to discourage Russia from helping Serbia and thus to localize the Austro-Serbian conflict. But the Germans were also ready to stand by Austria if the conflict should develop into a general war.

The decision whether the war was to be a local or a general one rested primarily with Russia. Germany's action throughout the crisis had given the impression, not unjustifiably, that far from trying to discourage Austria, the German government was actually urging it on into the showdown with Serbia. Since an Austrian victory over Serbia would be tantamount to a Russian defeat, Russian military authorities now began calling for mobilization. The question was: should such mobilization be partial, against Austria-Hungary only, or should it be general, against Germany as well? Plans for a partial mobilization had been abandoned some time ago and in any case would have entailed considerable disadvantages in case general mobilization should become necessary later on. But a general mobilization, it was understood, would make a European war inevitable. The internal debate over this issue went on for several days. Only when the tsar finally became

Archduke Francis Ferdinand of Austria and his wife at Sarajevo on June 28, 1914, about to enter the automobile that carried them to their deaths.

The arrest of the assassin.

The Unexecuted Schlieffen Plan
pre-1914

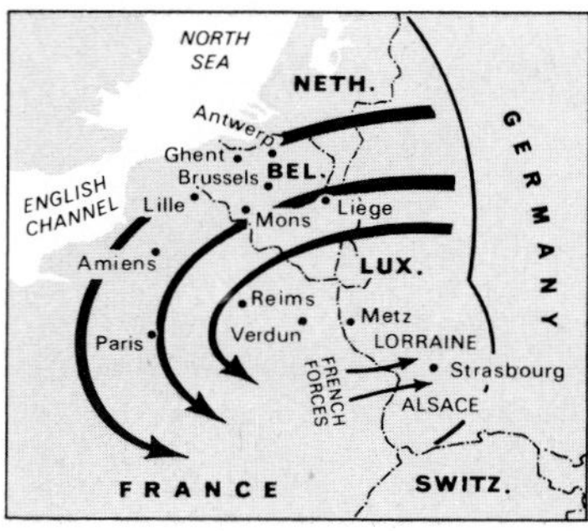

convinced, on July 30, that efforts to restrain Austria were futile, was the decision made to go ahead with a general mobilization.

The Outbreak of War

Germany's chief of staff, General Helmuth von Moltke, nephew of the great Moltke of Bismarckian times, was worried by reports from Russia. He therefore urged Austria, behind his government's back, to mobilize against Russia, promising unconditional German support. Austria ordered general mobilization on July 31, thus killing any chance for last-minute peace efforts. The same day Germany sent Russia an ultimatum demanding that the latter cease its preparations for war. When the tsar's government replied that this was impossible, Germany, on August 1, mobilized its own forces and a few hours later declared war on Russia. France, meanwhile, had also begun military preparations.To a German inquiry about its attitude in a Russo-German war, France replied that it would "act in accordance with its interests."

England Goes to War

August 4, 1914

It was 11 o'clock at night — 12 by German time — when the ultimatum expired. The windows of the Admiralty were thrown wide open in the warm night air. Under the roof from which Nelson had received his orders were gathered a small group of Admirals and Captains and a cluster of clerks, pencil in hand, waiting. Along the Mall from the direction of the Palace the sound of an immense concourse singing "God save the King" floated in. On this deep wave there broke the chimes of Big Ben; and, as the first stroke of the hour boomed out, a rustle of movement swept across the room. The war telegram, which meant "Commence hostilities against Germany," was flashed to the ships and establishments under the White Ensign all over the world.

I walked across the Horse Guards Parade to the Cabinet room and reported to the Prime Minister and the Ministers who were assembled there that the deed was done.

From Winston S. Churchill, *The World Crisis, 1911–1918* (New York: Scribner's, 1931), p. 128. [Churchill at the time was First Lord of the Admiralty.]

On August 3, Germany declared war on France.

The reason for Germany's haste in declaring war lay in the plans that its general staff had worked out for a war on two fronts. The basic idea of the "Schlieffen Plan"— named after its originator, Count Alfred von Schlieffen, who had been chief of the general staff from 1891 to 1906 — was for Germany's main forces to turn west, deliver an annihilating blow against France, and then turn east against the slowly mobilizing Russians. To succeed with its plan, Germany not only needed to mobilize as quickly as possible, but it also had to invade France at its most vulnerable spot, the northeastern frontier between France and Belgium. The Schlieffen Plan, in other words, called for German violation of Belgian neutrality, which, together with the rest of Europe, the Germans had guaranteed in 1839.

Germany's invasion of Belgium on August 3 brought England into the war the next day. Great Britain has subsequently been reproached for not making its position in the crisis clear enough from the start, the argument being that if it had come off the fence earlier, it would have deterred the Austrians from going to war against Serbia. Through the Entente Cordiale, especially its secret military and naval understandings, England was deeply committed to France. On the other hand, there had been a marked improvement in Anglo-German relations in the early months of 1914; and England's Entente with Russia had never been very popular. For reasons of its own security, Britain could not possibly afford to stand idly by while Germany won victories over France and Russia that would make it the dominant power on the Continent. But to get the British public to approve involvement in the war, some event was needed to dramatize the German danger. Such an event was Germany's violation of Belgian neutrality. Almost overnight it helped to convert Britain's indecisive neutrality into determined belligerency.

"War Guilt"

A word remains to be said about the question of "war guilt," a subject of controversy to the present day. Most historians agree that Germany, Austria, and Russia bear a major share of the responsibility. England clearly belongs at the other extreme, its errors being chiefly of omission; and France stands somewhere in between. This much is certain: no one power alone was responsible for the war, and none of the great powers was entirely free from responsibility. Many Europeans actually welcomed the war as a relief from the almost unbearable tension that had preceded it. Yet most of the leading statesmen, when faced with the certainty of war, were overcome by fear and desperation. It was as though they had a foreboding that the war they had failed to avert would be far more terrible than they could imagine, and that the world they had known would never be the same again.

Suggestions for Further Reading

The best works on the diplomacy of the late nineteenth century are still W. L. Langer's *European Alliances and Alignments,* 2nd ed. (1950) and *The Diplomacy of Imperialism, 1890–1902,* 2nd ed., 2 vols. (1951). Among the books on the origins of the First World War, L. Albertini, *The Origins of the War of 1914,* 3 vols. (1952–1957), is generally considered the best. There are numerous brief resumés of the controversy surrounding that issue, the latest of which by J. Joll, *The Origins of the First World War* (1985), points up its complexity.

The literature on the "new imperialism" is vast. The colonization of Africa is discussed in R. Robinson and G. Gallagher, *Africa and the Victorians* (1961). On East Asia, G. P. Hudson, *The Far East in World Politics* (1939), is the best brief account. See also J. T. Pratt, *The Expansion of Europe in the Far East* (1947). America's part in the scramble for overseas possessions is treated in H. W. Morgan, *America's Road to Empire: The War with Spain and Overseas Expansion* (1965). The motives of modern imperialism are examined in numerous books, among them the classics by J. A. Hobson, *Imperialism: A Study* (1902), and N. Lenin, *Imperialism: The Highest State of Capitalism* (1916), which still are worth reading. See also E. M. Winslow, *The Pattern of Imperialism* (1948), and A. P Thornton, *Doctrines of Imperialism* (1965).

The events of the last decade before the war are summarized in D. E. Lee, *Europe's Crucial Years: The Diplomatic Background of World War I, 1902–1914* (1974). The policy of two of the major powers is brilliantly analyzed in V. R. Berghahn, *Germany and the Approach of War in 1914* (1973), and Z. Steiner, *Britain and the Origins of the First World War* (1977). The influence of public opinion on foreign policy is explored in O. J. Hale, *Publicity and Diplomacy* (1940). On the July crisis of 1914, Albertini, cited above, is both detailed and fair. The controversy touched off by the German historian Fritz Fischer on the responsibility for the war is summarized in his brief book, *World Power or Decline* (1974).

	1815				1870	
SOUTHWEST ASIA AND AFRICA	**1818–28** King Shaka, apex of Zulu kingdom	**1836** Boers' Great Trek begins		**1860** French expansion in West Africa **1869** Suez Canal opens		
EUROPE	**1815** Congress of Vienna **1815–83** Karl Marx **1825** Decembrist Revolt, Russia **1825** First commercial railroad	**1829** Treaty of Adrianople **1830** France's "July Monarchy" **1832** Britain's Great Reform Bill **1848** *Communist Manifesto*	**1848–49** Europe in Revolt **1848–61** Unification of Italy **1848–70** Napolean III **1851** Crystal Palace Exhibition, London	**1859** Darwin, *Origin of Species* **1854–56** Crimean War **1861–71** Unification of Germany **1867** Austro-Hungarian *Ausgleich*	**1870–71** Franco-Prussian War **1876** First internal combustion engine **1878** Congress of Berlin	**1882** Triple Alliance **1894** Russo-French Alliance
SOUTH AND SOUTHEAST ASIA	**1819** British found Singapore		**1857–58** Indian Mutiny **1859** French seize Saigon			
EAST ASIA	**1825–30** Java War **1839–42** Opium War		**1850–64** Taiping Rebellion **1854** Perry opens US trade with Japan **1868** Meiji Restoration, Japan			**1893–1976** Mao Zedong **1894–95** Sino-Japanese War
THE AMERICAS AND PACIFIC	**1823** Monroe Doctrine	**1835–40** Alexis de Tocqueville, *Democracy in America* **1840** Britain annexes New Zealand **1846–48** Mexican War	**1849** Gold discovered in California	**1861–65** American Civil War **1867** Russia sells Alaska to US **1867** British North America Act	**1869** Opening of Transcontinental railroad	

Wood sculpture, Dogon tribe, Mali, West Africa.

Eiffel Tower, Paris, 1889.

***Empire State Express* No. 999, *ca.* 1890.**

Commodore Matthew Perry, a Japanese view, 1853.

British suffragette, *ca.* 1910.

Private Edwin Francis Jennison, Confederate Army.

1914	
1886 Gold discovered in Southern Africa **1889** Rhodesia colonized **1899–1902** Boer War **1910** Union of South Africa formed	
1894–1905 Dreyfus Affair **1905** Russian Revolution begins **1905** Einstein's Theory of Relativity **1907** Triple Entente **1912–13** Balkan Wars	
1885 Indian National Congress founded **1906** Muslim League founded	
1900 Boxer Rebellion **1904–05** Russo-Japanese War **1911** Chinese Revolution **1912–49** Chinese Republic	
1889 First Pan-American Conference **1898** Spanish-American War **1910** Mexican Revolution begins	**1914** Panama Canal opens

The Prince of Wales in Bangalore, India, *ca.* 1900.

Gold prospector, California, *ca.* 1850.

38 South Asia and Africa in the Nineteenth Century

For the peoples of Asia and Africa the nineteenth century was a time of unprecedented challenge and tribulation as Europe, transformed by economic and political revolution, extended its influence throughout the globe and European nations built vast empires straddling the world. As we have seen, the process of empire building culminated after 1870 in the New Imperialism which extended European sovereignty to the very heart of Africa and deep into the Pacific. It was a time when most Europeans were supremely confident that the superiority of their guns and ships was irrefutable proof of the superiority of their civilization as well—a time which came to an end only with the First World War.

The intrusion of Europe was a phenomenon common to the history of most of nineteenth century Asia and Africa, but the form and intensity of that intrusion differed over time and place. Furthermore, the presence of a common challenge and the increased interrelatedness of the world must not obscure the fact that the peoples of these two vast and varied continents were not merely responding to alien stimuli. Subject to the historical dynamics of their own regions and shaped by the historical circumstances of their particular societies, they participated in cultural traditions, each of which offered its own range of choices, opportunities, and constraints. The human enterprise remained wondrously varied and diverse.

SOUTH ASIA: THE BRITISH IN INDIA

After the defeat of the French by Robert Clive at Plassey in 1757 the British remained the prime European power on the Indian subcontinent. There they gradually created what became the largest and most important colony in the most powerful of the nineteenth-century empires.

India under Company Rule, 1786–1858

A new phase of the history of the British in India began in 1786 when Lord Charles Cornwallis, who five years earlier had surrendered at Yorktown to the Americans, was appointed governor-general of Bengal. In 1784 the British Parliament had established a Board of Control consisting of cabinet members to oversee the East India Company, whose reputation had been badly tarnished by scandal. The company, under its Board of Directors, continued to operate under a government charter, which after 1793 came up for renewal every twenty years. Although it lost some of its powers each time, it remained until 1858 the legal agent of the British government and continued to maintain the fiction that it was acting on behalf of the Mughal emperor still enthroned in Delhi.

Sent out as a reformer, Cornwallis, during his seven years in India (1786–93), put an end to the peculations of the Company's "servants" forever by establishing what was later known as the Indian Civil Service, staffed by well-paid, competent, prestigious, and supremely self-assured administrators. To pay their high salaries and generally place the government on a sound financial footing required a firm revenue base. This was provided by the Permanent Settlement of 1793, which transformed former Mughal revenue collectors *(zamindars)* into landowners regarded by Cornwallis as Indian equivalents of English gentry. Land previously governed by a system of traditional rights and obligations now became private property in the European manner. Cultivators lost their traditional rights, and absentee landlordism was to be a persistent problem. When English rule spread to other parts of India, the land was usually settled on the cultivators, but there too the British abolished the traditional system under which various parties held an interest in the land and replaced it with the European concept of unqualified possession, turning land into a commodity that could be bought and sold.

The area administered by Cornwallis already held a population greater than that of Britain, and the company directors were apprehensive about further expansion for which the company would have to foot the bill. However, Lord Charles Wellesley (governor-general 1797–1805), brother of the Duke of Wellington, had other ideas. Claiming that he was foiling French plans to expand beyond their Egyptian base, he involved the British in several wars, most significantly against the Marathas who were, after the eclipse of the Mughals, the strongest native power on the subcontinent. When he was recalled in 1805, Wellesley was censured. Peace followed for about eight years, but then the momentum of conquest resumed. A war fought during 1817–18 permanently eliminated Maratha power and left Britain paramount on the subcontinent. Beyond the areas under direct British rule, treaties with the individual native states gave the governor-general the right to appoint advisers whose views the local rulers disregarded at their peril, for the rulers themselves were subject to removal by the British.

Beginning in the late eighteenth century in Britain, opinion differed not only concerning the optimum size of the empire in India but also over what the British role there should be. Cornwallis's creation of the Indian Civil Service and his Permanent Settlement are examples of a European inclination to impose their own institutions and values on their colonies, but other influential statesmen, such as Cornwallis's predecessor Warren Hastings, felt that Britain should limit itself to maintaining peace and security much as the Mughals had once done. For many years, "Orientalists," frequently learned men who valued Indian traditions, debated "Anglicists" who insisted on the universal validity of British norms. To the Anglicists the Orientalists appeared to tolerate immoral practices such as *sati* (widows burning themselves on their husbands' funeral pyres) and child marriage, while the Orientalists could point to the ignorance and arrogance of their opponents and the disruptive effect their policies would have on Indian society. They could also point out that if Indians were transformed into Englishmen, they would claim the rights of Englishmen as had the Americans.

Those who wished to transform India represented divergent views. Some were religiously motivated (missionaries were first admitted to India in 1813) but especially influential were Utilitarians who sought to reform India even as they were pushing reform at home. William Bentinck (governor-general 1828–35), himself a Utilitarian, made great changes. *Sati* was outlawed (although not completely stamped out). Official funds previously used to support Hindu scholarship and education were redirected to further Western learning to create, in the words of Thomas Babbington Macauley, "a class of persons, Indian in blood and color, but English in taste, in opinions, in morals and in intellect." In the courts English replaced Persian as the official language.

British Expansion in India 1805–57

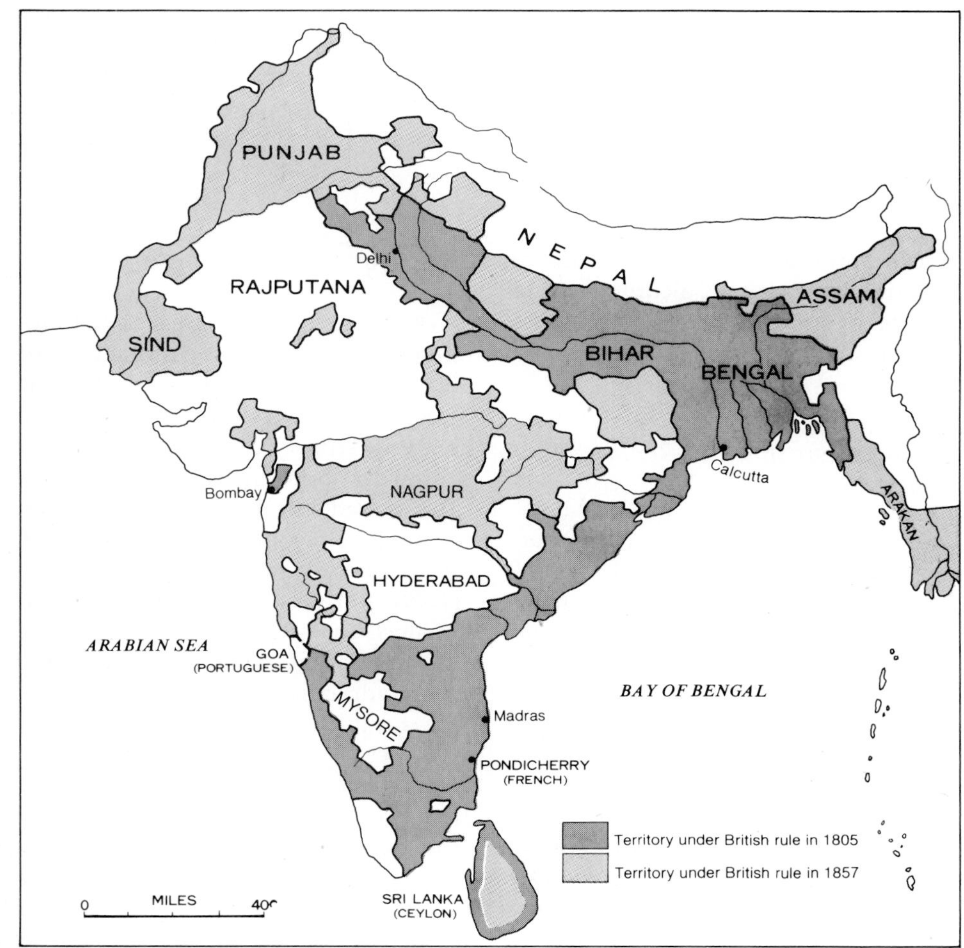

When its charter came up for revision in 1833, the East India Company lost its commercial monopoly (except on opium and salt) in line with Liberal belief in laissez-faire. By that time, however, the English market for Indian textiles had collapsed and the International textile trade had been reversed, because machine-made English cloth undersold the native product of Bengal. This destroyed the old cotton industry, created massive unemployment, and fostered economic dependence.

Indian responses to the British ranged from accommodation to hostility. A most constructive response was worked out by a group of Bengali intellectuals, followers of Ram Mohun Roy (1772–1833) often considered the father of modern India. Roy became fluent in English and more than held his own in religious debate with Englishmen. Affirming the essential validity of his Hindu heritage, he argued that all the major world religions had a monotheistic tradition that had been perverted and needed to be restored. For Hinduism, according to Roy, this involved a return to the Vedas, which provided no justification for untouchability or the subjugation of women. The Brahmo Samaj (Society of Brahma) founded by Roy in Calcutta in 1828 was never large, but it inspired a sense of pride in Hinduism as well as a will to reform.

Dalhousie and the Revolt of 1857

Lord James Dalhousie (governor-general 1848–56) combined Wellesley's expansionism with Bentinck's policy of cultural change. Not content with influencing native states through "advisers," he claimed the right to seize any territory whose rulers had no natural (as contrasted to adopted) heir. Even beyond India, he added territory in Burma. A firm believer in unification, he was a great builder of railways and telegraph lines and also gave India a modern postal system. At the same time he enacted policies that greatly alarmed traditionalists. His Widow Remarriage Act seemed to prove that the British were bent on destroying the traditional fabric of Indian life just as they were destroying Indian states.

The annexation of the state of Oudh in 1856 antagonized many at a time when numerous Indian soldiers *(sepoys)* were worried about a new regulation that provided they could be sent anywhere, even across the seas, regardless of the rules of their own *jati* (caste). The final outrage was the introduction by the British of a breechloading rifle with cartridges smeared in animal fat. The soldiers were supposed to bite off the top of the cartridges before loading. Muslims prohibited from tasting pork and Hindus for whom beef was taboo refused orders to use the new ammunition. Mutiny and revolt spread rapidly in northern India where Delhi and other cities were seized. Bitter fighting ensued, exacerbated by outbursts of racial hatred. The British emerged victorious, but the war brought on many changes including the final demise not only of the Mughal dynasty but also of the East India Company's rule.

India under the Crown, 1858–1914

As a result of the great revolt, authority over India was assumed by the British government and vested in the viceroy. Dalhousie's policy of increasing the territory under British rule by annexing princely states was now abandoned, but there were attempts at expansion beyond the Indian frontier. A second war against Afghanistan (1878–81) was as unsuccessful as its predecessor (1839–42). In contrast, the conquest of Burma was completed and it was administered as a part of colonial India until 1937.

After 1857 in India itself the British worked with and supported the princes and the traditional aristocracy while they retreated from the earlier policy of Anglicization. Most unfortunate was a change of tone and mood. Distrust and disdain poisoned the atmosphere as the imperialists assumed "The White Man's Burden" only to "watch sloth and heathen folly/bring all your hopes to naught." Kipling well expressed the sense of pride and futility of his contemporaries.

Caught in the middle, disliked both by the traditional elite and by the British was a growing "middle" class of English-educated men who worked in government, commerce, industry, and the professions. Although they made some progress, particularly during the viceroyalty of the liberal Lord Ripon (1880–84), they were often disappointed by British failures to work with them and treat them as equals. Educated Indians were keenly aware of the contrast between their own lack of power and the self-government enjoyed by the white citizens of the Canadian provinces (brought together in the Dominion of Canada, 1867) as well as those who lived on the Australian continent (Commonwealth of Australia, 1901).

A major case in point came in 1883 when the government gave in to the vociferous protests of the European community and withdrew the Ilbert Bill, which would have allowed Indian judges to supervise trials involving Englishmen. To the modern, educated Indian elite this not only provided a lesson in British racial arrogance but also demonstrated the importance of making oneself heard. As a result they organized the Indian National Congress in 1885. Its members were of high status, considerable financial means, and all spoke English.

The choices open to the Indian leadership were expressed in the rivalry between two remarkable leaders, Gopal Krishna Gokhale (1866–1915) and Balwabtral Gangadhar Tilak (1856–1920). Although they were both Maharastha Brahmans, they differed as much in personality as in their views. The gentle, mild, soft-spoken Gokhale drew strength from the strain of humanitarian social reform reaching back to Ram Mohun Roy and the Brahmo Samaj. Thus he welcomed measures to better the lot of women, improve hygiene, and so on. Furthermore, he believed in gradualism and was convinced that the British could be persuaded to make reforms and share power. His was the difficult and demanding role of serving as a bridge between India and Britain.

Crowded native quarters, Lahore, India (*ca.* 1905).

In contrast the robust and vigorous Tilak identified himself with the Hindu tradition, objected to the British introduction of vaccination into India (the vaccine being made from cows) and even opposed raising the age of marriage for girls from ten to twelve on the grounds that it was imposed by the British who had no right to interfere with Indian traditions. His virulent attacks on the reforms were combined with complete rejection of their British sponsor. Whereas Gokhale spent much time and energy in attempting to persuade the British, Tilak won a wide following by organizing festivals, including week-long celebrations of Shivaji, the great Maratha leader who helped destroy Mughal power. His stance, even as it attracted Hindus, naturally alarmed India's Muslims. Some, like Sayyid Ahmad Khan (1817–98), founder of a modern college for Mus-

Lord Curzon, Viceroy of India, 1899–1905.

lims, considered British rule preferable to living in a state dominated by a Hindu majority. Other Muslim leaders participated in a large-scale revival of Islamic learning and piety, demonstrating that tradition's capacity for self-renewal.

Gokhale's Moderates dominated the Congress, but their hopes for smooth, steady progress suffered a serious setback under Lord George Nathaniel Curzon (viceroy 1899–1905) who wrote, "My own belief is that Congress is tottering to its fall, and one of my greatest ambitions while in India is to assist it to a peaceful demise." By reducing the Indian voice on urban administrative boards, enacting an unpopular restructuring of the university system, and especially by partitioning the province of Bengal, he stimulated widespread resentment that found expression in a movement to boycott foreign goods, demands for self-rule, and calls for activism and violence.

Nationalism in India, which had its beginning with a small elite in the last quarter of the nineteenth century, was given a new impetus by Curzon, but the concept of self-rule *(swadeshi)* meant different things to different people both in terms of immediate demands to be made on the British and in terms of ultimate goals. The question whether all-India nationalism would prove sufficiently strong to bind together the diverse communities of the subcontinent would cast a shadow over the future.

Victoria Railway Station, Bombay, India (1907). The British legacy survives in India's excellent railroad system.

Muslim fears of Hindu dominance were stirred by the fact that one source for Hindu opposition to Curzon's partition of Bengal was that it would leave East Bengal with a Muslim majority. In response, in 1906, they formed the Muslim League as a vehicle for the expression of their interests and aspirations. Although the Moderates in Congress argued that their objectives were purely secular, they failed to convince the Muslims who, moreover, had British support. As a result, in the Morley-Minto Reforms (1909) under which propertied Indians were granted elected representation in an all-India Imperial Legislative Council as well as on provincial councils, special seats were reserved for Muslims. The Moderates in Congress had long sought for a greater voice in policy making. Reluctantly they accepted the new arrangement on the grounds that the reforms were a step in the right direction, and they made efforts to work with the Muslims, efforts which were welcomed by the Muslims who were losing British support largely because of Muslim-Christian conflicts in the Balkans.

During the First World War Indians supported Britain generously with high expectations of British goodwill. These expectations, like those of so many others, were destined to be shattered.

SOUTHWEST ASIA AND AFRICA

In contrast to the Mughals in India, the Muslim rulers of Iran and the Ottoman Empire were not displaced by Europeans nor were the heartlands of their states annexed by the imperialist powers. Instead, in both cases, weak and tottering regimes were propped up by European nations with their own reasons for upholding the status quo. Meanwhile religious and secular leaders tried to stem the tide of western power by traditional and modern means with varying degrees of success.

Iran (Persia)

The shahs of the Quajar dynasty, who ruled in Tehran from 1796 to 1925, never matched their Safavid predecessors in power or charisma (see pp. 521–27). No shah was ever to regain the status of Abbas I, political and spiritual authority remained divided, and the *ulema,* spiritually and financially independent of the state, exercised great influence; the authority of the *mujtahids* as true interpreters of holy truth was widely accepted and commanded great respect. Furthermore, the large territory of Iran with its arid, mountainous terrain encouraged the virtual autonomy of tribal peoples who also benefited from modern military technology as handguns became common and cancelled out the advantage the central government had once enjoyed by its possession of cannons. Furthermore, there was little to inspire loyalty to the rapacious court and a government that sold office to the highest bidder who then squeezed the people. Nor did the line of shahs produce outstanding leaders.

The predominant foreign powers in Iran were Britain and Russia. In 1801 Iran signed a treaty with Britain agreeing to support Britain against Afghanistan or France in return for receiving military equipment and technicians. These did not, however, prevent defeat by Russia in two wars, 1804–13 and 1826–28. As a result Russia won both territory (it had already seized Georgia in 1800) and concessions, as well as an indemnity. Particularly important were tariff concessions and extraterritoriality especially because they were extended also to other powers, foremost among them Britain in a treaty of 1841.

Tariff concessions meant that Iran was prevented from protecting its traditional handicrafts from foreign competition. Nor could it nurture its own modern industries. Skilled artisans such as carpet weavers were reduced to lowly paid laborers. Extraterritoriality provided for the exemption of Russians and British from Iranian law: they were to be tried by their own laws in their own consular courts. This special legal status was also extended to some Iranians, such as those in consular employ. The British treaty also included a Most Favored National Clause stipulating that any concessions Iran extended to any other country would automatically apply also to Britain. This provision, which became standard in the unequal treaties Britain imposed on other countries as well as Iran, made it difficult for Iran to play the imperialist powers off against each other.

Half of a stereographic print of a Durbar, or assembly of notables, held in Delhi, India (*ca.* 1900), showing the pomp of British Imperial India.

In the early nineteenth century an attempt was made at military modernization and was repeated in mid-century during the first three years of Naser ad-Din's long reign (1848–96) under the direction of Amir Kabir.

Kabir abolished sinecures, founded a school of higher learning, encouraged the translation of western books, and made an unsuccessful attempt to create modern industries. A very different response to the troubles of the times came from the Babi messianic socioreligious movement that Kabir helped to suppress. Kabir himself was dismissed and killed in 1851. The shah retained an interest in Europe but accomplished relatively little in modernizing and strengthening the country.

Pressures to make economic concessions mounted during the second half of the century. In 1872 concessions were made to Baron Julius de Reuter, founder of the Reuter news agency, so extensive that had they all been honored, they would have turned Iran into his private preserve. The government found ways to abrogate some of them, but Reuter did obtain the right to build the Imperial Bank of Persia with the exclusive power to issue bank notes and negotiable paper. The Russians, for their part, established a bank of their own.

While members of the *ulema* objected to departures from tradition, many others—bitterly resentful of the weakness and corruption of the government—joined more secular-minded men in opposing government measures. The first broadly based protest, joined in by the *ulema*, modernizers, merchants, and townspeople, came when the shah granted the English a monopoly on tobacco in 1890. The protest was so strong that he had to back down in 1892. Four years later, he was assassinated by a pan-Islamist. As throughout the century, the British and Russians saw to it that there was a smooth succession.

The movement for change was given a boost by Russia's defeat in the Russo-Japanese war of 1905, seen not only as a triumph of an Asian nation over a European power but also of a constitutional state over one lacking a constitution. As a result of revolution in Iran, the shah was forced to accept a representative assembly and a constitution that legally remained in effect until 1979 although disregarded in practice after 1912. When the government showed too much independence, the Russians sent in troops in 1911. By that time, as a result of the Anglo-Russian Entente (1907), Iran was divided into a Russian northern sphere, a British southern sphere, and a supposedly neutral area in the center. Significant for the future was the formation in 1909 of the Anglo-Iranian Oil Company. In 1912 the British navy switched to oil, and two years later the British government bought a majority of the company's shares.

In contrast to India where people enthusiastically supported the British effort in the First World War in expectation of concessions to follow, Iranians could expect only increased exploitation at the hands of the two dominant imperialist powers that governed their country without assuming actual responsibility.

The Ottoman Empire

The Ottoman Empire began the century under Sultan Mahmud II (r. 1808–39) who, like Russia's Peter the Great, sought to strengthen and modernize his state along European lines. After creating a modern army, he destroyed, once and for all, the Janissaries, who had so often stood in the way of change. Further, he abolished other institutions that were no longer functional, including the remaining *timars* (grants made to cavalrymen), and he generally reorganized his government to resemble those of Europe. A census and land survey were also among his accomplishments. Less successful was his attempt to control outlying provinces. The loss of the Ottoman hold on Moldavia and Wallachia as well as the formation of an independent Greek state occurred during his reign (see p. 701). Most serious was the threat mounted by Muhammad Ali (r. 1805–48), ruler of Egypt, whose forces were much superior to those of the Empire. In 1839 it took the intervention of the European powers to preserve the Empire.

This near disaster stimulated a period of reform, the Tanzimat Period (1839–78), which began with an imperial rescript promising the people individual rights to be extended equally to all inhabitants (including non-Muslims). Extensive reforms in law and justice, education, and government followed, but also persistent difficulties in foreign relations, especially the Crimean War. Government maladministration and extravagance as well as heavy foreign borrowings led to financial collapse in 1874, and trouble along the northern frontier led to war with Russia in 1877–78. But first, in 1876, as a logical culmination of the reforms but also with an eye on the impression it would make on European statesmen, the sultan promulgated a constitution including a proviso for a representative assembly. A leading figure in this as in other reforms was Midhat Pasha (1822–83), who envisioned the transformation of the Empire into a modern Ottoman state in which a sense of Ottoman nationalism would bind together the disparate peoples of the Empire. The constitution also seemed to fulfill the hopes of liberal writers and theorists, known as Young Ottomans, who had been advocating the establishment of a constitutional monarchy like that of Britain. Many of these men now returned from residence in Europe.

There were, however, competing loyalties. The Muslim devout were naturally offended by the secularization of the world's leading Islamic state, a state which for centuries had served as the bastion and champion of the faith, a state whose ruler was heir to the caliphs. It also provoked the righteous indignation of the *ulema* faced with the loss of their age-old control over the legal system as European law and jurisprudence were adopted. The backlash came under Sultan Abd al-Hamid II (r. 1876–1909), a supporter of the kind of pan-Islam that cost the Iranian Shah Naser ad-Din his life. While the sultan's emphasis on religious orthodoxy was welcomed by devout Arabs as well as Turks and other Muslims, it naturally alarmed his Christian subjects and helped to transform Christian Armenians from loyal subjects into revolutionaries. Beginning in 1890 they staged a series of uprisings culminating in the rising of 1894 which ended in a massacre of the Armenians.

Because the sultan ruled as an autocrat, opposition became very dangerous. He disssolved the legislative assembly, allowed the constitution to lapse, and employed spies and secret police to ferret out those who dared object. His rule did not, however, entail wholesale abandonment of modernization and its attendant secularization as the Empire drew physically closer to Europe with the opening of a railway to Hungary in 1888. He granted a concession to a German group to build a railway to Ankara (granted 1889, completed 1892) and a further concession to the Germans to extend it to Baghdad (1899). German officers had early on assisted in building a modern army, and Ottoman-German relations were further enhanced by two visits paid to Abd al-Hamid II by Germany's William II.

The Armenians were not the only ones who became militant in response to repression. In 1889 a secret society, called the Committee of Union and Progress, soon attracted a substantial following among army officers. Known as "Young Turks," the members of this movement became especially influential among the officers stationed in Salonika who took the lead in a revolt. The sultan was forced to reestablish the constitution in 1908 and was deposed in 1909 after he had attempted a military countermove. However, the earlier Ottomanism was not the only alternative to the sultan's pan-Islam. For many of the Young Turks their Turkish identity ultimately took precedence both over their loyalty to the multinational Ottoman state and to their multiethnic faith.

The years immediately after 1909 were particularly difficult, marred by still another massacre of Armenians in 1909, by insurrection in Albania (1910 and 1912), by the Balkan Wars (see pp.

Abd al-Hamid II, ruler of the Ottoman Empire, 1876–1909.

789–801), and by a coup d'etat by Young Turks in 1913. In November 1914 when the Empire joined Germany in the First World War, British Prime Minister Asquith said that it had committed suicide, and the war did administer the death blow. By that time, however, its control over its former domains in North Africa was long gone while the Arabs of Southwest Asia were, to say the least, seriously divided in their loyalties.

The Arabian Peninsula

Whereas in Islam there had long been those who were ready to accommodate the faith to local traditions and changing times, others, particularly from the seventeenth century on, insisted on purer and narrower adhesion to the original teachings of the Koran and the prophets. In places as far apart as Syria and Sumatra men of religion objected to medieval Muslim scholasticism and also to the development of mysticism as alien accretions and dangerous departures. Although the Sufi orders had been steeped in mysticism, the new fundamentalism won over some of these orders and thus gained increased vitality from their zeal. Fired with religious purpose, fervent fundamentalists were ready to do battle in holy war with the enemies of the faith.

In India the political implications of this stance became apparent during the reign of Emperor Aurangzeb (see pp. 536–38), but it had its greatest success on the Arabian Peninsula. There Muhammad Abd al-Wahhab (1703–92) preached against such corruptions of the true faith as saint worship and denounced anything that offended the strictest monotheism, even including homage paid to Muhammad's tomb at Medina. When he formed an alliance with Muhammad Ibn Saud, a chieftain based at Dariya near the center of the peninsula, once again, as in the early days of the faith, a potent fusion of faith and sword took hold. Soon the Wahhabis were able to challenge the Ottoman sultan not only theoretically by denying his role as universal caliph but militarily, seizing Mecca and Medina as well as advancing into Iraq and Syria. In control of the places of holy pilgrimage, they imposed their beliefs on anyone coming to pay homage at the sacred sites.

The Wahhabis were finally subdued after the Ottoman sultan called on Muhammad Ali to send an army against them. In 1818 his forces took and destroyed Dariya. However, both the faith and the house of Saud survived until Abd al-Aziz Ibn Saud (1880–1953) revived their fortunes and went on to found the modern state of Saudi Arabia. Elsewhere in the world of Islam, people continued to be attracted by the purity of an uncompromising fundamentalism. Those who did not share the Wahhabis' rejection of the modern world but sought instead to be both Muslim and modern were nevertheless attracted by the Wahhabis' example of going straight back to the source of the faith in disregard of all the interpretations and emendations of the subsequent millennium.

Egypt and the Sudan

The modern history of Egypt contrasts strikingly with that of the Arabian Peninsula. Victorious in the wake of Napoleon's withdrawal and the subsequent infighting complicated by British intervention, Muhammad Ali first came to Egypt as the commander of an Ottoman army composed of Albanians. After establishing his authority, this remarkable leader did much to lay the foundations for modern Egypt. Partly he accomplished this by sweeping away old institutions and power centers: his massacre of the Mamluks resembles the destruction of the Janissaries by Sultan Mahmud II. A mainstay of his power was the new army he created by conscripting Egyptians and employing foreign instructors. He also sent men to Europe to study technology and opened a polytechnic school at home. To collect the funds necessary to maintain his army and finance military expeditions, Muhammad Ali reformed the currency, fiscal, and tax systems and took steps to build up the economy by improving irrigation, encouraging commerce, and linking Egyptian trade with England.

After his modern army defeated the Wahhabis, he sent it south to conquer the Sudan in search of riches and slaves and then east again to fight for the sultan against Greek independence. When the sultan failed to reward him by turning over Syria, Muhammad Ali seized Syria and had his army march into Anatolia. But English intervention not only saved the Ottoman Empire but also forced Muhammad Ali to return Syria. The Treaty of London (1841) recognized him as hereditary ruler of an autonomous province.

In this way Egypt remained technically a part of the Ottoman Empire, but the threat of actual interference in its affairs came not from Istanbul but from London and Paris. Although the French built the Suez Canal (concession granted 1854, canal opened 1869), the British were vitally interested in this route that cut their travel time to India in half. Beleaguered by financial difficulties, the Egyptian government first sold a controlling interest in the canal to Britain (1875) and then (1876) turned over its finances to two commissioners, one British and one French. As already indicated (see p. 791), Britain intervened again in 1882 to crush a nationalist uprising. Henceforth France was excluded from Egypt which became for all intents and purposes a British protectorate controlled by a consul general.

During the lengthy administration of the capable but autocratic Lord Cromer (1883–1907) Egypt's ordinary people benefited from social reform (such as the abolition of routine flogging) and from the building of a dam at Aswan, but little was done to educate them nor did Lord Cromer believe in preparing Egyptians for self-rule. After a gross miscarriage of justice in the village of Denshawai in 1906 helped stimulate nationalist indignation, under Cromer's successors the British policy was one of using both the carrot of increased Egyptian participation in government and the stick of press censorship and imprisonment without trial.

In 1907 Egypt's First Nationalist Congress met, attended by over a thousand men from all over the country. While the beginnings of this movement can be traced back to the early 1880s and before, this marked a new stage in the opposition to foreign domination. The demand of Egypt for the Egyptians was a clear sign of things to come.

To the south, the fate of the Sudan remained tied to that of Egypt whose ruthless collection of taxes was greatly resented although Cairo's authority was spread very thin. In that vast and difficult land, slave traders and then ivory hunters long continued to prey on the surrounding peoples. In 1885, however, the fundamentalist Mahdist Movement spiritually akin to the Wahhabis, captured Khartoum and founded a theocratic state that lasted until 1898 when it was crushed in a terrible battle. When Lord Kitchener led Egyptian troops into a battle in which a good 20,000 men lost their lives, the stage was set for the Fashoda crisis with France (see p. 791), and when France backed down, the field was left clear for Britain to place the Sudan under joint Anglo-Egyptian administration. Further west, the Sanusis, a Sufi order, expanded in the Sahara

Building the Suez Canal (*ca.* 1865).

Desert to become the dominant force in Libya.

North Africa

In the Maghreb only Morocco had never been included in the Ottoman Empire. Its sultan, sanctified as a descendant of the Prophet, evoked wide loyalty as a religious leader and commander of the faithful even though he could never control the Berber tribesmen of the interior. However, based on the fertile Atlantic plains, the state maintained a precarious independence. Under Sultan Malay Hasan (1873–94) it experienced a wave of military and civil modernization, but this did not save it from becoming a pawn in European power politics nor from ultimate division into French and Spanish spheres.

Algeria lost its autonomy much earlier than Morocco. It had long had commercial relations with France, but in 1830 the French declared war on Algeria on the grounds that the Algerian ruler had hit the French consul in the face with a fly whisk. Although the Algerian government quickly surrendered, the peoples of the interior kept up a prolonged resistance fought as a holy war under the leadership of Abd al-Quadir (1808–83), himself the son of a holy man. Even after Abd al-Quadir was captured and deported in 1847 resistance continued until 1879. This resistance not only drew the French deeper and deeper into the interior but also induced them actively to encourage European colonization. In 1848 Algeria was designated a French territory and settlers, as French citizens, were allowed representation in the French

Major States of Africa *ca.* 1800

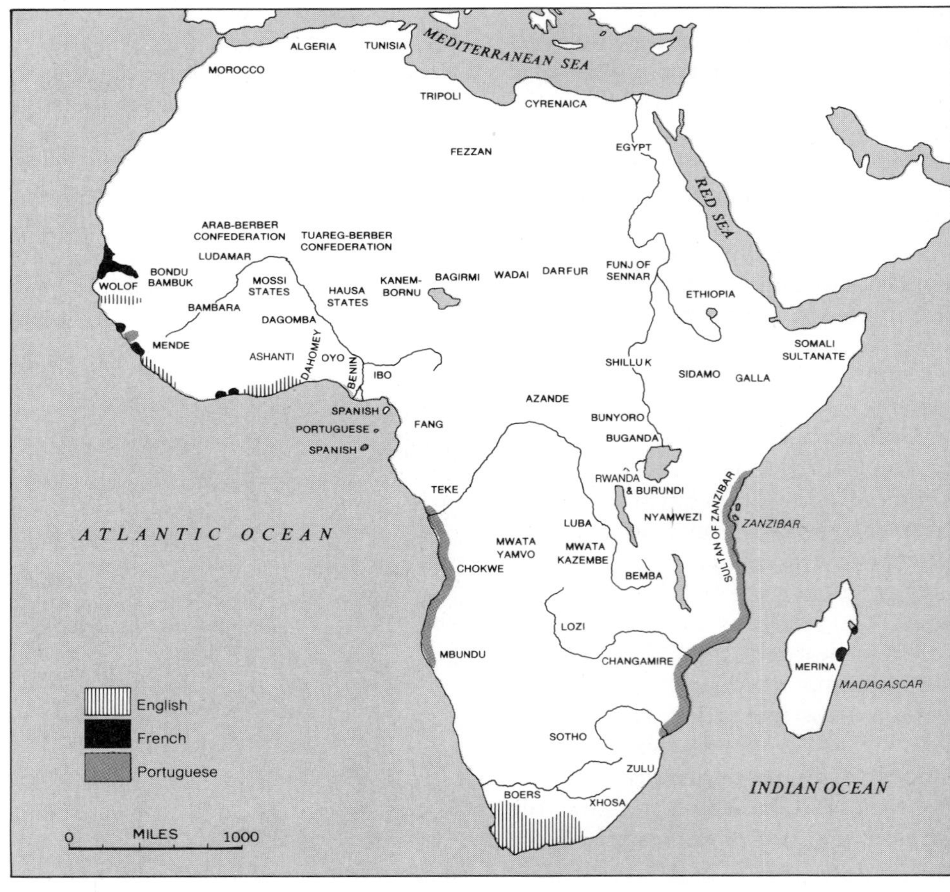

French Algiers, Algeria (*ca.* 1900).

parliament in Paris. As a result of these policies the inhabitants of Algeria were divided into a privileged Christian stratum and Muslims resentful at being economically and politically displaced by the infidels. After a rebellion in 1871, French became the only official language of Algeria and French law replaced Muslim law. Algeria was run for the benefit of the settlers who remained heavily dependent on the French market for the sale of their wine and other products. While the settlers looked economically and politically to France, the Muslims remained unintegrated in the new order—even those who chose assimilation and adopted French culture were denied the privileges enjoyed by the colonists.

Although the French also encouraged settlers to go to Tunisia after it became their protectorate in 1881, the European community there remained small. The French generally exercised control by ruling through the traditional elite, yet in the long run their powerful presence in itself undermined the authority of that elite.

West Africa

Until 1870, with the exception of French conquest of the Senegal River basin in the mid-fifties, formal European rule in West Africa was limited to coastal enclaves, although the effects of foreign trade were felt deep into the interior. Most vigorous of the African polities were those of the Muslim Fulani. In 1804, under the leadership of the deeply learned and devout Usman dan Fodio (1754–1817), the Fulani launched a religious war against the Hausa principalities and founded the Sultanate of Sokoto, an empire of 150,000 square miles divided on dan Fodio's death between his brother and

A World in Upheaval

Asante was changing. The leaders and people knew it could never be the same. The elders facing many problems, so many new and different things. Chiefs fought each other. Chiefs that the Asantehene ruled for a long time rebelled. They began to look elsewhere for a long time rebelled. They began to look elsewhere for their Lord. . . . Trading was hard in the north and in the coastal towns. Even trade in Kumase stopped for a time. How were Asante men and women to live their lives? And the whites were also coming closer to our lands. Every Asante—men, women, and children—looked to the young Agyeman Prempe to help the nation of our ancestors. But he too came to know that the whites were ambitious. They came to trade, to change our customs, to conquer, to rule. They would not allow Nana Asentehene's successes to continue. We waited. We watched. We heard the elders talk far into the night, every night. We wanted to live our lives. . . . It was a short, glorious time when Nana Prempe ruled our nation.

Domfe Kyere (b. *ca.* 1872), interview quoted by Thomas J. Lewin, *Asante Before the British: The Prempean Years, 1875–1900* (Lawrence, Kansas: The Regents Press of Kansas, 1978), p. 1.

his son. During 1810–15 another Fulani leader established the Muslim state of Masina on the upper Niger River. Dan Fodio's religious roots were in North Africa, but the background of another empire-builder, Jajii Umar Tall (1794–1864) included a pilgrimage to Mecca. In midcentury (1852–63) he embarked on a holy war and founded a theocratic state that stretched from Timbuktu to Senegal and lasted until it was absorbed by the French in 1893.

Two other vigorous states were the Ashanti Union and Dahomey. In midcentury the Ashanti Union made its power felt over most of modern Ghana but did not penetrate to the coast. Small coastal principalities cooperated with the British who repeatedly defeated the Ashanti in war. Smaller than the Ashanti and more exclusively tied to the slave trade was Dahomey. It did control its coastal area and profited as long as it could export slaves—a trade

Imperialism in Africa 1884 and 1914

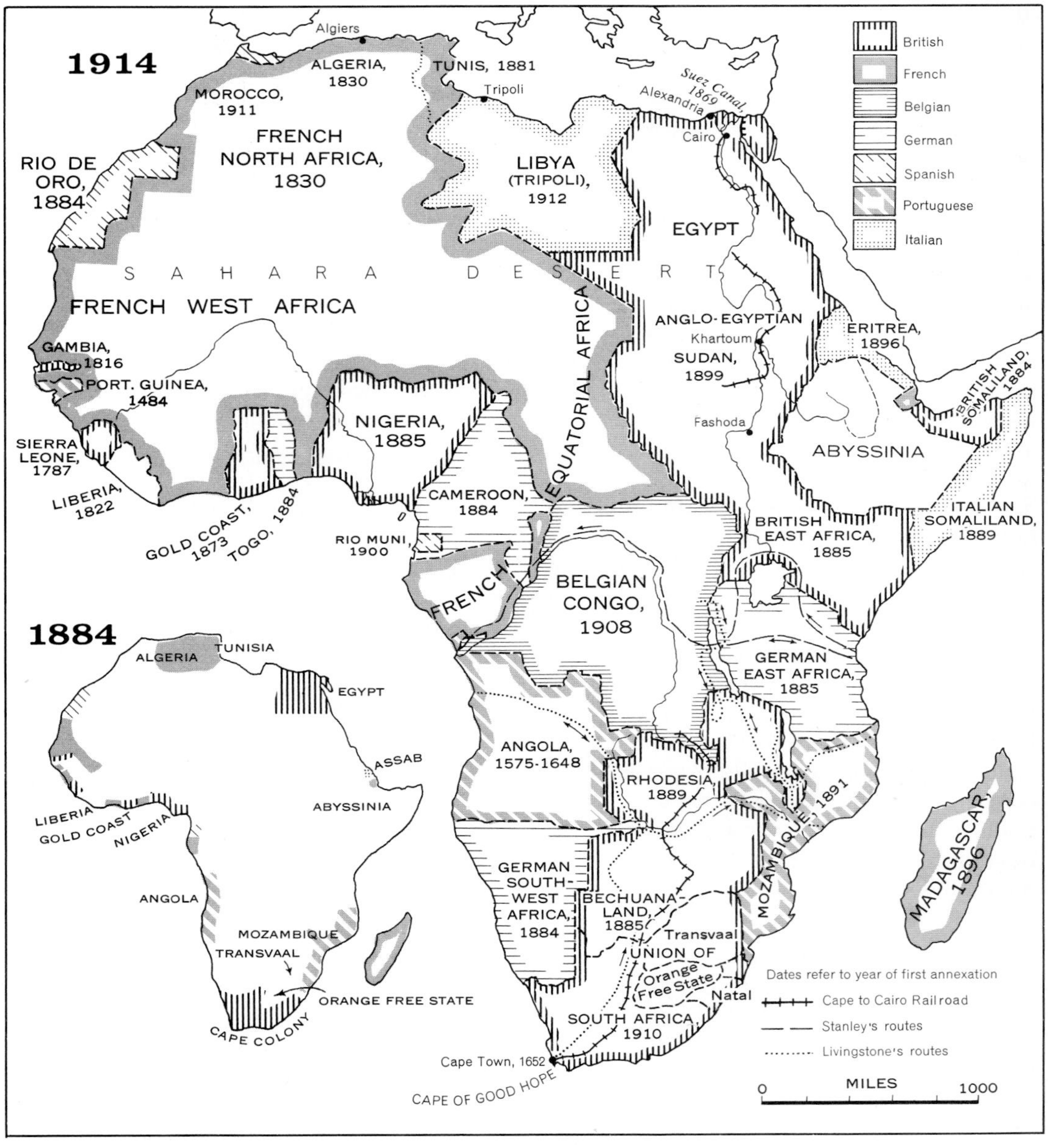

stopped less by British naval patrols than by the destruction of the market for slaves after the North won the American Civil War (1865) and the elimination of slavery in Cuba and Brazil in the 1880s. The demise of the slave trade brought economic dislocation to some states, and palm oil became West Africa's prime export.

The British objective in coming to Africa was trade but, as elsewhere, this easily led to political and military involvement. As Palmerston expressed it in 1860, "It may be true in one sense that trade ought not to be enforced by cannon balls, but on the other hand trade cannot flourish without security, and that security may often be unattainable without some degree of European control." With the backing of the British navy, the British interests in the enclaves were able to induce African rulers to accept commercial treaties, and gradually British influence penetrated into the interior until the competition for empire after 1870 spurred each colonial power to claim as much of the hinterland as it could.

In what later became the country of Nigeria, the main instrument of British penetration was the United Africa Company (later Royal Niger Company) formed in 1879 by Sir George Goldie by merging three other companies. In 1886 Goldie managed to obtain a charter giving his company a monopoly on trade, making it the de facto government. Then in the 1880s the British government and the company worked together to foil French ambitions. In 1900, the company was bought out and Nigeria became a crown colony.

First the company and then the government followed a policy of working with and ruling through native rulers such as the Fulani emirates in northern Nigeria. This policy of "indirect rule," as it was called after 1900, had the advantage of being inexpensive and accommodated humanitarian concerns at home while fitting in well with the abandonment of Anglicization as an objective of colonial policy after the Indian revolt of 1847. However, after 1900 in the African coastal cities, a new group of men—English in education and more western in outlook— began to challenge the traditional elite favored by the British.

The French possessions in West Africa were far more extensive than those of the English but less well endowed with natural resources. Economically the French invested more in developing their colonies, and politically too their policies were very different. In 1902 they organized all their holdings into a single entity under a governor-general at Dakar and built an administrative system directly linked to Paris. Local chiefs served merely as subordinate officials. French became the language of commerce and administration as well as education while native mores and traditions were regarded with disdain. However, those Africans who achieved fluency in the French language and a command of French culture could enter the administrative service and, after 1912, were eligible for French citizenship. In 1914 the first African was elected to the French National Assembly.

By 1914 the only independent state in West Africa was Liberia. It had been founded as a home for freed American slaves in 1822 and became a republic in 1847. There, as in British Sierra Leone, also founded as a home for freed slaves, the immigrants had little in common with the local peoples of the hinterland. Accordingly, their state was built along Western rather than African lines. Because of malaria and other diseases, no substantial number of Europeans settled in West Africa.

Southern Africa

In Southern Africa the interaction of native African elements and those initiated by Europeans produced conflict and instability on a vast scale as Africans, Boers, and English pursued their own ends.

The source of African instability was in Zululand. Starting in the eighteenth century land hunger among the Bantu-speaking peoples had led to conflict first among tribes, then among larger tribal groupings, and then to the creation of the powerful and aggressive Zulu kingdom. A major step in political as well as military integration was taken by Dingiswayo who created regiments composed of all young men of the same age with each regiment distinguished by its own dress and distinctive shields. By breaking up the old tribal warrior groups, he focused loyalty on himself as king. The apex of Zulu power was reached during 1818–28 under King Shaka, who also organized women into regiments. Men were forbidden to marry until they were forty, when their regiment was dissolved, and they were given wives from the corresponding female regiment. Before that any contact between the men and women was strictly prohibited. A military genius, Shaka reequipped his well-disciplined troops with short stabbing spears (replacing the throwing spear) and made skillful use of spies and surprise tactics.

The Zulu conquests set off an enormous upheaval known as the Mfecane ("havoc") with repercussions felt for thousands of miles as other peoples were stimulated to conquest, compelled to migration, or suffered grievous destruction. Some areas, as a result, were devastated by the ravages of war. Where previously people had been fairly evenly distributed over the land, now centers of population were separated from each other by a no-man's-land practically without inhabitants.

Into such lands the Boers advanced in what is known as the Great Trek in 1836. The primary motivation of the Boers' migration was land for their cattle. However, their move also had political dimensions because they resented British rule. It was alien to them and increasingly interfered with their way of life when it extended legal rights to the Hottentots (Khoi) and Coloured People (mulattoes) on whom the Boer farmers depended for labor. In 1828 when Hottentots were released from their condition of servitude and given the same rights as whites, the economy of the Boers and the legal order of their society were upset. To them the principle of racial equality was anathema, and when the Boers went on to establish the Orange Free State and the Transvaal Republic only whites were granted political participation.

The discovery first of diamonds at Kimberley and then gold in the Transvaal, the career of Cecil Rhodes, and the events leading to the Boer War have already been recounted (see pp. 792–93) and need not be repeated here. Although the British defeated the Boers in this bitter war, they had to compromise with Afrikaner (Boer) sentiments and demands. The ultimate result was that when the two former Boer states, Natal and the Cape, were combined in 1910 to form the United Federation of South Africa, nonwhites had political representation only in the Cape. Black Africans suffered from severe racial discrimination as did Indians originally

The Roots of Apartheid

The word Boer simply means "farmer" and is not synonymous with our word boor. Indeed, to the Boers generally the latter term would be quite inappropriate, for they are a sober, industrious, and most hospitable body of peasantry. Those, however, who have fled from English law on various pretexts, and have been joined by English deserters and every other variety of bad character in their distant localities, are unfortunately of a very different stamp. . . . They felt aggrieved by their supposed losses in the emancipation of their Hottenton slaves, and determined to erect themselves into a republic in which they might pursue without molestation the "proper treatment of the blacks." It is almost needless to add that the "proper treatment" has always contained in it the essential elements of slavery, namely, compulsory unpaid labor. . . .

I have myself been an eyewitness of Boers coming to a village, and, according to their usual custom, demanding twenty or thirty women to weed their gardens, and have seen these women proceed to the scene of unrequited toil, carrying their own food on their heads, their children on their backs, and instruments of labor on their shoulders. Nor have the Boers any wish to conceal the meanness of thus employing unpaid labour; on the contrary, every one of them . . . lauded his own humanity and justice in making such an equitable regulation. "We make the people work for us, in consideration of allowing them to live in our country."

David Livingstone, *Missionary Travels and Researches in South Africa* (London: 1857) as excerpted in Basil Davidson, *The African Past: Chronicles from Antiquity to Modern Times,* (New York: Grosset & Dunlap 1964), pp. 297–98.

brought to Natal to work on sugar plantations. It was in defending this Indian community that Mohandas K. (Mahatma) Gandhi (1869–1948) first developed the techniques of passive resistance he later applied so effectively in India. African opposition, after the suppression of the Zulu rebellion during 1906–07, also took political form with the foundation in 1912 of the African National Congress (called until 1935 the South African Native Congress).

Central and East Africa

In the nineteenth century, as earlier, the diversity of African societies in their patterns of interaction between people and environment, their social structures and mores, and their values and beliefs defy generalization. So far in our discussion of Africa it has been necessary to pass over in silence entire people and areas, including those under Portuguese rule in Angola and Mozambique, which expanded into the interior. The Portuguese dream of ruling from coast to coast was not realized, but Portuguese holdings were the third largest in Africa, exceeded only by those of Britain and France. South of Portuguese Angola, Germany, a latecomer, established German Southwest Africa (Namibia). Similar diversity in the vast regions not yet discussed prohibits detailed treatment. We can do no more than mention in passing the ancient Christian kingdom of Ethiopia, which managed to retain its independence despite the ambitions of Italian builders and note all too briefly that in the Congo, the very heartland of Africa, tribal peoples suffered cruel oppression under King Leopold of Belgium.

One of the more remarkable states of East Africa was the commercial empire constructed on the island of Zanzibar by the Arab Sultan Seyyid Said (r. 1806–56) based primarily on the lucrative trade in slaves and ivory. This trade prompted Arab slavers to penetrate deep into the African interior with devastating results for the local inhabitants. A clever diplomat, Said entered into diplomatic relations with western powers, establishing close relations particularly with Great Britain. An equally astute businessman, he turned Zanzibar into a major center for growing cloves (introduced from the Moluccas) and also had the foresight to encourage the growth of an Indian commercial community. However, after his death the state declined, and it suffered a severe blow in 1873 when the sultan was forced by the British to outlaw slavery. A Christian cathedral was

Zulu warriors (*ca.* 1900). The Zulus, militarily superior to their neighboring African tribes, were able to defeat British troops armed with rifles and artillery on several occasions until their final defeat in 1879.

Motives for Empire

Since history teaches that colonies are useful, that they play a great part in that which makes up the power and prosperity of states, let us strive to get one in our turn. Before pronouncing in favour of this or that system let us see where there are unoccupied lands . . . where are to be found peoples to civilize, to lead to progress in every sense, meanwhile assuring ourselves new revenues, to our middle classes the employment which they seek, to our army a little activity, and to Belgium as a whole the opportunity to prove to the world that it also is an imperial people capable of dominating and enlightening others.

From George Martelli, *Leopold to Lumumba: A History of the Belgian Congo, 1877–1960* (London: Chapman & Hall, 1962), p. 16 citing R.S. *Fondation de L'Etat Independent du Congo* (Brussels, 1933), p. 30.

built on the former site of Zanzibar's great slave market.

One approach to the history of this as of other parts of Africa is in terms of European expansionism. The explorers gradually enabled European geographers to fill in the blank spaces on their maps. They were a diverse cast of characters. David Livingstone (1813–73), a Christian missionary and a convinced apostle of the benefits of empire as an agency for peace and progress, was an implacable enemy of the East African slave trade. Henry M. Stanley (1841–1904), originally sent out by a New York newspaper to find Livingstone, subsequently led other expeditions that opened up the Congo for King Leopold.

The main theme of this period is the creation of European colonies, frequently by chartered companies. Heading one such company, Cecil Rhodes cheated King Lobengula of the Matabele out of his land and thereby laid the foundations for the British colony that bore his name. Another important British company was the East African Company, a counterpart to Goldie's West African Company although weaker because there was no East African equivalent of the Nigerian palm oil to make trade profitable in the postslavery period. For the Germans the most notable empire builder was Carl Peters (1856–1918), founder of German East Africa. The outcome of the process of European encroachment was the carving up of Africa into colonial territories (also see pp. 791–93).

From an African point of view one fact is noteworthy: Assignment of territories and the drawing up of boundaries took place in Europe and, although influenced by the situation in Africa, largely reflected the imperatives of European power politics. This resulted in superimposing boundaries on Africa that did not correspond to local realities and creating administrative structures not anchored in local traditions. Yet these artificial creations, which often brought under one roof people of very different cultures, outlasted the empires that had brought them into being.

Within the colonies the experience of the African people varied widely. Most notorious was King Leopold's Congo with its forced deliveries of rubber and the taking of hostages to ensure full payment. Even within a single empire's territory conditions could be very different: the Francophilia of West Africa contrasted greatly to the hatred for France found in France's equatorial colonies. Even within the same colony different peoples had very different experiences with colonial rule.

In understanding the experience and history of those subjected to colonization, we should distinguish between areas where few whites settled and those where their number was substantial. In areas like Algeria and South Africa, Southern Rhodesia, and Kenya the settlers tended to pursue their own interests regardless of what the wishes of the home government might be, and these interests usually conflicted with those of the native people. Frequently, as in Southern Rhodesia, the very idea of private ownership of land was alien to people who consid-

An East African Chief Refuses to Submit

This letter from Chief Macemba of the Yao people in southern Tanganyika is in reply to Hermann von Wissering, commander of the German forces in 1890.

I have listened to your words but can find no reason why I should obey you—I would rather die first. I have no relations with you and cannot bring it to my mind that you have given me so much as a *pesa* [fraction of a rupee] or the quarter of a *pesa* or a needle or a thread. I look for some reasons why I should obey you and find not the smallest. If it should be friendship that you desire, then I am ready for it, today and always; but to be your subject, that I cannot be. . . . If it should be war you desire, then I am ready, but never to be your subject. . . . I do not fall at your feet, for you are God's creature just as I am. . . . I am sultan here in my land. You are sultan there in yours. Yet listen, I do not say to you that you should obey me, for I know that you are a free man. . . . As for me, I will not come to you, and if you are strong enough, then come and fetch me.

From Basil Davidson, *The African Past: Chronicles from Antiquity to Modern Times,* (New York: Grosset & Dunlap 1964), pp. 357–58.

ered land to be the property of the tribe; even a chief could not give it away. In both Rhodesia and Kenya, as elsewhere, the people were forced to supply cheap labor for the European farmers who resolutely barred Africans from political participation. When the pressure of grievances built up to unbearable levels, rebellions erupted only to be suppressed by superior European arms.

The history of colonial Uganda where settlers were excluded provides a strong contrast. The oldest and most cohesive state in all of East and Central Africa was Buganda on the northwest shore of Lake Victoria. Ruled by its Kabaka with an elaborate system of chiefs, it had gained strength over the centuries until it predominated its neighbors. The British entered on the invitation of a group of Christian chiefs anxious for support against their enemies, and the association between the British and the Christian Buganda aristocracy continued and was extended throughout Uganda so that British administrators were usually accompanied by Buganda assistants. For the Buganda aristocrats the arrangement entailed a loss of their former independence, but they enjoyed political power within their kingdom, wealth based on land ownership, and prestige as cultural leaders. There were, of course, tensions latent in the relationship felt by the Africans, but hardly by the British. However, during the period we are concerned with in this chapter the arrangement remained solid.

Elsewhere too the imperial powers seemed deeply, if not permanently, entrenched. To be sure, during the decade prior to the First World War rebellions broke out in German Southwest Africa, in Natal (the Zulu rebellion), in northwest Nigeria, in Kenya, and in German Tanganyika, and there was political resistance in South Africa and Egypt. At home, too, imperialism was not without its critics. But the rebellions were examples of traditional resistance of a kind that was doomed. The future still seemed to belong to the nations of Europe, who, for better or worse and on their own terms, had drawn so many of the world's people into the current of world history.

Suggestions for Further Reading

Stanley Wolpert, *A New History of India* (2nd ed. 1982), is particularly strong on the modern period and his *Tilak and Gokhale: Revolution and Reform in the Making of Modern India* (1962), is also recommended along with Barbara D. Metcalf, *Islamic Revival in British India: Deoband, 1860–1900* (1982). For the British Empire as a whole see R. Hyam, *Britain's Imperial Century, 1815–1914* (1976), and Bernard Porter, *The Lion's Share: A Short History of British Imperialism 1850–1970* (1975).

Two pertinent books which analyze history from a global perspective are *Europe and the People without History* (1982) by the anthropologist Eric R. Wolf, and *Cross Cultural Trade and World History* (1984) by Philip D. Curtin, a noted historian of Africa.

Francis Robinson, *Atlas of the Islamic World since 1500* (1982), is a valuable source for bibliographic as well as other information on all the Muslim regions. P. J. M. McEwan, *Nineteenth Century Africa* (1968), offers a valuable selection of interpretive readings while Roland Oliver and J. D. Fage, *A Short History of Africa* (1962), is a useful survey.

	1815				1870	
SOUTHWEST ASIA AND AFRICA	**1818–28** King Shaka, apex of Zulu kingdom	**1836** Boers' Great Trek begins		**1860** French expansion in West Africa **1869** Suez Canal opens		
EUROPE	**1815** Congress of Vienna **1815–83** Karl Marx **1825** Decembrist Revolt, Russia **1825** First commercial railroad	**1829** Treaty of Adrianople **1830** France's "July Monarchy" **1832** Britain's Great Reform Bill **1848** *Communist Manifesto*	**1848–49** Europe in Revolt **1848–61** Unification of Italy **1848–70** Napolean III **1851** Crystal Palace Exhibition, London	**1859** Darwin, *Origin of Species* **1854–56** Crimean War **1861–71** Unification of Germany **1867** Austro-Hungarian *Ausgleich*	**1870–71** Franco-Prussian War **1876** First internal combustion engine **1878** Congress of Berlin	**1882** Triple Alliance **1894** Russo-French Alliance
SOUTH AND SOUTHEAST ASIA	**1819** British found Singapore		**1857–58** Indian Mutiny **1859** French seize Saigon			
EAST ASIA	**1825–30** Java War **1839–42** Opium War		**1850–64** Taiping Rebellion **1854** Perry opens US trade with Japan **1868** Meiji Restoration, Japan			**1893–1976** Mao Zedong **1894–95** Sino-Japanese War
THE AMERICAS AND PACIFIC	**1823** Monroe Doctrine	**1835–40** Alexis de Tocqueville, *Democracy in America* **1840** Britain annexes New Zealand **1846–48** Mexican War	**1849** Gold discovered in California	**1861–65** American Civil War **1867** Russia sells Alaska to US **1867** British North America Act	**1869** Opening of Transcontinental railroad	

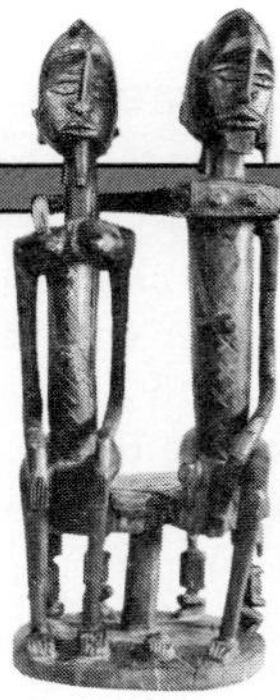

Wood sculpture, Dogon tribe, Mali, West Africa.

Eiffel Tower Paris, 1889.

***Empire State Express* No. 999, ca. 1890.**

Commodore Matthew Perry, a Japanese view, 1853.

British suffragette, *ca.* 1910.

Private Edwin Francis Jennison, Confederate Army.

1914	
1886 Gold discovered in Southern Africa **1889** Rhodesia colonized **1899–1902** Boer War **1910** Union of South Africa formed	
1894–1905 Dreyfus Affair **1905** Russian Revolution begins **1905** Einstein's Theory of Relativity **1907** Triple Entente **1912–13** Balkan Wars	
1885 Indian National Congress founded **1906** Muslim League founded	
1900 Boxer Rebellion **1904–05** Russo-Japanese War **1911** Chinese Revolution **1912–49** Chinese Republic	
1889 First Pan-American Conference **1898** Spanish-American War **1910** Mexican Revolution begins	**1914** Panama Canal opens

The Prince of Wales in Bangalore, India, *ca.* 1900.

Gold prospector, California, *ca.* 1850.

39 East and Southeast Asia in the Nineteenth Century

Some of the processes operating in the areas discussed in the last chapter were also at work in the vast regions of Asia not yet treated. Everywhere the internal dynamics of country and region were affected by the challenge of western arms and civilization. However, the interplay of the internal and external forces varied enormously. Of the three regions to be considered in the present chapter, Southeast Asia experienced full-scale colonization; Thailand alone retained its independence. For China the nineteenth century brought trials and traumas from which it did not recover until the middle of the twentieth century, yet it never lost its formal sovereignty. Japan, in sharp contrast, had by the end of this period so transformed itself as to become an imperial power itself rather than a target for the imperialist ambitions of others.

SOUTHEAST ASIA

Although the European presence in Southeast Asia goes back to the beginning of European expansion, it remained relatively confined and localized until the nineteenth century when it became more intensive as well as extensive. As in Africa, patterns of interaction between the colonial power and local communities varied even within the same empire.

The British in Burma and the Malay Peninsula

In the second half of the eighteenth century a new and vigorous dynasty, the Konbaung, came to power and imposed a degree of unity on Burma's diverse peoples. But it never developed an adequate policy for dealing with the British in neighboring India. The British, in accord with their European concepts of sovereignty, held the Burmese responsible for raids conducted by peoples in the frontier area (Assam, Manipur, Arakan) over whom the Burmese exercised only the loosest jurisdiction. Burmese failure to conform to British notions of proper trade and diplomatic relations added to the friction. Tensions led to war in 1824 – 26 initiated by a Burmese invasion of Bengal. The resulting peace in which Burma lost Arakan and Tenasseris (two coastal provinces) did not resolve the underlying issues. A second war in 1852 and a third war in 1885 led to the complete annexation of Burma and its incorporation into Britain's Indian empire in 1886, even though Burma had never been a part of India. One result of this arrangement was an accelerating influx of Indians into Burma. Some of the Indians were laborers, others moneylenders who extended rural credit. Economically the impact was particularly strong on Lower Burma where rice production increased enormously. From 1855 to 1881 alone there was a ninefold increase, and Burma became an important rice exporter. Although some Burmese landowners profited, Indians, including Indian workers, played an increasingly important role.

On the Malay Peninsula there had been a European presence ever since the Portuguese first established themselves in Malacca, but it hardly influenced the interior. This changed during the nineteenth century as British economic influence radiated from the three British settlements at Penang (1786), Singapore (1819), and Malacca (ceded to Britain in 1824). With the development of tin mining after 1850 and rubber cultivation late in the century, inland areas were drawn into the international economic network. This was accompanied by major ethnic change as Chinese and, to a lesser extent, Indians and Sri Lankans were found willing and able to perform tasks that Malays were either unwilling or unpre-

Singapore. These warehouses on the waterfront attest to the importance of the city as a British trading center (late nineteenth century).

pared to take on. Thus the Chinese supplied the labor for the tin mines and became an important element in the population of the peninsula. Even more dramatic was the transformation of Singapore from an insignificant fishing village into a major trade center with a clear Chinese majority by mid-century. Reflecting historical and functional differences, the three Straits Settlements were ruled as a crown colony whereas elsewhere local sultans continued to preside over their states but were required to accept a British Resident "whose advice must be asked and acted upon on all questions other than those touching Malay religion and customs." It was an arrangement not much different from that which prevailed in the Indian princely states and later on in Egypt and the emirates on the Persian Gulf.

The French Empire in Southeast Asia

In Vietnam the determination to maintain political independence from neighboring China had long gone hand in hand with admiration for Chinese culture and institutions. Thus the Nguyen dynasty (1802–1945) from its capital at Hue in central Vietnam ruled the country through a bureaucracy modeled on that of China and participated in the Chinese tributary system.

Vietnam's location in a cultural frontier area made for a rich and complex culture. A monument to the continued vitality of that culture as well as its debt to China was *The Tale of Thiu* by Nguyen Du (1765–1820), a much loved lengthy narrative poem which became a Vietnamese classic. One result, however, of the Chinese orientation of so much of Vietnamese high culture was that the social and cultural gap between village and bureaucracy was greater in Vietnam than in China. Another was the difficulty the Vietnamese state experienced in its efforts to incorporate the south, which had been gradually taken over from the Cambodians from roughly 1650 to 1750. Under the Nguyen dynasty this remained an area of large landlords and impoverished peasants, an area which also suffered from educational backwardness so that very few southerners were able to succeed in Vietnam's Chinese-style civil-service examination system.

French missionaries and soldiers early on showed an interest in Vietnam. Nearly four hundred Frenchmen served the Nguyen dynasty's founder and first emperor, Gia-long (r. 1801–20). After mid-century French interest became more intense. In 1859 France seized Saigon and by 1867 controlled all the southern provinces which it organized into the colony of Cochin China (1867). During 1862–63 the French also established a protectorate over Cambodia. The conflict between French ambitions to control central and north Vietnam, and Hue's traditional relationship to Beijing (Peking) led to war between France and China in 1884–85. In the peace agreement that followed, China was forced to abandon claims of suzerainty over Vietnam, leaving the French free to establish a protectorate over central and north Vietnam. The formation of French Indo-China was completed in the 1890s when France combined a number of petty states to form the new state of Laos, ruled indirectly as a protectorate.

The Tale of Kieu (Opening Stanza)

A hundred years—in this life span on earth
talent and destiny are apt to feud.
You must go through a play of ebb and flow*
and watch such things as make you sick at heart.
Is it so strange that losses balance gains?
Blue Heaven's wont to strike a rose from spite.

---

* A play of ebb and flow—"an event [in which] the sea [becomes] mulberry [fields]." A passage in the Chinese collection entitled *Stories of Gods and Fairies (Shen Hsien Chuan)* reads, "Every thirty years, the vast sea turns into mulberry fields and mulberry fields turn into the vast sea." Hence, the Vietnamese phrase "sea and mulberry" [*be-dau*] refers to some upheaval or profound change either in nature or in the affairs of men.

From Nguyen Du, *The Tale of Kieu* trans. by Huynh Sanh Thong (New Haven, Conn.: Yale Univ. Press, 1983), p. 3 and note p. 169.

Municipal theater and stand for rickshaws, Saigon, French Chochin China (*ca.* 1910).

ited as did Chinese businessmen engaged in the rice trade.

Thailand

As France and Britain each tried to expand its Southeast Asian empire, their ambitions clashed, thus providing an opportunity for Thailand to maintain its independence as a buffer state. It accomplished this first under the leadership of King Mongkut (r. 1851–68), a remarkable man deeply learned in Pali and the Buddhist scriptures but also a student of Latin, English, mathematics, and astronomy. His work was continued by his son King Chulalonkorn (r. 1868–1910), an enthusiastic modernizer. Faced with superior European might, the monarchs yielded when necessary. They accepted treaties granting the British and others extraterritoriality and a low fixed tariff. Thailand also had to cede territory to the French in Cambodia in the 1890s and in 1909 it lost four vassal states to the British in Malaya. At the same time, both rulers, assisted by capable ministers and open to foreign advice, restructured the government to make it more efficient, built canals, roads, and shipyards, fostered modern education, and generally strengthened the state without, however, effecting a transformation of society. In Thailand, as in Burma and Vietnam, new lands were brought under rice cultivation, but in this case the process was controlled by a native government with the result that ownership remained in the hands of the peasantry and the formation of large landlord holdings was avoided.

In the protectorates the French ruled as much as possible through existing institutions. Thus they maintained the Nguyen emperor in Hue. Even the old examination system was continued until 1919, thus outlasting its Chinese prototype. However, the evident dependency of the emperor on the French precluded the throne from becoming a symbol around which the Vietnamese could rally. In contrast, French intervention in Cambodia prolonged the life of a state in decline, a state that had steadily lost territory to its stronger neighbors, Vietnam and Thailand. Here the French helped to sustain rather than undermine the royal house.

Economically the most dramatic transformation took place in the south where a landscape of swamps and irregular waterways was transformed into a rich rice producing and exporting area. The beneficiaries of this development, however, were neither the Vietnamese peasants nor, contrary to their hopes, the French. Instead, a limited number of Vietnamese landlords prof-

The Indonesian Archipelago

By 1800 the Dutch had been in Batavia (Jakarta) for nearly two centuries and had developed commercial and political relations with much of Java, yet their influence had remained superficial as had their knowledge of Javanese civilization. They did not even know of the existence of that greatest of all Javanese monuments: Borobudur (see p. 211). Thus a major theme in

Imperialism in Southeast Asia Nineteenth Century

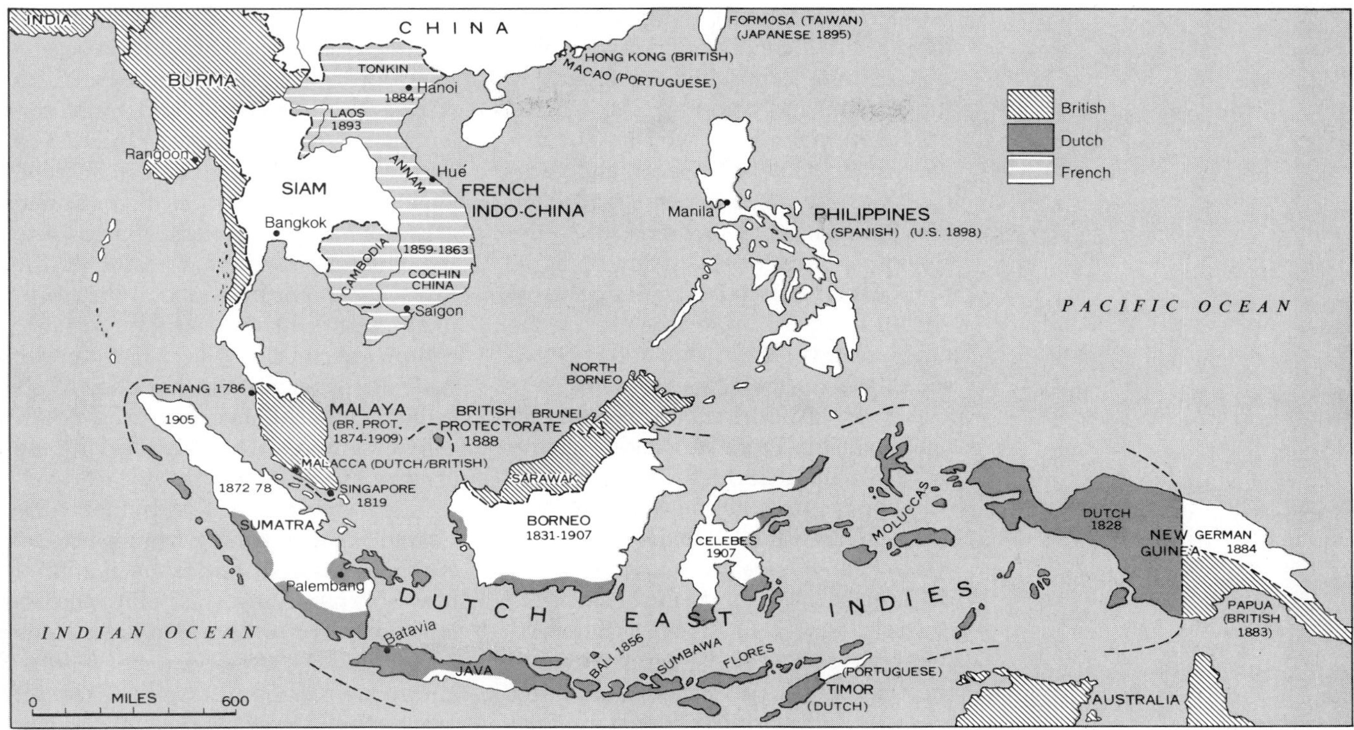

the modern history of the area is the process by which Dutch rule was extended and reached further down into society.

A turning point was the Java War (1825–30), the last attempt by the Javanese aristocracy to stem the tide of colonialism. Led by Pengerab Dipanagara (1785–1855), a prince and mystic drawing primarily on Javanese messianism but also on Islam, the Javanese were defeated. The end result was completion of the process by which once independent polities were reduced to the role of Dutch puppets while the old aristocracy increasingly became agents for the Dutch.

The Dutch empire on Java and the other islands was unusual among European colonies in directly benefiting the finances of the home government. Indeed, the income from Java became "the lifebelt on which the Netherlands remained afloat," saved from drowning in the sea of financial troubles after the costly and unsuccessful war against Belgian independence. What made the colony so profitable for Holland was the "Culture System" *(cultuurstelsel)* under which Javanese were forced to deliver to the colonial government such export crops as coffee, sugar, and indigo. Not exploitive in original intent, it was, nevertheless, oppressive in practice and weighed heavily on cultivators who had to divert land and labor from growing food crops. The system was particularly pernicious in areas where sugar production supplanted rice, producing spreading famines in the 1840s.

Despite subsequent reforms, the Javanese peasantry continued to lose ground during the period of economic liberalism, 1870–1900, as Dutch planters benefited while the peasants' standard of living declined. Population growth was a major problem because it exceeded gains in production. By 1900 the population of Java and nearby Madura was over 28 million, in contrast to a maximum estimate of 3 million prior to 1800. Even though the peasantry worked their land more intensively, production per area increased but per capita production remained constant. Meanwhile, enterprising Chinese, who had earlier profited from tax-farming, prospered during the liberal period by serving as commercial middlemen, operating industries, and running the official opium monopoly as well as government-controlled pawnshops and gambling dens. In 1901 the Dutch adopted the "Ethical Policy" epitomized in the slogan, "Education, Irrigation, Emigration." Emigration referred to a policy of encouraging Javanese to settle in the other islands, but it did not begin to solve Java's population problem.

Next to Java, the most important island was Sumatra. The London Treaty of 1824 delimited the British sphere of influence to include the Malay Peninsula and left Sumatra to the Dutch, but it took many years for them to force all of Sumatra into submission because for centuries centers of Islam on the island had provided a focus for resistance to the Europeans. Furthermore, Sumatra was also influenced by developments in the Islamic heartland. Thus leadership in the anti-Dutch Padri wars of the 1820s and 1830s was provided by three pilgrims who returned from Mecca where they had come under Wahhabi influence. Later, from 1872 to around 1908 the Dutch fought against Aceh, famed for its long history of Muslim learning and devotion. Altogether, the thousands of Indonesian pilgrims to Mecca helped to sustain Islam as a vigorous religion.

The Philippines

The Spanish presence in the Philippines goes back to the days of their imperial splendor in the sixteenth century. As elsewhere in the Spanish Empire, church and state went hand in hand spreading their influence among the population—only in the Muslim South was there prolonged, determined, and organized resistance. Like the Spanish colonies in the Americas and unlike any other Southeast Asian region, the Philippines came to have a Christian majority. When Filipinos and people of mixed blood (Spanish-Filippino or Chinese-Filippino), despite their Spanish education and Catholic faith, were denied equality with Spaniards, resentment found expression in the moderate nationalism of Jose Rizal (1861–96) and, more violently, in a nationalist revolution. The nationalist revolution began in 1896 against the Spanish and continued after the Philippines had been ceded to the United States as a result of the Spanish-American War of 1896. Suppression of this revolution was not completed until 1902. Then, under American rule, an official policy of ultimate independence gave the politically elite hope, while also serving the group's economic interests.

The transfer of the Philippines to the United States resulting from a war set off by events in distant Cuba illustrates how Southeast Asia was being increasingly drawn into world politics. One reason for the American decision to annex the Philippines was to preempt other powers (particularly Germany or Japan) from moving in at a time when it seemed that China was on the verge of disintegration. Because of China's sheer size, the prevalence of commercial ties with China, and the presence of communities of Chinese throughout Southeast Asia, what happened in China could not but affect the rest of Southeast and East Asia.

CHINA: THE EROSION OF THE OLD ORDER

Scholars date the beginning of modern Chinese history to the Opium War (1839–42), which radically changed China's relationship to the rest of the world. China's defeat by Britain brought to an end the Canton System under which trade was confined to that one port and all contact, political as well as economic, had to be channeled through a small number of Chinese monopoly merchants. British efforts to establish what they considered normal diplomatic relations were rejected as absurd by the Qing (Ch'ing) court which expected all foreign peoples to accede to the tributary system (see box p. 546). Both the Chinese and the English were supremely self-confident and proud of their civilizations. Both were narrowly culture-bound as they insisted that theirs was the only civilized way.

The Opium War

The British came to China to trade. Their main import from China was tea, which came to be considered a necessity for English life. Not only did the East India Company depend on the income from the tea trade, the British government itself derived about a tenth of its entire revenue from the tax on Chinese tea. The tea dumped from East India Company ships in the Boston Tea Party of 1773 came from China. The British problem was how to pay for the tea, because there was no market in China for European goods. Until 1823 the largest commodity imported into China was cotton, but this was never enough to balance the trade. That was accomplished by opium. Grown in India under East India Company auspices and shipped to China in the boats of private traders so that the Company could claim that it was not involved, the opium was distributed in China by a network of illegal wholesalers and retailers with the connivance of dishonest officials. The Chinese market for opium developed to the point that the balance of trade was reversed. During the 1820s and 1830s silver to pay for opium imports seems to have left China in large quantities. This, in turn, helped cause a decline in the exchange rate between copper coinage and silver, which upset the basis of the Chinese monetary system. Thus the opium trade became a fiscal as well as a public health problem for the Chinese government. When the government finally enacted a policy of strict suppression, it precipitated the war.

The war ended in China's defeat. The Treaty of Nanking (1842) set the pattern of China's relations with the West for the next century and also supplied the model for similar treaties imposed on Japan. The Canton system was abolished. Five ports—Guangzhou (Canton), Xiamen (Amoy), Fuzhou (Foochow), Ningbo (Ningpo), and Shanghai—were opened to western trade. Britain received the right to appoint consuls to these cities and to communicate with the Chinese government on a basis of equality. The Chinese were forced to pay an indemnity and to accept a low tariff on imports. The only territory that changed hands was Hong Kong Island, at the time the site of a tiny fishing village but well located with an excellent harbor. A supplementary treaty provided for two further concessions that were to become standard: Extraterritoriality gave British subjects the right to be tried according to British law in British consular courts. Most-favored-nation treatment obliged China to grant to Britain any rights China conceded in the future to any other power. Treaties China signed with the United States and France in 1844 also contained this provision.

The Treaty of Nanking did not mention opium, which was legalized in the next round of treaty settlements, 1868–70. The trade peaked in 1878 after which it declined as Chinese opium production increased. The 1868–70 documents, signed after a

Engraving of the East India Company's ships destroying the Chinese War Junks in Anson's Bay during the Opium War (1841).

China in Rebellion
Mid-Nineteenth Century

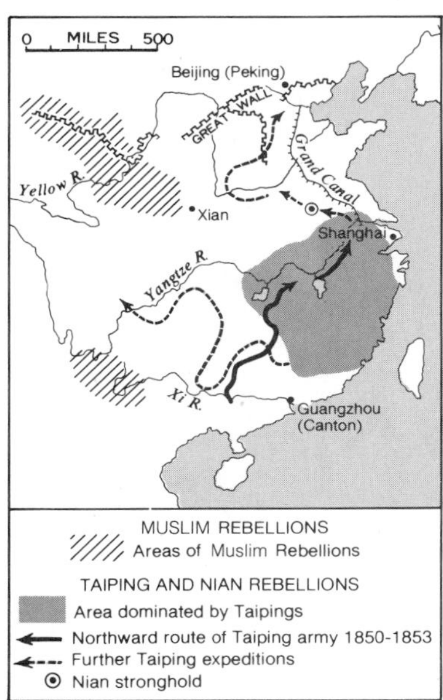

second war, also provided for the opening of eleven new ports, permitted foreign envoys to live in the Chinese capital, and granted foreigners the right to travel in the interior. Missionaries now were also granted the right to buy land and buildings anywhere in China. The Russians, who had acted as peacemakers, received the entire area north of the Amur River as well as lands east of the Ussuri River, which were incorporated into the Russian Empire as the Amur and Maritime Province.

Rebellion and Reform

The encroachment of the foreign powers was only one of the threats facing the Qing dynasty. An even greater danger to the regime developed internally as the government proved unable to deal with long-term problems that would have taxed even an honest and effective government. Foremost were the problems created by population pressures. By 1850 the population of China had risen to about 430 million without any comparable increase in productivity or resources. As ever, the poor suffered most, and they were legion, for the uneven distribution of land left many landless, destitute, and in despair. The situation was made worse by government neglect of public works. Thus, in 1852, a massive shift of the Yellow River, due to silting, spread flood and devastation over a wide area.

Famine, poverty, and corruption gave rise to banditry and armed uprisings as had so often happened in the past. Of the numerous rebellions, the most formidable was that of the Taipings (1850–64), who came close to destroying the Qing in a civil war. It has been estimated that more than 20 million people lost their lives during this war. The ideology of this rebellion was a combination of Old Testament Christianity and native Chinese utopianism propounded by Hong Xiuquan (Hung Hsiu-ch'üan, 1814–64), a religious visionary who was convinced that he was Jesus' younger brother with a divine mission to save humanity and exterminate the Manchu devils. Along with an egalitarian economic program, Hong and his followers stressed a strict, even puritanical, morality. Opium, tobacco, gambling, alcohol, prostitution, sexual misconduct, and foot binding were all strictly prohibited. Women were put on an equal basis with men in theory and, to a remarkable extent, also in practice.

Millenarian religious beliefs, utopian egalitarianism, moral righteousness, and hatred of the Manchus proved a potent combination when fused into a program of organized armed resistance. Starting from their base in Kuangxi (Kwangsi) province, the Taiping forces made rapid progress picking up strength as they went; it has been estimated they were over one million strong by the time they took Nanjing (Nanking) in 1853. There they paused to consolidate. Although expeditions were sent out to the west and north, the center of the rebellion remained in Nanjing, but instead of building unity and strength, the Taipings were plagued by divisiveness and failures of leadership. The dispar-

A camel caravan passing through one of the city gates in Beijing (*ca.* 1900).

ity between their promises and their performance became increasingly apparent. Furthermore, they alienated those who identified with the Confucian way of life and saw the Taiping program as subversive to the traditional social order. Not only did the Taipings fail to gain support of the gentry, but they antagonized this key element in Chinese society. To the literati, rule by "civilized" Manchus was preferable to rule by "barbarized" Chinese.

The dynasty was saved not by its traditional hereditary military forces, which had grown practically useless, nor by fresh Manchu and Mongol troops, but by newly formed provincial armies organized and led by gentry officers and officials. Most important was the army organized in Hunan by Zeng Guofan (Tseng Kuo-fan, 1811–72), a dedicated Confucian and reformer. Well led and highly motivated, honestly administered and true to its purpose, his army proved superior to the Taiping forces. Foreign support was also a contributory factor in the dynasty's victory.

The suppression of the Taipings and other rebels was only one aspect of a general effort to revitalize the dynasty, known as the Tongzhi (T'ung-chih) Restoration (1862–74). To cope with the dislocations wrought by war, old remedies were applied: Relief projects were instituted, public works projects initiated, land reclaimed and water controlled, granaries set up, expenses cut, and taxes reduced in the ravaged lower Yangtze Valley. Also dear to the hearts of its Confucian sponsors was a strengthening of scholarship by reprinting old texts, founding new academies, opening libraries, and the like. Examination system reform was similarly high on the list of priorities as was elimination of corruption from the bureaucracy. However, nothing effective was done about the solidly entrenched and notoriously corrupt subbureaucracy of clerks and other underlings.

The dynasty also could not reverse a shift of power from the center to the provinces where governors-general were able to pursue their own policies. Nor could the reformers control the central government itself after the court came under the domination of Empress Dowager Ci Xi (Tz'u Hsi, 1835–1908), mother of the Tongzhi emperor and aunt of his successor. An expert at political infighting and manipulation, her prime aim was to remain in power. Corruption again became a problem.

A Chinese engraving showing the attack on Nanjing, the Taiping celestial city (1864).

The Empress Dowager did not oppose the program of selective modernization initiated by the Tongzhi statesmen to deal with the challenge of the West, but neither did she commit herself to it. Its first phase (1862–74) was primarily a military program of building arsenals, a dockyard, and schools for teaching largely subjects with military applications. Its middle phase (1872–85) was widened to include projects in transportation, communication, and mining. Finally from 1885 to 1894 it was further broadened to include light industry. The fundamental idea behind this effort at self-strengthening was that Chinese learning would remain the heart of Chinese civilization, while western learning would have a subordinate supporting and technical role, in other words, western means for Chinese ends. The basic pattern of Chinese civilization was to remain sacrosanct, but protected by western techniques.

Empress Dowager Ci Xi, who resisted foreign encroachment by encouraging the abortive Boxer Rebellion (*ca.* 1900).

China in the Nineteenth Century

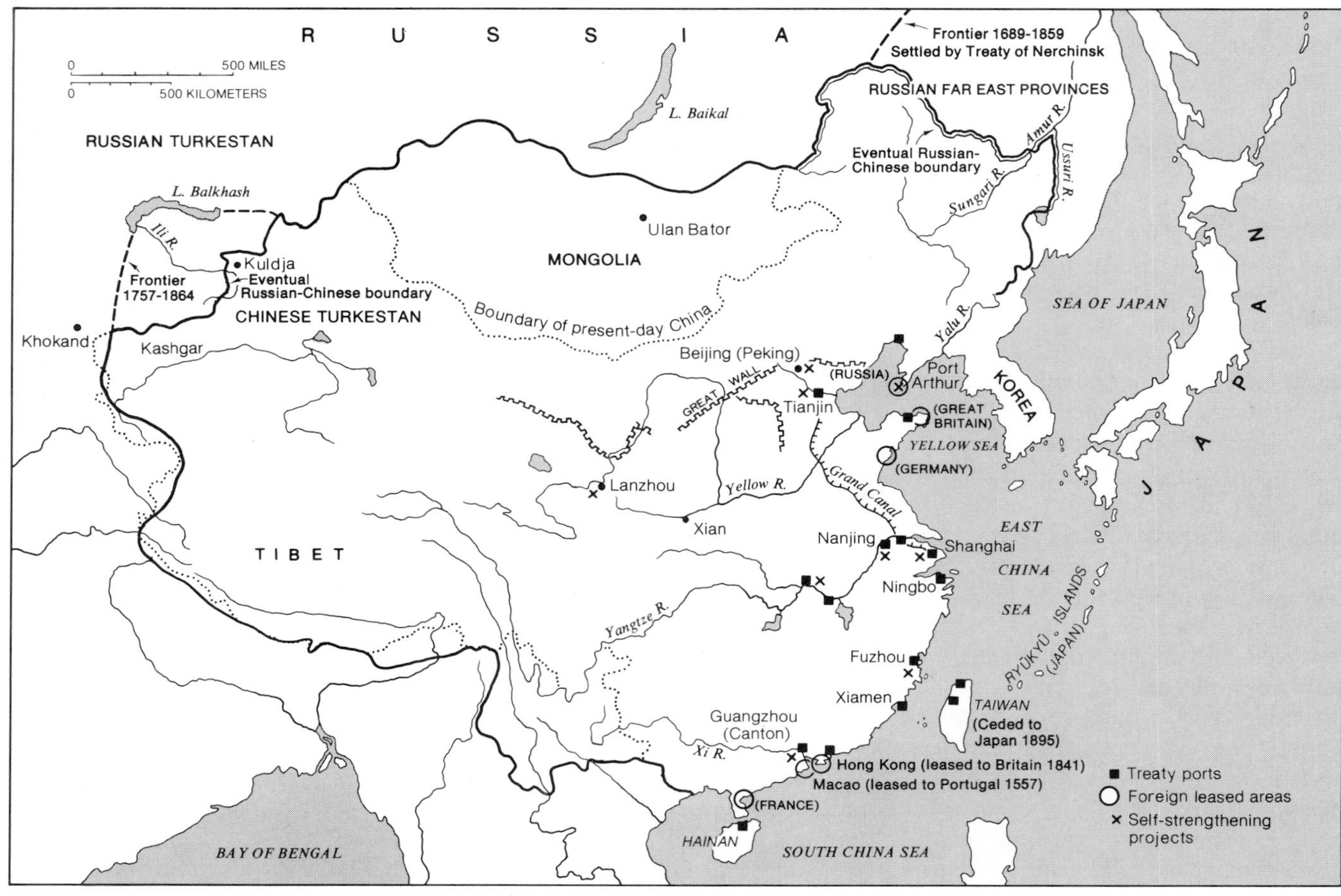

Conservative opponents of self-strengthening feared that Chinese civilization would be contaminated by borrowing from the West, that the ends would be compromised by the means. They held that China could not merely borrow the techniques of the West without becoming entangled in manifestations of western culture. Furthermore, the success of the Tongzhi Restoration appeared to demonstrate that the old means still worked.

Although the self-strengthening program did not lack in positive results, it failed to produce a new leadership both Confucian in basic commitment and competent in modern techniques. There were, to be sure, schools that taught the new modern subjects and students were also sent abroad for training, but a thorough command of the traditional curriculum remained the key to passing the examinations for entrance into the civil service. Traditional attitudes continued to make a military career unattractive and also inhibited the growth of a strong modern business and industrial sector.

China's international position remained weak. A war with France (1884–85) forced it to abandon claims to suzerainty over Vietnam, long a tributary, and in 1886 China also had to recognize the British conquest of Burma. The ultimate test for self-strengthening, however, came in a war fought over Korea. Japan was trying to pry Korea away from China even as China was trying to draw its tributary more closely into its own orbit.

China's defeat in the Sino-Japanese war of 1894–95 came as a great shock. In the resulting Treaty of Shimonoseki, it had to relinquish all claims to a special role in Korea, pay Japan an indemnity, cede Taiwan and the Pescadores Islands, and extend most-favored-nation status to Japan. Originally, Japan was also to receive the Liaodong (Liaotung) Peninsula but, after diplomatic intervention by Russia, Germany, and France, had to settle for an additional indemnity instead. Altogether, the treaty marked an unprecedented shift in the East Asian balance of power, a shift from China to Japan that was to continue until Japan's defeat in the Second World War.

China's defeat ushered in a period of accelerating change during which the forces of reform, reaction, and revolution competed, interacted, and interlocked in complex patterns. First came a movement for reform led by Kang Youwei (K'ang Yu-wei, 1873–1929), who provided a seemingly Confucian basis for ideas that went well beyond Confucius. His big chance came in 1898 when the emperor supported the reformers in an attempt to assert himself and shake off the control of the Empress Dowager. There ensued a flood of decrees reforming the examination system, remodeling the political apparatus, promoting industry, and otherwise modernizing state and society. It was an ambitious program, but most measures were never implemented because they aroused strong opposition among high-placed officials. The program also antagonized the Empress Dowager, who soon put an end to the "Hundred Days of Reform" and to the emperor's bid for power. A crucial role in these events was played by Yuan Shikai (Yüan Shih-k'ai, 1859–1916), a reform-minded military man who was trusted by the reformers but then sided with the Empress Dowager.

Also in 1898, external pressures on China reached a new intensity as the imperialist powers scrambled for economic and political concessions at China's expense. The powers forced loans on the Qing, which were secured by Chinese tax revenues, such as the maritime customs. Long-term leases of Chinese territory were granted to the powers, including the right to develop economic resources such as mines and railroads and frequently also the right to police the area. Often the powers combined leaseholds, railroad rights, and commercial rights, to create a "sphere of interest." Finally, "nonalienation" pacts were signed by which China agreed not to cede a given area to any power other than the signatory: the Yangtze Valley to Britain, the provinces bordering Vietnam to France, Fujian (Fukien) to Japan. In addition, Russia received special rights in Manchuria, and Germany in Shandong. The United States, then acquiring a Pacific empire of its own, adopted an "Open Door" policy in 1899 demanding equality of commercial opportunity for all powers in China and affirming a desire to preserve the integrity of the Chinese state and Chinese territory.

Antiforeign feelings ran high not only among officials but also among the commoners who resented the privileges granted to missionaries and their converts even as they feared the spread

A Boxer Notice

Attention: all people in markets and villages of all provinces in China — now, owing to the fact that Catholics and Protestants have vilified our gods and sages, have deceived our emperors and ministers above, and oppressed the Chinese people below, both our gods and our people are angry at them, yet we have to keep silent. This forces us to practise the *I-ho* magic boxing so as to protect our country, expel the foreign bandits and kill Christian converts, in order to save our people from miserable suffering. After this notice is issued to instruct you villagers, no matter which village you are living in, if there are Christian converts, you ought to get rid of them quickly. The churches which belong to them should be unreservedly burned down. Everyone who intends to spare someone, or to disobey our order by concealing Christian converts, will be punished according to the regulation when we come to his place, and he will be burned to death to prevent his impeding our program. We especially do not want to punish anyone by death without warning him first. We cannot bear to see you suffer innocently. Don't disobey this special notice!

Prepared by the *I-ho-ch'üan*.

Translated and reproduced in Ssu-yü Teng and John K. Fairbank, *China's Response to the West* (Cambridge: Harvard University Press, 1954), p. 190.

of railways. Cutting across the land regardless of ancestral graves, railways were accompanied by telephone poles carrying wires from which rust-filled rainwater dripped blood red. The Boxers, members of a militant religious society, relied on rituals, spells, and amulets to endow them with supernatural powers, including invulnerability to bullets. Their rebellion was originally directed against the dynasty, but Qing officials were able to turn the movement against the foreign powers. In June 1900 the Boxers entered the capital and for two months laid siege to the foreign legation quarter until it was rescued by a foreign military relief expedition. In the subsequent settlement the Chinese had to pay a huge indemnity and make other concessions.

After the Boxer debacle demonstrated the futility of old-style resistance, the Qing began an ambitious program of last minute reforms although it continued to denounce Kang Youwei and his associates, now in exile in Japan. In 1905 the examination system was abolished. Students were sent to study abroad (especially to Japan). Steps were taken to reform the army, to reconstruct the government along constitutional lines, and to centralize transportation, but nothing worked as planned. The students returned from abroad filled with revolutionary nationalism. The military were either influenced by antidynastic ideas or were loyal to their commanders, not the court. Provincial assemblies (1909) and the central legislative assembly (1910) became centers of opposition to the dynasty. Railway centralization alienated traditional provincial interests jealous of their autonomy even as it outraged nationalists because of the strings attached to foreign railway development loans.

The Boxer Rebellion. Prisoners captured by soldiers of the U.S. Cavalry, Tianjin.

Leadership of the disaffected shifted from Kang Youwei who still wanted to work through the dynasty to Sun Yat-sen (1866–1925) who advocated the overthrow of the Qing and the establishment of a republic. Sun, who had been educated in Hawaii and studied medicine in Hong Kong, had organized many unsuccessful insurrections but had gained important overseas Chinese moral and financial support. He was traveling in the United States when revolution broke out in October 1911.

In its crisis the Qing turned to Yuan Shikai as China's most powerful military man; but instead of saving the dynasty, Yuan arranged the abdication of its last infant emperor. Negotiations with the revolutionaries led to the formation of a republic with Yuan as president and a bicameral legislature. Yuan, however, rapidly became a dictator. The leader of the Nationalist Party (Guomindang, Kuomintang) was assassinated in March 1913, and that summer pro-Nationalist southern military governors were dismissed. When they revolted, Yuan crushed them easily. Once again, Sun Yat-sen found himself in exile.

Yuan continued a policy of centralization financed by foreign loans but won little support. During the First World War he managed to resist the most onerous Japanese demands, which would have reduced China to a virtual Japanese satellite, but was forced to make unpopular concessions. To reinvigorate his regime, Yuan set about restoring dynastic rule with himself as emperor. He may have been right in believing that a new imperial dynasty would meet the expectations of the great mass of the people, but he did not draw the people into politics. Those who did have a political say were overwhelmingly hostile. In March 1916 he gave way and officially abandoned his imperial ambitions, but he never regained his prestige and died a broken man in June of that year.

Yuan's failure to establish his dynasty was an indication of the passing of the old order, but the future remained precarious. At the center there was no obvious successor to sustain a measure of national unity. In the large cities along the coast new and foreign ways were gaining ground. In the countryside, the gentry, bereft of its political function, was losing its claim to moral leadership and becoming simply landlords. And the menace of imperialism was as threatening as ever. For China and its people, the transition from the old order to the new was to be exceptionally difficult and painful.

THE TRANSFORMATION OF JAPAN

Japan's modern history differed from that of China not only because Japan was much smaller and historically more open to foreign influence but also because the dynamics of Tokugawa history (see pp. 550–58) had already produced essential ingredients of change even though it took the threat from abroad to set them in motion.

Social and Political Change

A major source of instability was the inability of the ruling class to cope with a money economy. City merchants and rural entrepreneurs prospered, but the *daimyo* (feudal barons) and their domains were in serious financial straits. To cut the costs they frequently reduced the stipends they paid their samurai, reducing many of the lower ranking members of this social elite to lives of bitter poverty. Their swords in pawn, the poorest among them eked out a living by making umbrellas, sandals, and the like; on bad days they placed a toothpick in their mouths even though they had not eaten. To such men it seemed the height of injustice that society should reward the selfish moneymaking traders but condemn to indigence the warrior whose life was one of service. Furthermore, they deeply resented incompetence and corruption in high places and believed that ability, not birth, should determine a samurai's position in society.

There was also suffering and distress among the low-born rural and urban poor. Crop failures in the 1820s and 1830s caused great misery. Violent protests were never strong enough to threaten the system. However, they did signal the malfunctioning of the political economy.

The shogunate's attempts to solve its problems through reforms met with little success, but some of the individ-

China as seen from the West: The photographer labeled this picture "hordes of Chinese swarming along Canal Road," Guangzhou (*ca.* 1900).

ual domains *(han)*, more compact and less diverse than the Tokugawa holdings, did better. Particularly notable were Chōshū, located in southwestern Honshu, and Satsuma in Kyushu, whose *daimyo* raised to power capable and innovative young samurai of low hereditary rank. The strengthening of these two domains, however, did nothing to stabilize the political order because both had long traditions of hostility toward the Tokugawa.

The ideological foundations of the established order were also shaky because both Neo-Confucian and Shinto political thought emphasized the central importance of the emperor, who remained the final source of legitimacy of the shogun. While varieties of Neo-Confucianism and Shinto dominated the intellectual scene, the school of "Dutch Learning" (see pp. 557–58) continued to attract some very gifted and remarkable men, such as Sakuma Shōzan (1811–64) who studied chemistry, glassmaking, and the casting of guns. He also devised the formula, "eastern ethics and western science," as a way of preserving Confucian values while adopting western technology.

The intrusion of the West into Japanese politics came in July 1853 when Commodore Matthew C. Perry of the United States Navy arrived in Japan with a fleet of eleven ships and demanded the opening of the country. Having been under Russian and other foreign pressure for some time and aware of China's defeat in the Opium War, the *bakufu* (shogun's government) saw that it could not resist militarily. It took the unprecedented step of soliciting *daimyo* opinion, but the *daimyo* proved divided and unhelpful. When Perry returned for an answer in February 1854, the *bakufu* signed an initial treaty opening two ports to ships seeking provisions, assuring that anyone shipwrecked on the coast of Japan would receive good treatment, and permitting the United States to send a consul to Japan. Soon similar and then broader treaties with other powers followed. After 1858 Japan's international situation was similar to that of China as the *bakufu* acquiesced to the opening of selected ports, provisions for most-favored-nation treatment, extraterritoriality, and the surrender of Japan's tariff autonomy.

For the *bakufu* these were very difficult years; it was forced to accede to the foreign powers without enjoying support at home. Each failure in foreign affairs provided additional ammunition to its domestic enemies. To make matters even worse, the *bakufu* was itself divided by factionalism and policy differences, a situation making for the increased political importance of the imperial court.

Opposition now coalesced under the slogan "Revere the Emperor and Expel the Barbarians" and inspired men like Yoshida Shōin (1830–59) and his followers. Yoshida, who was born into a low-ranking Chōshū samurai family, condemned the *bakufu* for giving in to the western powers, which he felt reflected its incompetence, dereliction of duty, and lack of proper reverence for the emperor. Convinced that the *bakufu* must be eliminated, he plotted the assassination of a *bakufu* emissary to the court, but word leaked out and Yoshida was arrested and executed. Others, however, were stirred to kill and be killed for the cause. Men of extremist dedication terrorized the streets of Kyoto in the early 1860s and

The Americans' Arrival in Japan

Last summer the American barbarians arrived in the Bay of Uraga with four warships, bearing their president's message. Their deportment and manner of expression were exceedingly arrogant, and the resulting insult to our national dignity was not small. Those who heard could not but gnash their teeth. A certain person on guard in Uraga suffered this insult in silence, and having ultimately been unable to do anything about it, after the barbarians had retired, he drew his knife and slashed to bits a portrait of their leader, which they had left as a gift. Thus he gave vent to his rage.

From Sakuma Shōzan, *Reflections on My Errors (Seiken-roku)* as trans. in Ryusaku Tsunoda, Wm. Theodore de Bary and Donald Keene, *Sources of Japanese Tradition* (New York: Columbia University Press, 1958), pp. 614–15.

made the capital unsafe for moderates.

Foreigners too were subject to attack. When the *bakufu* proved powerless, western nations took matters into their own hands. In August 1863 the British bombarded Kagoshima in Satsuma in retaliation for the assassination of a British merchant by Satsuma samurai. In September 1864 Chōshū was attacked by a combined British, French, Dutch, and American fleet. These defeats stimulated modernizing military reforms in these two *han;* there was less talk now about immediately "expelling the barbarians" and more about "enriching the country and strengthening the army."

The politics of these years were very complicated. As long as Chōshū and Satsuma, traditionally unfriendly to each other, were on opposite sides, the situation remained fluid. Two *bakufu* wars were fought against Chōshū, one in 1864–65 when the shogun's forces were supported by the troops of many *daimyo* and a second in 1866 when Satsuma and other powerful domains refused to support the Tokugawa. The *bakufu*'s defeat in this war precipitated its downfall. On January 3, 1868, forces from Satsuma and other *han* seized the palace and proclaimed the restoration of the emperor. Fighting ended with the surrender of the *bakufu* navy in May 1869.

The Meiji Restoration

Although the emperor had been restored in name, actual power belonged to the men who had engineered the demise of the shogunate. These new leaders did not always see eye to eye, but they did share certain qualities: they were all of similar age (35–43) and rank, and came from Chōshū, Satsuma or two smaller *han* that had joined the coalition, or from the court aristocracy. Most important, for the sake of national self-preservation they were prepared to enact vast changes as prefigured in the Charter Oath issued in the name of the emperor in April 1868. In September of that year, the emperor was relocated to the shogun's

A Japanese view of Perry's landing.

old capital, now renamed Tokyo.

Thus began a period of rapid transformation. In 1871 the domains were abolished. The *daimyo* received generous financial compensation as well as honors leading to their elevation to a new peerage in 1884. Ordinary samurai fared much less well; their special status was abolished and even the wearing of swords was outlawed. With the creation of a modern conscript army under the leadership of Yamagata Aritomo (1838–1922), they lost their monopoly on military service, and they were cut loose economically when their stipends were converted into government bonds. This was a necessary economic move to place the new government on a sound financial basis.

Other financial measures included monetary and banking reforms and a new national tax system. The main source of government revenue remained agriculture, but instead of the old percentage of the crop payable by the village to the *daimyo,* the tax was now collected by the government in money on the basis of the assessed value of the land. It was payable by the owner, and for this purpose ownership rights had to be clearly established. This was not done in favor of the absentee feudal interests long divorced from the land, nor did ownership pass equitably to all peasants. Instead, certificates were issued to the cultivators and wealthy villagers who had paid the tax during Tokugawa times. Because poor peasants were often unable to meet their taxes, they were forced to mortgage their land. The rate of tenancy increased, rising from about 25 percent before the new system to about 40 percent twenty years later.

Not everyone approved of the new order. Peasants had cause for dissatisfaction and some of the large merchant houses found the transition very difficult, but most serious was samurai discontent. By 1873 the government itself was split between modernizers and conservatives, but the modernizers prevailed. However, the issue was not finally settled until the new conscript army crushed the Satsuma Rebellion of 1877, a samurai uprising led by Saigo Takamori (1827–77), the most charismatic of the original Restoration leaders.

After the Satsuma Rebellion occasional individual acts of political violence, particularly assassination attempts, were made, some of them successful. However, more important was the emergence of nonviolent political opposition directed not only against government policies but also against the political domination exercised by a few oligarchs from Chōshū and Satsuma. Antigovernment organizations voiced the discontent of local interests and demanded political rights, local self-government, and the formation of a national assembly. The advocates of a constitution and the leaders of what became known as the movement for political rights drew upon Western political theories but also argued that the adoption of representative institutions would create greater unity between the emperor and his people. This movement prompted the government to announce that a constitution would be granted, effective in 1890. It also prompted the formation of Japan's first political parties, the Liberal party (*Jiyūtō*) and the Progressive party (*Kaishintō*). These parties, however, were handicapped not only by a lack of internal cohesion but also by restrictive legislation, beginning with press laws in the mid-1870s and culminating in the Peace Preservation Law of 1887, which increased the Home Minister's power of censorship and gave the police authority to expel people from a given area (570 were shortly removed from Tokyo).

"Ladies Sewing," a woodblock print (1887). From the early 1880s sewing machines were used in the fashionable shops on the Ginza to produce the western dresses that were in great demand.

The architect of the constitution was Itō Hirobumi (1841–1909), a leading Meiji statesman from Chōshū, who spent a year and a half in Europe during 1882–83, mostly studying German theories and practices. Work was completed in 1889, and it was promulgated as a "gift" from the emperor to the people. Under this constitution, which remained in effect until 1945, the emperor retained the power to declare war, conclude treaties, and command the army. He could open, recess, and dissolve the legislature, veto its decisions, and issue his own ordinances. The cabinet was responsible not to the legislature but to the emperor. The Diet, as the legislature was called, consisted of two houses, the House of Peers and the House of Representatives. The representatives were elected by a constituency of about half a million out of a population of around forty million. The most consequential power of the Diet was the power of the purse, but, borrowing from the Prussian example, the constitution provided for automatic renewal of the previous year's budget whenever the Diet failed to pass a new budget. Only the emperor could take the initiative to revise the constitution.

By 1890 Japan had laid the foundations for a modern industrial economy. Agriculture remained very important. It had become more efficient due to the introduction of new seed strains, new fertilizers, and new methods of cultivation but the basic form of rural organization remained the same. In the modern sector, the government invested heavily in the public services that must be in place before an industrial economy can grow — education, transportation, communications, and so forth. Students were sent abroad, for example, to study western technology, and foreigners were brought to Japan to teach in their areas of expertise. A major investment was made in railroads. The government also took the lead in establishing and operating cement works, plants manufacturing glass and tiles, textile mills (silk and cotton), shipyards, mines, and munition works. It felt that these industries were essential, but private interests were unwilling to risk their capital in untried ventures with little prospect of profits in the near term.

The expenditure of capital required for this effort, the payments to the samurai on their bonds, the costs of the Satsuma Rebellion, and an adverse balance of trade combined to create a government financial crisis. The government's response was to cut back on expenditures, and late in 1880 as part of an economy move, it decided to sell at public auction all its enterprises with the exception of the munitions plants. The buyers were usually men who were friendly with government leaders and recognized the long-term advantages of buying the factories, which were selling at bargain prices. These enterprises did not become profitable immediately, but when they did the result was that a small group of well-connected firms enjoyed a controlling position in the modern sector of the economy. These were the *zaibatsu*, huge financial and industrial combines.

Especially in the early years after the Restoration there was great enthusiasm for western styles and ideas. Intellectuals like Fukuzawa Yukichi (1835–1901) were strongly influenced by the European Enlightenment, particularly the emphasis on reason as an instrument of progress. Then, after the mid-1870s, Social Darwinism gained influence. Most potent throughout was the force of nationalism which provided justification for all the sacrifices demanded of the people on the road to modernization. By appealing to old values and identifying itself with the Shinto tradition as the basis for the mystique of the emperor, the Japanese leadership sought and obtained the support of the Japanese people.

On the Ginza (*ca.* 1910), Tokyo's fashionable shopping area.

The appeal to the old to justify the new was also reflected in the education system designed to provide the people with the skills needed for modernization but also to preserve traditional virtues with a premium on service to state and throne. Thus the Rescript on Education (1890) memorized by generations of schoolchildren attributed "the glory of the fundamental character of Our Empire" to the Imperial Ancestors and called on his majesty's subjects to observe all the traditional virtues. The relationship between that past and the present, the tension between old and new, native and foreign, perplexed the Japanese psyche, stimulated soul-searching, and supplied the energy animating a modern literature of unusual distinction.

Japanese soldiers entering the city of Mukden, Manchuria, during the Sino-Japanese War.

Imperial Japan

From the very beginning, the foreign policy goals of the Meiji leaders had been to achieve national security and equality of national status, but these were elusive goals. While Japan's victory over China in 1895 was a great triumph, many nationalists felt cheated when Japan was forced to relinquish the Liaodong Peninsula. They did take satisfaction in the gradual elimination of the unequal treaty system (1889–1911), the acquisition of Taiwan (1895), and the formation of an alliance with Britain (1902). Yet it took another war, fought against Russia (1904–1905) and leaving Japan in control of Korea (annexed outright in 1910), to give the Japanese a greater sense of security. Even then they became bitterly resentful when they had to give up their demand for all of Sakhalin Island and forgo a large Russian indemnity in the Treaty of Portsmouth (1905). In Japan the treaty was greeted by riots even as in many Asian lands people were deeply impressed by the first victory of a non-western nation over a European power. Some of the Japanese elite saw no conflict between their nation's aspiration for a European-style empire and the well-being of their fellow Asians, but for the Koreans Japanese imperial rule brought harsh suppression of nationalist aspirations as well as economic exploitation. When Koreans protested, the Japanese repressed them ferociously.

Meanwhile, at home, the oligarchs discovered that even though the powers of the Diet were limited, they could not ignore the political parties that dominated the lower house. In 1900 Itō Hirobumi himself founded a political party that then developed sturdy roots by channeling funds into local projects thus building up a constituency among the local men of means who formed the limited electorate. The national financial and business community, including the *zaibatsu,* was interested in maintaining a political atmosphere favorable to itself, and political leaders welcomed business support. On the other hand, in 1900 Yamagata, Itō's chief rival among the oligarchs, had strengthened the already strong position of the military by obtaining imperial ordinances specifying that only officers on active duty could serve as minister of the army or minister of the navy thus, in effect, giving the military veto power over any cabinet. The army or navy could break any cabinet simply by ordering the army or navy minister to resign. Decision making under these circumstances was complicated, and government policies were determined by the interaction of various power centers, none of which could rule alone.

The system functioned reasonably well as long as there were sufficient funds to finance the military's and the politicians' highest priority projects, and as long as none of the participants felt their essential interests threatened. However, during 1912–13 a crisis occurred when the government, because of Japan's financial condition, had to cut back on spending. At a critical point the prime minister obtained an imperial decree prohibiting the passing of a non-confidence motion in the Diet, but

Japan Enters the Modern World

I was being dragged back more and more into the world of reality. Anywhere that you can find a railway train must be classed as the world of reality, for there is nothing more typical of twentieth-century civilization. It is an unsympathetic and heartless contraption which rumbles along carrying hundreds of people crammed together in one box. It takes them all at a uniform speed to the same station, and then proceeds to lavish the benefits of steam upon every one of them without exception. People are said to board and travel by train, but I call it being loaded and transported. Nothing shows a greater contempt for individuality than the train. Modern civilization uses every possible means to develop individuality, and having done so, tries everything to stamp it out. It allots a few square yards to each person, and tells him that he is free to lead his life as he pleases within that area. At the same time it erects railings around him, and threatens him with all sorts of dire consequences if he should dare to take but one step beyond their compass.

Natsume Soseki, *Kusa Makura* (1906) trans. by Alan Turney under the title *The Three Cornered World* (Chicago: Henry Regnery 1967, 1970). The quoted passage is found on p. 181, near the end of this short novel.

the politicians turned down the order. Out of this crisis a strengthened Diet and a two party system emerged that was to last until 1932. Another important symbol of change came in 1918 when the prime ministership for the first time went to a man who had made his career as a party politician.

Japan entered the First World War on the winning side and seized German holdings in Shandong and German islands in the Pacific. It also used the opportunity to obtain additional concessions from China but at the cost of stirring up strong Chinese resentment. Its largest and costliest effort, however, was its intervention during 1918–22 against the Russian Revolution. It sent 75,000 troops to Russia, three times the number sent by the Allies (United States, Britain, France, and Canada), and kept them there after the others had withdrawn in the vain hope that they could at least prevent the U.S.S.R. from controlling eastern Siberia. Japan was able to pay for this undertaking because of the great economic boom brought on by the First World War during which a withdrawal of European competition brought an unprecedented demand for Japanese products. However, the sudden economic expansion also brought major hardship as inflation raised the price of rice until many hungry people could no longer afford this most basic food and took to the streets.

Japan faced many problems as it entered the postwar world, but it had come a long way not only in its international position but also in its internal transformation. Opposition and protest was heard from both the left and the right, but politically it appeared to be following a liberal-democratic pattern of evolution that would culminate in 1924–26 with the granting of universal manhood suffrage. Economically the modern sector was growing although a traditional sector of small-scale business and industry remained very important and the vital agricultural base continued essentially untransformed. Intellectually, artistically, and spiritually this was a stimulating but also a confusing time. The twentieth century transition was fraught with strains and contradictions even as it brought Japan a large measure of successful accomplishment. The future would show that both despair and hope were justified.

Suggestions for Further Reading

Milton Osborne, *Southeast Asia: An Introductory History* (1979), is a good place to begin. D. J. Steinberg, ed., *In Search of Southeast Asia: A Modern History* (1971), is an excellent source for bibliography as well as insights and information. M. C. Ricklefs, *A History of Modern Indonesia* (1981), is reliable and factual. Alexander B. Woodside's *Vietnam and the Chinese Model* (1971), and his *Community and Revolution in Modern Vietnam* (1976), are indispensable for an understanding of that land.

The Cambridge History of China, Vols. 10 (1978) and 11 (1980), *Late Ch'ing,* 1800–1911, Parts One and Two, the first edited by John K. Fairbank and the second by Fairbank and Kang-ching Liu, contain excellent essays of synthesis on major aspects of nineteenth-century Chinese history as well as bibliographic essays. Also highly recommended is Paul A. Cohen, *Discovering History in China: American Historical Writings on the Recent Chinese Past* (1984), a reflective, probing account of the analytical frameworks and approaches employed by American scholars of modern Chinese history.

W. G. Beasley, The *Meiji Restoration* (1973), is a sound and careful study. The schooling of the men who became Japan's political, economic, and intellectual leaders is analyzed in Donald T. Roden, *Schooldays in Imperial Japan: A Study in the Culture of a Student Elite* (1981). *The Autobiography of Yukichi Fukuzawa* (1966), provides an "inside view" into the period. For the culture of business see Byron K. Marshall, *Capitalism and Nationalism in Prewar Japan: The Ideology of the Business Elite, 1868–1941* (1967).

	1815				1870	
SOUTHWEST ASIA AND AFRICA	**1818–28** King Shaka, apex of Zulu kingdom	**1836** Boers' Great Trek begins		**1860** French expansion in West Africa **1869** Suez Canal opens		
EUROPE	**1815** Congress of Vienna **1815–83** Karl Marx **1825** Decembrist Revolt, Russia **1825** First commercial railroad	**1829** Treaty of Adrianople **1830** France's "July Monarchy" **1832** Britain's Great Reform Bill **1848** *Communist Manifesto*	**1848–49** Europe in Revolt **1848–61** Unification of Italy **1848–70** Napolean III **1851** Crystal Palace Exhibition, London	**1859** Darwin, *Origin of Species* **1854–56** Crimean War **1861–71** Unification of Germany **1867** Austro-Hungarian *Ausgleich*	**1870–71** Franco-Prussian War **1876** First internal combustion engine **1878** Congress of Berlin	**1882** Triple Alliance **1894** Russo-French Alliance
SOUTH AND SOUTHEAST ASIA	**1819** British found Singapore		**1857–58** Indian Mutiny **1859** French seize Saigon			
EAST ASIA	**1825–30** Java War **1839–42** Opium War		**1850–64** Taiping Rebellion **1854** Perry opens US trade with Japan **1868** Meiji Restoration, Japan			**1893–1976** Mao Zedong **1894–95** Sino-Japanese War
THE AMERICAS AND PACIFIC	**1823** Monroe Doctrine	**1835–40** Alexis de Tocqueville, *Democracy in America* **1840** Britain annexes New Zealand **1846–48** Mexican War	**1849** Gold discovered in California	**1861–65** American Civil War **1867** Russia sells Alaska to US **1867** British North America Act	**1869** Opening of Transcontinental railroad	

Wood sculpture, Dogon tribe, Mali, West Africa.

Eiffel Tower, Paris, 1889.

***Empire State Express* *No. 999,* *ca.* 1890.**

Commodore Matthew Perry, a Japanese view, 1853.

British suffragette, *ca.* 1910.

Private Edwin Francis Jennison, Confederate Army.

1914	
1886 Gold discovered in Southern Africa **1889** Rhodesia colonized **1899–1902** Boer War **1910** Union of South Africa formed	
1894–1905 Dreyfus Affair **1905** Russian Revolution begins **1905** Einstein's Theory of Relativity **1907** Triple Entente **1912–13** Balkan Wars	
1885 Indian National Congress founded **1906** Muslim League founded	
1900 Boxer Rebellion **1904–05** Russo-Japanese War **1911** Chinese Revolution **1912–49** Chinese Republic	
1889 First Pan-American Conference **1898** Spanish-American War **1910** Mexican Revolution begins	**1914** Panama Canal opens

The Prince of Wales in Bangalore, India, *ca.* 1900.

Gold prospector, California, *ca.* 1850.

40 The Americas in the Nineteenth Century

From the Age of Discovery until the nineteenth century the world leadership of Europe had remained virtually unchallenged. As European nations established overseas commercial or colonial contacts, the ultimate conquest of the globe by western civilization appeared inevitable. But there had also been signs of a reverse trend, as some regions seemed to grow restive under European tutelage. The United States had been the first European overseas possession to gain independence, and soon similar movements for independence occurred in the other regions of the Americas where Europeans had settled. Despite the continued ascendancy of Europe during the nineteenth century, therefore, there were already some indications that the days of European supremacy were drawing to a close.

THE UNITED STATES IN THE EARLY NINETEENTH CENTURY

At the beginning of the nineteenth century, the United States was still a second-class power, playing only a minor role in international affairs. A century later, it had become the decisive arbiter in the greatest war Europe and the world had ever seen. The involvement of this newcomer in world affairs was a slow and gradual process. Through most of the nineteenth century America remained politically isolated, so much so that "isolationism" became a term commonly applied to American foreign policy.

America and Europe

In the Monroe Doctrine of 1823, America had warned Europe to desist from any further colonization in the Western Hemisphere. On several occasions during the nineteenth century, notably during the 1830s and 1840s, the United States became involved with its neighbors to the north and south over territorial issues. But these localized conflicts had no effect on the European balance of power. Even the international repercussions of the American Civil War did not lead to European intervention. Only at the close of the nineteenth century, in the war with Spain, did America once again go to war with a European power.

Despite the political isolation in which the United States shaped its destiny, cultural relations between the new republic and the old continent remained close, although America at first was a recipient rather than a contributor in this cultural exchange. In the 1830s and 1840s, foreign travelers still commented on the backwardness and boorishness of American manners and customs. But there were also some friendlier critics, like the young Frenchman Alexis de Tocqueville, whose *Democrary in America* (1835–40) predicted correctly the leading role that the United States would someday play in world affairs.

America had shared the European vogue of Romanticism, and some of Europe's early socialists had tried out their utopian schemes on American soil. By the middle of the nineteenth century, American writers like Washington Irving, James Fenimore Cooper, Henry Wadsworth Longfellow, and Edgar Allan Poe drew foreign attention to American literature, and the monumental works of the historians William H. Prescott, Francis Parkman, George Bancroft, and John L. Motley did the same for American historiography. There were other fields in which American influence made itself felt. The pioneering efforts of American reformers in advocating women's rights, pacifism, and temperance evoked responses overseas; and the gradual adoption in Europe of universal male suffrage and free public education profited greatly from the American example. In technical inventions America already showed signs of the genius that was ultimately to make it the leading industrial nation of the world. The cultural exchange between Europe and the United States thus became less one-sided. Better means of communication also played their part. By the 1860s the steamship had begun to compete successfully with the sailing vessel, and the laying of a transatlantic cable in 1858 speeded the exchange of news and ideas.

De Tocqueville on Russia and America

1835

There are at the present time two great nations in the world, which started from different points, but seem to tend towards the same end. I allude to the Russians and the Americans. . . . All other nations seem to have nearly reached their natural limits, and they have only to maintain their power; but these are still in the act of growth. . . . These alone are proceeding with ease and celerity along a path to which no limit can be perceived. The American struggles against the obstacles that nature opposes to him; the adversaries of the Russian are men. The former combats the wilderness and savage life; the latter, civilization with all its arms. The conquests of the American are therefore gained by the plowshare; those of the Russian by the sword. The Anglo-American relies upon personal interest to accomplish his ends and gives free scope to the unguided strength and common sense of the people; the Russian centers all the authority of society in a single arm. The principal instrument of the former is freedom; of the latter, servitude. Their starting-point is different and their courses are not the same; yet each of them seems marked out by the will of Heaven to sway the destinies of half the globe.

From Alexis de Tocqueville, *Democracy in America* (New York: Knopf, 1953), Vol. I, p. 434.

Immigration

The territorial growth of the United States was closely related to the phenomenal growth of its population.

From less than 4 million in 1790, the population shot up to over 60 million in the course of a century. Much of this increase was due to the ceaseless stream of European immigrants, totaling more than 35 million between 1815 and 1914. Many of them still came to escape political or religious persecution, but also the attraction of the economic opportunities of the New World appealed to many. The constant supply of cheap labor provided by immigration was a boon to America's growing economy. The rapid Americanization of these new citizens was aided by the fact that the United States had no privileged classes, no established church, and no military caste. American society had its sectional and occupational groupings, but they were not as rigid as the European hierarchies. Economic opportunity for all, an open society in which ability and hard work brought success — these were the ingredients of the "American dream," if not always the American reality.

Immigrants laden with baggage arriving at Ellis Island (1907).

Early Industrialization

Like most European countries, the United States in the first part of the nineteenth century remained predominantly agrarian. The abundance of land attracted land-hungry Europeans. But the vast increase of population required additional economic outlets, which were provided by industry. By the middle of the nineteenth century the eastern states had thriving industries. At the same time, the opening up of western territories provided an ever-expanding market. Full-scale industrialization did not take hold until after the Civil War. Prior to 1860, however, many of the social effects of industrialization that were seen in Europe had already made themselves felt. During the first half of the nineteenth century American labor unions began to organize, but a labor movement in the modern sense, in America as in Europe, did not develop until later.

In its economic philosophy, America shared the faith of European liberals in freedom from state control. The American Revolution had been fought against the mercantilist restrictions imposed by the mother country. Once these restrictions had been removed, few obstacles remained to free enterprise. A philosophy of laissez-faire thus came to permeate the economic life of the United States. Only in one field did American industry not only tolerate but demand government control — tariff legislation. With the world's largest free-trade area within their own borders, American manufacturers were eager to keep foreign competitors out.

The revolutionary turmoil in Europe after 1815 had its parallel in the unrest that prevailed in the United States during the 1820s. The source of this unrest was economic and social. As America's population increased, and as the new territories acquired with the purchase of Louisiana (1803) and Florida (1819) filled up with new settlers, a number of differences arose between the established interests in the East and the new forces on the western frontier. Discontent among the new immigrant workers of the East and among western settlers was expressed at the ballot box, thanks to the growth of the democratic process after the Revolution.

Andrew Jackson, by Thomas Sully.

The "Age of Jackson"

Democracy in the United States had been slow to reach all levels of society; not until the late 1820s had male suffrage been adopted in the majority of states. Largely as a result of this increased democratization, Andrew Jackson was elected president in 1828. More than any of his predecessors, Jackson could claim to be the people's choice. He was the first westerner to win the highest office, a popular hero of the War of 1812, and most important, a man who had risen from poverty by his own efforts. The road from log cabin to White House henceforth became part of the American dream.

The "Age of Jackson" was a period of major change in American life, more so even than the 1830s were in western Europe. The democratization of politics continued with the adoption of the patronage or "spoils system," and with the practice of having presidential candidates nominated by national conventions rather than by a handful of party leaders. Closest to Jackson's heart was the further development of the West. In a number of treaties concluded with Indian tribes, the federal government won title to millions of acres of virgin land. These were sold at auction at low cost, after free land for schools, roads, a state university, and other public purposes had been set aside. Jackson's opposition to eastern financial interests, furthermore, made him the advocate of state banks, whose lavish granting of credit helped develop the West.

"States' Rights"

With the opening of the West, sectional rivalry became one of the major issues in American politics. Not only

The Westward Expansion of the U.S. 1776–1853

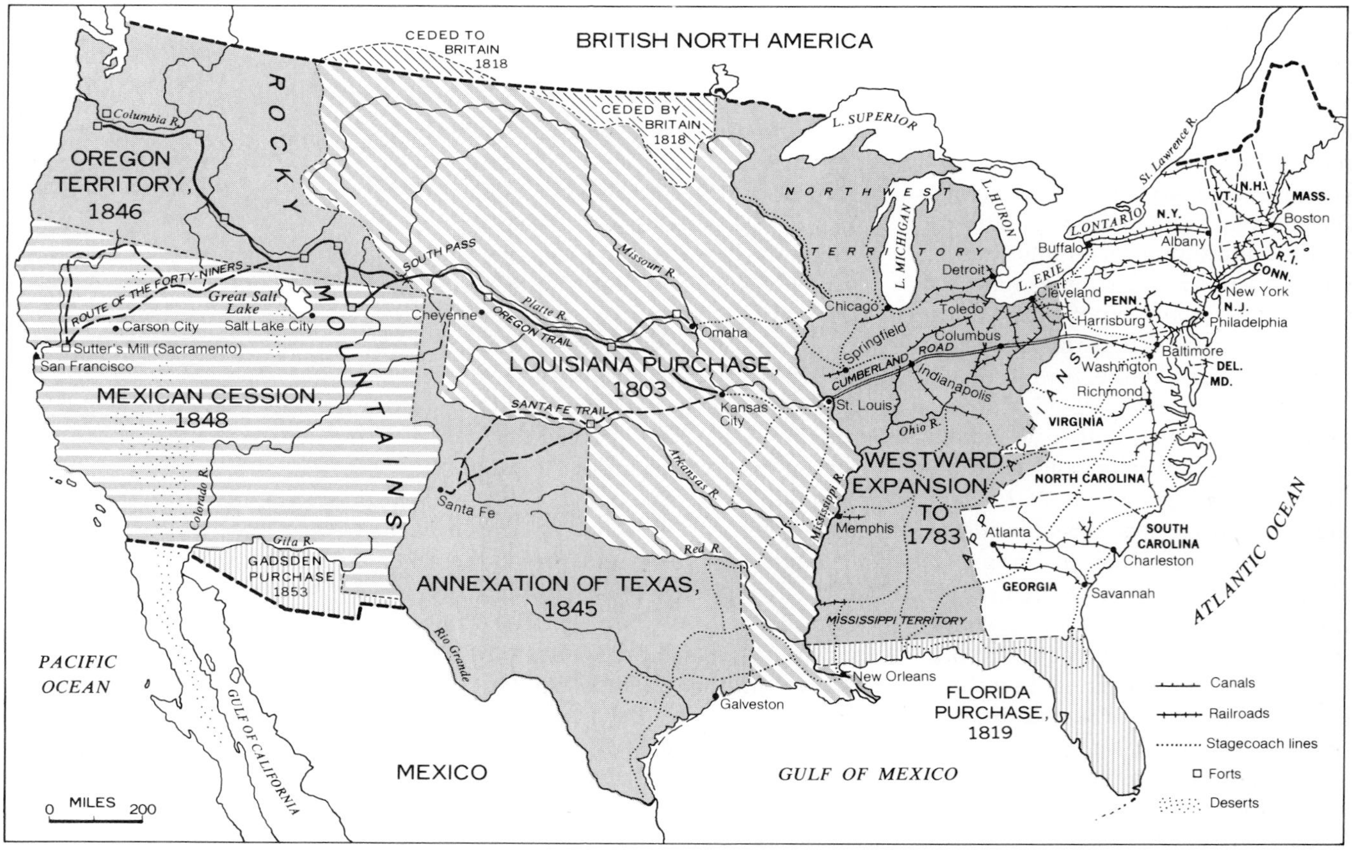

the West, but the South as well, found itself at odds with the North, especially over tariffs. The South, depending on cotton exports, favored free trade, while the North demanded high tariffs to protect its infant industries. Finding itself more and more overshadowed by the North, the South used the proposal of a high tariff in 1828 as an occasion for raising the vital question of "states' rights." The relationship between state and federal governments had been an issue in American politics since the early days of the Republic. The Constitution of 1787 had considerably widened the power of the central government over what it had been under the Articles of Confederation, and the policy since then had been to carry this centralization further.

But also strong sentiment was voiced against this tendency. Critics of centralization took the view that the Constitution was primarily a compact among sovereign states, and that the states had the right to nullify an act of Congress if it violated the terms of that compact. It was this idea of nullification that was used by Jackson's vice-president, John C. Calhoun, a southerner, to fight the "tariff of abominations." In the ensuing crisis Jackson broke with Calhoun and defended the sovereignty of the Union against the advocates of states' rights. A final showdown was averted by the compromise tariff of 1833. But this did not remove the underlying conflict between federal power and state sovereignty.

The Westward Expansion

In its domestic development the United States faced many of the same social and economic problems that confronted the nations of Europe. But America, unencumbered by feudal traditions and endowed with a rich and virtually empty continent, grew into something radically different from Europe. The American's belief in "Manifest Destiny"—the doctrine that the country's mission was to expand across the continent to the Pacific—helped to increase its territory more than fourfold within one century. To assimilate and integrate these new lands proved to be America's foremost political problem, and its final accomplishment contributed to the origins of a bloody civil war. Yet the abundance of fertile lands also helped to relieve economic and social pressures that might have had similarly violent repercussions.

As more and more settlers began moving westward, tensions developed with the British in the north and the Mexicans in the south over rival claims to western territories. These intermittent conflicts came to a head and were settled during the 1840s. American-British economic relations were so advantageous that it was in the interest of both to avoid a major crisis over the American-Canadian frontier. By the Webster-Ashburton Treaty (1842), therefore, the northeastern boundary was adjusted to mutual satisfaction, and a similar compromise was reached for the Northwest in the Oregon Treaty (1846).

Relations with America's southern neighbor, Mexico, were considerably more stormy. The main controversy

An 1846 daguerreotype showing United States General John Wool and his troops in Saltillo, Mexico, during the Mexican War.

California gold miners (1852).

here arose over Texas. The influx of American settlers into this Mexican border region had begun in 1821. Because of constant difficulties with Mexican authorities, the American settlers first demanded autonomy and then, in 1836, proclaimed their independence. The next logical step, admission of Texas to the Union in 1845, led to war with Mexico. As a result of the Mexican War (1846–48), Mexico relinquished its claims to Texas. Mexico also ceded California and New Mexico in return for $15 million. Six years later, with the Gadsden Purchase, the United States acquired another slice of Mexican territory.

The settlement with Mexico, together with the Oregon Treaty, gave the United States an extended frontage on the Pacific. The implications of this development for American foreign policy were to become evident only gradually. For the time being, the most pressing need of the vast regions of the new West was for settlers to substantiate America's claims. In a fitting climax to a decade of expansion, gold was discovered in the Sacramento Valley in 1848. The resulting gold rush profited only a few of the many thousands who streamed to California from all over the world. But these "forty-niners" helped to increase the population of California more than fourfold in a single decade.

THE SLAVERY ISSUE AND THE CIVIL WAR

The expansionism of the 1840s also aggravated the long-standing sectional conflict between proslavery and antislavery forces. What has been said about the democratic nature of American society did not apply to the large number of black slaves in the South or even to free blacks in the North. While almost everywhere in the world slavery was being abolished, it was gaining a new lease on life in the American South. In a nation dedicated to a belief in equality, there now arose an aristocracy of wealthy plantation owners

The Slavery Issue 1861

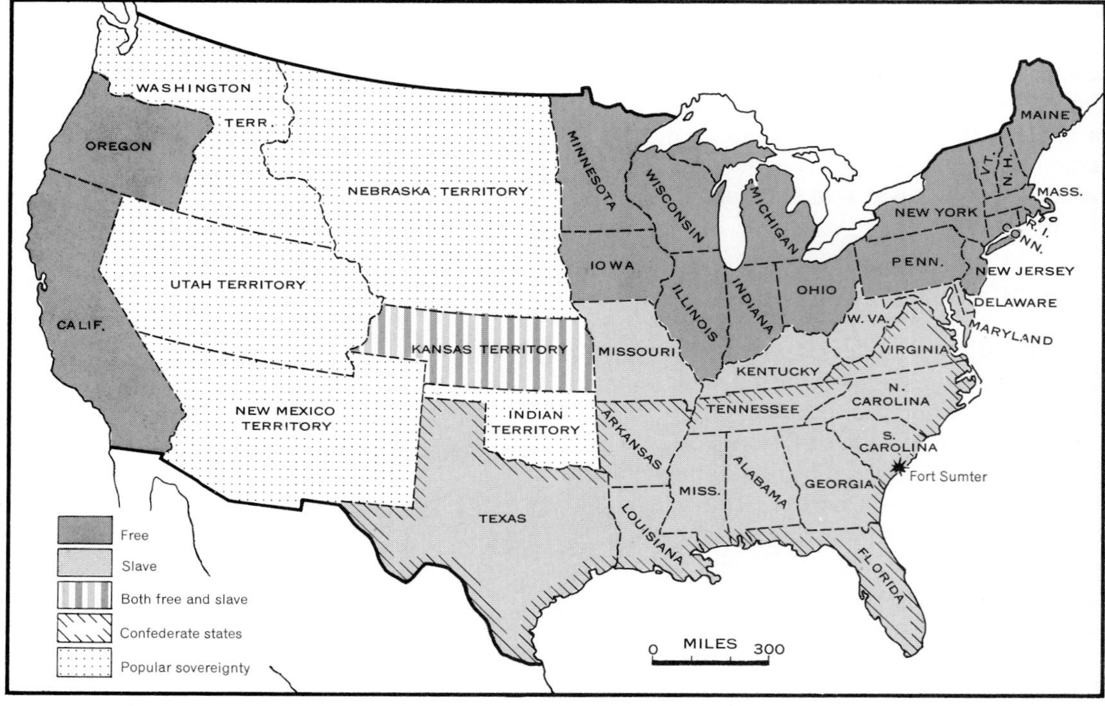

whose belief in their own superiority and the inferiority of the black race was not unlike the racist ideologies that already existed in Europe and became more widespread during the later nineteenth century.

Slave versus Free States

The main concern of southern politicians was to prevent antislavery legislation. This could be done only if an even balance between slave and free states was maintained. Such a balance in the past had been maintained by compromise. But compromise became increasingly difficult as more and more territories were added to the Union. With the petition of California in 1849 for admission as a free state, the issue reached a critical stage. If granted, the admission would upset the existing balance between slave and free states. After prolonged debates, differences were once more patched up. The Compromise of 1850 called for the admission of California as a free state, but it left the question of whether new territories were ultimately to be admitted as free or slave states up to their own decisions. This introduction of state option, or popular sovereignty, injected a new and disturbing element into the slavery controversy.

Beginning in the mid-1850s a series of tragic events and incidents drove the opposing factions on the slavery issue still further apart. The rivalry between proslavery and antislavery forces over whether Kansas was to be a free or slave state soon plunged that territory into a miniature civil war. The Supreme Court's Dred Scott decision (1857), which ruled that slaves were property and thus could not become free by moving to a free state, deeply antagonized the North. On the other hand, an attempt by the abolitionist John Brown to lead slaves in a raid on the arsenal at Harpers Ferry (1859) aroused the specter of a slave revolt in the South. The presidential campaign of 1860 was dominated by the slavery issue. The Democrats were divided into a southern, proslavery wing and a northern faction holding to the compromising policy of popular sovereignty. The Republicans stood united against any further extension of slavery.

The Republican candidate, Abraham Lincoln, was chosen as president by an electorate divided along sectional lines. Repeatedly in previous years the South had talked of secession as a last

Slavery

AN APOLOGIST'S VIEW

The negro slaves of the South are the happiest, and, in some sense, the freest people in the world. The children and the aged and infirm work not at all, and yet have all the comforts and necessaries of life provided for them. They enjoy liberty, because they are oppressed neither by care nor labor. The women do little hard work, and are protected from the despotism of their husbands by their masters. The negro men and stout boys work, on the average, in good weather, not more than nine hours a day. . . . Besides, they have their Sabbaths and holidays. White men, with so much of license and liberty, would die of ennui; but negroes luxuriate in corporeal and mental repose. With their faces upturned to the sun, they can sleep at any hour; and quiet sleep is the greatest of human enjoyments. . . . The free laborer must work or starve. He is more of a slave than the negro, because he works longer and harder for less allowance than the slave, and has no holiday, because the cares of life with him begin when its labors end. He has no liberty, and not a single right.

AN ABOLITIONIST'S VIEW

The slaves in the United States are treated with barbarous inhumanity . . . they are overworked, underfed, wretchedly clad and lodged, and have insufficient sleep . . . they are often made to wear round their necks iron collars armed with prongs, to drag heavy chains and weights at their feet while working in the field . . . they are often kept confined in the stocks day and night for weeks together, made to wear gags in their mouths for hours or days, have some of their front teeth torn out or broken off, that they may be easily detected when they run away . . . they are frequently flogged with terrible severity, have red pepper rubbed into their lacerated flesh, and hot brine, spirits of turpentine, etc., poured over the gashes to increase the torture . . . they are often stripped naked, their backs and limbs cut with knives, bruised and mangled by scores and hundreds of blows with the paddle, and terribly torn by the claws of cats, drawn over them by their tormentors.

From George Fitzhugh, *Cannibals All!* (1857); from Theodore Dwight Weld, *Slavery As It Is* (1839).

resort in defending its way of life. Calhoun, the defender of states' rights, had suggested that if compromise proved impossible the states should "agree to separate and part in peace." South Carolina, the home of the "great nullifier," now replied to Lincoln's election by passing its Ordinance of Secession. One after another, most of the slave states seceded from the Union and formed the Confederate States of America. In his inaugural address Lincoln strongly rejected the right of secession and vowed to maintain the Union. But he also left the door open for possible reconciliation. The issue of peace or war hung in the balance for a while longer. It was decided on April 12, 1861, when Confederate forces opened fire on the federal garrison at Fort Sumter in Charleston Harbor.

The American Civil War was fought initially to preserve and protect the Union. To that extent it belongs among the great wars of national unification that were being waged in Europe at the same time. The Civil War was expected to be a brief conflict in which the immense advantages of the North would prove decisive. But the South put up a valiant fight and in the early part of the war won some brilliant victories. Nobody would have predicted that the war would last four years and would turn into one of the most costly military ventures known up to that time.

Slaves working in a cotton field (*ca.* 1860).

Emancipation

Among the political developments of the war the most important was Lincoln's Emancipation Proclamation, a promise of freedom to come. The extension of northern war aims to include the abolition of slavery changed the war from a mere political struggle to an ideological crusade. This change was brought about more by the pressure of circumstances than by actual design. Lincoln himself would have preferred a more gradual and voluntary process of emancipation.

The granting of freedom to black Americans inevitably raised the closely related question of granting them equality as well. The abolitionist minority had never made any distinction between the two. But it took endless debates and several years before the country as a whole was ready to implement the gift of freedom with the guarantee of equality. This was done in several constitutional amendments and civil-rights acts. Beginning in the 1870s, however, the United States Supreme Court interpreted this postwar legislation in ways that violated its spirit, if not its letter, and that kept America's blacks in a position of inferiority for decades to come.

Europe and the Civil War

The Emancipation Proclamation made a very strong impression in Europe. The European powers had watched America's westward movement with disapproval. During the Mexican War, Great Britain actually considered joint intervention with France on behalf of Mexico, and during the 1850s these two powers helped to discourage American plans for the acquisition of Cuba from Spain. The outbreak of the Civil War led official European circles to hope that America would be permanently weakened by the secession of the southern states. Both the British and the French governments were decidedly cool toward the North. As far as Britain was concerned, the fact that its industry depended on southern cotton played its part. When a northern warship removed two Confederate commissioners from the British steamer *Trent* in 1861, a major crisis was averted only by America's readiness to give in to British protests and release the commissioners. Great Britain, on the other hand, had to heed the protests of the North against permitting southern privateers to be outfitted in, and to operate from, British ports.

American relations with France became strained when Napoleon III tried to bolster his position at home by establishing a puppet regime in Mexico. In 1863 French troops occupied Mexico City, and the following year Archduke Maximilian of Austria was proclaimed Emperor of Mexico. This was in open violation of the Monroe Doctrine, but the United States was too preoccupied to make any protest. Once the Civil War was over, however, it demanded the withdrawal of French troops (1866). Left without support, Maximilian could not last long. He was executed by a Mexican firing squad in 1867.

Not all the governments of Europe hoped to profit from America's domestic tragedy. The Prussian government was favorably disposed toward the North and wished to see the Union preserved as a counterweight to Britain's maritime supremacy. Russia took a similar attitude. The Russians had given up their settlements in California in 1844, and American fears that the tsarist government would take advantage of the Civil War to extend its sphere of influence southward from Alaska proved groundless. Russia sold Alaska, its last remaining colony in North America, to the United States in 1867 for a mere $7.2 million. The same year the United States also occupied the Midway Islands, thus signifying its new interest in the Pacific area.

The most wholehearted support of the northern cause during the Civil War came from the rank and file of Europe's population. To the Germans and Italians the war appeared as a struggle for national unity, and to people everywhere the Civil War was another phase in the universal fight for freedom and independence that had been waged in Europe ever since the French Revolution. Even before Lincoln's Emancipation Proclamation, most Europeans saw the American war entirely in terms of liberating the southern slaves. The victory of the North was widely hailed as a triumph of democracy, and some historians feel that it contributed to the liberalization of the British and French governments after 1865.

Archduke Maximilian of Austria, emperor of Mexico (1864–67).

Reconstruction in the South

America's reputation for liberalism and tolerance, however, was considerably tarnished by the Reconstruction period following the Civil War. The assassination of Lincoln had aroused worldwide indignation and sorrow, and the absence of his moderating influence was keenly felt in the U.S. government's efforts to deal with a recalcitrant South. In an attempt to overcome southern resistance to the political and social emancipation of southern blacks, the Reconstruction Acts of 1867 and 1868 placed the South under military rule, from which it could escape only after drafting new constitutions that accepted the constitutional amendments and civil rights legislation passed since the end of the war.

Added to the political tension were economic problems. The South emerged from the war with many of its cities destroyed, its economy disrupted, and one of its major economic assets, slavery, gone. The influx of northern "carpetbaggers," intent on making personal or political profit out of southern misfortune, kept alive the bitterness generated by war. The distinctive way of life on which southerners had prided themselves was gone forever; but the ideals on which it had rested remained alive. The slow process by which southern blacks were once again disenfranchised and, by a series of "Jim Crow" laws, segregated as well did not really gain momentum until the 1890s. Its cumulative effect was to perpetuate sectionalism by creating a "solid South" dominated by the Democratic Party and dedicated to keeping the black "in his place."

FROM SMALL POWER TO GREAT

While America was trying to heal the wounds of war during the last decades of the nineteenth century, it was also trying to fill its remaining "open spaces" and to realize its great industrial potentialities.

Economic Growth

Both these developments were aided by the continued influx of millions of immigrants. Of considerable help in attracting new citizens and in aiding American farmers were the Homestead Act of 1862 and successive land laws, as well as the easy access provided to the West by the construction of transcontinental railroads of which the first was completed in 1869. American agriculture already had profited from mechanization. The invention of barbed wire in 1873 made possible the fencing in of vast areas for cattle raising, and the introduction of the refrigerated boxcar proved a boon to the meat-packing industry. As a result of these and other improvements, western farming took on some of the characteristics of an industry, producing on a large scale for distant markets.

Even more important than the growth of America's agriculture after the Civil War was the expansion of its industries. Government procurement of war materials even at the cost of heavy federal deficits had caused an industrial boom, which continued once the war was over. Between 1860 and 1900 the amount of capital invested in American industry increased more than tenfold, and the export of manufactured articles by 1900 was four times what it had been in 1860. By 1890 the United States had emerged as the world's leader in the production of steel and pig iron, and with close to two hundred thousand miles of railroads in 1900 it had more mileage than the whole of Europe. It also excelled in mass-production methods based on standardization, interchangeable parts, and, ultimately, the assembly line.

Kansas Pacific Roundhouse, Armstrong, Kansas (1873). The railroads greatly facilitated the settlement of the West.

Government Regulation of Business

As often happens in rapidly expanding economies, America suffered a series of economic crises, of which the panics of 1873 and 1893 were the most significant. Both had their parallels overseas, and the withdrawal of European capital from American industry in each case precipitated matters. To modify the effects of competition, American heavy industry after 1873 began to combine its resources in order to ameliorate the cost of competition, to fix prices, and to control markets. The first of these "trusts" was the Standard Oil Company of John D. Rockefeller (1879). But since these large organizations evoked strong public protests, Congress in 1890 enacted the Sherman Antitrust Law, a dubious gesture toward remedy. Its enforcement was sufficiently lax to permit the continued concentration of control in industry and banking.

The federal government also had to intervene on other occasions in order to curb the excesses of unrestricted competition. Contrary to European practices, in which governments had taken an active hand in the construction and operation of railroads, American lines were built through private initiative, aided by lavish grants of public lands.

To realize maximum profits, American railroads charged exorbitant rates where there was no competing carrier. There had been earlier proposals for federal regulation of the railroads, but not until 1887 was the Interstate Commerce Act passed. The new law was chiefly concerned with rates, and to enforce its provisions it created an Interstate Commerce Commission that at first, however, was not very effective.

American business did not mind governmental intervention in protective tariffs, a major concern of industrialists during the early nineteenth century. Southern opposition to protectionism, together with Britain's abolition of the Corn Laws in 1846, had brought a brief interval of free trade. But the economic and financial demands of the Civil War reversed the trend. Beginning in 1861 America entered upon a new era of protectionism. Its high point came with the Dingley Tariff Act of 1897, which made the United States the most protectionist country in the world.

The unprecedented industrial expansion of the years after the Civil War gave an air of opulence and optimism to the "Gilded Age." Not all Americans, however, shared in the rise from rags to riches. The South in particular was slow to recover from its defeat and adjust to a world in which cotton was no longer king. The Panic of 1873, moreover, by causing price cuts among farmers and wage cuts among workers, bred widespread discontent. As a result, the 1870s saw the first serious efforts among these potentially powerful groups to assert their influence in national affairs.

Labor and Farm Unrest

American workers became increasingly aware that they might improve their status by combining their small local unions into a more powerful national organization. The first such body to wield any real influence, the Knights of Labor, was founded in 1869. At its height, it had more than seven hundred thousand members. In 1886 a wave of strikes culminated in the Haymarket Square riot in Chicago, in which several policemen were killed. The Knights of Labor, though not directly involved, were nevertheless blamed. Other reasons contributed to their decline, notably the strength of a new national movement, the American Federation of Labor, the spearhead of the American labor movement for the next half-century.

Members of the Knights of Labor (*ca.* 1880).

Workers' attempts at organization, however, did not at first materially improve their condition. With large numbers of impoverished immigrants swelling the labor market, working conditions continued to be harsh, hours long, and wages low. Repeated strikes, in which hired strikebreakers fought vicious battles with strikers, further widened the gap between capital and labor. After the Pullman strike of 1894, the Supreme Court ruled that the Sherman Antitrust Act applied to labor unions if they obstructed interstate commerce. Only after the turn of the century did workers' conditions improve, in large part because of the efforts of their unions, but also because of the intervention of a more sympathetic government.

Another large body of Americans who felt their interests neglected in a nation that was becoming rapidly industrialized were the farmers. In 1867 the National Grange of the Patrons of Husbandry had been formed, chiefly

Children working in a southern cotton mill (*ca.* 1910).

as a social organization, but also as a platform for agrarian discontent. The main grievance of farmers was the unfair practices of railways. The Interstate Commerce Act (1887) sought to improve the situation, but its initial effectiveness was limited. Suffering increasingly from protectionism abroad and falling prices at home, America's farmers during the 1880s formed regional groupings that ultimately grew into the National Farmers' Alliance and Industrial Union. Its purpose was to aid farmers by cooperative ventures and by bringing pressure against eastern industrial and banking interests who were held responsible for much of the farmer's plight. The climax of the farmers' discontent came with the formation of the People's party in 1891. The Populists, profiting from the unrest among workers as well, soon emerged as a powerful third force in national politics. Their demands included currency reform, a graduated income tax, and government ownership of the railroads. A particular issue long close to farmers' hearts was the free and unlimited coinage of silver, from which they expected an upturn of farm prices. When the Democratic party in 1896 adopted some of the Populist platform, including "free silver," the new party joined forces with the Democrats, thus making that party the spokesman of agrarian and labor interests.

Foreign Policy After the Civil War

There were few noteworthy events in American foreign policy between the Civil War and the end of the century. In 1889 America signed a treaty with Germany and Great Britain that established tripartite control over the island of Samoa. The following year Congress adopted a sweeping naval program, calling for a fleet that would place the United States among the world's leading naval powers. Various plans during the 1890s for an American-controlled canal across Central America failed to materialize, as did attempts to annex Hawaii.

Close to home the United States improved relations with the nations of the Western Hemisphere. In 1889 the first Pan-American Conference was held in Washington. In 1895, during a border dispute between Venezuela and British Guiana, Secretary of State Richard Olney reaffirmed the principles of the Monroe Doctrine in strong and belligerent tones. A few years later, in 1898, the United States caught the expansionist fever that was driving the European powers into imperialist ventures.

American Culture

In cultural matters the United States during the second half of the nineteenth century continued to share in the leading trends of Europe. American painters still went to study in Paris; American scholars were trained at foreign universities; and America's symphony orchestras and opera companies depended almost entirely on European talent. But a native American culture, making up in freshness and originality for what it lacked in refinement was coming into its own. The writings of Walt Whitman and Mark Twain, the paintings of Winslow Homer and Thomas Eakins, the compositions of Edward MacDowell, and the functional architecture of Louis Sullivan—all had an unmistakably American flavor. The most original and influential of America's intellectual contributions during the late nineteenth century was the philosophy of pragmatism. Its beginnings went back to the early 1870s, but it only attracted general attention with the writings of William James at the turn of the century. In the popular mind pragmatism justified America's preoccupation with practical pursuits and gave moral sanction to the fierce struggle for material success.

Most Americans were proud of this success. Yet some critical voices were heard. In a period of progress and prosperity, both seemingly the result of laissez-faire, the American journalist Henry George wrote his *Progress and Poverty* (1879), which challenged the free-enterprise system. Thorstein Veblen, in *The Theory of the Leisure Class* (1899), examined the role of the customer in the economy of his day and found that such materialistic considerations as "conspicuous consumption" and "conspicuous waste" were exerting an unhealthy influence on the existing price structure. Social criticism also found expression in the novels of Edward Bellamy, Theodore Dreiser, and Frank Norris. All these writers had considerable influence in Europe, where concern over the effects of unrestrained economic liberalism had long agitated socialists and social critics.

THE UNITED STATES AS A GREAT POWER

In the realm of ideas, as in politics and economics, America at the end of the nineteenth century was making its influence felt far beyond its frontiers. To all intents and purposes, the United States had become a great power with conditions and concerns not unlike those of the traditional great powers of Europe. In the political sphere, there was less need for further democratization than there was in some European countries, although the agitation of the Populists in the 1890s and of the Progressive party in 1912 showed that many Americans felt their interest neglected under the two-party system. In the economic sphere, the United States shared fully in the expansion that took place in Europe, and by 1914 America led the world in the production of coal, iron, and petroleum.

Mark Twain, American humorist of the "Gilded Age," in front of his boyhood home in Hannibal, Missouri.

In trying to cope with the social and economic problems resulting from rapid industrialization, the activities of both the labor unions and the government, in America as in Europe, brought a marked improvement of the worker's status. The efforts of Theodore Roosevelt (1901–1909) after the turn of the century, to secure a "square deal" for the workingman, and his attempts at "trust busting," helped to bridge the gap between capital and labor. Despite the opposition of many Americans to governmental intervention in economic affairs, the United States showed the same tendency toward becoming a "welfare state" that prevailed in most European countries. In tariff legislation the trend by 1914 was in the direction of lower tariffs. This was seen by some as a sign that American industry had come of age and was ready to compete with foreign imports on the home market.

The Spanish-American War

The United States at the end of the nineteenth century thus shared most of the major trends of Europe. This was nowhere more evident than in foreign affairs. Agitation during the 1890s to annex Hawaii and to construct a canal across Central America ran parallel to European expansionism during the same period. Under the administrations of Grover Cleveland (1885–89; 1893–97), such expansionist sentiments were kept under control. His successor, William McKinley (1897–1901), however, was less able to resist the pressures of American nationalism. One of the main subjects of agitation at the time was Cuba, where a revolt against Spanish rule had started in 1895. American sentiment sided with the Cuban rebels and demanded that the United States go to their aid. When the USS *Maine* mysteriously exploded in Havana harbor in early 1898, the clamor for war became too strong to be resisted any longer.

The Spanish-American War was the first war between the United States and a European power since 1814. The United States had little difficulty in winning the "splendid little war" against Spain. In the peace treaty signed at Paris in December 1898, the United States obtained Puerto Rico, the Philippines, and Guam. Cuba received its independence, though the Platt Amendment, adopted by Congress in 1901, made it a virtual American protectorate.

America made its influence felt in East Asia and elsewhere in other ways as well. In 1898 the United States finally annexed Hawaii and the following year divided the Samoan Islands with Germany. Also in 1899, Secretary of State John Hay proclaimed the "Open Door" policy, which called for equal opportunity in China for all powers, and in 1900 an American contingent participated in a joint expedition of the powers to put down the Boxer Rebellion in China (see p. 838). The United States also sent delegates to the First Hague Peace Conference in 1899, at which a Permanent Court of International Arbitration was created; and in 1905 President Roosevelt helped settle the Russo-Japanese War in the Treaty of Portsmouth (see p. 844).

Theodore Roosevelt and his Rough Riders atop San Juan Hill in Cuba (1898).

The United States and Latin America

America's first and foremost concern, however, was with affairs closer to home. Theodore Roosevelt in particular had long favored an active American policy in Central America. The Hay-Pauncefote Treaty of 1901 secured British consent for the construction of an American canal across the isthmus. In 1903 Panama, in a revolt sponsored by American interests, seceded from Colombia, and the United States was able to acquire the necessary land for its canal. The Panama Canal was opened shortly before the outbreak of war in 1914.

One of the chief dangers to peace in Latin America came from the loans that European investors in search of large profits had granted to the dictators of that region. Failures to meet payments invariably led to foreign intervention and threatened violations of the Monroe Doctrine. In 1902, Germany, Italy, and Great Britain sent warships to force Venezuela to pay its debts. Two years later another group of powers moved against the Dominican Republic. As a warning, and to forestall European intervention, President Roosevelt, in 1904, proclaimed a Corollary to the Monroe Doctrine. It gave the United States the exclusive right to exercise international police power in the Western Hemisphere. In line with its new policy, America sent marines to Cuba in 1906 and to Nicaragua in 1912.

The motive for America's intervention on these occasions was not merely to maintain order but also to protect its own financial interests. This "dollar diplomacy," as its opponents called it, caused much resentment in the countries concerned. America's policy, its Latin American neighbors charged, despite idealistic pronouncements, was every bit as imperialistic as that of the European powers.

The emergence of the United States as a world power was thus viewed with resentment by some of the other nations in the Western Hemisphere. The common use of "America" as synonymous with "United States" was symbolic of its preeminence. In comparison with the United States, events in the other American nations to the north and south attracted far less attention than they deserved.

CANADA: A NATION EMERGING

At the beginning of the nineteenth century, Canada was still a colony—British North America. It consisted of a number of regions or provinces: Rupert's Land, Upper Canada, Lower Canada, Newfoundland, and the Maritime Provinces of New Brunswick, Nova Scotia, and Prince Edward Island. The inhabitants were predominantly British, but there was a sizeable French-speaking minority. This ethnic dualism was never resolved and remained a divisive factor. Another problem facing the emerging nation was to reconcile its political fear of the United States with its economic dependence upon its southern neighbor. Internally divided and externally torn between the United States and the mother country, Canada had difficulty finding its national identity.

From Colony to Dominion

The influx into Canada of thousands of loyalist refugees during the American Revolution had strengthened the British element and thus antagonized further the already disgruntled French-Canadians. To counteract their discontent, in 1791 Britain's Parliament had passed the Canada Act, dividing Quebec province into Upper Canada (chiefly British) and Lower Canada (chiefly French). By allowing for local differences, the Act had helped to defuse ethnic tensions. But by creating oligarchic regimes in both Canadas, it led to mounting antagonism between the governors and their appointed councils on the one hand and the popularly elected assemblies on the other. The War of 1812 with the United States temporarily rallied the colonists behind the government in opposition to the American invaders. But once the fighting was over, domestic discontent reappeared, inspired in part by the example of Jacksonian democracy in the United States. Unrest finally came to a head in the rebellions of 1837. The uprisings were easily defeated by government troops, but they had called attention to the need for governmental reform.

To restore order, in 1838 Great Britain sent over Lord Durham as governor-in-chief. It was on the basis of his personal experience that Durham wrote his famous *Report on the Affairs of British North America* (1839). The *Report* suggested that Upper Canada (Ontario) and Lower Canada (Quebec) be reunited and given responsible self-government. Durham's proposals were incorporated in the Union Act passed by Parliament in 1840. The issue of

Lord Durham, governor of Canada (1838–40).

Sir John A. Macdonald, Canada's first prime minister.

self-government was evaded at first and not firmly implemented until the governorship of Lord Elgin in the late 1840s.

This new arrangement, however, still did not solve the differences between French and British settlers, nor did it sufficiently guarantee the protection of Canada's 3.5 million colonists against an almost tenfold number in the United States. It was a combination of political, economic, and military problems that after long debates finally resulted in a new federal constitution for Canada, the British North America Act, adopted by Britain's Parliament in 1867. Ontario and Quebec were once more separated and, together with the provinces of New Brunswick and Nova Scotia, were united in the Dominion of Canada. The new federation had complete control over its internal affairs, leaving the conduct of foreign policy to the mother country. The use of both English and French was guaranteed and Ottawa became the capital of the new central government.

The Dominion of Canada

The Dominion of Canada, like the United States and Great Britain, functioned under a two-party system — Liberals against Conservatives — with the latter predominant during most of the pre-1914 period. The Conservative leader, Sir John A. Macdonald, had been the main architect of confederation, and he continued to pursue the expansion of Dominion rule over the rest of the Canadian half of the North American continent. The first and foremost aim was the opening of the Canadian West, where claims to Rupert's Land and the North-West Territories were still held by the old Hudson's Bay Company. In 1869, the Company was bought out and in 1870 Manitoba became a Dominion province. The takeover caused an abortive rebellion in the Red River region by the local *Métis* (French/Indian half-breeds), who feared the loss of their lands. (Another flare-up, the Northwest Rebellion of 1885, was equally quickly suppressed.) The next member of the Dominion was British Columbia on the Pacific, joining in 1871. The accession of Prince Edward Island in 1873 concluded the early phase of confederation. The provinces of Alberta and Saskatchewan were not established until 1905, and Newfoundland did not join until 1949.

Next to extending Dominion rule, the Canadian government was concerned with tying together its diverse regions in the East and West. Some of the provinces had by no means been eager to join the federation and were induced to do so only in return for economic concessions. As in the United States the railroad proved a major aid to unification. The first transcontinental line, the Canadian Pacific Railway, was formally opened in 1887; it was followed by the Grand Trunk Pacific and the Canadian Northern. The easy transportation they provided aided the

John A. Macdonald on Confederation

1865

I have had the honor of being charged, on behalf of the Government, to submit a scheme for the Confederation of all the British North American Provinces — a scheme which has been received, I am glad to say, with general, if not universal approbation in Canada. . . .

One argument, but not a strong one, has been used against this Confederation, that it is an advance towards independence. Some are apprehensive that the very fact of our forming this union will hasten the time when we shall be severed from the mother country. I have no apprehension of that kind. I believe it will have the contrary effect. . . . When this union takes place, we will be at the outset no inconsiderable people. We find ourselves with a population approaching four millions of souls. Such a population in Europe would make a second, or at least, a third rate power. And with a rapidly increasing population . . . our future progress, during the next quarter of a century, will be vastly greater. (Cheers.) And when by means of this rapid increase, we become a nation of eight or nine millions of inhabitants, our alliance will be worthy of being sought by the great nations of the earth. (Hear, hear.) I am proud to believe that our desire for a permanent alliance will be reciprocated in England. . . .

From James J. Talman, *Basic Documents in Canadian History* (Princeton, N.J.; Van Nostrand, 1959), pp. 98–104.

settlement of the Canadian West by a rising number of immigrants — over two million between 1897 and 1912 — 40 percent of whom were of British origin, the rest coming from other North European countries and from the United States. These new citizens were attracted by generous grants of land under the Dominion Lands Act of 1872 and by other promises.

Easier communication and increased immigration, however, did not erase ethnic and regional differences. The American phenomenon of the "melting pot" remained unknown in Canada. Occasional outbursts of Canadian nationalism were sparked by opposition to outsiders — the United States or Great Britain — rather than by feelings of national unity or identity. In the early 1870s, a "Canada First" party tried to promote colonial nationalism; but it never received widespread support. Both Liberals and Conservatives advocated patriotism, but except in times of crises, ethnic differences, especially between the British and French founding races, prevented the emergence of a Canadian national consciousness.

Economic Developments

Whatever signs of nationalism or national purpose existed in Canada were often due to economic causes. In the early nineteenth century, Canada's economy was still predominantly one of hunting, logging, and fishing, with furs, timber, and cod as staples. In time other commodities — wood pulp, grain, oil, and minerals — were added to the list of raw materials for Canadian commerce. Agriculture, for climatic reasons, was limited to the southern latitudes along the American border, and industry did not take hold until late in the century.

As long as Canada remained a colony, its economic policy was influenced by that of the mother country. The abandonment of the British mercantile system between 1846 and 1849, therefore, and the shift to free trade had a deep effect on Canada's economy. Deprived of their preferential status in British markets, Canada's merchants now began looking for increased trade with the United States.

The economies of the two countries were interdependent in many ways, and there was interest in reciprocity on both sides. But a Reciprocity Treaty in 1854 lasted only until 1866, and subsequent attempts to revive it, while supported by Canada's Liberal party, were defeated by Macdonald's Conservatives. Instead of reciprocity, Macdonald in 1878 shifted to economic nationalism by instituting a protective tariff. The resulting prosperity assured the Conservatives of continued control until 1896.

Dominion versus Empire

In 1896, the Liberal Party under Sir Wilfrid Laurier took over. He was the first French-Canadian to become prime minister. The Liberals had won once before, in 1873, after Macdonald had resigned over a railway scandal. (He returned to power in 1878 and remained until his death in 1891.) The Liberals were in control until 1911. This was a prosperous era, witnessing the transition of the country into an industrialized urban society. As Canada became more mature and self-assured, it became less dependent upon the mother country and its Empire; and among French-Canadians in particular, a strongly anti-imperialist faction developed.

Economic relations between Dominion and Empire remained close, thanks to the British preferential tariff of 1897. In the area of defense the situation was less clear. Like the rest of the Empire, Canada sent a force of volunteers to fight in the Boer War at the turn of the century, but over vociferous French-Canadian protests. As tensions mounted in Europe during the pre-war years, the issue of Canada's contribution to imperial defense became acute. Instead of helping to finance the expansion of the British navy, in 1910 the Laurier government created its own small navy, but over strong Conservative opposition. Here was one issue that led to the Liberal defeat in 1911. Another was the Liberals' advocacy of economic reciprocity with the United States. On the question of whether Canada should draw closer to its neighbor or to the Empire, the majority of Canadians favored Britain as a more certain guardian of Canadian independence. It was thus under another Conservative prime minister, Robert Borden, that Canada entered the war in 1914 at Britain's side.

Canada and the United States

It is customary to view relations between the two major countries of North America as traditionally close and cordial. The contribution of American loyalists to Canada's early development, the constant migration in both directions, and the economic and cultural affinities between the two nations seem to support this view. But the fact that since the War of 1812 there has been no armed showdown, and that American-Canadian disputes have been settled peacefully, if not always amicably, must not blind us to the mixture of apprehension and envy that characterized the Dominion's attitude toward the colossus to the south. Having been twice invaded, Canadians feared that America's "Manifest Destiny" might not halt at their border. One of the motives leading to the consolidation of the Dominion had been to forestall such American expansion. Though at the same time America's insistence on observance of the Monroe Doctrine provided invaluable protection against threats or pressures from third powers. Especially in its dealings with the mother country, the alternative of "continentalism," that is, closer association with the United States, gave a strong bargaining point to the Dominion's quest for autonomy.

It is unnecessary to review the long series of Canadian-American disputes during the nineteenth century, mostly over borders and fishery rights. The last major such dispute before 1914 was the Alaskan boundary controversy of 1903. It was settled by arbitration in which the vote of the British commission member decided the issue in favor of the United States. On this as on other occasions, Canadian-American relations proved to be a function of American-British relations. This dependence on the support of the two great Anglo-Saxon powers imposed severe restraints on the Dominion's search for sovereign nationhood. Except in its foreign relations, however, Canada by 1914 had become a new and virtually independent nation.

LATIN AMERICA: AN AGE OF DICTATORS

Like Canada, Latin America in 1800 was still a vast colonial empire, controlled chiefly by Spain and Portugal. Thirty years later, the region was divided between some thirteen sovereign states, most important among them Argentina, Brazil, Chile, Peru, and Mexico. Subsequent partitions increased this number, to seventeen by 1850, and to twenty on the eve of the First World War. These countries had certain things in common. With the exception of Brazil (where Portuguese was spoken), they were Spanish in culture and language; they were all predominantly Catholic; and the majority of their people were Indians, with white minorities that grew larger as more and more immigrants arrived, chiefly from the Latin countries of Europe. Economically, Latin America throughout the nineteenth century remained predominantly agrarian and backward. Industrialization did not take hold until after the turn of the century, and then only slowly.

The Wars of Independence, 1807–30

The upheavals in Latin America were touched off in part by the aftermath of the French Revolution and their causes were not unlike those of the earlier American Revolution. Commercial activities were severely hampered by the mercantilist restrictions of the mother countries; taxes were high; and leading official positions were held by European-born rather than colonial Spaniards or Portuguese. Much of the revolutionary agitation originated among the colonials, the Creoles.

The immediate cause of the revolutions in Latin America was the invasion and occupation of the Iberian peninsula by Napoleonic troops in the first decade of the nineteenth century. The resulting separation from the mother countries could not help but foster colonial autonomy and a desire for independence. The wars of independence, mainly within the Spanish colonies, are a complex story of alternating victories and defeats. They were primarily civil wars between colonial patriots and Spanish royalists, with large numbers of foreign adventurers and volunteers, mostly British, fighting on the revolutionary side. Britain had long objected to the mercantilist practices of Spain and, together with the United States, favored the revolutions. The independence movement operated in four different regions—against Spain in the northern and southern part of South America as well as in Mexico, and against Portugal in Brazil.

Among the leaders of the revolutions, two names stand out: Simón Bolívar and José San Martín. Bolívar, the "Liberator," was the greater of the two. A wealthy Creole landowner, he was both an intellectual, deeply influenced by European and especially French ideas, and an extraordinary and charismatic leader of men. Due to Bolívar's untiring efforts, the northern portion of South America won its independence. By 1819 he had proclaimed the Republic of Colombia, with himself as president, and by 1822 included Venezuela and Ecuador as well. Meanwhile San Martín, an Argentine officer trained in Spain, had liberated a substantial part of southern South America. In 1816 an Argentine congress issued a declaration of independence. Chile was liberated by 1818; and in 1821 San Martín proclaimed the independence of Peru, making himself its "Protector."

San Martín was first and foremost a soldier, restrained in manner and devoid of political ambitions. By now the two liberation movements were beginning to coalesce. When San Martín continued to face royalist opposition in Peru, he turned to Bolívar for help. The two liberators met in 1822; but the meeting was not a success, in part because of temperamental differences between the two. Tired and discouraged, San Martín thereupon resigned and left politics. He died in French exile in 1850. His task in Peru was completed by Bolívar in 1824. In 1826, Upper Peru became an independent republic, named Bolivia after the great Liberator. But Bolívar's last years were far from happy. As his Colombian federation began to come apart, with Venezuela and Ecuador seceding, Bolívar likewise prepared for exile. In 1830 he died, ill and disillusioned, at age forty-seven.

The liberation of Spanish Latin America—except for Cuba and Puerto Rico—was thus completed. Mexico had become independent in 1821. Upheavals here were initially caused by unrest among the common people, Indians and *mestizos* (half-breeds), demanding land rather than independence. In 1810 a parish priest, Father Miguel Hidalgo, led a peasant rebellion against the government. It was ultimately defeated, and Hidalgo and some of the other leaders were executed. Beginning in 1814, the restoration of Spain's reactionary King Ferdinand VII strengthened the movement for independence. An ambitious and unprincipled Creole army officer, Augustín de Iturbide emerged as its leader. In 1821 Mexico proclaimed its independence, and the next year Iturbide had himself elected emperor. But he lasted for less than a year; in 1823 he was deposed and in 1824 Mexico, like the rest of Spain's former colonies, became a republic.

Compared to events in Spanish America, the independence of Brazil came about in a far less turbulent manner. When Napoleon's troops invaded Portugal in 1807, the Regent, Prince

Simón Bolívar, leader of the South American revolution against Spain and the greatest of Latin American heroes.

John, and his family left for Brazil, where they were warmly received. While there, John did much to improve the colony's administration and economy. In 1821, after a liberal revolution in Portugal, the now King John returned to Lisbon, leaving behind his son, Prince Pedro, as Regent. Once back in Portugal, the king reverted to some of the restrictive colonial policies of the past. In 1822, when he ordered his son back to Europe, the prince, supported by Brazilian patriots, refused. Soon thereafter he was proclaimed Pedro I, constitutional emperor of an independent Brazil. By the end of 1823, the remaining Portuguese troops had been forced to withdraw.

Disorder and Conflict

"America is ungovernable"— that is how Bolívar had summed up his life's work shortly before his death. He had hoped that from the turmoil of revolutions would emerge a united confederation of Spanish-speaking states, such as he had set up at Colombia. But this hope proved vain. Fragmentation rather than unity became the keynote of Latin American politics, leading to disorder within and to conflict among the new nations.

There were several reasons for Latin America's instability. Most important was the continent's ethnic diversity, with some 20 percent whites, 5 percent blacks, 45 percent Indians, and 30 percent *mestizos.* Because in most of the republics one of these races predominated, their differences were preordained. Racial differences, furthermore, were reflected in drastic economic disparities, with wealthy white minorities lording it over the poverty-ridden nonwhite masses. The resulting class hatred emphasized and intensified disunity. The dominant role of the Spaniards in colonial days was taken over by the main beneficiaries of the revolutions — the Creoles. Efforts to improve the situation through constitutions or decrees foundered upon the political inexperience and indifference of the vast majority of Latin Americans. As the Liberator had predicted: "There is no good faith in America, nor among the nations of America. Treaties are scraps of paper; constitutions, printed matter; elections, battles; freedom, anarchy; and life, a torment."

The revolutions had given prominence to military figures and virtues rather than to political leaders and aims. It is quite natural, therefore, that in times of crisis, the uniform should count more than the frock coat. The postrevolutionary era and beyond has rightly been called the age of the *caudillos,* or "strong men." With few exceptions, most Latin American countries lived in a state of perpetual revolution; frequently changed dictators, supported by military juntas, or cabals, tried to maintain order against anarchy. To the majority of the people — illiterate, poor, and incapable of representative government — this state of affairs was an inescapable condition or a necessary evil.

Much of the region's instability was due to wars among the Latin American states. The longest was the intermittent conflict between Argentina and Uruguay (1838–52). The War of the Triple Alliance (1865–70) between Argentina, Brazil, and Uruguay against Paraguay was the most costly, resulting in the annihilation of half of Paraguay's population. The War of the Pacific (1879–83), in which Chile fought her neighbors Peru and Bolivia for possession of the nitrate-rich Atacama Desert, left Chile the strongest nation on the Pacific coast. These were only the most spectacular conflicts; there were many other minor skirmishes. As far as conflicts with nations outside Latin America were concerned, France's attempts in the 1860s to make Mexico a satellite, and the simultaneous Spanish attacks against some Peruvian islands, were of little consequence. The war between Mexico and the United States (1846–48), on the other hand, was of great significance to Mexican-U.S. relations, but not to Latin America as a whole.

To discuss the individual history of each Latin American nation during the nineteenth century would be confusing and unjustified. We shall therefore concentrate on the most important countries—Argentina, Brazil, Chile, and Mexico.

Argentina

Like most Latin American republics, Argentina was troubled by conflicts between its capital city—Buenos Aires—and its provinces, the vast plains, or pampas, home of the South American cowboy, or gaucho. Tension between the liberal centralists of Buenos Aires and the conservative federalists of the provinces kept the country in a virtual state of civil war. In 1829, Juan Manuel Rosas, a wealthy landowner, became governor of Buenos Aires, a position he held until 1852. Rosas was Argentina's first national dictator, a typical *caudillo,* tyrannical and vain. He did contribute to the unification of the country, but was unable to break the spirit of gaucho independence. This was not achieved until the 1870s, when railroads began to penetrate the pampas, and wheat and cattle raising (sponsored by Great Britain) became Argentina's leading "industry." In 1853, a federal constitution was adopted, but universal male suffrage was not granted until 1912. With growing immigration from overseas, Argentina became more Europeanized than any other South American nation.

Brazil

The transition to independence in Brazil was more tranquil and orderly than anywhere else, due in large measure to the stabilizing influence of its monarchical regime. In 1824 a moderately liberal constitution was introduced, and while the emperor continued to enjoy much power, he was careful to observe at least the appearances of democracy. In 1831 Pedro I, whose profligate lifestyle had made him unpopular, abdicated. His son, Pedro II, did not reach majority until the 1840s, from which time on he became a much respected ruler until his abdication in 1889, when Brazil became a republic.

The immediate cause for the emperor's removal was the abolition of slavery in 1888, which conservative monarchists blamed on Pedro II, who had long been opposed to it. Slavery was a traditional institution in Latin America. Slaves there enjoyed some legal rights, but their lot was nevertheless dismal. In the early nineteenth century the abolitionist movement, spearheaded by Great Britain, gained ground, especially against the slave trade. Most of the new governments of Latin America abolished slavery in the 1820s. Brazil was a notable exception. Slavery there was less harsh, and at the time of its abolition there were at least three times as many free blacks in Brazil as slaves. Still, to the younger republican generation of the urban middle class, slavery, like monarchy, had no place on the American continent.

Under the new republican constitution of 1891, the president was granted considerable powers. The army, which had been instrumental in causing the emperor's abdication, continued to play an important role in Brazilian politics. After a turbulent period of transition, which saw several presidents overturned by revolts in the provinces and the navy, the republic at the turn of the century became more stable. Economic changes and growing prosperity played their part. Foreign trade, especially with Great Britain, increased, and European immigration supplied additional labor. For a while Brazil supplied most of the world's rubber, until overtaken by Southeast Asia. Coffee remained the mainstay of Brazil's economy and industrialization began to play an increasing role.

Chile

The first decade of Chilean independence was one of political disorder, with liberal federalists facing conservative centralists. A civil war in 1829–30 was won by the conservatives, under Diego Portáles. The constitution of 1833 established a strongly centralized

Benito Juárez, president of Mexico (1857–72).

regime under a virtually dictatorial president and with a restricted franchise. The rule of conservative landowners continued until the 1860s, when politics became more open and liberals gradually gained influence. The keynote of Chile's government was efficiency, allowing the country to win some minor conflicts and the major War of the Pacific (1879–83). As time went on, discontent with Chile's authoritarian system increased, leading to a brief civil war in 1891. The president's power henceforth was curtailed and he was made responsible to parliament. Chile's comparative stability aided its economic development. In contrast to most other Latin American countries, Chile's livelihood came from exploitation of natural resources—chiefly nitrate and copper—rather than from agriculture. As in the case of Argentina and Brazil, Chile's foremost trading partner and source of investments through most of the nineteenth century was Great Britain, the United States still being preoccupied with opening up its own territory.

Mexico

The history of Mexico was easily the most turbulent among Latin American nations and a prime example of *caudillo* rule. The leading figure until 1855 was General Antonio López de Santa Anna, president off and on and a dominant influence throughout. Treacherous and corrupt, but also astute and persuasive, Santa Anna ran the country for the profit of the Creole minority at the expense of the Indian and *mestizo* majority. As a general he was mediocre at best. In 1829 he defeated a Spanish expeditionary force and in 1838 he lost a leg fighting against a French punitive expedition, incidents used to bolster his heroic image. The disastrous defeat in the war with the United States forced him into exile, from which he briefly returned in 1853, only to be expelled again and for good two years later.

The liberal movement responsible for Santa Anna's fall was opposed to established privileges, especially of the Catholic Church. Its outstanding figure was Benito Juárez, a lawyer of Indian blood. In 1856 the Church was deprived of its landed wealth and in 1857 a liberal constitution introduced further reforms. Conservative and clerical opposition to these measures led to a fierce civil war, and not until 1860 did Juárez become the sole president of Mexico. But his troubles were not over. When he suspended payments on foreign loans in 1861, Napoleon III decided on intervention. The French venture ended with the execution of their puppet Emperor Maximilian in 1867 and the reelection of Juárez. But by then the domestic situation had so far deteriorated that Juárez was forced to rule by decree, like a *caudillo.* He died in 1872, a disillusioned man, his aims unfulfilled.

The next Mexican leader was a *mestizo,* General Porfírio Díaz, the most successful *caudillo* of all. He had served as a general under Juárez, but had later turned against him. In 1876 he took over by a military coup, and he remained in control for the next forty-five years. Using a mixture of bribery and force, he ingratiated himself with the established orders—landowners, the army, and the Catholic hierarchy. Díaz's main concern was with economic development. He started Mexico on the road to industrialization by sponsoring railways, developing the country's oil resources, starting new industries, and above all, encouraging foreign investment. But outsiders, especially from the United States, chiefly profited from Mexico's economic growth. Meanwhile the poverty-stricken Indian masses continued to demand land and social reform. Díaz was overthrown in 1911 by a revolution that was as much social as political. On the eve of the First World War, Mexico stood on the threshold of another turbulent era in its march toward social democracy.

SUMMARY

Considering the widely differing stages of development among the nations of the Western Hemisphere, North and

South, it is difficult to find any common denominators among them. Growth of democracy is one, more successful in North than in Latin America. The same holds for industrialization, which was more rapid in the United States and Canada than in Central and South America. Economic development in turn accounts for the preponderance of the Anglo-Saxon powers. The gap between the rich and poor certainly was more pronounced in South than in North America, and with accelerated population growth, it became more difficult to bridge. Finally, the nineteenth century saw a gradual recession of European influence from the Americas and a growing assertion of American, that is United States, leadership. The fact that such leadership also imposes responsibilities, the United States had yet to learn.

Suggestions for Further Reading

The vast literature on the history of the United States makes any selection of noteworthy works difficult. An excellent introductory survey is J. M. Blum et al., *The National Experience: A History of the United States.* 6th ed. (1985), with detailed bibliographies. On the pre-Jacksonian period, see G. Dangerfield, *The Awakening of American Nationalism* (1965). The westward movement is discussed in R. A. Billington, *Westward Expansion* (1967). Among studies on slavery, E. D. Genovese, *Roll, Jordan, Roll: The World the Slaves Made* (1974), stands out. On the Age of Jackson see J. C. Curtis, *Andrew Jackson and the Search for Vindication* (1976). J. G. Randall and D. Donald, *The Civil War and Reconstruction* (1961), covers the nation's most traumatic experience. C. V. Woodward, *Origins of the New South, 1877–1913* (1951), deals with its long-range impact. The involvement of the United States in world affairs is discussed in C. S. Campbell, *The Transformation of American Foreign Relations, 1865–1900* (1976), and H. K. Beale, *Theodore Roosevelt and the Rise of America to World Power* (1956).

Among general histories of Canada, the following stand out: D. G. Creighton, *Canada's First Century* (1970); A. R. M. Lower, *Colony to Nation,* 3rd ed. (1949); and E. McInnis, *Canada: A Political and Social History* (1947). C. W. New, *Lord Durham: A Biography* (1929), is a standard work. D. G. Creighton, *John A. Macdonald,* 2 vols. (1955), is a superb study of Canada's first prime minister and architect of the new nation. R. Cook, *Canada and the French Canadian Question* (1966), deals with a perennial issue in Canadian history.

One of the best general histories of Latin America is J. F. Rippy, *Latin America: A Modern History* (1958). Other good standard works are W. L. Schurz, *The New World: The Civilization of Latin America* (1954); J. L. Mecham, *Church and State in Latin America* (1934); L. Zea, *The Latin-American Mind* (1963); and W. C. Gordon, *The Economy of Latin America* (1950). On hemispheric relations, see J. L. Mecham, *A Survey of United States-Latin American Relations* (1965).

	1914				1950	
SOUTHWEST ASIA AND AFRICA	**1923** Kemal Attatürk, President of Turkish Republic			**1948** *Apartheid* in South Africa **1948** Founding of Israel, first Arab-Israeli war	**1954** Nasser takes control in Egypt **1956** Second Arab-Israeli war **1960–75** Independence movement sweeps Africa	**1967** Third Arab-Israeli (Six-Day) war **1971** Indo-Pakistani war **1973** Fourth Arab-Israeli war
EUROPE	**1914–18** World War I **1917** Bolshevik Revolution **1919** Paris Peace Conference	**1920** Keynes, *The Economic Consequences of the Peace* **1922** Mussolini's March on Rome **1923** French occupation of Ruhr	**1924** Death of Lenin, rise of Stalin **1924–25** Adolf Hitler, *Mein Kampf* **1924–29** Era of Locarno **1933** Hitler becomes Chancellor	**1935** Nuremburg Laws against Jews **1936–39** Spanish Civil War **1938** Munich Conference **1939** Hitler-Stalin Pact	**1939–44** World War II **1940** Fall of France **1941** Germany invades Russia **1941–45** Mass murder of Jews **1945** Yalta Conference	**1947** Marshall Plan **1949** Germany divided **1949** NATO Alliance **1953** Death of Stalin **1955** West Germany joins NATO **1955** Warsaw Pact
SOUTH AND SOUTHEAST ASIA	**1920–22** Gandhi's first Civil Disobedience Movement	**1927** Indonesian Nationalist party founded by Sukarno **1930** Gandhi's March to the Sea		**1947** Independence of India and Pakistan **1948** Mahatma Gandhi assassinated	**1949** Independence of Indonesia **1955** Bandung Conference, Indonesia	
EAST ASIA	**1927–37** Nationalist regime in Nanjing **1931** Japan seizes Manchuria **1934** Long March of Chinese Communists	**1937–45** Sino-Japanese War	**1941** Japan attacks Pearl Harbor **1945** Atomic bombing of Hiroshima and Nagasaki **1946–49** Civil war in China	**1949** People's Republic of China **1949–76** Mao Zedong's Chinese Revolution	**1950–53** Korean War **1951** US peace treaty with Japan	
THE AMERICAS AND PACIFIC	**1917** US enters World War I	**1929** The Great Depression begins **1933** Franklin D. Roosevelt's New Deal	**1941** US enters World War II **1945** First atomic bomb **1945** United Nations organized	**1946** First electronic computer **1947** Truman Doctrine **1948** Transistor invented	**1959** Fidel Castro's victory in Cuba **1962** Cuban Missile Crisis **1963** President Kennedy assassinated	**1968** Martin Luther King, Jr., assassinated **1969** Neil Armstrong, first man on moon

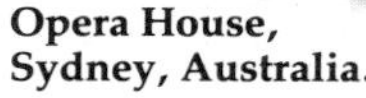

Opera House, Sydney, Australia.

British recruiting poster, World War I.

Signers of Egyptian-Israeli peace treaty: Sadat, Carter, Begin, 1979.

Official symbol of the United Nations.

Apollo 11 lands men on moon, July 16, 1969.

German inflation: two billion mark note, 1929.

1985	
1977 President Sadat visits Jerusalem **1978** Camp David Accords **1979** USSR invades Afghanistan **1979** Revolution in Iran	**1980–** Iran-Iraq war **1980** Black majority rule in Zimbabwe (Rhodesia) **1981** President Sadat assassinated
1957 First earth satellite, USSR **1957** European Economic Community	**1960** Yuri Gagarin, first man in space **1980** Solidarity movement in Poland
1961 Increasing US involvement in Vietnam	**1973** US forces withdraw from South Vietnam **1975** Communists take over Vietnam, Laos, Cambodia
1971 People's Republic of China joins UN **1972** Nixon visits Beijing **1976** Death of Mao Zedong	**1977** China begins liberalizing under Deng Xiaoping
1974 President Nixon resigns **1975** Helsinki Accords **1977** Panama Canal Treaty	**1979** Civil war begins in Nicaragua and El Salvador **1982** Falkland Islands War

Striking Solidarity union workers, Warsaw, Poland, 1981.

Emperor Hirohito of Japan, 1926.

41 World War, Revolution, and Peace, 1914–29

The "Great War," as it was called at the time, only gradually turned into a "World War." It was not the first worldwide conflict, but it was the largest. Before the war ended in November 1918, 49 million men had been mobilized in the "Allied" camp, against 25 million among the "Central Powers." More than any previous conflict, the war involved everyone, not only soldiers. The First World War was a truly "total war." The war lasted much longer than anyone had thought a modern war could, and it brought far more sweeping changes than anyone would have thought possible. Traditional empires collapsed and new nations arose from the wreckage. The New World, hitherto of little significance in European affairs, suddenly emerged as decisive to an Allied victory. Europe, which in the past had always settled its own affairs, apparently was unable to do so any longer.

The Great War was part of a transitional phase in modern history and will be treated as such here. There was no clear-cut end to the war—certainly not the peace settlements of 1919 and 1920. The problems that the statesmen at Paris wrestled with then continued to plague Europe and the world. It took a new series of crises, touched off by the Great Depression of 1929 and culminating in another World War, to complete the transition from nineteenth to twentieth century.

THE COMPARATIVE STRENGTH OF THE POWERS

Despite differences in numbers, the actual military strength of the Allies and the Central Powers at the start of the war was evenly balanced. The impressive size of the Allied armies was due to the ill-trained and poorly equipped Russian army. Germany's forces, on the other hand, were the best in the world. France and Britain matched the Germans in numbers, but the Germans excelled in the quality and quantity of their equipment. The Austrian army was weakened by its large Slav contingent. But since the main showdown was expected in the West, this handicap did not seem serious.

The Central Powers had other advantages, aside from their superior strength on land. Command of the interior lines of communication enabled them to shift their forces from one theater of war to another. The Allies, however, were widely separated; Russia in particular, with the closing of the Baltic and Black Seas, was cut off from much-needed aid. German industry, furthermore, was more readily converted to war production than the industries of its opponents. The Central Powers had more than enough coal and iron, and territories seized on the western front increased their resources. In their supplies of foodstuffs, however, Austria and Germany fell seriously short of their needs.

Had the war been as brief as most wars of the nineteenth century, Germany and Austria might have won it. But as the fighting dragged on, inherent Allied superiority made itself felt. Their manpower was greater; their industrial potential was superior; and, thanks to Great Britain, the Allies enjoyed naval supremacy. By keeping the sea lanes open, the British navy assured the uninterrupted flow of men and material; and by clamping a tight blockade on Central Europe, Britain aggravated Germany's and Austria's food problems.

Each side tried to strengthen its position further by seeking additional partners. Usually having more to offer, the Allies were more successful in this contest. At the end of the war, thirty "Allied and Associated Powers" were ranged against the Central Powers—Germany, Austria-Hungary, Turkey, and Bulgaria.

The most important additions to the Allied camp, aside from the United States, were Japan, Italy, Rumania, and Greece. Japan's entry into the war in August 1914 proved to be a most profitable move. Without delay the Japanese seized Germany's holdings in China's Shandong (Shantung) Province and occupied Germany's Pacific islands north of the equator. Italy did not join the war until 1915. It had refused to honor the Triple Alliance, claiming that its terms did not apply. To balance possible Austrian gains in the Balkans, moreover, the Italians had demanded territorial concessions from Austria. The Austrians agreed to some of Italy's demands, but the Allies were able to offer more. By the secret Treaty of London in April 1915, they promised Italy not only the Austrian regions inhabited by Italians but also considerable territory along the eastern Adriatic and in Asia Minor and Africa. Having received these promises, the Italians declared war against Austria-Hungary in May 1915, and against Germany in August 1916. At that time, Rumania also joined the Allies, and Greece followed in June 1917. In both these cases the pressure of military events and the hope for territorial gains were decisive.

The only two countries that joined the Central Powers were Turkey and Bulgaria. The Ottoman Empire had long maintained close economic ties with Germany, and its army had been trained by German officers. In August 1914 Turkey concluded an alliance with Germany; three months later a Turkish naval squadron bombarded Russia's Black Sea ports; and in early November 1914 the Allies declared war on the Ottoman Empire. As for Bulgaria, it had been wooed by both sides. But the Central Powers were able to promise more, and in October 1915 Bulgaria joined the Germans and Austrians in a major drive against Serbia.

THE GREAT STALEMATE, 1914–16

Both sides had prepared for a brief offensive war. In its grand simplicity, however, the German Schlieffen Plan promised a far quicker decision than France's Plan XVII, which called for an invasion of Alsace-Lorraine.

1914: The Allies Ahead

From the start of hostilities on the western front, Germany held the initiative. After one month of fighting, German forces had advanced to within twenty-five miles of Paris. In early September, however, the German drive was halted at the river Marne. The battle of the Marne was one of the decisive events of the war, because it dashed Germany's hope for an early victory. The battle was followed by a series of engagements in which each side hoped to outflank the other, and in the course of which the front was gradually extended to the sea. By November 1914 the fighting on the western front had changed from a war of movement to a war of position. Until the spring of 1918 the western front, except for an occasional thrust in one direction or the other, remained unchanged.

With the bulk of Germany's forces tied down on the western front, Russia was able to score some unexpected successes on the eastern front. In mid-August 1914 two Russian armies invaded East Prussia and within a few days overran almost half of Germany's easternmost province. At the height of danger, the kaiser recalled from retirement General Paul von Hindenburg and appointed as Hindenburg's chief of staff the younger and more capable Erich Ludendorff. These men soon reversed the situation on the eastern front. In two major battles, at Tannenberg and the Masurian Lakes, Russia lost close to 250,000 men. Russia's reversals in the north were balanced by successes in the southeast against Austria. In a sweeping campaign under Russia's commander in chief, Grand

Soldiers setting up a machine gun nest against the Germans on the western front.

Germany's warlords: Hindenburg, William II, and Ludendorff.

Duke Nicholas, Russian forces in September took most of Galicia and advanced to the Carpathian frontier of Hungary.

On the eastern front, as on the western, the end of 1914 found the Allied and Central Powers locked in a stalemate. But, because Germany had failed to deliver a knockout blow in the West and appeared to be stalled in the East, the advantage was felt to lie with the Allies. In addition, British naval superiority had been responsible for the sinking of a German naval squadron off the coast of South America and for the seizure of most of Germany's colonies.

1915: Allied Reverses

Allied dreams of victory, however, were premature. The new Italian ally proved to be of little use. Furthermore, a British attack against the Gallipoli Peninsula and the Turkish Straits failed. Had it succeeded, the Black Sea would have been opened to Allied shipping. Instead, the Straits remained closed for the rest of the war.

The most serious Allied reverses during 1915 were on the eastern front and in the Balkans. In the spring and summer, German forces in the north and combined Austro-German forces in the south advanced in a series of offensives that cost the Russians Poland, Lithuania, and Courland, drove them out of Galicia, and lost them almost a million men. All of central and eastern Europe was now in German and Austrian hands. In October the Central Powers turned against Serbia; and in November they moved into Montenegro and Albania.

By the beginning of 1916 the tide of war on land seemed definitely to have turned against the Allies. Even on the high seas the Germans were able to make some gains. To counteract Britain's blockade, the German government imposed a submarine blockade against the British Isles in early 1915. The first phase of German submarine warfare came to a head with the sinking of the British liner *Lusitania* in May 1915. The loss of 139 American passengers caused a serious crisis in American-German relations. It was settled only after Germany promised to restrict its submarine tactics.

1916: Stalemate

Since time was clearly on the side of the Allies, it seemed imperative to the Germans to force a major showdown. In February 1916, therefore, they launched an all-out offensive against the French stronghold of Verdun. The battle of Verdun was the most famous battle of the war. It lasted more than four months and caused more than seven hundred thousand casualties; yet it ended undecided. Its chief hero on the French side was General Henri Philippe Pétain. Like Hindenburg after the battle of Tannenberg, Pétain became the idol of his people. Both men were to play fateful roles in later years. The battle of Verdun was followed by an Allied counteroffensive along the Somme River. But the battle of the Somme, like that of Verdun, failed to force a final decision in the West.

Events elsewhere during 1916 were equally indecisive. In June, Russian forces under General Alexei Brusilov started a major drive against the Austrian lines and within a few weeks had taken most of eastern Galicia. These successes brought Rumania into the war. But its participation only made

The First World War 1914–18

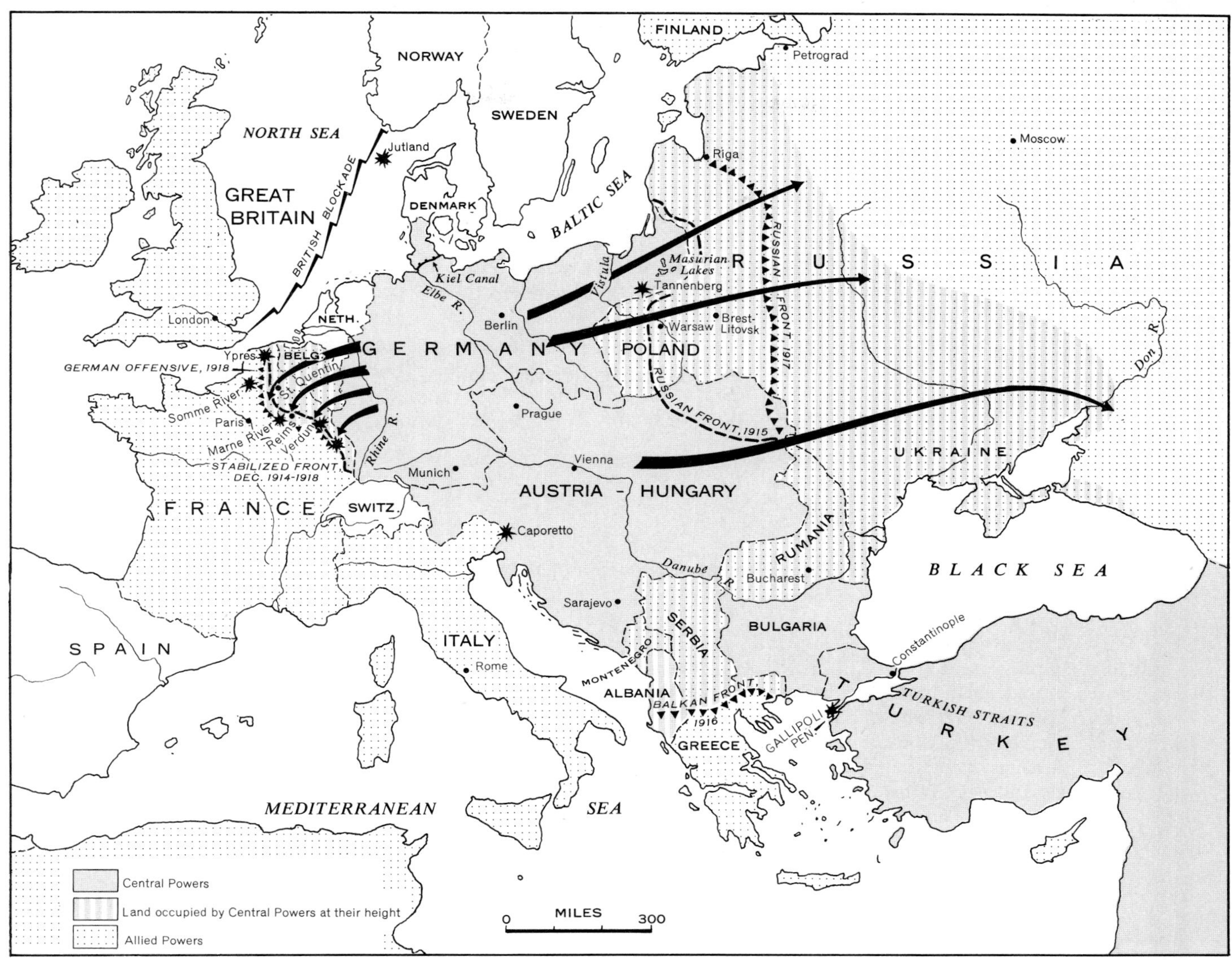

matters worse for the Allies. In late September, Austro-German forces invaded Rumania, and by January 1917 most of that country's rich resources were in the hands of the Central Powers. On both fronts the outcome of the war continued to hang in the balance.

The year 1916 also saw the one great naval battle of the war between Germany and Britain. The German navy, to have a chance of success, had to fight in its home waters. On several occasions the Germans went out into the North Sea, hoping to entice the British into battle. On one of these sallies the two fleets made contact off the coast of Jutland in May 1916. The battle of Jutland was indecisive. The British lost more naval tonnage than the Germans, but they could better afford to. The German fleet henceforth remained safely at home.

By the end of 1916 a stalemate had been reached on all fronts, and victory for either side seemed far away. Meanwhile losses and material costs of the war had been staggering, and the strain of war had begun to tell on the home fronts as well.

Nicholas II with Grand Duke Nicholas, commander in chief of the Russian armies until 1915.

THE HOME FRONTS

People everywhere had greeted the outbreak of war with enthusiastic demonstrations of national unity. Each side believed that it was fighting a "just war." In addition, the war was expected to be short. The Germans hoped to be in Paris before the summer was over, and the French were looking forward to Christmas in Berlin. When instead the war dragged on with no end in sight, enthusiasm gave way to depression.

One of the important conditions for victory was effective leadership. Both England and France found outstanding civilian leaders — the British in David Lloyd George, and the French in Georges Clemenceau. In Germany, Austria, and Russia, on the other hand, where the monarch was both chief executive and symbol of national unity, much depended on the leadership he provided. In none of the three countries did the ruler measure up to expectations. William II had neither the ability nor the energy to cope with the problems of a total war. As he gradually faded into the background, his role was taken over by Hindenburg and Ludendorff. In Austria, Francis Joseph was too old and his grandnephew Charles, who succeeded him in 1916, was too inexperienced to keep the crumbling Empire together. The saddest figure among Europe's monarchs was Nicholas II of Russia. In 1915 he assumed personal command of his armed forces, leaving the government in the hands of his wife and her sinister adviser, Rasputin.

Women in Wartime

In industry as a whole the total employment of women and girls over ten as between 1914 and 1918 increased by about 800,000, from 2,179,000 to 2,971,000. . . . It is in these arid statistics that we traverse a central theme in the sociology of women's employment in the twentieth century. . . . The growth of large-scale industry and bureaucracy would undoubtedly have brought this development eventually, but it was the war, in creating simultaneously a proliferation of Government commitees and departments *and* a shortage of men, which brought a sudden and irreversible advance in the economic and social power of a category of women employees which extended from sprigs of the aristocracy to daughters of the proletariat. . . .

Given the rigidities of the Edwardian class structure, there are difficulties in the way of summing up the consequences of the war for women as an entire sex. In the business, medical and military functions . . . the women concerned were very largely women of the middle and upper classes. Yet the major section of these women had been in pre-war years a depressed class, tied to the apron-strings of their mothers or chaperons, or the purse-strings of their fathers or husbands. Now that they were earning on their own account, they had economic independence; now that they were working away from home, in some cases far from home, they had social independence.

Obviously, then, women of all classes shared in a similar kind of emancipation. The suffragette movement before the war had . . . aimed simply at the same limited franchise for some women as was enjoyed by some men. The Women's Movement from 1915 onwards is a more unified movement than ever it had been previously.

From A. Marwick, *The Deluge: British Society and the First World War* (New York: Norton, 1970), pp. 91–94.

Total War

The demands of total war presented many new and difficult problems. All the powers experienced periodic munition shortages. Labor was scarce. Women were employed in growing numbers, and Germany "recruited" workers from Belgium. Except for the Russians, who were almost completely isolated, the Allies were able to supplement their domestic production of food and war materials with overseas imports. The Central Powers, however, cut off by the blockade, were chiefly dependent on their own resources. The Germans tackled the problem with customary efficiency, devising scores of ersatz, or substitute, products and perfecting new processes to obtain scarce materials. Austria-Hungary was far less successful in these respects. Its difficulties were made worse by continuous economic feuds between Austria and Hungary.

The most serious shortages of the Central Powers were in food and clothing. Germany began rationing in

1915. Shortages of labor and transportation reduced the coal supply, adding the misery of cold to hunger. Faced with these hardships, many Germans, especially among the working class, hoped for a speedy end to the war, even without victory.

War Aims and Peace Proposals

Neither side ever stated its war aims openly, except in the vaguest terms. Secretly, however, the Allies had agreed on a distribution of spoils: Russia was to get most of the Polish regions under German and Austrian rule, as well as control over the Turkish Straits; France was promised the left bank of the Rhine; England was allotted the German colonies; and Italy was to have parts of Austria and territories elsewhere. In supplementary agreements most of the Ottoman Empire was divided into Russian, Italian, French, and British spheres of interest.

The war aims of the Central Powers called for the "liberation" of the Poles and the Baltic peoples from Russian domination, the setting up of small satellite states under German and Austrian control, and the annexation of some regions outright. Germany hoped also to gain additional regions rich in iron ore from France and political and economic control over Belgium. There were also schemes for a central European federation under German leadership, a *Mitteleuropa,* and for a compact central African colony.

In view of these far-reaching Allied and German aims, it is not surprising that efforts to reach a compromise peace proved fruitless. The Central Powers took the first official step in December 1916, informing President Wilson that they were ready to enter into peace negotiations. Wilson thereupon asked both sides to state their terms. But this the Germans refused to do. There were other peace moves, notably one inaugurated by Pope Benedict XV in August 1917. All these efforts failed. Both sides wanted peace, but neither side wanted it badly enough to make any real concessions.

English women working at the Woolwich Arsenal munition factory.

The United States at first had made every effort to remain neutral. Isolationism was still a strong force; and although there were many Anglophiles in the East, there were also large numbers of German-Americans in the Middle West. America's abandonment of neutrality had several causes. Effective Allied propaganda was one. Another was the growing financial involvement of many Americans in the Allied cause. But more important than either of these factors was Germany's resumption of unrestricted submarine warfare early in 1917.

Unrestricted Submarine Warfare

Germany decided to step up the submarine campaign after its peace move of December 1916 had failed. Germany's civilian authorities opposed unrestricted submarine warfare, fearing that it might bring America into the war. But the real power now lay with the military. With time on the Allied side, Hindenburg and Ludendorff felt that only drastic submarine action could win the war. They realized that this might lead to American intervention, but they thought England would be defeated long before such intervention became effective.

Unrestricted submarine warfare began on February 1, 1917. America

World War I poster.

broke off diplomatic relations with Germany, and as German submarines began sinking American ships, public opinion became more and more interventionist. The publication of the intercepted "Zimmermann Telegram," a note sent by Germany's foreign secretary urging Mexico to make war on the United States, did the rest. On April 6, 1917, Congress declared war on Germany.

THE RUSSIAN REVOLUTION

America's entrance into the war was made more urgent by changes in Russia that weakened the Allied cause. Events there had long been pointing toward a major domestic upheaval. At first the Russian people had loyally supported their government's war effort. But the sufferings of war soon dampened their spirit. With insufficient arms and a chronic shortage of munitions, the army lost more than a million men during the first year of the war. While the armies lacked essential materials, the civilian population suffered from food shortages, despite Russia's agrarian economy. The blame for all these ills was rightly placed on the inefficiency and corruption of the government. The elected assembly, the Duma, repeatedly urged the adoption of reforms; but the tsar continued to meet discontent with repression.

The Background of the Revolution

Repression alternating with reform had been the policy for decades. There had been an earlier revolution in 1905, but it had brought few changes (see p. 776). To understand the sudden collapse of the tsarist regime in 1917, we must go back to 1861 and the emancipation of the serfs by Alexander II (see p. 757). The peasant liberated at the time provided the manpower for the belated industrialization of Russia. The resulting proletariat, uprooted and subject to the hardships of too rapid industrialization, provided a fertile breeding ground for revolution. By 1914 industrial workers made up less than 20 percent of the total population, but they were concentrated in the larger cities. It was here that the revolution started; but it found a ready echo in the countryside, where the peasants were leading a marginal existence, only a few of the more enterprising among them having profited from the emancipation.

The "February Revolution" and Provisional Government

The overthrow of the tsarist regime was the climax of a gradually mounting wave of popular protest. By 1917 more than a million soldiers had deserted; in the cities, food shortages led to strikes and riots; and in the countryside, landless peasants began to seize the lands of their noble landlords. In early March street demonstrations broke out in Petrograd (the name given to St. Petersburg at the beginning of the war). In the past the government had always been able to use the army against such disturbances. But the troops now fraternized with the rioters. From the capital, insurrection spread to the provinces. On March 12—or February 27 in the Russian calendar—the Duma established a Provisional Government under a liberal aristocrat, Prince George Lvov. Three days later, Nicholas II abdicated. He and his family were later murdered by the Bolsheviks in the summer of 1918.

The new Provisional Government was faced with problems for which it was unprepared. To meet the discontent of the masses some reforms were introduced, but these did not go far enough. The situation was complicated by the existence of a rival for political power, the Petrograd Soviet (Council) of Workers' and Soldiers' Deputies, consisting of Socialist Revolutionaries, Mensheviks, and some Bolsheviks.

The Provisional Government's main difficulty arose from its desire to continue the war. In July the new minister of war, Alexander Kerensky, launched a futile offensive against the Austrians. Its failure led to further riots in Petrograd. To restore order, Kerensky replaced Prince Lvov as prime minister on July 25. To strengthen his position, Kerensky appointed as commander in chief General Lavr Kornilov, who was popular with the army's rank and file. Kornilov succeeded in restoring some discipline but was unable to halt a German offensive. When there were signs that Kornilov wanted to make himself military dictator, he was arrested, and on September 14 Kerensky himself assumed supreme command of the army.

The revolution, meanwhile, which thus far had been free from terrorism, became increasingly violent, as workers sacked stores, peasants burned manor houses, and soldiers killed their officers. Revolution among the non-Russian nationalities in the borderlands, furthermore, threatened the unity of the country. Finally, the Petrograd Soviet, which until then had tolerated the Provisional Government, was gradually falling under the control of its most radical faction, the Bolsheviks.

The "October Revolution"

The exiled Bolshevik leaders—Lenin, Trotsky, Stalin, and others—had returned from abroad or from Siberia after the February Revolution. Their immediate aim was to gain control of the soviets in Petrograd and elsewhere. At first they only commanded a small minority within the Petrograd Soviet. Lenin advanced his radical program—immediate peace, seizure of land by the peasants and of factories by the workers—against the do-nothing policy of the Mensheviks and the Socialist Revolutionaries. Constantly reiterating this program, the Bolsheviks gradually increased their following within the Soviet and without. By September the Bolsheviks controlled the soviets in Petrograd, Moscow, and several other cities.

The only way for the Bolsheviks to gain control of the government was to use force. When Kerensky got wind of the Bolshevik plot and ordered the arrest of their leaders, Bolshevik forces began occupying strategic points in Petrograd on November 6. The main fighting took place around the Winter Palace, seat of the Provisional Government. On November 7 Kerensky took flight. The same afternoon an all-Russian Congress of Soviets convened. The majority of its delegates were Bolsheviks. As a first move they formed a new executive, the Council of People's Commissars, with Lenin as Chairman, Trotsky as Foreign Commissar, and Stalin as Commissar for National Minorities.

The "October Revolution"—so named because November 7 was October 25 old-style—was only the first stage on the road to a Bolshevik victory; a long drawn-out civil war was yet to follow. The followers of Lenin still numbered only a small percentage of the Russian people. When the constituent assembly was elected late in November, less than one-fourth of the delegates were Bolsheviks. But this was to be the first and last free election in Russia. When the assembly met for the first time in January 1918, it was dispersed by Bolshevik forces.

Lenin

November 7, 1917

It was just 8:40 when a thundering wave of cheers announced the entrance of the presidium, with Lenin—great Lenin—among them. A short, stocky figure, with a big head set down in his shoulders, bald and bulging. Little eyes, a snubbish nose, wide, generous mouth, and heavy chin; clean-shaven now, but already beginning to bristle with the well-known beard of his past and future. Dressed in shabby clothes, his trousers much too long for him. Unimpressive, to be the idol of a mob, loved and revered as perhaps few leaders in history have been. A strange popular leader—a leader purely by virtue of intellect; colourless, humourless, uncompromising and detached, without picturesque idiosyncrasies—but with the power of explaining profound ideas in simple terms, of analysing a concrete situation. And combined with shrewdness, the greatest intellectual audacity.

From John Reed, *Ten Days That Shook the World* (New York: International Publishers, 1919), p. 125.

The Treaty of Brest-Litovsk

The most important immediate result of the October Revolution was to end the war on the eastern front. On December 5, 1917, the Bolsheviks concluded an armistice with Germany, and on December 22 peace negotiations began at Brest-Litovsk. The Bolsheviks wanted a "just, democratic peace without annexations or indemnities." But the Germans were in no mood to forgo their advantages. At one point the Russians broke off negotiations, whereupon the Germans resumed their advance. On March 3, 1918, the Russians gave in and accepted Germany's terms.

Under the Treaty of Brest-Litovsk, Russia lost a quarter of its European territory, a third of its population, more than half of its coal and iron, and a third of its industry. The treaty was later invalidated because of the Allied victory. But for the moment, the Central Powers were freed from the burden of a two-front war and won access to the vast resources of eastern Europe. Their position was further strengthened by a peace treaty forced on Rumania at Bucharest on March 5, 1918, under which Germany received a ninety-year lease on that country's oil wells. The triumph of German expansionist aims served to warn the Allies of what to expect in the event of a German victory.

Lenin addressing the May Day demonstration in Moscow (1918).

CONTINUED STALEMATE IN THE WEST, 1917

With the Central Powers victorious in the East, the Allies more than ever depended on aid from the United States. A first small contingent of American troops under General John J. Pershing had landed in France as early as June 1917. But not until spring of 1918 did American units take any real part in the fighting. America's main contribution was material aid. To meet the submarine danger, a vast shipbuilding program was initiated. Unrestricted submarine warfare at first was a serious threat to the Allied cause. But in time ways of countering the submarine menace were devised, notably the convoy system.

While the Allies were holding their own at sea, the Central Powers were successfully resisting Allied attempts to force a decision on land. The campaigns on the western front in 1917 were among the bloodiest in the whole war. Yet the lessons of Verdun and the Somme still held true—a decision on the western front was impossible. The Central Powers, meanwhile, scored one of their greatest victories on the Italian front. The battle of Caporetto in October 1917 cost Italy close to half a million men. Only French and British reinforcements averted a greater disaster.

The Decline of Civilian Morale

Continuous heavy losses at the front and deprivations at home caused a serious decline in civilian morale. The British, suffering least, bore up best. The French, on the other hand, experienced a major military and political crisis. In May 1917 the senseless bloodshed on the front led to open mutiny among the troops. The French home front, too, was becoming more and more defeatist. In Italy, shortages of food and coal brought on a series of strikes. Only the disaster of Caporetto made people rally to the support of the government, realizing that the future of their country was at stake.

The Central Powers underwent similar crises. In Germany, differences between civilian and military leaders caused the resignation of Chancellor Theobald von Bethmann Hollweg and the assumption of virtually dictatorial control by Hindenburg and Ludendorff. In Austria the war gave new momentum to the separatist tendencies of the Empire's many nationalities. The Czechs and the Yugoslavs set up organizations abroad to work for Allied recognition of their cause, and Polish, Czech, and Yugoslav prisoners in Allied hands were formed into national legions to fight against their homelands.

The general weariness that affected all the belligerents quite naturally gave rise to further peace efforts. Like all the earlier attempts, however, they failed because neither side was ready to make the necessary concessions. The Bolsheviks published the secret treaties revealing Allied war aims, and western statesmen made highly idealistic pronouncements to counteract these revelations. In January 1918 President Wilson, in an effort to dissociate America from agreements to which it had not been a party, stated his famous Fourteen Points as the basis for a just peace. Briefly stated, they were:

(1) "Open covenants of peace" and an end to secret diplomacy; (2) freedom of the seas in peace and war; (3) "the removal . . . of all economic barriers and the establishment of an equality of trade conditions"; (4) the reduction of armaments "to the lowest point consistent with domestic safety"; (5) the "impartial adjustment of all colonial claims"; (6) the "evacuation of all Russian territory" and an attitude of "intelligent and unselfish sympathy" toward Russia; (7) the evacuation and restoration of Belgium; (8) the freeing of the invaded portions of France and the restoration to it of Alsace-Lorraine; (9) the "readjustment of the frontier of Italy . . . along clearly recognizable lines of nationality"; (10) "the freest opportunity of autonomous development" for the peoples of Austria-Hungary; (11) the evacuation and restoration of Rumania, Serbia, and Montenegro; (12) autonomy for the non-Turkish nationalities of the Ottoman Empire and the permanent opening of the Straits to all nations; (13) the creation of an independent Poland, including "the territories inhabited by indisputably Polish populations," and assurance to Poland of "a free and secure access to the sea"; and (14) the formation of "a general association of nations . . . for the purpose of affording mutual guarantees of political independence and territorial integrity to great and small states alike."

The Fourteen Points were to play an important role in the later negotiations for an armistice and peace, but for the time being they had little effect. The only way to get peace was to win the war. With time running against it, Germany, in the spring of 1918, decided to make an all-out bid for victory.

THE COLLAPSE OF THE CENTRAL POWERS

Ludendorff's plan for a large-scale spring offensive had some chance of success. The Germans were able to move large numbers of troops from the East. The Allies were still suffering from the heavy losses of their 1917 offensives, and reinforcements from America were only just beginning to arrive in sufficient numbers.

The Last Offensives

The gigantic "Emperor's Battle" was launched in March 1918. At first it was overwhelmingly successful. Within three months the Germans once again stood on the Marne, only fifty miles from Paris. But despite brilliant victories, they failed to breach the Allied front. On July 15, when the Germans mounted their last major drive, in the vicinity of Reims, the Allied front was held largely with the aid of American forces.

British tanks at Amiens in 1918. In the final months of the war the Allies effectively used large numbers of tanks under a smoke screen as a cover for advancing infantry.

On July 18, the Allies began their counteroffensive. On August 8, the German army suffered its "black day." Using for the first time large numbers of tanks, the British advanced almost eight miles. From here on the Allies never gave the Germans a moment's rest. By the end of September the German army had lost a million men in six months. Morale was low and desertions mounted. Germany's allies, moreover, were showing signs of imminent collapse. On October 4, finally, Germany and Austria appealed to President Wilson for an armistice based on the Fourteen Points.

Chaos in Central Europe

By the time prearmistice negotiations were completed a month later, all the Central Powers had collapsed. The first to give up was Bulgaria. The Bulgarian lines were broken in late September, and before the month was out the government had sued for an armistice. Next came Turkey. During the last year of the war, British forces had steadily advanced from the Persian Gulf into Mesopotamia and from Egypt into Palestine and Syria. With Bulgaria out of the war, Turkey was threatened from the north as well. On October 30 it concluded an armistice.

The Austro-Hungarian Empire, meanwhile, was falling to pieces. On October 21, 1918, the Czechoslovaks declared their independence, and a week later the Yugoslavs followed suit. On November 1, Hungary established an independent government. Ten days later, Emperor Charles renounced his throne, and by the middle of November both Austria and Hungary had proclaimed republics.

In Germany the government had reformed itself, in the hope of obtaining more favorable armistice terms. But the Allies would have no dealings with the kaiser. On November 3 mutiny broke out among Germany's sailors at Kiel. Within days the revolt spread through most of northern Germany. On November 7 revolution broke out in Munich and the king of Bavaria abdicated. On November 9, finally, revolution in Berlin overthrew the monarchy and a German republic was proclaimed.

The Allies, meanwhile, had agreed to accept the Fourteen Points as a basis for an armistice. Under its provisions Germany had to withdraw its forces beyond the Rhine; it had to renounce the treaties of Brest-Litovsk and Bucharest; and it had to surrender large quantities of strategic materials. The terms were designed to make any resumption of hostilities impossible. Fighting was officially ended on November 11.

The war that was to have been over in four months had lasted more than four years. At its height it had involved some thirty-four nations. It had killed close to ten million soldiers, wounded twice that number, and caused close to a million civilian deaths. Its total cost has been estimated at over $350 billion. It had brought revolution to central and eastern Europe and had swept away the last remnants of autocratic monarchism. The war's initial purpose — to determine the future of Serbia — had long since given way to far bigger aims. Germany had dreamed of hegemony in Europe and perhaps the world. The Allies had hoped to avert that German threat and in the process to round out their own possessions. Only the United States was seeking nothing. The Peace Conference was to show whether American idealism would prevail against the hardheaded nationalism of its European allies.

THE PARIS PEACE CONFERENCE

The Peace Conference opened on January 18, 1919. All the belligerents were present, except the Central Powers and Russia; this was to be a peace dictated by the victors. As in most peace conferences, the important decisions were made by the great powers who had contributed most to winning the war. The peace was thus made by a handful of men, the "Big Four": Wilson, Lloyd George, Clemenceau, and Orlando.

The star of the conference was Woodrow Wilson, a figure of hope to Europeans. The favorite aim of the American president was to set up a League of Nations. But his position had been weakened by the return of a Republican majority in the recent congressional elections. Great Britain was represented by its prime minister, David Lloyd George, the mercurial Welsh politician. Although his views on the peace were fairly moderate, he had recently won an election on the promise of a harsh peace. The most impressive figure of the conference was France's premier, Georges Clemenceau. He hated the Germans, and his foremost aim was to protect France by weakening its former enemy in every possible way. Italy's representative, Prime Minister Vittorio Orlando, played only a minor role.

Problems of Peacemaking

The problems before the Paris conference were without precedent. The last comparable meeting had been held at Vienna a century earlier. But while the Congress of Vienna had been concerned only with reordering the affairs of Europe, the problems before the Paris conference ranged over the whole world. The Allies had accepted the Fourteen Points as a basis for peace, but many of Wilson's principles differed from the provisions of the Allies' secret treaties. Other complications arose from the many foreign and domestic disturbances that occurred while the conference was in session, the popular clamor in the Allied countries for a speedy settlement, and the physical and nervous strain under which the delegates labored. It is not surprising that the peace they made was not perfect.

So long as the victors agreed among themselves, the negotiations went smoothly. But there were several questions on which they did not see eye to eye. The most important were Germany's colonies, the Rhineland, reparations, Fiume, and the Shandong Peninsula.

The Allies agreed that Germany's colonies should not be returned, but they did not agree on what to do with them. France, Japan, and Great Britain and its dominions wanted to annex Germany's holdings. President Wilson, on the other hand, felt that this would violate his Fourteen Points. The impasse was finally resolved by the adoption of the "Mandate Principle," which provided that the German colonies as well as a large part of the Ottoman Empire were to be placed under foreign control, subject to supervision by the League of Nations.

The crisis over the future of the Rhineland almost broke up the conference. The French demanded that the left bank of the Rhine be made into an autonomous buffer state for reasons of security. Such an arrangement, however, ran counter to Wilson's principles. The compromise arrived at after long and acrimonious debate called for the permanent demilitarization of the Rhineland and its occupation by Allied forces for fifteen years. In addition, the territory of the Saar was to remain under League administration for fifteen years, and France was given the region's coal mines. Finally, Great Britain and the United States promised France an alliance against possible German aggression.

In the discussion of reparations, an argument arose over the extent to which Germany was to make good damages done to the civilian population of the Allies. Wilson finally gave way to the pressure of his European colleagues and agreed that this should include pensions to victims of war and allowances to their families. To justify so large a claim, the Allies affirmed that German aggression had been responsible for starting the war. The controversial issue of "war guilt" was thus injected into the peace treaty.

The crisis over Fiume arose from Italy's demand that it be given the Adriatic port in place of the Dalmatian coast, which it had been promised in the Treaty of London but which had been incorporated into Yugoslavia. When Prime Minister Orlando finally left Paris in protest, the united Allied front showed its first open rift. Italy felt that it had been cheated out of its just reward.

The issue of Shandong involved Japan and China. China had entered the war on the Allied side in 1917. Japan's claim to succeed to Germany's former rights in the Shandong Peninsula clearly conflicted with China's own rights and with Wilson's principles. But the president had only just managed to resist French demands in the Rhineland, and the Fiume crisis was still at its height. So he gave in to Japan's demands. The Shandong solution was a serious defeat for the American president, and it lost the United States the traditional friendship of China.

Clemenceau, Wilson, and Lloyd George leaving the palace at Versailles after signing the peace treaty with Germany.

While the negotiations at Paris were in their final stages, the German delegation arrived at Versailles. The Germans were handed a draft of the treaty on May 7 and were given fifteen days in which to present their written observations. These resulted in only a few minor changes. The Germans, therefore, charged that this was a dictated settlement. The signing of the treaty took place on June 28, 1919, five years to the day after the assassination of the Austrian archduke at Sarajevo.

THE TREATY OF VERSAILLES

The peace treaty with Germany contained territorial, military, and economic clauses. It also called for the punishment of "war criminals," including the kaiser. Under the territorial terms of the treaty, Germany had to surrender 13 percent of its prewar area and population. This meant a loss of more than 15 percent of its coal, close to 50 percent of its iron, and 19 percent of its iron and steel industry. Besides giving up its colonies, Germany also had to recognize the independence of Austria. This last provision was to prevent a possible *Anschluss*, or union, for which there was much sentiment in both countries.

The military clauses of the treaty called for the reduction of Germany's army to one hundred thousand volunteers. The German navy was limited to six battleships of ten thousand tons and a few smaller ships. Germany was to have no offensive weapons—submarines, aircraft, tanks, or heavy artillery—and its general staff was to be dissolved. To supervise German disarmament, an Allied Military Control Commission was appointed.

In the economic field, the precise amount of reparations to be paid by Germany was left for a Reparations Commission to decide. In the meantime France was to receive large amounts of coal to make up for the wanton destruction of its coal mines by Germany's retreating armies, and Britain was given quantities of ships to compensate for the losses suffered from submarine warfare. German foreign assets of some $7 billion were confiscated; its rivers were internationalized; its patents were seized; and it was prohibited from raising tariffs above their prewar level. In short, everything possible was done to avert the threat of a renascent and vengeful Germany. The treaty was no worse than the treaties of Brest-Litovsk and Bucharest, which Germany had imposed on Russia and Rumania. Nor was it much better.

The Peace Settlements in Europe 1919–20

THE TREATIES WITH GERMANY'S ALLIES

The supplementary treaties with the smaller Central Powers were signed in 1919 and 1920. The Treaty of St. Germain with Austria was almost as harsh as that of Versailles. It called for the surrender of large territories to Czechoslovakia, Poland, Yugoslavia, and Italy. Not counting Hungary, the prewar area of the former Empire was cut to less than one-third and its population to one-fifth. In addition, Austria's army was limited to thirty thousand men. It also had to pay large reparations and agree not to become part of Germany.

Hungary signed its own treaty. Because of a brief communist interregnum under Bela Kun, Hungary did not sign the Treaty of Trianon until the middle of 1920. Its territorial provisions were the most severe of all the postwar treaties. After ceding lands to all its neighbors, Hungary was left with little more than a quarter of its former territory and a third of its population. It also had to pay reparations and reduce its army.

Bulgaria, in the Treaty of Neuilly, lost the outlet to the Aegean it had gained in 1913, agreed to reparations, and had to cut its armed forces.

Turkey concluded two peace treaties, one at Sèvres in 1920 and a later one at Lausanne in 1923. The first, which called for a virtual partition of the country, was superseded by the later agreement. In the interim, a revolt of Turkish nationalists under Mustapha Kemal Pasha had completed the revolution begun by the Young Turks in 1908 and overthrown the regime of the sultan. The Allies had favored the dismemberment of Turkey and in 1919 supported the invasion of Asia Minor by Greek forces. But Turkish resistance under Mustapha Kemal finally convinced the powers that their aim was unattainable. The Allies, therefore, revised the earlier peace settlement. Under the Treaty of Lausanne, signed in 1923, Turkey gave up everything except Asia Minor and a small foothold in Europe. It did not have to pay any reparations, and the "capitulations"—rights and privileges granted centuries ago to foreign powers—were abolished. The Straits were demilitarized and opened to ships of all nations in time of peace. Alone among the defeated countries, Turkey had thus been able to enforce a radical change in an initially harsh peace settlement. In October 1923 it was proclaimed a republic, with Mustapha Kemal "Atatürk" as first president.

THE AFTERMATH OF WAR

As might be expected, the defeated countries, foremost among them Germany, were deeply opposed to the postwar settlement. They attacked it not only as too harsh but also as unjust, because it violated Wilson's Fourteen Points. In its attempt to sort out the hopelessly intermingled peoples of central Europe, for instance, the principle of self-determination was often ignored. In countries like Poland, Czechoslovakia, and Rumania, from one-fourth to one-third of the population consisted of alien minorities, mostly German or Hungarian. The problem of national minorities, a source of much unrest before 1914, had not been solved by the war.

The situation looked more hopeful with respect to another prewar problem: The war, outwardly at least, had brought the victory of democracy. Popular governments replaced autocratic monarchies in eastern Europe and Turkey. But, because the political changes in countries like Germany, Austria, and Hungary were closely associated with military defeat, democracy in these countries carried a blemish that only time and success could erase. The tense and tumultuous atmosphere of postwar Europe, however, was not conducive to the peaceful consolidation of democracy. The chaos left behind by war and revolution soon proved too much for the inexperienced parliamentary governments. In their place there emerged new dictatorial and totalitarian regimes, better suited to cope with a world in crisis.

The first of these authoritarian systems arose in Russia during the 1920s. The victory of communism in that potentially powerful country introduced an entirely new and disturbing element into international affairs. The founding of the Third Communist International ("Comintern") in 1919 by Lenin's lieutenant, Grigori Zinoviev, seemed to confirm the western fear that communism was not content to remain in Russia. Short-lived communist regimes in Hungary and Bavaria showed that communism thrived on domestic disorder. After several attempts to engineer communist risings in Germany, Lenin finally decided to concentrate his efforts first on the communization of his own country. But the threat of communist Russia continued to haunt the statesmen of Europe until it was over-

National Minorities in Central Europe 1919

shadowed in the 1930s by the more immediate threat of Nazi Germany.

The tripartite division of Europe into victors, vanquished, and the Soviet Union was the cause of much international unrest. To remedy this situation the Allies had created the League of Nations. Here was something entirely new, a parliament of nations in which international problems could be discussed and solved. That was how the founders of the League had envisaged its mission. But events soon proved otherwise. When the League opened at Geneva in 1921, several of the great powers were missing: Germany was not admitted until 1926, the Soviet Union became a member only in 1934, and the United States never joined.

The failure of the United States to ratify the Treaty of Versailles, which included the Covenant of the League, showed that Americans were not yet ready to assume the role they were destined to play as the world's most powerful nation. America's absence from the League could not help but have unfortunate results. In an assembly dominated by the European victors, the United States would have served as an impartial arbiter. The League of Nations had many shortcomings; but none was as crucial as the void left by America's refusal to become a member.

THE LEAGUE OF NATIONS AND COLLECTIVE SECURITY

The general purpose of the League was "to promote international cooperation and to achieve international peace and security." It was founded on the concept of collective security, under which peace was to be maintained by an organized community of nations rather than by an uncertain "Concert of Europe." The specific tasks of the League were: to work for international disarmament; to prevent war by arbitration of international disputes; to apply sanctions against aggressors; and to register and revise international agreements. In very few of these tasks was the League successful.

Disarmament

The Treaty of Versailles had stated that the disarmament of Germany was intended "to render possible the initiation of a general limitation of the armaments of all nations." But general disarmament was tackled most hesitantly. Only in 1926 did a Preparatory Commission begin discussions of a Disarmament Conference, and the Conference itself did not meet until 1932. Its deliberations at that time proved entirely fruitless.

There were several causes for this failure. Shortly after the war, the Allied Military Control Commission began to report a long series of German violations of the Versailles disarmament provisions. Most important were secret contacts between the new German *Reichswehr* and the Russian Red Army. These German violations were alarming enough to keep the Allies from reducing their own forces. Another reason for Allied failure to disarm was the difficulty of finding a valid basis for determining a nation's military power. Geographic location, manpower, industrial development, and raw materials were far more significant factors than the actual size of armies. In most of these factors Germany and the Soviet Union excelled, and general disarmament would have been greatly to their advantage.

Arbitration of International Disputes

The second task of the League was to arbitrate international disputes. Members promised to bring any conflict "suitable for submission to arbitration" before the League Council. Any decision of the Council had to be unanimous. The League was able to settle a number of minor international conflicts. It was most effective in settling disputes between small powers. As soon as a major power was involved, however, the League proved powerless. In the "Corfu incident" of 1923, for instance, when Italy bombarded the Greek island of Corfu in retaliation for the murder of some Italians, the Italian government refused to acknowledge the League's competency.

Sanctions Against Aggression

The League's procedure for dealing with military aggression was laid down in Article 16 of the Covenant. As major punishment it provided for economic sanctions. To be effective, this policy needed the cooperation of all the great powers. But with two or more of them usually outside the League, the application of sanctions proved impossible. This became evident when Japan invaded China in 1931 and Italy invaded Abyssinia in 1935. Article 16 also provided for military sanctions, but these were left entirely to individual members. The League itself maintained no armed forces.

Treaty Revision

The registration and publication of international agreements called for under Article 18 of the Covenant were intended to prevent "secret diplomacy." Even so, most serious diplomatic negotiations after the war still went on behind closed doors, and the fear of secret treaties persisted. More significant was the provision made in Article 19 of the Covenant for the revision of existing treaties. Had the powers availed themselves of this opportunity, the Second World War might not have happened.

Clearly the League of Nations suffered from many weaknesses. Most of these could have been eliminated, had the great powers been ready to do so. Only in fields that involved none of their vital interests did the League score any gains. The League's Mandate Commission was able to improve the standard of colonial administration. The International Labor Organization, affiliated with the League, did much to raise the status of workers. Various other League agencies concerned themselves with matters of health, the illicit drug traffic, the international arms trade, and so forth. These agencies set important precedents for the activities of the United Nations today.

THE "WAR AFTER THE WAR," 1919–23

For several years after the Peace Conference, Europe underwent so many international crises that people wondered if the war had really ended. Until the fall of 1919, the Allies intervened against the Bolshevik regime in Russia. Poland fought with Lithuania over the town of Vilna, with Czechoslovakia over the region of Teschen, and with Russia over its eastern frontiers. Polish and German irregular forces fought over Upper Silesia in 1922. Intermittent conflicts between Italy and Yugoslavia over Fiume lasted until 1924. The Greeks invaded Turkey between 1919 and 1922 and almost came to blows with Italy in 1923. Austria and Hungary clashed over the Burgenland region in 1921. And in 1923 Germany's default in reparations led to the invasion of the Ruhr by French and Belgian troops. These were only the more noteworthy among an unending series of international incidents in early postwar years.

The French Search for Security

The greatest danger to peace was Germany's desire to escape the restrictions of Versailles. This worried the French in particular. The alliance between France and the Anglo-Saxon powers failed to materialize when America withdrew from the peace settlement. Because Germany was still superior in human and industrial resources, the French felt that their security demanded the strictest fulfillment of the peace terms. But this insistence on fulfillment caused a growing rift between France and Great Britain. To Britain, Germany was no longer a serious economic and naval rival; and because Germany had been one of England's best customers before the war, Britain wanted it to get back on its feet. Moreover, England felt that a healthy Germany was the best protection against the westward spread of communism. When France invaded the Ruhr in 1923, therefore, Britain expressed its disapproval. It had no desire to see France assume hegemony over the Continent.

The loss of British support forced France to look elsewhere for security. With Russia disqualified by communism and Italy dissatisfied with the peace settlement, only the smaller "succession states" of central Europe were left. In 1921 France concluded an alliance with Poland, in 1926 with Rumania, and in 1927 with Yugoslavia. In addition, Rumania, Yugoslavia, and Czechoslovakia organized the "Little Entente." All these countries were threatened by the revisionist agitation of Germany, Hungary, and Russia. As an attempt to isolate Germany, however, the French system failed, as the two outcasts of Europe—Germany and Russia—showed signs of drawing together.

Russo-German Rapprochement

Common economic and military interests led to a political rapprochement between Germans and Russians. The first outward sign was a treaty of friendship signed at Rapallo in April 1922. The world was startled and disturbed by what it suspected of being a military alliance. But the Treaty of Rapallo was merely a promise of cooperation between the two partners, important chiefly because it helped Germany escape its diplomatic isolation. There were people in both Germany and Russia who hoped that the treaty would develop into something more. But this hope was never fulfilled. Economically the two countries were complementary, and both stood to gain from mutual trade. But ideological differences made such an exchange difficult. Despite some later economic and neutrality agreements, Russo-German relations during the 1920s remained decidedly cool.

The Ruhr Occupation

The French occupation of the Ruhr in 1923 marked a turning point in the history of postwar Europe. Deprived of its major industrial region, Germany was thrown into an economic crisis, which was made more serious by the passive resistance the people of the Ruhr put up against the French. Financial pressures helped to escalate an already severe German inflation. By refusing to mine the coal France hoped to get from the Ruhr, the resisters contributed to French economic difficulties as well. The German government, fearing for the nation's existence, finally ended the Ruhr struggle. There were communist disturbances in central Germany and separatist uprisings in the Rhineland. In Bavaria an unknown ex-corporal, Adolf Hitler, was preparing his first try for power.

The Ruhr episode taught an important lesson to both French and Germans: rigid insistence on the fulfillment of the Versailles Treaty on the one hand, and stubborn resistance against such fulfillment on the other, helped neither side. Both, it seemed, had to give way if chaos was to be averted. For the next six years a group of dedicated statesmen devoted their efforts to bringing about such a compromise.

A trainload of coal on its way to France during the occupation of the Ruhr in 1923.

THE "ERA OF LOCARNO," 1924–29

The year 1924 saw important political changes in both France and England. In France the rightist cabinet of Raymond Poincaré, known for his vengeful attitude toward Germany, was replaced by a left-wing coalition in which Aristide Briand was foreign minister. In England the Labour party had a brief inning but soon gave way to a Conservative government with Austen Chamberlain as foreign secretary. In Germany the direction of foreign policy after the Ruhr crisis was in the hands of Gustav Stresemann. Together, Briand, Chamberlain, and Stresemann brought Europe a brief respite from fear and uncertainty.

The Locarno Pact

Europe's return to stability after 1924 was chiefly due to a more efficient handling of the reparations problem. Without these economic developments, the rapprochement between Germany and the western powers would hardly have come about. The first political result of this rapprochement was the Locarno Pact.

Under the terms of the Treaty of Versailles, the Allies were to begin withdrawing their forces from the Rhineland in 1925. But because of German disarmament violations, the Allies refused to leave. Stresemann realized that the basic reason for this refusal was France's fear of Germany. To dispel this fear, he now proposed a treaty by which not only France and Germany, but also England, Italy, and Belgium would guarantee the status quo in western Europe. Such a treaty was signed at Locarno in October 1925.

To a world torn for more than a decade by international strife, the Locarno Pact came as a harbinger of a new age. "We are citizens each of his own country," Stresemann said at Locarno, "but we are also citizens of Europe." This seeming conversion of Stresemann from a rabid German nationalist into a "good European" commanded the admiration of his contemporaries. But Stresemann was every bit as eager to abolish the restrictions of Versailles as were his nationalist compatriots. Where he differed was in his realization that the revision of Versailles could not be achieved by force but only through patient negotiation.

The rapprochement between Germany and the other western European powers, meanwhile, worried the Soviet Union. Despite Russia's resumption of diplomatic relations with France and Britain in 1924, it had remained an outsider in international affairs. England in particular resented the activities of the Comintern and in 1927 once again severed its connections with the Soviets. What Russia feared most was that Germany, as a member of the League, might be obligated to participate in sanctions against the Soviet Union. To quiet these fears, Stresemann, at Locarno, had obtained a modification of Article 16, allowing Germany to abstain from participating in any sanctions that endangered its own security. When this still did not satisfy the Russians, Stresemann in April 1926 signed a treaty of neutrality with them. Some saw this Treaty of Berlin as an attempt on Germany's part to play a double game between the eastern and the western European powers. But there is no doubt that Stresemann's foremost concern was always for closer relations between Germany and the West.

The Kellogg-Briand Pact

The efforts of the powers to guarantee Europe's security by treaties that would bolster the collective security system of the League climaxed in the signing of the Pact of Paris, or Kellogg-Briand Pact, in 1928. Its sixty-two signatories, which included the United States, promised "to renounce war as an instrument of national policy." Nothing was more characteristic of the spirit of hopefulness that pervaded the world after Locarno than this attempt to banish war simply by signing a treaty.

THE ECONOMIC CONSEQUENCES OF THE WAR

The economic results of the war were even more serious than its political aftermath. The territorial losses by themselves caused a major economic shock among the defeated powers. Added distress came from the seemingly limitless demands for reparations. But the victors, too, found the going far from easy. French and Belgian industrial regions had been devastated. In eastern Europe, lack of seed, fertilizers, and agricultural implements brought a marked decline of farm production. All the powers, particularly England, had lost important foreign markets. And a general return to protective tariffs retarded recovery everywhere.

The effects of the postwar economic crisis were felt in many ways. Five years after the war Europe's total industrial production was still at only two-thirds of its prewar level. Unemployment, never much of a problem in the past, now assumed alarming proportions. Another repercussion was felt in financial matters. All the major countries suffered from severe inflation. In Germany and Austria, inflation led to total devaluation.

The Reparations Problem

Much of the responsibility for Europe's economic difficulties rested with the peacemakers of 1919. In their efforts to solve the Continent's political problems, they often ignored the economic effects of their decisions. A member of the British peace delegation, the economist John Maynard Keynes, called attention to these oversights in his book *The Economic Consequences of the Peace* (1920), a sweeping indictment of the Versailles settlement on economic grounds. The most troublesome part of the treaty turned out to be reparations. In order to pay the large sums called for, the defeated nations needed surplus capital. This they could gain only through increased exports. But such exports competed with the products of the nations who hoped to profit from reparations. The transfer of large amounts of capital, furthermore, had unsettling effects on the economies of debtors and creditors alike. It was easy, in other words, to ask for huge reparations, but it was difficult to devise methods of paying them.

The reparations problem was further complicated by the mutual indebtedness of the victors. The easiest way out would have been the cancellation of all international debts. This solution was rejected by the United States, who would have ended up paying for the whole war.

The main source of reparations was Germany. The total amount of Germany's obligations was set at $32 billion in 1921. From the start Germany fell behind in its payments. The French, who were to receive more than half of the reparations, were adamant in their demands for prompt payment. The climax of France's insistence on fulfillment came with the invasion of the Ruhr in 1923.

The Dawes Plan and the Young Plan

America had already suggested that the reparations issue be studied by an international committee of experts. With the failure of the Ruhr venture, such a body was appointed. It worked out a plan, named after its chairman, the American banker Charles G.

A German housewife using inflated currency to light her stove. German inflation became so severe that money was not worth the paper on which it was printed.

The Economic Consequences of the Peace

The treaty includes no provisions for the economic rehabilitation of Europe—nothing to make the defeated Central Empires into good neighbors, nothing to stabilize the new states of Europe, nothing to reclaim Russia; nor does it promote in any way a compact of economic solidarity amongst the Allies themselves; no agreement was reached at Paris for restoring the disordered finances of France and Italy, or to adjust the systems of the Old World and the New.

The Council of Four paid no attention to these issues, being preoccupied with others—Clemenceau to crush the economic life of his enemy, Lloyd George to do a deal and bring home something which would pass muster for a week, the President to do nothing that was not just and right. It is an extraordinary fact that the fundamental economic problems of a Europe starving and disintegrating before their eyes was the one question in which it was impossible to arouse the interest of the Four. Reparation was their main excursion into the economic field, and they settled it as a problem of theology, of politics, of electoral chicane, from every point of view except that of the economic future of the states whose destiny they were handling.

From J. M. Keynes, *The Economic Consequences of the Peace* (New York: Harcourt, Brace, 1920), pp. 226–27.

Dawes, in September 1924. Under the Dawes Plan, Germany was to pay gradually rising amounts that were to reach a "standard annuity" in 1929. The Plan worked well. But more than was realized, Germany's ability to pay depended on the influx of foreign loans, mostly from the United States. This flow continued until 1929, when American investors began to speculate at home. Since at the same time Germany's yearly payments reached the "standard annuity," and no time limit had been set on such payments, it seemed a good idea to reconsider the whole reparations problem.

Meetings between German and foreign experts during 1929 finally led to the Young Plan, named after the American expert Owen D. Young. But the plan never went into effect. As the Great Depression spread from the United States to Europe, Germany ceased its payments altogether. At a final conference at Lausanne in 1932, Germany was relieved of any future obligations. Opinions differ on the total amount of reparations actually paid by Germany. A likely estimate puts it at $6 billion. This was not only far less than originally demanded, but in return Germany had received a far larger amount in foreign loans. The reparations settlement clearly had been a failure.

EUROPEAN RECOVERY

American capital played an important role in the economics of Europe. Most American loans were private and short-term. Their repayment was made difficult by America's tariff policy. Instead of helping foreign debtors to meet their obligations through increased exports, the United States surrounded itself with high tariff walls. This policy soon provoked a worldwide wave of protectionism. Insistent warnings by economists against such shortsightedness finally led the League of Nations to call a World Economic Conference in 1927. In their final report, the delegates urged their governments to lower tariffs as soon as possible. Before this advice was taken, the Great Depression began. Not least among its causes was protectionism.

Except for its warning on tariffs, however, the World Economic Conference was optimistic. France had rebuilt its devastated regions, had modernized its industry, and had stabilized its currency. Germany had recovered from the shock of inflation and had improved its production so that once again it was the industrial leader of Europe. England's recovery was slowed by adherence to the gold standard, antiquated production methods, and the high living standard of its workers. In Italy, the Fascist government of Benito Mussolini successfully raised food production. Even in Russia the "New Economic Policy," with its partial return to free enterprise, brought gradual economic improvement.

But this apparent economic recovery also had its weak points. It was chiefly restricted to industry. Agriculture continued to suffer from overproduction and foreign competition. The resulting decline in rural buying power reacted upon industry. Some producers, tempted by American loans and the example of American mass-production methods, expanded far beyond the need of their markets. When, after the American crash in October 1929, American loans ceased and old loans were recalled, Europe's economy, deprived of this financial infusion, collapsed.

Within one decade, Europe had thus come full cycle from despair through hope and back to despair. In the early 1920s it had seemed that the German Oswald Spengler had been right in his best-seller *The Decline of the West* (1918), which predicted the impending doom of western civilization. But then in the mid-1920s a "silver lining" had appeared on the horizon. The optimism of the Era of Locarno may appear unjustified in retrospect. But to contemporaries the decrease of international tension, the economic recovery, and the general air of stability and well-being seemed quite real. They were seen as proof that Europe at long last had found the peace it had been looking for. One may rightly wonder what would have happened if the recovery had lasted for another decade. In any effort to understand the unhappy events of the 1930s and 1940s, the Great Depression looms large.

Suggestions for Further Reading

Good recent books on the First World War are M. Ferro, *The Great War, 1914–1918* (1973), and G. Hardach, *The First World War, 1914–1918* (1977). The outbreak of the war is dramatically told in B. Tuchman, *The Guns of August* (1962). A. J. P. Taylor, *The First World War: An Illustrated History* (1963), adds a visual dimension. On the home fronts, see J. Williams, *The Other Battleground: The Home Fronts—Britain, France, and Germany, 1914–1918* (1972). The diplomatic history of the war is covered in Z. A. B. Zeman, *The Gentlemen Negotiators: A Diplomatic History of the First World War* (1971). On Germany's war aims, see F. Fischer, *Germany's Aims in the First World War* (1967). America's involvement in the war is discussed in E. R. May, *The World War and American Isolation* (1959).

The events of the Russian revolution are discusssed in detail in W. H. Chamberlain, *The Russian Revolution, 1917–1921,* 2 vols. (1953), and more briefly in R. V. Daniels, *The Russian Revolution* (1972). On the revolutions elsewhere in Europe, see F. L. Carsten. *Revolution in Central Europe, 1918–1919* (1972).

H. Nicolson, *Peacemaking 1919* (1933), vividly captures the atmosphere of the negotiations. The best book on the Versailles treaty is still P. Birdsall, *Versailles Twenty Years After* (1941). J. M. Keynes, *The Economic Consequences of the Peace* (1920), is a classic and most influential indictment of the settlement. The aftermath of the war is comprehensively covered in R. J. Sontag, *A Broken World, 1919–1939* (1971). On the diplomacy of the postwar years, see S. Marks, *The Illusion of Peace: International Relations, 1918–1933* (1976). The declining influence of Europe in world affairs is the theme of a small volume by H. Holborn, *The Political Collapse of Europe* (1954).

	1914				1950	
SOUTHWEST ASIA AND AFRICA	**1923** Kemal Attatürk, President of Turkish Republic			**1948** *Apartheid* in South Africa **1948** Founding of Israel, first Arab-Israeli war	**1954** Nasser takes control in Egypt **1956** Second Arab-Israeli war **1960–75** Independence movement sweeps Africa	**1967** Third Arab-Israeli (Six-Day) war **1971** Indo-Pakistani war **1973** Fourth Arab-Israeli war
EUROPE	**1914–18** World War I **1917** Bolshevik Revolution **1919** Paris Peace Conference	**1920** Keynes, *The Economic Consequences of the Peace* **1922** Mussolini's March on Rome **1923** French occupation of Ruhr	**1924** Death of Lenin, rise of Stalin **1924–25** Adolf Hitler, *Mein Kampf* **1924–29** Era of Locarno **1933** Hitler becomes Chancellor	**1935** Nuremburg Laws against Jews **1936–39** Spanish Civil War **1938** Munich Conference **1939** Hitler-Stalin Pact	**1939–44** World War II **1940** Fall of France **1941** Germany invades Russia **1941–45** Mass murder of Jews **1945** Yalta Conference	**1947** Marshall Plan **1949** Germany divided **1949** NATO Alliance **1953** Death of Stalin **1955** West Germany joins NATO **1955** Warsaw Pact
SOUTH AND SOUTHEAST ASIA	**1920–22** Gandhi's first Civil Disobedience Movement	**1927** Indonesian Nationalist party founded by Sukarno **1930** Gandhi's March to the Sea		**1947** Independence of India and Pakistan **1948** Mahatma Gandhi assassinated	**1949** Independence of Indonesia **1955** Bandung Conference, Indonesia	
EAST ASIA	**1927–37** Nationalist regime in Nanjing **1931** Japan seizes Manchuria **1934** Long March of Chinese Communists	**1937–45** Sino-Japanese War	**1941** Japan attacks Pearl Harbor **1945** Atomic bombing of Hiroshima and Nagasaki **1946–49** Civil war in China	**1949** People's Republic of China **1949–76** Mao Zedong's Chinese Revolution	**1950–53** Korean War **1951** US peace treaty with Japan	
THE AMERICAS AND PACIFIC	**1917** US enters World War I	**1929** The Great Depression begins **1933** Franklin D. Roosevelt's New Deal	**1941** US enters World War II **1945** First atomic bomb **1945** United Nations organized	**1946** First electronic computer **1947** Truman Doctrine **1948** Transistor invented	**1959** Fidel Castro's victory in Cuba **1962** Cuban Missile Crisis **1963** President Kennedy assassinated	**1968** Martin Luther King, Jr., assassinated **1969** Neil Armstrong, first man on moon

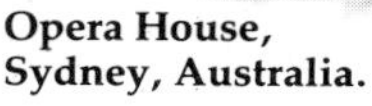

Opera House, Sydney, Australia.

British recruiting poster, World War I.

Apollo 11 lands men on moon, July 16, 1969.

Signers of Egyptian-Israeli peace treaty: Sadat, Carter, Begin, 1979.

Official symbol of the United Nations.

German inflation: two billion mark note, 1929.

1985	
1977 President Sadat visits Jerusalem **1978** Camp David Accords **1979** USSR invades Afghanistan **1979** Revolution in Iran	**1980–** Iran-Iraq war **1980** Black majority rule in Zimbabwe (Rhodesia) **1981** President Sadat assassinated
1957 First earth satellite, USSR **1957** European Economic Community	**1960** Yuri Gagarin, first man in space **1980** Solidarity movement in Poland
1961 Increasing US involvement in Vietnam	**1973** US forces withdraw from South Vietnam **1975** Communists take over Vietnam, Laos, Cambodia
1971 People's Republic of China joins UN **1972** Nixon visits Beijing **1976** Death of Mao Zedong	**1977** China begins liberalizing under Deng Xiaoping
1974 President Nixon resigns **1975** Helsinki Accords **1977** Panama Canal Treaty	**1979** Civil war begins in Nicaragua and El Salvador **1982** Falkland Islands War

Striking Solidarity union workers, Warsaw, Poland, 1981.

Emperor Hirohito of Japan, 1926.

42 Asia and Africa
The Twilight of Imperialism

Europe emerged from the First World War diminished in power and prestige, yet those responsible for imperial policies still regarded their empires as at least semipermanent. The war and its aftermath stimulated movements of national assertion throughout Asia and Africa, but that these represented the wave of the future did not become widely apparent until the Second World War speeded the erosion of empire. Moreover, the area included in the empires actually increased as regions formerly under Ottoman rule were turned over to Britain and France right after the First World War while during the 1930s the Japanese and Italian expansion of their overseas empires greatly contributed to international instability.

Furthermore, the history of Vietnam is a reminder that the process of decolonization even after the Second World War was sometimes bitter and prolonged. Yet, in this case too, the immediate roots of the revolution led by Ho Chi Minh (1890–1969) are to be found in the interwar period. In the case of Asia's two giants, China and India, the fruition of their very different revolutions came soon after the Second World War.

CHINA: THE STRUGGLE TO CREATE A NEW ORDER, 1916–49

After Yuan Shikai's failure to establish a new dynasty (see pp. 838–39), a na-

University students during the May Fourth Movement in Beijing (1919).

tional government in Beijing (Peking) continued to speak for China, but it was dominated by shifting alliances of regional strongmen (warlords). Of more lasting significance than the political maneuvers of the day was the intellectual and cultural revolution known as the May Fourth Movement, named after a massive student demonstration on that date in 1919 protesting the award to Japan in the Treaty of Versailles of Germany's possessions in China's Shandong Province. Embittered by China's failures, the leaders of the movement rejected not only the old political and social system but also most traditional values and ideas as well as the classical language in which they were expressed. They were, however, divided on what should replace the old. Many theories, doctrines, and philosophies were introduced; all had their champions, including Marxism, its prestige enhanced by the success of the Russian Revolution.

Mao Zedong during the Long March (1934).

The outstanding leader of China's own revolution until his death in 1925 continued to be Sun Yat-sen. In 1923 he led his Guomindang (Kuomintang = KMT) into an alliance with the fledgling Chinese Communist party (CCP) and received Soviet advice and assistance. At this time the revolutionaries had acquired a base in Guangzhou (Canton) where Chiang Kai-shek (Jiang Jieshi, 1887–1975) headed the Whampoa Military Academy training officers for the army of the revolution. From this power base Chiang was able to win the contest for leadership after Sun's death, and in the summer of 1926 he launched the Northern Expedition to reunify China. Suspicious of Communist intentions and desirous of reassuring Chinese bankers and industrialists as well as the foreign powers, Chiang turned against the Communists. In April 1927 he conducted a bloody campaign of suppression in Shanghai that was subsequently repeated in other cities.

In 1927 the new Nationalist regime established its capital in Nanjing (Nanking). Then in 1928 the Northern Expedition was resumed. Chiang quickly obtained the submission of northern warlords although often this merely entailed the formal incorporation of warlord armies into the government forces. National unification was accomplished in name but was actually far from complete. Warlordism remained an essential feature of Chinese politics until 1949. Furthermore, although Chiang had destroyed the CCP as an urban force, the Communists, after some false starts, were able to regroup and reorganize in a number of rural bases. The largest of these, the Jiangxi (Kiangsi) Soviet, was able to hold out against Nationalist armies until 1934. Then the Communists were able to break out of the Nationalist blockade and begin their incredible Long March covering some six thousand miles of frequently extremely difficult terrain before reaching their ultimate destination, Yenan in the Northwest.

During the Long March, Mao Zedong (Mao Tse-tung, 1893–1976) became the undisputed leader of the CCP. Long gone were the days when this was an urban party following Moscow's tactical advice. Mao not only saw the revolutionary potential of the Chinese peasantry, but, in a major innovation in Marxist theory, considered the peasants the primary force of China's revolution. His Marxism was fused with nationalism, with a belief in the power of sheer human will (as exemplified by the Long March), and with a populist faith in the peasant masses. It

China and the Northern Expedition 1926–28

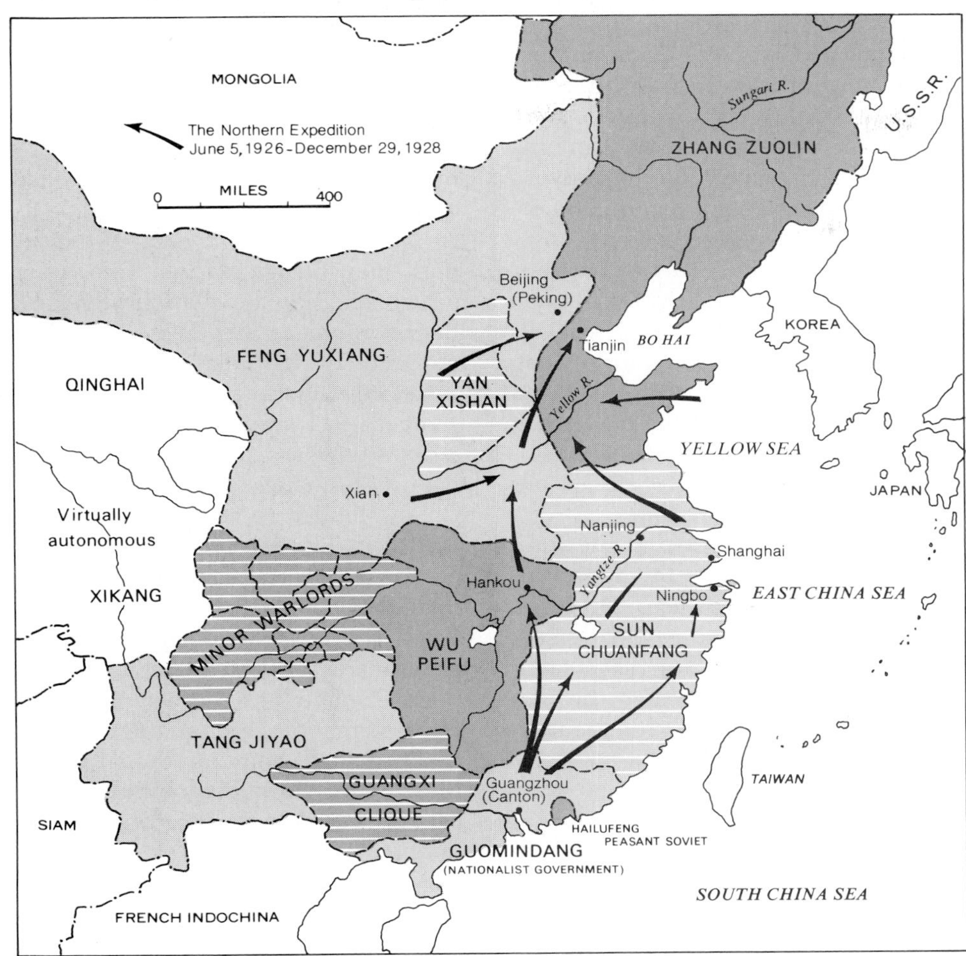

struck a responsive chord in the party and among those who felt that the KMT had betrayed, not fulfilled, the revolution. Faced with continued attack by the Nationalists, Mao and the CCP leadership called instead for a united national effort to resist the Japanese who continued to encroach on China after seizing Manchuria in 1931.

In Nanjing for ten years beginning with 1927, Chiang Kai-shek and the Nationalists attempted to consolidate the revolution and strengthen their regime. Their first order of priority—to build military strength—resulted in military spending and servicing the national debt consuming 60 to 80 percent of the government's annual expenditure. The military, however, was only one factor in a government composed of a number of factions and cliques ma-

Mao Zedong on Peasant Revolution

In a very short time, several hundred million peasants in China's central, southern, and northern provinces will rise like a tornado or tempest—a force so extraordinarily swift and violent that no power, however great, will be able to suppress it. They will break through all the trammels that now bind them and push forward along the road to liberation. They will send all imperialists, warlords, corrupt officials, local bullies, and evil gentry to their graves. All revolutionary parties and all revolutionary comrades will stand before them to be tested, to be accepted or rejected by them. To march at their head and lead them? To follow in the rear, gesticulating at them and criticizing them? To face them as opponents? Every Chinese is free to choose among the three, but circumstances demand that a quick choice be made.

Report of an Investigation into the Hunan Peasant Movement, 1927, translated in *Selected Works of Mao Tse-tung,* vol. 1 (New York, 1954) and included in Stuart R. Schram, *The Political Thought of Mao Tse-tung,* rev. ed. (New York: Praeger Publishers, 1963). p. 250.

Chiang Kai-shek (*ca.* 1935).

nipulated and kept in balance by Chiang Kai-shek. Given these circumstances it is not surprising that little economic progress was made in those years of worldwide depression. Similarly, although reform measures were passed, including a law in 1930 limiting rents to 37.5 percent of the harvest, there was no effective government organization to enforce them. Consequently, they remained dead letters. Ideologically too the KMT became more conservative. Whereas Sun Yat-sen had admired the Taipings, Zeng Guofan was Chiang's hero. Just as Zeng had stamped out the nineteenth century revolutionaries (see pp. 834–35), Chiang intended to stamp out Communism.

Unfortunately for Chiang, the army charged with attacking the Yenan regime had a different order of priorities. In December 1936, when Chiang flew to Xian (Sian) intending to breathe some life into the campaign, he was kidnapped by the army commander, himself the son of the warlord of Manchuria assassinated by the Japanese. After CCP intercession Chiang was released on the stipulation that he would lead a united Chinese effort against the Japanese. The conflict between Japanese ambitions and new Chinese resoluteness led to the outbreak of war in July 1937.

Chinese Communist soldiers entering Shanghai (1949).

The Japanese moved rapidly and in force. There was prolonged, bitter fighting with heavy casualties before Shanghai fell. After Shanghai, Nanjing was taken by the Japanese in December; the Japanese rampage of killing, raping, and burning left an estimated 100,000 dead. Pursuing a policy of trading space for time, the Nationalist government continued to retreat until they finally reached Chongjing (Chungking) in Sichuan (Szechuan), their wartime capital. There they held out until the entrance of the United States into the war against Japan in December 1941 shifted the overall balance of power.

After America entered the war, Chiang tended to rely on the United States while resisting American suggestions for reform. With the loss of Shanghai and other major eastern cities, the KMT was deprived of its most modern-minded sector of support. Confined to the Southwest, it came to rely on landlord support and did nothing about landlord abuses. Meanwhile within the military as well as the government, corruption was rampant. Although Chiang himself was personally austere, he valued personal loyalty more than ability and continued to govern by manipulation.

While the KMT deteriorated in popular standing and morale, the CCP grew enormously in strength as it spread its influence throughout occupied China by furthering socioeconomic reform even as it led the peasantry in resisting the cruel and heavy-handed Japanese. Having antagonized the Chinese but unable to patrol all of occupied China, the Japanese ended up controlling the cities and guarding lines of communication while the countryside belonged to the Communist-led guerrillas.

The end of the war did not bring peace to China. Postwar American efforts to mediate between the KMT and the CCP were hopelessly compromised by continued American support for the Nationalists, but it is doubtful that any reconciliation was possible. Even during the war against Japan, cooperation had turned into hostility. What surprised everyone, Communist as well as Nationalist, was the rapidity of the CCP triumph. On October 1, 1949, Mao was able to proclaim the establishment of the People's Republic of China in Beijing. By that time Chiang and his forces had fled to Taiwan where he continued to maintain that his was the legitimate government of China.

The CCP victory marked the end of a century of internal weakness and humiliation at the hands of foreigners. China's problems remained enormous, but the decisions on how to deal with them would now be made by Chinese leaders on Chinese terms. It was an end, and a beginning.

INDIA: THE TORTUROUS ROAD TO INDEPENDENCE AND PARTITION

When the First World War began, India supported Britain generously. Loyalty to the crown was so firm that Britain could afford to reduce its military presence on the subcontinent to as few as fifteen thousand troops while over sixty thousand Indian soldiers gave their lives for Britain, more than from any other part of the British Empire. In return, India expected commensurate political rewards, an expectation shared very widely by political leaders of different backgrounds and diverse views. Even the breach between Hindus and Muslims was temporarily healed late in 1916 when Congress and the Muslim League came to an agreement known as the Lucknow Pact. Both organizations agreed to work for self-government. Congress gave its consent to reserving certain seats in the national and provincial legislatures for Muslims while the League promised not to put up candidates for general seats. The Indian show of unity and Britain's own weakness helped strengthen the hands of Liberals in England with the result that in August 1917 the British promised India "representative government."

Indian nationalist aspirations, stimulated during the war, were seriously disappointed by the Montague-Chelmsford Reforms of 1919. Under an arrangement known as "dyarchy" certain government functions were turned over to Indians, but the vital areas of finance and revenue, police, and foreign affairs were retained under British control. To make matters much worse, these concessions were accompanied by the repressive Rowlatt Acts under which the government, among other things, received the right of preventive detention. One of the most vigorous in his denunciations of British policy was Mohandas Gandhi, who protested by organizing a cessation of all economic activity to express Indian outrage. As previously in South Africa, he insisted on nonviolent actions. Combining the personal mildness and moral scruples of Gokhale with the activism of Tilak, Gandhi transferred the locus of Congress activity from courtroom and council chamber to the market and the street.

Despite Gandhi, the protest movement spilled over into violence; at Amritsar, capital of the Punjab, troops commanded by General R. E. H. Dyer fired off 1,650 rounds into an unarmed crowd at a meeting, killing four hun-

Mohandas Gandhi, the Mahatma, sitting beside his spinning wheel.

dred and wounding another twelve hundred. To make matters infinitely worse, the home government, instead of reprimanding the general, raised him to the knighthood. Nothing could have been better calculated to outrage Congress and assure the leadership of Gandhi. Under his guidance the transformation of Congress was completed in 1922 when the membership fee was lowered to a few pennies so that everyone could afford to join what had originally been an elite organization.

Gandhi's response to Amritsar came in 1920 when he launched a campaign of total noncooperation including a boycott of all courts, universities, and government agencies. However, when violence erupted in 1922, he called it off convinced that the Indian people needed further spiritual training. He himself withdrew from active political life. Deeply religious, Gandhi lived the austere life of a holy man, relying on the moral power of truth and love, teaching by example, appealing to the best in all people — including his opponents. Seeking to purify Hinduism, he strove for the improvement of the Untouchables, whom he renamed "God's children" (Harijans). Symbolic of his commitment to tradition and the village was the spinning wheel on which he produced the homespun cloth worn by himself and his followers.

Gandhi was too political a saint to remain permanently aloof from national affairs. His political reemergence was occasioned by the fiasco of the Simon Commission (1927–29) sent out from Britain to evaluate dyarchy and not including a single Indian member. Congress, now under the leadership of Jawaharlal Nehru (1889–1964), responded by demanding total independence from Britain. In March 1930 Gandhi was joined by thousands as he led a 240 mile march to the ocean to make salt in defiance of the government monopoly. This was a stroke of genius because salt was a necessity, and the tax weighed heavily on the poor. Mass arrests soon filled the prisons, confronting the British with an impossible situation; they had to negotiate.

Unfortunately for the aspirations of Congress to represent all of India, Gandhi's very success in organizing and inspiring the masses had an impact not only on the British but also on Muslims. Muslims could not identify with Gandhi's person or style of leadership and feared that, the protestations of Congress notwithstanding, the goal of this nationalist movement was the creation of a Hindu rather than a secular state. In such a state they would be a minority, and they feared that despite all good intentions and legal safeguards, the Muslim community would suffer. Gradually the most notable Muslim leader, Muhammad Ali Jinnah (1876–1949), himself a highly cultivated secular-minded man who had once been a member of Congress much influenced by Gokhale, came to accept the view that Muslims would be secure only in a separate Muslim state. Muslim demands for a separate state were hardened after the 1935 reorganization of the government, when Congress won

Gandhi on Satyagraha

Truth (Satya) implies Love, and Firmness (Agraha) engenders and therefore serves as a synonym for force . . . that is to say, the Force which is born of Truth and Love or Non-violence. . . .

[There] is a great and fundamental difference between passive resistance and Satyagraha. . . . Again while there is no scope for love in passive resistance, on the other hand, not only has hatred no place in Satyagraha, but it is a positive breach of its ruling principle. While in passive resistance there is scope for the use of arms when a suitable occasion arrives, in Satyagraha, physical force is forbidden, even in the most favorable circumstances. . . . Satyagraha and brute force being each a negation of the other, can never go together. . . . In passive resistance there is always present an idea of harassing the other party, and there is a simultaneous readiness to undergo any hardship entailed upon us by such activity, while in Satyagraha there is not the remotest idea of injuring the opponent. Satyagraha postulates the conquest of the adversary by suffering in one's own person.

Excerpted from *Satyagraha in South Africa* (Triplicane, Madras, 1928) in Louis Fischer, ed., *The Essential Gandhi; His Life, Work, and Ideas: An Anthology* (New York: Vintage Books, 1963), pp. 87–88.

elections giving it control over provincial government and refused to share power with the Muslim League.

Politics during the 1930s and 1940s were consequently dominated by the threefold contest between Congress, League, and Britain, but during the Second World War British strength reached a new low. In India the war began badly as the viceroy declared India at war without consulting any Indians. Although they were basically sympathetic to the British side, Congress leaders were dissatisfied with British policy in India. Matters came to a head in 1942 when Congress launched the "Quit India Movement." Once again Congress leaders found themselves in prison. However, when the war ended it was apparent that the only way Britain could retain India was by force. Yet Britain, ravaged and drained by the war, no longer possessed that force.

Winston Churchill maintained that he had not become prime minister in order to preside over the dismantling of the Empire, but in 1945 he and his Conservatives were voted out of office, replaced by a Labour Government committed to independence for India. What remained was to negotiate the transfer of power. What ensued was an agreement on independence with Congress reluctantly agreeing to a partition that would create the Muslim state of Pakistan.

Independence came on August 15, 1946, but it was marred by mass suffering as an estimated twelve to fifteen million people migrated in and out of Pakistan to the accompaniment of widespread and terrible violence. Horrified, Gandhi did what he could to quell the violence only to fall himself, the victim of a bullet from the gun of a Hindu fanatic. That evening, January 30, 1948, Nehru told his radio audience. "The light has gone out of our lives and there is darkness everywhere." Like so many others, India's first prime minister, a sophisticated secular-minded believer in democracy and socialism, revered the "Mahatma" (Great Soul).

Thus even though India was spared a war of national independence, the attainment of that long desired goal was accompanied by all the pain of partition. Left unsettled was the fate of Kashmir where a Hindu prince ruled over a predominantly Muslim population, a problem compounded by the bitterness of the partition. The antagonism between the two new states became one of the constants of postwar international relations.

As elsewhere, the British bequeathed a mixed legacy to their successors on the subcontinent. They left an India provided with a fine railway network and with other public works. There was even a new capital at Delhi, planned before the first World War but not officially inaugurated until 1931, intended as a magnificent symbol of empire but confirming instead Curzon's prediction that it would end up merely as a "gilded phantom." Institutionally Britain left India with a bureaucracy and an army. Furthermore, despite efforts to the contrary, English remained the national language of the educated elite. Politically, India became the world's most populous democracy. But Britain also left a land plagued by poverty, divided by communalism and regional loyalties, a land of striking contrasts and enormous problems.

Sikhs fleeing to India from the new Muslim nation of Pakistan (1947).

An elephant working in a teak forest in Thailand.

THE TWILIGHT OF IMPERIALISM IN SOUTHEAST ASIA

During the period between the two world wars, Southeast Asia continued to be affected ever more deeply by global developments even while there remained striking differences between the experiences of its various peoples, differences stemming not only from their diverse heritages but also from differences in their treatment by colonial rulers — or in the case of Thailand, their ability to retain political independence. Within the individual lands, too, a wide gap developed between a traditional peasantry living much as had their forebears and a small but influential group of modern-minded people educated in the western style and residing in major cities. As in China and India, leaders appeared who attempted the heroic task of synthesis.

Among the global forces at work in the region were the dynamics of international commerce. Major exports from the Malay Peninsula and the Indonesian archipelago were tin and rubber, which was also shipped from French Indo-China. Both were vital for modern industry. By 1938 the region of modern Malaysia supplied 29 percent of the world's tin and 41 percent of the world's rubber (down from 53 percent in 1920). Meanwhile, the great delta regions of the major rivers, the Mekong in Vietnam, Chaophraya in Thailand, and Irrawaddy in Burma, continued to develop as major rice exporting areas. In all these areas the result was increased population growth, an uneven distribution of economic benefits, and dependence on the international market. Thus the great depression of the early 1930s sent shock waves throughout the region as the prices for tin, rubber, and rice collapsed. The effects were felt not only in Bangkok and Rangoon, Saigon and Singapore, but out in the country where substantial landowners were able to survive but laborers rioted in the face of starvation.

Modern ideas as well as modern economics affected the area more intensively after the First World War as people felt a widespread need to assert themselves against the imperialist powers. Throughout Southeast Asia an upsurge of nationalism took many forms, secular and religious. Colonies strove for independence while Thailand tried to gain international parity.

Thailand

In Thailand national unity was fostered by Buddhism and the groundwork for modernization had been laid by kings Mongkut and Chulalongkorn. By the mid-1920s the Thais, who had entered the First World War on the winning side, had brought extraterritoriality to an end leaving only minor aspects of the unequal treaties in place. Royal leadership in the process of modernization, however, depended on the wisdom and skill of the king. Both were lacking in the case of King Projadhipok (r. 1925–35) who based his government on a narrow group of largely princely advisers at a time when depression-induced retrenchment caused career frustrations among civil servants and army officers. As a result of the "revolution" of 1932 the monarch became a constitutional ruler. The government was broadened, but the military by virtue of their cohesion and discipline, became the controlling force in the land.

Burma

In Burma, as in Thailand, Buddhism provided a major focus for national cohesion. Not only did the Buddhist faith help define a Burmese identity, but Buddhism, most notably the General Council of Buddhist Associations (formerly the Young Men's Buddhist Association), provided an organizational framework for Burmese nationalism. Until 1935 Burma was governed as part of India and thus followed the Indian pattern of political development. There too, post-World War I dyarchy was modified in the light of the findings of the Simon Commission. Hampering the assertion of Burmese nationalism was the factionalism of the elite as well as Burma's communal diversity. For example, Burma's largest minority, the Karens, a substantial number of them Christians, were suspicious of the Burmese majority. Karen troops participated in the suppression of rural unrest, including most notably the peasant rebellion of 1930–32 led by Saya San, a former Buddhist monk and practitioner of traditional healing arts whose followers believed that magic amulets rendered them immune to bullets. Acting as legal counsel for Saya San at his subsequent trial for treason was European-educated Ba Maw, who became prime minister in 1936 under a new constitution that still reserved defense, foreign affairs, and monetary policy for the British governor.

The Philippines

Implicit in British concessions to India and Burma was the ultimate granting of complete independence. Already in 1900 the announced goal of the United States, was to prepare the Philippines for independence. Toward this end, Filipino participation in government was steadily expanded, but political power remained effectively concentrated in the hands of an urban, sophisticated intelligentsia (the *ilustrado*). Emanuel Quezon (1878–1944), leader of the Nacionalista party and president of the Commonwealth of the Philippines created in 1935, was content to leave it that way. The granting of full independence was delayed by the increasing likelihood of war in the Pacific. When war came, Quezon followed General Douglas MacArthur into exile. But in 1946 the Philippines became the first Southeast Asian colony to attain independence.

The Malay Peninsula

Elsewhere in the region the colonial powers seemed set to stay for a long, long time. British determination to remain a major force in Southeast Asia was conveyed by the plan to build a supposedly invulnerable naval base in Singapore. It was completed in 1938 at a cost of sixty million pounds. The great international seaport was linked by a system of roads and railroads to the rubber- and tin-producing Malay Peninsula while Penang and Kuala Lumpur grew as secondary economic centers. Until the Second World War the Chinese who formed the predominant ethnic element in all three cities continued to identify themselves with their homeland. Because the British worked with and sustained the traditional Malay authorities and imported labor (Chinese and Indian) worked in the mines and export industries, life in the Malay villages continued pretty much in its traditional ways; only among the more urban and educated population did a sense of Malay nationalism develop. Initially the Muslim component in this nationalism appeared not to have been as strong as in neighboring Sumatra or Java, but it was to prove stronger in the long run.

Indonesia

During the First World War the Dutch made concessions to Indonesian aspirations by appointing more Indonesians to government posts and established an advisory legislative body (*Volksraad*, People's Assembly) which, however, had little power and was not representative. On the Indonesian side, the Sarekat Islam (Islamic Association) founded as a mass movement in 1911, soon found itself challenged from left and right. On the left, the Communists (founded in 1920 as the Communist Association of the Indies, changed to the Indonesian Communist party in 1924) used traditional Indonesian symbols in appealing to the common people, but Communist-led risings in 1926–27 were easily suppressed.

Future leadership came to lie with the Indonesian National party founded in 1927 by Sukarno (1901–70), a charismatic and flamboyant leader once characterized as "a cross between Franklin Delano Roosevelt and Clark

Gable." A nationalist first and foremost, Sukarno also drew on Islam and Marxism in expressing his concerns for Indonesia's little people. In their eyes, as in his own, he became the embodiment of Indonesian unity. The Dutch response to Indonesian unrest was repression. Newspapers were suppressed; restrictions were placed on meetings; police surveillance was increased; leaders were arrested. Arrested in December 1929, Sukarno was released from prison two years later only to be arrested again in 1933. He was then exiled from Java and not allowed to return until the Japanese had ousted the Dutch.

Cambodia and Vietnam

In Cambodia the French remained content to work through the king who ruled pretty much in the traditional fashion, but the situation was very different in Vietnam; there as late as 1942 the proportion of Frenchmen to Vietnamese in government service was higher than that of Europeans in the government of any other Southeast Asian colony. The French were also particularly vigorous and thorough in suppressing nationalist movements, which began during the beginning of the century but gained in strength and militancy after the First World War. Nationalist aspirations that had fused with economic suffering fueled an uprising in 1930 led by the Vietnamese Nationalist party. In retaliation the French practically destroyed the Nationalists. The underground Communist party, however, was able to survive, led by Ho Chi Minh. He had acquired his Marxism in Paris and was a founding member of the French Communist party. Ho, like most of Vietnam's political leaders, was a northerner and the North remained the base for the Communists for many years, while in the South syncretic religious movements such as the Cao Dai provided a focus for the lives of masses of believers.

Southeast Asia After the Second World War

The Second World War was a watershed for most of Southeast Asia. Only Thailand, skillfully disentangling itself from its Japanese alliance, emerged essentially unchanged in domestic leadership and international status. Elsewhere Japanese victories at the beginning of the war destroyed the belief in the invincibility of the colonial powers. The Philippines and Burma became scenes of bitter fighting, but after the war they achieved independence rapidly and with ease. There, as elsewhere, the Japanese had initially roused nationalist hopes only to disappoint them in the end.

In Indonesia the Japanese decided to work with such nationalists as Sukarno, who used the opportunity to build organizations capable of independent political and military action once the Japanese departed. When they proclaimed an independent Indonesia in 1945, the Dutch were not ready to let go without a fight. However, although the Dutch seized the major cities, they did not have the means to dominate the land and had no prospects of obtaining outside assistance. In 1949 they yielded to the inevitable and recognized the new republic. In contrast to Indonesia, Malay independence came later (1957) but was accomplished without a war of national independence.

Sukarnoism

My grandfather inculcated in me Javanism and mysticism. From Father came Theosophy and Islamism. From Mother, Hinduism and Buddhism. Sarinah gave me humanism. From Tjokro came Socialism. From his friends came Nationalism.

To that I added gleamings of Karl Marxism and Thomas Jeffersonism. I learned economics from Sun Yat-sen, benevolence from Gandhi. I was able to synthesize modern scientific schooling with ancient animistic culture and to translate the end product into living, breathing messages of hope geared to the understanding of a peasant. What came out has been called—in plain terms—Sukarnoism.

Sukarno: An Autobiography, as told to Cindy Adams (New York: Bobbs-Merrill, 1965), p. 76.

Vietnam's wartime experience was different and unique. There the Japanese, recognizing Vichy France as an ally, left the European authorities in place. Nothing was done to defuse nationalist pressures directed at both French and Japanese until March 1945 when, six months before the end of the war, the Japanese ousted the French and took control themselves. By that time Ho Chi Minh had forged a broad nationalist coalition that constituted the dominant political force in the North and the strongest anywhere in Vietnam. In September 1945 he proclaimed the establishment of an independent state, but France, like Holland in Indonesia, was intent on reestablishing control. Vietnam was to become a bloody battleground before independence was secured (see pp. 994–95).

AFRICA SOUTH OF THE SAHARA

The outcome of the First World War did not radically alter the map of Africa, but Germany lost its colonies which were legally "mandated" by the League of Nations primarily to Britain and France. They were to be governed as "a sacred trust of civilization" until their peoples could "stand on their own feet in the arduous conditions of the modern world." The home governments had claimed all along that colonialism was beneficial for the subject people. No doubt there was much empty posturing, yet many missionaries and officials took their responsibilities toward the colonial people very seriously. It was generally accepted that the Europeans had moral obligations toward their subjects. At the same time, they also believed that they had a moral right to exploit the riches of the world. "The tropics," wrote Britain's foremost administrator in Nigeria, "are the heritage of mankind, and neither on the one hand has the suzerain Power a right to their exclusive exploitation nor on the other hand have the races which inhabit them a right to deny their bounties to those who need them."

In general, little was done to help the colonies develop modern economies. While roads and railways did facilitate trade and while the export of agricultural commodities was encouraged, the depression precluded substantial financial investment in the colonies while the decline in world commodity prices hurt all those in Africa, as in Southeast Asia, who depended on the international market. The colonial powers put special emphasis on education, but even in this aspect the results were hardly impressive. For example, in 1938 in Nigeria, Africa's most highly populated land, the number of children in school was still under 5 percent. Even so, in Lagos and other African coastal and international cities, a small, sophisticated elite continued to develop. In the case of France and the other continental colonial powers (Belgium, Portugal, Italy) the stated aim was to assimilate this elite into the culture of the home country with the eventual aim of incorporating the colonies into a greater France, Portugal, or Italy.

British Africa

In British West Africa and in the East and Central African colonies where white settlers were few (now including formerly German Tanganyika), the policy continued to be one of indirect rule through the traditional elite (although that did not preclude shifting from one group to another as happened in Buganda). British administrators preferred to work with tribal leaders rather than with the educated modern elite which one Chief Secretary of Nigeria characterized as "bad imitations of Europeans instead of good Africans." Yet among this new elite, men appeared who started to think of themselves in broader than tribal terms, as Nigerians rather than as Igbo, Hausa, or Yoruba. In Nigeria a minor concession to the coastal elite in 1922 allocated three seats in the colony's legislative council to elected representatives from Lagos. Here and elsewhere African leaders had formed political organizations that initially insisted on a greater African voice in government and became the focuses of movements for self-government and independence, as well as Pan-African aspirations.

Movement toward independence developed later in Africa than in South and Southeast Asia. African nationalists had not only to face the hostility of the colonial power but also to create a sense of national belonging among peoples of diverse cultures thrown together in a single polity by historical forces beyond their control. But in Africa as elsewhere the nation-state came to be accepted as the proper, and indeed natural, form of human political organization. A major legacy of the colonial period was to be the continued existence of territorial polities originally imposed on Africans from without. However, not until 1957 did the first black African colony, the Gold Coast, become an independent state, Ghana.

Although little was done by way of preparation for political or economic independence in the colonies without substantial communities of white settlers, they were at least spared the problems that arose in those areas where settlers were numerous enough to constitute a political force. A special case was South Africa where, after the formation of the Union of South Africa in 1910, the influence of the British government receded. The Union was accepted by a segment of the Afrikaner Boer community and welcomed by English-speaking whites, but Afrikaner nationalism remained a potent force.

The nationalistic Boers felt that their people were looked down upon and discriminated against but had no sympathy for similar feelings among black Africans. In 1912 they formed the Afrikaner National party and that same year black Africans organized the Native National Congress (later the African National Congress), which unsuccessfully tried to fight the political, legal, and economic disabilities being imposed on blacks at Boer instigation. Africans suffered discrimination in just about every aspect of their lives as the Afrikaners were intent to secure a way of life dependent on white supremacy and black labor. Yet with the growth of a black intelligentsia and a black labor movement in mines and factories there was still a prospect that the trend toward increasing discrimination and separatism could be reversed and progress made toward integration and equality. This hope was dashed as the elections of 1948 brought into power an all-Afrikaner government committed to apartheid.

During the interwar period white settlers also came to prevail in Southern Rhodesia (Zimbabwe), which was separated from Northern Rhodesia (Zambia) in 1923. At this time the all-white electorate of Southern Rhodesia voted to become a self-governing colony rather than join the Union of South Africa as some urged. These settlers were people from England who did not wish to join a state where they would be outnumbered by the Boers. Their decision had nothing to do with the treatment of black Africans on whom the settlers depended for their labor. Earlier they had already imposed on Africans a hut tax so that Africans would be compelled to earn money by working. Here, as in South Africa,

In the Copper Mines

Even though the African is educated [he] is . . . like a monkey to the Europeans. All the Africans who are at work at [the] mines are treated like this: when an African is carrying a heavy load, [and] a European is coming behind him without the notice of an African, the European kicks him. When the African says "What's the matter Bwana?" now the Bwana says, "Shut up, get away," and gives the African a very hard blow. When an African wants to know why he is beaten, the Bwana takes [his] number . . . so an African will have to be fined . . . for nothing. . . . Englishmen are thrifty like a python which swallows the animal without leaving anything out.

Kwafya Kombe, letter of May, 1940, as quoted in Robert I. Rotberg, *The Rise of Nationalism in Central Africa: The Making of Malawi and Zambia, 1873–1964* (Cambridge: Harvard University Press, 1965), p. 160.

black Africans were subjected to legal restrictions. Thus the Land Apportionment Act of 1930 divided the land into areas exclusively for European use and other areas reserved for the native Africans. During the early postwar years Southern Rhodesia remained firmly under white control.

In Kenya the white settlers were as ambitious as their confreres to the south, and an attempt was made in 1927 to merge all of Britain's East African colonies (Kenya, Tanganyika, Uganda, the Rhodesias, and Nyasaland) into a "Great White Dominion" dominated by Southern Rhodesia's whites, but this failed. Within Kenya the situation differed from that in Southern Rhodesia not only because there were fewer whites in proportion to native blacks (1 to 250 in Kenya as against 1 to 25 in Southern Rhodesia) but also because the whites were even outnumbered by Asian immigrants who were well organized, commanded considerable wealth, and had the backing of the (British) government of India. In 1923, the British government declared that in Kenya, as in Tanganyika and Uganda, native interests were to be paramount. That, however, did not prevent the settlers in the Kenyan highlands from forcing the native peoples into reserves and forcing them to work on European farms. To voice their concerns, the Kikuyu people organized. The most vital of their two organizations was the Young Kikuyu Association led by Harry Thuku, arrested in 1922 for sedition. Not until 1945 was an African admitted to membership in the Legislative Assembly.

The Impact of Christianity

In Africa, as elsewhere, the challenge posed by the West was intellectual/spiritual as well as political/economic: missionaries as well as soldiers, administrators, and merchants undermined old power structures and threatened traditional ways of life. Armed with the conviction that they possessed divine truth, the missionaries condemned polygamy and other well-established African practices at the very core of local cultures. An example of the disruptions thus caused is the intense dissension that followed the decision by missionaries in Kenya to ban female circumcision. On the other hand, missionaries in the British colonies and in the Congo fought to protect the African's basic human rights, and they played the major role in education by teaching people to read and write and by introducing them to the biblical doctrine of the brotherhood of man. From one point of view, they have been castigated as the prime agents of "cultural imperialism," but the case has also been made that "Christianity had not so much to drive out the old gods, which were already doomed, as to temper, by industrial and religious education, a social and economic revolution . . . which threatened to be physically and morally overwhelming."

In assessing the impact of Christianity in Africa we should note that its introduction had consequences not anticipated by the missionaries. One of these was "Ethiopianism," the establishment of African churches that retained traditional elements, such as polygamy, not accepted by western Christianity. Another was the development of national consciousness, for many of the nationalist movements were led and organized by men educated in the mission schools.

Christianity had considerable success in Africa but not in the areas where its traditional rival, Islam, was already established. On the continent as a whole Muslims then as now outnumbered Christians; we must consider their history in its relation to the history of the wider region dominated by Islam.

SOUTHWEST ASIA AND NORTH AFRICA

With the spread of European power, Muslims were confronted with the secularism that had long challenged Christians and Jews. Like the latter, their responses ranged from a fundamentalist rejection of anything seen as conflicting with the religious tradition to, at the other extreme, an unreligious if not outright irreligious adoption of modern values and ideas. In between were modernizers like Muhammad Abduh (1845–1906), rector of al-Amar in Cairo, founded in 972 as the premier Islamic institution of higher learning. Muhammad Abduh's conviction that Islam could and should be reconciled with modern scientific thought was widely influential from Morocco to Indonesia. It was compatible both with Pan-Islam and with nationalism. Thus his pupil, the Syrian Rashid Rida (1865–1935) is known primarily as an Arab nationalist.

For Muslims, as for Christians and Jews, the issues at stake were not only intellectual and spiritual but also involved the status and power of professional men of religion, the proper form of such basic social institutions as the family, and matters of everyday life and morality, including dress. The more deeply religion and society were integrated, the more far-reaching the issues.

Turkey

The most radical transformation took place in Turkey. The Ottoman Empire's entry into the First World War on the German side sealed its fate. It lost its non-Turkish territories, Istanbul itself was occupied, and it took several years of political and military maneuvering before the boundaries of the new Turkish state were finally defined by the Treaty of Lausanne, signed in July 1923 (see p. 885). By that time the government was controlled by the Ottoman's most successful wartime general, Mustafa Kemal (1881–1938), honored by his countrymen as "Atatürk" (Father Turk). In November 1922 Kemal had announced the abolition of the sultanate, and in October 1923 he became the first president of the new Turkish Republic.

Mustafa Kemal Pasha "Atatürk," first president of Turkey (1923–38).

It was Kemal's vision that out of the ashes of the old empire ruled by the sultan-and-caliph from imperial, cosmopolitan Istanbul with its mosques and palaces, there should rise a new modern, national Turkish state ruled by a president and an assembly from its new capital of Ankara deep in the Turkish homeland. With this in mind, Kemal began a program of radical modernization. In a drastic break with the past, in March 1924, the caliphate was abolished and the last of the Osmans (who had remained caliphs after being deprived of the sultanate) was shipped off to France. There could be no stronger statement of Kemal's determination to break with the past.

The abolition of the caliphate was not the only shock suffered by the *ulema.* They were now deprived of their monopoly on education and of law while the Sufi orders were suppressed. A highly symbolic move was the legal prohibition of the fez, the headgear that symbolized a Muslim identity. Denounced by Kemal as "an emblem of ignorance, negligence, fanaticism, and hatred of progress and civilization," it was replaced by the European hat. Slower to disappear and then more by suasion than by ordinance were the women's veils; the removal of the veil was generally accepted by educated people in the large cities but resisted in the traditionalistic countryside.

European laws were introduced to replace the old Islamic laws as Turkey adopted the Swiss Civil Code, the Italian Penal Code, and the German Commercial Code. Social legislation outlawed polygamy, and in 1934 women received the right to vote and to become members of the assembly. In another major change, the Latin alphabet was introduced, replacing the Arabic script. With the adoption of the first five-year plan in 1934, the state also took a lead in economic development—a textile factory built with Soviet Russian advice and a British-built iron and steel facility were its main achievements.

Anxious to avoid a repetition of its disastrous participation in the First World War, Turkey maintained an uneasy neutrality until near the end of World War II. Motivated by traditional distrust of Russia, the country remained westward in its political orientation during the postwar years.

Iran

Iran, like Turkey, suffered greatly during the First World War. Although a declared neutral, it became a battleground for Turkish, German, Russian, and British forces. When the Russians withdrew following their revolution of 1917, the British remained as the main foreign presence, but their attempt to turn Iran into a protectorate failed in the face of strong nationalist Iranian opposition supported by the United States and the Soviet Union. After the war Riza Shah Pahlavi (1877–1944) controlled the only modern military force in the country. In 1923 he became prime minister and in 1925 deposed the feeble Quajar dynasty, replacing it with his own Pahlavi dynasty (r. 1925–79).

The Shah's basic policy was to modernize Iran from above, and he initiated a program of reform modeled on that of Kemal Atatürk except that the Shah was a despot who harshly suppressed all opposition and that half of the government budget went to the army. Iran regained control over its banking, and a railway linking north and south was completed. There were advances in industry, education, and the rights of women and minorities. However, this was done at the expense of the poor, particularly the peasantry, and to the benefit of a relatively small urban upper and middle class. A dangerous gap developed in mental outlook as well as wealth between the modern urban elite on the one hand, and, on the other, the traditional "bazaar class" of the cities and the peasantry that continued to follow the *ulema.*

Oil production grew but royalties remained quite modest. The oil industry constituted a British enclave with little relationship to the rest of the country, but it enhanced Iran's geopolitical importance. Because Riza Shah was pro-German, British and Soviet troops entered the country in 1941. In September of that year Riza Shah was forced to abdicate in favor of his son, Mohammed Riza Shah. For the duration of the war, Iran was once again divided into three zones. The war brought disruptions and dislocations, economic difficulties, and bread riots in Teheran in 1942. After the war the new Shah continued to rule much in the pattern of his father.

Egypt and Arabia

During the First World War the British in Egypt, as in India, sought to marshal support by raising hopes for rapid progress toward independence, hopes that were not fulfilled once the war was safely won. This produced bitter nationalist protests and insurrection when the British deported Saad Zaghul (1860–1927), founder of Egypt's first mass nationalist party, the Wafd. In 1922 Egypt gained partial independence as a constitutional monarchy, but its foreign and military affairs remained under the control of the British who also retained a garrison to guard the Suez Canal, the lifeline to their Empire. Relations between Egypt and Britain remained strained—in 1924 the British even sent out gunboats—but in 1936 a new treaty was signed that granted Egypt full independence while still leaving the British Suez garrison in place. A motive for both sides in reaching this agreement was the threat of Fascist Italy that had seized neighboring Libya and was soon to invade Ethiopia. During the Second World War Egypt became the scene of bitter desert fighting.

In Egypt, as in Turkey and Iran, political leadership was provided by secular nationalists who looked to Europe for their models and challenged the values and authority of the *ulema.* The *ulema* came to regard the nationalists as their most bitter enemy and tended to turn their back on the modern state. In the 1930s and 1940s, however, a fervent Muslim nationalism was advocated by the Muslim Brotherhood, envisioning the formation of a theocracy.

If the idea of creating a strictly Islamic state held considerable attraction for those cast aside by modern secularism, it was realized only on the Arabian

Peninsula where it took the form of a resurgence of the Wahhabis (see p. 816) once again under the leadership of the house of Saud. From 1902 to 1925 Ibn Saud (1880?–1953) expanded his territory, forming the state that was renamed Saudi Arabia in 1932. Here, in the land where Islam began, Muslim law was again strictly enforced. In 1935 geologists discovered oil, thus foreshadowing Saudi Arabia's later economic importance.

The Levant

Nowhere was disappointment over Britain's failure to live up to wartime promises more bitter than among the Arabs who in 1914 were still under Ottoman rule in the Levant. Induced by British promises of independence, they revolted against the sultan and were of great help to the British forces advancing into Palestine and Syria where Arabs and British seized Damascus. Further east, British troops advanced into Iraq. In Damascus the Arabs joyfully proclaimed an independent state under King Faisal. The British, however, had secretly arranged with France (the Sykes-Picot Treaty, 1916) to partition the Ottoman lands between them. To complicate the situation still further, in the Balfour Declaration (1917) they promised, "the establishment in Palestine of a national home for the Jewish people."

After the war most of the Ottoman lands were mandated to Britain, but France received Syria and Lebanon. French troops then deposed King Faisal, who had ruled for twenty-two months. But the French soon faced armed resistance as well as political opposition. During the Druse Insurrection of 1925–27, they even lost Damascus, which they recaptured with tanks and airplanes. Thereafter, nationalist demands consistently exceeded French concessions and were only made more adamant when the French tried repression. After street fighting and a general strike in 1936, the French were obliged to recognize the formation of a nationalist cabinet, but it took another world war to get the French out of Syria. The last French left in 1946.

In 1920 the British in Baghdad also faced a great Arab insurrection protesting the assignment of Iraq as a British mandate. The pattern of subsequent Iraqi history resembled that of Egypt rather than Syria. Under King Faisal (r. 1921–33), who had fled from Damascus, Iraq became an independent state with special ties to Britain.

Britain also received a mandate over Palestine and Jordan, called Transjordan until 1949. Jordan was separated from Palestine in 1921 and placed under its own king. After 1928 it was recognized as an independent state, but the British retained military and some financial control. In Palestine the situation was most difficult because the Balfour Declaration in promising a Jewish homeland also stated "that nothing shall be done which may prejudice the civil and religious rights of existing non-Jewish communities in Palestine." The British were caught between the conflicting nationalist aspirations of Arabs and Jews, each convinced of the moral righteousness of their cause. In 1930 when the British restricted Jewish immigration to assuage the Arabs, Britain had to face Jewish protests; but when such restric-

George Orwell, Reflection in Marrakech

1939

When you walk through a town like this—two hundred thousand inhabitants, of whom at least twenty thousand own literally nothing except the rags they stand up in—when you see how the people live, and still more, how easily they die, it is always difficult to believe that you are walking among human beings. All colonial empires are in reality founded upon that fact. The people have brown faces—besides they have so many of them. Are they really the same as yourself? Do they even have names? Or are they merely an undifferentiated brown stuff, about as individual as bees or coral insects? They arise out of the earth, they sweat and starve for a few years, and then they sink back into the nameless mounds of the graveyard and nobody notices that they are gone. And even the graves themselves soon fade back into the soil.

George Orwell, "Marrakech," in *A Collection of Essays* (1954), p. 187 as quoted in Edward W. Said, *Orientalism* (1978), pp. 251–52.

tions were relaxed, it was confronted with equally vehement Arab opposition. After Hitler came to power in Germany, Jewish immigration markedly increased so that by 1936 there were 384,000 Jews in Palestine, more than double the 172,000 who had lived there only five years earlier. British efforts at conciliation proved fruitless, and a 1937 plan for partition was also unsuccessful. Feelings ran so strongly that by 1937 there were pitched battles in Jerusalem, and the British set up military courts to deal with terrorists. In 1939 the British issued a white paper that rejected partition and limited immigration to 75,000 during the next five years after which Arab consent would be required for any additional immigration. Restrictions were placed on Jewish land purchases from Arabs and provisions made for involving Jews and Arabs in administration. Although opposed by both Zionists and Arabs, Palestine remained relatively calm during the Second World War.

French North Africa

French North Africa was no exception to the spread of nationalism among the Muslim peoples. First to have a modern nationalist party was Tunisia (1923) where Habib ben Ali Bourgiba (b. 1903) followed a gradualist policy toward the eventual goal of independence, defined by him as "human dignity translated into political terms." In Morocco, where traditional resistance continued until 1930, Sultan Muhammad V (r. 1927–53) became a force as well as a symbol for nationalist aspirations.

Algeria presented a very different case. Here, as in Kenya and Palestine, a substantial community of European settlers considered the land their home. They resented the extension of French citizenship in 1919 to anyone who had fought for France during the First World War and feared that if the Muslim majority would ever come to power, they themselves would be dispossessed. Established in power in Algeria itself, they were able to block subsequent attempts to grant additional rights to Muslim Algerians. These included a proposal made by France's Popular Front in 1937 to extend French citizenship to about 21,000 distinguished Muslims without requiring them to renounce Islam and the jurisdiction of the *Sharia* (Islamic sacred law). Failure on the part of the French government to effect even such minor concessions undermined and disillusioned Muslim moderates thereby preparing the way for Algeria's bloody fight for independence after the Second World War.

Suggestions for Further Reading

John K. Fairbank, ed., *The Cambridge History of China,* vol. 12: *Republican China 1912–1949,* Part I (1983), is authoritative and includes bibliographic essays. James E. Sheridan, *China in Disintegration: The Republican Era in Chinese History 1912–1949* (1975), is excellent.

Susanne H. and Lloyd I. Rudolph, *Gandhi: The Traditional Roots of Charisma* (1967, 1983), is a perceptive study and a good place to begin further reading. Michael Brecher, *Nehru: A Political Biography* (1959), is highly recommended. Also see Hector Bolitho, *Jinnah: Creator of Pakistan* (1964). *Train to Pakistan* by Khushwant Singh (1956), is a novel that conveys the human tragedy of the partition.

Milton Osborne, *Southeast Asia: An Introductory History* (1979), discusses the individual countries of Southeast Asia and includes bibliographic information. In addition, the following are recommended: Nicki R. Keddie, *Roots of Revolution: An Interpretative History of Modern Iran (1981);* Michael Crowder, *The Story of Nigeria (1978);* Monica Wilson & Leonard Thompson, *The Oxford History of South Africa* (1971); A. J. Wills, *An Introduction to the History of Central Africa (1967);* W. E. F. Ward and L. W. White, *East Africa: A Century of Change 1870–1970* (1972). See also Suggested Readings for Chapter 46.

	1914				1950	
SOUTHWEST ASIA AND AFRICA	**1923** Kemal Attatürk, President of Turkish Republic			**1948** *Apartheid* in South Africa **1948** Founding of Israel, first Arab-Israeli war	**1954** Nasser takes control in Egypt **1956** Second Arab-Israeli war **1960–75** Independence movement sweeps Africa	**1967** Third Arab-Israeli (Six-Day) war **1971** Indo-Pakistani war **1973** Fourth Arab-Israeli war
EUROPE	**1914–18** World War I **1917** Bolshevik Revolution **1919** Paris Peace Conference	**1920** Keynes, *The Economic Consequences of the Peace* **1922** Mussolini's March on Rome **1923** French occupation of Ruhr	**1924** Death of Lenin, rise of Stalin **1924–25** Adolf Hitler, *Mein Kampf* **1924–29** Era of Locarno **1933** Hitler becomes Chancellor	**1935** Nuremburg Laws against Jews **1936–39** Spanish Civil War **1938** Munich Conference **1939** Hitler-Stalin Pact	**1939–44** World War II **1940** Fall of France **1941** Germany invades Russia **1941–45** Mass murder of Jews **1945** Yalta Conference	**1947** Marshall Plan **1949** Germany divided **1949** NATO Alliance **1953** Death of Stalin **1955** West Germany joins NATO **1955** Warsaw Pact
SOUTH AND SOUTHEAST ASIA	**1920–22** Gandhi's first Civil Disobedience Movement	**1927** Indonesian Nationalist party founded by Sukarno **1930** Gandhi's March to the Sea		**1947** Independence of India and Pakistan **1948** Mahatma Gandhi assassinated	**1949** Independence of Indonesia **1955** Bandung Conference, Indonesia	
EAST ASIA	**1927–37** Nationalist regime in Nanjing **1931** Japan seizes Manchuria **1934** Long March of Chinese Communists	**1937–45** Sino-Japanese War	**1941** Japan attacks Pearl Harbor **1945** Atomic bombing of Hiroshima and Nagasaki **1946–49** Civil war in China	**1949** People's Republic of China **1949–76** Mao Zedong's Chinese Revolution	**1950–53** Korean War **1951** US peace treaty with Japan	
THE AMERICAS AND PACIFIC	**1917** US enters World War I	**1929** The Great Depression begins **1933** Franklin D. Roosevelt's New Deal	**1941** US enters World War II **1945** First atomic bomb **1945** United Nations organized	**1946** First electronic computer **1947** Truman Doctrine **1948** Transistor invented	**1959** Fidel Castro's victory in Cuba **1962** Cuban Missile Crisis **1963** President Kennedy assassinated	**1968** Martin Luther King, Jr., assassinated **1969** Neil Armstrong, first man on moon

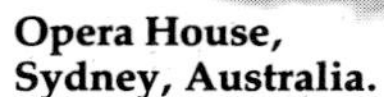

Opera House, Sydney, Australia.

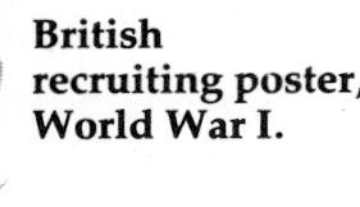

British recruiting poster, World War I.

Signers of Egyptian-Israeli peace treaty: Sadat, Carter, Begin, 1979.

Official symbol of the United Nations.

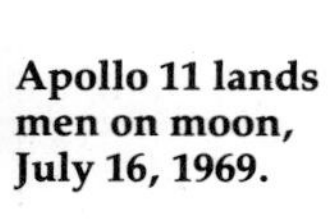

Apollo 11 lands men on moon, July 16, 1969.

German inflation: two billion mark note, 1929.

1985	
1977 President Sadat visits Jerusalem **1978** Camp David Accords **1979** USSR invades Afghanistan **1979** Revolution in Iran	**1980–** Iran-Iraq war **1980** Black majority rule in Zimbabwe (Rhodesia) **1981** President Sadat assassinated
1957 First earth satellite, USSR **1957** European Economic Community	**1960** Yuri Gagarin, first man in space **1980** Solidarity movement in Poland
1961 Increasing US involvement in Vietnam	**1973** US forces withdraw from South Vietnam **1975** Communists take over Vietnam, Laos, Cambodia
1971 People's Republic of China joins UN **1972** Nixon visits Beijing **1976** Death of Mao Zedong	**1977** China begins liberalizing under Deng Xiaoping
1974 President Nixon resigns **1975** Helsinki Accords **1977** Panama Canal Treaty	**1979** Civil war begins in Nicaragua and El Salvador **1982** Falkland Islands War

Striking Solidarity union workers, Warsaw, Poland, 1981.

Emperor Hirohito of Japan, 1926.

43 Democracy in Crisis and the Rise of Totalitarianism, 1919–39

Before 1914 the nations of Europe, despite national differences, still had much in common. What feeling of European community there had been then was gone by 1919. The Continent was now divided into victors and vanquished. Among the latter were not only the losers in the war but countries, like Italy and Russia, that felt dissatisfied with the peace settlements. In these "revisionist" powers new types of totalitarian governments arose, dividing Europe into democracies and dictatorships.

Another change was the decline of the Continent's central role in world affairs. As the United States gradually emerged from isolation, and as regions that hitherto had been dominated by Europe began to assert themselves, Europe's longstanding predominance faded. World politics gradually overshadowed European politics.

THE AFTERMATH OF WAR, 1919–29

One of the major aims of the western powers, the triumph of democracy, seemed to have been achieved. But the war left so many unsolved problems that even traditional democracies like France and England found it difficult to adjust to changed circumstances. Some of the new democratic states found their problems so insurmountable that their democracy turned out to be short-lived.

Stability in Great Britain

Among the western powers, Great Britain enjoyed by far the most stable domestic development. Democracy was completed when the franchise was extended in two further reform acts in 1918 and 1928. But while women were thus at long last granted political rights, the economic gains they had made during the war were soon again curtailed. Transition from war to peace was eased by the continuation of Lloyd George's coalition cabinet and by a brief economic boom. Beginning in 1920, however, England entered an extended economic crisis. Its effect was to shift power from the Liberals, first to the Conservatives and later to Labour. The Conservatives tried vainly to tackle the perennial problems of large deficits and growing unemployment. In 1929 Labour finally won its first major victory. But the solution to England's economic difficulties had to wait until after the Great Depression.

Despite its unsettled economy, Britain had no serious domestic disturbances. There was some unrest among the workers, and in 1926 trouble in the coal mines led to a general strike. But there was no violence. The Labour party, though accused of being "soft" on communism, was always moderate in its program and policy; and the Conservatives, though eager to curb the power of the unions, were sincerely concerned about the workingman's welfare. The government's policy of maintaining a stable currency was detrimental to British trade, but it saved the middle class from the demoralizing effects of inflation that were felt in most continental countries.

Instability in France

France led a more hectic existence. It was worse off economically, having suffered greater losses in money and manpower. Moreover, the French electoral system of proportional representation aggravated the instability of French politics. The interwar period saw more than forty different cabinets. After the war France was first governed by a "national bloc," with Raymond Poincaré as the leading figure. In 1924 the Ruhr fiasco brought to power a "cartel of the left," under Édouard Herriot and Aristide Briand.

The most urgent task before the French government was the reconstruction of the devastated regions. Because Germany until 1924 remained behind in its reparations, France had to pay for this reconstruction. Attempts to increase taxation ran into opposition from the right. Only the threat of runaway inflation finally led to drastic action. In 1926 a cabinet of "national union" under Poincaré was able to stabilize the currency and put France on the road to recovery. With reconstruction completed and German reparations paid regularly, France's economy improved rapidly. By 1928 the budget began to show a surplus, unemployment had vanished, and increased wages together with social legislation gave the lower classes a greater share in the nation's economy. France seemed well on the way toward resolving the long-standing conflicts between its rich and its poor.

The Weimar Republic

The new German republic was from the beginning plagued by disunity and disorder. In 1919 a constituent assembly at Weimar had drawn up an admirably democratic constitution. One of its weaknesses, however, was proportional representation, which contributed greatly to political instability. During the fourteen years of its existence, the Weimar Republic saw more than twenty different cabinets. The heavy legacy of war required a government that had the full support of its citizens. Throughout most of its brief life, the Weimar Republic failed to win such support.

The most loyal friends of the republic were the workers who had suffered most from political discrimination under the German Empire. The German working class, however, had been split before and during the revolution of 1918 into a moderate majority of Social Democrats and a radical minority of Communists, who several times threatened to overthrow the republic.

Most of the bourgeois parties professed loyalty to the new regime, although the parties of the right were hostile to it. This hostility was nourished by nationalist propaganda, which blamed the republic both for Germany's defeat and for the signing of the *Diktat* of Versailles. Soon after the war, rabidly nationalistic "free corps" embarked on a series of uprisings against the despised republic.

Considering the many attacks from every direction, it is surprising that the Weimar Republic was able to survive. In the early 1920s the antirepublican parties of the right attracted almost 30 percent of the vote. The most critical year was 1923, when the French invasion of the Ruhr, antirepublican risings on the right and left, and the total devaluation of the currency threatened the country's very existence. But as Germany's economy improved after 1924, the prorepublican parties made significant gains. Had this recovery lasted longer, the Germans might yet have become reconciled to their new republic.

The New Nations of Eastern Europe

Democracy faced even greater difficulties in eastern Europe. Most of the states there had gained their independence as a result of the war, and most of them faced similar problems. With the exception of Austria and Czechoslovakia, their economy was predominantly agrarian, and the division of large estates among the peasantry had long been a major issue. Where such land reform was carried out successfully, as in the Baltic states and Czechoslovakia, the rise of independent small proprietors contributed to political stability. In Poland and Hungary, where reform was obstructed by the landed aristocracy, domestic peace remained precarious.

Economic recovery in eastern Europe was slow. Widespread illiteracy, antiquated agricultural methods, and lack of capital funds for industrialization were the main obstacles. Efforts at regional collaboration ran into strong nationalist opposition. Nationalism in eastern Europe was intensified by the problem of minorities. Almost all the new nations included large numbers of foreign nationals.

All the new states started out with parliamentary governments. But this democratic trend was soon reversed. The first to change was Hungary. After a brief communist interlude under Bela Kun in 1919, conservative forces restored order under Admiral Nicholas Horthy, who founded Europe's first postwar dictatorship of the right. In Poland the rise of authoritarian rule came with Marshal Joseph Pilsudski's seizure of power in 1926. Elsewhere "strong men" suspended constitutions and silenced political opposition. None of these regimes was as totalitarian as the communist dictatorship in Russia or the fascist dictatorship in Italy. Only after Hitler's rise in the 1930s, did fascism gain control over most of central Europe.

Revolutionaries driving through the streets of Budapest in January 1919. This demonstration preceded the Communist takeover in March.

Of the few countries in eastern Europe where democracy took hold after the war, the most important were Czechoslovakia and Austria. Czechoslovakia, ably led by Thomas Masaryk and Eduard Beneš, was generally considered the model among the new democracies. Czechoslovakia's major problem was the desire for greater autonomy among its numerous minorities. Especially troublesome were the 3 million Germans living in the Sudeten region.

Austria since the war had only Germans within its borders. But the new republic was deeply divided between the industrialized and radical workers of Vienna, and the agrarian and conservative peasants of the provinces. Economically, the situation became so serious in 1922 that the League had to grant substantial loans for Austrian reconstruction. By 1926 Austria seemed to be out of danger. But the real cause of its difficulties—the loss of its economic hinterland—had not been resolved. As the least viable among the new states of Europe, Austria was the first to feel the effects of the Great Depression.

THE UNITED STATES

Isolationism and Nationalism

The recovery of Europe, though uneven, seemed well under way by 1929. It would have come earlier, had the United States been more aware of its new responsibilities as the world's richest power. But America preferred to keep aloof from European affairs. Most Europeans considered this isolationism extremely selfish. America, after all, had gained from the war economically, not merely by supplying the Allies but by penetrating into regions formerly controlled by European commerce. The least America could do was to forget the loans it had made to its allies during the war. But this the United States refused to do.

There were other sources of friction. The French resented America's and Britain's refusal to guarantee French security; the British were alarmed by America's growing commercial and naval competition; and neither France nor Britain welcomed the evident rapprochement between the United States and Germany. A further cause for concern was America's obvious intent of isolating itself economically by adopting some of the highest tariffs in its history.

America's isolationism had its domestic roots in a growing nationalist opposition to "foreign" and "radical" influences. Soon after the war the Ku Klux Klan claimed wide support for its persecution of racial and religious minorities; fear of radical elements in the early 1920s caused a "red scare" that led to several thousand arrests; and most important, restrictions on immigration severely limited immigrants from less desirable regions.

American International Involvement

Despite isolationism, America's humanitarian conscience and its economic interests could not help but lead to renewed involvement in international affairs. Right after the war, various relief organizations had dispensed millions of dollars' worth of supplies abroad. Beginning in 1924, American experts took the lead in tackling the reparations problem. With the return of economic stability, American investors lent vast amounts to various European countries, especially Germany.

In the political sphere America shared the general hope for peace and security with the warm reception of the Pact of Paris. But in other respects the country remained aloof. Even though many Americans had come to favor the League of Nations, the government refused to participate in any except the League's cultural and social work.

America was also concerned about disarmament, not so much on land as on sea. The rising influence of Japan and the large increase in Japanese naval expenditure made some limitation of naval forces seem highly desirable. Agreement on this point was reached at a naval conference in Washington in 1921 and 1922 that called for a ten-year naval holiday, the scrapping of large numbers of ships, and a fixed ratio for the capital ships of the major powers. But because Japan, France, and Italy remained dissatisfied with the results, these attempts at naval limitation were only partly successful.

Return to "Normalcy"

Economically, the United States, like Europe, found adjustment to peacetime conditions far from easy. The sudden cancellation of government contracts deeply upset the economy. As European industries resumed production, furthermore, United States exports declined. Attempts to cut costs by lowering wages were resisted by the workers, and labor unrest revived.

The American people were looking back with nostalgia to the peace and prosperity they had known before the war. The man who promised a return to "normalcy" was Republican President Warren G. Harding, elected in 1920. Under Harding America entered the era of hectic prosperity for which the 1920s are best remembered. The heyday of the "Roaring Twenties" came under Calvin Coolidge.

The Republicans' overriding concern was the American business community. High tariffs, the repeal of the excess-profits tax, the lowering of taxes on corporations and on high incomes, injunctions against strikes—all these measures benefited big business. America's phenomenal economic growth was also due to the ample capital resources and growing investments that were available from a broader segment of society. Big business, it seemed, was becoming everybody's business.

It was not quite everybody's, though. Neither the worker nor the farmer was getting his due share of prosperity. Labor had suffered from the postwar depression and from the hysteria that equated union protest with communism. As a result, union membership declined. Even so, most workers benefited from the nation's rising economy through better wages and full employment.

The stepchild of the American boom was the farmer. As a result of the war, America's farm output by 1919 had more than doubled. Then, as foreign demand decreased and surpluses accumulated, prices dropped. The government tried to help farmers by additional credit facilities and cooperatives, but the Republican administration shrank from direct subsidies. Protective tariffs, furthermore, led foreign countries to retaliate by cutting down their imports of American grain.

The "Jazz Age"

There was an air of frenzy about America's pursuit of business and pleasure during the "Jazz Age." As is common in periods of boom, America had its share of private and public scandals. The Eighteenth Amendment, introducing prohibition in 1920, invited violation of the law. The "speakeasy" and the "bootlegger" became part of American life, and "racketeering" was a common practice.

These features made the deepest impression abroad. Europeans professed to be shocked by the "materialism" of their nouveau riche American cousins, but Europe did not remain immune to American influences. American products and production methods found ready imitators abroad, and American styles and American jazz had their admirers among the young. For the first time in history Europe showed indications of becoming Americanized.

The American people themselves seemed well satisfied with their country's apparently endless prosperity. In 1928 they voted overwhelmingly for another Republican president, Herbert Hoover. Some developments, however, should have caused concern. Already before 1929 expansion in some basic areas had slowed down. Commodity prices had declined, and agricultural prices continued to fall. These signs of recession were obscured by a continuing boom on the stock market. Here prices were bid up by speculators to levels far out of proportion to actual values. In mid-September 1929, stock prices showed some decline. Failures of speculative companies in London later in the month caused some tremors on Wall Street, but still no panic. The collapse of the stock market came suddenly, on October 23. The next day, "Black Thursday," American investors sold close to twenty million shares at a total loss of $40 billion. The Great Depression had arrived.

THE GREAT DEPRESSION

"Business cycles"—that is, alternating phases of prosperity and depression—were a recognized feature of modern capitalism. But never before had a depression been quite so severe. The basic cause of the depression was the world's failure to solve the economic problems inherited from the First World War. Industrial expansion continued full force after the war and soon led to overproduction. Beginning in 1924 a brief, but artificial, recovery set in. As neither farmers nor workers really shared in the economic rise, purchasing power failed to keep up with production. In countries like Germany and Austria, furthermore, industrial expansion was largely stimulated by foreign loans. As these credits dried up, recovery ceased and the economy of these nations collapsed.

This, however, did not happen until the spring of 1931. In the meantime the situation in central Europe had become serious enough to demand radical remedies. One solution proposed in early 1931 was for an Austro-German customs union, strongly opposed by the French, who regarded it as a first step toward a political *Anschluss.* To put pressure on the Austrians, France began to withdraw its short-term credits. In May 1931 Austria's largest bank collapsed, beginning the European phase of the Great Depression. In July German suspended payments; in September the British government abandoned the gold standard. As other nations followed Britain's example, the only major European power to cling to

Soup kitchen in New York City during the Great Depression (1931).

the gold standard was France, where the depression was not felt until 1932.

Effects of the Depression

It is difficult to convey the staggering economic blow that the world suffered in the brief span of three or four years. World industrial production declined more than one-third, prices dropped more than one-half, and more than thirty million people lost their jobs. Some countries, especially Germany, were harder hit than others. In the United States, industrial production and national income by 1933 had decreased more than one-half, and unemployment was estimated at fourteen million.

Because of the worldwide scope of the depression, any remedy demanded cooperation among all the major powers. As debtor nations began to default, President Hoover in 1931 initiated a year's moratorium on all reparations and war debts to little avail. A year later an economic conference at Lausanne all but buried the troublesome problem of intergovernmental debts. A World Economic Conference in London in 1933 seeking to stabilize currencies failed when America refused to adopt its proposals.

International efforts to pull the world out of its economic slump thus were either too little or too late. Meanwhile governments everywhere reverted to the same practices that had brought on the depression in the first place. As America raised its tariffs to unprecedented heights, the rest of the powers followed suit, with even Britain abandoning its traditional policy of free trade in 1932. These and other restrictive measures hindered the revival of international trade.

THE DEMOCRACIES ON THE EVE OF WAR

The Great Depression belonged to both world wars — its roots went back to the First, and its effects contributed to the Second. While governments were still trying to repair the damages of the upheaval of 1929, clouds were already gathering for the far greater catastrophe of 1939. In this mounting crisis, resolute leadership was imperative. In countries like Germany and the succession states of Central Europe, democratic governments were no longer able to provide such leadership. As authoritarian regimes gained the upper hand, these nations were lost to the democratic cause. But even among the western democracies the crisis of the 1930s called for firm guidance. The need for leadership was felt particularly strongly in the United States.

The United States: The "New Deal"

Discontent with Republican half-measures was chiefly responsible for the Democratic sweep in the elections of 1932. For more than twelve years thereafter, the United States was

Roosevelt's New Deal

In our day these economic truths have become accepted as self-evident. . . :

> **The right to a useful and remunerative job in the industries or shops or farms or mines of the nation;**
>
> **The right to earn enough to provide adequate food and clothing and recreation;**
>
> **The right of every farmer to raise and sell his products at a return which will give him and his family a decent living;**
>
> **The right of every businessman, large or small, to trade in an atmosphere of freedom from unfair competition and domination by monopolies at home or abroad;**
>
> **The right of every family to a decent home;**
>
> **The right to adequate protection from the economic fears of old age, sickness, accident and unemployment;**
>
> **The right to a good education.**

All of these rights spell security. . . . For unless there is security here at home there cannot be lasting peace in the world.

From President Franklin D. Roosevelt, message to Congress, January 11, 1944.

President-elect Roosevelt greets President Hoover on the way to the Inauguration (March 4, 1933).

Ramsay MacDonald and Stanley Baldwin at a press conference in 1931, during their national coalition government.

guided by Franklin D. Roosevelt. The new president met the most difficult domestic and foreign emergencies with a boldness and confidence that earned him the admiration of the majority of Americans.

Some of Roosevelt's measures were intended for immediate relief, but others remain in effect to the present day. Republicans charged that government interference with free enterprise tended to corrupt America's pioneering spirit of self-reliance. In taxing the rich and aiding the poor, America certainly went far toward repudiating its traditional faith in laissez-faire. But the rising standard of living tended to hasten rather than retard the growth of American business; and if the "New Deal" entailed staggering financial burdens, the nation as a whole seemed willing and able to bear them.

Great Britain: Slow Recovery

The most successful holding action against the depression in Europe was waged in Great Britain. To rally parliamentary support, in 1931 Ramsay MacDonald transformed his Labour cabinet into a national coalition. Subsequent elections returned overwhelming Conservative majorities, and in 1935 Stanley Baldwin took over as prime minister. He was succeeded two years later by Neville Chamberlain. As might be expected from Conservative regimes, Britain sought to solve its economic problems by retrenchment rather than reform. Taxes were raised, government expenditures cut, and interest rates lowered. The devaluation of the pound stimulated exports. The Imperial Duties Bill of 1932 at long last introduced protectionism. The overall effect of these measures was a modest but steady recovery.

There were few important domestic events during the 1930s. King Edward VIII abdicated in 1936 to marry an untitled divorcée. Economic improvement helped to keep labor unrest at a minimum. Britain's main concern was with developments abroad, especially the actions of Italy and Germany.

France: A House Divided

In contrast to England and the United States, the French Third Republic during the 1930s was shaken to its very foundations. France until 1932 was an island of prosperity in a sea of economic misery. But disaster struck swiftly; by 1935 French industrial production had fallen almost one-third, and exports were declining rapidly.

It was not so much the severity of the economic crisis as the inability of the French government to cope with it that accounts for the political chaos that ended with the fall of France in 1940. The Third Republic had been deeply divided from the start. Workers and petty employees were virtual outcasts from French society, while the right-leaning wealthy classes and peasants had little enthusiasm for the Republic. The war had temporarily drawn the nation together, and once the difficult postwar transition had been made, French domestic tensions seemed to have eased. But the depression reopened wounds that had only just begun to heal.

Discontent flared up with sudden violence during the Stavisky scandal in early 1934. Rumors that an unsavory promoter, Alexander Stavisky, had enjoyed support in high places touched off a major rightist riot. Many of the rioters belonged to fascist leagues, right-wing and royalist organizations, similar to Hitler's storm troopers and Mussolini's Black Shirts.

The government's efforts to rally the country behind a cabinet of national union proved fruitless. In 1936 the parties of the left — Radical Socialists, Socialists, and Communists — buried their longstanding differences. Their "Popular Front" won a decisive electoral victory.

For almost two years various leftist coalitions, with Socialist Léon Blum as the leading figure, tried to halt the disintegration of the Republic. But to succeed, Blum's social reforms needed the cooperation of businessmen and bankers that was not forthcoming. Other obstacles to recovery were notably the unsettled state of international affairs, calling for costly armaments. But the basic reason for Blum's failure was that he was too radical for the right and not radical enough for the left.

While the Germans were preparing to fight the world, the French were fighting one another. Successive waves of strikes and a rigidly enforced forty-hour week slowed down industry when it should have been working overtime. In April 1938 a shift to the right brought Édouard Daladier to the premiership, with far-reaching powers to rule by decree. But Daladier could not do what abler men before him had failed to do: heal the breach between right and left, bourgeoisie and workers, capitalists and socialists, rich and poor. France was deeply divided when it went to war in September 1939.

AN AGE OF UNCERTAINTY

Before we turn from the democracies to the dictatorships during the "long armistice" between 1919 and 1939, we must briefly consider the intellectual climate of these critical years. The war and its aftermath had shaken many traditional beliefs and expectations, and the world had never regained the feeling of optimism that had prevailed before 1914. Growing doubts about hitherto accepted values changed the prevailing attitude during the postwar era from confidence to uneasiness and uncertainty.

Material Progress

Not everyone, of course, was sensitive to these changes. The majority of people were ready to enjoy the spectacular achievements that science had in store. Material progress certainly seemed as promising as ever with such new "miracles" as the radio and the talking motion picture, and constant improvements in production made these and earlier inventions, like the automobile, available to the average person. The veritable avalanche of labor-saving devices that combined to make for a "high standard of living" did not necessarily make life richer, but they made it easier.

Other technological and scientific achievements also changed everyday life. Improvements in transportation virtually eliminated distance as a barrier. The Old World and the New, formerly days apart, now were separated by only hours. Some of the most spectacular developments took place in medicine. Concentrated efforts brought many deadly diseases under control and lengthened the average lifespan in the advanced countries from less than fifty years in 1900 to almost sixty-five years by 1939. Modern science and industry thus continued to fulfill their promise of enabling people to live both better and longer.

Critics of Mass Culture

But material progress was not without its drawbacks. The growth of population now was seen more as a threat to cultural values than to the world's food supply. The Spanish philosopher José Ortega y Gasset, in his book *The Revolt of the Masses* (1932), warned that the increase in human beings was so rapid that it was no longer possible to educate people in the traditions of their culture. As a result, the gap between the cultured few and the uneducated many became ever wider. And because the masses exerted political power, their low standards would henceforth predominate.

Other voices were raised against the dangers of a civilization that envisaged progress entirely in material terms. The British novelist Aldous Huxley in his satirical novel *Brave New World* (1932) predicted many later "triumphs" of human ingenuity, from tranquilizers to brainwashing. Huxley pictured a well-adjusted society whose members were scientifically conditioned to whatever status they occupied, existing like animals on a well-tended experimental farm. Man as a slave to his technological inventions, as a mere cipher in a collectivist society, as a rootless, lonely, and lost being in a world of bewildering complexity—such were the subjects that increasingly occupied social critics, novelists, and poets.

The "Behavioral Sciences"

The study of man as an individual and as a member of society had for some time past been the task of the social sciences. This term had at first been used only for the traditional subjects: history, political science, and economics. But in time the field had come to include the new "behavioral sciences": psychology, sociology, and cultural anthropology.

The beginnings of modern psychology are associated with Sigmund Freud, a Viennese doctor who began formulating his theories at the turn of the century. Other psychologists before him, like Wilhelm Wundt and William James, had tried to discover the organic roots of human behavior, assuming that the brain, like any other organ, performed purely biological functions. Freud's approach, radically different, was that human behavior is directed by subconscious instincts, or "drives," of which the most important is the sexual impulse. These drives are inhibited, usually in early childhood, and such inhibition leads to frustrations, which in turn may cause serious neuroses. In an effort to cure his patients, Freud developed "psychoanalysis," an extended and deep probing of the patient's mind to get at its subconscious layers. The purpose of such probing was to make the patient understand the conflicts that caused his abnormal behavior and by such understanding remove the causes of his mental disturbance.

Other pioneers in modern psychology also tried to discover what made people act the way they did. Far from increasing man's self-confidence, however, modern psychology merely added to his feeling of uncertainty. Ever since the Enlightenment man had thought of himself as a wholly intelligent and rational being. Now suddenly he was faced with the realization that he was subject to dark instincts and drives and that these forces, rather than his intellect, determined his behavior.

The second of the behavioral sciences, sociology, originated in the nineteenth century with Auguste Comte, Karl Marx, and Herbert Spencer. But here, too, the twentieth century introduced new methods and provided new insights. One of the most important modern sociologists was the Italian Vilfredo Pareto, whose *Mind and Society* was published in English in 1935. Pareto accepted the findings of psychologists that men were swayed by emotion rather than guided by reason. The ideals or rationalizations that social groups set up were to him mere fronts that screened the basic irrational motives that really moved people. Pareto held that any clever leader or any elite capable of seeing through this human self-deception could use the basic motives of their fellow men to establish an authoritarian system in which the masses would obey slogans that appealed to their inner instincts. Pareto's analysis, if correct, held little hope for a rationally ordered, democratic society.

The third behavioral science, cultural anthropology, likewise tried to explain human behavior. By studying primitive tribes, anthropologists like Ruth Benedict and Margaret Mead hoped to determine what role environment played in shaping culture. One of their discoveries was that differences between cultures were due to environmental rather than inherent biological factors and that there was no basis for the belief in "superior" and "inferior" races. It was one thing, however, to study a small primitive tribe and another to apply the same techniques to larger and more complex societies. Some promising beginnings were made by students in the field of "human relations," who gathered valuable data on small segments of their own society, in the hope of determining what motivated its members.

Spengler and Toynbee

Most social scientists were concerned with the present rather than the past, but even historians often dealt with past events to gain a better understanding of the present. Some, notably Oswald Spengler and Arnold Toynbee, studied the rise and fall of past civilizations in order to predict the future. History had usually been viewed as a linear progress toward some faraway goal. However, Spengler and Toynbee held that civilizations had always risen and fallen in cycles or curves. But their grandiose predictions about where their own civilization was going were far from hopeful.

Oswald Spengler's *The Decline of the West* (1918) compared some twenty past "cultures," tracing each through identical phases down to a final phase of "civilization." European culture, being in the midst of this final phase, according to Spengler, would soon disintegrate and collapse. Other historical scholars warned that this "morphology of cultures" was based on incomplete or incorrect evidence. Yet it could not be denied that in his comparative study Spengler had uncovered many suggestive parallels, and in his predictions he seemed remarkably correct.

Following Spengler's example, Arnold Toynbee embarked on his own monumental work, *A Study of History* (1934–54). Toynbee also assumed parallel phases in major civilizations. The birth of a civilization Toynbee saw in man's successful "response" to a "challenge," usually by geography or climate. The growth of a civilization consists in man's gradually solving his physical problems, thus freeing his energies for more elevated pursuits. In this process, a creative minority takes the lead and makes its views prevail over the passive majority. The breakdown of a civilization, according to Toynbee, occurs when this minority loses its creative force to meet a particular challenge. Even though Europe was in the midst of this final phase, its "Time of Troubles," Toynbee held out some hope for western civilization, if it learned from its past mistakes.

The "New Physics"

While the social sciences were giving little comfort in an age of uncertainty, the natural sciences had been demolishing the rational and mechanistic view of nature that had prevailed since Newton. Already before the end of the nineteenth century, the findings of scientists like Wilhelm Konrad Roentgen, Pierre and Marie Curie, Ernest Rutherfold, and Max Planck had raised doubts concerning Newtonian physics. They made it clear that a whole new system of physics and mathematics was needed to supply the answer to questions on which Newton had been silent. Such a new system appeared in 1905 when the young German physicist Albert Einstein advanced his "theory of relativity."

According to Einstein's theory, time and space were not absolute, as Newton had assumed, but relative to the observer. Later he included gravitation and motion in his calculations. Mass in

Marie Curie in her laboratory (1906).

Albert Einstein in Berlin (1920).

Einstein's universe was thus a variable. The mass of a body depended on its rate of motion; its mass increased as its velocity increased, with the speed of light as the theoretical limit. The velocity of light, therefore, rather than time and space now emerged as absolute in the "new physics."

A further radical departure from accepted theory was Einstein's assumption of the equivalence of mass and energy. Experiments in nuclear physics already had shown that the dividing line between mass and energy was far from clear, and that matter slowly disintegrated into energy by way of radiation. The amount of matter thus lost was infinitesimal compared with the resulting energy. Einstein expressed this relationship between mass and energy in his famous formula $E = mc^2$, in which E is energy, m is mass, and c is the velocity of light. This formula implied that if a process were devised by which matter could suddenly be transformed into energy, only a small amount of matter would be required to produce a vast quantity of energy. A practical demonstration of the validity of Einstein's formula came with the first atomic explosion in 1945.

These and other revolutionary developments in science did not immediately affect the outlook of the average person. But as scientists began speaking of the "limitations of science," admitting that they no longer knew all the answers, their feeling of uncertainty could not help but enter general consciousness. A mysterious world (as the physicists said it was), inhabited by irrational man (as the psychologists said he was), caught in a civilization predestined for decay and disintegration (as Spengler and Toynbee said our civilization was)—this was a far cry from the happy and confident prospect that had existed only a generation before.

New Cultural Trends

The uncertainty of the age was also reflected in its literature and art. In literature, the common denominator was disillusionment—as seen in T. S. Eliot's *The Waste Land* (1922), Thomas Mann's *Magic Mountain* (1924), and Theodore Dreiser's *An American Tragedy* (1925). Some of the greatest literature of the years between the wars was escapist—the poetry of Rainer Maria Rilke, the tales of Joseph Conrad, and even the stories of Ernest Hemingway—and looked nostalgically to a simpler past—Marcel Proust, *Remembrance of Things Past* (1913–27), and Thomas Wolfe, *Look Homeward, Angel* (1929).

Though deeply tinged with disillusionment, postwar literature was also immensely creative. The insights of modern psychology proved a boon to writers in their quest to understand human nature. The Irishman James Joyce in his novel *Ulysses* (1922) introduced a method known as "stream-of-consciousness." The search into the subconscious also motivated dramatists like Luigi Pirandello and Eugene O'Neill. Sexual matters were now written about with far greater candor; still, an unexpurgated edition of *Lady Chatterley's Lover* (1928), by D. H. Lawrence, could not be published until thirty years later.

The mixture of uncertainty and creativity that characterized literature also prevailed in painting. Most artists still dealt with recognizable subjects, but more and more of them rebelled against the Realism and Impressionism of the prewar era. Instead, painters like Paul Klee, Vassily Kandinsky, and Pablo Picasso expressed on canvas their inner feelings and impulses, often in styles that reflected the chaotic world in which they lived. These "Expressionists" in time became so abstract that it was impossible any longer to recognize in them common aims and interests. Each artist had become a law unto himself.

This same creative uncertainty and search for new ways of expression had its parallel in modern music. Some composers—Jan Sibelius, Sergei Rachmaninoff, Richard Strauss, and Ralph Vaughan Williams—continued to follow traditional lines. But others

—Arnold Schönberg, Arthur Honegger, Béla Bartók, and Paul Hindemith—departed from familiar forms, developing a wholly new musical idiom.

Because modern art and music were highly individualistic, they appealed to only a few. Modern architecture had a somewhat wider following. Most architecture in the nineteenth century had been imitative of earlier styles. The inherent possibilities of new materials, steel and concrete, had been ignored by all but a few pioneers, such as Louis Sullivan and Frank Lloyd Wright. This changed after the First World War, as architects became increasingly concerned with the function as well as the appearance of their buildings. The doctrine of "functionalism" found its European exponents in Le Corbusier, Walter Gropius, and Ludwig Mies van der Rohe.

Anti-Intellectualism

It is difficult to gauge correctly the temper of a period as brief as the twenty years between the two world wars. Many of its accomplishments, especially in science, were impressive. But a paradox behind this extension of knowledge was: The more man found out about the world, the more he realized how little he had known before. From a feeling of supreme self-importance at the end of the nineteenth century, man's view of himself was pushed to the opposite extreme: He felt uncertain and insignificant, a creature of instinct, no longer able to shape his own destiny.

This uncertainty turned many people against the rationalist philosophy that had prevailed for the past two hundred years. As in the similar revolt of Romanticism against reason a century before, antirationalism now sprang from the disillusionment that followed a seemingly futile war. Modern anti-intellectualism took several forms. It brought a revived interest in religion, even among scientists, who not long ago had been ardent defenders of materialism. But far larger numbers turned elsewhere for guidance. There were many reasons for the sudden rise of totalitarianism after the First World War. Not least among them was that it provided its followers with simple beliefs in an age of bewildering uncertainty.

THE RISE OF TOTALITARIANISM

The Communist and Fascist regimes between the two wars have been variously called autocratic, authoritarian, dictatorial, and totalitarian. These terms are not synonymous. There had been autocratic and authoritarian regimes in the past, and there have been dictatorships from ancient times to the present. But none of these deserved to be called totalitarian. A totalitarian regime is one in which a determined minority, by use or threat of force, imposes its will on the total life of a society. The aims of this ruling clique are usually rooted in some all-embracing ideology. There were many ideological differences between fascism and communism. Communism was squarely based on Marxian socialism, while the outstanding characteristic of fascism was nationalism. But despite these ideological differences, fascism and communism were alike in many ways. Both controlled minutely the life of every individual; both ruled through propaganda and terror; both segregated and persecuted their opponents; and both sought to extend their power abroad through force or subversion. Why should totalitarian regimes have arisen when and where they did? The circumstances differed from country to country, but there were some similarities. Totalitarianism arose only in nations with little or no democratic tradition. Most of them underwent lengthy domestic crises caused by the First World War or the Great Depression. In all cases a resolute minority, headed by a leader with great demagogic gifts, initiated changes amounting to a revolution.

COMMUNISM FROM CRISIS TO TRIUMPH, 1917–41

It took several years for communism to gain full control in Russia. The initial difficulties faced by the new Soviet regime were so severe that its survival seems almost miraculous.

"War Communism" and Civil War

The Bolsheviks began by totally eradicating the tsarist past. In what was called "war communism" the nation's economy was socialized, where necessary through terror. But to Lenin, revolution in Russia was the prelude to world revolution; and the spread of the latter was seen as necessary to guarantee the success of the former. In March 1919, the Soviet-controlled Comintern was founded in Moscow, dedicated to inciting world revolution.

But these Bolshevik attempts to conquer Russia and the world simultaneously were premature. War communism, instead of bringing relief, actually brought further misery. Opposition to the new regime was helped by Allied intervention aimed at reviving Russian resistance against Germany. The Germans, still in control of much of Russia, encouraged separatism in the Ukraine and along the Baltic. And to complicate matters further, the Allies imposed a tight naval blockade.

As the antirevolutionary White armies converged on the Bolshevik Red army, its influence shrank to the region around Moscow and Petrograd. But the White armies lacked popular support, and the fact that they enjoyed Allied help further weakened their appeal. The White armies, furthermore, operated on widely separated fronts and under divided leadership. For all these various reasons, the White armies were no match for the newly created Red army. By the beginning of 1920, the Bolsheviks had defeated all the White forces except those in southern Russia under General Wrangel.

At this point a new danger arose. The Poles, who wanted to extend their border eastward beyond the boundary assigned to them at the Peace Conference, now joined forces with Wrangel in a concerted drive against the Red army. This was no longer a civil but a national war, and the Russian people rushed to the defense. In a brilliant counterattack, the Polish army was driven back to the gates of Warsaw. In August 1920, the Red army was halted again and thrown back. Under the subsequent Peace of Riga, Poland advanced its borders some 150 miles eastward into regions chiefly inhabited by Russians.

Lenin's "New Economic Policy"

The end of civil and foreign war did not relieve Russia's misery. Droughts and crop failures in 1920 and 1921 brought one of the worst famines in its history. The situation called for drastic measures. In March 1921, therefore, Lenin initiated his "New Economic Policy," or NEP, calling for a radical departure from war communism and a partial return to capitalist practices. Lenin's policy was justified by its results. In the seven years of NEP, agriculture and industry returned to their 1913 levels.

The modification of Soviet policy at home had repercussions abroad. The failure of communist uprisings in Central Europe had shown that world revolution was not imminent. And with Russia's recovery depending heavily on foreign trade and capital, the Soviets were eager to resume normal relations with the rest of the world. NEP was seen abroad as a sign that the Bolsheviks had learned the error of their ways. Foreign interests then hoped to avail themselves of Russia's vast market and resources. Economic rapprochement between Russia and the West began in 1921, and by 1925 all major powers except the United States had granted the Soviet Union diplomatic recognition. But relations between Russia and the West never became really close. The main obstacle was the well-founded suspicion that the Soviets had not really abandoned their aim of world revolution.

Lenin did not live to see the results of NEP. In 1922 he suffered a stroke, and in 1924 he died at the age of fifty-three. He had been a remarkable man, with a great mind and superior talents as an agitator and organizer. Without his leadership it is doubtful that Russia's revolution would have succeeded.

Stalin versus Trotsky

Lenin's death brought into the open a struggle for power that had been going on for some time. The two contenders Trotsky and Stalin were not unalike in their aims: Both looked forward to the ultimate victory of world communism. They differed in their methods. Trotsky believed that because Bolshevik Russia could not survive in a capitalist world, Russia should concentrate on fomenting revolutions elsewhere. Stalin, on the other hand, wanted to concentrate on "socialism in one country," and only then pursue the spread of communism elsewhere.

In the struggle between Trotsky and Stalin, their personalities and tactics were decisive. Both men had served the revolution well. But while Trotsky's importance as Commissar of War declined, Stalin's influence continued to grow. In 1922 he became general secretary of the Communist party, which gave him control over the entire party apparatus. Trotsky's doctrine of "permanent revolution," meanwhile, found little response in a nation exhausted by foreign and civil war. And while Trotsky's aloof manner offended his comrades, Stalin was careful to make friends with such "Old Bolsheviks" as Leo Kamenev, the party's chief ideologist, and Grigori Zinoviev, the head of the Comintern.

In 1925 Stalin's policy of conciliation and cunning succeeded in forcing Trotsky to resign from the Ministry of War. Soon thereafter, Kamenev and Zinoviev quarreled with Stalin and joined Trotsky, but Stalin proved the stronger. Allying himself with two other Old Bolsheviks, Alexei Rykov and Nikolai Bukharin, he had the "Trotskyites" expelled from the party. Trotsky was banished, first to Siberia and after 1929 abroad. He was assassinated in Mexico in 1940. In 1929 Stalin ousted Rykov and Bukharin. With the last potential rivals out of the way, Stalin emerged supreme.

A highly complex system, the Soviet government received its final form under the "Stalin Constitution" of 1936. The Soviet Union, a federation of states, was under strict control of the Supreme Soviet in Moscow. That body consisted of two chambers, the Soviet of the Union and the Soviet of Nationalities. They were headed by a Presidium of some twenty-seven members, but more important was the Council of People's Commissars, appointed by the Supreme Soviet.

Actual power rested in the hands of a few people. But a multiplicity of local, regional, and provincial soviets gave at least an appearance of representative government. Other features of the Russian constitution did the same. Franchise was universal, and a bill of rights guaranteed all kinds of freedoms. But these rights had to be exercised "in the interests of the working people." And the agency that interpreted these interests was the Communist party.

The Communist Party

Membership in the Communist party in 1918 was estimated at two hundred thousand. Ten years later it was over one million. Its function was to serve as "the vanguard of the working class." Undeviating faith in Marxian doctrine and blind obedience, these were the basic demands made of all party members. An All-Union Party Congress selected the Central Committee as the chief policy-making organ, and the Central Committee in turn delegated power to the Politburo, the party's highest authority.

The obedience demanded by party membership was highly rewarded. All leading positions in the bureaucracy went to party members, and they alone could hold political office. With the Communist party as the dominant force in Soviet life, control of the party ensured domination of the state. Stalin owed his absolute power to his leading role in the party rather than to any governmental position. And beginning in 1928 he used this power to carry the Communist revolution to its final triumph.

The Five-Year Plans

In order to survive in a hostile world of capitalist powers, the Soviet Union had to realize as rapidly as possible its inherent economic power. Stalin hoped to achieve this goal in three Five-Year Plans. Their aim was the large-scale development of basic industries and the increase of agricultural production through collective farming.

The first Five-Year Plan was launched in 1928. Even if one discounts Communist propaganda, the achievements of Stalin's policy were impressive. Between 1928 and 1940 Russia's industrial output grew more than sevenfold. Collectivization proved less successful because Russian agriculture was hampered by small holdings and antiquated methods. The conservative Russian peasant, who opposed large-scale farming and mechanization, resorted to passive resistance. To break this opposition, force was used. Executions and deportations, added to the severe famine of 1932–33, caused the death of some four million people. But even strong-arm methods did not bring the desired results. While by 1940 most Russian land had been converted into collective farms, the problems of Russian agriculture had by no means been solved.

Stalin's Five-Year Plans completed the victory of communism. The lot of the average Russian gradually improved. Free medical care and other social services, together with full employment, provided the workers with security at the expense of freedom. At the same time, some of the changes introduced after the revolution were abandoned. The family again became the basic unit of society. Education became less progressive but more universal. Religion was at least tolerated. One of the most surprising reversals of the Stalinist era was the renewed veneration of Russia's past. This new Russian nationalism ignored Marx's admonition that the proletariat had no fatherland and strengthened Stalin's regime by rooting it more firmly in the past.

The Sabotage and Treason Trials

Although communism under Stalin gained a firm hold, there were nevertheless frequent signs of internal unrest. Among its manifestations were the sabotage trials of 1928 and 1933 and the treason trials of 1934 to 1938. The sabotage trials involved Russian and foreign engineers who were accused of sabotaging Russia's industrial

Khrushchev on the Great Purge

Stalin originated the concept "enemy of the people." This term automatically rendered it unnecessary that the ideological errors of a man or men engaged in a controversy be proven; this term made possible the usage of the most cruel repression, violating all norms of revolutionary legality, against anyone who in any way disagreed with Stalin, against those who had bad reputations. This concept "enemy of the people" actually eliminated the possibility of any kind of ideological fight or the making of one's views known on this or that issue, even those of a practical character. In the main, and in actuality, the one proof of guilt used, against all norms of current legal science, was the "confession" of the accused himself, and, as subsequent probing proved, "confessions" were acquired through physical pressures against the accused. This led to glaring violations of revolutionary legality and to the fact that many entirely innocent persons, who in the past had defended the party line, became victims.

From *The Crimes of the Stalin Era: Special Report to the 20th Congress of the Communist Party of the Soviet Union by Nikita S. Khrushchev*, ed. by Boris I. Nicolaevsky (New York: The New Leader, 1956).

efforts. These trials were probably staged to hide or excuse the many instances of waste and inefficiency revealed during the early years of the Five-Year Plans.

The same explanation did not hold for the treason trials. These amounted to a major purge of thousands of leading Soviet figures. The reason given for the Great Purge was an alleged plot by Hitler and Trotsky directed at Stalin. In January 1935 Zinoviev and Kamenev were accused of conspiracy and comdemned to death, together with fourteen other "Trotskyites," in 1936. Many others followed, including Rykov and Bukharin. In 1937 the purge spread to the Red army and throughout the entire Soviet hierarchy. Tens of thousands were imprisoned, executed, or exiled.

Foreign observers were bewildered by this spectacle of the revolution "devouring its children." The Great Purge was seen as a sign of Russian weakness. That there was opposition in Russia cannot be doubted. In spreading his net as wide as he did, Stalin destroyed any possible danger of a future conspiracy.

Russia and the West

Prominent in Stalin's repressive policy was the fear of intervention from abroad. The memory of such intervention during the revolution was never forgotten. Outwardly, Russia's relations with the West improved during the 1930s. The Soviet Union was the only major power not affected by the Great Depression, and the Russian market offered welcome commercial opportunities. The rising threats of Nazi Germany in Europe and of Japan in East Asia established a further bond between Russia and the West. In 1933 the United States finally recognized the Soviet Union, and the following year Russia was admitted to the League of Nations. But despite the apparent rapprochement, both continued to distrust each other. This mutual suspicion had tragic consequences on the eve of the Second World War.

THE FASCIST REVOLUTION IN ITALY

The rise of fascism was in part a reaction to the real or imaginary threat of communism. But even without such threat, conditions in Italy after the war made major changes imperative. Italians had been divided about intervention in the war. But once the nation had joined the Allies, hopes for territorial rewards ran high, but were bitterly disappointed afterwards. Discontent was heightened by economic problems. Riots and strikes, together with a sharp increase in the Socialist vote, made Italy's propertied elements fear that a communist revolution was at hand. Parliamentary government had never worked well in Italy. Here was a situation in which some able and unscrupulous demagogue could promise a solution to Italy's problems. The man who saw and seized this opportunity was Benito Mussolini.

Mussolini was Italian fascism personified, and the movement would have been unthinkable without him. Born in 1883, Mussolini had become a Socialist in his youth. In 1912 he had become editor of *Avanti,* Italy's leading Socialist paper. When war broke out, Mussolini was still a pacifist, but soon advocated Italian intervention on the Allied side. This was the first of many radical reversals in the life of this accomplished opportunist.

Mussolini's first *Fasci di Combattimento* (groups of combat) were formed in 1919. They were initially made up of discontented veterans. These "Black Shirts" soon numbered many thousands. In the elections of 1919 the Fascists failed to get a single seat. But two years later they won thirty-five.

Mussolini's "March on Rome"

Meanwhile the Black Shirts were waging a virtual civil war against Socialists and labor unions, and Mussolini was mending his fences in preparation for his coup. Having changed his revolutionary movement into a regular political party, he proclaimed his loyalty to the monarchy and the Church. He also made certain that the army would not oppose him. In October 1922, Mussolini mobilized his Black Shirts for a dramatic "March on Rome." But King Victor Emmanuel had been well prepared and gave way easily. On October 29, 1922, Mussolini was invited to form a new government.

The change from democratic to totalitarian rule in Italy took several years. Mussolini was given full emergency powers for one year. These he used to tighten Fascist control. A new electoral law provided that any party gaining a plurality would receive two-thirds of the parliamentary seats. Even so, opposition continued. In 1924 one of Mussolini's severest critics, the Socialist leader Giacomo Matteotti, was kidnapped and murdered. At first it seemed as though popular indignation would sweep the Fascists from power. But when Mussolini realized how little united his opponents were, he stepped up his seizure of power. In a wave of arrests by a new secret police, enemies of the state were brought before a special tribunal and sentenced to prison or exile. Non-Fascist members of the cabinet were dismissed and Mussolini was given power to rule by decree. In 1926 all opposition parties were outlawed.

Mussolini was a charismatic speaker with carefully studied gestures.

The Fascist State

Political power, in Mussolini's "corporative state," was vested in some thirteen "syndicates." These confederations were initially organized to regulate labor conditions. Strikes and lockouts were declared illegal, and the final word in labor disputes rested with the government. Under a new electoral law in 1928, the syndicates drew up a list of candidates for the Chamber of Deputies, which had to be approved by the Fascist Grand Council, a body of some twenty party leaders appointed by Mussolini. As under communism, the party thus wielded complete political control. Parliament, under this new system, lost most of its former functions. In 1938 even the outward forms of democracy disappeared when the Chamber of Deputies was replaced by a new Chamber of Fasces and Corporations. With its members appointed, elections were no longer needed.

The Fascist party considered itself an elite. Its leader, or *Duce,* was Mussolini. Fascist youth organizations indoctrinated the young. The press and radio were under strict censorship, and every facet of intellectual and artistic life was made to fit the party mold. Only in his relations with the Church did Mussolini show leniency. One of his major achievements was the Lateran Treaty of 1929, settling the long feud between the Italian government and the papacy.

Mussolini's major efforts were aimed at improving Italy's economy. Reduction of government spending and increased taxation brought some financial stability. Italy shared in the general recovery of the late 1920s, but the Great Depression undid these gains. Even though the government by then had assumed full control over economic affairs, its policy was far less successful than Russia's planned economy. Not only was Mussolini less ruthless than Stalin, but Italy lacked the Soviet Union's vast natural resources. Beginning in 1935, furthermore, Mussolini embarked on a costly war.

One way of diverting domestic discontent was through a strong foreign policy. Mussolini's first attempt to try this remedy, the bombardment of the Greek island of Corfu, had brought him the protests of the great powers. For the next ten years he was careful not to appear too aggressive. Italy concluded treaties of friendship with a number of countries, especially those that, like Austria and Hungary, shared its opposition to the peace treaties. In 1924 Yugoslavia, in return for concessions elsewhere, agreed to Italy's annexation of Fiume. Mussolini's restoration of domestic order, meanwhile, endeared him to foreign visitors; his opposition to communism made him an ally of anticommunists everywhere; and his improved relations with the Church won him Catholic support. As a result, the new Italy and its leader commanded considerable respect abroad, at least until 1935.

NATIONAL SOCIALISM IN GERMANY

Mussolini's success in Italy was observed with keen interest in Germany, where a movement akin to Italian fascism had been active since the early 1920s. Its leader was an obscure Austrian rabble-rouser, Adolf Hitler, the moving spirit behind the National Socialist German Workers' Party (NSDAP). The brown-shirted members of the party—or "Nazis," as their opponents called them—were similar to Mussolini's first Black Shirts. Like their Italian counterparts, they hoped to seize power through a coup. But their Munich *Putsch* in November 1923 had failed.

Adolf Hitler and His Aims

The man who was soon to determine the fate of the world was still not taken seriously. Born in 1889, the son of an Austrian customs official, Hitler had gone into politics after the First World War, in which he had fought as a German soldier. Considering his background and haphazard education, Hitler's subsequent rise to power was remarkable. Circumstances played their part, but even they needed a master. The *Führer,* or leader, of the Nazi party was neither physically nor intellectually impressive. Yet he had certain qualities and abilities that enabled him to subject to his power first a whole people and ultimately a whole continent. There can be no doubt that Germany's past and the character of its people help to explain the rise of Hitler. But of equal if not greater significance were the evil genius of Hitler himself and the specific circumstances in the early 1930s that made his victory possible.

National Socialism, in contrast to Italian fascism, had a detailed, though internally contradictory, program. Its twenty-five points offered something to everyone. It was, of course, never completely implemented, and provisions that might scare off prospective

The Fascist Decalogue
1938

1. **Remember that those who fell for the revolution and for the empire march at the head of your columns.**
2. **Your comrade is your brother. He lives with you, thinks with you, and is at your side in the battle.**
3. **Service to Italy can be rendered at all times, in all places, and by every means. It can be paid with toil and also with blood.**
4. **The enemy of Fascism is your enemy. Give him no quarter.**
5. **Discipline is the sunshine of armies. It prepares and illuminates the victory.**
6. **He who advances to the attack with decision has victory already in his grasp.**
7. **Conscious and complete obedience is the virtue of the Legionary.**
8. **There do not exist things important and things unimportant. There is only duty.**
9. **The Fascist revolution has depended in the past and still depends on the bayonets of its Legionaries.**
10. **Mussolini is always right.**

From M. Oakeshott, *The Social and Political Doctrines of Contemporary Europe* (Cambridge: Cambridge University Press, 1949), pp. 180–81.

supporters were explained away. Yet with its Pan-German nationalism, its anti-Semitism, and its opposition to democracy, it clearly foreshadowed future Nazi policy. A still more important prediction was given in Hitler's autobiography, *Mein Kampf (My Battle)*, which he began in 1924. Besides Judaism and Marxism, Bolshevism emerged as a major target, and Russia was singled out as the chief victim of future German expansion.

Hitler's Assumption of Power

Before Germany had found time to recover from a lost war and a runaway inflation, it was plunged into the Great Depression. With millions of unemployed, political extremism flourished. Between 1928 and 1932 Nazi delegates in the *Reichstag* rose from 12 to 230, and Communists increased from 54 to 89. This radicalization made orderly government impossible. Democracy, which had never taken a firm hold in Germany, broke down.

President von Hindenburg in 1933. Visible directly behind him is Adolf Hitler next to a heavily decorated Hermann Göring.

Hitler's assumption of power was outwardly legal. On January 30, 1933, he was asked to form a coalition government. The men who helped Hitler gain power—the aged President von Hindenburg and his political advisers—felt confident that they could use the Nazi movement for their own ends: the establishment of an authoritarian regime. They failed to realize that Hitler was not a man to let himself be used.

To strengthen his poistion, Hitler first dissolved the *Reichstag.* Shortly before the new elections, the *Reichstag* building went up in flames, an event Hitler blamed on the Communists. But even so only 44 percent of the German people voted National Socialist. As a next step, Hitler manipulated the *Reichstag* into passing an Enabling Act that gave the government dictatorial powers for four years. These powers were then used to prohibit political parties. By July 1933 the National Socialists had become the only legal party. When President Hindenburg died in August 1934, Hitler combined the office of president with that of chancellor. The transition from democracy to dictatorship was complete.

Hitler did not introduce any constitutional changes. The *Reichstag* continued to meet, though infrequently, to endorse all measures put before it. There were no more elections, but occasionally the German people were asked in a plebiscite to support an act of the *Führer's.* The civil service was purged of Jews and political opponents. The legal system was overhauled, and justice elevated the welfare of the state above the rights of the individual. To ferret out enemies of the state, a secret police, the *Gestapo,* was given sweeping powers.

Nazism at Home

As in other totalitarian states, the Nazi party controlled every phase of

German life. Most of Hitler's lieutenants were rewarded with leading positions. But some of his old comrades failed to get what they expected. To forestall any "second revolution" on the part of these malcontents, Hitler, on June 30, 1934, instituted a major "Blood Purge." In a lightning move the *Führer* had several hundred of his possible opponents executed.

With government and party now under his firm control, there remained only one sphere in which Hitler did not wield complete authority. The armed forces had sworn personal allegiance to him after Hindenburg's death, and Hitler's renunciation of disarmament in March 1935 had further enhanced his standing with the army. But not until 1938, after a thorough purge of the army's top echelons, did the *Führer* feel he had a force on which he could fully rely. Henceforth Hitler himself was to wield personal command of all Germany's armed forces.

The same process of *Gleichschaltung,* or "coordination," that was carried out in government, party, and army, was extended to every other phase of German life. In many of his innovations, Hitler imitated Mussolini. He tried to make his country's economy strong and self-sufficient. Public works, rearmament, and military conscription eradicated unemployment. In 1934 the *Führer* launched the first of two Four-Year Plans to prepare Germany's economy for war. To finance such costly ventures, huge funds were raised through increased taxation, special levies, and rigid control of prices and profits.

The main sufferer of this policy of "guns instead of butter" was the German worker. His wages were low and his hours long. A German "Labor Front" took the place of the former unions. Strikes were forbidden, and all labor relations were controlled by the state. The farmer fared somewhat better. He was given various subsidies and protected against foreclosure. Food production increased, although Germany did not become self-sufficient. One of Hitler's aims was a large and healthy rural population. Artists and writers, regimented like everyone else, were called upon to glorify "blood and soil" and the "nobility of labor," and Nazi propaganda urged each and every German to place the welfare of the community before the good of the individual.

The majority of Germans readily complied with this appeal. Not that the German people were all ardent Nazis. The average German welcomed what he considered the "positive" features of the Nazi regime, and he secretly grumbled about the things he did not like. There was some active opposition —the thousands of prisoners in the concentration camps testified to that. But they were only a small minority. Before the outbreak of the Second World War, Hitler's many admirers abroad praised him, like Mussolini, for the miraculous improvements he had brought about, and in particular for the firm stand he had taken against communism.

Anti-Semitism

One aspect of Nazi policy, however, stirred deep concern among observers abroad, and that was the persecution of the Jews. Anti-Semitism was one of Hitler's earliest obsessions, and it was the aim that he pursued most persistently and ruthlessly to the bitter end. The first measures against Germany's Jews, about 1 percent of the population, were taken shortly after the Nazis came to power. In April 1933 all Jews were excluded from the civil service. Soon thereafter the Jews were excluded from universities, and lawyers and doctors were barred from practice. The "Nuremberg Laws" of 1935, deprived Jews of their citizenship and forbade their marriage to non-Jews. As a result of this "cold pogrom," many Jews went into exile. But worse was yet to come. In November 1938, a "spontaneous" demonstration against the Jews brought destruction to Jewish property and death to some of its owners. Jews henceforth had to wear a yellow Star of David and had to live in ghettos.

Hitler speaks.

Nazi picket during the boycott of Jewish-owned shops in 1933. The placard reads: "Germans! Strike back! Don't buy from Jews!"

The intensification of Jewish persecution was a sign that Hitler was getting ready for war. Hitler's ultimate aim was a "New Order" for Europe, under which the German people would expand into the unlimited *Lebensraum* (living space) to the east and rule over the "inferior" Slavic peoples. The unbounded ambition of Hitler's megalomania plunged the world into the most frightful war it had ever seen.

THE SPREAD OF AUTHORITARIANISM

One of the dangers of totalitarianism was its spread to nations that had been weakened by economic crises and political unrest. The rise of communism was generally considered the greater threat, and many a dictatorship of the right gained power in order to prevent a dictatorship of the left. The Soviet Union tried its best, with the aid of the Comintern, to help communist parties abroad. But its numerous attempts at fomenting leftist plots in Central Europe and in East Asia remained unsuccessful. Nowhere outside the Soviet Union did communism gain a decisive victory during the interwar period.

Efforts to set up rightist dictatorships proved more successful. We have already seen the rise of strong men in most of the smaller nations of Central Europe during the aftermath of the war. Similar regimes arose in Spain and Portugal. In Yugoslavia, Albania, Bulgaria, Greece, and Rumania, kings turned into dictators. In Hungary, Poland, and Spain, power was wielded by an alliance of military and agrarian groups. In Austria and Portugal, authority rested with parties supported by the Catholic Church. As in the case of Russia, Italy, and Germany, all these small nations lacked a strong democratic tradition. Their new regimes were authoritarian rather than totalitarian. In some instances Germany and Italy tried to aid the rise of such authoritarian regimes. In Austria a Nazi *Putsch* in 1934 failed, and Nazi victory was postponed until four years later. In Spain, however, General Francisco Franco defeated the republican government with the help of Italy and Germany. Like communism, fascism had its followers in the democracies as well. But with the exception of France, these native fascist parties never posed a serious threat. Only during the Second World War did fascist "Fifth Columns" become a real danger.

EUROPE ON THE EVE

Our survey of developments in the major powers before 1939 has shown some marked differences from the situation before 1914. On the earlier occasion, Europe had been split into two clearly defined and evenly matched camps, with only England and Italy remaining on the fence. In 1939 the situation was far less clear and the balance less even. Furthermore, ideology, which in 1914 had been a minor factor, in 1939 proved both a help and a hindrance in the international lineup. And finally, while in 1914 all the major powers had done their utmost to prepare themselves for a showdown, on the eve of the Second World War only Nazi Germany was in top form for what Hitler considered its champion fight. That there was to be such a fight, the *Führer* knew long before anyone else. The question was — when, where, and with whom was the war to be?

Suggestions for Further Reading

Among the few general surveys on the interwar period. R. J. Sontag, *A Broken World, 1919–1939* (1971), is one of the best. C. S. Maier, *Recasting Bourgeois Europe: Stabilization in France, Germany, and Italy in the Decade After World War I* (1975), is difficult, but worth the effort. Good books on the individual democracies are A. J. P. Taylor, *English History, 1914–1945* (1965); D. W. Brogan, *France Under the Republic* (1940); S. W. Halperin, *Germany Tried Democracy* (1946); and on the United States, W. E. Leuchtenburg, *The Perils of Prosperity, 1914–1932* (1958). The great depression is analyzed in J. K. Galbraith, *The Great Crash, 1929* (1955), and C. Kindleberger, *The World Depression 1929–1939* (1973).

Among works on totalitarianism, C. J. Friedrich and Z. K. Brzezinski, *Totalitarian Dictatorship and Autocracy,* rev. ed. (1965), provides a general theory, and C. W. Cassinelli, *Total Revolution: A Comparative Study of Germany under Hitler, the Soviet Union under Stalin, and China under Mao* (1976), compares its major manifestations. Books on Communist Russia are legion. E. H. Carr, *The Russian Revolution: From Lenin to Stalin* (1979), is a synopsis of the distinguished scholar's voluminous work. F. B. Randall, *Stalin's Russia: A Historical Reconsideration* (1965), is factual and objective. The best general account of Soviet foreign policy is A. B. Ulam, *Expansion and Coexistence: The History of Soviet Foreign Policy, 1917–1973* (1974). On Fascist Italy, C. Seton-Watson, *Italy from Liberalism to Fascism* (1967), is a good survey. Its key figure is the subject of D. M. Smith, *Mussolini* (1982). The best work in English on Nazi Germany is K. D. Bracher, *The German Dictatorship* (1970). J. C. Fest, *Hitler* (1974), is an excellent biography. On the treatment of the Jews, G. Reitlinger, *The Final Solution* (1953), is a pioneering and enduring study.

Among the innumerable books on intellectual history, J. Barzun, *The House of Intellect* (1959); C. Brinton, *Ideas and Men* (1950); and F. L. Baumer, *Modern European Thought: Continuity and Change in Ideas, 1600–1950* (1977), are recommended.

	1914				1950	
SOUTHWEST ASIA AND AFRICA	**1923** Kemal Attatürk, President of Turkish Republic			**1948** *Apartheid* in South Africa **1948** Founding of Israel, first Arab-Israeli war	**1954** Nasser takes control in Egypt **1956** Second Arab-Israeli war **1960–75** Independence movement sweeps Africa	**1967** Third Arab-Israeli (Six-Day) war **1971** Indo-Pakistani war **1973** Fourth Arab-Israeli war
EUROPE	**1914–18** World War I **1917** Bolshevik Revolution **1919** Paris Peace Conference	**1920** Keynes, *The Economic Consequences of the Peace* **1922** Mussolini's March on Rome **1923** French occupation of Ruhr	**1924** Death of Lenin, rise of Stalin **1924–25** Adolf Hitler, *Mein Kampf* **1924–29** Era of Locarno **1933** Hitler becomes Chancellor	**1935** Nuremburg Laws against Jews **1936–39** Spanish Civil War **1938** Munich Conference **1939** Hitler-Stalin Pact	**1939–44** World War II **1940** Fall of France **1941** Germany invades Russia **1941–45** Mass murder of Jews **1945** Yalta Conference	**1947** Marshall Plan **1949** Germany divided **1949** NATO Alliance **1953** Death of Stalin **1955** West Germany joins NATO **1955** Warsaw Pact
SOUTH AND SOUTHEAST ASIA	**1920–22** Gandhi's first Civil Disobedience Movement	**1927** Indonesian Nationalist party founded by Sukarno **1930** Gandhi's March to the Sea		**1947** Independence of India and Pakistan **1948** Mahatma Gandhi assassinated	**1949** Independence of Indonesia **1955** Bandung Conference, Indonesia	
EAST ASIA	**1927–37** Nationalist regime in Nanjing **1931** Japan seizes Manchuria **1934** Long March of Chinese Communists	**1937–45** Sino-Japanese War	**1941** Japan attacks Pearl Harbor **1945** Atomic bombing of Hiroshima and Nagasaki **1946–49** Civil war in China	**1949** People's Republic of China **1949–76** Mao Zedong's Chinese Revolution	**1950–53** Korean War **1951** US peace treaty with Japan	
THE AMERICAS AND PACIFIC	**1917** US enters World War I	**1929** The Great Depression begins **1933** Franklin D. Roosevelt's New Deal	**1941** US enters World War II **1945** First atomic bomb **1945** United Nations organized	**1946** First electronic computer **1947** Truman Doctrine **1948** Transistor invented	**1959** Fidel Castro's victory in Cuba **1962** Cuban Missile Crisis **1963** President Kennedy assassinated	**1968** Martin Luther King, Jr., assassinated **1969** Neil Armstrong, first man on moon

Opera House, Sydney, Australia.

British recruiting poster, World War I.

Signers of Egyptian-Israeli peace treaty: Sadat, Carter, Begin, 1979.

Official symbol of the United Nations.

Apollo 11 lands men on moon, July 16, 1969.

German inflation: two billion mark note, 1929.

1985	
1977 President Sadat visits Jerusalem **1978** Camp David Accords **1979** USSR invades Afghanistan **1979** Revolution in Iran	**1980–** Iran-Iraq war **1980** Black majority rule in Zimbabwe (Rhodesia) **1981** President Sadat assassinated
1957 First earth satellite, USSR **1957** European Economic Community	**1960** Yuri Gagarin, first man in space **1980** Solidarity movement in Poland
1961 Increasing US involvement in Vietnam	**1973** US forces withdraw from South Vietnam **1975** Communists take over Vietnam, Laos, Cambodia
1971 People's Republic of China joins UN **1972** Nixon visits Beijing **1976** Death of Mao Zedong	**1977** China begins liberalizing under Deng Xiaoping
1974 President Nixon resigns **1975** Helsinki Accords **1977** Panama Canal Treaty	**1979** Civil war begins in Nicaragua and El Salvador **1982** Falkland Islands War

Striking Solidarity union workers, Warsaw, Poland, 1981.

Emperor Hirohito of Japan, 1926.

44 The Second World War
Background, Ordeal, and Aftermath

The Second World War was quite different from the First. While the question of responsibility for the first war has caused much controversy, there was no doubt that the major responsibilty for the second rests heavily on one country, Germany, and on one man, Adolf Hitler. Still, it might be argued that Hitler would never have been able to go to war if the western Allies had stopped him in time. To that extent England and France may bear some responsibility. As for the Soviet Union, its pact with Hitler in 1939 made the war inevitable.

The war of 1939, far more than the war of 1914, was a world war. Japan had been fighting China for more than eight years, and before long the conflict spread to other parts of Asia and to Africa. The earlier war had been largely a war of position. The Second World War was one of almost constant movement. New weapons were chiefly responsible for the greater speed and mobility. The airplane in particular revolutionized warfare on land and sea. Its use against civilian targets, furthermore, eradicated all differences between the fighting and the home fronts. The Second World War was a truly total war.

THE MARCH OF FASCIST AGGRESSION, 1931–37

The series of international crises that culminated in the outbreak of the Second World War began as far back as 1931 in East Asia.

Japan Against China

Japan, for some time past, had been trying to gain control over Manchuria, China's border province in the Northeast. In September 1931 the Japanese army, using a minor incident along the South Manchurian Railway as an excuse, invaded the region and quickly defeated local Chinese forces. In 1932 the Japanese renamed their conquest Manchukuo and declared it a protectorate.

The Chinese government meanwhile protested to the League of Nations against the Japanese act of force. The League appointed a special commission of inquiry. Its report condemned Japan's aggression and proposed the establishment of an autonomous Manchuria. This was as far as the powers were prepared to go. Under the League Covenant they should have taken more drastic action. But China seemed far away and sanctions might prove costly at a time when the world was in the throes of depression.

Hitler's Visitors

Lloyd George visited Hitler in September 1936, discussed world affairs, and came away convinced that Hitler was a reasonable man with acceptable aims and no desire whatsoever to plunge Europe into war. Conservatives, Liberals, and Socialists alike sought out the Führer, and were mesmerized by him. Even Arnold Toynbee was reported to have been won over at his interview to a belief in Hitler's genuine desire for peace in Europe "and close friendship with England." George Lansbury, a pacifist, and earlier leader of the Labour Party, was convinced after their personal encounter that Hitler "will *not* go to war unless pushed into it by others." Lord Allen of Hurwood told the *Daily Telegraph* on his return from Germany that "I watched him with the utmost vigilance throughout our lengthy conversation, and I am convinced he genuinely desires peace." Halifax recorded after his own visit to Berchtesgaden: "He struck me as very sincere, and as believing everything he said." But all Hitler did at these meetings was to repeat to each visitor the same dreary monologue about the insults of Versailles, the need for German unity on an ethnic basis, the evils of communism which he as a German could appreciate more than they could, the stubbornness of the Czechs, the pugnacity of the Poles, and the long-suffering innocence of the Germans. . . . But . . . when Lord Allen of Hurwood, with greater courage than most of his fellow-visitors, raised the issue of Jewish persecution, Hitler had nothing to say.

From Martin Gilbert, *The Roots of Appeasement* (London: Weidenfeld and Nicolson, 1966), pp. 164–65.

Hitler Against Versailles

The moral of the Manchurian story was that if an aggressor acted quickly, nobody would stop him. This lesson was not lost on Adolf Hitler. In a series of dramatic moves between 1933 and 1936, he freed Germany from the most onerous restrictions of Versailles. In October 1933 the Germans withdrew from the Disarmament Conference and the League of Nations. In January 1935 the Saar region voted to return to Germany. Two months later Hitler denounced the disarmament clauses of the Versailles Treaty.

In order to forestall any opposition to his unilateral policy, Hitler at every step stressed Germany's peaceful intentions. In January 1934 he signed a nonaggression pact with Poland. In 1935 Hitler quieted Britain's fears of German rearmament by concluding an Anglo-German naval agreement. The British thereby acquiesced in the *Führer's* violation of the Treaty of Versailles and added to France's feeling of insecurity. It is hardly surprising, then, that France should have sought help elsewhere. In May 1935 it concluded an alliance with the Soviet Union. But this merely gave Hitler the pretext for his next major coup.

On March 7, 1936, Hitler ordered the German army to march into the demilitarized Rhineland, his most daring move to date. Had he been forced to back down at this crucial point, the future would doubtless have been far different. But again nothing happened. The French were afraid to act without the British. The British criticized Germany's act, but the general feeling was that the Germans merely did what any people would have done—establish mastery over their own territory. The implications of Hitler's action were overlooked. Should Germany want to move quickly, as it had done in 1914 and was to do again in 1940, there was no longer any protective zone to save the Lowlands from German invasion.

Mussolini Against Ethiopia

One reason why Hitler was able to get away with his daring move was that it coincided with a serious crisis elsewhere. On October 3, 1935, an Italian army had invaded Ethiopia, or Abyssinia, in northeastern Africa. This isolated region had escaped the scramble for colonies among the European powers before 1914. Once before, in 1896, Italy had tried to invade Ethiopia but had been repulsed. This humiliation was never forgotten. Mussolini now hoped to join Ethiopia with the existing Italian colonies of Eritrea and Somaliland into a sizable imperium.

Italy's forces were too powerful for the antiquated forces of Emperor Haile Selassie. On May 9, 1936, Mussolini proclaimed the annexation of Ethiopia. Meanwhile the League of Nations, after declaring Italy an aggressor, had imposed economic sanctions. But to be effective such a program had to be airtight. With several major powers outside the League, it could not be. Still, it might have been possible to stop the Italians if oil had been embargoed. But the fear that oil sanctions might lead to a general war made both France and England hesitate to take such a step. The French, who looked on Italy as a possible ally against Germany, did not wish to endanger their relations with Mussolini. The British feared that their navy would have to bear the brunt of a possible conflict. Without the support of its two leading members, the League was powerless.

Once again the western powers, instead of supporting collective security, had preferred to buy peace by making concessions at someone else's expense. But such concessions merely whetted the appetite of the dictators. Prior to this time, relations between Hitler and Mussolini had not been very close. Hitler's designs on Austria worried Mussolini, who was himself interested in the Danube region. But with the conquest of Ethiopia, Italy's energies had found an outlet elsewhere, and Germany's friendly attitude during the conflict had paved the way for closer relations. On October 15, 1936, the two powers concluded a formal agreement to coordinate their foreign policies. This "Rome-Berlin Axis" was later joined by Japan.

War in Spain

The significance of the Axis became evident in connection with the Spanish Civil War. Spain had become a republic in 1931, but the traditionally promonarchist forces—clergy, army, and aristocracy—still wielded considerable power. The Republican regime had been unable to cope with the economic consequences of the Great Depression. In 1936 a "Popular Front" of Republicans, Socialists, Syndicalists, and Communists won a major election victory. But this Republican success merely hastened the inevitable clash between Nationalists and Republicans. In July 1936 army units in Spanish Morocco, led by General Francisco Franco, rebelled against the Republic. The Spanish Civil War had begun.

Had the Spaniards been left alone, the war would hardly have become the tragedy it did. But Hitler and Mussolini favored Franco's Nationalists and sent them men and materials. The Russians in turn gave support to the Republicans, or Loyalists. But the Soviets alone were incapable of matching the aid supplied by the Fascists. To assure the survival of the Republicans, the help of the democracies was needed.

England and France were no more willing to risk a general war over Spain than they had been over Manchuria or Ethiopia. Public opinion supported the Republicans, and foreign volunteers fought in the International Brigades on the Republican side. But the governments were more cautious. In September 1936 a Nonintervention Committee in London could not prevent German and Italian "volunteers" from fighting on Franco's side. In an effort at neutrality, President Roosevelt in-

The Spanish Civil War 1936–39

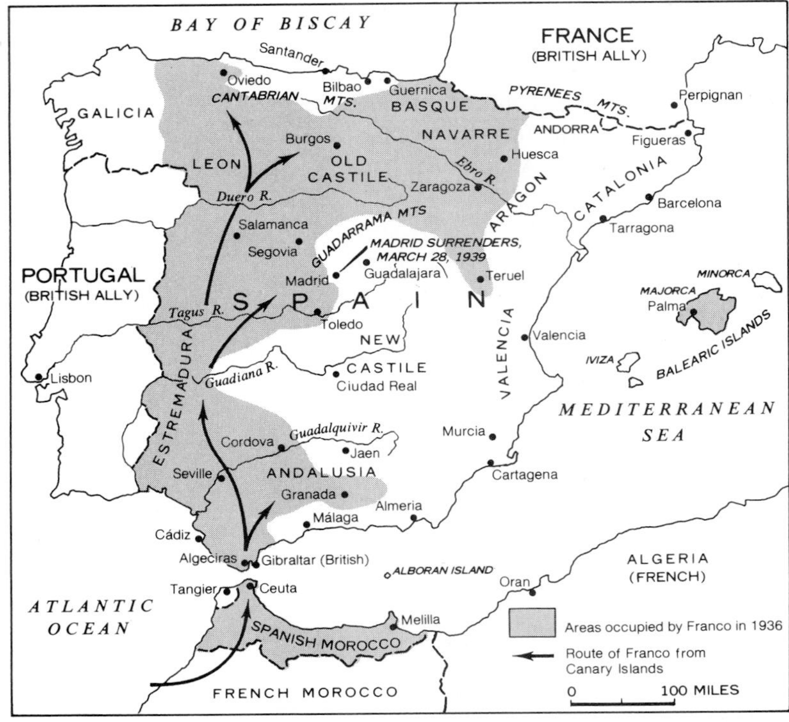

voked the Neutrality Act of 1935, prohibiting the export of arms and munitions. But this move mainly hurt the Loyalists, because Franco continued to receive supplies from Germany and Italy. The Spanish Civil War lasted for almost three years. By the time the last Republican forces surrendered in March 1939, events in Spain had long been overshadowed by more important developments elsewhere.

THE ROAD TO WAR

Except for the war in Spain, the international situation at the beginning of 1937 seemed hopeful. But this impression was mistaken. The preceding years had been crucial for the new German *Wehrmacht,* when determined outside resistance might still have put a stop to Hitler's plans. Now the balance of military power began to turn more and more in Germany's favor. In June 1937 Hitler issued the first directive to prepare for a future war. Five months later he met with his top advisers to present an outline of his strategy. First Germany would seek control over Austria and Czechoslovakia. Then it would be ready to pursue its major aim of eastward expansion to win the living space that Germany needed.

War in East Asia

While Hitler was making his plans in Europe, warfare had again broken out in East Asia. In July 1937 a minor incident near Beijing (Peking) touched off an undeclared war between China and Japan that lasted until 1945. By the end of 1938 the Japanese controlled most of northern China. Farther south, Japan had seized the city of Guangzhou (Canton) and surrounding territory. In March 1938 the Japanese set up a "Reformed Government of the Republic of China" at Nanjing (Nanking).

The government of Chiang Kai-shek, meanwhile, had taken refuge in Sichuan (Szechwan) province. The Chinese armies, while superior in numbers, were woefully short of equipment. To fight the invaders more effectively, Chiang Kai-shek and the Chinese Communists agreed to bury their differences. A "scorched earth" policy and guerrilla warfare on the part of the Chinese kept the Japanese from consolidating their gains. But despite the determined resistance of the Chinese, their ultimate survival depended on outside aid.

Chinese protests to the League of Nations brought little more than verbal condemnation of Japanese aggression. The French feared that resistance to Japan might lead to a Japanese attack on French Indo-China. And Britain hoped that by appeasing Japan it might maintain its commercial interests in China. The United States, too, was careful at first not to antagonize Japan. Only when it became clear that the "Open Door" policy was being threatened did the United States begin to aid the Chinese. Only the Soviet Union supported the Chinese from the start.

The Austrian Anschluss

Beginning in the spring of 1938, attention was diverted from Asia to Europe. Hitler's first victim was Austria.

Union with Austria, or *Anschluss,* had always been a major Nazi aim. The failure of a Nazi *Putsch* in 1934 did not end the Nazi conspiracy. In January 1938 the Austrian government uncovered another Nazi plot. To remove the resulting tension, Austria's chancellor, Kurt von Schuschnigg, went to see Hitler at Berchtesgaden in February. But instead he was presented with a set of demands that would have made Austria a virtual German protectorate. Refusal to accept, Hitler made clear, would result in a German invasion of Austria.

Faced with this ultimatum, Schuschnigg in March decided to rally the Austrian people in a plebiscite. Hitler's reaction was swift. Once more threatening invasion, he forced Schuschnigg to resign. On March 11, an Austrian Nazi, Artur Seyss-Inquart,

Europe Before the Second World War 1930–39

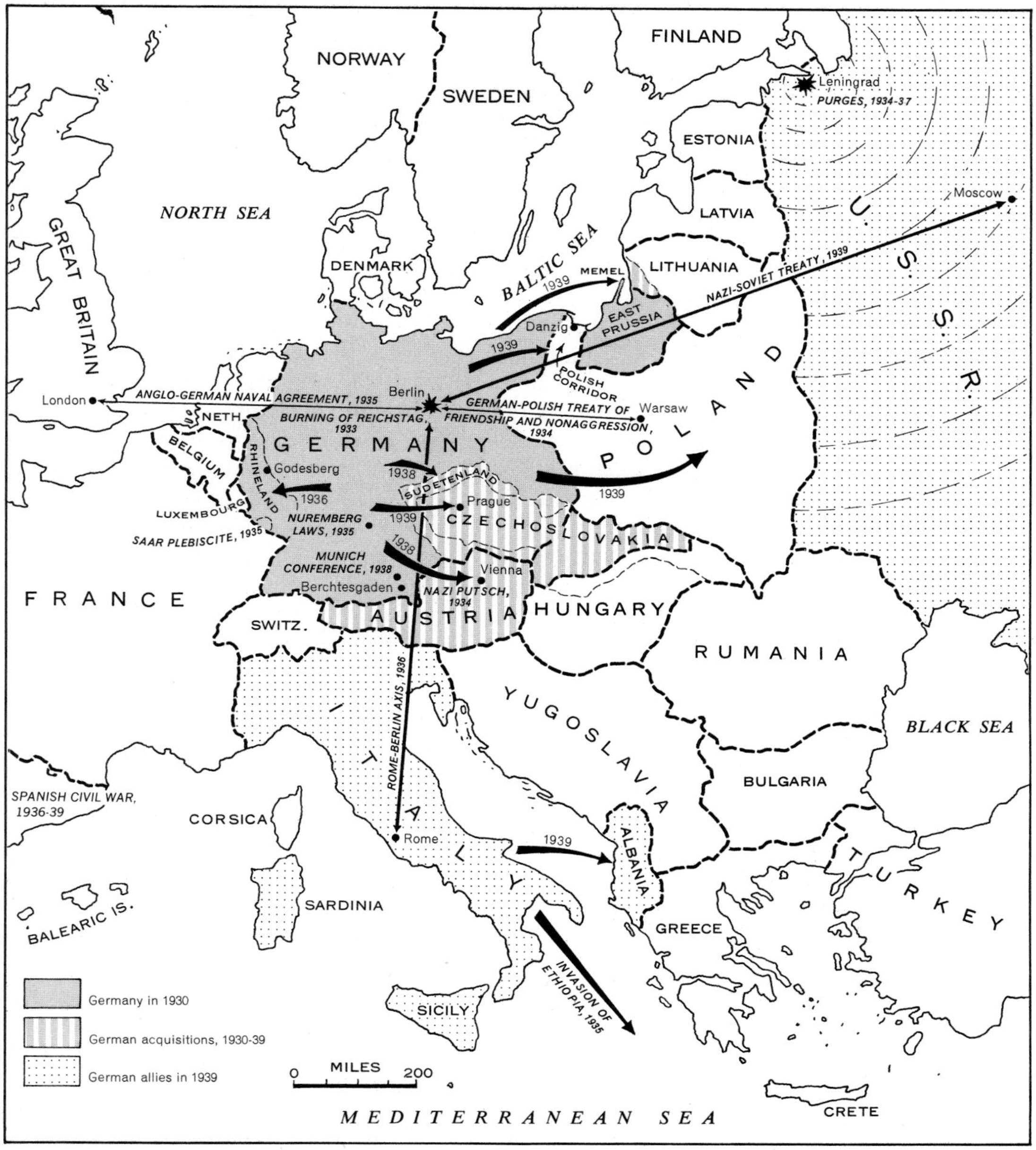

became chancellor; on March 12, German troops crossed the Austrian frontier; and on March 13, Austria was incorporated into the Greater German Reich.

The ultimate success of this latest act of aggression again depended on the attitude of the other powers. Again there were loud protests but no action. The French were in the midst of one of their perennial governmental crises and looked to the British to take the lead. But Britain, while deploring Hitler's methods, saw nothing wrong with an Austro-German *Anschluss,* so long as both peoples wanted it. And Italy, although long a champion of Austrian independence, was by now in the German camp. Some hoped that Hitler would be satisfied, now that his dearest wish had been fulfilled. The *Führer* did his best to confirm that hope by making his usual promises of peaceful intentions. The Soviet Union proposed a collective stand, but the western powers refused.

The Conquest of Czechoslovakia

The pretext for Germany's intervention in Czechoslovakia was the German minority in the Czech border regions. The three million Sudeten Germans had long been a source of trouble to the Czech government, especially since Hitler's rise to power. Beginning in 1936 their leader, Konrad Henlein, had begun collaborating with the Nazis; and as Germany's power increased, the demands of the Sudeten Germans became louder. In April 1938, after the fall of Austria, Henlein demanded autonomy for the Sudetenland. Nazi propaganda seconded this demand. The climax of Germany's campaign against the government of President Eduard Beneš came with Hitler's address to the annual party congress at Nuremberg on September 12, 1938, in which he threatened German intervention on behalf of the Sudeten Germans.

The German army had been spending the summer of 1938 preparing for the invasion of Czechoslovakia. The French and British, meanwhile, had been trying desperately to effect a compromise on the Sudeten problem. But the Czechs proved adamant, trusting in their own military strength and that of their French and Russian allies. When Hitler's speech intensified riots in the Sudetenland, the Czech government proclaimed martial law. War, it seemed, was imminent. It was narrowly averted by the action of Britain's Prime Minister Neville Chamberlain, who initiated a series of last-minute conferences with Hitler that sealed the fate of Czechoslovakia.

At their first meeting in Berchtesgaden, Hitler seemed to be satisfied with "self-determination" for the Sudeten region. But when Chamberlain returned a week later for a second meeting at Godesberg, the *Führer* upped his demands. He now asked for the surrender of the Sudetenland. This the Czechs declared unacceptable. But their protests were ignored at the final meeting in Munich on September 29–30. Hitler and Chamberlain, together with Mussolini and French Premier Édouard Daladier, now agreed on the Godesberg terms.

The first reaction when the Munich decisions were announced was one of relief that war had been averted. Deprived of its fortifications and most of its heavy industries, which were located in the Sudetenland, Czechoslovakia was now at Germany's mercy. The Russians, to be sure, had insisted that they would stand by their treaty obligations. But the strength of the Red army was not rated very high, and there was always the fear that the Soviet Union might try to embroil the West in a war with Hitler. The French, in betraying their Czech ally, bore a major share of the responsibility for Czechoslovakia's defeat. But how could they have acted without the support of Great Britain? And the British were neither morally nor materially ready for war. Appeasement, ever since Munich, has been an ugly word. But the purchase of peace at the expense of smaller or weaker nations had been going on for some time. The basic cause of the Czech disaster was the failure of the democracies to understand Hitler's true aims. Even at Munich these aims were not yet fully understood. It took one more of Hitler's moves to bring home the futility of appeasement.

On the eve of Munich Hitler had promised that the Sudetenland would be his last territorial claim. But even before the year was out he issued directives for the final liquidation of Czechoslovakia. On March 15, 1939, German army units crossed the Czech border, and the next day Hitler proclaimed a German protectorate over Bohemia and Moravia. Slovakia was to become an "independent" German satellite.

This final dismemberment of Czechoslovakia was an important turning point. Up until then, the desire to unite all German-speaking peoples had seemed to be the motive of Hitler's policy. Now suddenly the world realized his real aim: to gain living space and to subjugate foreign peoples. This latest act of Hitler's brought about a decisive change in the attitude of the western democracies. On March 31, 1939, Great Britain promised the Poles all possible support in defending their independence. And in April both England and France gave similar assurances to Rumania and Greece. What the western powers did not know was that on April 3, 1939, a secret directive to the German army ordered preparations for war against Poland anytime after September 1, 1939.

The Eve of the Second World War

That Hitler should turn against Poland next was hardly surprising. Of all the territorial provisions of Versailles, the loss of the Polish corridor and the city of Danzig had been the most resented by Germany.

The world had still not recovered from the demise of Czechoslovakia when the Fascist powers made two more quick moves. On March 21, 1939, Lithuania, in compliance with Hitler's demands, returned to Germany the small territory of Memel; and on April 8, Mussolini sent his troops to occupy the Kingdom of Albania, which since 1927 had been an Italian protectorate. A month later, Germany and Italy converted their Axis into a full-fledged alliance, the "Pact of Steel."

In late May 1939 Hitler informed his generals that war with Poland was inevitable. On August 22 he held another of his briefing conferences. The *Führer* expressed the hope that France and Britain might decide not to fight. Not that he feared their intervention. The western powers, he said, were completely unprepared. As a final surprise, Hitler then told his generals about the Nazi-Soviet Pact, about to be signed in Moscow.

The Nazi-Soviet Pact

The role of Russia in a future war had concerned Germany and the western powers for some time. Since April 1939 Russia had been negotiating with both sides. But France and Britain were unable to overcome their fundamental

Sullen Czechs watching German troops enter Prague (March 15, 1939).

Joseph Stalin.

distrust of the Russians; and still more significant, the western powers were unwilling to concede to Russia the predominance in eastern Europe that Stalin demanded. The Germans, however, did not hesitate to make concessions in the East if it meant gaining a friend. The Russo-German talks did not enter their decisive phase until mid-August. From then on events moved swiftly. On August 23 the two powers signed a nonaggression pact. Its most weighty part was a secret protocol that divided eastern and southeastern Europe into respective spheres of Russian and German influence.

The advantages of the Russian pact for Germany were obvious: it saved the *Wehrmacht,* once Poland had been disposed of, from having to fight on two fronts. Russia's motives were less clear. According to Stalin, the Soviet Union had long been afraid that the West was trying to turn Nazi aggression against communism. But it has also been argued that Stalin, by supporting Hitler, hoped to embroil Germany in a war with the western powers, allowing Russia to emerge as the decisive factor in the international balance.

With the signing of the Nazi-Soviet pact, the stage was set for the outbreak of war. It was still not clear whether the French and British would keep their word and come to Poland's aid. Negotiations for a last-minute compromise continued, and Hitler at one point postponed the start of hostilities to allow the West one more try at appeasement. But the lessons of the last few years had at long last been learned. On September 3, 1939, two days after the German invasion of Poland, England and France declared war on Germany. The Second World War had begun.

THE AXIS TRIUMPHANT, 1939–42

Since he had prepared his war for some time, Hitler at first enjoyed all the advantages of the aggressor. He expected the war to be short. Even though England and France had entered the war, he did not believe they would fight.

Blitzkrieg *in Poland*

Germany's forces crossed the Polish border on September 1, 1939. Everything went according to plan. The Poles were no match for the crack Nazi troops, and the fighting lasted less than four weeks. The Germans obviously had lost none of their skill at making war.

The world was stunned by Germany's rapid success. The Russians were hardly ready to avail themselves of the spoils that had fallen to them as a result of their recent deal with Hitler. At the end of September a treaty of partition was signed between the Reich and the Soviet Union. Poland was wiped off the map, Germany taking the western and Russia the eastern half. This operation completed, Germany and Russia announced that there was no longer any reason for Britain and France to continue the war.

War at Sea

This appeal for ending the war was directed primarily at France. The French were neither enthusiastic nor confident about the war. The French army had dutifully occupied the fortified Maginot Line along France's eastern frontier, but there it sat and waited in the "phony war." The British, for their part, expected a German air attack at any minute. But so long as Hitler thought that Chamberlain might give up the fight, the German air force remained grounded. England felt the first effects of the war at sea. On September 17 the aircraft carrier *Courageous* was torpedoed off Ireland, and in mid-October a German submarine sank the battleship *Royal Oak.* In December 1939 the British scored their first naval victory, against the German battleship *Admiral Graf Spee* off the coast of South America.

The Russo-Finnish War

The next aggression in Europe did not come, as was expected, from Germany but from Russia. No sooner had the Soviets shared in the Polish loot than they pressured the small republics of Estonia, Latvia, and Lithuania to sign "mutual assistance" pacts that allowed the Red army to occupy strategic bases along the Baltic coast. In June 1940, these states became members of the Soviet Union. The only country to resist Russian pressure was Finland. So on November 30, 1939, Russia renounced a seven-year nonaggression pact with Finland and crossed the Finnish border. The Finns were beaten in March 1940; but in the meantime the Red army suffered serious losses and showed itself woefully unprepared. In protest against Russia's attack on Finland, the League of Nations expelled the Soviet Union from membership. But attention was soon diverted away from Finland as the Germans embarked on a second round of aggression against the small nations on their periphery.

Germany Turns North and West

Both Norway and the Low Countries were of great strategic importance. Control of Norway would give German submarines a wider radius of action. The Low Countries, besides providing a protective glacis for the Ruhr, would offer the necessary bases for operations against France and England. Reports that Britain might occupy Norway made Hitler decide to move. Operations began on April 9, 1940. Simultaneously with their invasion of Norway, the Germans occupied Denmark. The main fighting in Norway took only a few days. Some pockets of resistance held out until early June, but by that time the Germans had already turned their attention elsewhere.

The war in the West was launched on May 10, 1940. It was one of the most awesome and frightening military performances ever witnessed. It took the Germans less than a week to overrun the Netherlands and little over two weeks to defeat the Belgian, French, and British forces in Belgium. The remains of the Allied armies were evacuated to England from Dunkirk. The Allied cause had suffered a resounding defeat.

On the day the Lowlands were invaded, Chamberlain resigned. He was succeeded by Winston Churchill, sixty-five years old and already famous, although his greatest contributions still lay ahead.

The Fall of France

There was no one to do for France what Churchill did for England. The man who was pushed into the limelight in the hope that he would unite the French people was Marshal Henri Philippe Pétain. Once before, in 1916, he had been the symbol of his country's resistance in time of national emergency. But in 1940 the old marshal was less concerned with continuing the war than with making peace. France, he felt, had been betrayed by its radical left and deserted by its British ally. Why not try and save what could be by collaborating with Hitler?

As the German armies reached the Channel coast in late May 1940, Hitler was faced with a major decision: Should he invade England or complete the conquest of France? He decided to do the latter, perhaps because he still hoped to reach a compromise with the British. There is no need to go into the melancholy details of the "Fall of France." When the French were at their lowest and German victory was beyond a doubt, Italian troops invaded southeastern France. Mussolini had stayed out of the war thus far, claiming that he was not ready for it. But the collapse of France was too good an opportunity to miss.

The official French surrender took place on June 22, 1940. Under the terms of the armistice Germany occupied three-fifths of France, including its entire Atlantic coast. There were no territorial provisions; these were to await a later peace conference. The unoccupied, southern part of France chose as its capital the town of Vichy. Besides Pétain, the leaders of the Vichy regime included Pierre Laval and Admiral Jean Darlan.

The Battle of Britain

With France out of the war, Britain now stood alone. Its most immediate fear was of a German invasion. But Hitler lacked the necessary naval power to launch his "Operation Sea Lion," and besides, he never gave up hope that England would capitulate without fighting to the finish. To break down British resistance, the German *Luftwaffe*, in July 1940, embarked on an all-out air offensive. The Battle of Britain lasted through the rest of the year. Several times the British reached the limits of their reserves in planes and pilots. But they did not give in. Meanwhile, halfhearted preparations for "Operation Sea Lion" continued. But a successful invasion of England required control of the sea and air, which the Germans never achieved. In the fall of 1940, invasion plans were postponed and Hitler decided to strike elsewhere.

Prime Minister Winston Churchill inspecting ruins of the House of Commons following bombing by the German *Luftwaffe* in 1940.

War in North Africa and the Balkans

An empire as large as that of Britain was vulnerable in many places. The British possession most coveted by Hitler was Gibraltar. To take this strongly fortified gateway to the Mediterranean, however, the *Führer* needed the support of Franco's Spain, which he failed to get. Another important region was Egypt. The task of ousting the British from there was given to the Italians. In September 1940 an Italian army invaded Egypt from Libya. It was stopped by a far smaller British force, which drove the Italians back into Libya. A major Axis defeat was avoided only by the intervention of the German *Afrikakorps* under General Erwin Rommel. By early April 1941 the Axis forces were once again on Egyptian soil.

The Italians, meanwhile, had become involved in another venture. In October 1940 Italian troops crossed from Albania into Greece. After some minor gains, they were soon pushed back again. Once more the Germans had to intervene and thus open another major front. Bulgaria and Hungary were already in the Axis camp. Yugoslavia was quickly overrun by German, Bulgarian, and Hungarian troops. Greece was defeated and occupied. In the spring of 1941 it seemed that Germany was looking still farther afield, toward the eastern Mediterranean. But before the *Führer's* schemes went very far, he became occupied with more important objectives in eastern Europe. Combined British and Free French forces were able, therefore, to keep the upper hand in the strategically vital eastern Mediterranean.

There were some other hopeful developments in the spring of 1941, while Britain was still fighting with its back to the wall. The United States was constantly increasing its aid to Great Britain, and ultimate American involvement in the war appeared a definite possibility. The British navy, meanwhile, won a major victory when it sank the German superbattleship

Bismarck on May 27. And, most important, there were persistent rumors that relations between Germany and Russia were rapidly deteriorating.

Hitler's Russian Gamble

Russo-German relations since the outbreak of the war had been far from smooth. Two totalitarian countries, each bent on expansion, could not avoid for long getting in each other's way. To be sure, the two partners maintained mutually beneficial economic relations. But on the political front Russo-German interests were far less complementary. Hitler was disturbed by Russia's expansion along the Baltic, and Stalin was taken aback by Hitler's unexpected success in the West. More serious still were Russo-German differences over the Balkans, where no clear line of demarcation had been worked out. Efforts to clarify these and other matters were made in November 1940 at a conference in Berlin. But the attempt failed, partly because of Russia's far-reaching demands for the control of eastern and southeastern Europe, partly because Hitler had already decided to attack the Soviet Union.

There were obvious reasons for Hitler's Russian gamble: He wanted *Lebensraum,* and he hated communism. But there was still another reason why he decided to strike at Russia. To defeat the Soviets while they were still weak from the Finnish War was the best way of inducing Britain to surrender. The first preparations for the invasion of Russia were made as early as July 1940. The final directives were issued the following December. Germany struck on June 22, 1941.

The German armies at first were disastrously successful, taking hundreds of thousands of Russian prisoners. But the Russians seemed to have inexhaustible manpower. Opposition to Stalin's ruthless regime disappeared in the face of foreign aggression. One of Hitler's gravest errors was not to have posed to the Russians as liberator from communist oppression. Instead, the *Führer* ordered Russian prisoners to be herded into vast camps where they died of starvation, or else had them transported to Germany as slave labor.

The Russian war closed the gap between the East and West. Great Britain now offered Stalin an alliance, and the Americans included the Soviets in their program of lend-lease. The Germans, meanwhile, were encountering unforeseen difficulties. Winter came unusually early in 1941, and the German army was not prepared for it. When Germany's commanders wanted to halt their advance, Hitler relieved them and took charge himself. The Germans suffered terrible hardships, but they continued their advance. In the fall of 1942 Hitler's generals once again urged him to shorten his lines, but the *Führer* remained unyielding. Since August, large German forces had laid siege to Stalingrad on the lower Volga. A German victory at Stalingrad would have given Germany control over the oil fields of the Caucasus. But instead of ejecting the Russians from Stalingrad, the Germans were caught in a Russian counteroffensive and suffered a major defeat by February 1943.

The battle of Stalingrad was not the first Nazi defeat. The western allies were simultaneously advancing and winning in North Africa. But the disaster in Russia was a decisive event. In a gradually mounting offensive, the Russians began to push Hitler's armies back across the plains of eastern Europe. It took almost two more years before the fighting reached German soil. Meanwhile the expansion of Japan in East Asia had also been halted in the winter of 1942/43, and the Japanese were being driven back to their home bases. By the spring of 1943 the tide of the war began to turn.

HITLER'S "NEW ORDER"

There was never any master plan for Hitler's "New Order," because the future depended on the final outcome of the war. Few of the territories under German domination were annexed outright, although the degree to which some of them were being Germanized left no doubt about their ultimate fate. The war had done its share in decreasing the population of eastern Europe. In addition, more than seven million foreign workers were forced to work in German factories. Into the areas thus vacated, ethnic Germans were sent as pioneers of Hitler's Germanization policy.

But Hitler was not content merely with taking land away from other peoples. The most frightful deed committed in the name of his "New Order" was the willful extermination of from six to eight million people, most of them Jews. Wherever the German armies went, the elite SS (*Schutzstaffel,* protective squad) followed to see that the party's racial policies were carried out. At first there was merely persecution of the Jews, in which the local populations often participated. But in time more drastic measures were adopted. Hitler's "Final Solution" called for nothing less than the complete extermination of all Jews. This was carried out by means of gas chambers in special extermination camps, such as Auschwitz. There were several such camps, not only for the extermination of Jews but for the "mercy killing" of the incurably ill and insane, and for the liquidation of political prisoners.

These were only the more gruesome acts committed by the Nazis. Additional millions were kept in concentration, slave labor, and prisoner-of-war camps, where many died more "natural" deaths by starvation. A great many Germans were involved in these crimes; yet after the war no one would admit having known what went on behind the barbed wire of these camps.

The "Final Solution"

The first train arrived . . . 45 freightcars with 6,700 people, of which 1,450 were already dead on arrival. . . . A large loudspeaker blares instructions: Undress completely, take off artificial limbs, glasses, etc. Hand in all valuables. Shoes to be tied together (for the clothing collection) . . . Women and girls to the barber, who cuts off their hair in two or three strokes and stuffs it into potato sacks. . . .

Then the line starts moving. . . . At the corner a strapping SS-man announces in a pastoral voice: Nothing will happen to you! Just breathe deeply inside the chambers, that stretches the lungs; this inhalation is necessary against the illnesses and epidemics. When asked what would happen to them, he replies: Well, of course the men will have to work, build houses and roads, but the women won't have to work. If they want to they can help in the household or the kitchen. For a few of these unfortunates a small glimmer of hope which suffices to have them take the few steps to the chambers without resistance—the majority knows what is ahead, the stench tells their fate. . . .

The wooden doors are opened. . . . Inside the chambers, the dead stand closely pressed together, like pillars of stone. . . . Even in death one recognizes the families. They still hold hands, so they have to be torn apart to get the chambers ready for their next occupants. The corpses are thrown out—wet with sweat and urine, covered with excrement, menstrual blood. Children's bodies fly through the air. . . . Two dozen workers use hooks to pry open mouths to look for gold. . . . Others search genitals and anuses for gold, diamonds and valuables. Wirth [an SS-guard] motions to me: Just lift this can of gold teeth, this is only from yesterday and the day before! . . .

From an eyewitness account of mass gassings, in *Vierteljahrshefte für Zeitgeschichte* (1953), Vol. I, pp. 190–91.

AMERICA ENTERS THE WAR

America's entrance into the war was by steps. The government had followed a policy of neutrality during the various acts of German and Italian aggression before the war. The question was whether this attitude could be maintained. As one country after another fell victim to the Axis, America's role in the war became of crucial importance. Axis domination of western Europe and North Africa would have posed a serious threat to the United States itself.

Benevolent Neutrality

On November 4, 1939, Congress had passed a revised Neutrality Act that lifted the embargo on all implements of war and put all trade on a "cash and carry" basis. This move favored the country with the strongest navy and the largest funds, Great Britain. But Britain's enormous need for material aid made its dollar credits dwindle rapidly. The two governments tried to overcome this difficulty in several ways. One was the "destroyer deal" of 1940, when the United States gave Britain some fifty ships in return for a lease of some British-held naval bases in the Western Hemisphere. Another way for America to help was through the Lend-Lease Act of 1941. It gave the president power to provide goods and services to any nation whose defense was vital to the United States.

There were other signs that America was getting off the fence. But in August 1941, Congress extended the military draft, established the previous September, by only the slimmest margin. The American people, it seemed, were perfectly willing to go to any limit in helping the Allied cause so long as they did not become involved in the war themselves. It took the Japanese attack on Pearl Harbor to push the United States across the line from nonintervention to belligerency.

War with Japan

The United States, for some forty years past, had stood in the way of Japan's major aim: to dominate China and to control the trading area of Southeast Asia and the neighboring Pacific. Since the start of the Sino-Japanese War in 1937, Washington had been concerned about Japan's violations of the "Open Door" policy in China. To put pressure on the Japanese, the United States, in July 1939, ended its thirty-year-old commercial treaty with Japan and subsequently imposed an embargo on certain strategic goods. By the middle of 1941 the embargo was seriously affecting the Japanese. Tokyo's demand for the cessation of United States restrictions was met with American counterdemands for Japan's withdrawal from China. As far back as January 1941 the Japanese government began to prepare for an armed showdown.

On December 7, 1941, the Japanese air attack against Pearl Harbor caught the American forces completely unprepared. The United States suffered one of the greatest defeats in its history. Yet the catastrophe of Pearl Harbor had one effect—it cut short the debate between isolationists and interventionists. As Italy and Germany declared war on the United States, the American people rallied wholeheartedly behind the war effort of their government.

Pearl Harbor, December 7, 1941.

THE DEFEAT OF THE AXIS

The European Allies were worried at first that America's involvement in the Pacific would prevent it from continuing its aid to Europe. The Russians in particular kept up a nagging insistence on the immediate opening of a second front on the Continent. Before such an operation could be thought of, however, large numbers of American troops had to be shipped overseas, and that was possible only after the threat of Germany's submarines had been overcome. The defeat of the submarine menace was due in part to the convoy system and to improved methods of detecting submarines. But the victory at sea could not have been won without the "battle of the shipyards," in which American workers built ships faster than the Germans could sink them.

German V-2 rocket, used against distant targets during the latter years of the war.

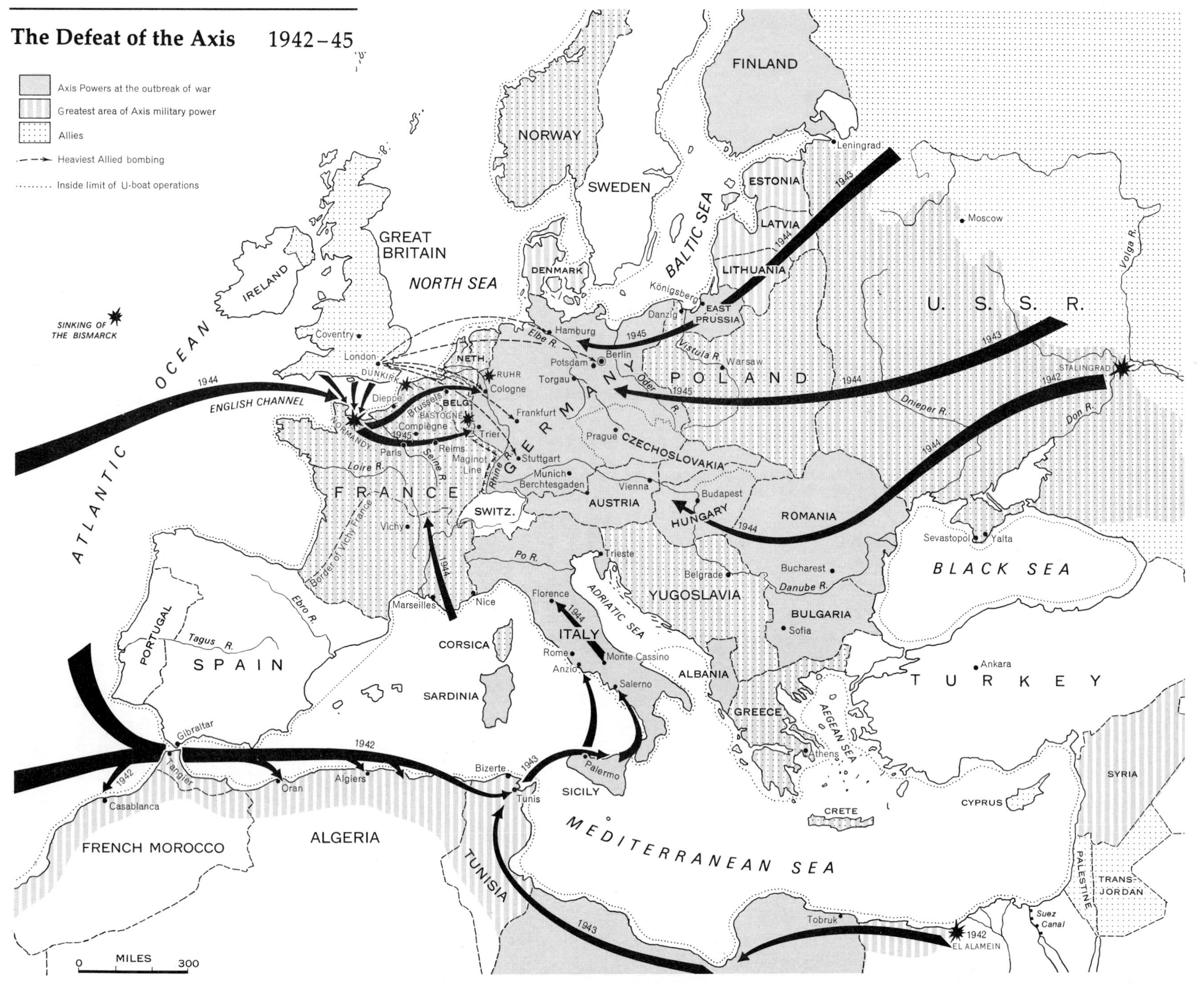

The Defeat of the Axis 1942–45
Axis Powers at the outbreak of war
Greatest area of Axis military power
Allies
Heaviest Allied bombing
Inside limit of U-boat operations
SINKING OF THE BISMARCK
ATLANTIC OCEAN
ENGLISH CHANNEL
NORTH SEA
BALTIC SEA
BLACK SEA
ADRIATIC SEA
AEGEAN SEA
MEDITERRANEAN SEA
IRELAND
GREAT BRITAIN
NORWAY
SWEDEN
FINLAND
DENMARK
ESTONIA
LATVIA
LITHUANIA
EAST PRUSSIA
U. S. S. R.
POLAND
GERMANY
NETH.
BELG.
FRANCE
SWITZ.
AUSTRIA
CZECHOSLOVAKIA
HUNGARY
ROMANIA
BULGARIA
YUGOSLAVIA
ALBANIA
GREECE
ITALY
CORSICA
SARDINIA
SICILY
CRETE
CYPRUS
TURKEY
SYRIA
TRANS-JORDAN
PALESTINE
SPAIN
PORTUGAL
FRENCH MOROCCO
ALGERIA
TUNISIA
Leningrad
Moscow
Stalingrad
Sevastopol
Yalta
Ankara
Königsberg
Danzig
Warsaw
Berlin
Potsdam
Hamburg
Torgau
Prague
Vienna
Budapest
Belgrade
Bucharest
Sofia
Athens
Trieste
Munich
Berchtesgaden
Stuttgart
Frankfurt
Cologne
RUHR
Trier
Brussels
BASTOGNE
Reims
Compiègne
Paris
Dieppe
DUNKIRK
NORMANDY
London
Coventry
Vichy
Nice
Marseilles
Florence
Rome
Anzio
Monte Cassino
Salerno
Palermo
Tunis
Bizerte
Algiers
Oran
Tangier
Gibraltar
Casablanca
Tobruk
EL ALAMEIN
Suez Canal
Volga R.
Don R.
Dnieper R.
Danube R.
Vistula R.
Oder R.
Elbe R.
Rhine R.
Seine R.
Loire R.
Po R.
Ebro R.
Tagus R.
Maginot Line
Border of Vichy France
1942
1943
1944
1945
MILES
0
300

The Invasion of North Africa

The first involvement of American ground forces in the war against the European Axis took place in North Africa. On November 8, 1942, an Anglo-American force under General Dwight D. Eisenhower landed at Casablanca in French Morocco and at various points in Algeria. The leading French representative in Morocco and Algeria at the time was Admiral Darlan. His cooperation helped keep Allied losses during the landing to a minimum, although the fact that Darlan was profascist caused some embarrassment. The North African campaign ended on May 13, 1943, with the Allied capture of Tunis and Bizerte.

In the meantime the German people were also feeling the effects of United States intervention nearer home. Almost daily, large fleets of American and British planes penetrated the antiaircraft defenses of the Reich, bombing industrial centers and strategic objectives. The much-advertised *Luftwaffe* of Reichsmarshal Göring, which had earlier failed to bomb the British into submission, now proved equally ineffective in defending German soil.

The Allied Invasion of Italy

Having won North Africa, the Allies next aimed for control of the rest of the Mediterranean. The invasion of Sicily and southern Italy was launched in the summer of 1943. Resistance in Sicily collapsed in mid-August, and on September 2 British and American troops landed on the Italian mainland. The campaign in Italy, which lasted until the end of the war, played a vital part in the final victory, because it helped tie down large German forces that might otherwise have been used on Hitler's two other fronts. But the Italian war also caused one of the first major crises between the Anglo-Saxon powers and their Russian ally.

Stalin had long been angry with the West for not opening what he considered a real second front. The invasion of Italy gave new cause for annoyance. During the Sicilian campaign in July 1943, a number of high officials within the Italian Fascist party staged a coup d'etat and forced Mussolini to resign. The new Italian government under Marshal Pietro Badoglio asked the Allies for an armistice. The agreement with Badoglio further aroused the suspicion of Stalin. What he feared was that the West might conclude a separate peace without the Russians.

"Operation Overlord"

The delay in opening a second front in the north was partly due to differences within the western camp on where the attack against Hitler's "Fortress Europe" should be launched. Some British experts favored the Balkans, expecting fewer losses from striking there. President Roosevelt and his advisers, on the other hand, saw France as the more suitable terrain for a second front. The American view prevailed.

The final decision for the invasion of France, "Operation Overlord," was made at a conference of the "Big Three" at Tehran in December 1943. The supreme command was given to General Eisenhower; the scene of the landing was to be the coast of Normandy; and D-Day was set for early June 1944. Because the Germans had expected the invasion nearer Calais,

D-Day: the invasion of Normandy, June 6, 1944.

the Allies were able to establish a firm beachhead. After three months of fighting, the Allies had driven the Germans out of northwestern France. On August 15 a second amphibious operation landed on the French Mediterranean coast and within a month made contact with the main invasion forces in the north. In mid-September the first American forces crossed the German frontier. Here they were halted by the fortified German "Westwall."

The German *Wehrmacht,* although on the run, was still far from beaten. During Christmas week 1944, Hitler staged his last big offensive of the war. Under cover of fog and snow in the difficult terrain of the Ardennes, German armored divisions drove a deep salient into the Allied lines. The "Battle of the Bulge" proved to be a costly failure for the Germans, but for a brief moment it seemed to threaten the Allied victory in the West.

Germany Invaded from East and West

The Russians, meanwhile, had been pressing slowly but steadily westward. By the end of January 1945 the Red army stood on the Oder River, less than a hundred miles from Berlin. These were terrible months for the Germans, who now felt what it was like to be the victims of invasion. As the fortunes of war began to turn, sporadic German opposition to Hitler gathered sufficient strength for a final attempt to rid the country of its tyrant. But the plot of July 20, 1944, miscarried, and the *Führer* took horrible vengeance. Thousands of decent men and women, who might have played a leading role in the postwar reconstruction of Germany, were put to death. The rest of the German people were urged on into suicidal resistance, especially since the Allied demand for "unconditional surrender" seemed to leave no alternative.

Early in 1945 the Allies stood poised for the final phase of the European war. The invasion of the Rhineland was launched on February 8, 1945. From here on events happened with lightning speed. By the end of March the Rhine had been crossed; by the middle of April the Ruhr district had been taken; and on April 25 the first American and Russian patrols met on the Elbe River. On April 30, while the Russians were fighting their way into the center of Berlin, Adolf Hitler committed suicide. On May 7, 1945, at the headquarters of General Eisenhower at Reims, a German military delegation signed the terms of Germany's unconditional surrender. May 8, 1945, was officially proclaimed V-E Day, victory day in Europe.

Dresden, Germany. In February 1945, the Allies launched a series of air raids on Dresden that destroyed the heart of the city and caused twice as many casualties as those caused by the first atomic bomb dropped on Hiroshima, Japan.

THE WAR IN THE PACIFIC

The war against Japan was primarily a naval war in which the United States carried the major burden. Considering America's losses at Pearl Harbor and its heavy commitment in Europe, the victory in the Pacific was a magnificent achievement. This was particularly true considering the extent of Japanese expansion. A few days after Pearl Harbor, the Japanese overran America's outposts at Guam and Wake Island. Early in 1942, they invaded the Philippines. The Dutch East Indies, the Malay Peninsula, and Burma went next. By May 1942 the whole area east of India and north of Australia, except for the southern part of New Guinea, had fallen into Japanese hands.

American Naval Victories Turn the Tide

The Japanese attempt to force the Allies out of New Guinea and to gain a base for the invasion of Australia triggered the first large naval battle between United States and Japanese forces. The battle of the Coral Sea in May 1942 cost heavy American losses, but it kept the Japanese from their objective. A still more decisive naval battle a month later at Midway Island brought a resounding Japanese defeat. For the first time America held a slight naval edge in the Pacific. The Japanese achieved some last successes when they occupied Attu and Kiska in the Aleutian Islands. But with the landing of United States marines in the Solomon Islands in August 1942, Japanese expansion was halted, and soon the tide began to turn.

In 1942 American naval supremacy was established in the Pacific; the next year brought the first breaks through the outer perimeter of Japan's defenses. Beginning with the battle of Guadalcanal, one after another of Japan's island outposts were retaken in some of the war's bloodiest fighting. Places most Americans had never heard of—Tarawa, Makin, Eniwetok, Iwo Jima, Okinawa—now suddenly became headlines. Meanwhile, United States submarines were taking a heavy toll of Japanese shipping, and the Japanese islands were put under a blockade. In June 1944 American superfortresses started their first bombing raids on Japan. In October 1944 United States forces under General Douglas MacArthur began their reconquest of the Philippines. And in Burma, British imperial forces under Lord Louis Mountbatten, supported by Americans

The Defeat of Japan 1942–45

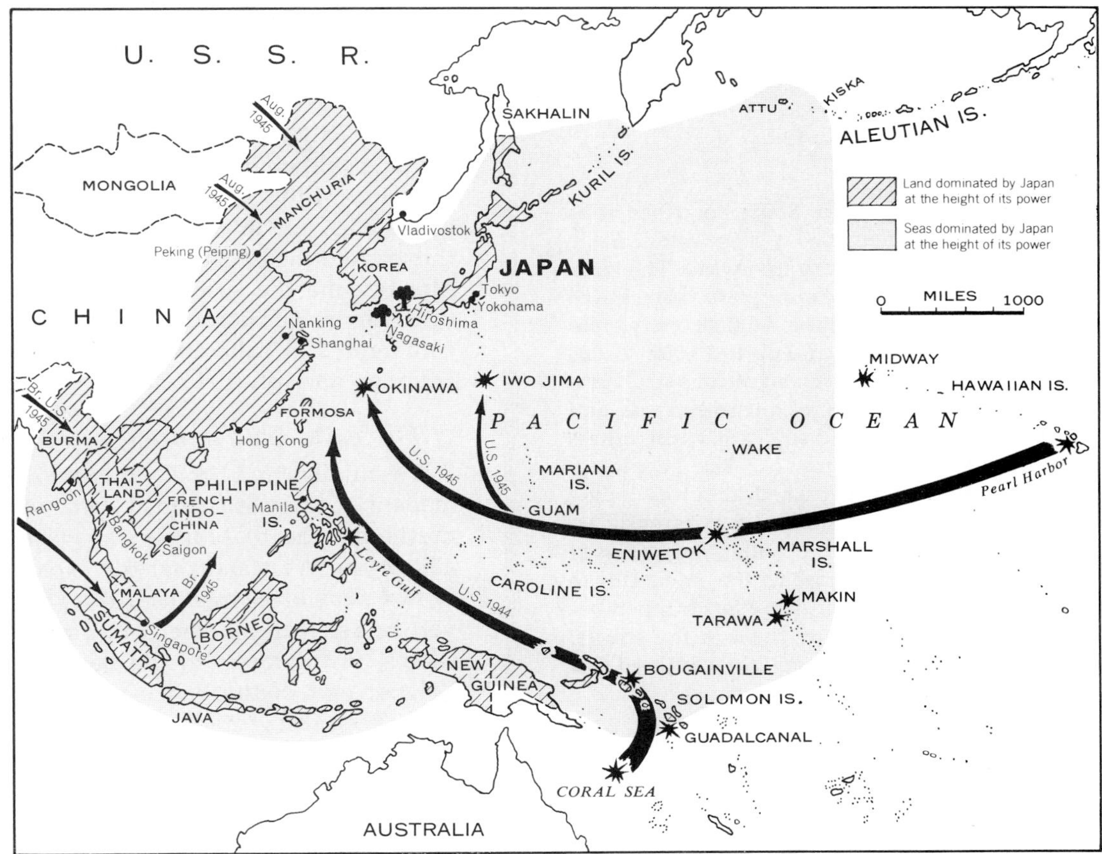

and Chinese, were rounding up the Japanese invaders.

The End of the War

The climax of the war in the Pacific came on October 21–22, 1944, with the battle of Leyte Gulf in the Philippine Sea, one of the biggest naval battles ever fought. Japanese losses were such that their navy henceforth was no longer a factor in the war. As Allied successes in Europe mounted, more and more strength could be diverted to the Pacific. In the spring of 1945 America's commanders in the Pacific were asked to prepare plans for the invasion of Japan. But while these preparations were still under way, on July 16, 1945, the first atomic bomb was successfully exploded at Los Alamos, New Mexico. The atomic bombing of Hiroshima and Nagasaki on August 6 and 9 led to the surrender of Japan on August 14, 1945 (V-J Day), and to the end of the Second World War.

The decision to use this terrible new weapon was not easy. Should not efforts be made to lay siege to Japan first? But President Truman and his advisers felt that an early surrender of Japan without invasion was unlikely. And an invasion, it was estimated, would cost more than a million Allied casualties and at least again that many Japanese. It was thought preferable, therefore, to bring the war to a quick, though horrible, end: 78,000 people were killed at Hiroshima and 50,000 at Nagasaki. The Atomic Age had begun.

Hiroshima

At about 0815 there was a blinding flash. Some described it as brighter than the sun, others likened it to a magnesium flash. Following the flash there was a blast of heat and wind. The large majority of people within 3000 feet of ground zero were killed immediately. Within a radius of about 7000 feet almost every Japanese house collapsed. Beyond this range and up to 15,000–20,000 feet many of them collapsed and others received serious structural damage. Persons in the open were burned on exposed surfaces, and within 3000–5000 feet many were burned to death while others received severe burns through their clothes. . . . The people appeared stunned by the catastrophe and rushed about as jungle animals suddenly released from a cage. Some few apparently attempted to help others from the wreckage, particularly members of their family or friends. Others assisted those who were unable to walk alone. However, many of the injured were left trapped beneath collapsed buildings as people fled by them in the streets. Pandemonium reigned as the uninjured and slightly injured fled the city in fearful panic.

From "The Effects of Atomic Bombs on Health and Medical Services in Hiroshima and Nagasaki," *The United States Strategic Bombing Survey* (Washington, D. C.: Government Printing Office, 1947), p. 3.

THE SEARCH FOR PEACE

Considering the tremendous political changes resulting from the Second World War, it is surprising how little advance thought had been given to the problem of peace. There were some general pronouncements, especially the Atlantic Charter, which President Roosevelt and Prime Minister Churchill had issued in August 1941. But this idealistic blueprint for the future, which aimed at a world free from want and fear, was drawn up before the harsh realities of the postwar world were known. Several conferences during the war—between Roosevelt and Churchill at Casablanca and Quebec, and among the western leaders and Stalin at Tehran—had dealt with immediate military matters and only incidentally with long-range political questions. Only in the final months of the war did the larger issues of the future become the subject of top-level discussions. These took place at two conferences at Yalta and Potsdam, in February and July 1945.

The Yalta Conference

To understand the concessions made to the Soviet Union at Yalta, we must remember that Russia was still an ally of the West and that the expansionist aims of communism were not yet understood. Some of Stalin's claims, furthermore, in the Baltic, in Poland, and in the Balkans, had already been recognized, at least by implication. And the fact that all these regions were already occupied by Red armies gave added strength to Soviet arguments. Most important, finally, was the conviction of western military leaders that Russia's continued contribution to the common war effort was essential to ensure an early victory.

The main issues discussed at Yalta dealt with the future of Germany, Poland, East Asia, and the United Nations. On Germany, the meeting achieved very little. The only firm agreement dealt with the postwar division of the country into four occupation zones, including a French one. A great deal of time was spent trying to determine the frontiers of Poland and to agree on the composition of its government. On both points the Russians scored a success. Poland's border was moved westward to where it had been fixed briefly after the First World War. Russia thus received almost 47 percent of Poland's prewar territory. The powers agreed, however, that Poland should receive compensations in the north and west. The new provisional government of Poland, meanwhile, was to be drawn from the Soviet-sponsored Committee of National Liberation rather than from the Polish government-in-exile, which the western powers favored; but to make sure that Poland was ruled democratically, "free and unfettered elections" were to be held.

The decisions about East Asia made at Yalta caused little difficulty at the time, although they came in for much criticism later. In return for Stalin's promise to participate in the Pacific war, the Soviet Union was granted large concessions at the expense of both China and Japan. Most of these repaired Russia's losses in the Russo-Japanese War of 1904–1905 (see p. 844).

The problem that most concerned the American delegation at Yalta was to get Russian and British agreement to final plans for a United Nations organization. Most of the details for such a body had already been worked out, except for two important points: the extent of the great powers' veto in the Security Council and the number of seats each was to hold in the UN Assembly. Both points were satisfactorily settled, a fact that greatly contributed to the success of the conference in American eyes. There was some hard bargaining at Yalta, but on the whole the atmosphere was friendly. It remained to be seen whether the powers could carry over their wartime unity of purpose into the postwar period.

The Yalta Conference. Churchill, Roosevelt, and Stalin sit for a formal picture-taking session with their advisers. Roosevelt clearly shows the strain of their meeting. He was to die two months later on April 12, 1945.

The United Nations

The first problem tackled after Yalta was the drafting of a charter for the United Nations. This was done at the San Francisco Conference in the spring of 1945. The United Nations owes much to its predecessor, the League of Nations. Like the League, the UN, at least at the start, was entirely dominated by the great powers. The most important agency of the UN is the Security Council, five of whose seats were assigned to the United States, Great Britain, the Soviet Union, France, and Nationalist (since 1972 Communist) China. Because each of these powers has an absolute veto, the effectiveness of the UN has been seriously hampered. The chief task of the Council is to maintain peace and security. Like the Council of the League of Nations, it can recommend peaceful arbitration or measures short of war, such as economic sanctions. But unlike the

The launching of the United Nations, as seen by the British magazine *Punch*.

League, the Security Council may also take "such actions by air, sea, or land forces as may be necessary to maintain or restore international peace."

The Potsdam Conference

While the San Francisco Conference was still in session, the end of the war in Europe called for another top-level meeting to settle the future of Germany. Russia's unilateral actions in eastern Europe, notably in Rumania and Poland, had already called forth repeated western protests. When the powers assembled at Potsdam in July 1945, therefore, the cordiality that had prevailed at Yalta had given way to coldness. The United States, after President Roosevelt's death in April 1945, was represented by President Harry S Truman; and Great Britain, after Churchill's defeat at the polls, was represented by Prime Minister Clement Attlee. This left Stalin as the only original member of the Big Three.

The main differences at Potsdam arose over the eastern borders of Germany and over German reparations. As compensation for the territories it had lost to Russia at Yalta, Poland had occupied about one-fifth of Germany, east of the Oder and Neisse rivers. Against Stalin's insistence that these lands become permanently Polish, the western powers at Potsdam won a postponement of any final decision until a later peace conference. As for German reparations, the Soviet Union held on to the high demands it had made at Yalta. But the West got Stalin to agree that Germany was to be treated "as a single economic unit." Here were several causes for subsequent friction.

During the closing days of the Potsdam Conference attention shifted to East Asia, where the war with Japan was drawing to a close. The Soviet Union entered the war at the last minute by invading Manchuria. When the fighting stopped, Russia took possession of the rights and territories it had been promised at Yalta. The United States claimed control over Japan itself, but Korea was divided into Russian and American zones. Here was another potential source of conflict.

Peace with the Axis Satellites

With the war finally over, peace negotiations could begin. The peace conference of the twenty-one nations that had fought against the Axis met in

Territorial Adjustments After the Second World War 1945

Paris in July 1946. The peace treaties with Italy, Rumania, Hungary, Bulgaria, and Finland were signed in February 1947. Italy was let off remarkably easy. It lost some territory to France, Yugoslavia, and Greece; its colonies were put under the trusteeship of the UN; and Italy had to pay reparations. The settlements with the rest of the powers were similar. Since, except for Finland, these countries were already under Russian domination, the details of the peace terms are not very important. The Soviet Union in each case was the main beneficiary, getting extensive territories and the major share of reparations. Some of these territories — the Baltic states, eastern Poland, and Bessarabia — had formerly belonged to tsarist Russia; but the Baltic states between the wars had been independent, and Bessarabia had belonged to Rumania. Stalin's aim, it seemed, was to restore Russia's borders as they had been before the advent of communism.

THE PROBLEM OF GERMANY

The signing of the Paris treaties ended peacemaking for the time being. Treaties with Japan and Austria were not signed until several years later, and there has yet been no peace treaty with Germany. It was over the issue of Germany that the Soviet Union and the West had their first real falling-out.

Germany, at Potsdam, lost about one-fourth of the territory it had held in 1937. But it still had almost seventy million people, and its industrial resources were considerable. The former Reich, therefore, would continue to be a vital factor. Beginning in 1946, Russia and the West tried to reach an agreement on the future of Germany. But it soon became clear that they did not see eye to eye on many crucial points. What each side hoped was to recreate a Germany in its own image. And when this proved impossible, each side reorganized its respective zones, eventually creating a Germany divided between East and West.

The Division of Germany

The first disagreements arose over economic matters. The division into occupation zones proved a serious obstacle to economic recovery. But western proposals for economic unification were met by Russian counterproposals for political unity first. Because it had been agreed at Potsdam that Germany was to be treated "as a single economic unit," the western powers, in December 1946, merged their zones economically. West Germany's recovery was then given considerable American aid. The result was a miraculous turn for the better. By 1950 the industrial output of West Germany had again reached its 1936 level.

While the West was integrating its two-thirds of Germany into the economy of western Europe, the Russians began the thoroughgoing "sovietization" of their eastern zone. In time these diverging policies could not help but lead to partition. At one point, from 1948 to 1949, the Soviet Union tried to force the West out of the former German capital by imposing a blockade on the Allied sectors of Berlin. But a gigantic western airlift foiled Russia's scheme. In May 1949 a West German

The Berlin airlift (June 1948 to May 1949).

Parliamentary Council adopted a constitution for the Federal Republic of Germany, with Bonn as its capital and with Konrad Adenauer as its first chancellor. In East Germany a Communist-dominated German Democratic Republic was founded in October 1949. By 1950 the struggle between East and West over Germany had resulted in the political division of the country, each part refusing to recognize the other and claiming to speak for the whole.

THE BEGINNING OF THE COLD WAR

As with most other wars, the origins and causes of the "Cold War" have been a subject of controversy. Most western historians still agree that the main responsibility for the Cold War lay with the Soviet Union's attempt to use the chaos of the postwar world to further its own expansionist and ideological aims. In the late 1960s, however, some "revisionist" historians in the United States began to see their own country's desire for economic predominance as having caused the Cold War by forcing the Soviets into communizing eastern Europe for reasons of self-protection.

The Spread of Communism

The communization of eastern Europe came gradually. At first some show of democracy was maintained, with "popular front" governments and "free" elections. But gradually the non-Communist members were ousted and coalition governments were transformed into "people's democracies." By 1947 this policy was causing deep concern in the West. Poland, Rumania, Yugoslavia, Albania, and Bulgaria all had either Communist or pro-Communist regimes, and the trend in Czechoslovakia and Hungary was in the same direction. The only way to halt this creeping expansion of communism, it was felt, was to meet force with force. The occasion to proclaim such a policy of "containment" came in the spring of 1947, when Russia tried to extend its influence near the entrance to the Black Sea.

The Truman Doctrine and the Marshall Plan

In Greece, a small Communist minority was waging a civil war against the government. The British, after the war, had supplied the Greek monarchy with financial and military aid. But Britain had serious economic problems at home, and it was also supporting Turkey's resistance to Soviet demands. In the spring of 1947, Britain announced that it could no longer give aid to Greece and Turkey. At this point the United States stepped in. In a message to Congress on March 12, 1947, President Truman called for American support to "free peoples who are resisting attempted subjugation by armed minorities or by outside pressures." A comprehensive scheme for American aid to Europe was announced three months later by Secretary of State George C. Marshall. By fighting the economic and social conditions that gave rise to communism, the United States hoped to contain it.

The Cominform and the Molotov Plan

The Truman Doctrine and the Marshall Plan opened a wholly new phase in United States foreign policy. America had broken with its isolationist past and had assumed the leadership of the free world. The significance of this break was not lost on the Soviet Union. To tighten its control over eastern Europe, Russia had already concluded mutual assistance pacts with most of its satellites. In order to coordinate the efforts of European communism, in 1947 the Russians founded the Communist Information Bureau (Cominform), as successor to the Comintern, which had been dissolved in 1943. In the economic field, finally, the Russians announced their "Molotov Plan" as counterpart to the Marshall Plan.

The Communist Coup in Czechoslovakia

While Russia and the West were consolidating their positions, the Russians scored another victory in the Cold War. Among the occupied nations of eastern Europe, Czechoslovakia alone had been able to maintain some democratic freedoms. But these were gradually undermined by the infiltration of native Communists with Russian backing. By February 1948 the country was ripe for a coup d'etat. In March, Foreign Minister Jan Masaryk, a friend of the West, was killed in a fall from his office window; and in June, President Beneš gave way to Communist leader Klement Gottwald. Except for Finland, all the countries of eastern Europe were now under Communist rule.

The North Atlantic Treaty

The Communist seizure of Czechoslovakia dramatized the need for military as well as economic integration of the West. Great Britain and France had already concluded a treaty of alliance at Dunkirk in 1947. As an additional safeguard, in 1948 they asked Belgium, the Netherlands, and Luxembourg to join them in the Brussels Treaty. But the nations of western Europe realized that effective resistance to Russia required the help of the United States. So on April 4, 1949, the United States joined the members of the Brussels Treaty, together with Italy, Portugal, Denmark, Iceland, Norway, and Canada, in the North Atlantic Treaty. These twelve powers were joined later by Greece and Turkey (1951) and by West Germany (1955). The gist of the treaty was contained in Article 5, which stated that "an armed attack against one or more" of its signatories "shall be considered an attack against them all."

THE UNITED NATIONS IN THE COLD WAR

The growing tension between Russia and the West was also felt within the United Nations. As long as one of the major powers, through its veto in the Security Council, could prevent joint action, the effectiveness of the UN was limited. Only when international disputes did not involve the interests of a major power could the UN make its influence felt. It was thus possible to stop the fighting between Dutch and native forces in Indonesia and between India and Pakistan over Kashmir. In trying to keep Russia from meddling in the affairs of Iran, however, or in calling a halt to the civil war in Greece, United States aid was more important than UN pressure. The United Nations did score one major success before 1950: the founding of the state of Israel. But this was possible only because both the Soviet Union and the United States supported it.

The Founding of Israel

There had already been intermittent clashes between Arabs and Jews in Palestine before the Second World War. When the British after the war found it increasingly difficult to keep peace within their mandate, they decided to withdraw. At this point, in 1948, the UN stepped in, hoping to bring about a peaceful partition of Palestine. The Jews proclaimed the independent state of Israel, which was recognized by the United States and the Soviet Union. But the Arabs resisted. In the ensuing war the Israeli forces proved superior. UN efforts for an armistice finally succeeded in 1949. But peace remained precarious and war was resumed in 1956.

Other UN Activities

The United Nations had other tasks besides settling international disputes. In some of these economic, social, and cultural activities, the UN was highly successful. In December 1948 the General Assembly adopted an ambitious technical assistance program for underdeveloped areas, for which the United States provided much of the necessary money. More important than economic and social problems, however, was the need for regulation of international armaments. Here the UN made little headway. The main concern was over the control of atomic weapons. In 1946 America proposed the establishment of an International Atomic Development Authority to which the United States would transfer its atomic knowledge and facilities. Because America still had a monopoly in the atomic field, this was a generous proposal. But the Soviet Union vetoed it, objecting in particular to its provisions for inspection. In July 1949 the UN Atomic Energy Commission adjourned. Two months later, Russia announced the successful explosion of its own atomic bomb.

THE COLD WAR IN EAST ASIA

The most momentous changes after 1945 occurred outside Europe. The emancipation of former colonial regions from foreign rule transformed the hitherto passive masses of Asia and Africa into active participants in international affairs. The most important change of the postwar period was the emergence of Red China as a major force in the global balance of power.

Postwar Japan

Because of its dominant role in the occupation of Japan, America's policy prevailed and there was no rivalry among occupying powers. With Japan's governmental machinery intact, furthermore, the transition from war to peace went more smoothly in Japan than in Germany. In May 1947, a democratic constitution transferred sovereignty from the emperor to the people. The Japanese army and navy had already been dissolved, patriotic organizations were banned, and education was reformed along democratic lines. In the economic sphere, plans to break up the great family trusts of Japan were abandoned when such dismantling was found to interfere with economic recovery. Most of the large holdings of absentee landlords, on the other hand, were divided among tenant farmers.

By 1951 the occupation of Japan had accomplished most of its aims and the time had come for a peace settlement. Peace with Japan was signed at San Francisco on September 8, 1951. The treaty was generous, restoring full Japanese sovereignty but permitting the United States to maintain military bases in Japan. America and Japan also concluded a defense agreement that ultimately became an alliance.

Communist Victory in China

While events in Japan were going largely according to American wishes, developments on the Chinese mainland were taking a different turn. The end of the war found most of China still divided between the government forces of Chiang Kai-shek and the Communist armies of Mao Zedong (Mao Tse-tung). Chiang had the backing of Chinese business and banking interests, while Mao's program of land reform brought him the support of the landless masses. Both sides began a fight for the regions formerly held by Japan. In this contest the Communists proved more successful. By the end of 1948 most of northern China was in Communist hands.

The United States had given large amounts of financial and military aid to Chiang Kai-shek. But as the Nationalists failed to introduce much-needed reforms, United States aid was curtailed and finally cut off. In the spring of 1949, Chiang Kai-shek began to withdraw to the island of Formosa. By early 1950 the whole Chinese mainland was in Communist hands. On October 1, 1949, the People's Republic of China was officially proclaimed at Beijing, with Mao Zedong as president. The Soviet Union immediately recognized the new regime, whereas the United States continued to recognize the Nationalist government of Chiang Kai-shek.

The East-West Conflict over Korea

The victory of Communism in China radically changed the balance of power between East and West. The effects of this change were felt almost immediately, as events in Korea transformed the Cold War in that country into an armed conflict. The Korean peninsula had been divided into American and Russian zones of occupation. Just as in Germany, this partition gradually brought about two quite different regimes. In 1948, elections in the U. S.-occupied southern part of Korea resulted in the founding of the Republic of Korea, with Syngman Rhee as president. The Russians sponsored their own Communist-dominated northern People's Democratic Republic, under the presidency of veteran Communist Kim Il Sung.

Late in 1948 the Soviet Union and the United States began to withdraw their troops from North and South Korea. A UN commission remained behind, trying to prevent a possible conflict between the two parts of Korea. Its efforts, however, proved in vain. On June 25, 1950, North Korean forces crossed the thirty-eighth parallel to "liberate" South Korea. Because Russia at the time was boycotting the Security Council, the United Nations could act without being hindered by a Soviet veto. When North Korea refused to halt its aggression, the Security Council asked the UN to go to the aid of South Korea. The United States had already intervened and was soon joined by contingents from other countries. For the first time, the United Nations had gone to war. The Cold War had turned hot.

Suggestions for Further Reading

Europe's diplomacy of the 1930s revolved around Germany's efforts to tear up the Treaty of Versailles. K. Hildebrand, *The Foreign Policy of the Third Reich* (1973), and C. Thorne, *The Approach of War, 1938–1939* (1967), are excellent brief discussions of the major events. On the wars in Ethiopia and Spain, see A. Del Boca, *The Ethiopian War, 1935–1941* (1969), and H. Thomas, *The Spanish Civil War* (1961). The role of the United States in European affairs is examined in C. A. Macdonald, *The United States, Britain, and Appeasement, 1936–1939* (1981).

The most monumental account of the Second World War is W. S. Churchill, *The Second World War*, 6 vols. (1948–1953). G. Wright, *The Ordeal of Total War, 1939–1945* (1968), is excellent. B. H. Liddell Hart, *History of the Second World War* (1970), deals authoritatively with military affairs. On American involvement, see R. A. Divine, *The Reluctant Belligerent: American Entry into World War II* (1965). The relations among the Allies are reviewed in H. Feis, *Churchill, Roosevelt, Stalin* (1957), and their wartime conferences are discussed in D. S. Clemens, *Yalta* (1970), and H. Feis, *Between War and Peace: The Potsdam Conference* (1960). N. Rich, *Hitler's War Aims*, 2 vols. (1973–74), unravels a complicated subject. The extermination of the Jews is treated in L. Poliakov, *Harvest of Hate* (1954), and B. Naumann, *Auschwitz* (1966).

The best general account of the early postwar years is D. Yergin, *Shattered Peace: The Origins of the Cold War and the National Security State* (1977). See also L. E. Davis, *The Cold War Begins: Soviet-American Conflict over Eastern Europe* (1974). W. A. Williams, *The Tragedy of American Diplomacy* (1972), is highly critical of American policy. A. Grosser, *The Colossus Again: Western Germany from Defeat to Rearmament* (1955), deals with the major battleground of the Cold War in Europe. Developments in Palestine are analyzed in E. Berger, *The Covenant and the Sword: Arab-Israeli Relations, 1946–1956* (1965), and in East Asia, by H. Feis, *The China Tangle* (1953), and *Contest over Japan* (1967).

	1914				1950	
SOUTHWEST ASIA AND AFRICA	**1923** Kemal Attatürk, President of Turkish Republic			**1948** *Apartheid* in South Africa **1948** Founding of Israel, first Arab-Israeli war	**1954** Nasser takes control in Egypt **1956** Second Arab-Israeli war **1960–75** Independence movement sweeps Africa	**1967** Third Arab-Israeli (Six-Day) war **1971** Indo-Pakistani war **1973** Fourth Arab-Israeli war
EUROPE	**1914–18** World War I **1917** Bolshevik Revolution **1919** Paris Peace Conference	**1920** Keynes, *The Economic Consequences of the Peace* **1922** Mussolini's March on Rome **1923** French occupation of Ruhr	**1924** Death of Lenin, rise of Stalin **1924–25** Adolf Hitler, *Mein Kampf* **1924–29** Era of Locarno **1933** Hitler becomes Chancellor	**1935** Nuremburg Laws against Jews **1936–39** Spanish Civil War **1938** Munich Conference **1939** Hitler-Stalin Pact	**1939–44** World War II **1940** Fall of France **1941** Germany invades Russia **1941–45** Mass murder of Jews **1945** Yalta Conference	**1947** Marshall Plan **1949** Germany divided **1949** NATO Alliance **1953** Death of Stalin **1955** West Germany joins NATO **1955** Warsaw Pact
SOUTH AND SOUTHEAST ASIA	**1920–22** Gandhi's first Civil Disobedience Movement	**1927** Indonesian Nationalist party founded by Sukarno **1930** Gandhi's March to the Sea		**1947** Independence of India and Pakistan **1948** Mahatma Gandhi assassinated	**1949** Independence of Indonesia **1955** Bandung Conference, Indonesia	
EAST ASIA	**1927–37** Nationalist regime in Nanjing **1931** Japan seizes Manchuria **1934** Long March of Chinese Communists	**1937–45** Sino-Japanese War	**1941** Japan attacks Pearl Harbor **1945** Atomic bombing of Hiroshima and Nagasaki **1946–49** Civil war in China	**1949** People's Republic of China **1949–76** Mao Zedong's Chinese Revolution	**1950–53** Korean War **1951** US peace treaty with Japan	
THE AMERICAS AND PACIFIC	**1917** US enters World War I	**1929** The Great Depression begins **1933** Franklin D. Roosevelt's New Deal	**1941** US enters World War II **1945** First atomic bomb **1945** United Nations organized	**1946** First electronic computer **1947** Truman Doctrine **1948** Transistor invented	**1959** Fidel Castro's victory in Cuba **1962** Cuban Missile Crisis **1963** President Kennedy assassinated	**1968** Martin Luther King, Jr., assassinated **1969** Neil Armstrong, first man on moon

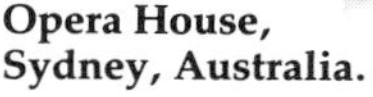

Opera House, Sydney, Australia.

"YOUR COUNTRY NEEDS YOU"

British recruiting poster, World War I.

Signers of Egyptian-Israeli peace treaty: Sadat, Carter, Begin, 1979.

Official symbol of the United Nations.

Apollo 11 lands men on moon, July 16, 1969.

German inflation: two billion mark note, 1929.

1985	
1977 President Sadat visits Jerusalem **1978** Camp David Accords **1979** USSR invades Afghanistan **1979** Revolution in Iran	**1980–** Iran-Iraq war **1980** Black majority rule in Zimbabwe (Rhodesia) **1981** President Sadat assassinated
1957 First earth satellite, USSR **1957** European Economic Community	**1960** Yuri Gagarin, first man in space **1980** Solidarity movement in Poland
1961 Increasing US involvement in Vietnam	**1973** US forces withdraw from South Vietnam **1975** Communists take over Vietnam, Laos, Cambodia
1971 People's Republic of China joins UN **1972** Nixon visits Beijing **1976** Death of Mao Zedong	**1977** China begins liberalizing under Deng Xiaoping
1974 President Nixon resigns **1975** Helsinki Accords **1977** Panama Canal Treaty	**1979** Civil war begins in Nicaragua and El Salvador **1982** Falkland Islands War

Striking Solidarity union workers, Warsaw, Poland, 1981.

Emperor Hirohito of Japan, 1926.

45 From Cold War to Coexistence

The Korean War might easily have sparked a third world war. The reason that it did not was due to the deterrent effect of the atomic bomb. With both the United States and Russia accumulating large stockpiles of nuclear weapons, the fear that some incident or accident might upset the precarious balance of terror became a dominant factor in world affairs. As a result, the perennial crises of the Cold War gradually gave way to a state of coexistence between the Communist and non-Communist worlds.

The years since 1950 have seen other significant changes. In its early phases, the Cold War was primarily a conflict between the United States and the Soviet Union. The rest of Europe seemed to have been relegated to a mere supporting role. Since then, however, the Continent has staged a remarkable comeback. At the same time, the rise of the former colonial regions to independence and influence has injected a whole new element, a "third world," into the international balance of power. The superpowers still play the leading roles, but the supporting cast has grown both larger and more influential.

THE DECLINE AND RISE OF WESTERN EUROPE

The decline of Europe's role in world affairs began during the First World War. Between the two wars, a semblance of the old European system of great powers was resurrected. But the Second World War brought the preeminence of Europe definitely to an end. The postwar problems facing the nations of Europe were alike in many ways. All the major powers of western Europe suffered territorial losses, either in Europe or overseas; several were threatened by communism from without or within; and they all were trying to recover from the economic effects of the war. In coping with these problems, the nations of free Europe had to modify their traditional nationalism and to cooperate. European recovery was retarded by the continued division of the Continent into Communist and non-Communist spheres. But in time the gulf between the two halves of Europe grew narrower and a reunion of the European continent again appeared possible.

Great Britain: Retreat from Empire

Great Britain after the Second World War had to cope with two related problems: economic recovery and the loss of its empire. In 1945 the British electorate for the first time returned a Labour majority. Under Clement Attlee, the government embarked on a program that Winston Churchill's Conservatives denounced as socialist. But most of the enterprises that were nationalized remained so even after the Conservatives returned to power in 1951. The most far-reaching measures introduced by the Labour government were the various State Welfare Acts that aimed at equality of opportunity for all citizens.

The tendency of these measures to make British society more egalitarian was enhanced by the austerity program by which the government hoped to balance the budget. Under Conservative rule from 1951 to 1964, the country experienced a temporary economic recovery. In 1964, however, dissatisfaction with a weak foreign policy and renewed economic stagnation once more brought a Labour victory. The second Labour cabinet was no more successful in overcoming Britain's economic paralysis than the first had been. When foreign loans, heavy taxation, and reduced government spending failed to improve matters, the government of Prime Minister Harold Wilson in 1967 devalued the pound, hoping thus to solve Britain's perennial trade deficit. But this and other drastic measures failed to improve matters. In 1970 the Conservatives won another chance to cope with rising inflation and unemployment. To economic unrest and strikes now were added bloody riots and bombings in Northern Ireland. In 1974 it became Labour's turn again. But neither party was able to halt the spiraling inflation, chiefly caused by wage demands.

One of the causes of Britain's depression was the rapid shrinking of its empire. Wherever colonial peoples demanded independence, British interests were usually involved. Most of the resulting new states remained within the Commonwealth of Nations, but the ties of this elusive organization grew weaker over the years. Within less than a generation, the once mighty British Empire virtually melted away.

One possible way of improving its position was for Britain to draw closer to the continental nations that had joined forces in the European Economic Community (EEC), or Common Market. But the island kingdom was reluctant to do so, for fear that such economic rapprochement might conflict with its Commonwealth ties. It was not until 1973 that Britain finally joined EEC, hoping to share in the organization's economic prosperity.

Economic difficulties continued to be Britain's major headache. In 1979 the Conservatives under Margaret Thatcher once again gained control. The first woman prime minister was a firm believer in free enterprise and laissez-faire. But as in most other industrialized nations, social services continued to require high taxation and retard economic growth. In addition, intermittent violence between Catholics and Protestants in Northern Ireland put a constant strain on Britain's finances. In 1982, a showdown with

Argentina over the Falkland Islands, while bringing an upsurge of national unity, further added to the country's economic ills and reminded the British people of how little was left of their once-mighty empire.

France: Search for Lost Grandeur

The French in 1946 gave themselves a new constitution. But the Fourth Republic was little different from the Third. As old enmities persisted and new ones arose, the traditional bickering among numerous small parties and interest groups continued. The chief beneficiary of this confusion were the French Communists, who until 1958 made up the largest party in the National Assembly. Only in foreign policy did the new republic show some consistency.

France, like Great Britain, found it difficult at first to regain its economic health. Financial problems were staggering, and their solution required taxation and a stable currency. But reluctant taxpayers, creeping inflation, and incessant strikes counteracted the beneficent effects of aid from the American Marshall Plan. When President de Gaulle began to dominate the national scene in the late 1950s, a broad austerity program, combined with careful economic planning, put France back on the road to prosperity.

France also faced the rapid dissolution of its colonial empire. In 1946 the Fourth Republic tried to maintain some control over its overseas holdings by founding the French Union. This federation, however, was far too centralized to satisfy the more developed territories, and a number of them — Syria, Lebanon, Morocco, and Tunisia — were given their independence. Indochina and Algeria won independence only after drawn out and costly fighting. In 1958 the French Union was transformed into the French Community, which included France proper, its few remaining overseas possessions, and most of the new African nations that formerly made up French Equatorial and West Africa. The Community was a loose federation whose main significance lay in whatever prestige it held for the former mother country.

Prestige was the main concern of the man who assumed direction of French affairs in 1958. Charles de Gaulle, leader of the Free French forces in the Second World War, had served briefly as provisional president in 1945. He was recalled in 1958 at the height of the Algerian crisis. Under de Gaulle's direction a new constitution was adopted that vastly increased the power of the president. In December 1958 de Gaulle was elected first president of the Fifth Republic, and for the next ten years, the general's towering figure dominated the French scene.

De Gaulle's most important achievement was the agreement of 1962, which gave Algeria its independence. Elsewhere, in Europe and overseas, de Gaulle's main ambition was to recapture some of France's past "grandeur." To strengthen his country's position in Europe, de Gaulle maintained close ties with West Germany and cemented relations with the Communist powers. To counteract Anglo-Saxon influence, he took France out of NATO and barred Britain from membership in the Common Market. Along similar lines, de Gaulle drew closer to Communist China, criticized American involvement in Vietnam, and encouraged separatist sentiment among French Canadians. Supporters of the French president defended his obstructionist policies as a reassertion not merely of French influence but of European influence as well against the United States.

In France itself, de Gaulle's preoccupation with foreign concerns at the expense of domestic ones gave rise to a wave of discontent, especially among workers and students, that almost led to revolution in May 1968. When some of his reform proposals were defeated in a national referendum the following year, de Gaulle resigned.

De Gaulle's successor was one of his close associates, Georges Pompidou. The new president's major concern

Konrad Adenauer of West Germany meeting with Charles de Gaulle of France (1962). They pursued policies of reconciliation between their two nations and a policy of a united Europe based on the Common Market.

was with domestic affairs; he tried to improve France's economy by overcoming its antiquated production methods and easing its transition into a highly industrialized and urban society. In foreign affairs, Pompidou at long last welcomed Britain into the Common Market. When Pompidou died in 1974, Valéry Giscard d'Estaing continued along a road of domestic reforms, fiscal austerity, and long-range economic planning.

Meanwhile gains in local elections by the parties of the left showed that many Frenchmen remained critical of their government's policy. This discontent came to a head in the elections of 1981, which gave a resounding victory to Socialist leader François Mitterand. The inclusion of some Communists in his new cabinet worried France's allies, but Mitterand's subsequent policies firmly endorsed the defense of western Europe against the Soviet Union. His domestic program of job creation, nationalization of major industries, and taxation of the rich ran into parliamentary opposition and did little to improve France's economy. By 1985, the parties of the center and right had begun to contest Mitterand's Socialist control, and the future of his government looked uncertain.

West Germany: The German Federal Republic

The most spectacular rise from rubble to riches in postwar Europe occurred in West Germany. The partition of the former Reich in 1949 as a result of the Cold War has already been discussed (see pp. 957–58). During the 1950s the western Federal Republic experienced a veritable "economic miracle." In contrast to the nationalization measures adopted by Great Britain and France, Germany followed a more traditional policy of laissez-faire. With a favorable balance of trade, a freely convertible currency, and hardly any unemployment, Germany's "free-market economy" aroused the admiration and envy of its neighbors.

Politically, developments in West Germany were remarkably steady. The country was fortunate in having as its first chancellor Konrad Adenauer, a conservative opponent of nazism and a sincere friend of the West. The "old man" virtually dominated German politics from 1949 until his retirement in 1963. His successor, Ludwig Erhard, popular as the author of the "economic miracle," was a man of lesser political stature. In 1966, the middle-of-the-road Christian Democratic Union (CDU), which hitherto had dominated the government, had to share power with the moderately leftist Social Democratic party (SPD). The shift toward the Social Democrats continued in 1969, with Willy Brandt as chancellor. He was succeeded in 1973 by the equally able Helmut Schmidt.

Next to economic development, the two most vital issues before the West German governments in the 1950s and 1960s were reunification and rearmament. To reunite not only East and West Germany but also the region beyond the Oder-Neisse line (occupied by Poland in 1945) was the fervent wish of every German. Repeated proposals of the western powers to achieve German unity through free general elections invariably met with Soviet opposition. Meanwhile the West German Federal Republic refused to recognize the East German Democratic Republic, in order to keep alive the idea of a united Germany. But as time went on, and as each section of Germany developed along widely divergent lines, most Germans became reconciled to the thought that they might not live to see their country reunited. As long as Adenauer was in control, however, any open acquiescence in the partition of Germany was out of the question.

This situation changed with the advent of Willy Brandt. Brandt had repeatedly stated his intention of bringing about a détente with the communist world. As first steps he signed treaties with the Soviet Union and Poland in 1970 that renounced force and resumed relations. The agreement with Poland also recognized the Oder-Neisse line as the German-Polish frontier. Of still greater significance was a treaty in 1972 between East and West Germany that recognized the existence of two sovereign German states and provided for closer collaboration between them. To round out his *Ostpolitik* (eastern policy), Brandt also resumed economic relations with a number of East European states and established diplomatic ties with Communist China.

Brandt's policy also helped to dispel whatever apprehension had remained over German rearmament. The creation of a West German army caused considerable debate in the 1950s. As the Russians at the time began training a German military force in East Germany, the western powers decided to permit the limited rearmament of West Germany. Under an agreement ratified in 1955, West Germany was to contribute a maximum of five hundred thousand men to the common defense of the West under NATO. In return, the Federal Republic was granted complete sovereignty.

The fear that rearmament would cause a revival of German militarism and nationalism proved groundless. Relations between Germany and its "traditional enemy" France were better than they had ever been, leading to a treaty of friendship in 1963. Collaboration with the Anglo-Saxon powers was close, and Brandt's *Ostpolitik* gave further proof of West Germany's peaceful intentions. In its domestic policy, furthermore, West Germany showed that it had made a clean break with the Nazi past. There were a few incidents of neonazism, but the majority of Germans disapproved of these activities. In the mid-1970s, a new type of leftist radicalism emerged in Germany, spearheaded by a small terrorist group. Their acts of violence against political and business leaders led the government to curtail the generous civil rights guaranteed by the Bonn constitution. The fear that such measures would lead to a revival of authoritarianism, however, proved groundless.

West Germany had thus emerged as the strongest nation in Europe (other than the Soviet Union) and most valued ally against the Russians. As West Germany's economy began to slow down, however, and share the fate of some of its industrial competitors, balancing the budget became increasingly difficult. With rising inflation and unemployment, many Germans felt that it was time for a change. That change came in 1983, when the CDU won a decisive victory over the SPD, and its leader, Helmut Kohl, suceeded Helmut Schmidt as chancellor. Kohl's domestic policy was more austere than that of his predecessor, but in his foreign policy he continued West Germany's close alliance with the West.

Helmut Kohl campaigning before the West German general election of 1983.

Italy: The Least Among the Great Powers

Italy came out of the Second World War with its already backward economy in a dismal state. After a slow start, however, the country staged a remarkable recovery. By 1965 Italy's industrial production had increased fourfold, and the nation's per capita income had doubled. With economic improvement came a period of political stability. The new Italian republic was launched successfully in 1946 under the capable leadership of Alcide de Gasperi and his Christian Democratic party. But with the onset of the Cold War, the government came under increasing attacks from a strong Communist party on the left and a growing neofascist movement on the right. Only when the Christian Democrats, beginning in 1962, allied themselves with the moderate Socialists did some measure of political calm return.

Even so, the fact that one out of every three Italians voted Communist showed that all was far from well. While there was prosperity, poverty persisted, especially in the agricultural South. Even in the North real wages did not keep up with the general rise in the economy, and the distribution of income remained uneven. In the late 1960s, economic discontent led to numerous strikes, which aggravated the economic crisis. In addition, the center-left coalition broke apart, as Christian Democrats and Socialists differed over the controversial divorce law of 1970 and other issues. Meanwhile, the Communists remained the country's second-largest party, and the neofascist Italian Social movement doubled its forces in the elections of 1972. From here on, Italy was governed by frequently changing minority coalitions that were still dominated by the Christian Democrats. The elections of 1976 brought further Communist gains, and Italy, like France, faced the possibility of having to let the Communists share in its government. In 1978 a wave of attacks by a small band of terrorists, the Red Brigades, against prominent political and business leaders were climaxed by the abduction and murder of a former Christian Democratic premier, Aldo Moro. The resulting grief and anger did much to reunite the deeply divided Italian nation.

Italy could ill afford to lose one of its ablest leaders. Its ailing economy, burdened by excessive social services, high unemployment, and astronomical inflation, led to continued instability. By 1980, Italy had had more than forty governments since World War II. The polarization between the Communist left and the neofascist right, furthermore, made viable coalitions difficult. The situation was exacerbated by continued terrorism, by scandals in high places, and by the disastrous earthquake of 1980. Among the leading industrial nations of the West, Italy was clearly the last and the least.

The Quest for European Unity

Given the similarity of their problems, especially economic, it was only natural that western European nations should try to devise means for common action. The Marshall Plan had shown that lasting recovery could be won only through economic cooperation; and the Brussels Pact, besides calling for a military alliance, had also stressed the need for collaboration in economic, social, and cultural affairs (see p. 958). The first major instance of such collaboration was the Schuman Plan, which established the European Coal and Steel Community. In 1952 France, Germany, Belgium, The Netherlands, Luxembourg, and Italy agreed to merge their resources of coal and steel in a common western European market. By 1957 enough progress had been achieved to extend the common market to other goods through the European Economic Community (EEC). It was not a closed organization, but any country could apply for membership. The admission of Great Britain was delayed until 1973, at which time Ireland and Denmark also joined. Later members or prospective candidates were Greece, Spain, Portugal, and Turkey. Representing close to 300 million people, the EEC is the most important and powerful trading area in the world.

Plans for European political union were less successful. Prospects looked bright in 1949, when the Council of

Toward a "European Consciousness"?

The adjective "European," which a century ago was understood only by a small minority, and which even in the early twentieth century was accepted perhaps only by the aristocracy, by the high bourgeoisie and by certain intellectuals, today has become an accepted adjective, a designation, a self-ascribed characteristic for the majority of the populations even in Central and Eastern Europe. To many a peasant in the Danube Valley the adjective "European" even twenty or thirty years ago meant either nothing at all or something that was vaguely and suspiciously alien. This is no longer so. Despite Communist political rule and regimentation, life for large masses of people in Warsaw and Belgrade and Budapest and Bucharest has now more in common with life in Berne and Brussels and Paris than it had fifty or one hundred years ago, and this is true of people in Lisbon, Madrid, Palermo, Athens. It is, let me repeat, by no means clear whether the increasing standardization of certain forms of life will, within Europe, lead to a further, and decisive, phase in the development of a European consciousness. That ten thousand Bulgarians watch television or that tens of thousands in Budapest experience their first traffic jam is unimportant. What is important, for our purposes, is to recognize that the collapse of the European state system did not mean the end of European history; that, indeed, we are facing two countervailing historical developments: decline—definite decline—of the European state system on the one hand; rise—vague rise—of a European consciousness on the other.

From John Lukacs, *Decline and Rise of Europe* (Garden City, N.Y.: Doubleday, 1965), pp. 169–70.

Europe was founded at Strasbourg. But it remained a purely consultative body, and the hope for a United States of Europe did not materialize. As Europe recovered economically and as the threat of Soviet expansion subsided, national differences once again came to the fore. Yet despite these disappointments, the general trend toward European unity was unmistakable. At their periodic summit meetings, the leaders of the European Community increasingly dealt not only with economic issues, but also discussed and took a stand on matters of common political concern, such as the defense of western Europe, to which they were committed as members of NATO.

THE AMERICAS

To the rest of the world the United States in 1945 appeared as a country of unbelievable wealth, untouched by the hardships of war. But to Americans themselves the picture looked quite different. Price controls, wage controls, incessant waves of strikes, and signs of widespread corruption — these were some of the problems faced by the United States. The Democratic administration's attempts to deal with the situation by further regulation found little support. It seemed that the country was tired of governmental controls and of a social service state that to most Republicans smacked of socialism.

The Truman Era

President Truman was reelected in 1948 chiefly because of his foreign policy: the Truman Doctrine, the Marshall Plan, and the Berlin airlift. Isolationism, of course, did not vanish overnight. But the fact that a Republican administration after 1952 continued substantially the same foreign policy showed that the shift from isolationism was a matter not so much of choice as of necessity. One aspect of American involvement abroad that was not universally popular was the foreign-aid program. During the first fifteen years after the war, United States economic and military aid amounted to more than $75 billion. Much of it was given in a spirit of genuine helpfulness. But foreign aid was also an important weapon in the Cold War, especially after 1955, when the Soviet Union began stepping up its own foreign-aid program.

In American domestic affairs, one of the major issues at the time was the fear of Communist infiltration. This fear reached its climax during the Korean War. Chiefly because of the agitation of Wisconsin's Senator Joseph McCarthy, the American public in the early 1950s was led to believe that its government had allowed Communists to get into key positions in the State Department and the army. These unfounded accusations created a climate of fear and distrust and did much to harm the reputations and careers of innocent people.

The reality of the Communist threat abroad, meanwhile, was brought home by events in Korea. As the war there bogged down in a bloody stalemate, critics of the administration demanded an escalation of the war, including the bombing of Communist bases in China. Foremost among these critics was America's commander in chief in Korea, General Douglas MacArthur. When efforts to silence him failed, President Truman relieved the general of his command in April 1951. The ensuing crisis was the most serious the United States had faced since 1945.

A unique photograph of the four men who occupied the American presidency between 1945 and 1968 — Kennedy, Johnson, Eisenhower, and Truman. The occasion was the funeral of House Speaker Sam Rayburn in 1961.

The Reverend Dr. Martin Luther King, Jr., at a civil rights rally in Washington, D.C., August 28, 1963: "I have a dream. . . ."

Together with a mounting wave of government scandals and continued suspicion of Communist influence in the government, the Korean War was a major cause of the defeat of the Democrats in 1952.

The Eisenhower Years

The victories of the Republican candidate, Dwight D. Eisenhower, in 1952 and 1956 were as much personal as partisan. He enhanced his popularity by concluding a Korean armistice in 1953. During his two administrations, bipartisan majorities in Congress produced much valuable social legislation. The nation's economy continued to flourish, except in the agricultural sector, where overproduction posed a serious problem. The administration's attempts to reduce price supports of agricultural products incurred the opposition of farm groups; this opposition was one of the reasons for the overwhelming congressional victory of the Democrats in 1958. Other reasons were the temporary economic recession and the antagonism that the Republican administration had aroused among organized labor.

A major issue that came to the fore during the Eisenhower years was desegregation. In *Brown* v. *Board of Education of Topeka* (1954), the United States Supreme Court ruled that American blacks had the right to attend the same schools as whites. Desegregation proceeded smoothly in most states, but in the Deep South every possible means was used to prevent it. In 1957 and 1958 President Eisenhower had to send federal troops to enforce desegregation in Little Rock, Arkansas. This was only the beginning of a drawn-out crisis, as blacks began to demand that desegregation be extended to other fields. The resistance of diehard "white supremacists" to these demands did much to tarnish America's image abroad.

From Kennedy to Johnson

The victory of John F. Kennedy in 1960 injected a fresh note into American politics. His administration got off to a promising start when Congress approved a series of social-service measures chiefly designed to aid the poor. When the president began to tackle the touchy subject of civil rights, however, he lost the support of southern Democrats and his domestic program came to a halt. Some improvement in the status of blacks was made under pressure of nonviolent protests directed by able black leaders. But as police in the South met peaceful demonstrations with violence, the situation became increasingly explosive. Much of President Kennedy's attention was taken up with crises in foreign affairs. In his efforts to counter Communist threats in Southeast Asia, Cuba, and Berlin, the president generally found the support that Congress withheld from his domestic program.

President Kennedy was assassinated on November 22, 1963. A major political crisis was avoided because of the firm manner in which his successor, Lyndon B. Johnson, took charge. Where Kennedy had labored in vain against congressional opposition, Johnson, a former majority leader in the Senate, was able to achieve some notable successes. By 1964 the new president had gained sufficient support to win a landslide victory.

From then on, however, President Johnson found the going increasingly difficult. Civil rights had become the key domestic issue. The Civil Rights Act of 1964 was the most sweeping legislation of its kind ever enacted. But its provisions were still disregarded in many parts of the South. Meanwhile black protests spread to the North, where the demand was for greater equality in employment, housing, and education. Demonstrations that hitherto had been orderly now became violent, as bloody riots swept through major American cities and as advocates of "black power" preached the use of force. To cope with the economic roots of black discontent, the Johnson administration stepped up the antipoverty programs initiated under Kennedy. But while the "war on poverty" called for vast amounts of money, more and more funds were being diverted to another kind of war.

The war in Vietnam, in which the United States had become involved since 1961, proved the most divisive issue in American politics. As "hawks" (advocating victory through war) ranged against "doves" (favoring American withdrawal), many young Americans chose to go to prison or abroad rather than to fight an "unjust" war. The cause of reform suffered a major loss with the assassination, in June 1968, of Senator Robert F. Kennedy, a leading Democratic contender for the presidency. Racial unrest, meanwhile, had flared up anew after the murder that April of the Reverend Dr. Martin Luther King, Jr., an outstanding black leader in the nonviolent civil rights movement. It was a deeply disturbed and divided nation that gave the Republican candidate, Richard M. Nixon, a narrow victory in November 1968.

The Nixon Administrations

The war in Vietnam continued to be the major cause of tension in American politics. The withdrawal of American forces beginning in 1972 and the subsequent start of armistice negotiations were largely responsible for President Nixon's reelection the same year by an overwhelming majority. An uneasy armistice was finally concluded in early 1973. Meanwhile the president and his dynamic secretary of state, Henry Kissinger, had embarked on new ventures elsewhere by paying visits to the Soviet Union and Communist China, thus easing tensions with the Russians and establishing first contacts with the mainland Chinese.

In his domestic affairs, President Nixon had a less fortunate hand. Most problems had already plagued previous administrations, but some of them worsened as time went on. One of these was crime. "Law and order," a key issue in the 1972 elections, was part of a larger question—the rapid decay of American cities into breeding grounds of crime, often connected with

An American soldier in Vietnam.

drug addiction. Another growing concern was protection of the environment against pollution by individuals and industries. Unrest among blacks decreased somewhat, as some of their demands were being met. There remained, however, the controversial issue of "busing" white or black students outside their school districts to achieve a better racial balance.

To slow the country's rising inflation, the Nixon administration, beginning in 1971, imposed wage and price controls, measures never before adopted in time of peace. To improve America's growing trade deficit, the dollar was officially devalued in 1972 and 1973. And to curtail government spending at home, President Nixon refused to spend some funds appropriated by Congress for purposes he considered wasteful. This action did not endear him to the legislature, and confrontations between the White House and Capitol Hill were frequent. The Nixon administration was also accused of showing less concern than its predecessors for minority groups; certainly, its support among blacks was minimal.

Far more disquieting than any of these issues, however, was the "Watergate Affair," in which leading members of the president's staff were found to have been involved in illegal acts against the Democratic party during the 1972 campaign. As judicial and Senate hearings uncovered a sordid story of intrigue and attempted cover-up, the question arose as to whether President Nixon had any part in these events. The president denied any such involvement. As more and more incriminating evidence came to light, however, and as congressional impeachment hearings got under way in early 1974, Nixon, on August 9, decided to resign rather than face further charges and revelations. He was the first president ever thus to leave office.

From Ford to Carter

The new president, Gerald Ford, had been appointed vice-president by Nixon when Spiro Agnew had resigned after being found guilty of income tax evasion. Ford's amicable manner made him many friends. His popularity suffered, however, when he first granted a general pardon to Nixon and then a limited amnesty to draft evaders during the Vietnam War. To ensure continuity in foreign policy, Ford retained Secretary of State Kissinger, who tended to overshadow him. In domestic affairs, economic issues and the effects of the energy crisis continued to loom large. Also, the nightmare of Watergate was not easily forgotten.

The race for the presidency in 1976 was the closest in recent times. The winner, Democrat James Earl ("Jimmy") Carter, was a dark horse, who owed most of his victory to his own efforts. President Carter's proposals for tax reform, reduced government spending, and legislation to deal with long-term energy requirements were innovative and addressed the nation's most urgent needs. In an effort to correct the "imperial" image of the presidency, Carter affected a more folksy style, which did not always enhance his popularity. To many Americans, the peanut farmer from Plains, Georgia, seemed to lack sufficient experience for his high office, especially in military and foreign affairs, where the Panama Canal Treaty and the decision to halt development of the neutron bomb met with widespread criticism.

From Carter to Reagan

Carter's defeat at the hands of Ronald Reagan in 1980 was due partly to his ineptitude, partly to circumstances beyond his control. The president's failure to cope with "stagflation" (an economy suffering simultaneously from stagnation and inflation) was no worse than the futile efforts of national leaders elsewhere or, for that matter, of his successor. Nor could Carter be blamed for the seizure of American hostages by Iran, although his bumbling attempts at their liberation contributed to his defeat. The Carter years did bring some positive achievements: the Camp David accords between Israel and Egypt, the Panama Canal Treaty, the stress on human rights for minorities and women at home and for political dissidents abroad.

Ronald Reagan won by a sizeable majority. Personal charm and skill as a politician played their part. His promise to balance the budget by reducing government spending and to stimulate production through tax cuts was appealing. But it was also inconsistent, and after some initial successes, ran into serious congressional opposition. Similar contradictions characterized Reagan's foreign policy, where efforts at détente conflicted with stepped-up military preparedness against the Soviet Union and growing involvement in Central America. Despite such shortcomings, however, Reagan's landslide victory in 1984 was due as much to his popularity as to his containment of inflation at home and his assertion of American power abroad.

The United States and Its Neighbors

With the global contest between communism and capitalism, the maintenance of harmony within the Western Hemisphere was of major concern to every administration after 1945. Relations with America's northern neighbor were, on the whole, cordial. Because of its tremendous economic growth, Canada ranked as one of the world's leading industrial powers. United States capital played an important part in this expansion, and the resulting American influence caused some resentment among Canadian nationalists. Military relations between the two countries were close, both within NATO and without. Continued membership in the (British) Commonwealth saved Canada from becoming too dependent on its powerful neighbor, although ties with Great Britain grew noticeably weaker. Canadian politics was dominated by the Liberal party, led until 1957 by Mackenzie King, thereafter until 1968 by Lester Pearson, and since then by Elliot Trudeau. One of the most burning domestic issues continued to be the division between French- and English-speaking Canadians. Trudeau resigned in 1984 and in the ensuing elections, the Liberals suffered their worst defeat ever at the hands of the Conservatives. The new prime minister, Brian Mulrony, promised to improve Canada's economy and unify the nation.

Relations between the United States and its southern neighbors were more complicated. The twenty republics of Latin America differed widely in size and significance, and the absence of a strong democratic tradition made many of them prone to authoritarian regimes of the right or left. The most pressing problem of the whole area was its alarming rise in population. Latin America had great economic potentialities, but financial and technical assistance were needed to develop them. The United States was expected to supply this aid. Prior to 1960 little such aid found its way to Latin America. Subsequently, a number of ambitious development schemes were launched, notably the Alliance for Progress, proclaimed by President Kennedy in 1961. But the results of such schemes were disappointing. Besides looking to the United States for help, the nations of Latin America increasingly looked to one another. The

President Reagan meeting former Presidents Nixon, Carter, and Ford at the White House. The former Chief Executives were about to leave for Egypt to attend the funeral of Anwar Sadat.

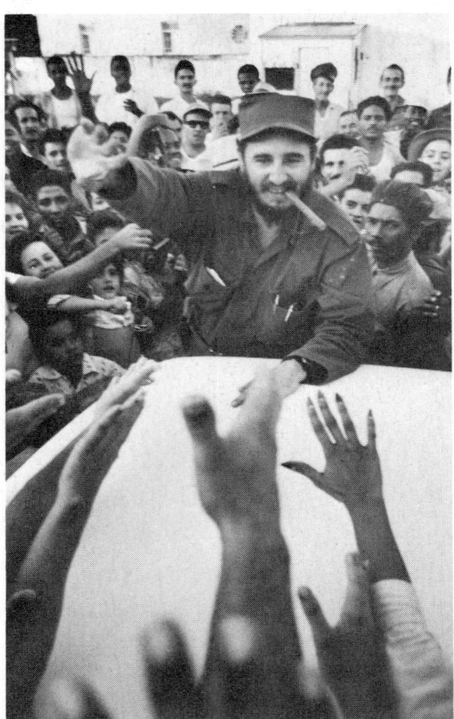

Castro arriving triumphantly in Havana (1959).

Latin American Free Trade Association (LAFTA), set up in 1960, called for the creation of a common market for all of Latin America, but its progress was slow. More successful in fostering economic cooperation were various subregional groups, especially the Central American Common Market.

The United States was much concerned with building a united military front against the threat of communism in the Western Hemisphere. In 1947 the Latin American nations and the United States signed the Rio Treaty, which called for mutual assistance in case of war. Subsequent agreements arranged for the exchange of United States arms against strategic raw materials. The most important agency of inter-American cooperation was the Organization of American States (OAS), founded in 1948. The Charter of the OAS proclaimed the equality of its members and laid down the principle of nonintervention in external and internal affairs. The OAS proved a major stabilizing influence.

The main threat to the security of the Western Hemisphere in the eyes of the United States was Fidel Castro's Cuba. After initially hailing the victory of his rebel forces in 1959, Castro's close relations with Communist China and the Soviet Union led the United States to break off relations with Cuba and make various attempts to overthrow the Castro regime. Tension between the two governments was kept alive through Cuba's involvement in various "liberation" movements in Central America and in Africa.

The United States was also involved in a number of other Latin American crises, notably in Chile and Panama. In Chile, the United States was justly accused of having engineered the violent overthrow of President Salvador Allende Gossens, a Marxist, by a military junta in 1973. In Panama, perennial demonstrations against American control of the Panama Canal finally led to the signing of a treaty in 1977, by which the waterway would come under Panamanian control by the end of the century. Under the Reagan ad-

Latin America, the U.S., and the Soviet Union

The Latin American policies of the United States should not be a by-product of U.S.-Soviet relations. In the past these policies have been too often shaped by U.S.-Soviet global rivalry and by misperceptions of Soviet actions in the region. Washington should deal with Latin American governments on their own merits. If U.S. ties with particular Latin American nations are healthy, strong, and mutually beneficial, the USSR will not be able to threaten Washington's interests there. . . .

Except for the Cubans and probably now the Sandinistas, most Latin American governments are not pro-Soviet. But they also believe that U.S. armed intervention in the hemisphere is more likely than Soviet intervention—not an unreasonable conclusion given the historical antecedents. For that reason many feel that the ultimate protection against U.S. intervention is countervailing Latin American power. This is not a Utopian prospect because Latin American power need not be equal to U.S. power, only sufficient to prevent intervention. In recent years the Latin American nations have been increasing their bargaining power with the United States, particularly in regional economic organizations. A Latin America that is truly independent of the United States will be most capable of remaining independent of the Soviet Union.

From Cole Blasier, *The Giant's Rival: The USSR and Latin America* (Pittsburgh: University of Pittsburgh Press, 1983), pp. 158, 164.

ministration, the main trouble spot in Central America was El Salvador, where leftist guerrillas, aided by Nicaragua and Cuba, waged war against a military junta supported by the United States. On this as on many earlier occasions, conservative Americans viewed popular unrest in ideological, anti-Communist terms.

THE COMMUNIST WORLD

For almost two decades after 1945, while the Cold War lasted, the Communist world appeared as a monolithic bloc dominated by Moscow. It took the rest of the world some time to realize how much this Soviet predominance depended on one man. In retrospect, the death of Joseph Stalin on March 5, 1953, was a major event in world history. It spelled the end of an era, not only for Russian communism but for world communism as well.

Russia under Khrushchev

The main features of the Stalinist era, which reached its high point after 1945, have already been discussed (see pp. 954–57). To repair the staggering damages of the war, two Five-Year Plans called for a new round of industrialization and collectivization. Simultaneously, strictest orthodoxy remained the keynote of Soviet political and cultural life. The slightest deviation from Stalinist-Marxist theory brought imprisonment, slave labor, or death. In a famous speech before the twentieth Party Congress in 1956, Khrushchev charged that Stalin, "a very distrustful man, sickly suspicious," had planned even to liquidate his most intimate political associates.

Stalin's reign of terror came to a sudden end with his death. For the first few years after Stalin's death, "collective leadership" prevailed. But it was only a matter of time before one of the most determined members of the group, Nikita S. Khrushchev, emerged as the recognized leader. As Stalin had done a generation earlier, Khrushchev used his key position as Secretary of the Central Committee of the Communist party to rid himself of his associates. The only novelty was that his rivals were not killed but merely ousted.

Khrushchev, a career party functionary, never achieved the absolute power that Stalin had wielded before him. Russia under Stalin had undergone not only an economic but a social revolution. From a nation of illiterate peasants, the Soviet Union had become a nation of educated workers. Although the basic Marxist concept of state ownership of the means of production remained in force, the concept of a classless society had been far from realized. Instead, a substantial upper class had grown up: the party elite, the top echelons of the vast political and economic bureaucracy, managerial personnel, technical experts, scientists, and the like. The Soviet Union, in other words, had become a far more complex society than it had been at the start. To run such a nation by regimentation based on terror was no longer possible.

The most dramatic change in the life of the average Russian came with the retreat from terror after Stalin's death. This did not mean that there were no longer any political prisoners. But it did mean that the number of punishable political crimes became smaller than it had been under Stalin. Henceforth it

Nikita Khrushchev delivering an angry diatribe at a United Nations debate in 1960.

was possible to criticize certain aspects of the regime without risking execution. The liberalization of Soviet life was felt in other ways. In factories and on collective farms, discipline was relaxed. Consumer goods became more plentiful, and the housing shortage was reduced. Education was broadened to admit more students to secondary schools and universities. With the easing of travel restrictions, Russians for the first time came in contact with the outside world. In Russian art and literature, the orthodox emphasis on "socialist realism" gave way to some modern trends. Initially, outside observers saw these changes as signs that Russia had abandoned its unbending opposition to the West. But Soviet leaders made no secret of the fact that the "new look" was merely a change in methods and that their aim remained what it had always been: the overthrow of capitalism.

Russia under Brezhnev

The return to virtual one-man rule under Khrushchev was suddenly reversed in 1964, when the Russian leader was purged by his party's Central Committee and his double role as premier and party secretary was divided between Alexei N. Kosygin and Leonid I. Brezhnev. The main reasons for Khrushchev's dismissal appeared to be domestic, notably his failure to live up to his boastful economic promises, although foreign reversals such as the Cuban missile crisis also played their part. Like Khrushchev and Stalin before him, Brezhnev, as General Secretary of the Communist party, gradually emerged as the key figure in Soviet affairs. Continuity in foreign policy was assured by the presence of veteran Foreign Minister Andrei A. Gromyko. In 1977 Brezhnev assumed the additional position of President of the Supreme Soviet, or head of state. A new constitution, meanwhile, attempted to project a more liberal image of the Soviet state by stressing individual rights; but like Stalin's effort in 1936, it was merely window dressing.

Economic growth in the Soviet Union during the 1960s and 1970s was at a slower rate than predicted, especially in the agrarian sector, where dependence on American grain imports gave the United States a limited means of exerting diplomatic pressure. With increased material gain came signs of spiritual unrest. The younger generation in particular seemed less and less willing to accept the intellectual restrictions of a totalitarian regime. The reaction of the regime to manifestations of dissent was twofold. On the one hand, critical writers like Alexander Solzhenitsyn and Andrei Sinyavsky, advocates of civil liberties like Yosif Brodsky and Andrei Sakharov, and various national dissidents in the Ukraine and Lithuania were arrested and in some cases forced to emigrate. But at the same time the government also tried to counter discontent by economic concessions, raising the living standard of the average Soviet citizen. The general tendency, however, was in the direction of repression rather than reform, leading some foreign observers to speak of a return to Stalinism.

From Brezhnev to Gorbachev

Leonid Brezhnev died in 1982. He was succeeded by Yuri Andropov, whose tenure was cut short, however, by his death in 1984 at age 69. His successor, Konstantin Chernenko, was 72 years old and lasted less than a year. At his death in 1985, the Politiburo appointed the much younger Mikhail Gorbachev to succeed him. This was seen as a possible turning point, away from the orthodox older generation toward a more liberal policy at home and a more accommodating position abroad. Gorbachev clearly had the ability and experience to make such changes. It remained to be seen if he also had the will and the power.

Unrest Among the Satellites

The effects of the post-Stalin "thaw" were also felt among the satellite nations of eastern Europe. The first defection from the Soviet bloc had occurred as early as 1948, when Marshal Tito of Yugoslavia, preferring "Titoism" to "Stalinism," had struck out on his own. By 1956, Stalin's successors had made peace with Tito and had acknowledged that there were "various roads to socialism." But the satellites were not satisfied with mere promises of greater independence. In the fall of 1956, revolts against Soviet domination broke out first in Poland and then in Hungary. Both revolts were motivated by nationalism. In addition, the Hungarian uprising was strongly anti-Communist. For that reason the Hungarian revolution was brutally suppressed by Russian intervention, while Poland's Communists, under Wladyslaw Gomulka, were given greater autonomy from Russian control.

For the next ten years, there were no violent attempts to resist Russian domination. The nations of eastern Europe were enjoying far greater freedom of action than they had had under Stalin. In 1961 growing tension between Russia and Albania over the latter's continued adherence to Stalinism led to an open break. In 1964 Rumania declared its virtual independence from Soviet influence, drawing closer to the West. The most dramatic change, however, occurred in Czechoslovakia, where, as a result of a peaceful revolution in the spring of 1968, the country regained briefly many democratic freedoms. The Soviet Union's armed intervention against the regime of Alexander Dubček emphasized the threat that these tendencies posed to Russia's leadership in the Communist world.

Crisis in Poland

The country that posed the greatest threat to that leadership was Poland. The periodic unrest of 1970 and 1976 had been caused by economic problems, but in time grievances had become more general, demanding individual freedoms and participation in governmental decisions. As intellectuals and other dissidents made common cause with the workers, their protest gained momentum. The latest crisis was touched off by a massive strike among shipyard workers at Gdansk in 1980. Major violence was avoided when the government granted demands for an independent union, "Solidarity," headed by Lech Walesa.

Mikhail Gorbachev (right) and Andrei Gromyko at the opening meeting of the Supreme Soviet (1985).

But this was only the beginning. Farmers now also demanded a union, while workers asked for further liberalization of Communist rule. The Soviet Union was deeply concerned over these developments. Using economic aid and the threat of military intervention, the Russians tried to contain a movement that might spread to other parts of their empire. As opposition to Russia's influence in Poland became more open, the prime minister, General Wojcieck Jaruzelski, imposed martial law, leading to the arrest of thousands of dissidents. The West, from the start, supported Poland's fight for freedom, now also backed by the Catholic Church and Poland's most illustrious son, Pope John Paul II.

"Socialist Pluralism"

Despite Russia's efforts to maintain its leadership over world communism, the unity that had once prevailed among Communist states and parties had given way to diversity. At a Communist world conference in 1976, the Communist parties of western Europe proclaimed their own brand of "Eurocommunism," asserting their allegiance to democratic principles and their readiness to join in parliamentary governments. Instead of a monolithic Communist bloc directed from Moscow, there now existed a plurality of socialist states.

The most important split within the Communist camp developed between Moscow and Beijing (Peking). While Stalin was alive, the potentially powerful People's Republic of China had not contested Russia's claim to leadership. But after 1953 the Chinese gradually began to assert themselves. At first it seemed as though China's influence was to be on the side of moderation. Beginning in 1957, however, and especially after 1963, Beijing showed signs of a new, hard line. The Sino-Soviet dispute was primarily ideological, each side accusing the other of deviating from true "Marxism-Leninism." Following the principles of Mao Zedong's "cultural revolution," China preached "liberation" of peoples everywhere through force rather than peaceful competition, as advocated by Moscow. After Mao's death in 1976, China's policy became less ideological and more pragmatic, emphasizing its role as a member of the "third world" rather than the Communist bloc. The general effect of this shift was a further step along the road of "socialist pluralism."

American soldiers in Korea.

COLD WAR OR COEXISTENCE?

While Russia's leadership in the Communist world was thus becoming a thing of the past, America's leadership in the Free World was likewise undergoing a change. As western Europe became once again a factor in world affairs, the role of the United States within the western alliance became more one of first among equals. As a result of these changes, the most clearly discernible trend in international relations during the 1960s and 1970s was the gradual shift away from the angry confrontations of the Cold War to an equally competitive but more peaceful state of coexistence.

The Korean War

Peaceful coexistence came only after a decade of intermittent sparring during the 1950s, in which each side felt out the strength of the other. The years immediately after 1950 brought to a climax the international tensions that had been building up since 1945. In the fall of 1950, United Nations forces fought their way into North Korea. But when victory seemed almost in sight, the Chinese Communists intervened and drove the UN forces back into South Korea. By the spring of 1951, the front had become stabilized along the thirty-eighth parallel, and there it substantially remained. Armistice negotiations were begun in 1951 and completed in 1953. The resulting armistice merely established an uneasy truce in which North Korean troops continued to face South Korean and American forces across a demilitarized zone.

Escalation in Both Camps

One of the effects of the Korean conflict was a substantial buildup of western military strength. The United States increased its military spending fivefold, doubled its armed forces, and extended its military bases abroad. During the Korean War NATO perfected its organization and increased its membership by adding Greece and Turkey. Plans were also made for adding West Germany. In 1952 the United States exploded its first hydrogen bomb, thus regaining its nuclear lead.

The change from a Democratic to a Republican administration in 1953 brought forth a man who was determined to use America's military strength not merely to contain but to challenge communism. Until his death in 1959, Secretary of State John Foster Dulles was the leading political strategist in the western camp. But his policy of "massive retaliation" and "brinkmanship" did not always have the support of America's allies, nor did it have the desired effect of scaring the Russians into making political concessions.

More decisive than the changing of the guard in Washington were the events touched off by Stalin's death in 1953. While the new Soviet rulers were consolidating their position at home, they adopted a more conciliatory policy abroad. At the same time, however, the Russian government announced its first testing of a hydrogen bomb. And while the West was rallying its forces behind NATO, the Soviets were lining up their eastern satellites behind the Warsaw Pact of 1955.

The Search for Coexistence

The first sign that Russia might be willing to negotiate East-West differences was seen in the Korean armistice, which would have been impossible without Soviet acquiescence. In January 1954 the foreign ministers of the United States, Britain, France, and the Soviet Union resumed their talks in Berlin after an interval of several years. In April the Geneva Conference on Far Eastern Affairs, with Communist China attending, temporarily divided Vietnam, where the French had recently been defeated by the Vietminh Communist insurgents. Elections for the whole of Vietnam were to be held in 1956, but these never took place.

The culmination of the initial search for coexistence came with the Geneva Summit of 1955. This was the first time since Potsdam, ten years earlier, that the heads of state had assembled. On the eve of the meeting, the Russians agreed to an Austrian peace treaty, another hopeful sign of growing Soviet moderation. Relations at Geneva were cordial, but the results of the conference were disappointing. On none of the major issues—German reunification, European security, and disarmament—was any understanding reached.

Mushroom cloud from a 1952 explosion of a hydrogen bomb in the Marshall Islands of the Pacific.

Continuation of the Cold War

While the "spirit of Geneva" appeared to have dissipated some of the suspicions of the Cold War, events in Southwest Asia soon showed that war to be far from over. President Nasser's nationalization of the Suez Canal in the summer of 1956 (see p. 997) was seen as a victory for Egypt and its backers in the Communist camp. The Soviet Union's reputation as a champion of anticolonialism, however, was immediately tarnished by its brutal intervention against the uprising in Hungary. Both the Suez crisis and the Hungarian revolution might have led to a major showdown had it not been for the fear of nuclear war.

The year 1957 was relatively peaceful. America's proclamation of the Eisenhower Doctrine served notice that the nation was ready to oppose the spread of Soviet influence in Southwest Asia. In the Soviet Union, meanwhile, Khrushchev emerged as the supreme leader of communism. The most spectacular event of the year, however, was the launching of Russia's first earth satellite, *Sputnik I.* This event proved that the Russians had rockets powerful enough to make a nuclear attack on the United States. The balance of power had apparently shifted in Russia's favor.

To the Brink of War

For the next five years the initiative in international affairs rested with the Soviet Union. The United States launched its first satellite, *Explorer I,* in 1958. But the Russians maintained their lead by placing heavier satellites in orbit. Continued Communist attempts to stir up trouble in Southwest Asia were foiled by American and British landings in Lebanon and Jordan in 1958. Next came a crisis in East Asia, where Chinese Communist attacks on the offshore islands of Quemoy and Matsu were halted only because America stood firmly by its Nationalist Chinese ally. In November 1958 the Soviet Union again challenged the western position in Berlin.

While East-West relations were thus being kept in a state of tension, there were feelers from both sides for another try at summit diplomacy, but the conference scheduled for 1960 never materialized. On the eve of the Paris meeting the Russians shot down an American U-2 reconnaissance plane over the Soviet Union. Eisenhower's refusal to make amends for this incident led Khrushchev to withdraw from the conference before it started.

There was much concern over the increasingly aggressive Soviet stance in foreign affairs. Besides trying to scare the United States into making concessions, Russia's policy was also influenced by the growing rift between Moscow and Beijing. Much of the conflict between the two was over the allegiance of nonaligned countries. It was to reassert his claim to leadership over world communism that Khrushchev delivered his boastful threats of "burying capitalism."

The advent of the Kennedy administration in 1961 at first seemed to bring a lessening of tension. The new president was faced by a perplexing array of foreign problems. In April 1961 the ill-fated Bay of Pigs invasion of Cuba—undertaken by anti-Castro refugees with American backing—was quickly suppressed by Castro's forces. In South Vietnam, meanwhile, Vietcong guerrillas, supported by Communist North Vietnam, were stepping up their "war of liberation." A similar war was going on between the Communist Pathet Lao and the government forces in Laos. The most serious problem Kennedy inherited, however, was the continued Russian demand for western withdrawal from Berlin. Here the Russians threatened to sign a peace treaty with the East Germans that would give the latter control over access to West Berlin. Only Kennedy's obvious determination to go to war rather than give in made Khrushchev finally back down. To stop the stream of refugees from East Germany into West Berlin, the Communists, in August 1961, built the Berlin Wall, which henceforth made East Germany a virtual prison.

There were other signs that negotiations might replace confrontations. In July 1962 a foreign ministers' conference in Geneva agreed on the formal neutralization of Laos. This, it was hoped, would calm the situation in Southeast Asia. But at the same time the Russians were involved in secret activities in Cuba that soon brought the United States and the Soviet Union to the very brink of war.

The Cuban crisis built up during the summer of 1962 as Washington learned about Russia's stepped-up military support for Castro. In September a Soviet-Cuban security treaty was announced. In October the United States gained proof that the Soviets had supplied Cuba with missiles capable of delivering nuclear warheads. President Kennedy imposed a strict blockade on further arms shipments to Cuba and demanded that all Soviet weapons be withdrawn and all missile bases dismantled. Faced with pressure from the United Nations and American threats of retaliation, Khrushchev backed down. The most serious confrontation of the Cold War was over.

East-West Détente

The Cuban crisis, surprisingly, ushered in the first genuine détente in the East-West conflict. To reduce the risk of accidental war, Washington and Moscow in early 1963 established a "hot line" of direct communication. In July 1963 the two powers, together with Great Britain, signed a Nuclear Test Ban Treaty outlawing all but underground tests. There were other agreements on minor issues. The détente did not at first resolve any of the major issues of the Cold War. The most serious crisis in the 1960s was the drawn-out war in Vietnam. The United States poured thousands of men and millions of dollars into a conflict that was not unlike the war in Korea. Just as in that earlier war, the United States perceived Communist China as the ultimate threat. But while at the time of Korea the Soviet Union, as leader of world communism, had been instrumental in helping end the war, such mediation was difficult now that Moscow's leadership was being challenged by Beijing.

But even the Vietnam War did not seriously alter the climate of coexistence. One of the more hopeful results of détente was the Nuclear Non-Proliferation Treaty of 1968, which tried to halt the spread of nuclear weapons. It was not only the fear of nuclear war that made peaceful coexistence appear preferable to warlike confrontation. Another factor was the loosening of ties within the eastern and western camps and the emergence of the nonaligned nations as a "third force" in world affairs. The trend toward "polycentrism," or many-centeredness, was also evident in the United Nations, where the new countries of Asia and Africa increasingly challenged the predominance of the superpowers.

The most dramatic moves toward a more pragmatic, nonideological foreign policy came in the 1970s. Most of

On the Brink of War

1962

Sunday, October 28, was a shining autumn day. At nine in the morning Khrushchev's answer began to come in. By the fifth sentence it was clear that he had thrown in his hand. Work would stop on the sites; the arms "which you described as offensive" would be crated and returned to the Soviet Union; negotiations would start at the UN. Then, no doubt to placate Castro, Khrushchev asked the United States to discontinue flights over Cuba. . . . Looking ahead, he said, "We should like to continue the exchange of views on the prohibition of atomic and thermonuclear weapons, general disarmament, and other problems relating to the relaxation of international tension." It was all over, and barely in time. If word had not come that Sunday, if work had continued on the bases, the United States would have had no real choice but to take action against Cuba the next week. No one could discern what lay darkly beyond an air strike or invasion, what measures and countermeasures, actions and reactions, might have driven the hapless world to the ghastly consummation. The President saw more penetratingly into the mists and terrors of the future than anyone else. A few weeks later he said, "If we had invaded Cuba . . . I am sure the Soviets would have acted. They would have to, just as we would have to. I think there are certain compulsions on any major power.". . . When Kennedy received Khrushchev's reply that golden October morning, he showed profound relief. Later he said, "This is the night to go to the theater, like Abraham Lincoln."

From Arthur M. Schlesinger, Jr., *A Thousand Days: John F. Kennedy in the White House* (Boston: Houghton Mifflin, 1965), p. 830.

the important events have already been noted: West Germany's improved relations with eastern Europe, President Nixon's historic visits to Moscow and Beijing; and the many instances of improved relations between other Communist and non-Communist countries. In 1972, a four-power treaty on Berlin removed another perennial source of friction by guaranteeing access to and easing communications within the city. American withdrawal from South Vietnam, while not ending the troubles, at least helped to ease the tensions in that part of the world.

But while an improved international climate thus helped solve or at least defuse some explosive issues, others continued and new ones arose. Arab-Israeli differences in the Holy Land and black-white confrontations in southern Africa remained a constant threat to peace in both areas. In an effort to limit the arms race, the United States and the Soviet Union in 1972 concluded the first Strategic Arms Limitation Treaty (SALT I); but efforts at further SALT talks in the late 1970s made slow progress. By that time a new issue had arisen, as President Carter began to criticize the Soviet Union and other regimes for violating the basic human rights guaranteed by the Helsinki Accords of 1975. Some Americans, pointing to the continued buildup of Russia's military forces, criticized détente for letting down America's guard; but others welcomed the feeling of relief that normalization of East-West relations had brought.

Détente or Disaster?

In the 1980s, détente still had far to go. There were no violent confrontations, but there were still many areas of disagreement between the United States and the Soviet Union. Only the fear of a nuclear catastrophe keeps these differences from escalating into war. In this latest phase of antagonistic coexistence, the Russians were still the aggressors. Their invasion of Afghanistan to aid a pro-Soviet regime was seen as an indication that the Soviet Union possessed the military superiority some critics of détente feared. Russia's pursuit of a hard line on Poland and its support of leftist movements in Africa and Central America further interfered with détente.

There was much verbal recrimination between the Americans and the Russians, but there were also frequent and serious talks. The issue that loomed largest was the nuclear arms race. Both sides controlled the most advanced nuclear weapons and the most perfected means of delivering them. The United States, fearing that the Russians held a quantitative advantage, aimed at catching up. It is unnecessary to go into the countless proposals and counterproposals for mutual arms reduction. Meanwhile the rivalry between the superpowers had reached a stage where the only choice was between détente or disaster.

At this point a new element entered the picture. The general public in the past had been mainly spectators in the sparring between the nuclear giants. This now changed, as sporadic antinuclear demonstrations grew into mass protests. This spontaneous fear of a nuclear disaster was more visible in the West; but there were signs of it also in the East. In 1985, the United States and the Soviet Union resumed their negotiations on the limitation and reduction of nuclear arms. But at the same time, each side continued to build up its forces, and the United States, with its "star wars" concept, added a whole new dimension to the nuclear contest. Successful arms limitation, moreover, will merely reduce the effects, but not the possibility, of a nuclear catastrophe.

Suggestions for Further Reading

The most reflective book on the postwar history of western Europe is J. L. Lukacs, *Decline and Rise of Europe* (1965). W. Laqueur, *Europe Since Hitler* (1970), is admirably comprehensive. On the search for European unity, see P. Scalingi, *The European Parliament: The Three-Decade Search for a United Europe* (1980). Europe's role in the East-West conflict is analyzed in A. W. DePorte, *Europe Between the Superpowers* (1979), and in A. Grosser, *The Western Alliance: European-American Relations Since 1945* (1980).

On the United States, there are numerous books on each administration, from Truman to Reagan. For a recent general overview, see R. Polenberg, *One Nation Divisible: Class, Race, and Ethnicity in the United States Since 1938* (1980). S. E. Ambrose, *The Rise to Globalism: American Foreign Policy Since 1938* (1971), is first-rate. On Canada, see N. L. Nicolson, *Canada in the American Community* (1963), and A. H. Malcolm, *The Canadians* (1985). For the southern hemisphere, see S. Clissold, *Latin America: New World, Third World* (1972).

Works on the communist world suffer from restricted access to sources. S. Bialer, *Stalin's Successors: Leadership, Stability, and Change in the Soviet Union* (1980), is a recent assessment. On Russia's satellites, see Z. K. Brzezinski, *The Soviet Bloc: Unity and Conflict* (1967). Two major crises among the satellites are discussed in J. Valenta, *Soviet Intervention in Czechoslovakia, 1968* (1981), and D. Singer, *The Road to Gdansk: Poland and the USSR* (1981). "Socialist pluralism" is treated in W. Leonhard, *Three Faces of Communism* (1974). A. B. Ulam, *The Rivals: America and Russia Since World War II* (1972), is an excellent survey. See also, A. Z. Rubinstein, *Soviet Foreign Policy Since World War II* (1981). On the most crucial issue in Soviet-American relations, W. Epstein, *The Last Chance: Nuclear Proliferation and Arms Control* (1976), and A. Myrdal, *The Game of Disarmament: How the United States and Russia Run the Arms Race* (1977), stress the mortal dangers of the arms race.

	1914				1950	
SOUTHWEST ASIA AND AFRICA	**1923** Kemal Attatürk, President of Turkish Republic			**1948** *Apartheid* in South Africa **1948** Founding of Israel, first Arab-Israeli war	**1954** Nasser takes control in Egypt **1956** Second Arab-Israeli war **1960–75** Independence movement sweeps Africa	**1967** Third Arab-Israeli (Six-Day) war **1971** Indo-Pakistani war **1973** Fourth Arab-Israeli war
EUROPE	**1914–18** World War I **1917** Bolshevik Revolution **1919** Paris Peace Conference	**1920** Keynes, *The Economic Consequences of the Peace* **1922** Mussolini's March on Rome **1923** French occupation of Ruhr	**1924** Death of Lenin, rise of Stalin **1924–25** Adolf Hitler, *Mein Kampf* **1924–29** Era of Locarno **1933** Hitler becomes Chancellor	**1935** Nuremburg Laws against Jews **1936–39** Spanish Civil War **1938** Munich Conference **1939** Hitler-Stalin Pact	**1939–44** World War II **1940** Fall of France **1941** Germany invades Russia **1941–45** Mass murder of Jews **1945** Yalta Conference	**1947** Marshall Plan **1949** Germany divided **1949** NATO Alliance **1953** Death of Stalin **1955** West Germany joins NATO **1955** Warsaw Pact
SOUTH AND SOUTHEAST ASIA	**1920–22** Gandhi's first Civil Disobedience Movement	**1927** Indonesian Nationalist party founded by Sukarno **1930** Gandhi's March to the Sea		**1947** Independence of India and Pakistan **1948** Mahatma Gandhi assassinated	**1949** Independence of Indonesia **1955** Bandung Conference, Indonesia	
EAST ASIA	**1927–37** Nationalist regime in Nanjing **1931** Japan seizes Manchuria **1934** Long March of Chinese Communists	**1937–45** Sino-Japanese War	**1941** Japan attacks Pearl Harbor **1945** Atomic bombing of Hiroshima and Nagasaki **1946–49** Civil war in China	**1949** People's Republic of China **1949–76** Mao Zedong's Chinese Revolution	**1950–53** Korean War **1951** US peace treaty with Japan	
THE AMERICAS AND PACIFIC	**1917** US enters World War I	**1929** The Great Depression begins **1933** Franklin D. Roosevelt's New Deal	**1941** US enters World War II **1945** First atomic bomb **1945** United Nations organized	**1946** First electronic computer **1947** Truman Doctrine **1948** Transistor invented	**1959** Fidel Castro's victory in Cuba **1962** Cuban Missile Crisis **1963** President Kennedy assassinated	**1968** Martin Luther King, Jr., assassinated **1969** Neil Armstrong, first man on moon

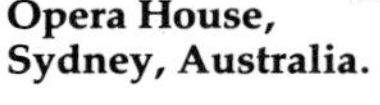

Opera House, Sydney, Australia.

British recruiting poster, World War I.

Apollo 11 lands men on moon, July 16, 1969.

Signers of Egyptian-Israeli peace treaty: Sadat, Carter, Begin, 1979.

Official symbol of the United Nations.

German inflation: two billion mark note, 1929.

1985	
1977 President Sadat visits Jerusalem **1978** Camp David Accords **1979** USSR invades Afghanistan **1979** Revolution in Iran	**1980–** Iran-Iraq war **1980** Black majority rule in Zimbabwe (Rhodesia) **1981** President Sadat assassinated
1957 First earth satellite, USSR **1957** European Economic Community	**1960** Yuri Gagarin, first man in space **1980** Solidarity movement in Poland
1961 Increasing US involvement in Vietnam	**1973** US forces withdraw from South Vietnam **1975** Communists take over Vietnam, Laos, Cambodia
1971 People's Republic of China joins UN **1972** Nixon visits Beijing **1976** Death of Mao Zedong	**1977** China begins liberalizing under Deng Xiaoping
1974 President Nixon resigns **1975** Helsinki Accords **1977** Panama Canal Treaty	**1979** Civil war begins in Nicaragua and El Salvador **1982** Falkland Islands War

Striking Solidarity union workers, Warsaw, Poland, 1981.

Emperor Hirohito of Japan, 1926.

46 The "Third World"

Many historians object to the term "third world" as being too sweeping, vague, or even condescending. It means different things in different contexts. In politics, it often refers to powers that are nonaligned with either the United States or the Soviet Union; in economics, it denotes nations that are still underdeveloped, in contrast to the world's highly industrialized countries, including the Soviet Union; historically, most of the third world was once colonized by the former great powers; and geographically, many of the third world's people inhabit the southern part of the globe. This overlapping of criteria makes any concise definition of the term "third world" impossible. Yet the term has won sufficient currency to justify its use to describe the world beyond Europe and North America.

One of the most revolutionary developments since the Second World War was the liberation of all the world's former colonial territories. This independence movement had already begun in the years between the two world wars. It was hastened by the weakening of the mother countries in the Second World War and the subsequent rivalry between the free and Communist worlds. Although the various native revolts differed from country to country, they all had one thing in common—intense opposition to any form of colonialism. Some of the new nations took sides in the Cold War, but most of them preferred a "neutralist" stand. The most urgent need for all was economic and technical assistance. At first, most of this aid came from the United States. But in time the other industrialized nations of the West as well as the Soviet Union and Communist China began to set up foreign aid programs and compete for the allegiance of these uncommitted regions.

THE END OF COLONIALISM IN SOUTH ASIA

The first major additions to the nations of the third world came with the partition of the subcontinent of India in 1947 into the independent states of India and Pakistan (see pp. 899–901). Although both were republics, they continued as members of the (British) Commonwealth. India was predominantly Hindu and Pakistan mostly Muslim. In the process of separating the two religions, many bloody riots broke out. India and Pakistan also clashed repeatedly over the northern state of Kashmir, to which both laid claim. In addition, there were intermittent border incidents between India and Communist China.

India

The Republic of India was by far the more important of the two states. The new nation suffered a tragic loss in 1948, when its political leader, Mohandas K. Gandhi, was assassinated by a religious fanatic. The task of guiding India through its formative years fell to Gandhi's disciple, Jawaharlal Nehru, leader of the ruling Congress party. India's main problems were economic. The only way to support its huge population was through long-range development of the country's abundant natural resources with outside aid. India's dependence on such aid from all sides, together with its closeness to the centers of communism and its recent experience with western imperialism, led to a neutralist stand on most international issues. With Nehru's death in 1964, domestic affairs became less stable, especially under his daughter, Indira Gandhi, who became prime minister in 1966. Whatever economic growth the country experienced was neutralized by its high birthrate, despite costly birth-control programs. Periodic famines, epidemics, and riots between Hindus and Muslims, together with a renewed Indo-Pakistani clash in 1971, led to a permanent state of crisis.

In 1971, India veered away from its nonalignment by signing a treaty of friendship with the Soviet Union. This was followed two years later by an economic and trade agreement. In 1974, the world was startled by the explosion of a nuclear device, showing that India was ready to join the nuclear club. Meanwhile Prime Minister Indira Gandhi, who had been accused of illegal activities in connection with her reelection, became increasingly authoritarian, declaring a state of emergency, arresting political opponents, and suspending civil liberties. With Mrs. Gandhi's electoral defeat in 1977, constitutional government was restored.

Colonial Nationalism

The West, having sown its own national wild oats in the past, is now sometimes inclined to look with a combination of dismay and superior wisdom on the upstart countries which assert an allegedly anachronistic desire to follow the same course. . . . However great the disenchantment of Europe with nationalism, the colonial nationalist is little likely to be persuaded by an argument so easily identifiable with the interest of the West in maintaining some facsimile of its older relationships in a world swiftly sliding out of its grasp. . . . Even if it be conceded that nationalism fails to furnish the foundations for an acceptable world order and has outlived its usefulness for the advanced, thoroughly "nationalized," countries of the West . . . it has by no means exhausted its contribution to the development of the non-Western peoples. Nationalism . . . has a chronology of its own derived not from the calendar but from the stages of the gradually spreading impact of the revolution which originated in Western Europe. . . . One can plausibly argue that in the different but related stages of the cycle in which Asia and Africa are now engaged nationalism intrudes itself not only with an aura of inevitability but also as the bearer of positive goods.

From Rupert Emerson, *From Empire to Nation: The Rise to Self-Assertion of Asian and African Peoples* (Cambridge, Mass.: Harvard University Press, 1960), p. 379.

The departure of Prime Minister Gandhi from the national scene, however, was only temporary. Her successor, Morarji R. Desai, was initially quite successful, especially abroad, where he drew close to the United States under President Carter. But economic problems at home and disarray within his own Janata party cut short his tenure, and in 1980 Mrs. Gandhi staged a spectacular comeback. There were continued problems—bureaucratic inefficiency and corruption, party strife, social unrest, and religious violence. But India's economy was on the upswing, despite the energy crisis and continued rise in population. In 1984, Mrs. Gandhi was assassinated by Sikh terrorists, a religious minority. She was succeeded by her son, Rajiv Gandhi, who vouched to follow in his mother's footsteps. In its foreign policy, India tried to steer a middle course between the superpowers, leaning now in one, now in the other direction, especially on the issue of Afghanistan. With a population of 700 million, India is the world's largest democracy. It ranks as the tenth industrial nation and has the world's fourth largest army. It is clearly a major power.

Pakistan

In contrast to India, popular government in the Islamic Republic of Pakistan was much slower in taking root. Like India, Pakistan suffered a serious loss in 1948, when its outstanding leader, Mohammed Ali Jinnah, died. The country's economy was mainly agricultural, and trade with India, its natural market, suffered from political tensions. Economic difficulties in turn led to political instability. When democracy was no longer able to cope with bureaucratic inefficiency and corruption, the head of Pakistan's armed

Prime Minister Indira Gandhi with her son, Rajiv, who succeeded her after she was assassinated in 1985.

South and East Asia Since the Second World War

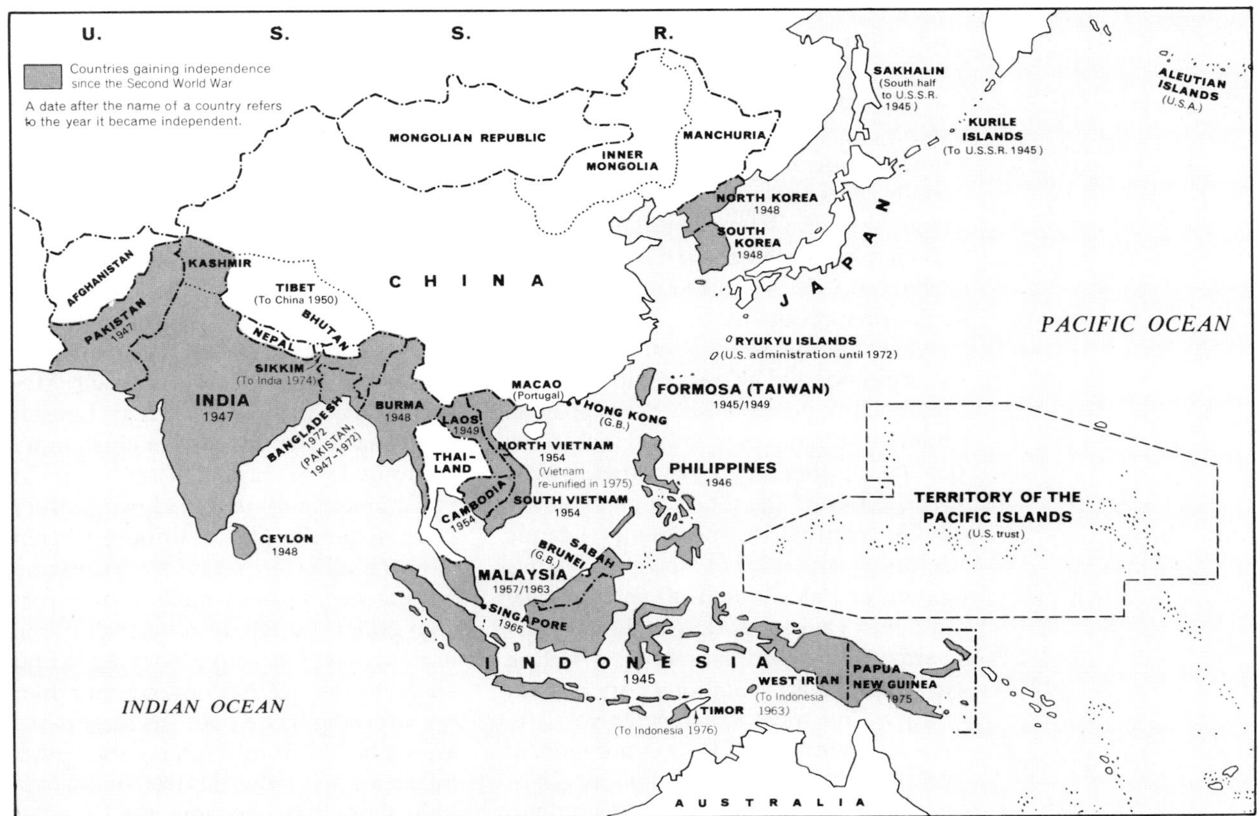

forces, General Ayub Khan, took over and ruled as virtual dictator from 1958 to 1969. Pakistan's foreign policy, at first firmly prowestern, during the 1960s became increasingly neutralist in an effort to attract aid and trade from both sides.

One of Pakistan's major difficulties derived from the fact that it consisted of two parts, separated by a thousand miles of Indian territory. Relations between the two regions were far from smooth; the more numerous and poverty-stricken Bengalis of East Pakistan felt exploited by the affluent and influential Punjabis of West Pakistan. The only bond between the two peoples was their common Muslim religion. Differences between East and West Pakistan came to a head in 1971, when civil war broke out between Bengali and government forces, leading first to the defeat of the Bengalis and then, after intervention by India, to the defeat of West Pakistan. East Pakistan now seceded, taking the name of Bangladesh. In 1972 the new nation signed a treaty of friendship with India, and in 1974 it was recognized by (West) Pakistan. The latter was now headed by Prime Minister Zulfikar Ali Bhutto, who valiantly tried to cope with Pakistan's economic backwardness under a new democratic constitution. In 1977, Bhutto was ousted by the army, whose chief of staff, General Mohammad Zia ul-Haq, proclaimed martial law to help overcome the country's political and economic problems.

The regime of General Zia, which was intended to be only temporary, remained in power into the 1980s. Its main problem was to find a viable form of representative government. Zia, who assumed the office of president in 1978, instituted a number of Islamic reforms, which led to increased Islamization of Pakistan's legal and political system. These reforms included barbaric criminal punishments, resulting in numerous violations of human rights. The most spectacular was the execution in 1979 of former premier Ali Bhutto for the murder of a political opponent while he was in office. Under a new provisional constitution of 1981, an appointive Federal Council was set up to give at least the appearance of popular participation in government. Economically, Pakistan has fared better under President Zia's rule. Much of this improvement was due to foreign aid, especially from the United States. America views Pakistan as a potential supporter in its conflicts with Iran and with the Soviet Union over Afghanistan. Still, Pakistan tries to follow a course of nonalignment. Relations between Pakistan and India continued to be watchful, although both sides have made efforts to allay tension. Pakistan's main problems continued to be domestic — with political repression leading to protests of increasing violence and the continuation of military dictatorship.

Bangladesh

Compared to India and Pakistan, the People's Republic of Bangladesh played only a minor role in the affairs of South Asia. The first ten years following its independence in 1971 were characterized by political and economic instability. The leading figure during this period was General Ziaur Rahman, who ruled under martial law since 1975 and became president in 1977. Elections in 1978 and 1979 further aided transition to civilian rule. When Ziaur was assassinated in 1981, Vice-President Abdus Sattar succeeded, as provided by the constitution. But in 1982 the army once again interfered, with General Hossein Mohammad Ershad declaring himself chief martial administrator. Instability continued.

Economically, Bangladesh is very poor, depending on continuous foreign aid to maintain its rapidly increasing population of ninety million. In its foreign policy, Bangladesh belongs to the nonaligned bloc, active in trying to find ways for the rich nations to share their resources with the poor. Its closest ties are with Communist China and India. Relations with the Soviet Union, initially close, have become less so, especially after the government of Bangladesh criticized the Soviet invasion of Afghanistan.

Afghanistan

The Democratic Republic of Afghanistan is one of the least developed countries in the world. It deserves mention here chiefly as the latest scene of Soviet aggression. Russia's efforts to gain influence over Afghanistan go back to the early nineteenth century. After the First World War, the kingdom of Afghanistan still retained its sovereignty, and during the 1920s it maintained cordial relations with the Soviet Union. After a dormant period, when Russia was preoccupied with events in Europe, the Soviets in the mid-1950s again turned their attention to Afghanistan, establishing economic and military ties. In 1973, a coup of military officers, influenced by Russia, overthrew the monarchy and set up a leftist government. Subsequent coups in 1978 and 1979, openly directed by the Soviets, brought in more pliable Marxist leaders. The last, Babrak Karmal, was installed as president by a Soviet invasion force in 1979.

One reason why the Soviets thus openly abandoned détente was to challenge American influence in the Indian Ocean, while the United States was involved with Iran; in addition, Afghanistan had large natural resources; and finally, Russia's drive was merely the latest phase in its century-old encroachment on Afghanistan. Soviet involvement, however, did not achieve its purpose. Widespread popular resistance to the Marxist government of Babrak Karmal necessitated the deployment of large numbers of Soviet troops. At the same time, the Soviet Union was accused of aggression by most of the rest of the world and was asked to withdraw its forces.

THE EMERGENCE OF COMMUNIST CHINA

The most significant development in the emergence of a third world was the return of China as a major factor in world affairs. The People's Republic of China was founded in 1949 (see pp. 895–99). Its government at that time was closely modeled on that of the Soviet Union. As in Russia, all power in China rested with the Communist party and its leader, Mao Zedong (Mao Tse-tung). Under the constitution of 1954, the main task of the state was "to bring about, step by step, the socialist industrialization of the country," a goal that was to be achieved in several Five-Year Plans. As was the case in other underdeveloped nations, the rapid increase in China's production resulted in some impressive achievements. Symbolic of the country's scientific and technical achievements was the detonation of its first atomic bomb in 1964, followed by a hydrogen bomb in 1967.

The Mao Zedong Era

In the long run it was only through industrialization that China could solve its most pressing problem of too many people and too little land. With an estimated yearly population growth of more than sixteen million, the one-billion mark would be reached by 1990. Yet the backbone of the Chinese economy was still agriculture, and the government tried by every possible means to boost agricultural production. The second Five-Year Plan of 1958 called for a "great leap forward" in both agriculture and industry. The population was organized in gigantic "people's communes" including as many as one hundred thousand persons and embracing farms and factories.

But the "great leap" not only failed to reach its goals, it actually brought a decline in production. The cause for this failure was seen in the continued moderation of many leading officials. To purge Chinese communism of these "revisionist" elements, another sweeping revolutionary movement was initiated in the 1960s, the "great proletarian cultural revolution." Spearheaded by younger members of the party, the "Maoist" revolution re-

Mao Zedong with steel workers (1959).

Deng Xiaoping during his trip to Washington, D.C. (1979).

pudiated traditional cultural values, emphasized collectivization and austerity, and elevated the figure of Mao Zedong to unprecedented heights of personal adulation. Through indoctrination, brainwashing, and terror China hoped to produce the most regimented society the world had ever seen. At first, these drastic measures aggravated rather than solved China's economic problems. But eventually the discipline and industry of the Chinese people did achieve new high levels of production and make China a major economic power.

As a result of these achievements, the pace of China's development became less hectic as time went on. In 1976 Mao Zedong died, and his more radical followers, including his widow, were purged in favor of a more moderate faction, headed by the new Chairman of the Communist party, Hua Guofeng.

China under Deng Xiaoping

The leading figure in China's domestic and foreign affairs since then was Deputy Premier Deng Xiaoping. Temporarily ousted under Mao, he was rehabilitated in 1977 and he soon became active in party reform, economic liberalization, and the improvement of China's relations with the capitalist nations of the West, especially the United States. In 1980, one of his supporters, Zhao Ziyang, an economic planner, replaced Hua Guofeng as Premier, and in 1981, Hua's position as Chairman was taken over by Hu Yaobang. These new leaders followed a more pragmatic and flexible policy, free from the ideological restrictions of Maoism. In 1978, a new constitution emphasized civil rights, and at subsequent party meetings Mao's "cultural revolution" was severely criticized. A further outlet for popular dissent, however, the "democracy wall," where individuals could proclaim their views without censorship, was soon again curbed.

China's foremost concern continued to be with economic modernization. Under a new Ten-Year Plan, agriculture was further improved through mechanization, stepped-up fertilizer production, and experimentation with high-yield seeds. Various incentives to peasants and communes resulted in overall food increases, but continued population growth prevented a simultaneous rise in per capita consumption. Efforts to curb the problem of population increase have culminated in an official one-child-per-family policy, more successful in urban areas than in the countryside. In the industrial area, the new plan called for a doubling of annual steel production, substantial increases in coal mining, where China ranks third among the world's producers, and the further exploration of oil resources, which provide a valuable

Time Bomb or Myth: The Population Problem

After centuries of steady acceleration, overall growth rates during the last decade and a half have turned downward. This decline in the rate of population growth has led many observers to believe that the world in general, and most individual countries as well, no longer face serious population problems and, therefore, that efforts to deal with such problems can be relaxed. . . . But this assessment is simply wrong. The fertility change which has occurred during the last decade or two has been very uneven. In particular, the statistical decline for the developing countries as a whole, and indeed for the world, is heavily skewed by the special experience of China. In many other parts of the developing world, including much of Africa, a large part of South Asia, and some countries of Latin America, no measurable or significant drop in fertility has occurred. . . .

India will more than double in the next 45 years, becoming almost 40 percent larger than China is today. Bangladesh in the same time will have nearly tripled and will have 259 million people jammed into an area, alternately swept by flood and drought, the size of the state of Wisconsin. Mexico, which today has the most rapidly growing labor force of any large country in the world, will more than double in size. And Kenya, in which 17 million people are already putting heavy pressure on the limited supply of arable land, will have quintupled. The total population of developing countries as a group, 3.3 billion in 1980, will rise to over seven billion by 2025, and to over 8.5 billion by 2050. Of this total, Africa's population will be 2.3 billion, representing a tenfold increase during the course of the preceding 100 years. A century from now the world's population will total about 11 billion. So much, then, for the supposed end of the population explosion.

Robert S. McNamara, "Time Bomb or Myth: The Population Problem," *Foreign Affairs,* vol. 62, no.5 (Summer 1984), pp. 1112, 1115.

World Population

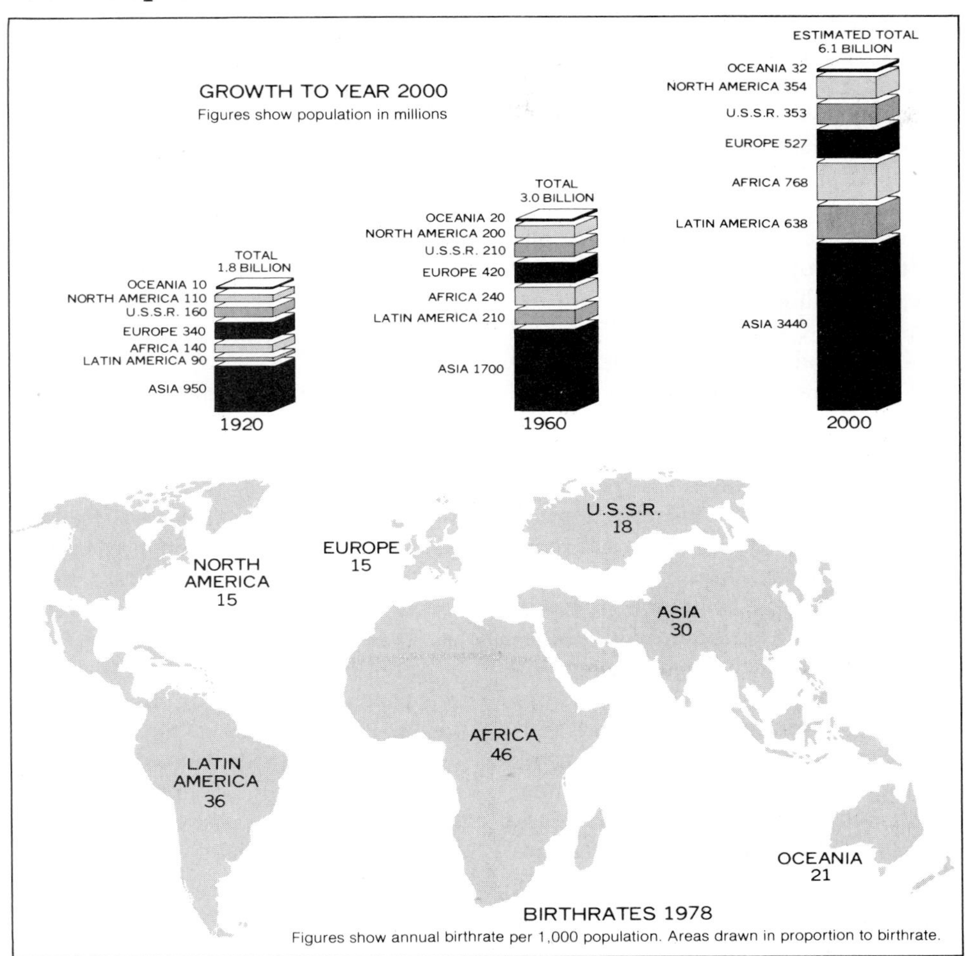

BIRTHRATES 1978
Figures show annual birthrate per 1,000 population. Areas drawn in proportion to birthrate.

export commodity. Another major source for exports is the country's growing textile industry. Despite spectacular growth, China's economy still depends on foreign investments and technical assistance. The shift toward liberalization at home thus also called for a parallel liberalization of China's policy abroad.

China's Foreign Policy

In foreign affairs, Communist China was at first deeply anti-American. The two countries were on opposite sides in the Korean War and in most other conflicts in Asia. Washington's support of the Chinese Nationalists in Taiwan, its alliance with Japan, and its refusal to recognize Beijing (Peking) were major targets for Communist attacks. This situation changed dramatically in 1972, when the United States, having abandoned its opposition to Communist China's membership in the United Nations the year before, reciprocated Chinese feelers for normalization of relations and President Nixon visited Beijing. Full diplomatic relations between the two countries were not established until 1979, after the United States had abrogated its defense treaty with Taiwan. The following year, when the Sino-Soviet alliance of 1950 ran out, it was not renewed.

Relations between China and the Soviet Union, initially very close, had become increasingly hostile. In 1969 the two countries had actually waged a brief border war. Ten years later, when

China invaded Vietnam and the Soviets invaded Afghanistan, each protested the aggression of the other. China's global strategy was to seek a "united front" with the second and third worlds as well as the United States against the Soviet Union. In 1978, China and Japan concluded a treaty of peace and friendship, and economic relations with Japan and western Europe were very active.

In its dealings with third world nations, China during the 1950s and 1960s had alternated between kindness and threats. There were repeated clashes along the borders with India, Burma, and Nepal, and Tibetan resistance to communization was ruthlessly suppressed. As relations with the Soviet Union worsened, China's attitude toward the third world came to be guided by national rather than ideological motives, supporting non-Communist countries, like Pakistan and Egypt, that opposed the Soviet Union and opposing Communist countries, like Vietnam and Cuba, that supported the Russians. Given its economic potential and its anti-Soviet alignment, the People's Republic of China occupied a special position within the third world.

THE NATIONS OF THE PACIFIC

There are several other countries in East Asia and the Pacific — Taiwan, the Philippines, and the two Koreas — that are part of the third world.

Taiwan

The "Republic of China" was founded when Generalissimo Chiang Kai-shek retreated to Taiwan in 1949. After his death in 1975, his son, Chiang Ching-kuo, succeeded him as head of state and of the leading Kuomintang or Nationalist party. The keynotes of Taiwan's domestic policy have been economic growth and political stability. The effects of the oil crisis and growing dissatisfaction with one-party rule caused occasional unrest, but never a serious crisis. The main concern has been over Taiwan's international role. As the United States established close relations with Communist China, a Chinese invasion of Taiwan became a possibility. Washington at the time warned that such an act would be "of grave concern to the United States"; but Beijing asserted that Taiwan's relations with the "motherland" were entirely a Chinese internal affair.

The Philippines

Taiwan's neighbor, the Republic of the Philippines, is in a far less fortunate position as far as economic development and political stability are concerned. More than half of its fifty million people live in dire poverty and its economy depends heavily on foreign loans. Since gaining its independence in 1946, the Philippines has been plagued by constant civil, ethnic, and religious unrest, causing thousands of deaths. The country is kept from utter chaos by the "constitutional authoritarianism" of President Ferdinand Marcos, who assumed power in 1965 and imposed martial law in 1972. His undemocratic and repressive regime has been accused of economic corruption and political fraud. There are a number of opposition parties and a large guerrilla force, the New People's Army. The main support of Marcos has come from the United States, which maintains some seventeen thousand troops on its twenty-two military bases in the Philippines and has more than $3 billion invested there. With so much at stake, the United States seems ready to overlook the gross violations of human and civil rights of which the Marcos regime has been accused.

South Korea

In its close ties to the United States, the Republic of Korea is not unlike the Philippines or, for that matter, Taiwan. Under a mutual defense treaty of 1953, America in 1982 still had thirty-eight thousand troops stationed in Korea. Economically Korea, thanks to large-scale American aid, has made considerable strides since the Korean War thirty years ago. Its main problems have been with the unequal distribution of wealth. The early years of the new republic were dominated by its first President, Syngman Rhee, who was elected in 1948 and resigned in 1960, in the face of growing disorders. The following year General Park Chung Hee staged a coup. His rule, while economically beneficial, became increasingly authoritarian. Under a new constitution in 1972, Park assumed the presidency for life and stepped up repression of the growing opposition, especially among intellectuals and students. In 1979, Park was assassinated by the director of his own Central Intelligence Agency. His place, after another coup, was taken by General Chun Doo Hwan who, under a new constitution, had himself elected president for a seven-year term. Chun enjoyed the support of the Reagan administration, despite reports of continued unrest and violations of human rights.

North Korea

While all the nations discussed in this section thus far have closely tended toward the United States, the other part of Korea, while dependent on its Communist neighbors for economic and military support, has tried to steer a more nonaligned course. The Democratic People's Republic of Korea for close to forty years has been ruled by its Communist party under the "Great Leader Comrade Kim Il Sung." Like Mao Zedong, Kim has been the center of a personality cult bordering on deification, and to insure continuity and stability, his eldest son, Kim Jong Il, has been groomed for succession. North Korea's economy, highly centralized and strictly planned, has made much progress on its own, and its hardworking people enjoy a satisfactory standard of living. There are no official relations with the United States, and relations with the Soviet Union have been closer than with China. The North Koreans, however, have refused to take sides in the Sino-Soviet dispute. Occasional proposals from one or the other of the two Koreas for reunification have failed to find a satisfactory solution.

Japan

The most important among the nations of the western Pacific, Japan is clearly not a member of the third world. As one of the leading economic powers, it rather belongs to the industrialized second world. Because of its geographic location, however, and its importance in East Asian affairs, it seems justified to include Japan in our discussion here.

Japan regained its full sovereignty in the peace treaty signed in 1951. At that time the divine monarchy of Emperor Hirohito had already been transformed into a democratic government. The most influential figure in early postwar reconstruction was General Douglas MacArthur as America's military governor. With one brief interruption, Japan has been ruled by the moderate Liberal Democratic party. Because of its rapid industrialization, the country has suffered from the usual problems of massive urbanization, housing shortages, air and water pollution, and such. There have been occasional disturbances, especially among students and the parties of the left. But the majority of Japanese — well-trained, highly disciplined, and hardworking — have been willing instruments in their country's miraculous economic growth.

In its foreign policy, Japan has been a close ally of the United States. Under a Treaty of Mutual Cooperation and Security, concluded in 1960 and extended in 1970, the United States guaranteed Japan's defense in return for continued bases there. Under the constitution of 1946, Japan forswore any military force of its own, but it later developed a 240,000-man self-defense force. The United States would like to see a still greater contribution to common defense. The main problems between the two countries have been economic: the increasingly unfavorable balance of American trade vis-à-vis Japan. Efforts to improve the situation through voluntary restraints on the part of Japan have been only partly successful.

Relations with the Soviet Union have been correct rather than cordial. Diplomatic ties were resumed in 1956, but continued Soviet occupation of the Kuril Islands, added to traditional rivalries, has prevented closer relations. In dealing with its other Asian neighbors, Japan has followed a policy of trade and aid, in an effort to eradicate the memories of Japanese aggression in the Second World War. Relations with China were resumed in 1972 and a treaty of friendship was signed in 1978. In its ceaseless search for markets and access to raw materials, the major concerns of Japan have been with economic rather than military security.

SOUTHEAST ASIA

The region east of India and south of China saw more political changes after the Second World War than any other part of Asia. Prior to 1945 only Thailand (Siam) was fully independent. In the years that followed, Burma, Indonesia, Vietnam, Laos, Cambodia, Malaysia, and Singapore gained their sovereignty. Southeast Asia was a wealthy region, producing most of the world's natural rubber, and more than half its tin and rice. Like all third world areas, Southeast Asia was predominantly agricultural; but except for Indonesia, it did not suffer from overpopulation. Despite its rich natural resources, the living standard of the region was very low. What Southeast Asia needed was a better-balanced regional economy with more varied commodities and increased industrialization.

Ho Chi Minh, Vietnamese Nationalist leader and president of North Vietnam (1954).

Vietnam, Laos, and Cambodia (Kampuchea)

With the exception of Thailand, every country of Southeast Asia experienced Communist revolts of varying severity. In the countries that formerly made up French Indo-China — Vietnam, Laos, and Cambodia — Communist takeovers were finally successful after drawn-out and bloody civil wars.

The most important of these countries, Vietnam, owed its liberation from French colonial rule to the veteran Communist leader Ho Chi Minh and his independence movement, the Vietminh. The final defeat of French forces came in 1954 with the battle of Dien Bien Phu. The same year a conference in Geneva divided Vietnam at the seventeenth parallel, calling for reunification after elections in 1956.

These elections were never held. In 1955 a non-Communist nationalist, Ngo Dinh Diem, established a Republic of (South) Vietnam. He had strong American support, but his repressive regime was opposed by the Communist Viet Cong, supplied from the North. As time went on, American personnel increased from a few hundred to half a million men. In 1963 a military coup, supported by the United States, killed Diem, in the vain hope of setting up a more popular regime. Beginning in 1965, major bombing attacks were launched against North Vietnam. But American involvement prolonged rather than resolved the Vietnam conflict. In the light of mounting criticism at home and abroad, President Nixon in 1969 began a policy of gradual withdrawal. A peace settlement was finally reached in 1973, and two years later Vietnam had become reunited under Communist rule.

Ho Chi Minh had died in 1969 and his position taken over by a system of collective leadership, in which Pham Van Dong, premier in Hanoi since 1955, and Le Duan, first secretary of the Vietnam Communist party, were prominent. The Socialist Republic of Vietnam since 1975 has found its going more and more difficult. Ambitious plans to improve its economy required massive foreign aid, but such aid was curtailed because of Vietnam's intervention against Laos and Cambodia, and the expulsion from Vietnam of large numbers of refugees, the "boat

Refused permission to settle in Malaysia, these "boat people" are set adrift on the South China Sea (1979).

people," mostly Chinese. In retaliation, China in 1978 terminated its aid and in 1979 briefly invaded Vietnam.

The other two states of Indochina, Laos and Cambodia, were significant chiefly as pawns in a power struggle between Vietnam and the Soviet Union on the one hand, and Thailand and Communist China on the other. Both countries had traditionally been buffers between Vietnam and Thailand. After gaining control over all of Vietnam in 1975, the government of Pham Van Dong ousted the fanatic Communist regime of the Khmer Rouge under Pol Pot in Cambodia, using Laos as a staging area. The Khmer Rouge, moving into Thailand, helped rekindle the old conflict between that country and Vietnam. To China and to a lesser extent the United States, the Vietnamization of Indochina appeared as a further step in the expansion of Soviet power in Asia.

The Association of Southeast Asian Nations (ASEAN)

To counteract the spread of communism in Southeast Asia, the non-Communist nations of the area took various countermeasures. Some of them joined the Southeast Asia Treaty Organization (SEATO), of which the United States was a member. It was established in 1954 for mutual defense against aggression and subversion, but did not prove very effective and was dissolved again in 1977. The Association of Southeast Asian Nations (ASEAN), a nonmilitary alliance of Indonesia, Malaysia, Thailand, Singapore, and the Philippines, formed in 1967, was more useful. Its members cooperated on international, political, and economic issues, and in 1979 ASEAN protested Vietnam's invasion of Cambodia.

In looking at the individual nations of Southeast Asia, we find a wide variety of political and economic problems that defy generalizations. The largest country is Indonesia, with some 13,000 islands and more than 150 million people. The Republic of Indonesia proclaimed its independence in 1945, after more than three centuries of Dutch rule. The leading figure during its first two decades was President Achmed Sukarno, whose "guided democracy" was but a thinly veiled and not always benevolent dictatorship. Economic difficulties at home and intermittent clashes with the new federation of Malaysia abroad finally led to Sukarno's ouster by the army in 1966 and his replacement as president by General Suharto, army chief of staff. While Sukarno had been moving closer to Communist China, Suharto followed a policy of nonalignment and closer relations with the non-Communist members of ASEAN. His "new order" program of austerity and economic development depended heavily on Western aid, mostly from the United States. Suharto's several reelections provided political stability, but Indonesia's economic situation, despite its vast natural resources, especially oil, remained precarious.

Among the remaining nations of Southeast Asia, the Kingdom of Thailand holds a unique position. Never having been subject to colonial rule, it is a constitutional monarchy with a king who is revered but has little power. In the last forty years, the country has seen a succession of more or less corrupt military regimes. Constitutional changes in 1979 reconfirmed the power of the prime minister, usually a general, but increased his dependence on elected civilian representatives. Thailand's economy remains largely agricultural. Industrialization has brought a high living standard to urban Thailand, but the majority of its forty-eight million people are still farmers.

Thailand's overriding concern in recent years has been with foreign affairs. Up to 1975, economic and military relations with the United States had been close. This changed with the collapse of South Vietnam. Thailand now established diplomatic relations with China and American forces were asked to withdraw. Incursions of large numbers of refugees from Laos, Cambodia, and Vietnam in the late 1970s, and clashes with Vietnamese forces along the Thailand-Cambodian frontier, once again strengthened Thailand's ties with the United States. Vastly outnumbered by seasoned Vietnamese forces, Thailand depends on American and Chinese aid to hold its own.

SOUTHWEST ASIA IN THE "THIRD WORLD"

Our discussion of events in East Asia since the Second World War has shown the term "third world" to be quite vague at best. It describes nations that vary so widely in economic development and political orientation that it is difficult to find common terms to describe them. To call them "less developed countries," as some authors euphemistically do, covers too wide a range, as does the term "nonaligned." The latter, as we have seen, applies to very few Asian countries. These ambiguities we must keep in mind as we turn to the nations of Southwest Asia and their position in the third world.

Arab Nationalism

One of the most turbulent scenes of rebellion against western influence after the Second World War was the mostly Arab nations of Southwest Asia, the area bridging Asia and Africa, from Egypt in the west to Iran in the east. Before 1945, the only independent Arab states were Egypt, Saudi Arabia, Yemen, and Iraq. Since then all the rest have won their freedom. Most of the region was extremely backward and desperately poor. But it was also of great strategic importance; it contained half the world's oil resources; and it was the religious center of hundreds of millions of Arab and non-Arab Muslims. Outwardly, the Arab world was united by its opposition to foreign domination and its resentment of Israel. But below the surface there were many divisive forces. To present a united front to the outside world, the Arab nations in 1945 organized the Arab League. But behind this front, Arab differences persisted.

To meet the threat posed by Communist support of Arab nationalism, Britain, Turkey, Iran, Iraq, and Pakistan in 1955 signed the Baghdad Pact. When Iraq dropped out of the alliance in 1958, a new Central Treaty Organization (CENTO) was formed. It included the United States, which, under the "Eisenhower Doctrine" of 1957, had already promised armed assistance against Communist aggression to any nation in the region that requested it.

The Arab Republic of Egypt

The most vociferous proponent of Arab nationalism was President Gamal Abdel Nasser of Egypt, who had taken over in 1954, a year after the Egyptian monarchy was abolished. Following a neutralist course, Nasser's Egypt accepted large-scale aid from the West and East alike. When the western powers in 1956 withdrew their support for the Aswan Dam, a huge power project on the Nile, Nasser retaliated by nationalizing the Suez Canal. The ensuing invasion of Egypt by England, France, and Israel might have resulted in a major war, had not the United Nations insisted on the withdrawal of foreign troops. Meanwhile Egypt was left in control of the Canal, and the Aswan Dam was completed in 1970 with financial aid from the Soviet Union. By that time Nasser was receiving large-scale Soviet military support as well, and thousands of Russian "advisers and experts" were reported to be in Egypt.

Nasser died in 1970 and was succeeded by Muhammad Anwar el-Sadat. The new president proved to be far more moderate and conciliatory toward the western powers. In 1972 he ordered the expulsion of virtually all Russians from Egypt and secured far-reaching economic aid from the United States and some oil-rich Arab states. Sadat's most courageous and statesmanlike act was his visit to Jerusalem in 1977 and the subsequent Camp David negotiations, leading to the Egyptian-Israeli peace treaty of 1979. Before it could be fully implemented, however, Sadat, who had been forced into a more authoritarian position by economic and social problems, was assassinated late in 1981. His successor, Hosni Mubarak, continued to be faced with economic difficulties and opposition from Muslim fundamentalists at home, and troubles with Israel abroad.

Arabs Against Israel

The main danger to peace in the region was the intermittent war between the Arabs and Israel. The war started in 1948–49, when Israel's neighbors invaded the newly independent country, only to be beaten and evicted. From here on an uneasy armistice prevailed. The Arabs refused to recognize Israel,

Anwar el-Sadat Addresses the Israeli Knesset

November 20, 1977

I have chosen to set aside all precedents and traditions known by warring countries. In spite of the fact that occupation of Arab territories is still there, the declaration of my readiness to proceed to Israel came as a great surprise that stirred many feelings and confounded many minds. Some of them even doubted its intent. . . .

I have chosen to come to you with an open heart and an open mind. I have chosen to give this great impetus to all international efforts exerted for peace. I have chosen to present to you in your own home, the realities, devoid of any scheme or whim. Not to maneuver, or win a round, but for us to win together, the most dangerous of rounds embattled in modern history, the battle of permanent peace based on justice.

It is not my battle alone. Nor is it the battle of the leadership in Israel alone. It is the battle of all and every citizen in all our territories, whose right it is to live in peace. It is the commitment of conscience and responsibility in the hearts of millions.

When I put forward this initiative, many asked what is it that I conceived as possible to achieve during this visit and what my expectations were. And as I answer the questions, I announce before you that I have not thought of carrying out this initiative from the precepts of what could be achieved during this visit. I have come here to deliver a message. I have delivered the message and may God be my witness.

I repeat with Zacharia: Love, right and justice. From the holy Koran I quote the following verses: "We believe in God and in what has been revealed to us and what was revealed to Abraham, Ishmael, Isaac, Jacob and the 13 Jewish tribes. And in the books given to Moses and Jesus and the prophets from their Lord, who made no distinction between them." So we agree, Salam Aleikum—peace be upon you.

From Anwar el-Sadat, *In Search of Identity: An Autobiography* (New York: Harper & Row, 1977/78), p. 343.

Israel in 1985

and hundreds of thousands of Arab refugees, made homeless by the partition of Palestine, helped keep the conflict alive. Full-scale fighting was briefly resumed during the Suez crisis in 1956, when Israeli forces made a quick dash for the Suez Canal. In 1967, in a furious six-day war, Israel took the Sinai Peninsula and some other territory. Egypt's and Syria's attempts to regain these lands led to another bloody conflict, the Yom Kippur War of 1973, in which Israel won another resounding victory.

The Israelis vowed to retain their conquests until a final and stable peace could be agreed on; they believed that they were fighting for the very survival of their nation. Yet the occupation and possible annexation of Arab lands only exacerbated the Arab-Israeli conflict. Beginning in 1972, a rash of bombings, airplane hijackings, and assassinations by Palestine Arab terrorists and retaliations by Israeli commandos intensified the crisis. The Palestine Liberation Organization (PLO) under Yasir Arafat demanded the return of the Arab lands occupied by Israel and the creation of a separate Palestinian state.

The stalemate that had existed since 1973 came to an end in 1977, when President Sadat approached Israel with a series of peace proposals. His counterpart in Jerusalem was Prime Minister Menachem Begin, whose coalition of conservative parties, the Likud, had recently defeated the Labor party under Shimon Peres. Hopes for a final settlement, however, proved premature. Israel lived up to some provisions of the peace treaty of 1979, such as the evacuation of the Sinai Peninsula. But when it came to evacuating the West Bank taken from Jordan, and the Golan Heights taken from Syria, the Begin government hesitated.

The main obstacle proved to be the PLO. Israel refused to recognize that organization and discuss Palestinian autonomy, unless in return the PLO ceased its activities and recognized Israel's right to exist. In 1981, Israel started bombing PLO headquarters in Beirut and in 1982 invaded Lebanon. Begin's belligerency, meanwhile, including a preemptive air strike against an Iraqi nuclear reactor in 1981, led to Israel's condemnation by the U.N. Security Council and to sharp criticism from its most loyal and steadfast friend, the United States.

Sadat, Carter, and Begin after signing the Egyptian-Israeli Peace Treaty (March 26, 1979).

The Republic of Iraq

The most serious danger to Israel in the past has come from Egypt and Syria. The rest of the Arab states were too small to pose much of a threat. There was one exception. Iraq at all times has been strongly anti-Israel, and according to most observers it has the most promising future of all Arab states. The government of Iraq, repressive politically, has been enlightened economically, using its large oil revenues for industrial development, of which the nuclear reactor destroyed by Israel was an example. Since the overthrow of the monarchy in 1958, Iraq has been ruled by a number of military strongmen of whom the latest, Sadam Hussein, took over in 1979. In 1980

Hussein launched an attack upon neighboring Iran hoping that it would settle a long-standing border dispute and other differences. But the war did not bring the easy victory Iraq had expected, and it added further to the tensions of the region.

The Islamic Republic of Iran

The turmoils in Southwest Asia, of course, were of deep concern to the two superpowers. The break between Egypt and the Soviet Union, and America's key role in the efforts to resolve the Arab-Israeli conflict, sharply curtailed Soviet influence in the region. Throughout that conflict, the Russians closely sided with the Arabs and the PLO, and they continued to supply arms to Syria and Iraq, to whom they were linked by security treaties. In 1978, furthermore, the Soviet Union gained influence on the periphery by supporting the newly emerged pro-Soviet regimes in Afghanistan, Ethiopia, and the People's Democratic Republic of Yemen. But at the same time the United States was strengthening its ties not only with Egypt, but with the two other leading states of the region, Saudi Arabia and Iran. The sudden turn of Iran against the United States in 1979, therefore, could not help but seriously affect the balance between the superpowers, especially when followed by the Soviet invasion of Afghanistan.

Iran (called Persia until 1935) was a constitutional monarchy, ruled since 1941 by Shah Mohammed Riza Pahlavi. He was known as the "reform shah" because of his radical attempts to modernize his country. The rapid pace of these changes and the authoritarian manner in which they were introduced caused mounting opposition among vested interests and religious leaders. Iran maintained close relations with the United States, which provided massive economic and military aid. When financial difficulties forced curtailment of reforms, opposition spread to the urban masses. Attempts to meet protests by ruthless repression alternating with token concessions proved useless. In early 1979, the Shah and his family left Iran for a "vacation." He never returned. The leading figure in the ensuing revolution was a religious leader, the Ayatollah Ruhollah Khomeini, who had been exiled by the Shah. He was widely revered by the masses and, while holding no official position, had the decisive voice in all matters. The new government immediately cut all military relations with the United States and nationalized large segments of the economy. Khomeini's special concern was with the revival of Islamic traditions. Belonging to the fundamentalist Shi'ite branch of Islam (see p. 267), in contrast to the more numerous Sunnites, Khomeini injected a strongly religious note into Iranian politics. Stressing the Shi'ite-Sunni split, which existed in other Islamic nations as well, emphasized a further source of tension in the region.

Ayatollah Khomeini in Tehran (February 1979).

The most startling act under the Khomeini regime was the seizure by revolutionary militants of more than fifty hostages in the American Embassy in Tehran in November 1979, to try to force the surrender of the Shah. They were not released until January 1981, after worldwide protests, ineffective boycotts, and an abortive rescue effort. Meanwhile in 1980 Iran had for the first time elected a president. Abol Hassan Bani Sadr was a moderate and for that reason caught between the religious extremists of the right and their radical opponents on the left. He was dismissed in 1981 after serving only seventeen months. Since then Iran has been in a virtual state of civil war. Only the war with Iraq brought some diversion. Relations with the United States remained interrupted; but Muslim opposition to "godless communism" also worked against closer relations with the Soviet Union. Iran was thus one of the world's truly nonaligned powers.

The Republic of Turkey

There is one other third-world power in Southwest Asia that deserves a brief mention. Like Iran, Turkey is a non-Arab state. Nominally a democracy, the army has frequently intervened in times of crisis and there have been several prominent military premiers and presidents, notably General Ismet Inönü, close friend of Kemal Atatürk, the founder of modern Turkey. The latest military coup was by General Kenan Evren, who became president in 1980. Economically Turkey has depended heavily on economic aid from the United States and from the European Economic Community, of which Turkey hopes to become a member. In its foreign policy, Turkey has tried to get along with both superpowers. But despite occasional strains with the United States, the Turks have always leaned closely to the West, as shown by their membership in NATO. Turkey's main foreign disputes have been with Greece, over their respective claims on the island of Cyprus. These differences have lessened the military effectiveness of the two NATO partners in the Mediterranean.

THE AWAKENING OF AFRICA

As we turn from the third world of Asia to that of Africa, the situation becomes infinitely complex. The dark continent was the last to be swept by the tide of nationalism. From only four sovereign states in 1950, the number by 1983 had grown to fifty-one. The former colonial powers had virtually eradicated tropical diseases, but the resultant population growth had not been matched by a similar increase in food supplies. Most of Africa, therefore, remained underfed, and several regions have been plagued by catastrophic famines. Added to poverty was extreme diversity, with no tradition of political unity and with some seven hundred different native dialects. The one sentiment common to all Africans was anticolonialism. Just as it did everywhere else, nationalism in Africa demanded immediate independence, even though people might not be ready for it. This rush into freedom caused severe growing pains for most of the new nations.

The Islamic States of North Africa

The countries along the southern coast of the Mediterranean Sea form another logical subgroup within the third world. They have much in common. As part of the Roman Empire, their region had early contacts with western Europe; its people were mostly Islamic; and during the colonial era the majority were under French rule. One major difference is between those countries with large oil resources—Algeria and Libya—and the rest. Belonging to the Arab world, all these states shared in the conflict with Israel. Most of them were nonaligned, but some tended more toward one or the other of the superpowers.

American relations have been closest with Morocco, Tunisia, and the Sudan. Morocco, under King Hassan II, has received considerable military aid from the United States and has favored the Egyptian-Israeli peace treaty. Its main problem has been with the adjacent and as yet unassigned Western Sahara, which is claimed by both Morocco and Mauritania. Tunisia, since 1957 under President Habib Bourguiba, has been prowestern, except on the issue of Israel. The Sudan under President Gaafar Nimeiri was one of Egypt's few Arab friends. Several attempts against his regime, instigated by Libya with Soviet involvement, led to tension between the Sudan and these two countries. In 1985, Nimeiri was ousted by his defense minister, who promised free elections and better times.

The most troublesome country in the region has been Libya. Once among the poorest nations of North Africa, it is now, thanks to the discovery of oil in the Libyan Desert, the richest. Its president, Colonel Muammar al-Qaddafi, has been an unpredictable troublemaker. After concluding a major arms deal with the Soviet Union in 1975, he began supporting international terrorists and intervened in Egypt in 1977 and in neighboring Chad in 1980. But while the United States considers Libya

Africa and Southwest Asia in 1985

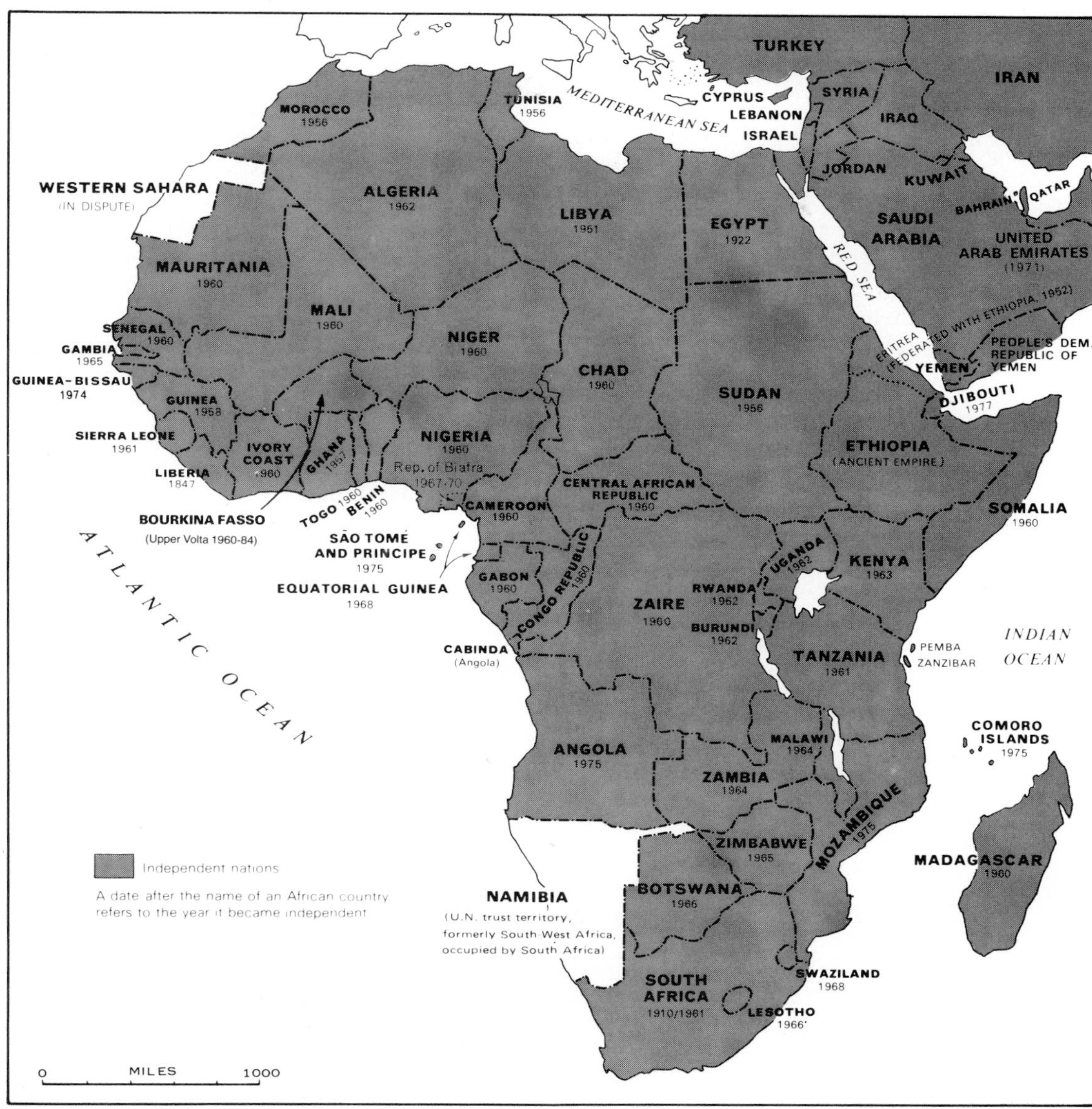

to be in the Soviet camp, America still buys 40 percent of that country's oil, and Libya continues to employ some two thousand American technicians. Political relations were virtually broken in 1981, but mutually advantageous economic contacts continued.

Next to Egypt and Libya, the most prominent country in North Africa is Algeria. In an effort to reduce traditional ties to France, Algerians, under President Chadhi Bendjedid, in 1979 began moving closer to the United States. In 1980, Algeria was instrumental in negotiating the release of American hostages from Iran. The United States in return continued as the largest purchaser of Algerian oil. On some issues, such as Israel, the two countries differed, with Algeria remaining the strongest supporter of the PLO. Like most African states, Algeria tries to steer a middle course, reaping advantages from both East and West.

Africa South of the Sahara

Most victories of African nationalism occurred in the central part of the continent, south of the Sahara Desert, in areas inhabited by poverty-stricken, primitive, and largely illiterate native tribes. All African states were founded as democracies, but lack of political experience and ethnic disunity soon gave rise to one-party systems and strongman rule. American involvement in Central Africa was less active than elsewhere. Under a policy of "noninterventionism," the United States preferred to have the African states solve their own problems. The Soviet Union and its ally Cuba, on the other hand, were less hesitant and in states like Angola, Ethiopia, and Somalia gained considerable influence.

It is impossible here to discuss more than a few of the new central African states. One of the largest and most troubled was the Republic of Zaire. It was ruled since 1965 by President Mobuto Sese Seko and his Popular Movement of the Revolution (MPR). Zaire is rich in natural resources, especially copper, but has been beset by regional strife, especially in Katanga province. As Mobuto's regime became increasingly corrupt and repressive, the economy, due to haphazard socialization, or "Zairization," became more and more dependent on foreign aid. Zaire has been kept alive by the former colonial powers, Belgium and France, and by the United States. To let its economy collapse would lead to utter chaos.

In contrast to Zaire, the Federal Republic of Nigeria was one of the most successful of the new African states. Its major problem was to cope with its ethnic and linguistic diversity. Between 1967 and 1970, civil war between Hausa-Fulanis and Ibos led to the short-lived secession of the Ibo Republic of Biafra. Nigeria initially was under military rule. It was not until 1979 that President Shehu Shagari, a civilian, was elected under a new democratic constitution; but it was short-lived. In 1983, General Mohammed Buhari staged another military coup. Much of Nigeria's initial economic success was due to the production and export of oil. The resulting wealth made possible far-reaching reforms, such as the introduction of free universal primary education. But unequal distribution of prosperity, mismanagement, and corruption caused economic and social unrest. Relations with the United States were close and mutually beneficial, with America buying the major share of Nigeria's oil.

As the two examples above show, it is impossible to generalize about the states of black Africa. The Republic of Kenya is a further illustration. Its evolution from a British colony plagued by Mau Mau terrorism in the 1950s into a free republic in the 1960s owed much to its first president and "Father of the Nation," Jomo Kenyatta. Upon his death in 1978, he was succeeded by Daniel Arap Moi. Both of them were leaders of the only political party, the Kenya African National Union (KANU). While Kenya is thus a one-party state, compared to other such states it has enjoyed relative tolerance and the rule of law. In contrast to neighboring Tanzania, its economy remains free and attractive to outside investors. As in Zaire, there has been corruption at the top, and as in Nigeria, the

Jomo Kenyatta of Kenya, one of the most revered leaders of the independence movements in Africa.

gap between rich and poor remained wide. It was economic rather than political discontent that caused a rare outbreak of violence in 1982. Kenya's foreign and economic orientation was clearly toward the West.

The early history of third-world countries was often associated with some leading figure—Joseph Mobuto of Zaire, Jomo Kenyatta of Kenya, Kwame Nkrumah of Ghana, Julius Nyerere of Tanzania. One of the most notorious of these strong men was Idi Amin of Uganda. The first decade of that new nation had been dominated by the incompetent Milton Obote and his Uganda People's Congress (UPC). In 1971, Obote was ousted by a charismatic army sergeant, Idi Amin. There followed an eight-year nightmare of lawlessness and terror, costing thousands of lives. Amin was ousted by Tanzanian troops in 1979, and constitutional government under Milton Obote was restored in 1980. In the meantime, Uganda's potentially healthy economy had been wrecked almost beyond repair, an example of the dangers of too rapid transition from colonialism to freedom.

Southern Africa: Whites Against Blacks

There was one region in Africa where the black quest for political power continued to be resisted. In the Republic of South Africa, as in Rhodesia and in the Portuguese colonies of Angola and Mozambique, small white minorities controlled political and economic affairs. Increasingly, however, this white power came under attack from black nationalism.

In South Africa, where the white minority constituted only 18 percent of the total population, the government in 1948 introduced a policy of strict racial segregation, or *apartheid.* It provided for complete separation of the races, restricted franchise for nonwhites, forced resettlement of Africans, and separate schools with lower standards for black children. In 1966 Prime Minister Henrik V. Verwoerd, a leading advocate of apartheid, was assassinated; but his successors, Balthazar J. Vorster and, since 1978, Pieter W. Botha, continued the policy of segregation. South Africa's racist policies, meanwhile, led to increasingly violent confrontations at home and the censure of most of the civilized world abroad. In the face of such protests, the South African government somewhat alleviated the worst abuses of urban apartheid. But these measures will merely postpone the inevitable showdown between blacks and whites.

South Africa has followed similar delaying tactics with respect to neighboring Namibia, formerly South-West Africa. A German colony before the First World War and a League of Nations mandate thereafter, Namibia has been ruled by South Africa for over half a century. Agitation by the South-West African People's Organization (SWAPO) for Namibia's independence found support among the governments of Western Europe, Canada, and the United States, but has been resisted by South Africa. The emergence of an independent state in the area could not help but have repercussions among blacks in South Africa.

As far as Rhodesia was concerned, its ruling white minority constituted only 3 percent of the population. Outside pressures to gain political equality for the black majority ran into stubborn resistance from the white regime of Ian Smith. It took a bitter seven-year civil war before the new nation of Zimbabwe came into existence in 1980. Its first prime minister was Robert Mugabe, head of the Zimbabwe African National Union (ZANU). A Marxist, Mugabe nevertheless maintained a free market economy; and though a former guerilla leader, he pursued a policy of conciliation with the white minority. Whites continued to play an essential part in the economy, producing nearly half of the country's exports. Mugabe's moderation attracted substantial economic aid, especially from western Europe. His reliance on persuasion rather than force made him one of Africa's most respected leaders.

However by 1985, his plans for single-party rule caused considerable concern among white and black minorities.

By the time Zimbabwe was founded, the oldest two colonies in Africa, Mozambique and Angola, had already won their independence from Portugal. They each became a people's republic in 1975, Marxist in their domestic affairs and aligned with the Soviet Union and Cuba abroad. This left the escalating conflict between whites and blacks in South Africa as the major problem on the African continent.

LATIN AMERICA IN THE THIRD WORLD

The last major area in the third world that we must briefly consider is Latin America. Again it differs from the other regions. Except for some islands in the Caribbean, the nations of Latin America gained their independence more

Central and South America 1952–85

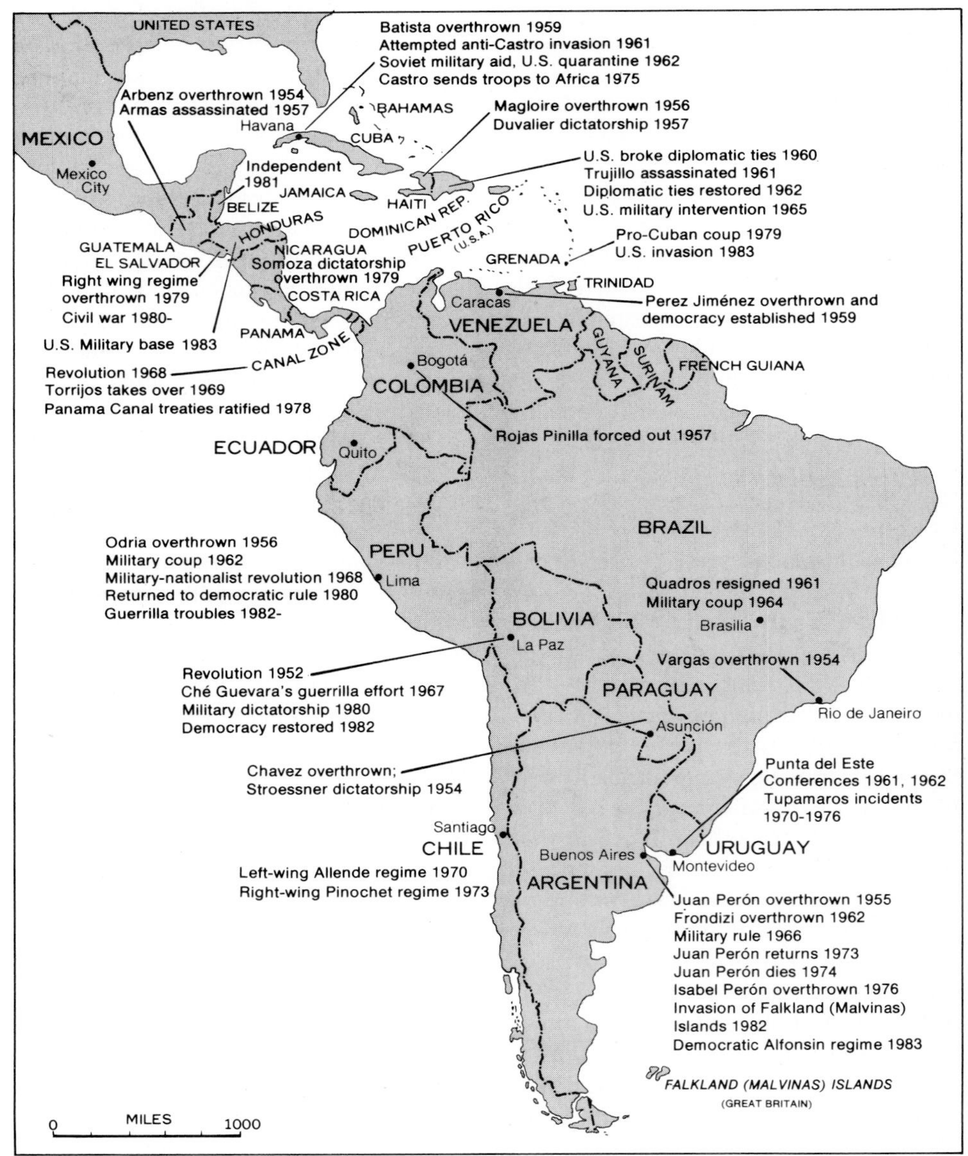

than a century ago. They include a number of industrial states that do not fit the pre-industrial model of most third-world countries; and their economies range from the dire poverty of Haiti to the easy affluence of Venezuela. We have already touched on some of the problem areas and their relations with the United States and shall add to what we have said earlier (see pp. 973–75).

Cuba

The most worrisome country in the western hemisphere for the United States continued to be Castro's Cuba. For a while after the confrontation of 1962, there were some signs of improvement in American-Cuban relations and in time de facto contacts were reestablished. But in the 1970s and early 1980s, as Cuba intervened first in Africa (Angola and Ethiopia) and then in Central America (Nicaragua and El Salvador), the rapprochement came to a halt. In 1980 when Castro permitted Cubans to join relatives already in the United States, the resulting exodus testified to widespread opposition, aggravating the situation. Cuba's economy continued to fall short of its goals and it depended heavily on Soviet aid. By necessity as well as inclination, therefore, Cuba continued to be firmly within the Russian orbit.

Mexico

The major power in Central America, Mexico, while leaning toward the United States, considers itself nonaligned. In the 1970s and early 1980s, its foreign policy became quite independent, maintaining friendly relations with Cuba, and favoring radical movements in Nicaragua and El Salvador. Mexico's government has been described as a six-year presidential dictatorship, under which a president is elected for a nonrenewable six-year term, usually from the leading Institutional Revolutionary party (PRI). Mexico underwent a sudden boom with the discovery of extensive oil deposits in the 1970s. Its overall economic health, however, leaves much to be desired. While a few Mexicans became extremely wealthy, the masses remained dismally poor. Declining agriculture and a rapidly increasing population make food a major concern. There has been growing unrest, some of it relieved by Mexican migration to the United States. The two countries are linked by close economic ties; but memories of past "American imperialism" continue to cast their shadows.

Argentina, Brazil, Chile

One of Latin America's main characteristics has been its long tradition of military dictatorships. We shall deal here only with the three largest countries; but their experiences could be duplicated by virtually all the rest.

Argentina has a long tradition of strongman rule. Its best-known dictator, Juan Perón, ruled for ten years after World War II, and again briefly in the 1970s. In 1976 a military junta seized power. The regime of General Jorge Videla (1976–80) was accused of numerous murders and human rights violations; but under his successors, repression became somewhat less. In 1983 a democratic government under Raúl Alfonsín was finally elected, and several of the country's former military rulers were put on trial. Argentina was plagued by huge deficits and record inflation, leading to social unrest and terrorism. The Falkland crisis of 1982 created a brief diversion, but defeat at the hands of the British further aggravated the situation.

In Brazil, the army took over in 1964, installing a series of military leaders, most important among them Ernesto Geisel (1974–79) and his successor, João Baptista Fugueiredo. Beginning in 1977, there were some slight signs of democratization. In 1985, a respected moderate, Tancredo Neves, was elected president. He died, however, before taking office, and was succeeded by the equally moderate, but less capable, José Sarney. After much economic progress in the early 1970s,

Brazil's development again slowed down and discontent mounted. In the early 1980s, violent crimes, land seizures and looting were frequent. Like Argentina, Brazil was strongly anti-Communist, yet nonaligned. Relations of both countries with the United States were correct, rather than cordial.

While Argentina and Brazil had frequently experienced dictatorships in their past, Chile had been rare among Latin American nations for having almost always had elected governments. The last such, under Salvador Allende, came to power in 1970. An avowed Marxist, Allende embarked on a program of socialization and resumed relations with Cuba and Communist China. In 1973, he was overthrown and killed in a military coup. The United States, as was later shown, had supported the opposition to Allende. The new president, General Augusto Pinochet, soon emerged as a full-fledged dictator. In its economic measures, his regime was surprisingly liberal, hoping to solve Chile's difficulties through free market policies. Pinochet's brutal violations of human rights led to estrangement under President Carter, but his strong anticommunism was welcomed by the Reagan administration.

"THE NORTH" AND "THE SOUTH"

The third world, as our discussion has shown, includes a wide variety of countries—some of them rich, most of them poor; some of them old, most of them new; some of them on the threshold of the second world, and others still so desperately poor that one might speak of a fourth world—some twenty-eight of the poorest nations with a quarter of the world's population and a per capita income of less than $200 per year.

The history of the third world is closely related to decolonization. As more and more nonwhite peoples gained their independence, common concerns naturally drew them together. There were a number of Asian-African conferences in the 1950s, the first at Bandung, Indonesia, in 1955. They were still concerned with ideological and racial issues. Only in the 1960s, when deliberations shifted to economic problems, did these meetings become more purposeful. As time went on, they brought together not only Asians and Africans, but people from other parts of the world, especially Latin America. The next step was a further widening of the debate, not only within the third world but between the poorer nonindustrial nations of the South and the rich industrial nations of the North.

In time there have developed a large number of international organizations devoted wholly or in part to economic improvement. There are the large regional bodies: the Organization of American States (OAS); the Organization of African Unity (OAU); the Association of South East Asian Nations (ASEAN); and the League of Arab States. Then there are the smaller economic groupings devoted to economic planning and marketing in specific areas, more than twenty all told. And finally there are hundreds of mostly private agencies—from the African Groundnut Council to the Zinc Development Association—all of them trying to make an economically more successful world. If planning could do it, we would be living in paradise.

But we are not. When it comes to sharing, nations, like individuals, are selfish. Why do the OPEC nations, once poor themselves, not share their newfound wealth with their poorer brethren? Why does the United States give aid only where it profits most? Why do former colonial countries like France and Great Britain prefer to help their one-time dependencies? How long will it be before both East and West realize that poverty is a global disease calling for universal cures?

From time to time, doctors and patients meet to see what can be done, as

The Wealth — and Poverty — of the Third World

SELECTED COUNTRIES	BALANCE OF PAYMENTS* (*in millions of dollars*)	GNP PER CAPITA (*in dollars, 1978*)	DAILY CALORIE SUPPLY PER CAPITA (*as percent of requirement 1977*)	AVERAGE ANNUAL POPULATION GROWTH (*in percent, 1970–78*)
LOW-INCOME COUNTRIES				
Bangladesh	−302	90	78	2.7
Ethiopia	−98	120	75	2.5
Somalia	−63	130	88	2.3
India	915	180	91	2.0
Sierra Leone	−96	210	93	2.5
Zaire	88	210	104	2.7
Pakistan	−550	230	99	3.1
Tanzania	−442	230	89	3.0
Afghanistan	38	240	110	2.2
Haiti	−39	260	93	1.7
Uganda	−129	280	91	2.9
Sudan	−54	320	93	2.6
Kenya	−474	330	88	3.3
Senegal	−114	340	95	2.6
Indonesia	−773	360	105	1.8
MIDDLE-INCOME COUNTRIES				
Egypt	−540	390	109	2.2
Ghana	32	390	86	3.0
Southern Yemen	−20	420	81	1.9
Zambia	−191	474	88	3.0
Thailand	−1,098	490	105	2.7
Philippines	−991	510	97	2.7
El Salvador	−230	660	90	2.9
Ivory Coast	−533	840	105	5.6
Colombia	305	850	102	2.3
Ecuador	−54	880	92	3.3
Guatemala	−192	910	98	2.9
Tunisia	−411	950	112	2.0
Malaysia	284	1,090	117	2.7
South Korea	−455	1,160	119	1.9
Turkey	−1,121	1,200	115	2.5
Algeria	−2,977	1,260	99	3.2
Mexico	−896	1,290	114	3.3
Taiwan	1,979	1,400	120	2.0
Chile	−659	1,410	109	1.7
South Africa	2,010	1,480	116	2.7
Brazil	−5,310	1,570	107	2.8
Argentina	2,512	1,910	126	1.3
Portugal	−337	1,990	126	1.0
Venezuela	−4,973	2,910	99	3.3
Israel	−732	3,500	122	2.7
CAPITAL-SURPLUS OIL-EXPORTERS				
Iraq	1,209 (1977)	1,860	89	3.3
Iran	5,370 (1977)	2,160 (1977)	130	2.9
Libya	1,024	6,910	126	4.1
Saudi Arabia	12,793	7,690	88	3.5

* Current account balance before interest payment on external debt.
Source: World Bank data.

they did at Cancun, Mexico, in 1981. On that occasion, the South's richest nation, Saudi Arabia, with a per capita income of $7,300 faced the North's poorest nation, Great Britain, with a per capita income of $6,300. But both of them were confronted with the *world's* poorest nation, Bangladesh, with a per capita income of $90. How will it end?

Suggestions for Further Reading

Good general works on the "Third World" are M. Harrington, *The Vast Majority* (1977); G. Myrdal, *The Challenge of World Poverty* (1970); and A. Hoogvelt, *The Sociology of Developing Societies* (1977). For a survey of conditions in South Asia see W. Wolpert, *Roots of Confrontation in South Asia* (1982). On individual nations see A. Lall, *The Emergence of Modern India* (1981); L. Ziring, *Pakistan: The Enigma of Political Development* (1981); and L. Dupree, *Afghanistan* (1973).

The literature on Communist China is extensive. W. S. Morton, *China: Its History and Culture* (1981), is a good introduction. J. C. Wang, *Contemporary Chinese Politics: An Introduction* (1980), is a valuable source of information. V. Shue, *Peasant China in Transition, 1949–1956* (1980), covers the period of communization. J. F. Copper, *China's Global Role* (1980), assesses China's rank among world powers. On Japan, E. O. Reischauer, *Japan: The Story of a Nation* (1974), is an excellent introduction. L. E. Williams, *Southeast Asia: A History* (1976), is a good general survey. C. A. Buss, *Southeast Asia and the World Today* (1980), places the area in a wider perspective.

P. Mansfield, *The Middle East: A Political and Economic Survey* (1980), is a useful general work. On individual countries see R. W. Baker, *Egypt's Uncertain Revolution under Nasser and Sadat* (1978); M. Khadduri, *Socialist Iraq: A Study in Iraqui Politics Since 1968* (1978); B. Rubin, *Paved with Good Intentions: The American Experience and Iran* (1980); W. F. Weiker, *The Modernization of Turkey: From Atatürk to the Present Day* (1981); and H. M. Sachar, *A History of Israel* (1976). Some good general works on Africa include R. Gibson, *African Liberation Movements*; J. Dunn, ed., *West African States, Failures and Promise* (1978); and R. W. Hull, *Southern Africa: Civilizations in Turmoil* (1981). On Latin America, see R. W. Duncan, *Latin American Politics* (1976); S. B. Tanzer, *Economic Nationalism in Latin America* (1976); and B. Loveman and T. M. Davies, *The Politics of Antipolitics: The Military in Latin America* (1978).

Appendix *Principal Rulers and Periods*

ROMAN EMPIRE

Augustus	27 B.C.–14 A.D.
Tiberius	14– 37
Caligula	37– 41
Claudius	41– 54
Nero	54– 68
Vespasian	69– 79
Titus	79– 81
Domitian	81– 96
Nerva	96– 98
Trajan	98–117
Hadrian	117–138
Antoninus Pius	138–161
Marcus Aurelius	161–180
Commodus	180–193
Septimius Severus	193–211
Caracalla	211–217
Elagabalus	218–222
Severus Alexander	222–235
Philip the Arab	244–249
Decius	249–251
Valerian	253–260
Gallienus	260–268
Aurelian	270–275
Diocletian	284–286

WEST		EAST	
Maximian	286–305	Diocletian	284–305
Constantius	305–306	Galerius	305–311
		Maximius	308–313
		Licinius	308–324
Constantine	308–337	Constantine	324–337
Maxentius	307–312		
Constantine II	337–340		
Constans	337–350		
Constantius II	351–361	Constantius II	337–361
Julian	360–363	Julian	361–363
Jovian	363–364	Jovian	363–364
Valentinian	364–375	Valens	364–378
Gratian	375–383		
Valentinian II	383–392		
Theodosius	394–395	Theodosius	379–395
Honorius	395–423	Arcadius	393–408
		Theodosius II	408–450
Valentinian III	425–455	Marcian	450–457
		Leo	457–474
Romulus	475–476	Zeno	474–491

BYZANTINE EMPIRE

Anastasius	491– 518
Justin I	518– 527
Justinian I	527– 565
Justin II	565– 578
Tiberius	578– 582
Maurice	582– 602
Phocas	602– 610
Heraclius I	610– 641
Constans II	641– 668
Constantine IV	668– 685
Leo III	717– 741
Constantine V	741– 775
Leo IV	775– 780
Constantine VI	780– 797
Irene	797– 802
Nicephorus	802– 811
Leo V	813– 820
Michael III	842– 867
Basil I	867– 886
Leo VI	886– 912
Constantine VII	912– 959
Nicephorus II	963– 969
John I	969– 976
Basil II	976–1025
Theodora	1042–1056
Alexus I	1081–1118
Michael VIII	1259–1282
Constantine XI	1448–1453

ISLAMIC EMPIRE

Muhammad	622–632
Abu Bakr	632–634
Omar	634–644
Othman	644–656
Ali	656–661

UMAYYADS

Muawiya	661–680
Marwan I	684–685
Marwan II	749–750

ABBASIDS

Abu'l-Abbas	750–754
al-Mansur	754–775
al-Mahdi	775–785
al-Rashid	786–809
al-Amin	809–813
al-Mamun	813–833
al-Mu'tasim	833–842
al-Wathik	842–846
al-Mutawakkil	846–861
al-Muktafi	902–908
al-Mugtadir	908–932

CAROLINGIAN KINGDOM

Pepin, Mayor of the Palace	680–714
Charles Martel, Mayor of the Palace	715–741
Pepin the Short, Mayor of the Palace	741–751
Pepin the Short, King	751–768
Charles the Great, King	768–814
Charles the Great, Emperor	800–814
Louis the Pious, Emperor	814–840

WEST FRANKS

Charles the Bald	840–877
Louis II the Stammerer	877–879
Louis III	879–882
Carloman	879–884

LOTHARINGIA

Lothar	840–855
Louis II	855–875
Charles	855–863
Lothar II	855–869

EAST FRANKS

Louis the German	840–876
Carloman	876–880
Louis	876–882
Charles the Fat	884–887

THE PAPACY

Leo I	440– 461
Gregory I	590– 604
Nicholas I	858– 867
Silvester II	999–1003
Leo IX	1049–1054
Nicholas II	1058–1061
Gregory VII	1073–1085
Urban II	1088–1099
Paschal II	1099–1118
Alexander III	1159–1181
Innocent III	1198–1216
Gregory IX	1227–1241
Boniface VIII	1294–1303
John XXII	1316–1334
Gregory XI	1370–1378
Martin V	1417–1431
Eugenius IV	1431–1447
Nicholas V	1447–1455
Pius II	1458–1464
Alexander VI	1492–1503
Julius II	1503–1513
Leo X	1513–1521
Clement VII	1523–1534
Paul III	1534–1549
Pius V	1566–1572
Pius VII	1800–1823
Pius IX	1846–1878
Pius X	1903–1914
Benedict XV	1914–1922
Pius XI	1922–1939
Pius XII	1939–1958
John XXIII	1958–1963
Paul VI	1963–1978
John Paul I	1978
John Paul II	1978–

HOLY ROMAN EMPIRE

SAXONS

Henry the Fowler	919–936
Otto I	962–973
Otto II	973–983
Otto III	983–1002

SALIANS

Conrad II	1024–1039
Henry III	1039–1056
Henry IV	1056–1106
Henry V	1106–1125
Lothar II	1125–1137

HOHENSTAUFENS

Frederick I Barbarossa	1152–1190
Henry VI	1190–1197
Philip of Swabia	1198–1208
Otto IV	1198–1215
Frederick II	1198–1250
Conrad IV	1250–1254

OTHER DYNASTIES

Rudolf of Habsburg	1273–1291
Adolph of Nassau	1292–1298
Albert of Austria	1298–1308
Henry VII of Luxemburg	1308–1313
Ludwig IV of Bavaria	1314–1347
Charles IV	1347–1378
Wenceslas	1378–1400
Rupert	1400–1410
Sigismund	1410–1437

HABSBURGS

Frederick III	1440–1493
Maximilian I	1493–1519
Charles V	1519–1556
Ferdinand I	1556–1564
Maximilian II	1564–1576
Rudolf II	1576–1612
Matthias	1612–1619
Ferdinand II	1619–1637
Ferdinand III	1637–1657
Leopold I	1658–1705
Joseph I	1705–1711
Charles VI	1711–1740
Charles VII	1742–1745
Francis I	1745–1765
Joseph II	1765–1790
Leopold II	1790–1792
Francis II	1792–1806

OTTOMAN EMPIRE

Muhammed II	1451–1481
Selim I	1512–1520
Suleiman I	1520–1566
Selim II	1566–1574
Muhammed III	1595–1603
Mahmud II	1808–1839
Abu al-Hamed	1808–1839
Abdul-Hamid II	1876–1909
Muhammed V	1909–1918
Muhammed VI	1918–1922

SAFAVID EMPIRE

Ismail I	1501–1524
Abbas I	1588–1629
Abbas II	1632–1666

AFRICA

Salma, king of Kanem	1194–1221
Sundiata, ruler of Mali empire	1230–1255
Mansa Musa, ruler of Mali empire	1307–1332
Sonni Ali, ruler of Songhai empire	1464–1492
Mai Ali, king of Bornu	1476–1507
Askia Mohammed, ruler of Songhai	1493–1528
Usman dan Fodio, sultan of Sokoto	1804–1817
Seyyid Said, ruler of Zanzibar	1806–1856
Shaka, king of the Zulu	1818–1826

INDIA

Mauryan Empire	321–181 B.C.
Chandragupta	321–301 B.C.
Bendusara	302–269 B.C.
Ashoka	269–232 B.C.
Gupta Empire	320–550
Samudra Gupta	335–375
Chandra Gupta II	375–415
Sandra Gupta	455–467
Delhi Sultanate	1206–1526
Muhammad	1325–1351
Mughal Empire	1526–1739
Babur	1526–1530
Akbar	1556–1605
Jahangir	1605–1627
Shah Jahan	1628–1657
Aurangzeb	1658–1707
British East India Company	1757–1858
British *raj*	1858–1947
Self-governing dominions of India and Pakistan	1947
Republic of India	1950–
Republic of Pakistan	1956–

CHINA

Shang	*ca.* 1600–1027 B.C.
Western Zhou	*ca.* 1027–771 B.C.
Eastern Zhou	771–256 B.C.
Spring & Autumn Period	722–481 B.C.
Warring States Period	403–211 B.C.
Qin	221–206 B.C.
Qin Shi Huangdi	221–210
Former Han	202 B.C.–8 A.D.
Liu Bang	206–194 B.C.
Emperor Wu	140–86 B.C.
Xin [Wang Mang]	9–23
Later Han	25–220
Guangwu-di	25–58
Period of the Three Kingdoms	220–280
Jin	280–316
Period of Division	316–588
Northern Wei	386–534
Sui	589–618
Wen-di	589–605
Yang-di	605–617
Tang	618–907
Tai-zong	626–649
Xuan-zong	713–756
Five Dynasties	907–960
Song	960–1279
Northern Song	960–1127
Shen-zong	1068–1086
Hui-zong	1101–1126
Jin	1115–1234
Southern Song	1127–1279
Yüan	1279–1368
Khubilai Khan	1260–1290
Ming	1368–1644
Zhu Yuanzhang	1368–1398
Shen-zong	1573–1627
Qing	1644–1911
Kangxi	1662–1722
Yongzheng	1723–1735
Qianlong	1736–1795
Tongzhi	1862–1874
Guangxu [Empress Dowager Ci Xi]	1874–1908
Chinese Republic	1912–1949
Yuan Shikai	1912–1916
Warlords	1916–1927
Nationalist [Guomindang]	1928–1949
The People's Republic of China	1949–
Mao Zedong	1949–1976

JAPAN

Tomb Period	250–552
Late Yamato	552–710
Shōtoku Taishi	592–622
Nara Period	710–784
Heian Period	794–1185
Fujiwara Michinaga	995–1027
Taira	1156–1185
Kamakura Period	1185–1333
Ashikaga Period	1336–1467
Kenmu Restoration	1333–1336
Yoshimitsu	1368–1408
Yoshimasa	1443–1473
Period of Warfare	1467–1573
Period of Reunification	1573–1600
Oda Nobunaga	1568–1582
Toyotomi Hideyoshi	1582–1598
Tokugawa Ieyasu	1598–1616
Tokugawa Period	1600–1868
Modern Period	1868–
Meiji	1868–1912
Taishō	1912–1926
Shōwa	1926–

ENGLAND

ANGLO-SAXONS

Alfred the Great	871– 899
Ethelred the Unready	978–1016
Canute *(Danish)*	1016–1035
Harold I	1035–1040
Hardicanute	1040–1042
Edward the Confessor	1042–1066
Harold II	1066

NORMANS

William the Conqueror	1066–1087
William II	1087–1100
Henry I	1100–1135
Stephen	1135–1154

ANGEVINS

Henry II	1154–1189
Richard I	1189–1199
John	1199–1216
Henry III	1216–1272
Edward I	1272–1307
Edward II	1307–1327
Edward III	1327–1377
Richard II	1377–1399

LANCASTERS AND YORKS

Henry IV	1399–1413
Henry V	1413–1422
Henry VI	1422–1461
Edward IV	1461–1483
Edward V	1483
Richard III	1483–1485

TUDORS

Henry VII	1485–1509
Henry VIII	1509–1547
Edward VI	1547–1553
Mary I	1553–1558
Elizabeth I	1558–1603

STUARTS

James I	1603–1625
Charles I	1625–1649
Charles II	1660–1685
James II	1685–1688
William III and Mary II	1689–1694
William III alone	1694–1702
Anne	1702–1714

HANOVERIANS (FROM 1917, WINDSORS)

George I	1714–1727
George II	1727–1760
George III	1760–1820
George IV	1820–1830
William IV	1830–1837
Victoria	1837–1901
Edward VII	1901–1910
George V	1910–1936
Edward VIII	1936
George VI	1936–1952
Elizabeth II	1952–

FRANCE

CAPETIANS

Hugh Capet	987– 996
Robert II	996–1031
Henry I	1031–1060
Philip I	1060–1108
Louis VI	1108–1137
Louis VII	1137–1180
Philip II Augustus	1180–1223
Louis VIII	1223–1226
Louis IX	1226–1270
Philip III	1270–1285
Philip IV	1285–1314
Louis X	1314–1316
Philip V	1316–1322
Charles IV	1322–1328

VALOIS

Philip VI	1328–1350
John	1350–1364
Charles V	1364–1380
Charles VI	1380–1422
Charles VII	1422–1461
Louis XI	1461–1483
Charles VIII	1483–1498
Louis XII	1498–1515
Francis I	1515–1547
Henry II	1547–1559
Francis II	1559–1560
Charles IX	1560–1574
Henry III	1574–1589

BOURBONS

Henry IV	1589–1610
Louis XIII	1610–1643
Louis XIV	1643–1715
Louis XV	1715–1774
Louis XVI	1774–1792

1792–1870

Napoleon I, Emperor	1804–1814
Louis XVIII *(Bourbon)*	1814–1824
Charles X *(Bourbon)*	1824–1830
Louis Philippe *(Bourbon-Orléans)*	1830–1848
Napoleon III, Emperor	1851–1870

1870–PRESENT

Third Republic	1870–1940
Pétain regime	1940–1944
Provisional government	1944–1946
Fourth Republic	1946–1958
Fifth Republic	1958–
de Gaulle	1958–1969
Pompidou	1969–1974
Giscard d'Estaing	1974–1981
Mitterand	1981–

SPAIN

Ferdinand	1479–1516
and	
Isabella	1479–1504

HABSBURGS

Philip I	1504–1506
Charles I (Holy Roman Emperor as Charles V)	1506–1556
Philip II	1556–1598
Philip III	1598–1621
Philip IV	1621–1665
Charles II	1665–1700

BOURBONS

Philip V	1700–1746
Ferdinand VI	1746–1759
Charles III	1759–1788
Charles IV	1788–1808
Ferdinand VII	1808
Joseph Bonaparte	1808–1813
Ferdinand VII (restored)	1814–1833
Isabella II	1833–1868
Amadeo	1870–1873
Alfonso XII	1874–1885
Alfonso XIII	1886–1931

1931–PRESENT

Republic	1931–1939
Fascist Dictatorship	1939–1975
Juan Carlos I	1975–

ITALY

Victor Emmanuel II	1861–1878
Humbert I	1878–1900
Victor Emmanuel III	1900–1946
Fascist Dictatorship	1922–1943
Humbert II	1946
Republic	1946–

PRUSSIA AND GERMANY

HOHENZOLLERNS

Frederick William the Great Elector	1640–1688
Frederick I	1701–1713
Frederick William I	1713–1740
Frederick II the Great	1740–1786
Frederick William II	1786–1797
Frederick William III	1797–1840
Frederick William IV	1840–1861
William I	1861–1888
Frederick III	1888
William II	1888–1918

1918–PRESENT

Weimar Republic	1918–1933
Third Reich	1933–1945
Allied occupation	1945–1952
Federal Republic of Germany (west)	1949–
German Democratic Republic (east)	1949–

AUSTRIA AND AUSTRIA-HUNGARY

(Until 1806 all except Maria Theresa were also Holy Roman Emperors.)

Maximilian I, Archduke	1493–1519
Charles I (Emperor as Charles V)	1519–1556
Ferdinand I	1556–1564
Maximilian II	1564–1576
Rudolf II	1576–1612
Matthias	1612–1619
Ferdinand II	1619–1637
Ferdinand III	1637–1657
Leopold I	1658–1705
Joseph I	1705–1711
Charles VI	1711–1740
Maria Theresa	1740–1780
Joseph II	1780–1790
Leopold II	1790–1792
Francis II	1792–1835
Ferdinand I	1835–1848
Francis Joseph	1848–1916
Charles I	1916–1918

1918–PRESENT

Republic of Austria	1918–1938
Annexed by Germany	1938–1945
Republic restored (Allied occupation)	1945–1956
Free Republic	1956–

RUSSIA

Ivan III	1462–1505
Basil III	1505–1533
Ivan IV the Dread	1533–1584
Theodore I	1584–1598
Boris Godunov	1598–1605
Theodore II	1605
Basil IV	1606–1610

ROMANOVS

Michael	1613–1645
Alexius	1645–1676
Theodore III	1676–1682
Ivan IV and Peter I	1682–1689
Peter I the Great alone	1689–1725
Catherine I	1725–1727
Peter II	1727–1730
Anna	1730–1740
Ivan VI	1740–1741
Elizabeth	1741–1762
Peter III	1762
Catherine II the Great	1762–1796
Paul	1796–1801
Alexander I	1801–1825
Nicholas I	1825–1855
Alexander II	1855–1881
Alexander III	1881–1894
Nicholas II	1894–1917

1917–PRESENT

Soviet Republic	
Lenin	1917–1924
Stalin	1928–1953
Khrushchev	1957–1964
Brezhnev	1977–1982
Andropov	1982–1984
Chernenko	1984–1985
Gorbachev	1985–

UNITED STATES

George Washington	1789–1797
John Adams	1797–1801
Thomas Jefferson	1801–1809
James Madison	1809–1817
James Monroe	1817–1825
John Quincy Adams	1825–1829
Andrew Jackson	1829–1837
Martin Van Buren	1837–1841
William H. Harrison	1841
John Tyler	1841–1845
James K. Polk	1845–1849
Zachary Taylor	1849–1850
Millard Fillmore	1850–1853
Franklin Pierce	1853–1857
James Buchanan	1857–1861
Abraham Lincoln	1861–1865
Andrew Johnson	1865–1869
Ulysses S. Grant	1869–1877
Rutherford B. Hayes	1877–1881
James A. Garfield	1881
Chester A. Arthur	1881–1885
Grover Cleveland	1885–1889
Benjamin Harrison	1889–1893
Grover Cleveland	1893–1897
William McKinley	1897–1901
Theodore Roosevelt	1901–1909
William H. Taft	1909–1913
Woodrow Wilson	1913–1921
Warren G. Harding	1921–1923
Calvin Coolidge	1923–1929
Herbert C. Hoover	1929–1933
Franklin Delano Roosevelt	1933–1945
Harry S Truman	1945–1953
Dwight D. Eisenhower	1953–1961
John F. Kennedy	1961–1963
Lyndon B. Johnson	1963–1969
Richard M. Nixon	1969–1974
Gerald R. Ford	1974–1977
Jimmy Carter	1977–1981
Ronald W. Reagan	1981–

Copyrights and Acknowledgments

For permission to use copyrighted material reprinted in this book, the authors are grateful to the following publishers and copyright holders:

COLUMBIA UNIVERSITY PRESS For the poems on p. 58 "My Lord's Gone to Service," on p. 196 "Pitying the Farmer," and on p. 359 "Confiscating Salt," reprinted from *The Columbia Book of Chinese Poetry: From Early Times to the Thirteenth Century* by Burton Weston. Copyright © 1984 by Columbia University Press. By permission.

DOUBLEDAY & COMPANY, INC. For the poem on p. 194 "Recruiting Officer of Shi-hao" by Tu Fu, translated by Irving Yucheng Lo from *Sunflower Splendor,* edited by Wu-chi Liu and Irving Yucheng Lo. Copyright © 1975 by Irving Yucheng Lo and Wu-chi Liu. Reprinted by permission of Doubleday & Company, Inc.

GROVE PRESS, INC. For the poem on p. 342 "Climbing Kagu-yama and Looking Upon the Land" from *Anthology of Japanese Literature* by Donald Keene. Reprinted by permission of Grove Press, Inc. Copyright © 1955 by Grove Press, Inc. For the poem on p. 547 "Books" from *Yuan Mei: Eighteenth Century Poet* by Arthur Waley. Reprinted by permission of Grove Press, Inc. Copyright © 1956 by Grove Press, Inc.

YALE UNIVERSITY PRESS For the excerpt and note on p. 829 from *The Tale of Kieu,* translated by Huynh Sanh Thong. Copyright © 1983 Yale University Press. Reprinted with permission.

ILLUSTRATION CREDITS

Time Line 1 (left to right): Venus of Willendorf, Courtesy Department Library Services, American Museum of Natural History; Pont du Gard, The Bettmann Archive; Jade disk, Nelson Fund, Nelson-Atkins Museum of Art, Kansas City, Missouri.

Time Line 2 (left to right): Chinggis Khan, The Metropolitan Museum of Art, Gift of Mrs. Edward S. Harkness, 1947; Mosque lamp, The Metropolitan Museum of Art, Bequest of Edward C. Moore, 1891; Justinian coin, Reproduced by Courtesy of the Trustees of the British Museum; Crusaders, The Bettmann Archive; Crown, Kunsthistorisches Museum, Vienna.

Time Line 3 (left to right): Aztec calendar stone, Neg. #318168, Courtesy Department Library Services, American Museum of Natural History; Dante, Photo W. Speiser, Basel; Benin mask, Reproduced by Courtesy of the Trustees of the British Museum; Cathedral of Florence, Alinari/Art Resource, New York: Alpaca, Neg. #106713, Courtesy Department Library Services, American Museum of Natural History.

Time Line 4 (left to right): Merchant, By Courtesy of the Board of Trustees of the Victoria and Albert Museum; Napoleon, Giraudon/Art Resource, New York; Fan, The Metropolitan Museum of Art, Purchase, 1951. Rogers Fund, 1951.

Time Line 5 (left to right): Suffragette, The Press Associated, Ltd.; Confederate soldier, Library of Congress; Dogon sculpture, Photograph © copyright 1986 by The Barnes Foundation; The Prince of Wales, Keystone-Mast Collection, California Museum of Photography, University of California, Riverside.

Time Line 6 (left to right): UN symbol; Official United Nations Photo; Astronaut, NASA; Poster, The Trustees of the Imperial War Museum, London; Bank note, Courtesy of Chase Manhattan Archives; Peace treaty, UPI/Bettmann Newsphotos; Hirohito, © 1980 Black Star.

Chapter 1 Page 9 (top): S. Halperin/Animals Animals; 9 (center): Transvaal Museum, D. Panagos; 9 (bottom): Neg. #315446, Courtesy Department Library Services, American Museum of Natural History; 10 (top): National Museums of Kenya; 10 (bottom): Ralph S. Solecki; 11 (top): Courtesy Department Library Services, American Museum of Natural History; 11 (center): Neg. #310705, Courtesy Department Library Services, American Museum of Natural History; 11 (bottom left): Neg. #39686, Courtesy Department Library Services, American Museum of Natural History; 11 (bottom right): Ralph S. Solecki; 12: Caisse Nationale des Monuments Historiques, Paris; 16: British School of Archaeology in Jerusalem; 21: © Loren McIntyre/Woodfin Camp.

Chapter 2 Page 26: The Metropolitan Museum of Art, Acquired in exchange with J. Pierpont Morgan Library, 1911 (11.217.24); 31 and 32: Hirmer Fotoarchiv, Munich; 33 (top): Courtesy of the Oriental Institute of the University of Chicago; 33 (bottom): Cliché des musées nationaux; 34 (top): HBJ Collection; 34 (bottom): Hirmer Fotoarchiv, Munich; 35: Reproduced by Courtesy of the Trustees of the British Museum; 36: The Metropolitan Museum of Art, Museum Excavations, 1928–1929 and Rogers Fund, 1930 (30.3.31); 37: Hirmer Fotoarchiv, Munich; 40: The Metropolitan Museum of Art; 44: Courtesy of the Oriental Institute of the University of Chicago; 45: HBJ Collection.

Chapter 3 Page 51: Courtesy, Museum of Fine Arts, Boston; 52 (top): Freer Gallery of Art, Smithsonian Institution (Acc. no. 39.42); 52 (bottom): Courtesy of the Cultural Relics Bureau, Beijing, and the Metropolitan Museum of Art; 53: East Asian Library, Columbia University; 54 (both): Freer Gallery of Art, Smithsonian Institution (Acc. nos. 51.18 and 36.6); 55 (top): Reproduced by Courtesy of the Trustees of the British Museum; 55 (bottom): Courtesy Harry N. Abrams, Inc.; 57 (top): Freer Gallery of Art, Smithsonian Institution (Acc. no. 39.53); 57 (bottom): Avery Brundage Collection, Asian Art Museum, San Francisco; 63: From *Chinese Portraiture* by Eli Lancman, published by Charles E. Tuttle Co., Inc., 1966.

Chapter 4 Page 69 (top): Hirmer Fotoarchiv, Munich; 69 (bottom): Society of Antiquaries of London; 70 (top): Reproduced by Courtesy of the Trustees of the British Museum; 70 (bottom): Ashmolean Museum, Oxford; 71: TAP Service; 72: Alinari/Art Resource, New York; 75: The Metropolitan Museum of Art, Purchase, 1947, Joseph Pulitzer Bequest (47.11.5); 76: Courtesy, Museum of Fine Arts, Boston; 83: E. M. Stresow-Czakó; 84 (top): © Alison Frantz; 84 (bottom): Reproduced by Courtesy of the Trustees of the British Museum; 85: Brogi/Art Resource, New York; 86: Alinari/Art Resource, New York; 87 (top): American School of Classical Studies at Athens: Agora Excavations; 87 (bottom): Reproduced by Courtesy of the Trustees of the British Museum; 88: Phot. Bibl. nat. Paris; 89: The Mansell Collection.

Chapter 5 Page 94: Art Resource, New York; 98: Reproduced by Courtesy of the Trustees of the British Museum; 99 and 106: Alinari/Art Resource, New York; 108: Collection H. Roger-Viollet; 109: Alinari/Art Resource, New York; 110: Brown Brothers; 111: Courtesy, Museum of Fine Arts, Boston; 117: Deutsches Archäologisches Institut, Rome.

Chapter 6 Page 118: Musei Vaticani; 120: HBJ Collection; 123: Kunsthistorisches Museum, Vienna; 125: Hirmer Fotoarchiv, Munich; 127: Guglielmo Giaretta/Musei Capitoline; 131: Fototeca Unione at the American Academy in Rome; 132: Giraudon/Art Resource, New York.

Chapter 7 Page 141: Cleveland Museum of Art, gift of George P. Bickford; 145 and 146: Archaeological Survey of India; 148: Courtesy, Museum of Fine Arts, Boston; 150: Freer Gallery of Art, Smithsonian Institution; 151: Photo by Eliot Elisofon © Life Picture Service; 152 (top): HBJ Collection; 152 (bottom): Archaeological Survey of India; 153: Vishnu, Gupta, Fifth Century. Courtesy, Museum of Fine Arts, Boston, Ross Collection.

Chapter 8 Page 158: American Numismatic Society; 161 and 164: HBJ Collection; 165 and 166 (top): Courtesy Cultural Relics Bureau, Beijing, and the Metropolitan Museum of Art; 166 (bottom): Royal Ontario Museum, Toronto; 168: Nelson-Atkins Museum of Art, Kansas City, Missouri; 169: From R. C. Rudolph, *Han Tomb Art of West China,* University of California Press, 1951; 171: Magnum Photos; 172: The Scientific Academy, Leningrad. Photo by A. C. Cooper; 173: Courtesy of the Cultural Relics Bureau, Beijing, and the Metropolitan Museum of Art; 174: The Metropolitan Museum of Art, Rogers Fund, 1917.

Chapter 9 Page 180: Reproduced by Courtesy of the Trustees of the British Museum; 184 (top): Rubbing from the Collection of Conrad and Lore Schirokauer. Photo by Lore Schirokauer; 184 (bottom): Photo by Lore Schirokauer; 185: SCALA/Art Resource, New York; 187: Photo by Lore Schirokauer; 191 (bottom): Collection of Mr. and Mrs. Ezekiel Schloss; 192: Freer Gallery of Art, Smithsonian Institution (Acc. no. 09.98); 193: Reproduced by Courtesy of the Trustees of the British Museum; 195: Palace Museum Collection, Taipei.

Chapter 10 Page 202: The Asia Society, Collection of Mr. and Mrs. John D. Rockefeller III, photo by Otto E. Nelson; 203: Archaeological Survey of India; 204: Photo by Eliot Elisofon; 205: HBJ Collection; 206: Eliot Elisofon, *Life* Magazine © Time Inc.; 211: HBJ Collection; 212: Photo by Lore Schirokauer; 214: Eliot Elisofon, *Life* Magazine © Time Inc.; 215: Photo by Lore Schirokauer; 216: Keystone-Mast Collection, California Museum of Photography, University of California, Riverside.

Chapter 11 Page 220 (top and bottom): The Metropolitan Museum of Art; 221: Alinari/Art Resource, New York; 222: (top): Hirmer Fotoarchiv, Munich; 222 (bottom): Alinari/Art Resource, New York; 224: Hirmer Fotoarchiv, Munich; 226: SCALA/Art Resource, New York; 230: Reproduced by Courtesy of the Trustees of the British Museum; 231: Bayer. Staatsbibliothek, Munich; 232: The Metropolitan Museum of Art, Purchase 1895, Administrative Fund; 233: Giraudon/Art Resource, New York; 236: Edinburgh University Library.

Chapter 12 Page 242: SCALA/Art Resource, New York; 243: The Louvre, Paris; 245: Historical Pictures Service, Inc., Chicago; 247: Phot. Bibl. nat. Paris; 250: The Bettmann Archive; 254: Hirmer Fotoarchiv, Munich; 256: Biblioteca Apostolica Vaticana; 257: Culver Pictures; 258: The Mansell Collection; 260: Lincoln College, Oxford; 261: The Mansell Collection.

Chapter 13 Page 266 (top): Edinburgh University Library; 266 (bottom): Courtesy of the American Numismatic Society, New York; 268: Berlin Museum; 269: The New York Public Library, Astor, Lenox and Tilden Foundations; 270: The Metropolitan Museum of Art, Bequest of Edward C. Moore, 1891; 271: Edinburgh University Library; 274: The Metropolitan Museum of Art; 281: HBJ Collection; 283: The Metropolitan Museum of Art; 284: Bildarchiv Österreichische Nationalbibliothek, Vienna.

Chapter 14 Page 290: Reproduced by Courtesy of the Trustees of the British Museum; 296: National Archives, Paris; 297: Bildarchiv Österreichische Nationalbibliothek, Vienna; 298: Marburg/Art Resource, New York; 299: The Louvre, Paris; 300: Phot. Bibl. nat. Paris; 301: Reproduced by Courtesy of the Trustees of the British Museum; 303: The Bettmann Archive; 305: Reproduced by Courtesy of the Trustees of the British Museum; 307: Colorphoto Hans Hinz, Allschwil-Basel; 308: Phot. Bibl. nat. Paris.

Chapter 15 Page 313: The Bettmann Archive; 314: Reproduced by Courtesy of the Trustees of the British Museum; 317: The Bettmann Archive; 320: Burgerbibliothek, Bern; 323: The Metropolitan Museum of Art; 326: HBJ Collection; 327: Reproduced by Courtesy of the Trustees of the British Museum; 329: The Houghton Library, Harvard University; 331: Jean Roubier; 332: Marburg/Art Resource, New York; 333: Caisse Nationale des Monuments Historiques, Paris.

Chapter 16 Page 336 (top): Osaka University; 336 (bottom): Tokyo National Museum; 337 (top): Katherine Young; 337 (bottom): Photo by Lore Schirokauer; 338 (left): National Commission for the Protection of Cultural Properties of Japan; 338 (right): Cleveland Museum of Art, Norweb Collection; 340 (top): Japanese Consulate General; 340 (bottom): National Commission for the Protection of Cultural Properties of Japan; 343: Shashinka Photo; 345: Photo by Lore Schirokauer; 347 (top): Sakamoto Photo Research Lab; 347 (bottom): Kyoto National Museum; 349 and 350: National Commission for the Protection of Cultural Properties of Japan.

Chapter 17 Page 354: From Samuel Wells Williams, *The Middle Kingdom,* vol. 1, 2nd ed., Charles Scribner's Sons, 1883; 357: The Qing Ming Festival Scroll, Imperial Palace Museum Collection, Beijing; 358: Sir Percival David Foundation of Chinese Art, University of London; 360: Commission for the Protection of Cultural Properties of Japan, Tokyo National Museum; 361 (top): Palace Museum Collection, Taipei; 361 (bottom): The Metropolitan Museum of Art; 362: The St. Louis Art Museum; 363: Jingo-Ji Kyoto; 366: Courtesy, Museum of Fine Arts, Boston; 367: Todaiji, Nara; 369: The Metropolitan Museum of Art.

Chapter 18 Page 373: The Mansell Collection; 374: The Bettmann Archive; 375 (top): Reproduced by Courtesy of the Trustees of the British Museum; 375 (bottom): The Mansell Collection; 378; Robert Hardy Picture Library; 381: The Cleveland Museum of Art, Purchase Leonard C. Hanna, Jr. Bequest; 382: Indianapolis Museum of Art; 383: The Art Institute of Chicago; 384: The Cleveland Museum of Art, Purchase Leonard C. Hanna, Jr. Bequest.

Chapter 19 Page 390: Giraudon/Musée de l'Eveche, with Permission of the City of Bayeaux; 392: A. C. Cooper, Library, Inner Temple; 396 (top): HBJ Collection; 396 (bottom): SCALA/Art Resource, New York; 399 (top): The Mansell Collection; 399 (bottom): Giraudon/Art Resource, New York; 400: Caisse Nationale des Monuments Historiques, Paris; 402: Uffizi Gallery, Florence; 407: Culver Pictures; 408: Alinari/Art Resource, New York; 409 (top): HBJ Collection; 409 (bottom): Reproduced by courtesy of the Trustees, The National Gallery, London; 410: Brancacci Chapel, Sta. Maria del Carmine, Florence.

Chapter 20 Page 414: Trustees of the Science Museum, London; 418: SCALA/Art Resource, New York; 422: Gabinetto Fotografico, Florence; 424 and 425: Alinari/Art Resource, New York; 426: The Bettmann Archive; 427: Giraudon/Art Resource, New York; 428 (top): Herzog Anton Ulrich-Museum, Braunschweig, Fotonachweis: Museumsfoto B. P. Keiser; 428 (bottom) Giraudon/Art Resource, New York; 430: Giraudon/Art Resource, New York/Musée Conde, Chantilly; 434: New York Public Library Picture Collection.

Chapter 21 Page 439: Courtesy Staatliche Lutherhalle Wittenberg; 441: Bildarchiv Österreichische Nationalbibliothek, Vienna; 442: National Portrait Gallery, London; 443 (top): Caisse Nationale des Monuments Historiques, Paris; 443 (bottom): Bayerische Staatsgemäldesammlungen, Munich; 448: Bibliothèque publique et universitaire, Geneva; 449: By permission of the British Library; 451: Reproduced by Courtesy of the Trustees of the British Museum; 453: Historical Pictures Service, Inc., Chicago.

Chapter 22 Page 459: The Metropolitan Museum of Art (31.6.40); 463: HBJ Collection; 464: Library of Congress; 465: HBJ Collection; 467: Courtesy of the Robert S. Peabody Foundation for Archaeology, Philips Academy, Andover, Mass.; 468: Arizona State Museum, University of Arizona, Photo by E. B. Sayles, Photographer; 470: By Richard H. Stewart © 1940 National Geographic Society; 472: © Kuiko Y. Ante; 473: Neg. #330105, Courtesy Library Services Department, American Museum of Natural History; 474: Museo Nacional de Antropologia, Mexico City; 478: © Andrew Rakoczy.

Chapter 23 Page 483 (top): The Metropolitan Museum of Art; 483 (bottom): Asia Society, Collection of Mr. and Mrs. John D. Rockefeller III, photo by Otto E. Nelson; 485: The Metropolitan Museum of Art; 487: Nelson-Atkins Museum of Art, Kansas City, Missouri (Nelson Fund); 489: Cleveland Museum of Art; 492: Tokyo National Museum; 493 (top): Photo by Lore Schirokauer; 493 (bottom): Hakone Art Museum, Gora-Hakone Machi, Kanagawa Prefecture, Japan; 494: Tokyo National Museum; 495 (top): Photo by Lore Schirokauer; 495 (bottom): Plate 59 from Suzuki, Diasety T., *Zen and Japanese Culture,* Bollingen Series LXIV © 1959 Princeton University Press; 496: Hamban Bunka Kan, Osaka, Japan.

Chapter 24 Page 501: Norwegian Information Service; 503 (top and center): Culver Pictures; 503 (bottom): Giraudon/Art Resource, New York; 506: Alinari/Art Resource, New York; 507: Library of Congress; 509 (top): Library of Congress; 509 (bottom): Museo di Capodimonte, Naples; 513: The Royal Library, Stockholm; 514: Reproduced by Courtesy of the Trustees of the British Museum; 515: By kind permission of the Marquess of Tavistock, of the Trustees of the Bedford Estates; 516: Musée Cantonal des Beaux Arts, Lausanne.

Chapter 25 Page 525: The Bodleian Library, Oxford; 526: The Metropolitan Museum of Art; 527: Reproduced by courtesy of the Trustees, The National Gallery, London; 528: HBJ Collection; 530 (top): Giraudon/Art Resource, New York; 530 (bottom): Reproduced by Courtesy of the Trustees of the British Museum; 532: Turkish Information Office; 534: By Courtesy of the Trustees of the Victoria and Albert Museum; 536: Freer Gallery of Art, Smithsonian Institution; 537: California Museum of Photography, University of California, Riverside.

Chapter 26 Page 542 (top): © Bruno Barbey/Magnum Photos; 542 (bottom): Honolulu Academy of Arts, Wilhelmina Tenney Memorial Collection, 1956; 543: The Metropolitan Museum of Art; 544: Photo by Lore Schirokauer; 547: Gest Oriental Library of East Asian Collections, Princeton University; 548: University of Sussex, Barlow Collection; 549: Fujii Museum, Photo by Lore Schirokauer; 551: From *Hiroshige's Tokaido in Print and Poetry,* ed. by Reiko Chiba. Charles E. Tuttle Co., Inc. of Japan; 553: Seattle Art Museum; 554: From *Hiroshige's Tokaido in Print and Poetry,* ed. by Reiko Chiba. Charles E. Tuttle Co., Inc. of Japan; 556: Nezu Museum, Tokyo; 557 (left): Collection W. Boller, Photo by R. Spreng; 557 (right): Sharaku, Toshusai, *The Actor Otani Oniji as Edhoei,* Japanese print,

Clarence Buckingham Collection, The Art Institute of Chicago.

Chapter 27 Page 563: Phot. Bibl. nat. Paris; 564: Reproduced by courtesy of the Trustees, The National Gallery, London; 565: Wallace Collection, London; 567: Colonial Williamsburg Collection; 568: The Metropolitan Museum of Art, Gift of George A. Hearn, 1906; 569 (top): The Bettmann Archive; 569 (bottom): The Mansell Collection; 572 (top): The Bettmann Archive; 572 (bottom): Culver Pictures; 578: Rijksmuseum, Amsterdam; 580: The Bettmann Archive.

Chapter 28 Page 584: Giraudon/Art Resource, New York; 585: Caisse Nationale des Monuments Historiques, Paris; 586: Historical Pictures Service, Chicago; 589: By permission of the British Library; 590: Museum of the City of London; 592: The Granger Collection, New York; 593: Reproduced by Courtesy of the Trustees of the British Museum; 595: National Portrait Gallery, London; 596: Réunion des Musées Nationaux, Paris; 597: Photo Hachette; 599: Rijksmuseum, Amsterdam; 600: Novosti Press Agency.

Chapter 29 Page 604: Phot. Bibl. nat. Paris; 605: National Portrait Gallery, London; 606: David Eugene Smith Collection, Rare Book and Manuscript Library, Columbia University; 607 (top): The Bettmann Archive/BBC Hulton; 607 (bottom): Culver Pictures; 609: © Helga Schmidt-Glassner; 610: The Metropolitan Museum of Art; 611: HBJ Collection; 614: John R. Freeman, London; 618: Culver Pictures; 619: Reproduced by courtesy of the Trustees, The National Gallery, London; 620 (top): Culver Pictures; 620 (bottom): Mozart Museum, Salzburg.

Chapter 30 Page 627: Bord Failte Photo; 628: The Mansell Collection; 629: Reproduced by Courtesy of the Trustees of the British Museum; 630: National Galleries of Scotland, Edinburgh; 631: Bildarchiv Foto Marburg; 633: Giraudon/Art Resource, New York; 634: The Granger Collection, New York; 635: Library of Congress; 637 (top): Staatliche Münzsammlung, Munich; 637 (bottom): The Bettmann Archive; 638: Historical Pictures Service, Chicago; 641: Bildarchiv Österreichische Nationalbibliothek, Vienna.

Chapter 31 Page 647: Rare Books Division, The New York Public Library, Astor, Lenox and Tilden Foundations; 649: Hispanic Society of America; 652: Stokes Collection, The New York Public Library; 655 (top): Rare Books Division, The New York Public Library, Astor, Lenox and Tilden Foundations; 655 (bottom): Jamestown-Yorktown Foundation; 656 (top): Rare Books Division, The New York Public Library, Astor, Lenox and Tilden Foundations; 656 (bottom): South Caroliniana Library, University of South Carolina; 659: Courtesy of the New-York Historical Society, New York; 661: Library of Congress; 663: Courtesy, Pennsylvania Academy of Fine Arts; 664: Rare Books Division, The New York Public Library, Astor, Lenox and Tilden Foundations; 665: By Courtesy of the Trustees of the Victoria and Albert Museum, London; 666: Slavonic Division, The New York Public Library, Astor, Lenox and Tilden Foundations.

Chapter 32 Page 672: Art Resource, New York; 673: Library of Congress; 675: Phot. Bibl. nat. Paris; 677: Fotomas Index, London; 678: The Bettmann Archive; 679 (top): The Granger Collection, New York; 679 (bottom): Phot. Bibl. nat. Paris; 683 and 684: Art Resource, New York; 687: Photo © Musée de l'Armée, Paris; 688: The Granger Collection, New York.

Chapter 33 Page 693 (top): The Bettmann Archive; 693 (bottom): Teresa Fitzherbert Print Room, Royal Library, Windsor Castle; 697: National-Gallery, Berlin (destroyed

1945); 701: Reproduced by permission of Her Majesty the Queen. Phoebus Picture Library; 703: The Bettmann Archive; 705: The Pierpont Morgan Library, New York; 706: Courtesy of the City of Manchester Cultural Services, Manchester, England; 707: The Mansell Collection; 708: The Bettmann Archive; 710: HBJ Collection; 712: Reproduced by permission of Her Majesty the Queen.

Chapter 34 Page 718: The Bettmann Archive/BBC Hulton; 719: The Mansell Collection; 720: HBJ Collection; 722: The Mansell Collection; 723 (both): The Bettmann Archive/BBC Hulton; 725: Brown Brothers; 729: The Granger Collection, New York; 730: Library of Congress; 731: Historical Pictures Service, Chicago; 734 (top): By courtesy of The Dickens House Museum, London; 734 (bottom): Sovfoto.

Chapter 35 Page 738: Culver Pictures; 740: Mayer and Pierson, Gernsheim Collection, Harry Ransom Humanities Research Center, The University of Texas at Austin, Texas; 741: The Bettmann Archive; 742: Photo Ferrier and Solier, Courtesy of the International Museum of Photography at George Eastman House, Rochester, NY; 745: Alinari/Art Resource, New York; 746: The Bettmann Archive; 747: Bildarchiv Preussicher Kulturbesitz, Berlin; 751: HBJ Collection; 752 and 755: Gernsheim Collection, Harry Ransom Humanities Research Center, The University of Texas at Austin, Texas: 756: The Granger Collection, New York; 757: Katherine Young, Archiv für Kunst und Geschichte.

Chapter 36 Page 762: Culver Pictures; 766: The Bettmann Archive; 768: Phot. Bibl. nat. Paris; 771: Culver Pictures; 773: Gernsheim Collection, Harry Ransom Humanities Research Center, The University of Texas at Austin, Texas; 774: Brown Brothers; 776: Sovfoto; 777: The Bettmann Archive; 778: National Portrait Gallery, London; 781: Gemäldegalerie Neue Meister, Staatliche Kunstsammlungen, Dresden.

Chapter 37 Page 786: Culver Pictures; 788 and 791: The Bettmann Archive/BBC Hulton; 792: UPI/Bettmann Newsphotos; 793 (top): Brown Brothers; 793 (bottom): Keystone-Mast Collection, California Museum of Photography, University of California, Riverside; 794: The Bettmann Archive/BBC Hulton; 801: The Press Association, London; 803 (top): UPI/Bettmann Newsphotos; 803 (bottom): The Bettmann Archive/BBC Hulton.

Chapter 38 Page 811: Keystone-Mast Collection, California Museum of Photography, University of California, Riverside; 812 (top): The Bettmann Archive/BBC Hulton; 812 (bottom) and 813: Keystone-Mast Collection, California Museum of Photography, University of California, Riverside; 815: The Bettmann Archive; 817: The Bettmann Archive/BBC Hulton; 819: Collection H. Roger-Viollet; 823: The Bettmann Archive/BBC Hulton.

Chapter 39 Page 828: Popperfoto; 830: Keystone-Mast Collection, California Museum of Photography, University of California, Riverside; 833: The New York Public Library, Astor, Lenox and Tilden Foundations; 834: Keystone-Mast Collection, California Museum of Photography, University of California, Riverside; 835 (top): Collection H. Roger-Viollet; 835 (bottom): Brown Brothers; 838 and 839: Keystone-Mast Collection, California Museum of Photography, University of California, Riverside; 841: Courtesy U.S. Naval Academy Museum; 842: Courtesy, Museum of Fine Arts, Boston; 843 and 844: Keystone-Mast Collection, California Museum of Photography, University of California, Riverside.

Chapter 40 Page 849: Museum of the City of New York; 850: Courtesy of the

New-York Historical Society, New York; 851: Western Americana Collection, Beinecke Rare Book Room and Manuscript Library, Yale University; 852: Sutter's Fort State Historical Monument; 854: Courtesy of the New-York Historical Society, New York; 855: Library of Congress; 856: Courtesy Amon Carter Museum, Ft. Worth, Texas; 857: Department of Archives and Manuscripts, The Catholic University of America; 858: Photo Lewis W. Hine, Courtesy of the International Museum of Photography at George Eastman House, Rochester, NY; 859 and 860: Library of Congress; 861: Culver Pictures; 862: C-8735 Public Archives of Canada; 865: Culver Pictures; 868: The Bettmann Archive.

Chapter 41 Page 873: National Archives; 874, 876, and 877 (top): The Trustees of the Imperial War Museum, London; 877 (bottom): National Archives; 880: Culver Pictures; 882: The Trustees of the Imperial War Museum, London; 884: The Bettmann Archive/BBC Hulton; 889: Gernsheim Collection, Harry Ransom Humanities Research Center, The University of Texas at Austin, Texas; 891: UPI/Bettmann Newsphotos.

Chapter 42 Page 896 (top): © Eve Arnold/Magnum Photos; 896 (bottom): Collection J.A.F./Paris/Magnum Photos; 898 (top): AP/Wide World Photos; 898 (bottom): UPI/Bettmann Newsphotos; 899 and 901: Margaret Bourke-White, *Life* Magazine © Time Inc.; 902: Philip Gendreau, N.Y.; 908: Culver Pictures.

Chapter 43 Page 915: *L'Illustration*/Sygma; 918: The Granger Collection, New York; 920 (top): AP/Wide World Photos; 920 (bottom): © Dr. Erich Salomon/Magnum Photos; 923: The Bettmann Archive/BBC Hulton; 924: Brown Brothers; 930: Culver Pictures; 932: Library of Congress; 933: UPI/Bettmann Newsphotos; 934: Gernsheim Collection, Harry Ransom Humanities Research Center, The University of Texas at Austin, Texas.

Chapter 44 Pages 943 and 944: AP/Wide World Photos; 946: Times Newspapers, Ltd.; 949 (top): National Archives; 949 (bottom) and 951: The Trustees of the Imperial War Museum, London; 952: Bildarchiv Preussischer Kulturbesitz; 955 (top): © Ewing Galloway; 955 (bottom): © 1961 *Punch* (Rothco); 957: © Fenno Jacobs/Black Star.

Chapter 45 Page 965: UPI/Bettmann Newsphotos; 967: © Regis Bossu/Sygma; 969: AP/Wide World Photos; 970: *Ebony;* 971: © Donald McCullin/Magnum Photos, Inc.; 973: UPI/Bettmann Newsphotos; 974: Grey Villet, *Life* Magazine © Time Inc.; 975: United Nations; 977: AP/Wide World Photos; 978: U.S. Army Photograph; 979: AP/Wide World Photos.

Chaper 46 Pages 987, 989, 990, and 994: UPI/Bettmann Newsphotos; 995: © J. Pavlovsky/Sygma; 998 and 999: UPI/Bettmann Newsphotos; 1002: © Ian Berry/Magnum Photos, Inc.

Index

A

B

C

D

E

H

I

J

K

L

M

N

O

P

Q

R

S

T

A 6
B 7
C 8
D 9
E 0
F 1
G 2
H 3
I 4
J 5